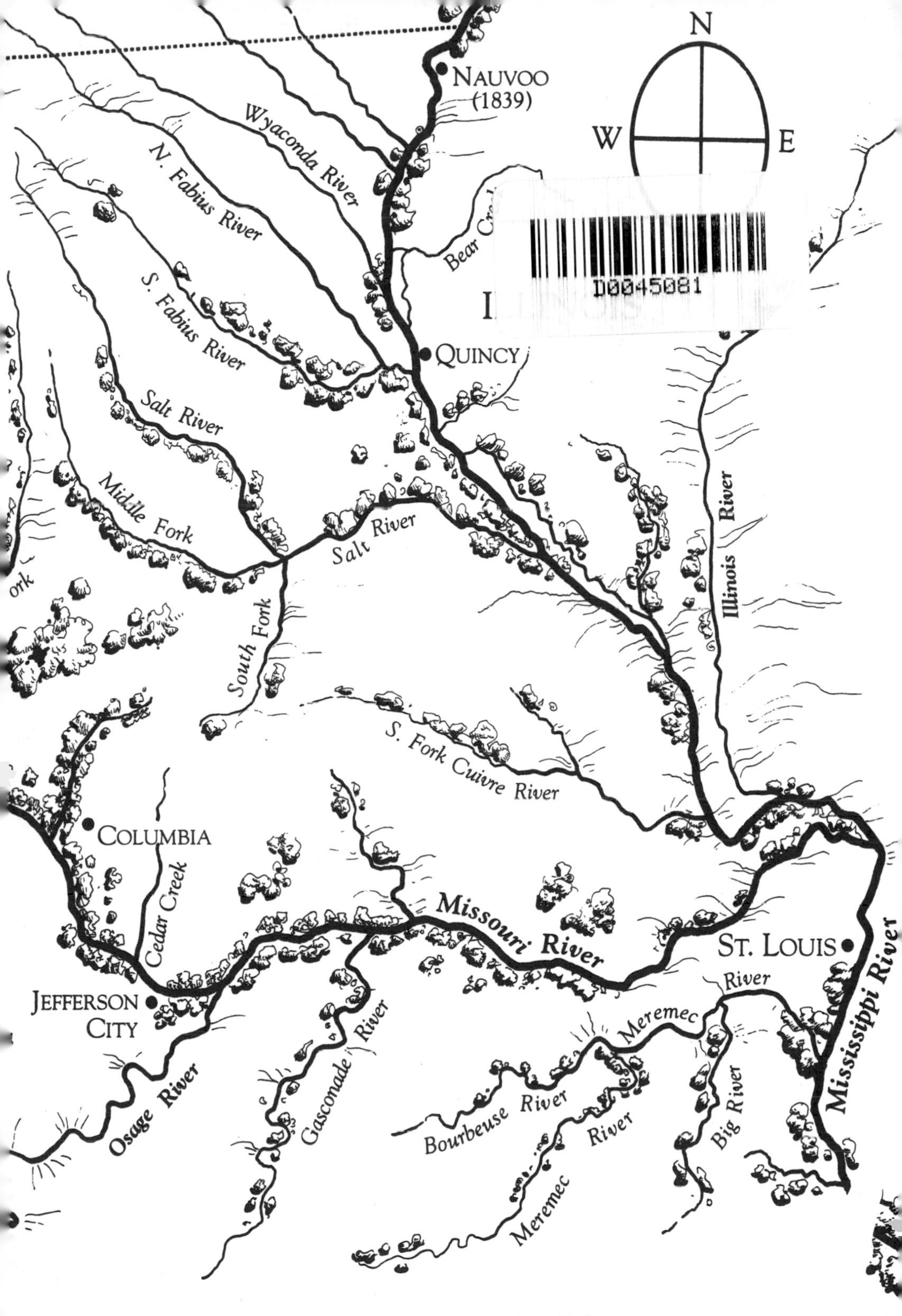

WESTERN ILLINOIS 1838–39

THE
WORK
AND THE
GLORY
Thy Gold to Refine

"Majesty in Chains"

Gerald N. Lund

BOOKCRAFT
Salt Lake City, Utah

THE WORK AND THE GLORY

Volume 1: Pillar of Light
Volume 2: Like a Fire Is Burning
Volume 3: Truth Will Prevail
Volume 4: Thy Gold to Refine
Volume 5: A Season of Joy
Volume 6: Praise to the Man
Volume 7: No Unhallowed Hand
Volume 8: So Great a Cause
Volume 9: All Is Well

First printing in hardbound 1993
First printing in paperbound 2001
First printing in trade paperbound 2006

Visit us at deseretbook.com

Library of Congress Catalog Card Number: 95-81231

ISBN-10 0-88494-893-5 (hardbound)
ISBN-13 978-0-88494-893-3 (hardbound)
ISBN 1-57345-873-2 (paperbound)
ISBN-10 1-59038-652-3 (trade paperbound)
ISBN-13 978-1-59038-652-1 (trade paperbound)

Printed in the United States of America
Edwards Brothers Inc., Ann Arbor, MI

20 19 18 17 16 15 14 13

For behold, this is my work and my glory—to bring to pass the immortality and eternal life of man.

—Moses 1:39

Preface

In the prefaces to the previous three volumes, I have concluded by expressing my appreciation for all of those who have made important contributions to this series. It is not necessary to repeat all of those expressions again, so I say only this: Without Kim and Jane Moe and their vision, without the competent and efficient staff at Bookcraft, without the researchers and secretaries and trusted manuscript readers and artists, *The Work and the Glory* would not be a reality today. And my wife, Lynn—the only one besides myself who knows what writing this series has required because she has paid much of the price—not only puts up with my long hours at the computer but also completely and totally believes in this project. How can one ever give adequate thanks for that?

In prefacing this volume, I should like to add only two additional expressions of thanks. To the numerous readers who have been following the saga of the Benjamin Steed family and who have come to think of the Steeds as I do—as real and living people whom we care about a great deal—thank you for your unflagging support. It has been a most gratifying project for me to work on, but it is especially gratifying to know that others are enjoying it as well.

Second, I express a deep and reverential gratitude to those early Saints who provided the raw material from which this novel gets its life. Not only have they inspired me, but they have kindled in me a renewed determination to put away the petty and temporal things that so often clutter our lives and to willingly submit myself to whatever the Lord sees is necessary in the refining and forging of the gold I hope he has in mind for me someday.

One other comment of a more practical nature: As I wrote volume 4, I decided to do the endnotes as I completed each chapter, rather than wait and do them all at once as I had done in previous volumes. For convenience, on the manuscript I added them to the end of each chapter. To my surprise, those who read the manuscript found this to be a welcome change. They said they really liked knowing immediately which portions of the chapters were based on historical events.

So in this volume the chapter notes are found at the end of each chapter.

With the coming forth of *Thy Gold to Refine*, volume 4 in the series *The Work and the Glory*, the saga of the Steed family and their intimate involvement with the events of the Restoration continues.

Volume 1 (1827 to 1830) introduced the Steeds, who had moved into upstate New York in 1826. There, in the spring of 1827, they met Joseph Smith, the young man the Lord had called to open the work of the last dispensation. Through Benjamin's doubting eyes and Nathan's and Mary Ann's believing eyes, we witnessed the opening scenes of God's great work of the latter days.

In volume 2 (1830 to 1836), the development of the infant Church began, and we saw how that development profoundly impacted the Steed family members as the Church swelled rapidly in numbers and moved from New York to Ohio and Missouri.

Volume 3 (1836 to 1838) saw the first major internal challenge to the Church as many of the recent converts—including several important leaders—became disillusioned and disaffected with the exacting standards the Lord requires of his people, and left the Church. Not only did they apostatize, but in many cases they became bitter enemies and fought with untiring ferocity against Joseph Smith and their former associates. Driven from Kirtland, the Church and the Steeds ended up in northern Missouri. Old wounds that had left rifts in the Steed family fabric began to heal, and through marriage and childbirth the Steed clan more than doubled in numbers.

Surprisingly, volume 4 covers the smallest period of time of any of the volumes so far—from July 1838 to March 1839, a period of less than nine months. I say "surprisingly" because as I began work on *Thy Gold to Refine*, I was determined to pass over swiftly the first few months that the novel would cover. Why? Because this period of Church history is one of the grimmest in the whole story of the Restoration. It is a time of continuous adversity, grinding opposition, intense tribulation, and frightening violence. Gallatin, Crooked River, Far West, Adam-ondi-Ahman, DeWitt, Haun's Mill—the very geography reeks with blood and horror and sorrow. I feared that the story was so depressing and so dark that readers would find it a burden to wade through it in any detail. So my original plan was to treat those few months swiftly. We would get the Steeds out of Missouri and into Nauvoo as quickly as possible and go on to more pleasant times.

But stories have lives of their own sometimes, and to my own surprise—and wonder!—this turned out to be the case with volume 4. The story is too rich, the events are too momentous, the tragedies too moving, the pathos and the poignancy too wonderful and too terrible and too inspiring to simply brush over lightly. These Saints were real people, and their story is one of incredible loyalty and faith in the face of staggering adversity.

Why was the price so high for these early Church members? Why was the call to conversion so fraught with challenges? If the Saints were God's people, as they believed they were, why did he allow their enemies to run amok among them? Why didn't God intervene in their behalf? These are questions of pressing relevance for our generation as well. Sometimes we, as modern Latter-day Saints, wonder why adversity and trials and setbacks and tragedies become our lot. "Why is this happening to me?" we cry. "What am I doing wrong? Why isn't the Lord answering my cries for help?"

As I delved into the details of those threshing days in Missouri, I began to find answers to those questions not only in the scriptures and the revelations but in the fleshy chapters of individual hearts. Such chapters were written by people who, without question, considered themselves in no way unusual or remarkable, other than in their faith and their calling to serve God. And grim though those chapters may sometimes be, they nevertheless teach powerful lessons about choices and chastisement, about challenges and change, about cherishing and charity, about tribulation and triumph. They are lessons of pressing relevance for today's stress-filled, harried world. They can stiffen the will and lift the heart and bring consolation in answer to our ardent cryings.

Speaking through the prophet Isaiah, the Lord said, "Behold, I have refined thee, but not with silver; I have chosen thee in the furnace of affliction" (Isaiah 48:10). A few chapters later in the same book, similar imagery is used: "Behold, I have created the smith that bloweth the coals in the fire, and that bringeth forth an instrument for his work" (Isaiah 54:16).

The furnace and the forge. In those two images there are great lessons to be learned.

First, the fire itself is a refining, purging, cleansing agent. The impurities are consumed, the dross burned away until only the purest of the metal remains. Speaking of Christ's second coming, Malachi asked: "But who may abide the day of his coming? and who shall stand when he appeareth? for he is like a refiner's fire . . . : and he shall sit as a refiner and purifier of silver: and he shall purify the sons of Levi, and purge them as gold and silver" (Malachi 3:2–3).

There is a work to be done in preparation for the second coming of Christ, and the Lord needs a people who are not only willing but also strong enough (and pure enough!) to do what must be done. And for all their wonderful and wondrous determination to be good and faithful Latter-day Saints, those early converts brought into the Church considerable overburden along with the ore of their faith. They were guilty of very human lapses in their commitment to God—not all were, but enough to bring a lessening of divine power and protection. In the fateful nine months covered in volume 4, the examples of minor pettiness and major abandonment of covenants abound. In one place we find a leader of a settlement too stubborn to listen to a prophet's counsel. He lives to see the tragic folly of his pride. In another, there is the myopia of a senior member of the Quorum of the Twelve who sides with his wife against the First Presidency. Within days his bitterness burns so hot, he leaves his brethren and swears out an official and slanderous deposition against Joseph Smith and the Saints. That deposition becomes a major factor in Governor Boggs's decision to issue his infamous extermination order. The examples are legion.

Are they so different from us? We look back on some of those early members and say, "How could they have been so foolish? How could they have been so blind?" And even as we speak, some of us are stung by real or imaginary wrongs—some petty, some momentous—and we chafe and murmur and sour and sometimes take ourselves out of the Church. Will future generations look on our lives and wag their heads: "How could *they* have been so foolish?"

Those few terrible months in Missouri bring a lesson that should cause us sober reflection. There are no warranties against wavering. Aligning ourselves with the Lord and his cause is a commitment that must be made again and again, day after day. Unless we ground ourselves in faith, sink down our foundations to the bedrock of Jesus

Christ, and commit ourselves to follow those whom he has called to lead us, we too may falter and fall.

The second image—that of the forge—carries an equally powerful lesson for modern Saints. Through Isaiah, the Lord spoke of bringing forth an instrument from the coals to do God's work. As any blacksmith can tell you, you don't get steel without fire, and you don't make steel instruments without hammer, tongs, and anvil.

Missouri was the Lord's forge! A raging inferno swept across those northern plains, but emerging from the smoke and the flames to cross the river into Illinois was a people of steel—a people who would abandon homes and farms and livestock and even their very lives before they would abandon their faith; a people who no longer thought only of their own survival but covenanted to take their poor with them or not survive at all; a people who would carve a city from a swamp and send emissaries out far enough and wide enough that they would see their numbers double in the next six years.

Joseph was the "Smith" the Lord chose to lead the Saints through the fire and to help forge an instrument for achieving what He himself called "my work and my glory" (Moses 1:39). And Joseph Smith was not exempt from the process of being made into steel. He too was an instrument to be hammered out in the forge of the Lord so that God could use him for his divine purposes. Joseph felt the scathing fires of apostasy in Kirtland. He saw betrayal and treachery in Far West. He sat for months in the hellhole of a place ironically named Liberty Jail.

From that loathsome dungeon in Liberty, he himself cried out in anguish, "O God, where art thou?" (D&C 121:1.) The answers came, as recorded in a letter to the Saints, and a century and a half later they still ring like the hammer striking steel:

"Peace be unto thy soul."

"Thine adversity and thine afflictions shall be but a small moment."

"If thou endure it well, God shall exalt thee on high." (See D&C 121:7, 8.)

In that same letter (the letter from which sections 121, 122, and 123 of the Doctrine and Covenants are taken), Joseph summed up how he saw what was happening to them: "Inasmuch as God hath said that He would have a tried people, that He would purge them as gold, now we think that this time He has chosen His own crucible, wherein we have been tried; and we think if we get through with any degree of safety, and shall have kept the faith, that it will be a sign to this generation, altogether sufficient to leave them without excuse; and we think also, it will be a trial of our faith equal to that of Abraham, and that the ancients will not have whereof to boast over us in the day of judgment, as being called to pass through heavier afflictions; that we may hold an even weight in the balance with them" (*History of the Church* 3:294).

Thy Gold to Refine covers only nine months of history, yet it is the longest, by several pages, of all the volumes so far in this series. It is my hope that when you, the reader, have finished reading this book, you will understand why. The story could not be told in any less detail and still do honor to those who lived it.

Vilate Chambers Raile captured the essence of what these wonderfully normal and completely unassuming pioneers of the Restoration did for us:

> They cut desire into short lengths
> And fed it to the hungry fire of courage.
> Long after—when the flames died—
> Molten gold gleamed in the ashes.
> They gathered it into bruised palms
> And handed it to their children
> And their children's children.
>
> (As cited in Asahel D. Woodruff, *Parent and Youth* [Salt Lake City: Deseret Sunday School Union Board, 1952], p. 122.)

GERALD N. LUND

Bountiful, Utah
August 1993

Characters of Note in This Book

The Steed Family

Benjamin, the father and grandfather; age fifty-three as the book begins.
Mary Ann Morgan, the mother and grandmother; fifty-one.
Joshua, the oldest son; thirty-one as the book begins.
Caroline Mendenhall Steed, Joshua's wife; almost thirty-two as the story opens.
William Donovan Mendenhall, Caroline's son; fourteen.
Olivia Mendenhall, Caroline's daughter; about three and a half years younger than William.
Savannah Steed, daughter of Joshua and Caroline; fifteen and a half months old as the story opens.
Jessica Roundy Griffith, ex-wife of Joshua and now married to John Griffith; thirty-four as the book begins.
John Griffith, husband of Jessica.
Rachel, daughter of Joshua and Jessica; six years old as the story opens.
Luke and Mark Griffith, sons of John from his first marriage; five and three years old, respectively, as the book begins.
John Benjamin Griffith, son of John and Jessica; three and a half months old.
Nathan, the second son of Benjamin and Mary Ann; twenty-nine.
Lydia McBride, Nathan's wife; almost twenty-nine as the story opens.
Joshua Benjamin, older son of Nathan and Lydia; seven years old.
Emily, older daughter of Nathan and Lydia; thirteen and a half months younger than Joshua.

Nathan Joseph, younger son of Nathan and Lydia; not yet three years old.

Elizabeth Mary, younger daughter of Nathan and Lydia; two months old.

Melissa Steed Rogers, older daughter of Benjamin and Mary Ann; twenty-seven.

Carlton Rogers, Melissa's husband.

Rebecca, younger daughter of Benjamin and Mary Ann; age twenty.

Matthew, the youngest son of Benjamin and Mary Ann; two years younger than Rebecca.

Note: Melissa and Carlton ("Carl") Rogers have children, but they do not figure prominently in this volume.

The Smiths

*Joseph, Sr., the father.

*Lucy Mack, the mother.

*Hyrum, Joseph's elder brother; almost six years older than Joseph.

*Mary Fielding, Hyrum's second wife.

*Joseph, Jr., age thirty-two as the story opens.

*Emma Hale, Joseph's wife; a year and a half older than Joseph.

*Lucy, Joseph's youngest sister; about fifteen and a half years younger than Joseph.

Note: There are other brothers and sisters to Joseph, but they play no part in the novel. Also, both Joseph and Hyrum have children that are mentioned briefly but who are not listed here.

*Designates actual people from Church history.

Others

Obadiah Cornwell, Joshua's business partner in Independence, Missouri.

Derek Ingalls, a factory worker from England; nearly twenty-one.

Peter Ingalls, Derek's younger brother; fourteen.

* Heber C. Kimball, friend of Brigham Young's and a member of the Quorum of the Twelve Apostles.

Nancy McIntire, a nonmember widow living outside of Gallatin, Missouri.

Jennifer Jo McIntire, older daughter of Nancy; sixteen years old.

Kathryn Marie McIntire, Jennifer's sister; four years younger than Jennifer.

* Thomas B. Marsh, a member of the Quorum of the Twelve Apostles.

* Parley P. Pratt, an early convert and a member of the Quorum of the Twelve Apostles.

* John Taylor, an early convert from Canada.

* Mercy Fielding Thompson, sister to Mary Fielding Smith.

* Brigham Young, an early convert and a member of the Quorum of the Twelve Apostles.

Though too numerous to list here, there are many other actual people from the pages of history who are mentioned by name in the novel. Sidney Rigdon, David W. Patten, Sampson Avard, Edward Partridge, Amanda Smith, and many others mentioned in the book were real people who lived and participated in the events described in this work.

*Designates actual people from Church history.

The Benjamin Steed Family†

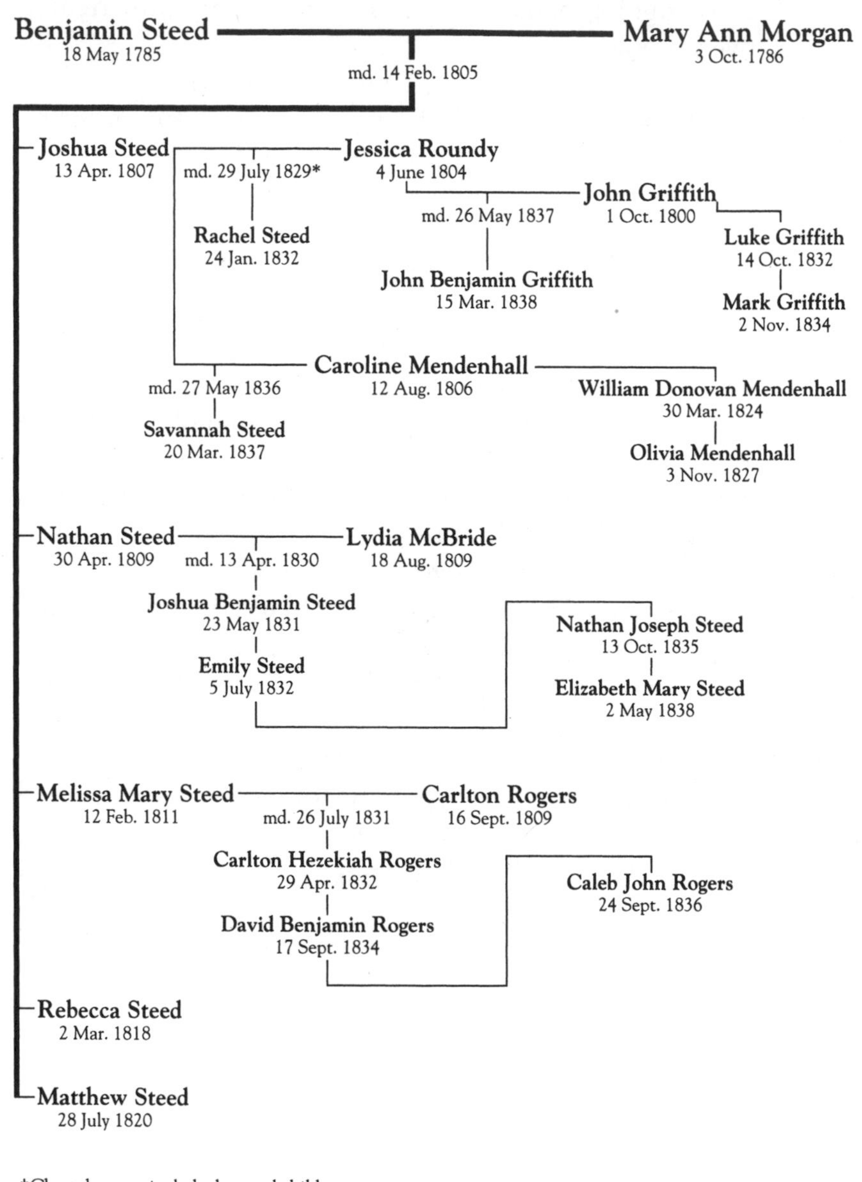

†Chart does not include deceased children
*Divorced Jan. 1833

Key to Abbreviations Used in Chapter Notes

Throughout the chapter notes, abbreviated references are given. The following key gives the full bibliographic data for those references.

American Moses	Leonard J. Arrington, *Brigham Young: American Moses* (New York: Alfred A. Knopf, 1985.)
By Their Fruits	Jeanine Fry Ricketts, comp. and ed., *By Their Fruits: A History and Genealogy of the Fry Family of Wiltshire, England, and Their Descendants, Including the Allied Lines of Harwood, Ramsden, Toomer, Thruston, Bosen, and Maddox* (Salt Lake City: Privately published, n.d.)
CHFT	*Church History in the Fulness of Times* (Salt Lake City: The Church of Jesus Christ of Latter-day Saints, 1989.)
Far West Record	*Far West Record: Minutes of The Church of Jesus Christ of Latter-day Saints, 1830–1844*, ed. Donald Q. Cannon and Lyndon W. Cook (Salt Lake City: Deseret Book Co., 1983.)
HC	Joseph Smith, *History of The Church of Jesus Christ of Latter-day Saints*, ed. B. H. Roberts, 7 vols. (Salt Lake City: The Church of Jesus Christ of Latter-day Saints, 1932–51.)

HR	Milton V. Backman, Jr., *The Heavens Resound: A History of the Latter-day Saints in Ohio, 1830–1838* (Salt Lake City: Deseret Book Co., 1983.)
JD	*Journal of Discourses*, 26 vols. (London: Latter-day Saints' Book Depot, 1854–86.)
LHCK	Orson F. Whitney, *Life of Heber C. Kimball* (1888; reprint, Salt Lake City: Bookcraft, 1992.)
Mack Hist.	Lucy Mack Smith, *History of Joseph Smith by His Mother*, ed. Preston Nibley (Salt Lake City: Bookcraft, 1954.)
MFS	Don Cecil Corbett, *Mary Fielding Smith: Daughter of Britain* (Salt Lake City: Deseret Book Co., 1966.)
Persecutions	B. H. Roberts, *The Missouri Persecutions* (1900; reprint, Salt Lake City: Bookcraft, 1965.)
PPP Auto.	Parley P. Pratt, *Autobiography of Parley P. Pratt*, ed. Parley P. Pratt, Jr. (1874; reprint, Salt Lake City: Deseret Book Co., 1985.)
Redress	*Mormon Redress Petitions: Documents of the 1833–1838 Missouri Conflict*, ed. Clark V. Johnson (Provo, Utah: Religious Studies Center, Brigham Young University, 1992.)
Restoration	Ivan J. Barrett, *Joseph Smith and the Restoration: A History of the Church to 1846* (Provo, Utah: Brigham Young University Press, 1973.)

Thy Gold to Refine

When through the deep waters I call thee to go,
The rivers of sorrow shall not thee o'erflow,
For I will be with thee, thy troubles to bless,
And sanctify to thee thy deepest distress.

When through fiery trials thy pathway shall lie,
My grace, all sufficient, shall be thy supply.
The flame shall not hurt thee; I only design
Thy dross to consume and thy gold to refine.

. . . .

The soul that on Jesus hath leaned for repose
I will not, I cannot, desert to his foes;
That soul, though all hell should endeavor to shake,
I'll never, no never, no never forsake!

—From "How Firm a Foundation"

Chapter One

Mary Ann Steed stepped out onto the small porch, slowly and carefully shutting the cabin door behind her. For a moment she stood there, letting the early-morning sunshine bathe her face, feeling the warmth of it on her skin, even though it was not yet six o'clock. Then, stepping quietly so as not to awaken those sleeping inside, she moved off the porch and out toward the front gate. She crossed the road to the split-rail fence that enclosed the pasture across from the cabin and for a moment watched the two milk cows that stood there. They gave her an inquiring look. Their udders were full to the bursting and the two animals were anxious that someone should come and relieve them.

She turned around and leaned against the rail, letting her head tip back. Off to the west a row of starchy white cumulus clouds lined up unevenly, ready to start their race eastward. She closed her eyes and breathed deeply. A gentle breeze still carried the freshness of the night. The heat and humidity of the previous three days had softened somewhat, and the Missouri prairie seemed glad for the temporary respite.

Behind her, a meadowlark began its chirping, lilting cry. She opened her eyes and turned, trying to spot it. Mary Ann had once heard Lydia tell her children that if you listened very carefully to a meadowlark's song, you could hear him singing the words, "Caldwell County is a pretty little place." As Mary Ann listened now, she smiled. The rhythm of the words did perfectly fit the bird's song. She sang along softly the next time the bird burst forth.

She straightened and turned back to face the cabin, pushing down a momentary twinge of guilt. She should be starting breakfast. It wouldn't be long before the Steeds were up, and they would be hungry. All twenty-three of them! Her mouth pulled into a wry expression. Twenty-three. That's how many were here now, if you counted Derek and Peter Ingalls as part of the family—which everyone did, especially now that Derek and Rebecca were talking about marriage in the spring.

Twenty-three! Nine of them were children under the age of ten, and two of those were infants less than six months old. And all were crunched into two one-room cabins that were crowded even without extra guests. Nor was it as though they could turn to their neighbors for help. Tomorrow was the Fourth of July. Not only were the Saints going to have a grand celebration of the nation's birthday, but Joseph had announced that they were also going to lay the cornerstones for a new temple in Far West. With the temple in Kirtland lost to the enemies of the Church, that news was greeted with great joy. Now virtually every Latter-day Saint within a radius of a hundred miles had come to town to be present. Far West was like Bethlehem on that first Christmas. Every home had two or three families crammed into it. There was not a vacant lot that wasn't filled with tents or wagons or both. Not only was there no room at the inn, there was no room anywhere!

Not that Mary Ann would have had it any other way. She reached up and touched her face, remembering a few nights back when she had stood in front of the mirror and gazed at her reflection. She would be fifty-two years old in October. The lines were starting to show around her eyes and mouth, and the first touches of gray were spreading through her hair. She was starting to look more and more like a grandma. It had come to her then, there in front of the mirror, with a clarity so sharp it hurt, how fortunate she was. Many a frontier woman never lived to see forty, let alone fifty. Childbirth, disease, accident, and sometimes just the sheer exhaustion of trying to survive took a heavy toll on the women of America. How many women had she known personally who had never had the privilege of living to see their grandchildren? She could count a dozen or so easily. No doubt those women would gladly have accepted the extra work that came with feeding and housing twenty-three people if those twenty-three were family.

No, on this day, Mary Ann had only one regret, and that was Melissa. The twenty-three could have been more if Melissa and Carl had come to Missouri with them. But Carl was not a member of the Church and had strong feelings against it. Melissa had finally backed away from her commitment to full activity—though she averred that her testimony was still as strong—in order to achieve some peace. And so when the Steeds had left Kirtland, the family had not quite been whole. That was a constant source of sadness to Mary Ann. And yet, other than that, her life was one of great gladness. One had been left in Kirtland, but now another had been found.

Gladness! Suddenly her eyes were burning. If she had died earlier—even a week ago—she would have missed the miracle. After more than a decade of tears and prayers and yearning, Joshua had returned. The son who was lost had been found. Blinking quickly to stay the tears, Mary Ann bowed her head. *I thank thee, Father. Oh, how I thank thee for this wondrous gift!*

She stood that way for several moments, letting the flood of joy infuse her soul. Then suddenly there was a soft sound off to her left and she opened her eyes. They widened in surprise. "Joshua! Good morning."

Her oldest son was nearly to her, his boots making almost no sound in the soft dust of the road. He smiled as he came up to her. He took her by the shoulders and gave her a quick kiss on the cheek. "Good morning, Mother."

"What are you doing up already? I was hoping you could sleep for a while this morning," she said. "It was so late by the time we finished talking last night."

He laughed quietly. "And Caroline and I lay there and talked for another hour or two after that."

Mary Ann's hand shot out and touched his arm. "You're not going back this morning, are you, Joshua? You can't. Not this soon. You just got here." Last night he had said something about having to get back and see to his freight business.

Joshua stood almost a full head taller than his mother. His hair, still wet from the water he had used to comb it back, was jet black and thick. He had not taken time to shave though, and so his chin was covered with the dark stubble of his heavy whiskers. He rubbed one hand across his jaw, looking a little rueful. "If I try to get my family out of here before Thursday, I'll be drawn and quartered and left on the prairie as wolf bait. No, we'll stay for tomorrow's celebrations."

Mary Ann threw her arms around him and hugged him tightly. "That's wonderful! I couldn't bear it if you turned around and left again right now." She peered up at him. "You and your father need to spend time together."

He shook his head ruefully. "We were both kind of tongue-tied last night." In all the hours of talking the family had done after Joseph Smith had finally left yesterday, there had been only limited conversation directly between Joshua and Benjamin.

Mary Ann cocked her head to one side. "Joshua, you and your father haven't spoken for a long, long time. It mustn't surprise you too much if there is still a little awkwardness there."

"I know, I know," he said quickly. She was right. There was awkwardness, but he sensed that it was more from a sense of strangeness—almost shyness—than from any residual strain between them.

He turned and leaned back against the fence as she had been doing when he first saw her. "I really wasn't very serious about going back so soon, Mother. I want to be with the family. It's been so . . ." He shook his head suddenly, his voice becoming gruff. "It's been long enough."

She slipped an arm into his, nodding, but also too touched to trust herself to speak. Finally, she cleared her throat. "How did Savannah sleep?"

Joshua chuckled. "That little imp. She was awake at the crack of dawn, wanting to go see her grandpa."

Mary Ann's eyes softened mistily. "She is so adorable, Joshua. That red hair, and those big blue eyes. You can just see her mind working quicker than a fox's."

He was smiling now too. "I've never seen her take to anyone like she has taken to Pa. Even Caroline can't believe it."

Nodding, Mary Ann looked up at him. "I was thinking about that last night. Do you know what I decided, Joshua?"

"What?"

"Heavenly Father gave you Savannah to help heal the breach between you and your father."

One eyebrow went up, but then almost immediately his head bobbed up and down. "You may be right."

Again they lapsed into silence; then finally Joshua looked around. "Everyone still asleep in there?"

"Oh, I think they're beginning to stir. Actually, I need to go in and start breakfast."

"Caroline and Lydia are getting the children up and dressed. I thought I would come help you until they can get here."

That obviously pleased her greatly. "Why, thank you, Joshua. I would like that very much."

She straightened and stepped away from him. Joshua reached out and took her hand. "How's Melissa, Mother?"

Mary Ann's shoulders lifted slightly, then fell again. "She seems to be doing fine. She married a fine man. He and his father own a livery stable in Kirtland." She faltered momentarily, then went on more quickly. "They have three wonderful little boys."

"Why didn't they come with you?"

She bit her lip. "Carl—Melissa's husband—isn't a member of the Church. As things started getting bad in Kirtland, he turned quite bitter against us. Melissa finally decided she had to let the Church go if she was going to save their marriage. I think it came as a relief to Carl when we all left to go west."

Now her head dropped slightly, and she was staring at the ground. When she spoke, her voice was barely a whisper. "If only they were here now, the family would be complete."

Joshua stepped to her and put his arm around her waist. "I've never had a need to go as far north as Cleveland," he said, "but we're often sending teams back and forth along the Ohio Turnpike. The next time I go that way, I'll detour and go up and see her."

She laid her head against his shoulder. "Melissa would like that very much, Joshua. You and she were always especially close."

He laughed softly. "She always took my side when Pa and I were battling. She would try to get me so that I wasn't so angry, but she always took my side."

"I know." She slipped her arm around his waist now as well, and they started walking slowly toward the cabin. As they reached the gate, Mary Ann stopped. Her voice grew very soft. "Do you remember little Jacob at all, Joshua?"

For a moment he looked puzzled; then it clicked. "Of course. I was about twelve when he died."

There was a long pause before she went on. "I lost four children at birth—they were either stillborn or died within a few hours after they were born—but none of those hurt so fiercely as Jacob's death. We had him for four precious years. He was such a wonderful little boy, with his long blond hair and sparkling blue eyes." She laughed lightly. "You and Nathan used to tease him mercilessly, and he loved it."

"I remember. What was it he died from?"

She shrugged. "Pneumonia probably. It was an early, terrible winter. We couldn't get the doctor out in time to help him."

She looked away, her hand dropping away from his waist. "I sat and held him while he died."

She turned back now and looked up at her son. To his surprise, she was smiling. It was radiant, and all the more so because it shone through the glistening in her eyes. "But that pain was nothing compared to losing you."

"Mother, I—"

She reached up quickly and put her hand over his mouth. "For eleven years you were as dead to me as little Jacob. And now God has brought you back to us. If I were to die this moment, I would die a happy woman. Thank you, Joshua."

He started to speak, but she laughed lightly and took him by the hand. "Come on," she said. "We've got some cooking to do."

Jessica Griffith sat in a rocking chair on the narrow front porch of the Steed cabin, humming softly to the infant sleeping peacefully in her arms. The family had dispersed after breakfast. Rebecca and Derek had finished the breakfast dishes and gone for a walk, hands entwined and heads close together as they moved away. The other men had gone to the northern outskirts of the city to help one of the new settlers put up a barn. Lydia's baby was asleep inside, and so she and Mary Ann and Caroline had gone to the center of town to see if there was any mail or any new arrivals at the dry goods store. The children had trooped after them, excited to be together and hoping for a piece of rock candy or maybe even a licorice stick.

Being alone, Jessica had come out into the fresh air to nurse little John Benjamin. He quickly fell asleep, but she did not get up. She was grateful for the chance to have a quiet, undisturbed moment with him. Smiling, eyes filled with love, she reached down and gently stroked his cheek with the back of her finger.

A movement out of the corner of her eye brought her head around. Peter Ingalls was standing at the corner of the cabin, his hands behind him. "Why, hello, Peter," she said in surprise. "I thought you left with the others."

He shook his head, not moving except to shift his weight back and forth between his two feet. He gave her a tentative smile, then ducked his head. With a quick flash of insight, Jessica realized he wanted to speak with her. "Come sit down, Peter. Get out of the sun."

Eagerly Peter moved toward her and sat down on the step, not caring that he was still in the sun. Jessica saw that he was holding a sheet of paper in his hand but half trying to keep it out of sight behind his back. She smiled to herself, sensing that asking him about it too quickly would not be wise. "Tell me about Adam-ondi-Ahman, Peter. Do you like it?"

"Oh, yes, Jessica. It's lovely."

His face had lit up, and his blue eyes danced with pleasure. Even though he was now fourteen, there was still a boyishness about him that Jessica loved. His face would always have a youthful look about it, and one shock of his thick, dark hair was continually falling down into his eyes. It did so again now, and he brushed at it impatiently, barely aware that he had done it. His skin was a deep brown and slightly freckled from the sun. That made her smile. When he and Derek had first arrived from Kirtland the previous December, they both were so pale they almost looked sickly. Now that was gone completely, and Peter looked as healthy as a young colt.

"Is your house finished?" Jessica asked.

"No. We're living in it now, but we've spent a lot of time getting the land ready for planting. Grandpa Steed says he thinks we ought to put in winter wheat so we'll have an earlier crop next summer."

She nodded and they talked on, Peter enthusiastically describing the work they were doing and the joy he and Derek had in owning land in America. Jessica was surprised at how much affection she felt for this lad with the wonderful British accent. He was truly part of their family.

Finally, in a lull in the conversation, Peter began to fidget again. "May I ask you a question, Jessica?" he asked after a few moments.

"Of course, Peter. What is it?"

"Matthew says you teach school."

"Yes. Well, actually I go around to people's homes and teach their children. We don't have a schoolhouse in Haun's Mill yet."

"Oh." He took a quick breath and let it out slowly. "We have a school in Di-Ahman."

"Yes, I heard. I heard that Sister Brownley is teaching it."

"Yes, but it's only for the younger children."

Then Jessica understood. "Would you like to go to school, Peter?"

"Oh, yes," he breathed. "I went to the factory school in England until Derek and me were fired."

"And you loved to learn, didn't you." Jessica didn't make it a question. The answer was too obvious.

"Yes." He looked down, rubbing a smooth place in the dirt with the toe of his boot. "I . . . I was wondering . . ." He shook his head, and she could see that color had filled his cheeks.

"You were wondering if I might teach you, Peter?"

His head jerked up. "Yes," he burst out. "I know we won't get to see each other very much, but if you could tell me what to do, I'd study real hard at night, after the work is done."

"I would very much like that, Peter. Very much."

"Really?" His eyes were wide, almost disbelieving.

"Yes, really. I wish I had brought some of my books with me, but let me put the baby down and we'll talk about some things you can do until we see each other again."

He nodded happily as she carefully stood and took the baby in the house. She laid him down and covered him with a light blanket. After she was sure he wasn't going to awaken, she stepped to the other cradle. Elizabeth Mary had been born to Lydia and Nathan just six weeks after Jessica's baby. She too was still sleeping soundly, so Jessica turned and went quietly back out.

As she came out on the porch again, Peter jerked up. He had been reading the paper. Now he lowered it, looking embarrassed.

"Have you written something, Peter?"

"I . . ." Impulsively he held it out toward her. "I've written a poem."

Jessica nodded, taking it from him with the same amount of gravity in her face as he showed. "A poem? That's wonderful, Peter. May I read it?"

He nodded, the shyness making him seem more like he was ten than fourteen.

She brought the paper up. Two things struck her almost immediately. He had written it in cursive, but it was neat and clearly legible. More impressive, the words were correctly spelled. In frontier America, even many adults spelled out things as they sounded when spoken rather than as they were properly written—*whare* for *where*, *Missuri* for *Missouri*, *mooveing* for *moving*, and so on.

And then as Jessica began to read what Peter had written, she forgot all about the handwriting and the spelling.

Home

Softer than a kitten's step,
Dawn steals across Diahman's plain;
Wondrous as a secret kept,
A new day paints the broad terrain.

Tree and flower, fox and fawn,
All now share in Adam's home;
Fish in crystal waters spawn,
Geese and duck the heavens roam.

England had its beauties fair:
Meadow, river, glade, and tree,
And misty morns with frosty air;
But man and boy were never free.

'Tis no surprise that Adam came
And built these altars with his hand.
Now English lads kneel at the same
And call this place their motherland.

She lowered the paper slowly, looking at him with wide eyes. Peter was watching her anxiously. "Is it all right, Jessica? You can tell me true." Before she could answer, he went on in a rush. "There are some things I don't like. The second line, about dawn stealing across the plain, the rhythm isn't exactly right. It sounds funny and . . ."

He faltered as Jessica stepped up to him. She was still staring at him in wonder. She laid her hand on his shoulder. "Peter, I would consider it a very special honor to be your schoolteacher."

Olivia Mendenhall would turn eleven years old in November. She still had the look of a young girl, but even now there were things in her appearance that held out the promise of what she would look like when adolescence passed and she matured. She was going to be tall and slender like her mother. And she also had her mother's hair—inside in dim light it looked dark brown, almost brunette, but when she was out in the sun, the reddish highlights gleamed like burnished copper. Olivia knew her hair was the envy of many of her friends, so she wore it long and straight and brushed it every morning till it glowed. She refused to wear a bonnet except on the hottest of days. She also had her mother's eyes. They were large and round and green as a field of new corn, but flecked with light brown in spots.

It would have been easy for her to take pride in her appearance, for she keenly sensed that she was a very pretty girl. She loved to stand before the full-length mirror Joshua had bought for her and examine how her clothes fit, or make sure her hair was just right. But Caroline constantly reminded her that outer beauty was a gift of God, for which she should be ever thankful, but that what mattered most was to be beautiful inside. Olivia accepted that, and believed it. But she was also very glad God had chosen to make her pretty on the outside too. What she did not yet fully appreciate was the fact that once womanhood came, she was going to be remarkably beautiful.

She was outside the dry goods store waiting for the others to finish. Surprisingly, she had tired quickly of the shopping, something not in character for her, and had come outside and sat down on a barrel of dried cod that sat on the porch. For a girl of not quite eleven, there were heavy things weighing on her mind.

She looked up as the door opened and Lydia came out. She had a small bag with some material for a dress for Emily. She smiled at Olivia. "They're still not finished in there, but I'm afraid Elizabeth Mary is going to be waking up. I'm going to go on back."

Olivia felt a little jump of excitement. She needed to talk with someone, but was very much concerned that if she shared her problem with the wrong person, that person might misunderstand, and that would be devastating. She stood up quickly. She felt a special bond with Lydia. "Can I go with you, Aunt Lydia?"

Lydia was tying the ribbons of her bonnet beneath her chin. She turned. "Don't you want to stay with the others? I think they're going to go to a couple of other stores as well."

Olivia shook her head. "No, I'm ready to go home."

Lydia eyed her sharply. "Are you feeling all right?"

"I'm fine. I'm just"—she shrugged—"bored. Please?"

Lydia laughed. "That's fine. Stick your head inside and tell your mother. I'd love to have some company."

It was only about a ten-minute walk back to the house, so Olivia plunged in as soon as they were away from the store. "Aunt Lydia?"

"Yes, Livvy?"

"I would like to speak with you about something."

Surprised at the adultness of Olivia's tone, Lydia looked down at her in surprise. "All right."

"You've got to promise not to tell anyone."

Lydia suppressed a smile. "All right, I promise."

Suddenly the adult was gone and it was all little girl again. Her hand flashed back and forth across her chest. "Cross your heart and hope to die, poke a stick in your eye?"

Lydia laughed aloud. She emulated Olivia's movement with her hand. "Yes, cross my heart and hope to die. I won't tell a soul."

"Good." Olivia's chest rose and fell. Now that the moment had come, she wasn't sure she had the courage. Lydia walked more slowly, watching Olivia out of the corner of her eye, not wanting to push but fully curious now.

"Is it all right . . . I mean, can a person . . ." Olivia shook her head, her cheeks coloring.

"What, Livvy? It's all right. Just ask me straight out."

Olivia swallowed once, then blurted it out. "Can relatives ever marry each other?"

Lydia stopped walking, staring at her in surprise.

"I mean, I know they can, but is it all right? Sometimes people say they shouldn't and . . ."

Lydia was smiling broadly now. "Are you thinking about Matthew?" she asked softly.

Olivia blushed even more deeply and looked away quickly. But there was a quick bob of her head.

Lydia was sorely tempted to laugh right out loud at that. The whole family had noticed that Olivia was totally smitten with Matthew. She followed him around, hung upon his every word, watched him with sad, longing eyes, and tried not to act hurt when he seemed not to notice any of those things. But Lydia knew this was not a laughing matter to Olivia, so she kept her face impassive and spoke gravely. "Some people say it's not a wise thing to do, Livvy. Especially for close relatives, like first cousins."

Olivia turned back. "*First* cousins? What's that?"

"When brothers and sisters in a family have children, the children are first cousins to each other. So Emily and Rachel are first cousins."

"What about others?"

Lydia reached out and took Olivia's hand and began to walk again, moving slowly now. "Most people would consider it improper for an uncle to marry his niece or for an aunt to marry her nephew."

Olivia's face fell. "Oh."

Lydia squeezed her hand. "However, in your case Matthew is only your stepuncle."

Olivia's head snapped up. "My stepuncle?"

"Yes. That means you're related only through marriage. Like Joshua is your stepfather. If Joshua were your real father, then Matthew would be your real uncle, but he's not. Actually you're not really related to each other at all. Not by blood."

"Really? Then it would be all right?" Olivia nearly shouted it.

Again keeping her voice very serious, Lydia nodded. "In that way it would. But there might be other problems."

It barely registered. Olivia's face was infused with joy. An insolvable problem had just been resolved.

"Matthew's seven years older than you, Olivia."

"I know," Olivia said defensively, "but I'll wait for him until I'm old enough to marry. That's only a little over five years away."

Lydia nodded sagely. "I see. You plan to marry at sixteen, then?"

There was not a moment's hesitation. "Yes."

Lydia smiled. How simple was life to a child!

The weight had been lifted from Olivia's shoulders. She began to walk more swiftly now, moving out ahead of Lydia. There was almost a skip to her step. Then she turned around, walking backwards so she could face her aunt. "You promised not to tell."

"I did. And I won't tell a soul."

"Not even Mama?"

"Not even your mother."

Olivia's lips pulled into a pout. "I told Will the other night and he laughed at me. He said Matthew would be married long before I turn sixteen."

"That's possible, Livvy," Lydia said gently. "He's nearly eighteen now. Some young men are married by his age already."

Olivia frowned, brushing that aside. "But some don't get married until they're old. Like twenty-five or twenty-six."

"That's true," Lydia chuckled.

"Will said I was being stupid. Do you think I'm being stupid, Aunt Lydia?"

"No, Olivia, I think you are being wise beyond your years. And very, very sweet."

By three o'clock that afternoon, the last of the roof planking was put into place and fastened with wooden tenons and mortises. The roof shingles and some of the finish work—framing in the windows and hanging the doors—would have to wait until Thursday, after the Independence Day celebrations, but the heavy work was done.

The Steed men stood together, eyeing their handiwork and relaxing for a moment before they started home. Matthew and Will Mendenhall were off to one side talking quietly. John Griffith had seen a family from Haun's Mill and gone over to say hello. Benjamin, Joshua, and Nathan stood around the water bucket, their tools in their hands or at their feet. Brother Alexander Cope, whose barn it was, was shaking hands all around, thanking everyone profusely for their assistance.

As Cope moved on to the other men, Joseph and Hyrum Smith appeared from around one corner of the barn. They had been working a two-man saw out back cutting the planks. It seemed like that was the job they always drew. Brigham Young said they were the best sawing team west of New York City. Joseph had the long blade balanced on one shoulder, and it bounced up and down with a soft, metallic hum as he walked. When he saw the Steeds they changed direction and came over.

"A good day's work, I'd say," Joseph said, looking at the barn.

"Agreed," said Benjamin. "Brother Cope should have it finished in plenty of time to get some meadow hay in before winter."

"We especially appreciate your help, Joshua," Hyrum said with a laugh. "Hardly seems fair that a man comes north to see his family and gets put to work building someone else's barn."

Joshua was shaking his head even before Hyrum finished. "Don't apologize. It's been almost a dozen years since I had the chance to work alongside my father and brother." He looked at Benjamin. "It feels good again."

Benjamin nodded, meeting and holding his gaze. "Very good," he murmured.

Then Joshua shot a quick glance at Nathan. "Besides, things haven't changed much. Nathan still doesn't pull his full weight unless I'm there to see to it."

"Oh ho!" Nathan cried. He slapped his stomach, which was flat and hard. "It's not the little brother who's become a rich businessman and gone soft in the belly from too little grunt work."

Joshua sucked in his gut with exaggerated effort. "Don't know what you're talking about."

Will and Matthew came over to join them. Will was grinning. He jabbed playfully, touching his father's waist. "Want some help, Pa?"

Joshua whirled and took a swipe at him, missing by a yard as Will jumped back with a yelp and a laugh.

"My own son, even," Joshua grumbled. "It's bad enough to have your brother insult you, but my own son . . ."

As the laughter subsided, Joseph turned to Joshua. "Ben says you're going to stay over for the celebration tomorrow."

"Yes. We won't leave until Thursday morning."

"Good. How would you and your wife like to come over to our house for supper tonight?"

Joshua's jaw dropped slightly. "I . . ."

"Emma would like to meet you again. She was thrilled when I told her all that has happened with your family and you."

"Uh . . ." He didn't know what to say. Joseph had completely stunned him.

"If you're worrying about old times in Palmyra, don't give it a second thought. Neither Emma nor I hold a grudge."

That took him aback even more. Back in Palmyra, in 1827, Joshua had turned quite sour about Joseph Smith and his so-called "experiences." He had not been too reticent about expressing those feelings to Joseph. One day in the village there had been a confrontation with Emma—some of the local toughs trying to give her a bad time. Joshua had been there, not really taking the lead but not doing anything to stop it either. And then there had been the night when Joseph had gone for the golden plates. Joshua had been waiting in the woods for him, and there had been an exchange of blows. That was the same night Joshua had left Palmyra, but he was pretty sure that Emma knew that it had been him who had jumped Joseph in the woods.

Joshua wasn't worried now about Joseph's feelings. When he and Nathan had come to Far West from Independence the day previous, with the intent to reunite Joshua with his family for the first time in eleven years, Nathan had gone straight to Joseph for help. And Joseph had been amazing. There wasn't the slightest hint of any bad feelings. Instead, Joseph had made them wait while he called the Steed family together and talked with them about forgiveness and acceptance. Then he had called Joshua in. It had made all the difference and paved the way for the marvelous reunion which had taken place between Joshua and his father.

But Emma. Joshua was embarrassed at the thoughts of having to face her again after how he had treated her.

"It's true, Joshua," Nathan said softly. "There aren't any bad feelings. Emma is a wonderful woman. She and Lydia have become the best of friends."

"That's right," Joseph boomed. "Shall we say seven o'clock, then?"

"Well, I . . . I'll have to talk with Caroline."

"She'll come," Joseph said with confidence. He turned to Will. "You tell your mother to bring you and your sisters too. Emma especially wants to meet this little red-headed girl who has Benjamin Steed bragging about her all over town."

Holding on to the saw with one hand to steady it, Joseph reached out and clapped Joshua on the arm. "Till seven, then." And he and Hyrum strode away, leaving Joshua to stare after them.

Chapter Two

"Grandpa! Make them hurry. We're gonna miss the Fourth of July parade."

Benjamin looked down at Emily and smiled, pulling away from his thoughts. "What was that, Emmy?"

"We're gonna be late. Go in and tell Mama to hurry up." Her hands were on her hips, and her head was cocked to one side. She would celebrate her sixth birthday on the morrow, but sometimes she seemed much older than that. Her dark eyes were crackling with impatience, and her mouth was drawn into a pout. At times like this she looked so much like Lydia, with her jet black hair and her large brown eyes and the long lashes that fluttered like a debutante's, that it always made her grandfather smile. He fought to keep it from broadening. "They're coming, Emmy," he soothed. "Your papa is helping your mother get the baby dressed."

"Papa said the soldiers were gonna be first," she wailed. "I don't want to miss the soldiers."

"Yeah, Grandpa." Young Joshua, just fourteen months older than his sister, was usually much more mature, but now there was a touch of petulance on his face too. "Pa says there's gonna be cavalry. We can't miss that."

"Children, children," Benjamin laughed. "We have plenty of time. We're not going to miss anything."

Emily's face mirrored sharp disappointment. There were sacred responsibilities here that were not being fulfilled. With a toss of her head and a sniff of disgust, she stomped away. "I'll just get them myself."

Her brother gave his grandfather a sharp, challenging look, but when it was obvious he wasn't going to take action he spun on his heel. "Wait, Emmy, I'm coming too."

Joshua came out of the cabin just as Emily and young Joshua came stalking toward him. He stepped aside, holding the door for his niece and nephew. His look was one of faint surprise, then amusement. Emily didn't so much as give him a passing glance. "Mama!" came the plaintive cry as she entered the cabin. "Hurry up!"

The elder Joshua saw his father. There was a momentary look of surprise, and then he walked over to join him. "Where's Mother?"

"Helping Jessica get the picnic lunch ready. I thought I'd come and see if I could hurry things along here, but the children said you were nearly ready, so I thought I'd just wait out here."

Joshua nodded, then turned to look back at the cabin. "What's the matter with Emily?"

Benjamin chuckled softly. "She thinks she's going to miss the parade."

Joshua laughed now too. "She is so excited. She was up at six and has been cracking the whip over us ever since. I think I'm going to take her back to Independence with me and make her one of my drivers."

"She's a strong-willed one, that's for sure."

Joshua nodded. "It serves Lydia right to get one who's just like her."

Just then Caroline came out the door. Will was with her, carrying Savannah in his arms. For a moment they squinted at the brightness of the sunshine, then saw the two men standing near the front gate. Savannah saw them too, for instantly she held out her arms and started crying, "Gampa! Gampa!"

Pleased more than a little, Benjamin dropped to one knee as Will put her down and Savannah raced to him and threw herself into his arms. He hugged her tightly and nuzzled his face in against her cheek. "Hello, little sweetheart." He scooped her up and stood to face Caroline.

"Mornin', Caroline. Mornin', Will. Are you ready for a great day?"

"*I* am," Will said in disgust. "If we can ever get Olivia to stop primping."

Caroline rolled her eyes in mock despair. "The curse of the Steed men—waiting for the women in the family to make themselves presentable."

"Well," her son grumbled, "she's been in front of the mirror all morning."

Benjamin smiled gravely. "After a time, Will, one learns patience."

Joshua laid a hand on his stepson's shoulder. "Speaking of the Steed men, Will made me a very happy man yesterday afternoon."

"Oh? Why's that?" Benjamin asked.

Caroline was watching her oldest closely now, her eyes filled with warm pride and affection. "Do you want to tell Grandpa, Will?"

Will pulled back his shoulders as he turned to his grandfather. "Olivia and me, we want to be adopted so Pa is our real pa. We want to become Steeds."

"Really?" Benjamin exclaimed.

"Yes," Will said simply. "We're gonna do it as soon as we get back to Independence."

Benjamin started to speak, then had to blink quickly. Finally he cleared his throat. "What a wonderful thing," he said quietly. "Then that means you'll really be my grandson."

Will was beaming. "Yes, Grandpa. I would like that."

"I would like that too," Benjamin said. "Very much."

"It is a wonderful present for us," Caroline said, stepping to Will and giving him a quick hug. "It has made us very happy."

"Very happy," Joshua murmured, looking deep into the boy's eyes.

Embarrassed a little now by the depth of their emotions, they fell quiet. Benjamin finally turned and looked toward the cabin. "Are they about ready in there?"

Caroline nodded. "The baby spit up, so Lydia had to change her again, but they should be right out."

Again they fell silent. Then, after a moment, Benjamin gave Joshua a sideward glance. "How did it go last night?"

Both Joshua and Caroline spoke together. "It was fine," he said. "It was wonderful," was her response.

"Joseph has a very nice family," Joshua went on. "They're very well-behaved children. I was impressed."

"And Emma," Caroline broke in, "what a lovely and gracious woman!"

"Yes, she is, isn't she?" Benjamin agreed, with relief. He took his coin purse from his pocket and held it out for Savannah. She took it and began turning it over and over, intrigued by the soft clinking of the coins and the shifting weight within it. Finally he looked up again. "Young Joshua said you didn't get home until late."

Caroline laughed. "Yes. It was nearly ten o'clock. I couldn't believe it. Joseph and Emma made us feel so comfortable, we just talked and talked."

"Oh." He kept his voice casual and disinterested. "What did you talk about?"

Joshua hooted softly at his father. "All right, you win. Joseph didn't try to preach at us."

Benjamin nodded in satisfaction. After they had returned

home the previous afternoon and Joshua told Caroline about the invitation, Joshua started waffling about going. After the role Joseph had played in reuniting Joshua with his family, Joshua was sure Joseph was going to try and get him converted to Mormonism and make the reconciliation complete. The whole family had protested, vowing that Joseph was not that way, but Joshua hadn't believed them. Joshua owed Joseph big. It was too good an opportunity for Joseph to pass up. And so the argument had seesawed back and forth until Caroline stood up, gave Joshua a long look, and said simply, "Joshua, we *are* going, and that settles the matter."

"Joseph's not that way," Benjamin said now. "He really respects a person's right to believe what he wishes. Or not to believe, for that matter."

"Well, there was one point where he talked religion," Joshua said.

"Only because I asked him a question," Caroline retorted.

"What question was that?" Benjamin asked.

Caroline suddenly looked a little embarrassed. "Some of the people down in Jackson County say that Joseph Smith claims to be God. I didn't want to offend him, but I asked him if that was true."

"I'll bet he laughed right out loud at that," Benjamin chortled.

Caroline was a little surprised. "Yes, that's exactly what he did. He wasn't offended at all."

"And so, what else did he say?"

"I know it's silly, but since everyone calls you Mormons, I've just thought all along that was the name of your church. He told us that was a nickname, from your Book of Mormon, that the full name of the Church is The Church of Jesus Christ of Latter-day Saints. He then got very serious. He said that name was very important, because it showed that this was Christ's church. It isn't Joseph's church. He is only the Lord's prophet, called to direct his work on the earth. Christ is the head of it and the center of all you believe."

Joshua was frowning slightly by the time she finished, but Caroline was not looking at him and did not notice. Benjamin was pleased with the fact that even now as she retold the conversation, she seemed impressed with what Joseph had told them. "That is exactly how we believe," he said earnestly. "We love Brother Joseph, but we worship the Lord."

Caroline now seemed to sense Joshua's disapproval. "But," she went on, "once he had answered my question, the subject of religion did not come up again."

"No," Joshua admitted grudgingly. "He really was a very pleasant and thoughtful host."

"He's one of the most congenial men I've ever met," Caroline said. "It was a delightful evening."

"Good," Benjamin said. He was silent for a moment, then turned to his son. When he spoke, his voice was musing. "Joseph made a most unusual statement here a month or so ago. It really shocked us."

"What was that?"

"He said that before this year was over, one of the elders of the Church would have the opportunity to preach a gospel sermon in Jackson County once again."

"Really?" Caroline blurted.

"Yes. I find it difficult to understand how that could be, given the current situation, but . . ." He shrugged.

Joshua opened his mouth, but just then the door to the cabin opened and Emily came out leading the rest of the family. As they all called out their greetings to Benjamin, Joshua stepped close to his father.

"Pa," he said in a low voice, "you know I don't hold any bad feelings for Joseph anymore."

Benjamin's head came around quickly. "Yes, I know that."

"So tell him from me, as a friend now, that that would not be a good idea. They'll kill any Mormon who steps foot across the river."

By the summer of 1838, the Mormon population in northern Missouri had passed five or six thousand people. That number went up almost daily as the Saints from branches of the Church in the South and the East and from Canada left their homes to join the main body of the Saints. Lying about sixty miles north of Jackson County, Far West was the largest city, with almost half of all the Mormons living there. But other settlements, like Adam-ondi-Ahman to the north in Daviess County and Haun's Mill out to the east, were growing rapidly as well. And more and more homesteads were springing up out on the open prairie.

Joshua Steed had come through Far West for the first time in April. He had been surprised then. The newspapers talked about the rapid growth of the Mormons in the north, but he had not been prepared to see a whole city sprung up on what had been, just a few months earlier, empty countryside. Since his arrival on Monday, the surprise had deepened even further. In the three months since his last visit, there had been visible and startling growth. Buildings were going up everywhere. Lumber wagons rattled past constantly. The sounds of hammer and saw were almost omnipresent. And in any direction one looked, the long prairie grass had surrendered to the plow. The Mormons were transforming this portion of the Great Plains into a garden spot.

But even after having witnessed all that, Joshua was still dumbfounded by what he was seeing now. As the Steed family moved slowly toward the end of the main street that had been designated as the assembly point, it was as if they had become part of some vast tributary system in which every spring and fountain, every rivulet, brook, and creek were feeding into a growing stream of people, combining and joining and swelling until they became one mighty river of humanity. There was no way to estimate accurately, but he guessed that virtually every one of those five or six thousand people was converging on Far West this morning.

Somehow Joshua had gotten it into his mind that Mormons

all carried a dreary sameness about them. Now he saw how far from the truth that notion was. There were the tall and there were the short. There were the lean and the plump. Some had hair as black as tar; others were as blond as bleached muslin. Most of the faces were pleasant and wreathed with smiles, but here and there he saw the pinched look of the worriers, the scowls of the perpetual whiners, and the deeply lined faces of those who had seen sorrow and tragedy.

They came as families for the most part, with children as numerous as chicks in the barnyard. They came in wagons and they came on foot. They came with shoes and they came without. Some were clothed in store-bought or tailor-made suits; others sported homespun shirts and deer-hide suspenders. They wore sunburned faces and cracked lips, calluses thick as a twenty-dollar gold piece, pants worn shiny at the knees, or dresses which had been washed and ironed and patched, then washed and ironed again.

Joshua turned to Caroline in wonder. "Can you believe this? I always thought Jackson County drew a crowd for the Fourth of July, but this . . ." He swept out one arm, trying to take it all in.

Caroline was equally impressed. "We never saw the likes of it in Georgia either."

Nathan and Lydia were walking beside Joshua and Caroline. Lydia carried the baby. Nathan held young Nathan in his arms. Lydia leaned forward so she could see Joshua. "Remember, it's not just the holiday bringing them in."

"Oh, yes," Caroline said, "the laying of the cornerstones. I'd forgotten that."

Joshua nodded but didn't answer. In actuality, he would have been much more pleased if it were only the Fourth of July celebration. The thoughts of being in the middle of a religious service left him feeling a little uneasy.

Matthew, Peter, and Will were walking on the other side of Joshua and Caroline. Matthew joined in the conversation. "But they're not all Mormons," he said. "I expect 'bout every man, woman, and child in the county has come in." He grinned, his blue eyes filled with fun. "Up here, there's not much going on, so the old settlers will even come in for a Mormon party."

"Oh," Rebecca cried, pointing, "there's Mary Smith."

"Who?" Derek asked, looking around, trying to see who it was she had singled out of this sea of people.

"Hyrum's wife, Mary Smith. Come on, I want to say hello to her." She took him by the hand and looked back over her shoulder at her mother. "We'll meet you by the temple site."

Derek pulled a face. Since word had gone out about his and Rebecca's engagement, he had been dragged off by Rebecca and Mary Ann to more than one introduction where he then stood around feeling like a fool while the women talked about him as if he were an ox on display at the sale yard. He definitely did not find these to be enjoyable encounters.

Sensing his reluctance, Rebecca tugged on his hand. "Come on, you old stick-in-the-mud," she laughed. "Mary's not going to bite you."

"I know that. It's just that—"

"She's British too, you know."

"She is?"

"Yes. She and her sister moved to Canada to live with their brother. She was one of those that Nathan and Parley Pratt converted on their mission to Toronto."

"Oh," he said, brightening a little. "Mary Fielding. Her brother is Joseph Fielding. He came to England with Elder Kimball and Elder Hyde."

"Yes. He's still over there in fact."

Derek felt a little better now. "I've seen her once or twice since coming here, but I've never really met her."

"Well, now you will. Even though they are quite a bit older than me, when she and her sister Mercy came to Kirtland from Canada last summer, we became best friends." She was searching the crowd now. "There she is." She raised a hand and started waving. "Mary! Mary!"

Mary Fielding had been thirty-six and destined in everyone's mind to be an old maid when she moved to Kirtland in the summer of 1837. Attractive and well educated, she became a live-in governess for some of the more well-to-do families in the city. Then in October, while Hyrum and Joseph were out of state on Church business, Hyrum Smith's wife, Jerusha, died eleven days following the birth of their sixth child. A few days after the two brothers returned in mid-December, while Hyrum was still grieving over his loss, Joseph said it was the Lord's will that Hyrum marry the English convert. Stunned but obedient, Hyrum had sought her out and explained what had happened. No less shocked than Hyrum, Mary Fielding nevertheless believed Joseph was a prophet and accepted the will of the Lord. She and Hyrum were married a few days later on Christmas Eve.

She was a relatively tall woman, with long dark hair that she usually wore pulled back and tied in a bun at the crown of her head. A woman of unshakable faith and deep spiritual leanings, she was seen by many as somewhat somber of nature. But those, like Rebecca, who knew her well knew that beneath the outward English reserve was a keen—though dry—wit; a natural love for life; a penchant for rollicking fun, given the right setting and group; and a warm compassion for those in need. In the six months since her marriage, she had won the respect and love of most of the Saints in Caldwell County.

The two women hugged each other tightly as Derek watched. The crowd flowed around them. Derek heard a few people grumble at the blockage of their movement, but when they saw who it was, they smiled and called out their greetings.

"Where are the children?" Rebecca asked as they fell into step with one another, Derek right behind, and began to move with the crowd.

"Mother Smith has the baby. The others are with Joseph's children and Eliza." Eliza Snow lived with the Smiths and helped Emma care for the children. Mary stuck out her stomach, which Derek now saw was quite round, and patted it firmly. "I guess they thought my carrying one baby was enough for right now."

"How are you feeling, Mary?"

There was a soft chuckle, nearly lost in the noise of the crowd. "Very heavy with child. And I've still got four more months to go. Or maybe I should say, four more months to grow."

Derek was content to tag along. He was listening carefully to Mary's voice. It felt wonderful to hear English spoken properly again. When Mary suddenly stopped and took him by the arm, it startled him. Immediately she pulled him across the stream of people until they were out of the main flow.

"There now," she said soberly, "let's get a look at this man you have reeled in for yourself, Sister Rebecca."

Rebecca giggled a little at Derek's dismayed expression. "Mary, this is Derek Ingalls, my fiancé. Derek, this is Mary Fielding Smith."

"How do you do?" Derek said, extending his hand.

Mary took it and curtsied slightly. "Very well, thank you." She stepped back, looking him up and down with unabashed directness. Derek blushed as Rebecca took his hand, smiling and waiting for the verdict.

Finally, Mary gave one curt nod. "My congratulations, Rebecca. While I find these North Americans to be an acceptable lot for the most part—my husband being one of the best, of course—you have shown wisdom beyond your tender years by selecting a man privileged-born in the mother country. Very wise. Very wise indeed."

Derek was startled. Then, as Rebecca laughed happily, he realized he was being teased—and being approved.

"I understand you're from Preston, in Lancashire, where my uncle James has a congregation."

"Yes," Derek said. Then, emboldened, he cocked his head to one side, as though listening to her more carefully. "And I would dare say you're from Bedfordshire."

Mary clapped her hands. "Well done, sir. You are absolutely correct. I was born in the hamlet of Honidon. You have a good ear."

"My brother and I lived in Bedfordshire for a time, before we came to Preston."

She sized him up and down one more time, this time with open approval in her eyes. Then she turned to Rebecca. "You have done very well for yourself, Miss Rebecca Steed. He's a handsome lad, this one."

Rebecca slipped her arm through Derek's, who was now blushing furiously. "I know, Mary," she said. "I know."

Caroline once again found herself impressed. At first it hadn't seemed possible that order could be brought out of the milling ocean of people, but at ten minutes to the hour of ten, Joseph Smith climbed up on a box and began shouting instructions. Immediately design began to impose itself upon chaos and the procession started to form.

"You know the order of march, brothers and sisters," Joseph was saying. "Everyone take your place."

First came the infantry, meaning those in the militia who did not have horses. There were no uniforms, and their weapons represented a diversity of arms. One or two of the men even carried muskets that dated back to Colonial times. They lined up in semi-neat rows with some good-natured jostling for positions. But uniforms or no, Lydia's Emily was so excited to see them, she kept running back and forth, looking up into their faces and calling back excitedly to her parents.

Immediately behind the infantry, a distinguished-looking older gentleman took his place, standing all alone. It was instantly obvious from the comments among the crowd and the few calls to him that he was held in great respect and deference.

Lydia leaned over to Caroline. "That's Joseph Smith, Senior, Joseph's father. He's the Patriarch to the Church."

"Patriarch?"

Lydia laughed. "I keep forgetting that we Mormons sometimes have a language of our own. I'll try to explain it later to you. It's just an important office in the Church."

"Look," young Joshua cried, "there's Brother Joseph and Brother Hyrum."

"Sure enough," Nathan said.

Benjamin had Savannah up on his shoulders. He turned to Joshua and Caroline. "Brother Joseph was elected president of the day's festivities; Hyrum is vice president."

"They look alike, don't they?" Will Mendenhall said.

"Yes, very much so," his mother agreed.

"The man in the blue suit," Benjamin went on, "that's Sidney Rigdon. He's the orator for the day. He'll speak to us after the cornerstones are laid. The man behind him is Reynolds Cahoon. He's the chief marshal. The others are assistant marshals and the clerk for the day."

Savannah babbled something and reached out for her mother. Caroline took her and gave her a quick hug. Nathan picked up where his father had left off. "The next group is the Quorum of the Twelve. They are the Apostles for the Church. After that, you—"

Olivia, always the practical one and always one to speak her mind, looked up to her uncle. "But I only count eight."

"Olivia!" Will said quickly, embarrassed by his sister's boldness.

She gave a toss of her head, causing her hair to flash as it rippled in the sunlight. "Well, I do. Uncle Nathan said there were twelve."

Nathan laughed. "You are exactly right, Livvy. There are only eight." Then he sobered. "Sadly enough, in the problems that arose in Kirtland, even some of those closest to Joseph turned on him. Four members of the Quorum of the Twelve were excommunicated." He looked at Olivia. "That means they left the Church. So now there are only eight. Joseph is in the process of selecting replacements for them now."

"Oh."

Mary Ann smiled. "You're very observant, Olivia."

"Sometimes she's very impudent, too," Will growled.

Before Olivia could retort to that, a cry rang out. It was Joseph Smith. "It's ten a.m. Let the procession begin."

Instantly a cheer went up. Someone beyond their sight started beating a measured cadence on a bass drum. Then suddenly band music began. It was noticeably rough, but it was band music nevertheless. Joshua was surprised. He swung around to his father. "You have your own band?"

Benjamin grinned, trying not to look too pleased. "It's not much yet, but yes, we have a band. Only four or five instruments, but as you can hear, we also have a drum." He looked at the children. "And you can't have a parade without a drum now, can you?"

There was a chorus of assent. Jessica's daughter, Rachel, started clapping in time to the drumbeat. The two Griffith boys, her stepbrothers, picked it up, and in a moment even the adults joined in. Off to their left, Joseph Smith raised one arm, turned to see that everyone had their eyes on him, then dropped it. "Forward march," he shouted.

It may not have been much in a city like New York or Boston, but for being no more than forty miles from the western border of the United States, it was a grand parade. The militia moved out slowly. For a moment a few were out of step, but there were some quick hops and shuffling and then they went forward in rhythm to the music. Following the Quorum of the Twelve came other Church officers and dignitaries—the presidencies of the Far West and Di-Ahman stakes and the members of their two high councils, the bishop and his counselors, and the architects for the new temple. Then the crowd fell into line. Ladies and gentlemen marched arm in arm; children ran alongside them excitedly, calling to one another.

The Steeds waited until near the end so that young Joshua could have his wish. As the last of the thousands moved away, the men on horseback—the cavalry portion of the militia—wheeled into line behind them. The horses were dancing, their hooves throwing up small chunks of dirt, their shuddering whinnies betraying their excitement.

Young Joshua kept turning around to watch them, his seven-year-old eyes wider than a startled owl's. His uncle couldn't help but note his enthusiasm. Finally he moved over and laid a hand on young Joshua's shoulder. "You like horses?"

"Yes, Uncle Joshua. I love horses. I think they're just grand."

Joshua smiled. "Tell you what. When you come down to Jackson County—" He stopped as Nathan's head jerked around. "The next time me and Will come north to St. Jo," he corrected himself quickly, "we'll come by this way and get you." He turned to Nathan and Lydia. "Think you could spare your boy for a day or two? I could use another driver to get that freight delivered."

Young Joshua's jaw dropped. "Really?" he cried.

His uncle laughed. "Really." He stepped over closer to Nathan and elbowed him in the side. "What do you say, Pa? Maybe you could even come. I could give you a lesson or two in driving a wagon. As I remember, you never could keep a team moving in the right direction."

Nathan's face twisted. "Oh, now, that hurts. As *I* remember, it was me who first taught you how to handle a horse."

Matthew joined in now. "Why don't you let me come too? Then me and Will and young Joshua can drive, and you old men can sleep in the back of the wagon."

They were all laughing now. Except for Jessica. She was watching Joshua in wonder. This was a side of this man she had never seen when she was married to him. There was a momentary stab of sadness, then instantly she pushed it aside. Joseph was right. Joshua had changed. And what she had never had with Joshua she now had with John Griffith. It was right to put the past aside. She reached out and took her husband's hand and joined in the laughter.

Joshua finally sobered a little and turned to Lydia. "How 'bout it, Mrs. Steed? Can we borrow your husband and son for a few days and try to teach them a few things?"

Lydia's mouth softened, and suddenly her eyes were shining. "Nathan said he told you how we came to give Joshua your name?"

One eyebrow came up. That was not the answer Joshua had expected. "Yes, he did."

"Well, I think it would be only fitting and proper that the man for whom my Joshua was named should be the man who teaches him how to drive a team of horses."

Chapter Notes

The marriage of Mary Fielding to Hyrum Smith shortly after the death of Hyrum's first wife is accurately described in the novel (see *MFS*, pp. 43–44).

Chapter Three

The original plat for the city of Far West had been one square mile, but additions were quickly made as the population swelled. A large public square lay right at the heart of the original plat, and it was approached by four main roads, one coming from each of the four principal directions. The other streets of the city were more in keeping with other towns and villages, but these four main roads were a full one hundred feet wide. The effect was to open up the central part of the fledgling city with a great sense of spaciousness. And since Far West stood atop the highest swell of any of the surrounding prairie, one could see for miles in every direction.

As the great procession reached the center of Far West, Joshua Steed nodded to himself. You had to give it to the Mormons for that. They had picked a great site for a new home. They were moving slowly now as the people began to form a great circle around the outside of the square. The women and smaller children took the front places; the men and older children filled in behind. The cavalry then moved their horses up behind them to complete the ring.

As the Steeds found their places, Joshua was suddenly staring. Over the heads of the women he could see mounds of rich, black prairie soil. He stretched a little and then realized that the people had surrounded a shallow but massive excavation right in the center of the square. It was no more than a couple of feet deep, but it was huge! He let his eye run along it, trying to estimate its size.

Beside him his father was watching him, sensing his amazement. "It's one hundred ten feet long and eighty feet wide," he said in a low voice.

"A hundred and ten feet?" Joshua echoed. That was as big as some of the warehouses he and his partners owned in St. Louis. "You're really going to build something that big?" Joshua whispered back.

"Yes. When we built the temple in Ohio, it was one of the largest buildings in the state. But this will be even bigger than that one—longer by about forty feet and wider by twenty."

Matthew was standing next to Olivia. Or better, Olivia had made sure that once they got into place she was standing next to him. Now he took her by the arm. "See that pole, Olivia?" He was pointing to a tall, narrow, and carefully trimmed tree trunk buried in the ground to make a flagpole. At the top of it, barely stirring in the light breeze, flew the stars and stripes of America.

She glanced quickly at Matthew's hand on her arm; then, obviously pleased, turned to where he was pointing. "Yes, I see it."

"That's the liberty pole."

"The liberty pole?"

"Yes." He gave a sidelong glance at Peter. "We put it in special just for this day. This day we celebrate whupping the British and kicking them out of our country." He grinned mischievously, looking straight at Peter now. "No offense intended, mate."

Peter kept his face impassive. This was a running joke between him and Derek and Matthew. "It's all right, bloke. I think it's nice that the colonies finally got their own flag. They need *something* to make them feel important."

Before Matthew could retort to that, Joseph stepped to the makeshift pulpit that had been placed at the north edge of the excavation. He raised his hands and instantly a hush swept over the crowd. Even the children fell silent. The air of expectation was strong.

"Brothers and sisters." He was speaking loudly, turning his head so his voice would carry to the surrounding crowd. "It is time for the laying of the temple cornerstones. We shall begin by having our choir sing that wonderful hymn written by Brother W. W. Phelps, 'Now Let Us Rejoice in the Day of Salvation.' At the conclusion of the singing, our brother Hyrum Smith, vice president for today's celebration, will lead us in prayer."

Savannah, who was in Rebecca's arms for the moment, suddenly turned and looked up at her father. "Hold me, Papa," she mumbled. She held out her hands, trying to wiggle free.

Joshua reached out and took her. Immediately she snuggled against his chest and her eyes began to droop. As he began to stroke her hair gently, Caroline's eyes found him. Her lips never moved, but he read the question on her face as clearly as if she had spoken. "Are you leaving?"

He shook his head slightly and saw the relief in her face. The night before, as they had lain in bed discussing the upcoming day's activities, Joshua had warned her that once the parade was over, he was going to take Savannah home for a nap. It was one thing to go to a Fourth of July celebration; it was quite another to participate in a Mormon worship service.

Caroline had gotten a little angry. They were sleeping at Nathan's cabin, which at night was partitioned off with blankets to give them separate sleeping quarters, so she had gone up on one elbow and leaned over to speak directly into his ear. "That will really hurt your family," she said firmly. He started to protest, but she hissed at him with even greater vehemence.

"You're not going to die if you stay through the whole thing." So he had backed off, not giving in to her but not absolutely refusing either. He would wait and see.

But now Joshua wasn't thinking about leaving. At least not yet. In spite of himself, he was somewhat curious about what was about to happen.

By the time the hymn and invocation were over, Savannah was asleep against his chest, so Joshua turned his attention back to the proceedings. Joseph began to explain who would set in place each cornerstone. He used words that were not always familiar to Joshua—*priesthood quorums*, *stake presidencies*, *bishop*, and *bishopric*—but as Joseph spoke, men stepped out of the congregation and came forward. They divided themselves into four groups of three each, and Joshua realized these were the presidencies to which Joseph referred.

"Would those twelve who will be assisting the presidencies and the bishopric also step forward," Joseph called. To Joshua's surprise, far more than twelve men came forward to stand behind the four groups. He counted quickly. There were forty or more stepping out now. Then, as they grouped themselves equally behind the leaders, Joshua understood. There were twelve men in each group beside the presidency.

Will had evidently seen the same thing. He turned to Benjamin. "Why are there twelve in each group, Grandpa?"

Benjamin smiled. "How many tribes of Israel were there in the Bible?"

"Twelve," Olivia blurted, following along closely with the conversation.

"So?" Will said, still not understanding.

Benjamin glanced out of the corner of his eye toward Caroline and Joshua, who were watching them now. "To have twelve men on each corner reminds us that we are God's covenant people and that he is restoring the house of Israel in the last days, just as was prophesied in the Old Testament."

"Oh," Will said, still not fully understanding but satisfied now.

Joseph gave a signal and the four groups moved off in solemn processions, splitting so that they were soon headed for each of the four corners of the excavation. Only then did Joshua notice that there were four large, flat boulders, each nearly three feet long and at least two wide, waiting for them there.

Joseph waited until the four groups had lined up behind each of the four great stones; then he called out again. "All right, brethren, it may not take every one of the twelve of you to lift each stone, but I would like all to participate anyway. The architect for the temple will see that the stones are laid precisely in place. We will proceed in the following order: The presidencies of the Caldwell County and Di-Ahman stakes will go first, laying their stone at the southeast corner. The elders will follow, laying theirs at the southwest corner. Bishop Partridge, you and your brethren of the Aaronic Priesthood will lay your stone next, at the northwest corner where you now stand. The northeast cornerstone will then be laid by the teachers quorum."

The men in the first group started to move forward, but Joseph raised his hand. They stopped and he instantly sobered again. "Before we proceed, I would like to say a word or two about the importance of cornerstones. Brethren and sisters, as you know, the cornerstones are used to lay out the rest of the building. If they are not put precisely and correctly in place, the rest of the structure will suffer. Today we lay the cornerstones for another temple to our Lord and God. This will be the house of the Lord. May we never forget for whom we build it. The Apostle Paul tells us that if we make Jesus Christ the chief cornerstone the whole building will be fitly framed together. That is true of this temple, which will be his house. It is true of the temple of our lives. Jesus is the chief cornerstone. May we ever look to him as the model for building lives worthy of all acceptation to him." He paused for a moment, letting his eyes sweep the congregation and finally come to rest on the group at the southeast corner. He nodded. "Brethren, you may proceed."

From the time he was small, Joshua Steed had chafed under the touch of spiritual things. When his mother read the Bible to the family in the evenings or on the Sabbath, his span of attention was the shortest of any of the children's, even though he was the oldest. He had found some of the stories, especially those in the Old Testament, compelling, but the long sermons, the doctrinal expositions, and some of the interminable "begat" passages left him squirming like a worm in an ant bed.

Adult life had done little to change that. His experience with organized religion left him feeling something between faint disdain and total disgust. If pressed, Joshua probably would have admitted that he did believe in a supreme being, but that did not mean he believed in a deity that took an active role in the lives of men. Divine Providence. That title best fit how he saw God. Somewhere in the distant past some Divine Providence had created the universe, including the world on which men now dwelt, and then basically had given it a shove to get it started, and that was that. The world and the men in it were left pretty much on their own to work and wear out their lives.

So Joshua found himself a bit taken aback by the feelings he was experiencing now. There were grunts and soft groans of exertion as the men in the first group stepped forward, went into a crouch, then hefted the large stone to waist level. Moving forward with a great reverence, they laid the stone in place, not setting it down until the man who Joshua assumed was to be the architect gave them the signal. One by one the other groups followed suit. Then, with a mighty shout, the people thundered out their response.

"Hosannah! Hosannah to God and to our liberty!"

He had come prepared to feel disapproval at all this. He might not have been too surprised even at open curiosity. But . . . What? He couldn't think of a good word to describe his reactions. Admiration? Maybe even a touch of envy? For years he had nursed a deep rage toward Joseph Smith and his followers. Then two days ago Nathan had brought him home, home to his family, home to a whole clan of Mormons. Now he was honest enough to admit that that was what his previous feelings had been—blind, hatred-driven prejudice. Suddenly it wasn't so easy to accept the idea that these Mormons were the wild fanatics or deluded fools he had assumed them to be.

His mind jumped back five years. In November 1833, Joshua had ridden with about fifty armed and angry Missourians out to the Big Blue River west of Independence with the avowed purpose of driving the Mormons out of Jackson County once and for all. They had fully expected the Saints to scatter like a flock of chickens at the sight of the fox. But they didn't. Outnumbered two to one, the Mormons marched straight into the muzzles of the Missourian guns. Two had been hit almost immediately; one was fatally wounded. But they did not falter. On they came. Then, much to Joshua's disgust, it had been his men who broke ranks and fled, leaving their dead and wounded behind in their wild retreat.

His eyes moved to the northwest corner where Bishop Edward Partridge stood with his group; then he looked away quickly. Earlier that same year of 1833, Joshua and a man named George Simpson had stood face-to-face with this quiet man and another Mormon, Charles Allen, and demanded that they deny their belief in the Book of Mormon or be tarred and feathered and run out of town on a rail. Not only had Partridge and Allen not denied their faith, they submitted to the violence and humiliation with such a calm and peaceful demeanor that the mob had finally slunk away in shame, leaving Joshua and Simpson to face the two Mormon men alone.

You could say what you wanted about the craziness of Mormon teachings. You could talk all day about their being strange and different. But you couldn't so easily dismiss their faith. Joshua knew for himself. It was a faith strong enough to die for. He could not help but admire that.

Yesterday at the barn raising, Edward Partridge had showed up a few minutes after Joshua and his family had arrived. Joshua had nearly turned and walked away, afraid that Partridge would remember his past tormentor. He did. But instead of recoiling in horror, Partridge dropped his hammer and came straight for Joshua, smiling warmly and stretching out his hand!

It *was* just a touch of envy he was feeling, Joshua realized now. He knew that he wasn't man enough to do what Edward Partridge had done. And he realized that for all his skepticism, all his unwillingness to believe in a deity that spoke to men and told them what to do, he recognized there must be something very comforting in this kind of devotion, this kind of simple, life-directing faith.

He turned to his family. Every eye was on the four groups of men who were marching back to their places. He let his gaze move from one family member to another. Nathan was holding little Nathan. The faces of father and son were equally alive with excitement. Mary Ann held Emily's hand, a look of deep contentment infusing her features. He turned to his father. Benjamin was solemn, but Joshua could see the joy in him as well. Lydia, Jessica, John Griffith—one by one he searched their faces in profile. It was present in all of them. Even Caroline. She wasn't a Mormon, and Joshua suspected that she found aspects of this ceremony as strange as he did, but she had the same look in her face. It was what had brought her back to prayer and church and Bible study after years of bitterness over the loss of her first husband.

And then a great sadness filled Joshua's soul. He realized now with painful clarity that it was this that made him different from the rest of them. This was the underlying factor in the years of alienation, the years of separation.

He turned, not able to look at them any longer. For at that moment he realized something else. There might be admiration. There might even be a touch of envy for such simple faith. But down deep, rooted in his soul so firmly that it would never come out, he knew that this part of him would never completely change.

Sidney Rigdon had been elected as the orator of the day. Lydia explained to Caroline that Sidney had been a popular

Campbellite preacher before joining the Church. The moment he began to talk, Caroline saw why. His voice was clear and pleasant, and he articulated his words precisely. Having grown up in Baltimore and then having spent several years in culture-conscious Savannah, Caroline had found the rough and profanity-filled language of the Missourians jarring to her sensibilities. But here was a man who knew what words were for and took pleasure in the use of them.

The podium was only a short distance from where the Steeds stood, so Caroline got a good look at him. He was a middle-aged man, slightly on the stout side but quite distinguished-looking. He had a full head of hair, though his hairline was quite high, and he wore a beard in the Greek style—full and thick and running from ear to ear under his chin and jawline, but leaving his face clean shaven. Her eyes jumped for a moment to Joseph for a comparison. Sidney was considerably shorter, and he didn't have that striking grandeur of Joseph's that was so arresting, but nevertheless Caroline was impressed.

Sidney spoke briefly of the laying of the cornerstones and the importance of what had just taken place, but then opened a sheaf of papers and moved on to his subject. This day was the sixty-second anniversary of the signing of the Declaration of Independence, and Sidney began by making reference to that fact and noted that they were there assembled, isolated from former friends and associates because of their religion.

As he moved into his topic, his voice rose both in volume and in passion. He spoke of the flag of freedom and how it stood for the Constitution and for liberty from oppression. As he spoke of those freedoms he spoke also of those who were oppressed and persecuted for their religion and how the banner stood for their rights as well.

He turned and looked at the liberty pole. Almost every set of eyes in the congregation followed. Any breeze there had been had died out now, and the air was hot and muggy. The flag of the United States of America hung limply, without stirring.

Fourth of July

Caroline felt suddenly uneasy. This was not what she expected. She stole a glance at Joshua. Rigdon was now loudly reviewing the history of their persecution as Latter-day Saints. Savannah was sound asleep now, and Joshua swayed back and forth slowly to keep her that way. He did not see Caroline look at him. His head was down, his mouth drawn in a tight line.

"And how did we respond to this violation of all human decency?" Sidney cried in indignation. "I'll tell you how we responded. We bore it patiently. In the words of Isaiah, we gave our cheeks to the smiters and our heads to those who pluck off hair. When smitten on one cheek, we not only turned the other, but we did it again and again, until now we are wearied of being smitten, and tired of being trampled upon. We have proved the world with kindness. Though it was without cause, we have suffered their abuse with patience. We have endured their actions without resentment until this day."

Caroline saw that many heads, especially those of the men, were nodding their assent. From the pinched look around their eyes, it was clear that Sidney Rigdon's words were striking home.

"And what has this submission gotten for us? Have the persecutions and violence ceased? I say unto you, No, they have not ceased. Even now the Missourians talk about dealing with the 'Mormon problem.' Even now there are those who clamor for the chance to drive us from this state."

He paused, his chest rising and falling. "Well," he bellowed, "I say that from this day on, we shall suffer these things no more. We call on God and all the holy angels to stand as witnesses of what we say. We warn all men to come against us no more forever, for from this very hour we say, *We will bear it no more!*"

"Amen!" someone behind Caroline shouted. "Amen!" shouted another. She turned her head to see who it was, but there was no way to tell.

Joshua reached out and touched her arm. "I'm going to take Savannah home and put her to bed."

Mary Ann, watching her son anxiously, stepped forward. "I'll take her, Joshua," she whispered.

He shook his head quickly. "No, that's all right." And without waiting for a response, he turned and began pushing his way through the crowd.

Mary Ann looked at Caroline, and shook her head sadly. Caroline nodded, feeling suddenly desolate. Things had been going so well.

"I say again," Sidney was thundering, "from this very day, we declare our independence. Our rights shall not be trampled upon with impunity. Any man or set of men who attempt to do so, do so at the risk of their lives. And that mob that comes on us to disturb us, it shall be between them and us a war of extermination; for we will follow them until the last drop of their blood is spilled, or else they will have to exterminate us, for we will carry the seat of war to their own houses and their own families until one party or the other shall be utterly destroyed."

The answering murmurings and mutterings that had been punctuating Sidney's speech had completely stopped now. Utter silence hung over the crowd. The words were like thunderbolts being hurled at them, and they were starting to shock and stun now. Wanting to cry, Caroline turned and craned her neck, hoping that Joshua was out of earshot. But he was not. Over the heads of the people she caught a glimpse of his face. He had stopped at the edge of the crowd and was peering intently at the speaker.

Rigdon's voice dropped, though it still carried clearly in the still air. The contrast was dramatic. "Remember it, then, all men," he muttered. "We will never be the aggressors, we will infringe on the rights of no people; but we shall stand for our rights until the death. We claim our own rights, and are willing that all others shall enjoy theirs. No man shall be at liberty to come into our streets, to threaten us with mobs. If he attempts to do so, he shall atone for it before he leaves the place. No man shall be at liberty to vilify and slander any of us again, for in this place we will not suffer it. We shall not be the victims of vexatious lawsuits designed to cheat us of our rights. We say woe to any man who tries it.

"Do you hear me, my brothers and sisters?" he shouted triumphantly. "On this sacred day, we proclaim ourselves free and independent, with a purpose and a determination that never can be broken." He raised one arm, his hand clenched in a fist. "No, never!" He punched the air again, his face twisted with passion, his voice nearly a scream now. "I say, *No, never!*"

For a moment the silence was startling. Not a person stirred. Even the children seemed mesmerized. Then Sidney let his hand fall to his side and stepped back, bowing his head.

Above them, high on the liberty pole, the stars and stripes of the United States of America hung majestically, silent witness to the thunderous words acclaiming freedom on this day of Independence.

Chapter Notes

The depicted events held on the Fourth of July, 1838, in Far West, including the laying of the cornerstones for the temple, follow the accounts of that day (see *HC* 3:41–42; *Far West Record*, p. 197), though some specifics—such as conversations, the hymns that were sung, and so on—are interpolations made by the author.

Only a small portion of Sidney Rigdon's oration is given in the novel. The fiery words about the Saints' determination to endure no more persecution are taken almost word for word from the original (for the complete text of the oration, see Peter Crawley, "Two Rare Missouri Documents," *BYU Studies* 14 [Summer 1974]: 517–27).

Sidney Rigdon's speech was later published by the Saints and was widely circulated. Unquestionably it became an important factor in the inflaming of the bitterness against the Mormons.

There is some question as to the Prophet's reaction to the speech. There is no doubt that it was enthusiastically received by the crowd. One source says that Joseph approved the publication of the speech (see Crawley, "Two Rare Missouri Documents," p. 504). B. H. Roberts wrote that Joseph later corrected some of the things that Sidney said, since the latter, "stirred with indignation in contemplating the sufferings the saints had endured, allowed his eloquence to carry him beyond the limits of calm wisdom" (*Persecutions*, p. 192).

Perhaps it was both. That is, Joseph did approve of the general message, that the Saints had rights that had been ignored, but thought that Sidney went too far in his saying that the Mormons would follow any mob that came against them "till the last drop of their blood [was] spilled."

Chapter Four

"Your brother Joshua didn't like what was said today, did he?"

Rebecca and Derek Ingalls were walking along the northern outskirts of Far West. Rebecca had her arm through his as they moved slowly along the dusty road. She looked out to the west. The sun hung low in the sky, obscured now by a line of clouds but sending golden shafts skyward against an upper level of cirrus. In a little less than an hour now, it was going to provide a spectacular sunset.

Finally she looked up into Derek's face. "I'm not sure *I* liked what was said today. Did you?"

Derek, as was his usual habit, considered the question carefully, his eyebrows pulling down, his lips pursing slightly. "Well, I'm not sure Brother Rigdon's choice of words was the best."

"But?" She had to smile. This was one of the things she so loved about him. Many men made up their minds on an issue too quickly, letting their emotions be their guide. But Derek had an innate fairness about him that made him want to examine both sides of an issue, keeping an open mind so he could see all of the implications more clearly. Rebecca was not judgmental by nature, but neither was it her tendency to so carefully weigh the various points before deciding. It was a trait she very much liked and wanted to learn from this man.

He blew out his breath slowly, choosing his words with deliberation. A shock of his thick, rough-cut hair slipped down over one eye. "But there is some truth to his message," he said, pushing it back again. "Do we always have to suffer persecution and plunder to be acceptable to God? Is there ever a point where we are justified in saying, 'It is enough'?"

"Of course, but—"

"*But!*" he cut in quickly, grinning at her.

She laughed up at him. "Yes, but what?"

He sobered almost instantly. "To call for a war of extermination? To talk about pursuing our enemies until the last drop of their blood is shed? If the people of Missouri hear that?" He shook his head. "I don't think that was wise at all."

"I know," she said soberly.

They were approaching a site where someone had begun digging the foundations for a cabin. There was a pile of logs nearby. Rebecca tugged on Derek's arm, gesturing toward the wood. "Let's sit down for a while."

He glanced at the western sky. "Your mother will be getting supper soon. Shouldn't we go back and help?"

Rebecca smiled shyly up at him. "Didn't you hear what Mama said as we were leaving?"

"I heard her say good-bye, but that was all."

"She said, 'Rebecca Steed, Derek and Peter will be leaving for Di-Ahman in the morning. It may be several weeks before you will see this man again. Normally I would expect you to be here to help get supper ready, but I think you and Derek need some time alone together. So if you're back just in time to eat, it will be all right.' "

"Eh, what?" Derek blurted. "She said all that?"

Rebecca laughed merrily. "She did. You just have to learn how mothers talk."

They walked to the stack of logs and Derek brushed one off for her. Then they sat down, facing north, where they had an unobstructed view of the rolling prairie land stretching off to the horizon. They were both silent for a time, simply enjoying each other's presence. Derek watched her out of the corner of his eye, marveling again at the sight of her. Her hair was long and light brown, combed straight, so that it caught the light every time she moved. When she smiled or was concentrating deeply as she was now, a dimple in her one cheek showed. He had learned to watch for it, loving to see it come and then disappear again. But it was her eyes he loved the most—wide and trusting, pale blue, the color of the Wedgwood china he had seen in the windows of the finer shops of England.

"Tell me about Di-Ahman," she said.

His head came up in surprise, but then his eyes lightened and a softness played around the corner of his mouth. "Aye," he murmured, "it's beautiful, Becca."

She looked at him sharply. For a moment he was startled by her expression, then he blushed. "Would you rather I not call you that?"

Her head went back and forth, and quickly. "No, it's just that . . . you haven't called me that before. Only my family ever calls me Becca."

"If you'd rather I—"

She put a finger to his lips. "I like it," she said firmly.

Satisfied, he leaned back, pulling up one knee. "Peter and me, we were real lucky to go up north that soon. There are so many people coming now, the best of the land is already gone. But we got us a real nice piece. It overlooks the Grand River. Everything is so green and beautiful." His voice took on a wistful note. "In some ways it reminds me of England."

"You miss it sometimes, don't you?"

He looked surprised. "England? Not really."

"Not at all?" she teased. "Weren't there girls there?"

He laughed, but it came out as a short, mirthless bark. "If there were, I didn't notice." His eyes narrowed, and there was a quick look of pain. "England didn't offer much to Peter and me. Twelve-hour days workin' for old Mr. Morris. Sharin' a hole in a cellar with two drunks and a family of rats. Winters so cold and damp and us with nothin' more than a sweater and wooden clogs for our feet." There was a quick explosion of disgust. "Nah, I don't miss England much at all."

His words saddened her. This was something he rarely talked about. She had even grown so used to his accent that she often forgot he had not been raised American. "Well, I'm glad it didn't offer you much, or you would never have come here."

He brightened. "Aye. And then look what I'd be missin'. Ownin' a piece of my own land. Me and Peter with our own house. True, right now it's only a sod hut, but it's still ours. Being here with the Church. Having the privilege of knowing Brother Joseph."

Rebecca was watching him closely, nodding with each item he mentioned. When he stopped she frowned. "And?" she prodded.

"And what?" he asked innocently.

She slugged him on the shoulder. "What else?"

He laughed, and slipped an arm around her waist. "And most important, I'd be missin' Miss Rebecca Steed, fairest lass in all the land."

"That's better." She leaned her head against his shoulder. "So describe Di-Ahman for me. Pa says he'll take us up there sometime soon, but I want to be able to picture it in my mind."

"Well," he started, half closing his eyes, "as you know, it's about twenty-five miles north of here. The Grand River runs through a valley with bluffs on both sides. The river makes a sharp bend right below our cabin and goes almost northward for a mile or two before it turns again."

"And your cabin is near there?"

"Yes. We look right down to where the river bends."

"On the north or south side of the river?"

"On the north. The south bluffs are limestone outcroppings and they're pretty steep. Ours are more gently sloped."

She pounced on that. "Ours," she echoed. "I like the sound of that."

"Yes." He got a faraway look in his eyes. "By spring, Peter and me will have built a front porch on the house. Then we can sit out there in the evenings and look out over the valley. Just like Adam and Eve probably did."

"I know," she murmured. "I think about that almost every day. Brother Joseph says it's no wonder they went to Adam-ondi-Ahman after the Fall. He says it's as close to the Garden of Eden as anything he's ever seen."

"It is." Derek surprised her by reaching out and taking her hand. He squeezed it gently. "You're going to love it there, Becca."

She squeezed back. "I know."

"When Father Steed brings you up, I want to take you and show you around. It is a thrill to walk that land and know it is the same land where father Adam walked."

"Yes!" Rebecca breathed, trying to picture it in her mind. She leaned forward, folding her arms and putting her chin on her knees. "It's hard to imagine, isn't it? Six thousand years ago Adam and Eve and Cain and Abel and all the other children roamed these hills."

"Yes, it is. And yet . . ." His eyes grew thoughtful. "There is a really special feeling up there."

"And then," Rebecca added, "when you think about what's going to happen there sometime in the future. Adam gathering all of his righteous posterity together once again. The Son of Man coming down among them, getting things ready for his second coming, just like Daniel saw in vision so many years ago. It leaves me a little bit breathless."

"So you think you might like to live there?" Derek asked softly.

She turned fully to him now. "Oh, Derek, I don't know if I can wait until spring. The thoughts of you leaving again now leave me so empty inside."

Derek nodded. With the sun behind the clouds and low in the sky, the light was muted and soft and made her skin glow. When he thought about leaving in the morning, what he felt was not emptiness but a powerful, permeating pain all through him. How he longed to take her back now! But there was a house to finish, and land to break and sow. Feelings for a woman weren't enough. You also had to be able to care for her. Suddenly, a little taken aback at his own daring, he reached out and touched her hair.

He could tell he had surprised her, but she didn't move. He began to stroke it softly. "I'm gonna miss you, Becca," he finally said in a whisper.

She shook her head quickly beneath his touch. "Don't talk about it. I don't know if I can bear it."

She straightened and Derek put one arm around her shoulder. She moved closer and snuggled against him. He wanted to stare at her in wonder. He still couldn't believe that this gentle, wonderful, lovely woman could really be feeling this way about him, an unlearned, rough-cut, coal shoveler from the poorest section of Lancashire, England.

He turned slightly and she looked up at him, her eyes wide and luminous. His heart was pounding, but with every ounce of courage he could muster he leaned down and kissed her softly on the lips. He pulled back, a little dazed. She smiled at him, and there was so much tenderness and love in her eyes, he kissed her again, this time harder and with more intensity.

When he straightened, his voice was fierce and husky. "When next spring comes, Miss Rebecca Steed, I'll have that house ready. I'll have ten acres of crops in. I'll have that front porch on the house. Then I'm coming back to Far West, and there'll be no more good-byes. Not ever."

Supper that evening at the Benjamin Steed cabin in Far West was a grand celebration in its own right. Since there was no possible way all of them could fit inside, they laid planks across sawhorses and ate outside beneath a sky that was filled with azure blues, rich turquoise, and shafts of gold. The sun was just setting, and it was as though the Lord wanted to put his own seal of approval on the nation's birthday.

There was much laughter and happiness as the food was served and consumed, but there was also a touch of sadness. By morning the family of twenty-three would be down again to ten. Joshua and Caroline and their three had the farthest to go. It was nearly sixty miles south to Independence, a full two-days' trip. Jessica and John Griffith and their four would return to Haun's Mill, twelve miles to the east, and Derek and Peter would head north with the Di-Ahman group.

But that was tomorrow. For now they pushed away the melancholy, determined to make the most of their remaining time together. Talk of the day—especially any reference to Sidney Rigdon's speech—was studiously avoided. This was family time, and it would be a while before it happened again, so they made the most of it.

After the leftovers were cleaned up and the dishes dumped into an iron washtub to soak, the children went off to play "run, sheepie, run" and "red rover," with Matthew, Will, Olivia, and Peter in charge. Lydia and Jessica nursed their babies and put them to sleep head to head on Benjamin and Mary Ann's double bed. Savannah, exhausted from the day's activities, curled up in her grandpa's lap and fell asleep, and Benjamin resisted every effort to have her taken away and put on a bed.

As the sunset gradually fell and the lingering prairie twilight settled in, the children trailed back and played more quietly around the perimeter of the circle of adults. Occasionally one of the women would go in to check on the babies, but other than that, everyone was content to sit and talk quietly. Sometimes the circle of conversation would widen to include everyone; at other times, the talk would break up into smaller subgroups.

In one of those times, Joshua and Caroline were sitting quietly listening, not actively participating for the moment. After a time, Joshua leaned over and whispered something in

Caroline's ear. She turned in surprise, then immediately nodded.

"You're sure?" he said.

She touched his hand. "Yes, I'm sure, Joshua. You need to do it."

His head bobbed once, and then he turned to John Griffith, who sat on the step just below Jessica's knee. He and Jessica and Nathan were discussing the winter wheat crop and how soon it would be ready to harvest.

"John?" Joshua said, when there was a break in the conversation.

Jessica's husband turned.

Joshua hesitated for a moment. Except for Father and Mother Steed, John Griffith was the oldest person in the family. He was four years older than Jessica, which made him nearly thirty-eight, about seven years older than Joshua. But he was a gentle man, a man of decent goodness, a man of the soil. He had bright blue eyes and big hands and a face sunburned deeply up to the line where his hat covered his balding head. From there up, his skin was as white as a baby's tummy.

When Nathan had persuaded Joshua to come north with him and make his reconciliation with the family, Joshua had come with two great sources of dread. The first was that first meeting with his father. The second was to have to face his ex-wife, the woman he had driven first from his home and then from his county. He had desperately hoped that Jessica and her new husband would not be at Far West. After Joseph had talked to the family about forgiveness and putting the past aside, they had all welcomed him back without restraint—Jessica as quickly and as warmly as any of the others. And he had found that John Griffith was completely secure in his marriage with Jessica. There had not been the slightest hesitancy on his part in accepting Joshua's return to the family.

"Yes?" John said.

Joshua realized he had been lost in his thoughts. He smiled, feeling a little foolish. "I would like to ask you a question."

"All right."

"I need an honest answer."

John looked a little surprised. Jessica was watching Joshua closely now too, obviously puzzled as well. "Fair enough," John replied.

Joshua took a quick breath. "I would like to speak with Jessica alone for a time. Would you be offended if I did so?"

Jessica jerked forward slightly, staring at Joshua. The others had all stopped talking now too. Every eye was on him. Finally, Jessica looked down at her husband and he looked up at her. Something passed between them, then John turned back to Joshua. He smiled. "Not at all."

Jessica stood slowly. She was looking at Caroline. "Do *you* mind, Caroline?"

Caroline reached out and touched Joshua's arm. "Joshua was thoughtful enough to ask me first," she said, her voice soft. "No, I don't mind in any way, Jessica."

"All right." Jessica came down the step and started down the dirt path that led to the roadway. Joshua fell in behind her. Rachel was sitting on the grass a few feet away, playing some kind of hand games with Olivia and Emily. She looked up, a quick look of alarm darkening her eyes. "Mama?"

"It's all right," Jessica said. "Joshua and I are just going to talk for a few minutes."

"Would you like to come?" Joshua asked.

Rachel considered that for a moment. Then, sensing that there was no tension in any of this, she shrugged. "No, that's all right. I'm winning right now."

Joshua laughed, as did the others. He waved briefly and they moved away. They went down the road about a hundred yards from the cabin and stopped near the far limits of Benjamin's wheat field. Darkness was gradually stealing in from the east, pushing the twilight back, but there was still enough light to see that the shafts of grain were showing their first signs of yellowing. The full heads of wheat were still green, but in another few weeks the whole field would be like a waving sea of gold.

He pulled his mind back to the present, knowing full well

that he was just stalling. Finally he looked at Jessica. The night had gotten suddenly warmer, and Joshua felt the first tiny beads of perspiration breaking out on his forehead. She was aware of his discomfort, but was also wise enough to know that he had to do this without her prodding.

He straightened. "Jessica?"

She waited.

"I don't know exactly where to start. Or how to . . ." He let it trail off, and looked away again.

"You don't have to say anything, Joshua. It's really not necessary. The past is gone now."

"No, I need to. I want to." His chest rose and fell as he sought for the right beginning. "Words are cheap, Jessie. I know that. After all I did, saying I'm sorry seems so inadequate. But I am sorry. Every time I think of that night when I hit you—I keep blaming it on being sodden drunk, but being drunk was only part of it. I was so frustrated with everything. Losing almost all of my business in the poker game. You and me fighting all the time. Not being able to have babies."

"I know," she murmured.

He didn't seem to hear. "And then when you went to the Mormons. Joseph Smith represented all that had driven me from my father and my family. I hated him. I hated them." He looked down at his hands. "I hated you." He blew out his breath in frustration. "Now I also realize that I hated myself too."

Jessica was watching him, nodding slowly. When he didn't continue she straightened a little. "Joshua, I want to say this, and I don't want you to interrupt. All right?"

He looked up. "All right."

"You say that words are cheap, and that's true. Remember that night you came out to the Lewises where I was staying? That was just after you came back from Santa Fe. Rachel was about six months old then."

"Yes, I remember it very clearly."

"You said you were sorry then too. And those words *were* cheap. Why? Because you didn't mean them. Not really. Oh, you were sorry, all right, but not sorry enough to change. Not sorry enough to let me be what I wanted to be."

He stirred, but she went on hastily. "Now here you are once more, standing before me again, saying you're sorry." A look of the gentlest compassion filled her eyes. "But the words aren't cheap anymore, Joshua. They're exactly the same words. But it's a very different man saying them." She shook her head slowly, remembering so many things. "I guess no one else in the family knows that like I know it. Not even Caroline."

Her words touched him deeply. It was true. Jessie was the only one who had known the old Joshua intimately, up close, day by day.

She gave him a fleeting smile. "As I've watched you these past three days"—there was a soft, throaty laugh—"I keep wanting to pinch myself. Is this the Joshua I married? Is this the man I—"

"No. I was a fool back then."

"No, it's more than that. Lord knows, I wanted it to work. I wanted to make you happy. I wanted to give you babies. But we were just too different. I was too . . ." She shrugged. "I don't know what I was. I'm not sure what you were. We just didn't match, that's all."

"Jessie—"

"No, let me finish." She went on in a rush now, wanting it said so they could put it behind them once and for all. "In one of the revelations given to Joseph Smith, the Lord made a most interesting promise. He said that if we are faithful and diligent and strive to keep our covenants with him, all things will work together for our good."

"I'm not sure what that means."

"It means that even though those times were ugly in some ways, for the both of us, even though they were hurtful times, for the both of us, even with all that, the Lord has turned things around for our good. Look at me. Rachel's fine. She's healthy and a happy child."

"She's lovely. She is very much like you, you know."

"Yes," she said simply and with pleasure. "She is. She's very much like I was as a child, but much happier." She peered up at him for a moment. "I also have two wonderful stepsons. I have a baby that makes me want to shout for joy every time I think of him." She turned and looked back towards the house. "I've married a wonderfully decent man."

Joshua nodded, understanding now. "He's a good man, Jessie. You did well."

"No, the Lord did me well," she corrected him. "And that's what the promise means. And look at you. Caroline." She shook her head in amazement. "She's wonderful, Joshua. You are very lucky to have her."

"She is the finest thing that ever happened to me," he said with great softness and great feeling.

"And so the past is past," Jessica finished. "I am touched that you care enough to try and make it right. It says again how much you have changed. And that's enough for me."

For a long moment, Joshua considered that, then he finally nodded. "There is one other thing."

"What?"

"Rachel."

Jessica watched him, trying to read his face in the darkness, but she couldn't, so she waited.

"I've been thinking about this a great deal. When I came up with Nathan, I was determined to make up for all those years. I planned to take her aside. Spend some time with her. Let her know that her father hasn't stopped caring, even though he's not seen her since she was a baby."

"You sent us money. I know some of the questions about Rachel my father asked in his letters were from you."

"It wasn't much. Even the money. Not when she was my own flesh and blood."

Jessica didn't want to focus on the past. "And now?"

"I watch her with you and John—" His voice caught, and he shook his head, angry that his emotions had broken through. He let out a quick breath, fighting to gain control again. "I watch her with her cousins. If I try to be another father to her, it will only confuse her."

"I've not hidden any of this from her, Joshua."

"I know that, and I appreciate it. But we have to think of what's best for her. John is wonderful with her, and it's obvious she loves him."

"Yes, she does," Jessica said, not able to soften that fact for him. It was true. John Griffith had taken Rachel as his own.

"Then I think it's best if I just become her Uncle Joshua. When we come up to visit, we'll be friends and let it go at that. I don't want John to be worried about me stepping in either." He hesitated. "Do you think that will be all right?"

For several moments, Jessica did not answer. Then, finally, she turned to face him squarely. Now it was her voice that was husky. "You started by saying that words are cheap, Joshua. But I think I know what they must have cost you, and I thank you." On an impulse, she stepped to him, went up on tiptoe, and kissed him quickly on the cheek. "I thank you very much."

Not long after Joshua and Jessica returned to the cabin, the parents began to stand and make noises about it being time to think about getting the children to bed. At that point it became obvious that the younger members of the Steed clan had been doing more than simply playing games together. They had formed a conspiracy and laid some careful plans. What if all of the children, except for the youngest ones, slept outside at Grandpa's house? There were immediate parental protests—tomorrow would be a long day, especially for Joshua's family, who had two long days of riding ahead of them; the children needed their sleep; Grandma and Grandpa were tired. But they had planned well. Matthew and Will volunteered to chaperon. Rachel and Emily and Olivia turned the full extent of their charm on Benjamin and quickly enlisted his support. Mary Ann capitulated with an accepting smile. After all, it was their last night together for a time. Finally it was agreed. All but the two babies, Savannah, and two-year-old Nathan were granted permission. The boys would sleep on the prairie sod, the girls on straw spread out on the floor of the nearly finished smokehouse.

By nine o'clock, Joshua and Caroline were back at Nathan's cabin. Savannah, young Nathan, and baby Elizabeth Mary were quickly put to bed and fell asleep. Knowing this was their last time together for a time, the couples went back out on the porch and sat down to talk. The last of the twilight was gone now, and it was full dark. The crickets were chirping in a combined chorus that filled the air. Occasionally the hum of a mosquito near the ear would bring a hand up to shoo it away. Lydia and Caroline sat in chairs. Nathan and Joshua were on the step.

"Do you really have to leave tomorrow?" Lydia asked. "You couldn't stay for another day or two?"

Caroline looked to her husband. "I don't think so."

Joshua nodded, pulling a face as he looked at Lydia. "As you remember, this husband of yours came calling on me like some thief in the middle of the night. He dragged me out of Independence at first light. I barely had time to leave a note for my partner and tell him I was leaving."

Nathan sniffed, feigning hurt pride. "I *dragged* you out?" He looked at his wife. "This man was so afraid of being seen with some of his poorer relatives, we had to sneak out of town while everyone was still asleep." He shook his head and spoke to his wife again. "And by the way, you ought to see the house this man has built for Caroline. It's a mansion."

Caroline laughed in embarrassment. "I kept telling him I didn't need that much room, but he wouldn't hear of it."

"It's a lovely home," Nathan said, more soberly now. "I think you deserve it."

Caroline swung around and grabbed Lydia's arm. "Why don't you come to Independence and see it? Bring your family and come for a visit."

Joshua straightened sharply. Nathan too was staring at her.

"Young Joshua will love the freight yard. Will would burst his buttons showing him around."

"Caroline."

She stopped and turned to Joshua, her face flushed with enthusiasm. "We have plenty of room, don't we, Joshua?"

He cleared his throat awkwardly. "Uh . . . I'm not sure that would be wise right now."

Dismay flashed across her face. "Joshua!"

Nathan jumped in quickly. "Joshua's right. It might not be the best time, Caroline."

"But why?" There was just a touch of anger now too. "Everything's fine now between you and your family. I can't believe you would say that, Joshua." She turned to Lydia, the excitement returning. "You could bring Father and Mother Steed. And Rebecca. There are some wonderful dress shops. We could look for something for the wedding. It's not a bit too early."

"Caroline!" Joshua spoke more sharply now, trying to pull her back.

She swung on him, her eyes flashing. "Stop it, Joshua! I won't hear of this. I want your family to come visit us."

His mouth opened, then shut again.

Nathan cut in to help him. "Caroline, what Joshua is trying to say is . . ." He stopped, looking for a good way to say it. Then he went on, more quietly, but determined. "This is probably not a good time for Mormons to go to Jackson County, Caroline."

There was a momentary flash of surprise, as if she had been stung by an insect; then her face fell. "Oh," she murmured.

"Especially after today," Nathan finished. "If word gets out about that speech . . ." He let out a heavy sigh, the concern evident around his mouth. "The Missourians are already at a flash point. We need to be very careful for a while."

Lydia was watching her husband's face closely. It was soft in the lamplight coming from one window, but there was no mistaking the worry that was written there. And that gave her a sudden chill. She turned to her sister-in-law. "Nathan's right, Caroline. It sounds wonderful, and the children would love it. But maybe this isn't the best time."

There was pain on Caroline's face as she turned back to

Joshua. "They are your family, Joshua. You are highly respected in Independence. Surely no one would dare—" She stopped. Faces of various neighbors and associates of Joshua flashed before her mind. She didn't finish. She wasn't so sure anymore. She knew how deeply the feelings against Mormons ran in that town.

Lydia cleared her throat. "You've got to understand, Caroline. You heard the response of our people to what Sidney said. It's not that we want to start a war of retaliation, but we are tired of being pushed and driven and . . ." She hesitated for a moment. "And killed. So to hear Sidney say we have had enough struck deep chords within us. But Nathan's right. Sidney's speech is going to stir a lot of emotion now."

"Sidney has become a bit of a hothead of late," Nathan said grimly. He was thinking of events that had taken place in just the last two weeks or so. Sidney Rigdon had preached a sermon on the Sabbath day, June 17. The "Salt Sermon," it had been dubbed. He had used the passage from Matthew in which the Savior likened his disciples to the salt of the earth. And if the salt had lost its savor, it was thenceforth good for nothing but to be trodden under foot of men.

Memories of the apostasy in Kirtland were still vivid and painful. And now apostasy was rising among some of the most prominent members here as well. Oliver Cowdery had been excommunicated. David Whitmer, another of the Three Witnesses to the Book of Mormon, had withdrawn his name from fellowship before they could do the same to him. He was excommunicated anyway. In Kirtland, such apostasy had cost the Church dearly, so feelings ran very deep.

Sidney didn't say so directly, but the implications of his sermon were clear. The unfaithful were like salt without savor. Perhaps they too needed to be trampled underfoot. Shortly thereafter, a circular was distributed around Far West. In specific and threatening terms, it warned the apostates to flee the city or face dire consequences. It still wasn't clear who had written it. Some said Sidney himself. But it was signed by enough prominent Latter-day Saints to give it a terrible credibility.

Oliver Cowdery had come to Nathan's house like a fugitive in the night. He begged him to watch over his wife and children until he could send for them. And so they had fled, fearing the wrath stirred up by Sidney's fiery sermon.

It had sobered Nathan greatly, to think maybe it had come to that again. Nathan sighed and turned to Joshua. "In calling for blood, Sidney doesn't represent how the rest of us feel."

Joshua looked at him for a long time, then spoke. "Nathan, I don't think your people have any idea how deeply the feelings against you still run in the state. Your coming up north here hasn't solved anything. Not permanently."

"So much for the land of liberty," Nathan said bitterly.

"Nathan," Joshua said wearily, "I'm not here to argue these points with you. I'm just telling you, this is not the kind of news that settles people. The mood in Jackson County—in Clay County, in Ray and Carroll counties, all around you—it's not good. Not good at all."

Nathan nodded, his eyes morose. "I know."

"And some people are nervous about the fact that you have your own militia now, your own judges and law officers. You even have a cavalry. There are those who are saying if they don't stop you now, pretty soon you'll be unstoppable."

"That would be nice for a change," Nathan said dryly.

But Caroline had been struck by another thought, and it left her feeling slightly sick. "You hold a commission in the Jackson County militia, Joshua. What if they call it out against the Mormons again?"

He looked away. "I've tried not to think about that."

"But surely you wouldn't go," she cried.

With a snap his head came back around. "Caroline, a commission from the governor is not a thing of convenience. I am an officer in the military. You think I can just shuck that aside?"

Her eyes were stricken. "What will you do, then, if it comes to that?"

Nathan was staring at the ground. "He'll have to go," he said, his voice barely audible. "There will be no choice."

Chapter Notes

Derek's description of the area around Adam-ondi-Ahman is taken from Joseph's history (see *HC* 3:34–35, 39–40).

The prophecy that Adam—or the Ancient of Days, as the prophet Daniel calls him—will return prior to Christ's second coming is found in Daniel 7:9–14, 22. The fact that this will happen in the valley of Adam-ondi-Ahman was given to the Prophet Joseph through revelation in 1838 (see D&C 116). The Lord also revealed to Joseph that Adam gathered his righteous posterity in that same place three years before his death and blessed them and prophesied many things concerning the future (see D&C 107:53–56).

Chapter Five

Thursday morning was a long series of farewells all around Far West. Families began moving out at dawn and continued in a steady stream through most of the morning. Most lived in scattered homesteads, but there were a considerable number from Di-Ahman and several families from Haun's Mill. At the Steeds, Derek and Peter were the first to leave. They had come down in Lyman Wight's wagon with other families from Daviess County. Brother Wight was anxious to make the twenty-five-mile trip before dark, and the wagons were out front of Benjamin's cabin by the time the sun was fully up. With everyone looking on, Derek and Rebecca said their farewells with a brief touch of their hands, and with longing eyes.

John Griffith and Jessica were next. Theirs was the shortest trip, but John was anxious to get back in time to get in half a day's work. As he and Jessica loaded Rachel and the two boys into their small wagon, the children wailed and made solemn vows to each other about all they would do when they got back together again. The women hugged Jessica. The men shook hands with John. Jessica's baby was chucked under the chin and held up and cooed at, and then they were off, heading east.

Though he had the farthest to go, Joshua seemed the least concerned about getting an early start. Benjamin, Nathan, and Matthew helped him pack the wagon and hitch the team. Lydia and Caroline stayed at Mary Ann's, gathering the leftovers from the night before—fried chicken, corn bread, some apple pie—along with the first of the season's sweet corn and tomatoes from the garden. By the time the men returned with the wagon, the Steeds from Independence had enough food to take them safely on to New Orleans.

Finally it was time to load up. Matthew stepped forward and stuck out his hand to Will. There was four years' difference in age, and technically they were stepuncle and nephew, but they paid that no mind, for they had become close friends. "Remember," Matthew said, "you and your pa promised to take me to St. Joseph the next time you go that way."

"We will," Will vowed.

"Count on it," Joshua added firmly. "We'll be back through here in four to six weeks."

Olivia went to Mary Ann and threw her arms around her waist. "Good-bye, Grandma."

Mary Ann held her tight. At almost eleven years old, Olivia was growing fast now and was only an inch or two shorter than Mary Ann. Mary Ann bent down and kissed her cheek. "Good-bye, Olivia."

"I'm so glad I have a grandpa and grandma now," Olivia said fiercely.

Mary Ann had to blink quickly. "And we're so glad that we've got such a lovely granddaughter as you."

Olivia hugged Rebecca, her grandfather, and Nathan and Lydia and their children in quick order. But when she turned to Matthew she became suddenly quite demure and merely held out her hand. Matthew gave her a hurt look. "What? No hug for your Uncle Matthew?" He swept her up, swinging her off her feet, making her squeal in surprise. When he set her down finally, she shot a quick glance at Lydia, who smiled and nodded with a knowing look, then climbed up on the wagon, quite out of breath.

Savannah was in the arms of her grandfather. She was talking in a steady stream of her peculiar jabber, speaking to no one in particular. Caroline came to them. "All right, Savannah. It's time to go. Say bye-bye to Grandpa."

Savannah's blue eyes surveyed her mother's face gravely, but she didn't move. Then she turned away, pointing over Benjamin's shoulder and launching into a nonstop explanation about something that caught her eye. Benjamin chuckled. "You want to just stay here with Gampa?" he said. The red head bobbed up and down vigorously without turning around.

"Benjamin," Mary Ann chided, "don't make it harder than it is."

Benjamin reached in his pocket and withdrew a small piece of hardtack candy. "Here, Savannah, this is so you'll remember Gampa and come back soon."

Savannah snatched it and popped it in her mouth, looking very smug about the whole thing. Caroline shook her head at her father-in-law. "You are shameless. You know that, don't you?"

"Yes," Benjamin said cheerfully. Then suddenly he pulled Savannah to him. "Good-bye, little sweetheart. You come back and see Gampa real soon."

He stepped forward and handed Savannah to her mother. For a moment, he stood there awkwardly. Then he put his arms around mother and daughter. "Thank you, Caroline," he whispered. "Thank you for not giving up on an ornery old man. Thank you for what you've done for all of us."

Caroline's eyes widened, then instantly filled with tears. She started to speak, but couldn't get it out. She just went up on tiptoes and kissed his cheek.

Mary Ann was to them now as well. Then Lydia and Rebecca were there, all trying to hold one another. Caroline reached out and touched Mary Ann's face. "Dear Mother Steed. I feel like I've known you for years. And my children do too. Thank you. Thank you for everything."

Mary Ann could barely speak. "If you hadn't come, none of this—" She couldn't finish. She finally sniffed back the tears and looked at her little granddaughter. "And maybe if you come up here often enough, I'll even get this little scamp to pay some attention to someone besides her grandfather."

Savannah was watching her grandmother with those same wide eyes. The soberness of her expression suggested a much greater age than her fifteen months. Then she startled everyone. "Bye, Gamma," she said, and leaned forward and gave Mary Ann a wet and sticky kiss smack on the lips.

"Oh, you precious little thing!" Mary Ann cried, holding her hands. "Grandma will buy you a whole bag of candy for that."

Pleased with the delight she had caused, Savannah proceeded to dole out kisses to the rest of the family. Finally Caroline turned and walked to the wagon. Joshua took Savannah from her, and Nathan helped her up onto the wagon seat. Then Joshua handed up the little girl.

He turned to Nathan. For several seconds, the two brothers just looked at each other, then suddenly they were embracing, pounding each other on the back. Nothing was said. Nothing needed to be. Joshua moved swiftly now. He gave Rebecca a huge bear hug, whispering something into her ear about Derek that made her laugh and nod happily. He grabbed Matthew's hand and shook it firmly. "St. Jo. No later than the middle of next month. Agreed?" Matthew grinned back his answer.

Nathan's firstborn son stood beside his father, waiting expectantly for his turn. Joshua walked to him and stuck out his hand. "Young Joshua?"

He took it and gripped it firmly. "Yes, Uncle Joshua?"

"You make me very proud of my name. I promise you I will not do anything to bring it shame."

"Me too," the boy said, beaming proudly.

"And I haven't forgotten my promise to have Will teach you how to drive a team of horses, either."

"Great!" Young Joshua said, nearly whooping it out.

Joshua took a step to the left and stooped down. He took Emily by the hand. "And here's our birthday girl, a big six years old today."

"Yep," she crowed.

His voice got very soft. "A little Lydia, as pretty and wonderful as your mother. If I had known it was going to be your birthday, I would have brought you something. But next time I come I'll bring you whatever you want. What will it be?"

There was not an instant's hesitation. "A dress!"

"Done!" he laughed.

"Emily!" Lydia said in dismay.

"Now, Mother," Joshua said, "you stay out of this. This is between me and your daughter."

He straightened, and in doing so came up to face Lydia. Neither moved for a moment, then she opened her arms. He stepped into them and hugged her tightly. "If my brother doesn't treat you right," he growled, loud enough for Nathan to hear, "you let me know, and I'll set him straight."

She laughed. "I will." Then she was instantly serious. "We're so glad you're back, Joshua. This has been a wonderful three days."

He nodded. Then at last it was time for his parents. They were standing together now, watching him. Mary Ann was still weeping quietly, but there was no sadness in her eyes, only joy. Joshua swept her up, lifting her off her feet. "Oh, Mama, forgive me," he whispered. "Forgive me for all those stupid, terrible years."

When he set her down she took his face in both hands, pulled his head down so she could whisper in his ear. "All what years?" she said.

They hugged again, then Joshua stepped back. The hesitancy was evident in his eyes. Benjamin saw it too. Three days before, when they had stood like this, facing each other across the room in Nathan's cabin, Benjamin hadn't had the courage to move until Joseph prompted him. Now, however, he did have it. He simply stepped forward and put his arms around his son. For almost a full minute, they held each other like that, not speaking, not moving, just holding each other.

Finally they separated. Benjamin stuck out his hand and Joshua gripped it hard. "Thank you, Pa."

"No. Thank *you*, son. Thank you for coming home."

"It felt like home," he said softly. "It really felt like home again." He stepped back and looked around. He took a deep breath, then let it out slowly. He scanned the faces of the family forming a half circle around him; then he turned and smiled up at his wife, who was crying openly now. "I think we'd better get out of here before we're all bawling like babies."

They were about two hours out of Far West. The team was moving steadily southward, not needing much urging, for they seemed to know they were on the way home. Caroline, Olivia, and Savannah had stretched out on the mattress in the back of the wagon and were asleep. Joshua sat beside Will, who held the reins lightly in one hand. They had not spoken for several minutes. Then Will looked at his father. "Pa?" He spoke softly so as not to wake the women.

"What, Will?"

"When is Grandma's birthday?"

One eyebrow came up.

"I'd like to get her something for her birthday."

Joshua looked at his son, not trying to hide his pleasure. "What a fine idea, son!"

"But when is it?"

He thought for a moment. "October. October third." He was nodding. "We could get her something nice, then come up to Far West and throw a real birthday party for her."

"I'd like that."

"That's a wonderful idea, Will. We'll talk to Mother when she wakes up."

"What about Grandpa? When is his birthday?"

This time Joshua had to search his memory a little more diligently. It had been a lot of years. "It's in May," he finally said. "The eighteenth, I think."

Will's face fell. "Oh."

"What's the matter with that?"

"We missed it, then."

"Ah," Joshua said, seeing the problem. Then he brightened. "But what if we celebrated it with Grandma's? I think that would be all right, don't you?"

Will was instantly relieved. "Yes. What shall we get them?"

That was not an easy question to answer, and Joshua thought about it for a minute. "For your grandmother, I think we'd better trust your mother's judgment. For Grandpa?" He shook his head. "That's a more difficult question."

They fell silent as they considered it.

It was almost five minutes later when Joshua straightened with a jerk. "That's it!"

Will's eyes had started to droop, and his father's voice startled him. "What?" he said in confusion.

"I know what to get your grandpa for his birthday."

"You do?"

"Yes. It's perfect."

"What is it?"

Joshua smiled slowly, savoring the idea. "Next week, how would you like to make a trip to St. Louis? Then you and me will pick out a gift that will make Grandpa's eyes pop right out of his head."

Late the following day, just before sundown, Rebecca stuck her head in the door of the cabin and called to her mother. "Mother, it looks like it's going to rain."

"Wouldn't you know," Mary Ann moaned. They had spent most of the day doing the laundry and had finished getting it all hung out on the line only a couple of hours previously.

"It's coming fast," Rebecca said. "And it looks like it's going to be a real gully buster."

Mary Ann put down the dish of peas she had been shelling and walked to the door. As she stepped out on the porch and looked to the west, her eyes widened. There had been a few clouds when they had started hanging the wash, but now the whole western sky was one solid mass of black, punctuated by rippling flashes of light. The great mass was moving toward them even as she looked.

"Get Matthew and your father," she commanded. "We're going to have to hurry."

They barely made it. The first big drops came slashing in as Matthew ran in with the last of the sheets. Any vestiges of daylight were gone. Then the heavens opened. The rain came in horizontal sheets, pounding against the windows like bird shot. For the first few minutes, the lightning would flash, then six or seven or eight seconds later the thunder would crackle and roll across the prairie. But then the interval between flash and sound began to narrow rapidly.

Matthew stood at the front door. When the lightning flashed, he would begin counting slowly. "One, two, three. . . ." A rule of thumb was about one mile away for every five seconds counted.

"For heaven's sake, Matthew, get away from that door."

He turned to face his sister, grinning. "Ain't gonna strike here. I'm just counting to see how close they are. I love a good thunderstorm."

But as he turned back, there was a tremendous flash of light. Every detail in the cabin was thrown into brilliant relief. Matthew jerked violently, but even before his mind could react, the sound hit them. It was like a giant tidal wave smashing against the walls. Even the logs seemed to rattle with the blast of the thunder. Instantly there was the smell of ozone in the air.

Matthew fell back a step, half-blinded. "Heavenly days!" he cried. "What was that?"

Benjamin was up and to the door. He too was a little dazed.

"That hit somewhere close. Real close." He moved quickly to the back window and peered out to see if the outbuildings were all right.

Matthew stepped back inside. He gave Rebecca a long look. "Maybe you're right. I think I will shut the door."

The next morning, Rebecca and Mary Ann were about halfway through hanging the wash out to dry again when they heard someone calling. Rebecca turned, squinting a little in the bright sunlight. Then she smiled. "It's Lydia."

Nathan's wife was in a hurry. She was coming from the direction of town and had her skirts held up enough to stop them from dragging through the puddles. Mary Ann put the wash back in the basket and turned. She raised one hand to wave, then dropped it again slowly. She could see Lydia's face more clearly now. It looked frightened and filled with concern.

Alarmed, Mary Ann dropped the clothespins into the basket now as well and started walking toward her daughter-in-law. Rebecca had seen it too and joined her mother. "Lydia," Mary Ann called as they approached each other. "Is everything all right?"

Lydia only quickened her step until she came up to the other two women.

"What is it, Lydia?" Rebecca asked anxiously.

Lydia had to stop for a moment and catch her breath, but finally she turned and looked back over her shoulder. "I've just been to the main square."

"Yes?"

"You know that terrible lightning strike we got last night?"

"Yes, we heard it," Mary Ann said. "Was anyone hurt?"

Lydia shook her head, still breathing heavily. "It hit the liberty pole."

For some reason, that news jolted Rebecca as hard as if Lydia had said it had struck someone's home. "The liberty pole?" she echoed.

"Yes. It shivered it from top to bottom. There's nothing left but a few splinters."

"But—," Rebecca started. She stopped, not even knowing what she was going to say.

The liberty pole had been more than just a flagpole. The Saints had come to Missouri and tried to settle in Jackson County. They were driven out with whip, gun, and bayonet. They crossed the river into Clay County, only to be asked to leave two years later or face a similar fate. They fled from Kirtland in the dead of winter, robbed of their land and homes, hated by their neighbors and former friends. So they had come to northern Missouri, to the open, unsettled prairies. They had built their cabins and their barns and their settlements and tried to mind their own affairs.

And then, just three days before, they had gathered in the central square around the liberty pole. On it they raised the Stars and Stripes to fly over their fledgling city. Sidney Rigdon had spoken with passion of the liberties that that flag stood for. When he had finished, some five or six thousand voices had shouted hosannahs and collectively vowed that they would defend those liberties, even to the death if necessary.

And now the liberty pole was in splinters.

Lydia was very subdued. "Some of the people are saying this is an omen, that this is God's way of saying we strive in vain to maintain our liberties in a state where law is set by mob rule and where those who govern care nothing for the rights of the Mormons."

Mary Ann looked startled for a moment, then her jaw set. "The liberty pole was a symbol of our freedom and independence. We'll put up another one."

Rebecca shook her head slowly, feeling a great sense of desolation sweep over her. "The liberty pole is gone, Mama. It's gone."

By Eastern standards, the lumberyard at Far West left much to be desired. The selection was limited, and much of it was unfinished beams or just plain logs. On the Great Plains, where the almost endless forests that covered much of the continent east of the Mississippi were nonexistent, lumber was always at a premium. And to make matters worse, Far West was in a building boom. Even Kirtland at the height of its greatest boom time had not rivaled this.

The smokehouse Benjamin and Matthew Steed were building behind their cabin was small and it was nearly finished. But they still needed some good, solid hardwood for the smoke racks on which they would hang the long strips of bacon or the fat and heavy ham shanks. Benjamin went to the lumberyard nearly every day to see what might have come in. Finally, in mid-July, he found what he was looking for. Or rather, Matthew found it for him.

"Pa, come look at this."

Benjamin walked around a pile of logs and joined his son. Eight or ten planks lay on the prairie sod.

"It's ash," said Matthew. "Probably white ash, I'd guess."

"Hmm. Sure is."

"It still looks pretty fresh. It will probably take a week in the kiln to get it cured properly, but it looks like good wood."

Benjamin raised his head. Brother Thomas Billings, manager of the yard, was already watching them. "How much for the ash?" Benjamin called.

Billings came over and looked down at the lumber. "Oh yes, this stuff. Lucky to get it. Came up river to DeWitt, then one of the newcomers brought it the rest of the way in to help pay his way once he got here." His mouth twisted a little as he concentrated. "How 'bout four dollars fifty for the lot?"

Benjamin blew out his breath. "Really only need about half of it, actually. Just need to finish a rack in the smokehouse."

The lumberman frowned. "Hate to break up the lot. It's the only ash I've got right now."

"I'm going to have to take it to the kiln and have it dried some more. Can't wait for it to cure out by itself. Expect that will cost me another dollar at least."

Billings nodded. "All right, tell you what. Take the bunch and I'll let it go for three dollars even."

Now it was Benjamin who was thoughtful. It was more than a fair price, but with the kiln fees his total cost would be four dollars, and that would be a hefty hit on his cash reserves.

"Pa," Matthew broke in, "I could make Ma that dish cupboard she's been wanting with the rest of it."

"And I'll help him do it," a voice boomed from behind them.

They all turned, and Benjamin immediately smiled. "Brother Brigham. Good mornin'."

"Mornin', Brother Ben. Matthew." Brigham Young turned and shook hands with Billings as well. Then he dropped into a crouch and picked up the end of one board. He ran his hand along the grain of the wood. "Very nice," he murmured.

"Needs some more curing," Matthew volunteered.

"Yep. It does that," Brigham agreed. "Two days at most, though. You don't want to overdry this. Especially if you're gonna put it into furniture."

Benjamin nodded. That would make a difference. It wouldn't take a full dollar to dry it. He pulled at his lower lip. He trusted Brigham's judgment. Brigham Young was one of the finest, if not *the* finest, of master carpenters and glaziers in all of Far West. If he said two days, two days it would be.

Benjamin turned to Billings. "Done," he said. "Can I bring you the money this afternoon?"

"Of course."

Brigham laid a hand on Matthew's shoulder. "I've already seen some of the things you've done, young man. You've got a gift for working with wood. But I meant what I said. I'd be pleased to help you with a cupboard for Mary Ann. I may have some tools you don't."

Matthew was beaming. "I'd be right pleased to have your help, Brother Brigham."

"Good. You know where I live. Out about four miles on Mill Creek. Why don't you bring the lumber over once you've got it out of the kiln."

“You’ve got to remember that wood is a living thing, Matthew. Even after it’s been cut down and made into lumber, it’s still a living thing.”

“I’ve noticed that.” He was standing at Brigham’s side near the workbench. They were in the carpenter’s shed behind Brigham’s cabin. “The first door I made for Pa, I used a mitered joint on the corners. By the time summer was finished, the joints had big cracks in them.”

“That’s right,” Brigham boomed cheerfully. “And I’ll bet the cracks were bigger in some places than others, right?”

Matthew thought for a moment. That had been back in Kirtland, almost four years ago now. But he could picture the door in his mind. “That’s right. They were wider on the outside and inside corners.”

“Exactly. Wood either shrinks or swells *across* the grain. So a mitered joint pulls apart at the ends. That’s why a shiplap joint is best for doors. It holds the door at a ninety-degree angle to the grain.”

“Yeah,” Matthew said ruefully, “I learned that the hard way.”

Brigham had the first of the long boards of white ash on the bench and was planing it down smooth with long, even strokes. It was already hot in the shed, and beads of perspiration were forming on his upper lip. He stopped for a moment and looked at Matthew. “I like to think of it as breathing. It’s like the wood actually breathes.”

Matthew was nodding, knowing at once what he meant. “I never thought of it quite that way, but that’s really true.”

Brigham chuckled as he went back to work. “The softwoods do it much more than something like this, of course, but they all do. They breathe in, they breathe out. I remember back in New York we had barn roofs that you could see starlight through, but when it got stormy they’d swell right up, and by the time it actually rained you’d not get a single leak through them.”

"My grandpa died before I was very old, but Nathan says he used to teach him and Joshua about different kinds of wood. He said any man who wants to get along with nature needs to develop a reverence for wood."

The stroking stopped for a moment as Brigham looked at him. "That's a good way to put it." One of the callused hands ran along the wood lovingly. "It's like an old friend. Treat him with respect and he'll give you his best."

He stepped back and handed Matthew the wooden plane with its steel blade. "Here, you finish this. Do the others as well. Be careful you don't get one thinner than the others. I'll get some paper and a charcoal stick. We don't want to be building something until we know what it will look like."

When he returned, Brigham asked Matthew a few questions about what Matthew's mother desired in terms of a dish cupboard, then began to sketch as Matthew continued planing the boards. As he worked, Brigham began to hum to himself; then he started to sing softly.

> There's an old mouse chewin' on my pantry door,
> He must have chewed for a month or more.
> When he gets through he'll sure be sore,
> For there ain't a durn thing in there!

Matthew laughed. "That's one I've not heard before."

Brigham looked up. "An old New England folk song." His head dropped again, and he chewed on his lower lip as he continued sketching. Matthew watched him, remembering. His father had once told him that during the early years in Kirtland, Brigham had spent so much time doing missionary work that he had been unable to earn money for his family. One winter he had gone to one of his friends, hat in hand, and begged for a loan so he could get enough food to feed his family until he could earn some money. Benjamin said he had wept in humiliation, for Brigham prided himself on making his own way in the world.

Brigham's blue-gray eyes were filled with a soft amusement as he began to hum again, and Matthew wondered if he was thinking of the same thing. Though Brigham was often of sober demeanor, Matthew had learned that the Apostle had a keen sense of humor and a smile that flashed easily and quickly when he was around his friends. He was clean shaven and had broad, pleasant features. He wore his reddish hair combed straight back and at shoulder length. He was four years older than the Prophet Joseph, which made him around thirty-seven. He was almost four inches shorter than Matthew's six foot two, and had a tendency to be a bit stoop-shouldered, which made him seem even shorter. But he was solidly built, with broad shoulders, and would tip the scales at close to two hundred pounds, Matthew guessed.

Matthew's father and mother had a great deal of respect for Brigham Young and spoke very warmly of him. Matthew knew that he had been a staunch defender of the Prophet during those last harrowing months in Kirtland and had finally fled for his life even before Joseph had left. Benjamin had also told Matthew about the time that Brigham had spoken in tongues while offering the prayer in a meeting with some of the brethren. Afterwards, Joseph had told a few of them that someday Brigham would lead the Church. Matthew wondered if Brigham was aware of that. If so, he seemed totally unaffected by it.

Matthew cleared his throat as he turned back to the bench and began to work. "May I ask you a question, Brother Brigham?"

"Of course."

"How did you first come to hear about the Church?"

Brigham sat back, laying the lapboard and paper down for a moment. His features softened as his mind went back. "Samuel Smith, the Prophet's brother. Haven't you ever heard the story about how he went out trying to sell copies of the Book of Mormon?"

"Oh, yes. That's right. He gave one to your brother-in-law or something."

"Well, he gave one to John Greene, husband of my sister Rhoda. And then my brother Phineas also ended up buying one from him."

"And that's how you got it?"

"Yes. They started passing them around. After my older sister Fanny read Phineas's copy, she gave it to me. Heber also read the same copy."

"You and Brother Kimball are related too, aren't you?"

"Yes, my sister Fanny is Heber's mother-in-law." He leaned back, bringing his knee up and holding it. "Before we were through, those two books went through quite a few hands."

"Did you believe it right away?"

"Well, yes and no. I knew this was a very unusual book. It felt like scripture to me. Just as the Bible feels like scripture. But you got to remember, I was born in Vermont. Us Yankees are pretty hardheaded. I actually took about two more years before I was absolutely sure I accepted the doctrines found therein and whether the Saints—those that followed Joseph—really acted like they had been converted to Christ. But once I was sure, there's been no turning back."

Matthew nodded. That was for sure. He had seen the confidence that Joseph had in Brigham Young and Heber C. Kimball. They were two of his staunchest defenders. Matthew made a determination to corner Heber C. Kimball the next time he saw him and hear his version of how they had come to join the Church.

Brigham picked up the charcoal and the lapboard and the paper and set back to work again. Matthew turned and began to smooth the wood again too. About five minutes later, Brigham spoke.

"Matthew?"

He turned. "Yes?"

"I've been thinking about taking on an apprentice here in my shop."

Matthew set the plane down slowly, not daring to hope. "Yes?"

"I have more work than I can handle. I need someone who's a good worker and dependable." He grinned. "And one who likes to listen to my stories. You ever be interested in that?"

Matthew was staring now. "Do you mean it?"

There was a full-bellied laugh. "Of course I mean it. If you agree, I'll speak with your father about it this evening."

For a moment Matthew fought down the temptation to whoop right out loud. "I would like that, Brother Brigham," he said slowly. "I would like that very much."

Chapter Notes

The liberty pole, which played an important part in the Fourth of July celebration, was struck by lightning a day or two later and was completely destroyed. Parley P. Pratt later wrote that its loss "seemed to portend the awful fate which awaited that devoted city, and the county and people around" (in *Redress*, p. 74).

Brigham Young was a renowned carpenter and glazier (see *American Moses*, pp. 13–17). He supervised or did much of the finish work in the Kirtland Temple.

Joseph's prophecy that Brigham would one day lead the Church is true (see *CHFT*, p. 116).

Chapter Six

On July fourth, 1838, Sidney Rigdon gave his famous Independence Day speech. It was published a short time later. Supposedly it was meant for distribution only among the Saints, something to stiffen their backs and strengthen their will, but within days copies were circulating among the non-Mormons, and portions of the speech were reprinted in some of the Missouri papers. By mid-July, Sidney's ringing cry for nonsubmission was being read by tight-lipped and angry men in the marbled halls of the state capital, Jefferson City.

Sidney Rigdon was a skilled orator. On that early July day he had hoped to fire the emotions of his people. As it turned out, as the month of August got under way, he helped fire far more than that.

The first white settlers in what would later become Daviess

County were a family by the name of Peniston. They built a gristmill on the Grand River and called their little settlement Millport. That was in 1831. By 1836, there were still no more than a hundred settlers in the area, but the county was formed anyway and a town platted to become the county seat. That town was three miles west of Millport and was called Gallatin.

When the Saints began moving into northern Missouri in 1836 and 1837, they settled primarily in Caldwell County to begin with. But as they continued to pour in, they spread north as well. When the Prophet went north looking for sites for additional settlements in May of 1838, he quickly settled on Adam-ondi-Ahman. It was then affectionately dubbed Di-Ahman by the Saints who moved there. Branches, or small congregations of up to a hundred or more, began to form. Very soon there was enough for one branch, then a second. By the last of June, barely a month later, there were enough branches in the Di-Ahman area that Joseph came back and formed a stake—a collection of branches covering a larger geographical area. The Di-Ahman Stake was the second one to be formed in Missouri.

Thus in a matter of weeks the old settlers went from being the majority in the county to being a minority, by a ratio of about four or five to one. They watched the change with growing alarm. Eighteen thirty-eight was an election year. Daviess County set August sixth for its local elections, with the voting to take place in the county seat of Gallatin. There were two candidates running for state representative from the county. Neither were Latter-day Saints, but the Saints had a definite favorite. John Williams was known as a fair-minded and well-respected man. William Peniston was another matter altogether. A hard-drinking, hot-tempered man, he felt he deserved the office by virtue of being the earliest settler in the county. Many of the old settlers supported his bid because they wanted one of their own to represent them in the state legislature. The Mormons vehemently opposed the idea. Peniston was a colonel in the Missouri militia. During the mobbings of 1833, he had led a group of men from Clay County to help drive the Saints out of Jackson County. He made no secret about his bitter and violent hatred for the Mormons.

As election day drew near, Peniston began to lay his plans to make sure the Mormons did not spoil his chances for election.

"But you can't vote, can you, Derek?"

"No, Peter. I don't turn twenty-one until October."

"But even if you were twenty-one, we're not Americans."

Derek sighed and turned over on his side. The inside of the sod hut was nearly pitch black. The windows were small and covered with pieces of a blanket to keep out the mosquitos. They let in very little light. But even if they had, it had been cloudy and overcast for the past two days, and outside there was neither moon nor stars. There was no way he could see Peter in the darkness, but he could picture his face as clearly as if a candle were held right over his head. His blue eyes would be wide and innocent, not challenging what Derek was saying but curious, wanting to know.

He took a breath. "We *are* Americans, Peter, and don't you forget it."

"But—"

"Do we ever plan to go back to England?"

"No."

"Do we own land here?"

"Yes."

"Then we're Americans. And once I turn twenty-one, I will vote." He said it flatly, not willing to accept any further argument. It was one of the few things of which Derek Ingalls was truly proud.

It was quiet for a while, then Peter spoke again. "Are the brethren going to take arms with them, then?"

"No!" It came out as a bark, betraying Derek's own uneasiness about the whole situation.

"But that judge said the people in Gallatin are gonna be waiting for you. He said if you did go, to be sure and—"

"I know what the judge said, Peter," Derek snapped. "But we are not going up there looking for a fight. It's election day. A few of the brethren are going to go up and vote. Then we're going to turn right around and come back home."

"But if you can't vote, why are you going?"

Derek blew out his breath in exasperation. Peter was so blooming logical, always chewing on things, like a dog worrying over an old boot. "I'm going with them, that's all. If there's enough of us, no one's gonna give us any trouble."

There was no answer. Derek waited for the next question to come, but evidently he had finally satisfied his brother. After a few minutes, Peter's breathing deepened and slowed and Derek knew he was asleep. Derek lay back again, putting his hands behind his head, and stared into the blackness above him. He had been there for the council that made the decision to go vote in spite of the rumors that were flying now. A friendly judge had told them that Peniston planned trouble. He counseled them not to go. If they did, he said, they should be sure and go armed.

The council had decided otherwise. They would go, but they would go south without arms of any kind. Derek had raised his arm to the square to sustain the decision. And when he was asked to accompany them—because he was young, and strong, and had no family besides Peter—he immediately agreed, proud that they had that kind of confidence in him.

He felt strongly that it was the right thing to do. But knowing that their cause was just did little to stop the feelings that were tightening his stomach into one large and very tight knot and driving any hope of sleep this night far from his mind.

The sixth of August was a dark, overcast day. It had rained off and on for almost a week, and the roads were muddy and difficult to travel. Gallatin's main street—actually, its only street—was a rutted mud hole, with puddles everywhere and no boardwalks to escape to. It was hardly fit to be called the county seat. It was one straggling row of about nine or ten buildings. And three of them were saloons.

As the small group of Mormons—about an even dozen—trudged into Gallatin just before eleven a.m., their boots made soft sucking noises in the thickness of the "Missouri goo." Several carried umbrellas in expectation of rain again later in the day. Two members of the Di-Ahman stake presidency led the group—Reynolds Cahoon, the first counselor, and Lyman Wight, second counselor. The stake president was John Smith, the Prophet Joseph's uncle. He was an older man, and it was felt that it was not wise for him to come. The rest of them were just the fathers and husbands and brothers who had come in the last few weeks to make a home in Adam-ondi-Ahman. They weren't violent men. The thought that it might come to that left them with a sick feeling in the pits of their stomachs. But they were citizens of a free republic. The Constitution guaranteed them the right to vote. They were determined to exercise that right on this day.

Derek walked between John D. Lee, a man of quiet strength, and John L. Butler, a large man about ten years older than Derek. John and his wife had befriended the two English boys when they came to Di-Ahman and on more than one occasion had shared tools and food with them. John was a soft-spoken man, often preferring to listen rather than to speak. Derek felt a sense of comfort being next to him.

As they approached the first of the buildings, Derek's heart began to thump a little harder. There was a crowd of men already gathered on the steps of the first saloon. A shout went up, and several of them started pointing.

"Lookee there!" a raucous voice cried. "Here come the Mormons."

"Steady, brethren," Reynolds Cahoon said quietly. "We'll just be going in to vote, then we're going right back home."

The man who had first cried out darted to the door of the saloon and shouted through the door. Jeers and catcalls were starting to fly now. Down the street, men were milling around the two other saloons. At the sound of the commotion, they started up the street to join the first group. Derek eyed them quickly. When they joined, there would be over a hundred, perhaps as many as a hundred and fifty. That meant the Mormons were going to be outnumbered ten to one.

As they got closer, any hopes Derek had for a quick in and out plummeted. There was a rough, hand-scrawled sign tacked over the door of the first saloon. "Polls," it read. Derek knew that the polls had to be in a public place. The saloons in Gallatin were about as public as it got.

The doors to the saloon pushed open and a heavyset man in a long coat, ruffled white shirt, and string tie stepped out. John D. Lee turned his head. "That's William Peniston," he said to the others. "Let's go easy now, men."

"Well, well," Peniston sneered as the Mormons came up to the crowd and stopped. "Who let this sorry lot of misfits into town?"

"We've come to vote," Lyman Wight said boldly, stepping forward and elbowing aside the first man. "We don't want no trouble."

"No trouble!" Peniston snarled. "Don't fun me, boy! I read that speech about you waging a war of extermination against us. Is that your idea of no trouble?"

"I don't know what you saw or didn't see," Wight said evenly, "but we're not here for trouble today. All we want is to vote."

Peniston turned. Beside the door to the saloon was a small nail keg turned upside down to hold the door open in hot weather. He leaned down and pulled it forward. The men around him pushed back. One held his elbow and he climbed up on the barrel. Wight had started for the door of the saloon, but instantly a wall of men closed in, blocking his way. For the first time Derek saw that several men were holding stout clubs or short lengths of boards in their hands. He felt his knees go weak. He had seen this kind of thing in Preston once or twice, when liquor fueled massive brawls in the streets. It was not going to be pretty.

The Mormons crowded closer together. Derek's pulse was racing wildly now, and his senses were keenly aware of things around him. The smell of whiskey was ripe in the air. Several of the men were smoking cigars or chewing tobacco, and the acridness of that added to the foul odor. There was also the unmistakable touch of fear in the air, like the static electricity that precedes a violent thunderstorm. A large man with huge hands was half dancing in the front of the circle surrounding Peniston. His hands were up, his fists clenched like a pugilist's.

John Butler leaned over to Derek. "Watch that one. That's Dick Welding."

Derek had already been watching him, feeling the open malice in the man's eyes. Perry Durphy, a convert from Kentucky who was farming a plot of land down next to the river, was on the other side of Derek. "He's the town bully," he whispered. "Thinks he's a real tough. And, as usual, he's drunk."

"Men," Peniston shouted, raising his hands. "This is election day. And these here Mormons have said they've come to vote. Are we gonna let just anyone come into our town and vote today?"

There was an instant roar of response. "No!"

"You know and I know that the leaders of the Mormons are a set of no-good horse thieves, liars, and counterfeiters."

Derek shook his head. If accusations fit your prejudices, truth is easily pushed aside. The crowd howled their agreement with Peniston's words, one or two men shaking their fists or their clubs at the brethren.

"They claim to heal the sick and cast out devils," Peniston continued. "Do you believe they can do that?"

"No!"

"Then does that make them liars?"

"Yes!"

"And Joe Smith, he's the biggest liar of them all. He's duped these poor people into thinking he's got the truth. Does he have the truth?" Peniston roared.

"No!" the crowd roared back.

"Can you count on a Mormon to swear a false oath against us when it suits their needs?"

"*Yes!*" The crowd was stoking up now, and Derek sensed that if the men he had come with didn't move now, it was going to get ugly. But the others seemed paralyzed by Peniston's harangue.

"When the Mormons are around, is your property safe?"

"No!"

"Will they steal you blind the minute you turn your back?"

"Yes!"

"Is that the kind of people we ought to let vote today?"

"No! No! No!" The questions were coming fast and hard now, Peniston pausing only long enough to let the crowd grab a breath between each shouted response.

Suddenly his voice dropped and he turned directly to the Mormons, jabbing his finger at them. "We don't want you here. Nobody asked you to come to Daviess County. Get out!"

"We own land here, same as you," John Butler called out. "That gives us the right to vote, same as you. We came here in peace, and as soon as we vote we'll be gone again."

Such audacity only enraged Peniston all the more. His face was a mottled red now. His nostrils were flared, and his neck was swollen against his shirt collar. "You think we're gonna let you take away our suffrage? If we let you vote, we'll lose everything."

At one point during the mobbings at Independence, Lyman Wight had been chased by the mob who had vowed to kill him. For seven days and seven nights he had eluded them, sleeping in the open, living on little or no food. Lyman Wight was not an easy man to intimidate. He stepped forward, his chin thrust out, his mouth twisted with anger. "You have no right to stop us," he yelled into Peniston's face. "We're citizens of the United States. We have every right to vote."

"I'll see you in hell before we let you vote," Peniston screamed. "I led a mob that drove the Mormons out of Clay County and I can do it again."

Dick Welding, the town bully, had had enough. "Mormons are not allowed to vote," he muttered loudly, "no more than the Negroes are." He started to swear, cursing and raging, and then lumbered forward. The first Mormon he faced was Samuel Brown, a small man from Georgia who had just arrived in Di-Ahman no more than a week before. One arm cocked back and the fingers tightened into a massive fist.

Alarmed at the sight of this mountain bearing down on him, Samuel Brown backed up hastily. He carried an umbrella and lifted it to defend himself. "I don't want any trouble," he blurted.

"Liar!" Welding screamed. He swung at him. Brown jumped back, parrying the blow with the closed umbrella. Welding was just drunk enough that his movements were slow and cumbersome. "Liar!" he shouted again, throwing one blow after another now but only connecting with the air.

The sudden action had frozen both the Missourians and the Mormons. They were all staring at the two men—Brown backing away from the crowd, Welding stumbling after him, his arms flailing. Then Perry Durphy, who stood next to Derek, jumped into action. He darted forward and grabbed Welding's arm as it came back in a swing. "Leave him alone!" he shouted.

Welding roared like a bear that had been stuck with a pike. He swung around, throwing off Durphy's grasp. That broke the spell that gripped the crowd. With a shout, five or six Missourians swarmed at Durphy, clubs and boards swinging. "Kill him! Kill him!" they screamed.

Instantly it was a melee. Lyman Wight swung an uppercut from below his waist and caught the man nearest him full on the chin. The man slammed backwards against the saloon wall and collapsed with a groan. But Derek didn't see the end of that, for a man leaped at him and rode him to the ground, pounding at his face, trying to get through his guard.

Derek Ingalls had shoveled coal twelve hours a day, six days a week for four years in the boilers of old Mr. Morris's factory. For the past month, he and Peter had been cutting and hauling fifty- and sixty-pound slabs of sod and heaving them up to make walls. Any softness he might have developed since leaving England was completely gone again. With a cry of his own, he lunged upward, sending the man on top of him hurtling away. In an instant he was on his feet, backing up to get into the open.

Now the greater numbers of the mob began to pay off. The Mormons were being separated and lost the advantage of staying together. As Derek swung around, he saw Abraham Nelson knocked to the ground by half a dozen men. In an instant they were all over him, ripping at his clothes. The Nelson family lived two plots over from Derek and Peter, and they too had been very kind to the two English lads. A great anger welled up inside Derek. Roaring like a bull, he shoved forward, aiming at the men who were pounding and kicking at Brother Nelson.

But before he had gone two steps, he was caught from behind in a great bear hug. Even as he fought to break the grip that held him, he watched in horror. The Missourians backed away from Nelson momentarily. He moaned once, then pushed himself up on his knees. His face was bloody, his eyes dazed. When they saw he wasn't finished, the man closest to him raised his club and stepped in again. Then there was a shout of rage and Nelson's younger brother, Hyrum, came running in full tilt. He lowered his head, catching the man full in the chest, and sent him sprawling.

Derek gave a shout of his own. He reached back over his head and grabbed the hair of the man that had pinned him. He yanked hard. There was a scream of pain and then he was free. He raced forward again, determined to help his neighbors. But he didn't make it. Someone grabbed Derek's arm. He spun around, a fist coming up to strike at his attacker. He was too late. He saw the flash of the club. The blow caught him just below the elbow. He screamed as the pain shot clear through his body. Stumbling backwards, he fought to keep his balance in the sucking mud. In doing so, his arms flew out to catch himself, leaving his upper body unguarded. The second blow caught him right at the hairline. White lights and flashes of red exploded before his eyes. He went down hard, barely aware of the soft plopping sound he made as he hit the mud and slid backwards a foot or two.

Fortunately his attacker did not attempt to assault Derek further but whirled and went after another Mormon. Moaning with the pain, conscious of the cold wetness through the back of his clothes, dazed by the incredible pain in his head and arm, Derek staggered back to his feet. Blood streamed down his face, and he wiped at his eyes with the sleeve of his shirt.

He stood there for a moment, gasping at the pain. Then a movement off to his right caught his eye. It was John Butler, running hard. For a moment, Derek felt a sharp jab of bitter disappointment. Butler was running away, leaving his brethren to the mob. But the disappointment lasted only for a moment, for even as Derek watched, the gentle giant of a man reached a nearby woodpile. He picked up one piece of wood, hefted it, then hurled it away. The second piece he brought up was a two-foot length of oak. In three leaps he was back into the fray, swinging the club like an Indian warrior with his tomahawk.

It was like watching a master reaper going through a wheat field. The club flashed. One man was knocked rolling. The next one raised his club to defend himself and had it knocked flying out of his hand. A second blow to the side of his head took him down without a sound.

Derek straightened, feeling a surge of pride. Just in front of Butler, another Mormon was down with eight or ten men swarming over him, hurling blows and kicks at his face and ribs. Butler gave one mighty roar, and waded in. He gave the first man a blow across the back that sounded like an ax hitting a tree stump. The man screamed and dropped writhing to the ground. The next two Missourians swung around. He caught them both with one sweeping blow that sent them sprawling. A fourth man, then a fifth were cut down, helpless before the onslaught. The rest turned and ran.

That didn't stop Butler. He jumped to the next group. Down

went another, then another. A cry went up. Peniston was running down the muddy street, his coat flying, screaming for others to follow him. A few men tried to regroup enough to face this slashing fury. Like a lion attacking a flock of sheep, Butler went after them. With a yell, they turned tail and fled.

Wincing, Derek wiped at his head. His sleeve came away a bright red, and only then did it register that he was seriously injured. Awkwardly, unable to use his left arm—it was totally numb now—he fished in his pocket for the rag he used as a handkerchief. As he pressed it to his head, he could feel the long gash in his scalp. He looked around. It was a scene to chill the blood. Men were down everywhere, Mormons and Missourians alike. There was a brief flash of satisfaction as Derek saw that one of them was Dick Welding, the loudmouthed bully who had started the whole thing. Lyman Wight had a cut on his cheek, and his face was bloody. Reynolds Cahoon was holding the back of his head. He grimaced as he waved his other hand. "Brethren, we'd best move out of here."

With the townspeople who had not joined in the fracas looking silently on, the battered group began to move out. John Butler came to Derek and took his elbow. As they moved slowly up the street, Derek looked up at his friend in awe. "I didn't know you could do that."

Butler held up the piece of oak in a bit of a daze, then turned to Derek. "Neither did I," he murmured. He dropped the club in the mud, and took Derek's arm. "Come on. We'd better get out of here. You know they'll be coming after us as soon as they find their courage."

Derek felt his heart drop. He hadn't thought about that. Di-Ahman was a scattered settlement and not easily defended. If the Missourians really gathered their strength, it could prove to be a very long and difficult night.

By midnight, the rain was coming down in sheets, slicing through the thicket of hazel bush and drenching all those trying to hide in it. The temperature had dropped to the mid-sixties, and there was a stiff wind blowing. With clothing, shoes, and blankets completely soaked and the ground as sodden as a swamp, the Saints could do little more than huddle together in misery. Children whimpered pitifully; women hunched over tiny babies, trying to keep them dry; older youth hugged themselves tightly, trying to get warm.

Peter Ingalls had turned fourteen in May and was now almost as tall as Derek. That left him too young for guard duty but too big to be treated as a child anymore. And he had no family but Derek. So he stood alone, shivering violently, feeling the water running off his cap and down the back of his neck. Any thought of sleep was completely insane.

Finally, he could bear it no longer. He straightened and stepped to where Sister Butler held two of the younger children in her arms, pulling themselves together to share what little body warmth the three of them had. A third child was lying in front of her on the ground, crying softly. "Sister Butler?"

She looked up. "Yes, Peter?"

"I can't bear this waiting any longer. I'm going to find Derek and stand with him for a time."

"All right, Peter. Please be careful."

He nodded, and began pushing his way through the thick tangle of brush, feeling the branches scratching at his arms. As he came to the edge of the thicket, he stopped, peering into the darkness. It took a moment, then he made out the dark shape standing a few feet away. "Derek?" he whispered loudly. "Is that you?"

"No, son," came the answering whisper, "Derek's the next man down."

Peter didn't recognize the voice, nor could he make out any identity in the darkness. He walked slowly along the edge of the thicket until he saw the second shape. He called again.

"Peter," came the welcome answer, "I'm over here."

"Aye." He went quickly to him, and for a moment the two brothers embraced.

"No sign of them?" Peter finally said, pulling back.

"None so far."

"What time is it?"

Derek looked up, as if the lightless sky might reveal some clues. "I'm not sure. Around midnight, I guess."

The thicket was down in the river bottoms, about a mile from the main part of Di-Ahman. Peter was gazing in that direction. "Do you think they came?"

Derek had wondered the same thing only about a hundred times in the past three hours. Di-Ahman was completely empty now. Before the men who had gone to Gallatin had even gotten out of sight of the town, they had seen the riders leaving to call for help. Rumors quickly spread. The old settlers were going to ride against Di-Ahman and have their revenge. So there had been no delay. When the Mormon men returned to Di-Ahman, they had gotten the few arms they had, taken their families to the thickets along the river, and posted guards.

Derek's mind kept conjuring up images of drunken men going from house to house, looting what little of value there was, vandalizing what couldn't be carried away. It left him feeling hollow and empty inside. But he couldn't share those images with Peter, so he tried to keep his voice cheerful. "I don't think so, Peter. I know the rain is making us miserable, but I think it will discourage them too. They get wet and cold and it'll sober them up. Then I'm sure they'll think twice about comin' after us."

"I hope so."

Peter moved close enough that their shoulders touched. He did not like the blackness of the night, not knowing what was out and about in it. For several moments he stood there, then finally he turned to his brother. "Derek?"

"Yes, Peter?"

He took a breath, shoving his hands deep into his soggy pockets. "Why do things like this happen?"

How do you answer a question like that? Derek reached out with his good hand and touched the huge welt and the rough bandage on his forehead. Finally he shook his head. "I don't know, Peter. I really don't know."

Chapter Notes

Election day at Gallatin is described by Joseph in great detail (see *HC* 3:55–58; see also *CHFT*, p. 194). Peniston's speech against the Saints; the start of the fight by Dick Welding; John Butler's courageous defense with an oak club; the Saints hiding all night in a thicket for safety—all these events really occurred and are accurately portrayed here, though of course fictional license has allowed the author to fill in some of the details and to sustain a smooth narrative flow. The names of both Saints and Missourians used in this chapter are the actual names of people involved in the events depicted, with the obvious exception of the novel's fictional characters.

Chapter Seven

Mary Ann brought a heaping plate of eggs and thin slices of ham over from the small cookstove and set them on the table. She turned. "I think the corn bread should be ready now, Rebecca."

Nodding, Rebecca opened the oven, reached in and touched the top of the bread lightly with her fingertip. "Yes, it's done."

"Good," Matthew crowed. "I'm starving."

Rebecca carried the heavy pan over and set it on a towel Mary Ann had folded and placed on the table, then both mother and daughter sat down. Benjamin looked around at his family briefly, then bowed his head. They all followed suit.

"God in heaven," he began, "we thank thee for this bounteous food which thou hast given us this day. We thank thee for the goodness of life and the beauties of the earth. We thank thee for the rain that has come and for the richness of our coming crops."

There was a momentary pause. "We are mindful of our family

this day. We pray for Carl and Melissa and their children back in Kirtland. Bless them and keep them in our absence from one another. We rejoice again in the reuniting of Joshua and his family to us. We know that it was thy hand that brought that about, and we thank thee for it. Bless Jessica and John and their children and our two English boys in Di-Ahman. We ask thee to bless our food as we partake of it with gratefulness. In the name of Jesus, amen."

"Amen!" Matthew immediately reached for the plate of ham and eggs, winning a quick look from his mother. When he saw it, he was immediately sheepish. He handed the plate across the table to Rebecca. "Ladies first," he said gallantly.

Rebecca laughed and pushed it back. "Go ahead. I would hate to see you faint away before the food gets to you."

"Good," Matthew said, pulling four eggs and several slices of ham onto his plate. Then he carved out a huge chunk of corn bread with his fork, steadying the steaming portion quickly with his hand to get it back to his plate.

Mary Ann just shook her head. "I hope it is a bounteous harvest," she said ruefully to Benjamin. "Otherwise we won't have enough to feed this boy through November."

Benjamin just smiled, remembering when Joshua and Nathan had gone through the same cycle of voraciousness. "Good thing we get a little work out of him, or we couldn't afford to feed him."

"Speaking of work," Matthew said between mouthfuls, "do you think we can start cutting the wheat this week? Brother Brigham says I can take whatever time I need to help you."

Benjamin shook his head. "No, not this week. Maybe early next week."

"How about if we—"

But Matthew didn't finish. There was a sharp knock on the door. Benjamin looked at Mary Ann in surprise. It was barely seven o'clock in the morning. He got up and went to the door, opened it, then stepped back. "Well, Brother Joseph. Brother Hyrum. Good morning."

"Good morning, Brother Benjamin," Joseph said. He looked

past him. "Morning, Sister Steed. Rebecca. Matthew. How are all of you this morning?"

"Fine," Mary Ann responded, standing now. "We're just sitting down to breakfast. Will you join us?"

Joseph smiled briefly, shaking his head. "Thank you anyway, Mary Ann, but we've already eaten." He turned back to Benjamin, his face sobering. "Brother Ben, we need your help."

"All right."

"Do you still have your rifle?"

There was a sharp intake of breath from Mary Ann.

"Yes." Benjamin was watching the Prophet very closely now.

Hyrum stepped forward to stand beside his brother. "We have received some bad news. From Di-Ahman."

Instantly Rebecca was on her feet, her face tight.

"A rider, Vinson Knight, came in about half an hour ago," Joseph went on. "Some of our brethren went to Gallatin yesterday to vote."

"In spite of the warning they received?" Matthew blurted.

"Yes," Joseph said grimly. "We have a right to exercise our franchise. They didn't want trouble, so they went without arms." He stopped, the worry heavy in his eyes.

"And?" Benjamin prompted.

"There was a mob waiting," Hyrum said softly. "Trouble broke out."

Rebecca came forward in three quick steps. "Derek?" she whispered. "Did Derek go with them?"

Joseph hesitated, then finally bobbed his head once. "I knew that would be your first question." The blue eyes clouded momentarily. "Vinson says Derek went with them."

A hand flew to her mouth.

Mary Ann came quickly to her and put an arm around her. "How bad?" Mary Ann asked Joseph.

Joseph sighed, obviously reluctant to share what he knew. "The report is sketchy right now. But not good."

"How bad?" Benjamin demanded, watching his daughter closely now.

Hyrum also had an eye fixed on Rebecca. He looked at Joseph once, then back to Benjamin, avoiding Rebecca's burning stare. "Two or three dead," he said slowly.

Rebecca gasped, then swayed as her knees gave way a little. Mary Ann steadied her, holding her tightly.

Hyrum rushed on. "We don't know who they are as yet. The mob has refused to let our people get the bodies for burial."

Joseph turned to Benjamin. "Hyrum, Sidney, and I are leading a group of men." He took a quick breath and let it out again. "Brother Knight says the people of Daviess County are arming themselves to drive our people right out of the county. We're going north to give assistance. We've already stopped at Nathan's. He'll be going."

"I want to go too, Pa," Matthew said.

"No!" Mary Ann cried.

Matthew swung around. "It's not just Rebecca who cares about Derek."

Benjamin had turned now too.

"Mother"—Matthew was pleading now—"this is Derek and Peter. They are my friends. I want to help."

Mary Ann looked to Benjamin, her eyes imploring him to sustain her on this one. Benjamin searched her face, then turned to look at his youngest son, now almost a full head taller than his mother. "He's a man now, Mary Ann," he said simply.

Her lip started to quiver and her head dropped. Joseph walked to her. "It'll be all right, Sister Steed," he said with great solemnity. "We shall see that no harm comes to Matthew." Half turning, he reached out and laid a hand on Rebecca's arm. She was weeping quietly now. "It will be all right!" he said, more firmly now. "You must have faith."

Then he stepped back and turned to Benjamin. "We're gathering at the public square. If you bring your horse, we'll have a second mount for Matthew."

"We'll be there in five minutes," Benjamin said.

Shoal Creek lay about a half mile north of Far West. It was not a large stream, no more than four or five feet across in most places. It flowed eastward in a meandering path, through Haun's Mill twelve miles to the east, and eventually into the Grand River. There was not a lot of timber along its bank, but enough trees and brush to provide a place of privacy.

It was to those thickets that Rebecca came as the sun began to break through the clouds and climb toward its zenith on this August morning. She pushed her way through a patch of river birch and wild raspberry and found a small clearing beneath a group of medium-size cottonwood trees.

She looked around to make sure she was alone; then, brushing at the corners of her eyes, she dropped to her knees and bowed her head.

It was almost a half hour before she came out of the trees and started back up the gentle rise to her father's cabin, head bowed, walking slowly.

"Mama! Mama!"

The voice carried clearly all the way through the house. Caroline looked up from her task of kneading a large clump of bread dough. Savannah, sitting on the floor playing with a set of blocks Joshua had bought for her, was jabbering away happily. At the sound, she looked up. "Livvy?"

"Yes," Caroline said, wiping the flour from her hands onto her apron. "It's Olivia."

The front door burst open and Olivia came tearing through the house. "Mama!"

"We're back in the kitchen," Caroline called.

Olivia came sliding in, her face flushed, her chest rising and falling. "Mama, Papa's back."

Caroline's head came up. "He is?"

"Yes, he and Will. The steamboat got in early this morning. They're at the freight yard."

Savannah pushed to her feet. "Papa?"

Olivia picked her up, lifting her above her head so she looked down into Olivia's face. "Yes, Savannah, Papa's home. Papa's home."

"Wanna see Papa," Savannah said matter-of-factly.

Caroline started to untie her apron, feeling a rush of excitement. Joshua and Will had left for St. Louis on the twentieth of July. That was better than two weeks ago. She always hated it when Joshua was gone on these extensive trips, but this was particularly bad, for Will had gone with him.

"Wanna see Papa," Savannah repeated, more forcefully.

"You and Mama both, Savannah," Caroline said. "The bread can wait."

"What do you think?" Joshua said. He had Savannah in one arm, but he put the other one around Caroline's waist and pulled her against him. He was grinning like a kid who had just discovered he could tie a bow in his own bootlaces for the first time.

Caroline hugged him, looking up at the large crate that sat in the wagon. "I think it's wonderful, Joshua. The perfect gift. Your father is going to be very pleased."

"I think so too," he said, not trying to hide his pride. "So, get your things. We've got to get going."

For a moment it didn't register, then Caroline's head came around. "What?"

"If we get started right away and push hard, we can make it by tomorrow night."

"Today? Joshua, I'm not ready to leave. I . . . There's food to get. Clothes to pack. I'll have to wash—"

He put a finger to her lips, cutting her off. "Did you get your part of the buying done?"

"Yes. Olivia and I have bought everything, but . . . the roads, they're going to be a mess."

He gave her an incredulous look. "You think muddy roads are a threat to a man who makes his living hauling freight? Besides, the weather is clearing. They'll be drying up fast."

"Mama," Will jumped in, siding with his father, "if we don't get Grandpa's present up there soon, it will be too late for this year."

"Oh, yes, Mama," Olivia cried, "let's go. I want to see Grandma and Grandpa again."

Now it was Savannah's head that came around. "Gampa?" she said, looking around.

Joshua chuckled. "Do you want to go see Gamma and Gampa?"

"Yes. Wanna see Gampa."

"Then it's unanimous," Joshua declared. "Cornwell will have a fit, but we'll only stay a day or two. And we'll help you get ready, won't we kids?"

Will and Olivia answered in a single chorus. "Yes!"

Joshua took both her hands, his eyes half pleading now. "What do you say?"

Caroline knew she had lost. And she didn't resent it. His excitement was infectious. She threw up her hands in surrender. "All right, today it is."

There were about twenty armed men who left Far West with Joseph and Hyrum at their head. As they moved north, their numbers swelled as brethren living in isolated homesites between Far West and Di-Ahman joined them. Word of the disaster had spread rapidly, and there was much concern among these Saints who lived out and away from everyone else. The whole countryside was in an uproar. County officials were trying to calm people. Two ministers were trying to do just the opposite. Emotions were running hot and rumors flying faster than a Missouri twister.

As they passed the various homesteads of non-Mormons, there was fear on that side as well. About a mile south of Gallatin, they approached a cluster of two or three cabins. From a distance they could see a woman out hanging wash on her line. Several children were playing here and there around her. Then there was a faint cry. One of the children was pointing in their direction. The woman stood frozen for a moment, then dropped the dress she was holding and started shouting. In moments the woman, the children, and any others who had been outside were into the cabins, and Benjamin could see the shutters slamming shut. And then, before the group of Mormon men had gone fifty more yards, a man darted out of the back of the farthest cabin and ran hard toward the small barn behind it. A moment later a horse came pounding out. The man leaned low over the horse's neck, whipping him hard with a riding crop. He turned north and, in a moment, disappeared behind some trees.

Benjamin felt a tightening in his chest. In five or six minutes Gallatin would have its warning. The Mormons were coming. And they were coming in numbers and they were armed. Without saying a word, Joseph jerked his head toward the east and reined his horse to the right. They would give Gallatin a wide berth.

It was midafternoon when the brethren, now nearly fifty strong, rode up the valley of Adam-ondi-Ahman, following the long bend in the Grand River. Benjamin and Matthew were up near the front, not far behind Joseph and Hyrum and Sidney Rigdon. They were tired, and now that they were on the outskirts of Di-Ahman, their vigilance relaxed a little. Several of the men were half dozing in their saddles.

Then Joseph reined in his horse, pointing. "That's Tower Hill," he called back over his shoulder, "and the cabin you see there, that's Lyman Wight's. We're almost there."

Matthew leaned forward eagerly. About three hundred yards ahead, a ridge from the bluffs jutted sharply out into the valley. Signs of settlement were now everywhere evident—lean-tos, tents, sod huts, a log cabin or two.

Word of their coming had evidently reached the Mormons as well, for as they rode along now, people began to stream out to greet them. Several of the men carried arms, but the sight of Joseph and Hyrum and this many of their brethren was cause for great rejoicing.

Then suddenly Matthew turned. Someone was calling their names. He searched the growing crowd.

"Matthew! Nathan! Father Steed!"

"Peter?" Matthew reached across to punch his brother's arm. "Nathan, it's Peter." He craned his neck. "And Derek. It's Derek, Pa!"

Benjamin was staring as he reined in the horse. "It *is* Derek." The relief washed over him in a great rush. "Thank the Lord!" he breathed.

Joseph had turned in his saddle. He was smiling broadly. "This will be welcome news for Mary Ann and Rebecca." He laughed right out loud at the thought of that. "Give those two boys my best, Benjamin. We'll meet you at Brother Wight's place later."

Father and sons pulled their horses out of line and swung down as Derek and Peter hurried up to them. Matthew was to Derek in four great strides and threw his arms around him. Derek gave a little yelp and winced in pain. "Easy, lad," he cried, pulling free and holding his arm.

Matthew was instantly contrite. Then as he stared at Derek, his eyes got wide. The arm was in a sling, and the bandage tied to Derek's forehead was soiled and bloodstained.

Nathan's mouth was tight. "Are you all right, Derek?"

Derek stuck out his good hand and firmly gripped Nathan's, then Benjamin's. "I'm fine. What a welcome sight you are."

"What happened?" Matthew blurted.

"Are you sure you're all right?" Benjamin asked, peering at the bandage.

Peter answered for his brother. "Brother Wight thinks the bone in his arm may be cracked. But even though he took a nasty blow to his head, it's just cut bad." An impish grin split his face. "But I know he's gonna be all right. He's been snappin' at me all afternoon. Peter, do this. Peter, fetch that. Peter, stop makin' so much noise."

The burden of worry and dread that had ridden on Benjamin's shoulders for the past twelve hours lifted, and a dizzying sense of euphoria swirled in around him. He was still holding Derek's hand. He gripped it fiercely. "We are so glad to see you, Derek. When we heard that some of you were killed—"

"Killed?" Derek interrupted. He shook his head. "No one was killed."

"No one?" Nathan repeated.

"Not on either side." There was a fleeting smile. "There's more than one set of cracked ribs and some whopping headaches today in Daviess County—and I'm not talking just about the Saints—but that's about all. And thank the good Lord for that."

Benjamin quickly told them about the report that had come south.

"How swiftly rumor flies," Derek said with a grimace. "We heard the whole county was arming against us, so we spent the night down in the river bottoms hiding the women and children. But no one ever came."

"Well," Matthew said, with just a touch of defiance, "there are over four dozen of us now. Those old settlers had better think twice about trying something."

Suddenly overcome with the emotion he was feeling, Nathan laid a hand on Derek's good shoulder. "Rebecca is worried sick about you. To see you in no worse shape than this . . ." He shook his head. "We're very grateful."

Derek nodded, understanding immediately how such news would have struck his beloved Rebecca. "I shall write a letter tonight for you to take back with you."

Benjamin shook his head firmly. "No letters. You're not going to be doing much farmin' with that arm, so you're coming home with us. Becca won't be convinced you're all right until she sees you for herself."

Matthew grinned at his friend. "And I'll just warn you now. When she sees you, you may end up with another broken arm and a set of cracked ribs, because you're going to get the hugging of your life."

Rebecca sat on a thick clump of prairie grass between the two wagon tracks that were the road that led out of Far West. She was about a quarter of a mile beyond the last house, just enough off the brow of the hill on which the city sat to get a panoramic view of a wide expanse of the countryside. With her eye she could follow the road as it snaked its way down the gradual decline, then on across the rolling folds of prairie. Though she couldn't see it, about five miles from where she sat the north-south road intersected this one.

She closed her eyes, trying to shut out the images that followed. Derek's description of Di-Ahman had been too explicit. She could picture the wandering line of trees that marked the banks of the Grand River, the bluffs on either side of the beautiful little valley. And on the northern bluff there was a partially finished sod hut. A boy was off to one side of it. It was Peter, on his knees in front of a freshly turned square of dirt. A roughly painted slab of board stuck in the ground at one end of the gravesite served as a tombstone. Other Saints were standing around, heads bowed.

Angrily, Rebecca stood up, kicking at the soft dirt that two days ago had been thick mud and by tomorrow afternoon would be dust again. It had been yesterday morning when Brother Joseph and Hyrum had come to the house. Even though she had known there was little chance they could return the same day, the moment her chores were over, she had come out on the road and sat there until twilight. Watching to the east and north. Hoping against hope.

Today she had been here since nine o'clock, her mother finally shooing her out of the house, knowing that nothing else would help. Now it was almost sundown again. Several times Rebecca's hopes had soared when she saw figures in the distance, but her hopes were quickly dashed as they approached and then passed her by. She was growing numb now, exhausted in both mind and spirit at the thoughts of having yet another night and day of not knowing.

A movement caught her eye. Her heart jumped, and then just as quickly fell again. Some figures had appeared on the top of one of the gentle ridges that stretched out to the east of her. At first she had thought there were only two of them, both on horseback. But then she could see there were five people—two on horseback and three others walking beside them. It was too few to be the brethren returning and too many for it to be her father and Matthew and Nathan.

She turned away, the pain knifing through her. She would go home. Better to sit in the cabin staring at the chinked walls and rough-cut furniture than to feel this constant leaping and then dashing of her hopes. But she didn't move. Finally she turned back to look at the figures again. The low sun was at her back, but she still raised one hand to shade her eyes.

Then suddenly she was staring. They were about two hundred yards away now. The lead horse had a white blaze on its face, just like the sorrel mare that her father owned. She took a step forward, going up on tiptoe, as if that might help her see better. The man riding that horse sat tall and straight and wore a large straw hat.

"Papa!" she whispered. She didn't dare believe. She told herself her eyes were playing tricks on her. They had done it before. But she shook it off. This time there was something unmistakably familiar about the man. It was her father.

She started walking now, at first slowly, then more swiftly. The man walking closest to the horses was Nathan. And beside him was Matthew. She was almost certain now. Suddenly she stopped, staring, her heart leaping. The person beside Matthew was short and slender. She leaned forward. It was Peter!

Her eyes jumped back to the second horseman. She barely dared to breathe. Then, with a cry of joy, Rebecca broke into a run, waving. The figure on the second horse had straightened now in the saddle and one arm came up and waved. Then the sound came floating toward her on the late afternoon air. "Becca! Becca!"

Mary Ann laid the bandage back across Derek's forehead and tied it into place. "It's going to scar."

He pulled a face. "I know." Then, turning to Rebecca, he grinned. "That won't make you change your mind about me, will it?"

Seeing the ugly gash in Derek's forehead had made Rebecca sick to her stomach. She shook her head, forcing a wan smile.

Now he looked genuinely concerned. He lifted the arm that was in the sling. "It *is* going to make a difference to her, Mother Steed. Your daughter doesn't want a broken-down husband."

Rebecca moved over to the bench where Derek was sitting. She sat down next to him, slipped an arm through his good arm, and laid her head against his shoulder. "Please don't joke about it, Derek. Every time I think about what happened to you . . ." She gave a little shudder.

He put his arm around her, sobering. "It's all right, Rebecca. It's over now."

"Is it?" she cried.

No one answered. Benjamin stared at his hands. Matthew looked at Peter, then away. Mary Ann was watching her husband. Finally, Benjamin looked up. "Joseph is still up north. He's going to hold a meeting tomorrow at noon in Di-Ahman with a delegation of some of the county officials—there *are some* cooler heads in the county. They'll try and work out some kind of truce."

He smiled at his daughter with great tenderness. "The brethren wanted us to wait and come home with them tomorrow, but we decided you and your mother would be very anxious to receive the news that everything was all right."

Rebecca snuggled up against Derek. "I would have died if you hadn't come until tomorrow."

"Me too," Peter said, pretending petulance. "One more day of Derek's cooking and it would have been me they were burying."

"What?" Derek cried. He tried to swat at his brother, but Rebecca blocked his arm. The others all broke out in laughter.

Mary Ann stood, still smiling. "I think we'd better get this poor, starving boy fed and happy again. I have a chicken already boiling in the pot, so it won't take long." She looked to her youngest. "Matthew, you go tell Nathan and Lydia to come over for supper. I think this deserves a family celebration."

"Right." As Matthew stood and started for the door, Derek sat up, pushing Rebecca back slightly. "Uh . . . Matthew, could you wait just one second?"

Matthew stopped. Derek stood now too. He shot a panicked look at Benjamin, then a fleeting, sickly smile at Mary Ann. Then, taking a quick breath, he looked down at Rebecca and took her hand. "Uh . . . Becca, I was going to talk with you about this, but maybe right here is as good as anything."

Rebecca looked surprised. "What?"

Derek gulped nervously. "I wanted to get the farm started good. Have a nice place. Make sure I could make a go of it. I thought that by next spring . . ." He trailed off, struggling.

Eyes widening, Rebecca straightened slowly. Mary Ann had turned back around and was staring at Derek.

Suddenly the words came out in a rush. "And I was thinking, after what happened up there, that sometimes it might not be the best thing to do. To wait, I mean. Sometimes you just have to seize the moment. Sometimes waiting just makes it worse. I mean, it might be tough this first winter, but after that I . . ."

He had turned to look at Benjamin, and his voice trailed off when he saw the older man's face. The heavy brows had pulled downward; the pale blue eyes were noticeably grim. "What are you trying to say, boy?" Benjamin said gruffly. "Come on, spit it out."

"Benjamin!" Mary Ann said, slapping at his arm.

Rebecca had come to her feet. Her eyes were large and filled with shining wonder as she stared at Derek. He took her hand now and drew her a step closer to him. "I'm . . . I'm wonderin' if you might consider getting married now. Not waiting until spring."

Before Rebecca could react, Benjamin stepped to the two young people. "Right now?" he barked. "You're asking to marry her right now?"

"Uh . . . yes, sir. I guess that's what I'm suggesting. With your permission, sir."

"That wouldn't be possible right now." It came out flat and hard.

Derek looked like he had been struck. Rebecca's mouth dropped. There was a sharp gasp from Mary Ann.

Then a twinkle stole into Benjamin's eye. "You can't marry him right now. Jessica would never forgive us if she weren't here."

Derek was staring, comprehension not yet coming. Then Rebecca laughed. In one step she was to her father. "Oh, Papa, thank you!"

Benjamin brought up a hand and brushed her hair, smiling now into her eyes. "And Joshua. It will probably take a week by the time we send a letter down and get them back up here." He put his hand under her chin and lifted her face to his. "Think you two could bear to wait a whole week?"

Her eyes were shining. "Oh, yes, Papa. Yes. Thank you." And then she turned and threw herself into Derek's arms as Mary Ann and Matthew came swarming in to congratulate them.

They had finished the chicken stew and started on Mary Ann's rhubarb pie when Benjamin's head suddenly came up and he held up one hand. The conversation around the table stopped immediately. Then they all heard it—the jingle of harness and the creaking of a wagon. Even as they listened, it stopped.

"Someone's here," Benjamin said, swinging his legs out and around the bench. He stood and went to the door. All eyes in the room followed him. As he opened the door, his body filled the frame. They tried to see past him, but couldn't.

"Well, I'll be!" Benjamin exclaimed. Then he turned back to look at his family, grinning broadly.

"What?" Mary Ann asked.

"You two must be living right," he said to Derek and Rebecca.

Mary Ann stood quickly. "What is it, Ben?"

He still stood in the doorway, blocking their view to the outside. "Matthew," he said gravely, "you'd better plan an early start to Haun's Mill. We'd best fetch Jessica and John here as soon as possible."

Mary Ann stood up, walking toward the door. She was trying to see past her husband. "Ben, for heaven's sake, what is it?"

Before she could reach him he stepped forward and took her by the shoulders. He kissed her on the cheek soundly. "You think you could get a wedding together by Friday?"

"Friday?" Mary Ann said, half-shocked.

"Friday?" Rebecca echoed, standing up quickly. "But that's day after tomorrow. I want to wait for Joshua and Caroline."

Benjamin laughed right out loud. "But that's just it. Joshua and Caroline are here," he said. He stepped back, throwing the door open wide. "Joshua and Caroline are here right now."

Chapter Notes

The first reports reaching Far West were that two or three brethren had been killed. Joseph led a party north to aid the Saints but thankfully found that the reports had been wildly exaggerated. (See *HC* 3:58–60.)

Chapter Eight

The midday meal was finally finished. With everyone home again, the Steeds had once again moved the table outside and laid some planks across four sawhorses to accommodate the whole family. But even then the older children had to eat from their laps. Nathan and Lydia had come over right after breakfast and spent the morning visiting with Joshua's family. Matthew had left for Haun's Mill before dawn and returned with Jessica and John Griffith and their four children in midafternoon. The initial excitement of the reunion had tempered a little now, but the children were still talking excitedly with one another, making grand plans for the day. The women were clustered together, laying out the details of the wedding. Benjamin, Matthew, Derek, and Nathan were talking crops and harvesting. Savannah sat on her grandfather's lap playing with a small braided leather snake Matthew had made for one of Jessica's boys. She was so fascinated by its sinuous movements that she was totally engrossed and, for the moment, was completely quiet.

Joshua sat on the front step watching it all with some impatience. Finally, he could bear it no longer. He looked at Caroline until he caught her eye. He gave her a quizzical look. For a moment she was puzzled, then she laughed softly at him and nodded. "Yes, Joshua, I think it's time."

He stood and raised his hands. "All right, everybody," he called, "we've waited long enough." And then as all heads turned toward him he grinned. "We've got a birthday party to do."

That stopped all conversation instantly. "A what?" Mary Ann exclaimed.

"A birthday party?" young Joshua echoed.

"You heard me," Joshua laughed. "I think we ought to have a birthday party."

"Whose party, Uncle Joshua?" Emily said, any thoughts of play now forgotten.

"Yours," he said, walking to her and touching his finger to her nose. As she squealed, he turned to her brother. "And yours, Joshua." He moved from child to child. "And yours, Rachel."

Olivia jumped in now too. "And yours, Matthew," she cried.

"What are you talking about?" Matthew asked. "It's not my birthday. In fact, nobody has a birthday today."

Will had come to stand by his father. The smile on his face nearly split his face from ear to ear. "Yes they do," he crowed. "It's everybody's birthday today."

Joshua waved his hands for silence as that brought an eruption of noise. Gradually they quieted down again. He swung around to face his mother, his eyes softening. "It's been eleven years since I was there for anyone's birthday. That's a lot of birthdays! Well, today we're going to celebrate every one of them."

Caroline was standing next to her mother-in-law. "He means it, Mother Steed," she said happily. "You wouldn't believe it. He and Will and Olivia have been like little kids at Christmastime about this."

"But I don't think—," Mary Ann began.

Joshua cut her off. "Didn't it occur to anyone to ask why we brought up two wagons with us this time?"

"Why, Uncle Joshua?" Rachel called. "Why did you bring two wagons?"

Jessica jerked around. Rachel, normally so shy and quiet, especially around Joshua, was fairly dancing with excitement. Her two stepbrothers were beside her. Luke was almost six now, but Mark was not yet four. He was too young to fully follow what was going on, but he sensed that something exciting was about to happen. Their eyes were as wide as Rachel's. Jessica couldn't help but laugh right out loud at the magic Joshua was working with the children.

He reared back, looking very solemn. "Why did we bring two wagons?" he intoned. "I thought you'd never ask." He turned his head. "Olivia, would you like to tell Rachel why we brought two wagons?"

"Because one of them is full of presents!" she sang out, jumping up and down.

The eyes of the children widened, but not much more than those of the parents. "You're funning with us," Nathan exclaimed, more surprised than disbelieving.

"Really, Uncle Joshua?" Emily shouted. "Are there really presents in it?"

"Really, Emmy. Cross my heart."

Three-year-old Mark Griffith stepped forward to face Joshua, his face grave, the brown eyes large and expressive. He tugged on Joshua's coat until Joshua stopped and looked down at him. "Yes, Mark?"

"Did you bring me a present, Uncle Joshua?"

Joshua clapped his hands. "I did indeed, young man. So what say we get around back to that wagon and see just exactly what's in it?"

Caroline was fascinated. She had watched Joshua slowly changing since they had married, and she had been especially amazed at the transformation since he had returned and been reunited with his family. But now, as he and Will untied the lashings on the wagon canvas, she saw a Joshua she had never seen before. He was more like one of the children. He laughed and teased and cajoled as he played the surprise to its very limits. Not only was he a complete part of the family again, but right now he was the very center of it.

She wanted to be by his side, holding his hand, letting some of his electricity seep into her. But, of course, she couldn't get within ten feet of him. He was completely thronged with children. Even Peter and Matthew hung close, eager to see what secrets the wagon held.

"Olivia, you want to be the first?"

Olivia was hopping with excitement. "Yes, Papa." She climbed up on the back step of the wagon and rummaged among the packages that lay there. She retrieved a large, flat box and jumped down again.

Joshua let his eyes run across the children's faces until they stopped on six-year-old Emily. She began to wiggle and squirm before he could say anything. Joshua laughed. "When I left here a month ago, did I or didn't I make you a promise?"

"Yes," she fairly shouted, "you said you'd bring me a pretty dress. Did you? Did you?"

"Emily," Lydia called, trying to be stern even as she smiled. "Mind your manners, now."

"Now, Mother," Joshua said to Lydia, "a promise is a promise." He reached out and took Emily's hand and drew her forward. "Emmy, you and Olivia became special friends, didn't you?"

Emily looked to her cousin and nodded. There was five years' difference between the two girls, but it was really true. The two of them and Rachel had gotten very close.

"Well, that's why we decided to let Livvy pick your present for you." He turned to his daughter. "Okay, Livvy."

Olivia held it out to Emily. "Happy birthday. I hope you like it."

With a cry of joy, Emily snatched the box and pawed it open. She almost ripped the lid off it once it was unwrapped. There was a gasp. Then very slowly she pulled out the dress that lay there. There were instant oohs and aahs and a smattering of applause as Emily dropped the box and held the dress up to her. She twirled slowly around. The dress was bright red, with a white pinafore and white lace at the collar and sleeves. There was a matching bonnet with long ribbons.

Emily looked up at her mother in awe. "Oh, Mama!" she breathed. "Look at me."

"It's beautiful, Emmy." Lydia stepped over to Caroline. "It is, Caroline. It's perfect for her, with her dark hair and eyes."

Caroline was watching her niece with a pleased smile. "I was there, but Livvy really did pick this one out all by herself. And she is getting to be quite the seamstress. She helped me fix some things on it so it will fit better."

"Well, it's wonderful. Look at Emmy's eyes. I've never seen her so happy."

Joshua was again searching the faces of the children. "Let's see." He pulled at his lip thoughtfully. "Will, you think we might have something for these Griffith boys?"

Luke and Mark looked to Will with great, hopeful eyes. Will nodded and went to the wagon. He came back with two pairs of fine leather boots. Again there were cries of surprise and pleasure. Boots were typically for men only. Most boys went barefoot all summer—except for Sunday, and then they only wore shoes. But these were small miniatures of the kind of boots Joshua himself wore. The two boys took them reverently and walked back to the others in half a daze.

And so it went. Joshua was having the time of his life. There was a finely sharpened hunting knife for Nathan, two wonderfully clever folding prams for Lydia's and Jessica's babies, a double-bladed ax for John Griffith, sets of hand-carved walnut mixing bowls for Jessica and Lydia, a dress of royal blue for Rachel. Mary Ann got four bolts of cloth and a cleverly designed sewing box full of thread and lace and needles and buttons.

Joshua had purchased ten pairs of boots altogether from the boot maker in St. Louis. In addition to the two pairs he'd given Luke and Mark, there were three pairs for Nathan and his two sons, one for John Griffith, a pair each for Derek and Peter, and two more pairs for Matthew and Benjamin. When he finished, everyone had to sit down and try them on. Young Joshua and Luke Griffith had to trade, but other than that, Joshua and Will had guessed pretty accurately.

Mary Ann was shaking her head. "Joshua, you've spent a small fortune on these. You shouldn't have."

"Now, Mother," he chided her. "After eleven years of no presents, I figure this is a bargain at twice the price."

"Well, it's wonderful," Nathan said. "I can't believe it. No wonder you had to bring a second wagon."

Looking suddenly perplexed, Joshua scanned the circle. "Have we missed anyone?" His eyes stopped on his younger sister, who held nothing. "Why, dear me. We seem to have missed Rebecca."

Beaming now, he turned again to the wagon and drew out a very large, flat box. It was tied carefully with a red ribbon. He turned. "Rebecca?"

She came forward, shyly now, suspecting what it might be. He reached out and took one hand. The corners of his mouth softened. "Dear, sweet Becca. Caroline and I never dreamed you would need this so soon. We thought it would be next spring before you would be married. How grateful we are that we decided to come up now." He handed her the box. "I hope you like it."

She opened it slowly, untying the ribbon and then folding it neatly and placing it in the pocket of her apron before proceeding. Then she lifted the lid of the box. There was a quick intake of breath, then a long "Ohhhhh." The family echoed it almost instantly.

She took the dress by the shoulders and held it up, pushing the box aside. The dress was high necked with a tight-fitting bodice. The sleeves were Victorian, coming straight off the shoulder and then puffing out at each elbow. The skirt was full, pleated at the waist and long to the ground. But it was the colors that made it most striking. They were the colors of an early spring sunrise. The taffeta was a light pink; the collar, cuffs, and bowknots that fastened down the front were white.

"Oh, Joshua! Caroline! It's . . ." There were no words she could find that were adequate.

Caroline stepped to the wagon and got a smaller box, this one round and stiff. Smiling, she brought it to Rebecca. "As Emily well knows, no dress is complete without a matching bonnet." She lifted the lid.

The bonnet was simple, matching the elegance of the dress. It was also pink and white, with a white bow at the throat and long white ribbons trailing down from that.

Derek was staring. "That's the most beautiful dress I've ever seen," he said. Then suddenly his face fell. "You will look absolutely lovely in it." *And me standing next to you in my patched cotton pants and worn shirt.*

Joshua read his face as clearly as if he had spoken. "Seems to me a gentleman needs something more than a pair of new boots to get married in." He looked at his wife. "Caroline?"

"Come here, Derek," Caroline said.

As Derek stepped forward, she eyed him up and down. "This was a lot harder for me," she said. "I'm not used to buying clothes for men."

"The boots are more than enough," Derek started, embarrassed to be the center of attention now.

"Nonsense," Caroline said. She looked over her shoulder at Joshua. "All right, Joshua, let's see how I did."

This time Joshua brought out a large leather valise. He unbuckled the straps, opened it, and began handing things out to Caroline. First came a white shirt with a ruffle down the button line. A dark brown silk cravat was fastened to the top button just below the high collar. The trousers were fawn colored, with tight-fitting legs and straps at the bottom to hold them down. Finally out came a man's frocked coat. It was cut at the waist in the front but had long tails in the back. The broadcloth was dyed a tobacco brown and trimmed out with a darker brown velvet shawl collar. It was handsome indeed, and Derek just gawked at it.

As Joshua held it up against Derek, Caroline nodded. "I think we may have done it right," she said, obviously pleased. She turned to Rebecca. "It was made for a taller man, so I had the tailor shorten it a little. I think it will be fine."

"Fine?" Derek cried. "I have never worn anything half so fine, let alone owned it for myself."

Lydia clapped her hands in delight. "I think we need a modeling show. Rebecca, go in the house and try on your dress. Derek, you can change in the smokehouse."

"Yes," Mary Ann said. "If we have to fix anything, we'd better know it now so we can have everything ready for tomorrow."

Joshua cut in. "Hold it, everyone. Before you run off, let's make sure everyone has a present."

Everyone turned. No one was without something. Young Joshua answered for them all. "Everybody's got something, Uncle Joshua."

"What about Grandpa?" Will said.

Benjamin's head came up and he looked startled. Then he held up his boots. "I've got these."

Joshua waved that off. "Go on, Pa. I just got you the boots because we were getting them for everyone else." He swung around. "What do you think kids? Does Grandpa deserve his very own present?"

An instant chorus rang out. "Yes! Yes!"

"Actually, this will kind of be for Grandma too. But mostly it's for Grandpa."

"What is it?" Emily called, her own dress forgotten now.

"You come look and tell me," Joshua answered. She ran to him and he lifted her up to the wagon. She lifted the flap and peered inside. When she turned back she was puzzled. "What is it, Uncle Joshua?"

"I wanna see," young Joshua said, running up to join them.

He too looked in the wagon and swung back with a strange look on his face. "It's big. What is it?"

Joshua turned to his son. "Will, let's get the canvas down."

Working swiftly, they untied the ropes along the side of the wagon that held the canvas cover down over the metal hoops. They swung the cover high over the top and let it drop to the other side, revealing the inside of the wagon. There was very little room in it. The back few feet, which had been filled with all the other presents, was now empty, but the rest of the large wagon box was filled with a huge wooden crate.

Benjamin moved forward, his eyes going over it carefully. "I'm with the grandchildren, Joshua," he finally said. "What is it?"

"Come around this side, Pa," Joshua said softly. He took his father's elbow and walked him around to the opposite side. He pointed. On one of the wooden slats there were stenciled red letters. They ran vertically, and Benjamin tipped his head to read them, pronouncing the words slowly.

" 'McCormick Company, Chicago, Illinois.' " He turned to Joshua. "McCormick Company? I don't get it."

Joshua's grin was nearly splitting his face now. "Cyrus Hall McCormick. Doesn't that name mean anything to you?"

Benjamin started to shake his head, then he stopped, stunned. "The reaping machine?" he said in a hoarse whisper.

Joshua laughed right out loud. "Exactly!"

"This is one of them reaping machines?" Benjamin repeated again, barely able to comprehend. "But how . . . ? Where . . . ?"

Caroline laughed. She stepped forward to Benjamin and laid her cheek against his. "Joshua and Will went to St. Louis for it. Happy birthday, Father Steed."

Benjamin turned to his son, his eyes still looking dazed and bewildered. Then in a moment he realized all that the gift meant, all that was being said. Instantly there were tears in his eyes. "Thank you, son."

And then just as swiftly Joshua's eyes were glistening too. "Happy birthday, Pa," he said gruffly. "I hope you like it."

It was in the fall of 1826 when Benjamin Steed moved his family from Vermont to the wheat-rich country of Palmyra Township in western New York. By that simple act, the Steed family were brought into contact with Joseph Smith and were swept up in the grand events of the Restoration. They were participants from the beginning and thus began a series of associations with a group whose names would someday read like a veritable who's who of early Church leadership. Oliver Cowdery, David Whitmer, Martin Harris, Sidney Rigdon, Emma Smith, Lucy Mack Smith, Newel K. Whitney, Edward Partridge, Eliza R. and Lorenzo Snow, Orson Pratt, Parley P. Pratt, Brigham Young, Heber C. Kimball, Orson Hyde, John Taylor—they knew them all.

So it came as no surprise that when word was sent out to the Saints living in Far West and its environs that Rebecca Steed and Derek Ingalls were to be married at ten a.m. on Friday, the tenth day of August, 1838, the numbers who turned out to honor them were legion.

Originally the plan had been to hold the wedding in the largest place in Far West—the building that served the community as courthouse, schoolhouse, and meetinghouse. But by nine-thirty that morning, it was evident that there was no possible way—either sitting or standing—that everyone who had come could be accommodated. So, after a brief consultation with Mary Ann and Benjamin, Joseph declared that the ceremony would be moved to the public square.

Now Derek and Rebecca stood at the east end of the square, between two of the cornerstones for the temple that had been laid more than a month earlier. Derek kept brushing at his clothes, feeling like he had to smooth them down, though the fabric was of such quality that it showed no wrinkles whatever.

Rebecca reached out and took his hand, smiling at him. "You look wonderful," she whispered.

He pulled a quick face. "I'm not used to being dressed like this."

"You look wonderful," she said again, the happiness making her face glow.

Brother Joseph was standing right behind them. "We'll wait a few more minutes," he said, "let everyone get their places." He looked at Derek. "In the meantime, we have a surprise for you."

"You do?"

Joseph swung around. "Ben. Mary Ann. You didn't spoil it, did you?"

Benjamin shook his head. "We were sorely tempted, but no, we didn't."

"What is it?" Rebecca asked, curious now too.

Without speaking, Joseph half turned, raised a hand, and motioned someone forward. In a moment, two men came through the crowd. The first was short and stocky, built somewhat along the lines of a hundred-year-old oak tree. He was balding, and a large smile split his rather plain and open features. The second was slimmer and about three years younger than the first.

Derek took half a step forward, smiling broadly. "Elder Kimball?" he exclaimed. "Elder Hyde? We heard you were back and we were going to look you up the next time we came down."

" 'Lo, mate," Heber C. Kimball said in a perfect Cockney accent. Then in a moment he was to Derek and shaking his good hand vigorously.

Elder Hyde was right behind him, slapping Derek on the shoulder. "Where's Master Peter?" Orson asked.

But Peter, who was standing with the rest of the family, had already seen what was happening and was pushing his way forward, calling excitedly.

Over in the family circle, Joshua leaned over to Nathan. "Who is that?" he asked.

"It's Heber C. Kimball and Orson Hyde," Nathan answered.

"They are two of our twelve Apostles. But more to the point, they were the two missionaries who went to England and found Peter and Derek. Derek hasn't seen them since he came to America. They just arrived in Missouri about two weeks ago, and with Derek and Peter being up in Di-Ahman this is their first chance to meet."

"Oh," Caroline said, "no wonder they're so happy to see each other."

Derek finally broke loose from Heber's grip. He stepped back, looking proud, and took Rebecca's arm. "Brother Kimball, Brother Hyde, I'd like you to meet my bride-to-be."

Heber laughed right out loud at that, and stepped over to put one arm around Rebecca's shoulder. He pulled her up tight against him. "You don't have to introduce me to this one," he said. "She's been one of my special people ever since I met this family." He looked into her face. "Thank you for not spoiling our surprise and telling Derek we were going to be here this morning."

Rebecca looked a little sheepish. "To be honest, I was so worried about what happened at Gallatin, and so glad when Derek came home safely, I never even thought to tell him."

Heber looked wounded. "Well, I suppose that's why they say love is blind." Instantly he brightened and looked back at Derek. "We bring you and Peter greetings from your friends in Preston, and we have much to tell you about the work there, but there'll be time enough for that later. I think that for right now you have more important things to do."

Joseph laughed. "Brother Heber is right. A lot of people have come to see you two married. So I think we'd best proceed."

Rebecca was positively radiant. Though she loved the bonnet Caroline had chosen for her, she had chosen not to wear it for the wedding. Her hair was brown and long, coming down below the shoulder blades. Lydia and Caroline had taken turns brushing it, and now it gleamed in the sunlight. The pink taffeta of her dress only heightened the fairness of her skin, and the white trim seemed to make her eyes all the more pale and lovely.

And Derek was a near match for her. The cut of the coat emphasized the broadness of his shoulders and the strength of his features. Caroline had taken the new scissors that came with Mary Ann's sewing box and trimmed back the thickness of his hair so it looked as if he had been to the barbershop. The only thing that marred his overall appearance was the dark bruise and thick scab on his forehead and the fact that his one arm was in a sling and had to be placed beneath the jacket instead of in the sleeve.

Matthew stood next to Derek as best man, almost as proud and happy as Derek himself. Rebecca had asked that all three of her sisters-in-law stand as matrons of honor, and so she was flanked by Lydia, Jessica, and Caroline. Her only regret was that there was one other who should also have been there yet wasn't—Melissa. But her older sister was still in Kirtland. If only she were here too . . . Rebecca shook it off and looked around. The rest of the family, including all of the children, were gathered directly off to the left of them so they could see Joseph's face and also Derek's and Rebecca's.

A brief prayer was offered; then, at Joseph's invitation, Benjamin stepped forward to affirm that he did, indeed, accept Derek Ingalls of Preston, England, as a suitable husband and did, indeed, give the hand of his daughter to him in marriage. Since Derek had no father, Heber C. Kimball spoke in his behalf. He spoke as warmly as if Derek had been his own son and solemnly averred to Benjamin that Derek was a worthy bridegroom.

As they finished their fatherly speeches, Joseph straightened to his full height—about half a handspan taller than Derek's stocky five feet nine inches—and let his gaze sweep across the assembled faces, then to the family members, and finally to Derek and Rebecca. There was deep pleasure in the blue eyes that seemed to see right through the both of them. He cleared his throat. When he spoke, he spoke directly to Derek and Rebecca, but it was loud enough for all the assembly to hear.

"Marriage is ordained of God and was instituted with Adam and Eve in the Garden of Eden. It is always pleasing to God to see a righteous man and woman joined together in matrimony." A smile played briefly at the corners of his mouth. "But in this case, it seems that God also took a direct hand in bringing the two of you together." He swung around. "Isn't that right, Nathan Steed?"

"Absolutely," Nathan answered without hesitation. Lydia and Mary Ann were nodding too.

"This is not the place to retell that whole story," Joseph went on, "but suffice it to say that two years ago now, Nathan was present when Elder Kimball gave a blessing to Parley P. Pratt and told him to go to Canada. Elder Kimball made some remarkable promises to Parley—about his wife, about a new child to be born, about the missionary work in Canada. Nathan Steed was asked to accompany Parley and was told that if he did so it would prove to be a great blessing to his family.

"Well, here we are now, seeing the fulfillment of that promise. As you know, among those whom Nathan and Parley converted in Canada there was a man by the name of Joseph Fielding and his sisters, Mary and Mercy. And it was none other than Joseph Fielding who went with Brother Heber to England. They went to Preston, where James Fielding, Joseph's brother, had a ministry. And there in Preston there were two young men who were ready to hear and accept the gospel."

He turned back to Rebecca and his voice dropped, as though he were speaking only to her. "And now we come full circle. Derek is here and the promise is fulfilled." He chuckled softly now. "It took the Lord to get Derek to the home of Benjamin Steed, where Rebecca was the first one to open the door. From that point on, the Lord didn't have to do much else. Rebecca did the rest."

To everyone's surprise, Rebecca was not blushing. She just

looked at Derek with those wide, blue eyes and nodded. "It took some doing, but with a little help from Mother and Matthew we went and did it."

That really pleased the crowd and they roared their approval. Finally, as the laughter died, Joseph sobered again. "Well, the Lord has done his part. Rebecca has done her part. I guess it's time I do my part and get you two married."

"Joshua?"

"Mmm."

"Are you asleep?"

"If I say yes, will you believe me?"

Caroline jabbed him in the back with her fist.

"Ouch!"

She punched him harder.

"All right! All right!" he grumbled good-naturedly. "I'm awake." He rolled over to face her, and she moved into his arms.

"That's better," she said.

"Yes," he agreed lazily.

"Wasn't today wonderful?" she said, after a moment.

"Yes," he agreed. "I thought it couldn't have gone better. Rebecca looked like she was going to lift right off the ground."

"I'm so glad for her. Derek is a wonderful young man."

"Yes. Yes, he is. I'd hire him in a minute."

She looked up at him in the darkness, and there was a faint teasing note in her voice. "Is that all you men ever think about? Who would make the best workers?"

He considered that for a minute, then answered seriously. "For a man, to say that you'd like to have another man work with you is . . ." He thought about it some more. "I don't know. It's our way of saying that we like what he is."

"I know," she murmured, snuggling in against his cheek. "I didn't mean to tease you. But a woman thinks differently. If you asked me what I thought of Derek . . ."

She paused. When he didn't answer, she shook her head and

let out her breath in mock exasperation. "But if you asked *me* what I thought of Derek . . . ," she said again.

"Oh," he said, laughing now. "And what do you think of Derek?"

"I think he'll make Rebecca a wonderful husband. He's kind and gentle and a good worker—"

"That's what I said."

"I know, but for me that means he'll take care of her. Give her a good home."

"He will," Joshua responded. "And she will be a good woman for him. Maybe even as good for him as you are for me."

Her head came up in surprise at the unexpected compliment. From his voice, she knew he had really meant it too. "Why, thank you, Joshua."

He leaned down and kissed her on the forehead. "I mean it."

"I know you do," she answered happily.

For almost a minute they were quiet, and Caroline began to wonder if she had lost him to sleep, but then he shifted his weight a little.

"Joshua?"

"Mmmm."

She hesitated, suddenly unsure of herself.

His head came up slightly. "What?"

"What did you think about what Joseph said? Before he married them."

Joshua laid his head back down. "I don't know. What in particular?"

"About Brother Kimball's prophecy to Nathan?"

"*Brother* Kimball?" he asked pointedly.

She blushed a little. "That's what everyone else calls him. But don't change the subject. Tell me what you think about that whole story. You heard Nathan give us all the details tonight. So what do you think?"

Joshua shrugged. "*Story*? Yes, I guess that's a good word for it."

"You don't believe it?"

"Oh, I believe something happened back then. I believe the

part about Nathan and . . ." He groped for the right word. "Mister Kimball," he finally settled for. "But the mind's a funny thing. When you want something badly enough, you can start seeing things that way. After a year or two passes"—he shrugged again—"it's easy to remember things differently."

She rolled onto her back, off his arm. "And you think that is an explanation?" She was clearly miffed.

"Maybe," he said, a little defensively now. "There could be a dozen others."

"Tonight, while you were putting Savannah to bed, I was with your mother and Lydia and Jessica."

"Yes?"

"I asked them about it. I asked them specifically about Parley's wife. She did have consumption, Joshua. They said she was near death. And what about the baby? After ten years of being childless, she had a baby within a year of the blessing. That's a little hard to deny, isn't it?"

There was a momentary flash of irritation. Here it was again. This wanting to attribute everything to some supernatural power. Always looking for some spiritual explanation for things. "Caroline, look, I don't doubt that. I don't think Nathan and Mother and the others would lie about a thing like that. I think they did give Pratt one of these so-called blessings. I'll even grant you that they probably told him they hoped his wife would get better."

"Hoped?"

He ignored the barb in her voice. "Do you remember what time of year it was?"

That took her aback a bit. "I don't remember if . . . Oh, yes. Nathan said it was in the spring."

"Exactly. And when is the worst time for problems with your lungs? In the winter, right? So spring comes. Warm weather arrives." He didn't have to finish.

"And what about the baby?" There was doubt in her voice now.

That was easy. "The consumption finally leaves. She gets

stronger and healthier. What could be more natural? Finally, she is well enough to conceive and have a child."

"Hmm." She felt a strange sense of disappointment that it made sense to her. But then another thought came. "But Lydia said that when Nathan came home that night, he told her about Brother Kimball's prophecy, exactly as Nathan described it. So it's not just Nathan's memory tricking him."

Joshua fought down the temptation to be sarcastic. He sensed his wife was struggling with this and that if he made light of it, it might come back to bite him. "Did Brother Kimball actually say that someone in England would come and marry Rebecca?"

"Well, no, but—"

"Did he even say that this promise to the family would have anything to do with Rebecca?"

"No."

"See, that's what I mean. I don't doubt but what something was said, but that's the point. This prophecy"—he pronounced the word with just a touch of derision—"was so general that it's possible to put almost any kind of interpretation on it. Especially two years after the fact, when it's hard to remember exactly what was said." He paused for a moment, and when she didn't answer, he asked, more softly now. "Does that make sense, Caroline?"

There was silence for some time, then a soft sigh. "Yes, it does."

He reached out and touched her cheek. "That doesn't make it any less wonderful that Derek and Rebecca found each other. I'm still really happy for them."

"I know," she murmured. "So am I." She squeezed his hand and then turned onto her side, half away from him. She didn't want to pursue it further. What Joshua said made sense. In a way it was easier to believe his interpretation than to believe what Nathan and Lydia believed. But nevertheless she couldn't shake off a sense of loss. She wished she had not started the conversation.

After some time she turned back. "Good night, Joshua," she murmured.

There was no answer. This time he really was asleep.

Chapter Notes

Cyrus Hall McCormick successfully demonstrated his new harvesting machine in 1831. In 1834 he patented an improved model and began manufacturing it. Many historians mark this as the beginning of the mechanical revolution in agriculture. It came at a time when the vastness of the Great Plains was opening up to settlement and when fields of wheat, far too large for one man to harvest them, started to become commonplace. McCormick was a millionaire by the time he was forty.

The blessing given by Heber C. Kimball to Parley P. Pratt was treated in detail in chapter 4 of *Truth Will Prevail*, the third volume of this series. Parley's account of it is found in his autobiography (see *PPP Auto.*, p. 110).

Chapter Nine

Are you sure you can't stay long enough to see Pa use that reaper for the first time?"

Joshua was reaching under the horse's belly and cinching the girth strap that snugged down the shaft tugs. He gave it one last pull, then looked up. "I'd like to, but even with you and Matthew helping, he'll be lucky to have it assembled by dark tonight. That means you won't be able to try it until tomorrow at the earliest."

Without thinking, Nathan immediately said, "Tomorrow is the Sabbath. Pa won't work on the Sabbath."

"Exactly," Joshua said. "That means it will be Monday before he can try it out. We just can't wait that long." He moved around to the off horse and began the final check of the harnessing there. "We'll be back in a couple of weeks. I've got that load of hardware going to St. Joseph. I promised I'd let Matthew and young Joshua go with me." He finished and gave the horse a pat on the rump. "Well, that's it. Let's see if Mother has the food packed, then we'd best be leaving."

Nathan had known what the answer would be before he asked Joshua to delay the departure. "Well, what's most important, you were here for the wedding. That worked out so well."

"Yes. We had no idea, of course, but it was perfect timing."

Nathan went around to the front of the team to check the bridles and make sure the bits were comfortable in the horses' mouths. As he did so, a movement caught his eye. A boy was coming toward them at a quick trot. Nathan stopped and straightened, squinting a little. It was Bishop Partridge's oldest son. Joshua saw him now too and stopped what he was doing to watch.

"Brother Steed," the boy called even before he was to them.

"Yes."

"My pa said to come and fetch you quick. And Father Steed too."

"What's the matter?"

"A group of men from Daviess County just rode into town. They're at the courthouse."

Nathan's jaw went slack, and there was a quick little jolt of fear. "Daviess County? Are they armed?"

"No," the boy said quickly. "But they've brought a paper. It don't look good. Pa wants as many men as I can find to come quick."

The boy hadn't gotten it quite right. The group of men who had ridden into Far West were from Ray County, to the south of Caldwell County. But they came in behalf of the citizens in Daviess County. Unfortunately, Joseph Smith and some of the other leading brethren weren't there to meet them. A group of Saints from Canada, supposedly on their way to Far West, had decided to stop and settle at DeWitt, down on the Missouri River. That was contrary to Joseph's counsel, and he and some other leaders had left that morning to go to DeWitt and straighten the matter out.

By the time Benjamin, Nathan, Derek, and Joshua arrived at the building that served as the courthouse—Joshua said there was no way he was going to ride out of town when there might be trouble—there was a substantial group of brethren milling around in front of the building. Someone had brought a small table out, and Bishop Edward Partridge and a man Nathan did not recognize were sitting at it. Nathan also saw five or six others he didn't know.

Newel Knight was standing near the table watching the proceedings. As the Steed men arrived he leaned over and said something to Bishop Partridge. The bishop nodded, retrieved a piece of paper that sat in front of him, and handed it to Knight. Newel pushed his way through the surrounding crowd and came toward the three men.

"What's going on, Newel?" Nathan asked.

"This!" Newel exclaimed as he waved the paper at them. "It's an affidavit. Signed by William Peniston and three or four others."

"Peniston!" Derek exploded in disgust.

"Who's that?" Joshua asked his father.

"He's the one who whipped up the mob at Gallatin," Derek snorted.

Benjamin was grim. "He's the cause of all the trouble."

"That's right," Newel said, "so listen to what he has to say." He held the paper out and began to read, squinting a little at the flowery handwriting. " 'On this day, the 10th of August, 1838, personally appeared before me, judge of the Fifth Judicial Circuit, the undersigned, William P. Peniston—' "

"Which judge is it?" Benjamin cut in.

"Austin King," Newel replied.

"That explains a lot," Nathan muttered. "He's one of them too."

Newel's head bobbed once, then he went on. " 'The undersigned, William P. Peniston, makes oath that he has good reason to believe, and that he verily does believe, that there is now collected and embodied in the County of Daviess, a large body of armed men, whose movements and conduct are of a highly insurrectionary and unlawful character—' "

"Well, he's right on that count!" Benjamin muttered. "Only that large body of armed men aren't Mormons, they're Missourians."

Knight continued without comment. " 'That they consist of about five hundred men, and that they, or a part of them, to the number of one hundred and twenty, have committed violence against Adam Black—' "

"Adam Black?" Nathan cut in in surprise. "The man we asked to sign the petition?"

"The same," Newel Knight answered shortly. "And listen to this. 'Have committed violence against Adam Black, by surrounding his house, and taking him in a violent manner, and subjecting him to great indignities, by forcing him, under threats of immediate death, to sign a paper of a very disgraceful character—' "

"That's a lie!" Nathan said hotly to Joshua. "We were there. This was the day after the problems in Gallatin. We went to Black. Joseph had written a paper stating that as justice of the peace Black would see that our rights were protected. Black refused to sign it, but he offered to write one of his own. There were no threats against him. No force of any kind." He turned and spat on the ground. "Threats of immediate death? That man's a bald-faced liar."

Joshua nodded, not saying anything. He believed his brother, that there were no overt threats on Black's person, but he also knew that if a large body of hostile men—or men that you *thought* were hostile—rode up to your house, there was threat present whether it was intended or not. It didn't surprise him that Black changed his tune once he felt safe.

Knight was too angry to continue. He shook the paper at the Steeds. "This says we are threatening violence on all the old settlers in Daviess, that we have threatened to put to instant death Peniston himself." He shook his head, still not quite believing the audacity of the man. "He says that Joseph Smith and Lyman Wight are the leaders of this supposed army that is going to kill everyone. He says we're going to take vengeance for"—he peered at the paper again, finding his place—" 'for some injuries, or imaginary injuries, done to some of their friends.' "

Derek reached up and lightly touched the ugly scab on his forehead. "That makes me feel better, to know this is just an imaginary injury."

Knight lowered the paper, his eyes hooded and darkly troubled. "It's signed by William Peniston and three others, and attested to by Judge King." He gestured toward the table where the meeting was taking place. "The delegation from Ray County is here to demand that we answer these charges."

Nathan was fuming. Derek's fists were clenching and unclenching. He had been there at Gallatin. He knew as well as anyone how unjust these accusations were. Matthew was almost dancing, he was so indignant.

Joshua watched them, then spoke, choosing his words carefully. "This is an official affidavit and these are formal charges. You don't have any choice but to answer them." Then as they turned on him in amazement, he rushed on. "But you've got your own statement to make. You have witnesses who were there. You simply answer these charges with the truth."

"You're right, of course, Joshua," Benjamin said grimly. "We have to answer." He paused, then looked away. "But it's been our experience that truth doesn't buy too much for Mormons in Missouri."

Benjamin reached down and picked up some dirt from the first furrow of the wheat field. He rubbed it slowly between his fingers. The last three days had been hot and dry. Any vestiges of the heavy rains that had blanketed Missouri a week ago were completely gone now.

His eyes lifted to the sea of wheat that waved before him. All traces of green were gone now too. The grain stood like an undulating sea of golden brown. The heads on each stalk were full and starting to droop.

Trying not to look too proud, he turned to face the people who stood along the edge of his field. He was faintly surprised by the size of the crowd. It was as if it were another holiday. Most were from Far West, but somehow word had spread and Benjamin saw several from outlying settlements, including some who were not Mormons. There was a slight preponderance of men, but there were numerous women as well. Mary Fielding Smith was there with Hyrum. Vilate Kimball and Mary Ann Young had come with Heber and Brigham. Emma Smith was there with Joseph's mother and one of his sisters. To Benjamin's disappointment, Joseph had not returned from DeWitt and so would not be there to witness it.

Benjamin's family stood together in a half circle around the reaper. Matthew hovered protectively, looking as though he might pop anyone who dared to touch it prematurely. The machine itself looked like an awkward and ungainly beast, and yet it also had a certain majesty about it. Two draft horses borrowed from Micah Staples, the owner of Far West's one livery stable, were hitched to the reaper and were waiting, their heads down in patient surrender to the heat.

In spite of himself, Benjamin's eyes were drawn to a wooden panel on the reaper. Joshua had given his father one more surprise, not discovered until they had the machine out of its crate. Neatly burned into the slat that ran directly in front of the iron driving seat were four words: "Property of Benjamin Steed." He knew it was a worldly emotion, but each time he saw that, he felt a little thrill of pride.

Benjamin finally met the expectant gaze of the crowd. He let the dirt blow away now, then brushed his hands off against his trouser legs. "I think it's ready," he said simply. Mary Ann was watching him proudly. She smiled as he climbed slowly up into the seat and took the reins of the horses. An expectant hush fell over the group. He smiled briefly back at Mary Ann, then clucked softly, snapping the reins. Creaking slightly, the machine began to move.

Trying to keep his face impassive, he swung the horses

around to face directly north. He already knew where he wanted to start and how he planned to transverse the field. Cutting wheat on the Sabbath might be against the Lord's law, Benjamin had decided, but *thinking* about how to do it didn't seem to qualify as work. So he had spent a great deal of time the previous afternoon working it all out in his mind.

The people walked alongside, talking animatedly now. Some were talking about what a wondrous day and age it was they lived in. Others were still skeptical, saying that even if it worked, it would be hard for any machine to beat what a good man with a sharp scythe could do. Benjamin paid them no mind. He lined the horses up so they would be on the sod for the first pass but would take the machine right along the edge of the wheat field. He was careful to leave a band of wheat along the edge. Joshua had warned him that the thick tangle of prairie growth could jam the blades or foul up the feeder wheel.

As the front of the machine reached the first of the stalks, Benjamin grabbed the engaging lever and pulled it toward him. Instantly the machine began to clatter as the metal blades along the front edge of the machine began sliding back and forth. It was like three dozen shears working in perfect synchronization. The round feeder wheel also began to turn. It was similar to the paddle wheel on a steamboat, only it was about six feet wide and the paddles were narrow boards. Its purpose was not to drive anything but simply to pull the wheat stalks evenly into the cutter blades.

A gasp went up, then shouts and cries. Benjamin did not turn. He was concentrating intently. This first pass was the most important, and he had to make certain he kept it straight along the edge. But he couldn't help but dart glances downward. It was amazing. The wheat was falling in neat, even layers onto the conveyor system and moving through the machine and out the back.

At the end of the return pass, Benjamin stopped the horses. Slowly he dismounted, keenly aware of the silence of the crowd. Mary Ann came over quickly and took his hand. Together they turned and surveyed what he had done. In a twelve-foot swath, the wheat lay in even layers, waiting for someone to come gather it up and tie it into sheaves for the threshers.

"It's amazing," Mary Ann said softly. "It really works."

He nodded in dazed wonder. What he had done in just two passes—three or four minutes total—would take a single man half a day to cut. Then, without a word, he turned, took Mary Ann by the shoulders, and kissed her soundly.

A cheer went up from the crowd and there was wild applause. Benjamin leaned over and put his mouth to Mary Ann's ear. "I've got to write, Joshua," he said. "I want to tell him all about it."

The sun was low in the sky and seemed twice as large as it did at its zenith by the time Derek and Rebecca and Peter came around the shoulder of the small hill on the Wednesday after the wedding. Derek pulled up the horse, and the small wagon rolled to a stop. The wagon was borrowed from Heber Kimball. The horse had been given by the Pratts, the Youngs, the Kimballs, and the Smiths as their wedding present to the young couple. Derek still could hardly believe he now owned his own horse.

Peter, standing up in the back of the wagon, was already pointing. "There it is," he cried in excitement. "That's our place right there."

Derek nodded, watching Rebecca closely for any signs of disappointment. The sod hut that stood on the hillside about twenty or thirty yards away suddenly seemed terribly small. The sunlight was coming from the west and backlighting the closest wall. For the first time Derek noticed how uneven the slabs of prairie sod were.

But there was no disappointment in Rebecca's eyes. Her face lit up as she leaned forward, peering. "Oh, Derek, what a lovely setting."

He looked around, greatly relieved. "It is lovely, isn't it?"

Arrival in Di-Ahman

The valley of Adam-ondi-Ahman spread out before them, and the line of trees along the Grand River was a darker green against the valley crops. He lifted an arm in a sweeping motion. "Our land goes nearly to the top of the ridge, and then out to about where that large clump of grass is."

She slipped her arm through his. "*Our* land," she murmured. "I like the sound of that." Then with excitement she nudged him. "Hurry, I want to see inside."

Derek helped his bride from the wagon, then walked quickly to the door, which was made of rough slabs of lumber and hung on leather hinges. He took a quick breath and pushed it open, the anxiety clearly clouding his features. They stepped into the gloomy interior. "It's not much yet," he started. "I planned to do a lot of work during the winter when we can't work the fields. The floor still needs some more smoothing, and we'll have to get something to divide off a place for Peter to sleep. I was planning to have it all ready for you by spring and—"

She clamped her hand over his mouth, looking around. "The only thing this place needs is a woman's touch. If you had waited until spring to marry me and bring me here, I'm not sure I could have saved it."

He removed her hand. "Really?" he said. "You think it's all right?"

She went up on tiptoes and kissed him quickly. "Really. It's wonderful, Derek. And thank you for not making me wait to move in."

Joshua groaned and rolled over in bed, burying his head deeper in the pillow. Caroline shook him again. "Joshua, someone's knocking."

He came up on one elbow, realizing it was a knocking from downstairs that had awakened him. Someone was pounding heavily on their front door, and whoever it was, they weren't going to go away.

He sat clear up, peering at the clock on the wall. It was eighteen minutes after seven. He groaned again. After they had returned from Far West, he had been home only three days before leaving for Springfield, Missouri, about a hundred and seventy-five miles south of Independence. There he had picked up four wagonloads of deer, elk, and cow hides for the new tannery. The round trip had taken a full seventeen days, and he had not arrived back at Independence until late the previous evening.

Caroline nudged him again. "Hurry, Joshua, or they're going to wake Savannah."

Nodding, still grumbling to himself, he swung his feet out of bed, grabbed his pants from the chair where he had tossed them a few hours previously, and pulled them on as he hopped his way across the room.

"I'm comin'!" he muttered as he stomped down the stairs, combing through his hair with his fingers. "I'm comin'."

The man outside—and he could see it was a man through the thinness of the curtains—evidently heard his footsteps on the stairs, for now the pounding stopped. Still barefoot and shirtless, Joshua walked to the front door and yanked it open. He was not in much of a mood for visitors.

Outside, the sun was bright and about two hours high in the sky. Joshua had to squint a little to make out who it was. Then he recognized the familiar figure. "Cornwell?" he said.

Obadiah Cornwell, once Joshua's yard foreman and now his full partner in the freight business, nodded. "Mornin', Joshua."

Joshua blew out his breath and stepped back, opening the door wider and motioning for Cornwell to come in. "Can't a man even have one day off?"

Cornwell ignored that, took his hat off, and followed Joshua inside. He was dressed as though he were ready for church, but then, that was how Cornwell always dressed. When Joshua had brought him in as a full partner in the business, Cornwell's dressing habits had changed dramatically. He didn't want people remembering he had once wrangled horses, cleaned stables, and manhandled freight into the wagon beds. He wore a well-tailored jacket and trousers, white shirt, cravat at the collar, and hand-tooled boots.

He tossed his hat on the table and walked to the center of the room. "Sorry to bother you so early, Joshua. What time did you get in?"

"It was after one by the time we got the horses cared for and I got to bed."

Cornwell's face was somber as he reached inside his coat and withdrew a folded paper. He held it out for Joshua. "This came late yesterday. I thought you'd want to see it as soon as possible."

Fifteen minutes later when Caroline heard the front door close again, she came out of the bedroom, tying her robe around her, and went to the stairs. From the landing she could see Joshua sitting in a chair, staring at a sheet of paper.

"Joshua?"

He looked up.

She started down the stairs. "Was that Obadiah?"

"Yes." He folded the paper and laid it in his lap.

"What did he want so early?" And then she saw his face more clearly. "What is it?" she asked in alarm. "What's the matter?"

"You'd better come sit down," he said softly.

Feeling a quick chill, she hurried across the parlor and sat in the chair beside him. "What is it, Joshua? What's wrong?"

For several moments, he didn't answer; then finally he picked up the paper and unfolded it slowly. "This came yesterday. From Jefferson City. It's signed by Lilburn W. Boggs."

"The governor? But what is it?"

He lifted it, and his eyes scanned the top few lines. His voice was low and filled with pain. "It's from the adjutant general's office and dated two days ago, August thirtieth. It's addressed to General David R. Atchison, commander of the Third Division of the Missouri militia."

She was completely baffled. "The militia?"

Joshua lifted the paper higher and started to read, slowly and with some emotion. " 'Sir—Indications of Indian disturbances on our immediate frontier, and the recent civil disturbances in the counties of Caldwell, Daviess, and Carroll, render it necessary, as a precautionary measure, that an effective force of the militia be held in readiness to meet either contingency.' "

Open fear registered in Caroline's eyes now. "The Indians? Has there been more trouble?"

"Yes."

One hand came up to her mouth. Like many other residents of western Missouri, Caroline had a deep paranoia about the Indian tribes living just to the west of them. In the earlier part of the decade, Congress had passed a law setting up what was called Indian Territory. It was just beyond the western borders of the United States. That was only ten or twelve miles away from Independence. The government moved tens of thousands of the native populations westward to make way for white settlers. It was an unnatural and forcible resettlement, and the Indians had not taken well to it. Intertribal clashes were frequent, and sometimes the anger exploded against the whites who oppressed them. In an incident just a week earlier, a trading post had been burned and the Indian agent killed before the soldiers had arrived to quell the uprising. Joshua had deliberately avoided telling Caroline about it.

"Is there any chance they'll break out of the reservation?" she asked with a little shudder.

Joshua blew out his breath. "Caroline, this is not about the Indians. At least, not very much."

"It's not? But it said—"

He jerked up the paper again, waving it at her half angrily. "It said Indian disturbances *and* recent civil disturbances in Caldwell, Daviess, and Carroll counties."

For a moment it still didn't click; then in a flash, understanding dawned. The horror that leaped across her face now was worse than the first. "The Mormons?" she whispered.

He nodded slowly.

Now she was very intent. "Read it again, Joshua," she demanded.

Wearily he lifted the paper and started again, this time reading more slowly. " 'Sir—Indications of Indian disturbances on our immediate frontier, and the recent civil disturbances in the counties of Caldwell, Daviess, and Carroll, render it necessary, as a precautionary measure, that an effective force of the militia be held in readiness to meet either contingency. The Commander-in-Chief therefore orders that you cause to be raised immediately, within the limits of your division, to be held in readiness, and subject to further orders, four hundred mounted men, armed and equipped as infantry or riflemen, and formed into companies according to law, under officers already in commission.' "

He stopped, not looking up at her.

"Officers already in . . ." She couldn't bring herself to finish it.

Still not meeting her eyes, he continued. " 'The Commander-in-Chief suggests the propriety of your causing the above to be carried into effect, in a manner calculated to produce as little excitement as possible, and report your proceedings to him through the Adjutant General.' It's signed by order of Governor Boggs."

For a long time after Joshua finished and put the paper back on the table, they both sat there. Finally, Caroline straightened. She had pushed her emotions back to the point where she could begin to think more clearly. "So," she asked calmly, "is it just a bluff to frighten the Mormons, or do you think they'll actually take the field against them?"

It was a question that had come to Joshua's mind as well. He was sorely tempted to soften it for her, but he was fighting a cold fear of his own and knew he was going to need her to help him work through it. "Similar letters have been sent to Samuel D. Lucas and five other generals of the militia. That's seven altogether. If they've been asked to raise what Atchison has, that's nearly three thousand men."

She shuddered at that, but then, still composed, asked again. "But will they take the field against the Mormons?"

He stood up and began to pace slowly, his eyes concentrated in thought. "As you know, Governor Boggs is a resident of Jackson County. What you may not know is, when the troubles here erupted in '33, Boggs was right in the middle of it. He was lieutenant governor then, and had to keep a low profile about it, but he was here, whipping us up and goading us on."

"I had heard that," Caroline said. Then with a trace of asperity she added, "I also heard that he benefitted quite handsomely by taking over some of the abandoned properties."

Joshua shrugged. It was true, but Boggs wasn't the only one. There were others. Joshua himself had been offered a choice parcel because of his role in the matter, but he had turned it down. In his mind he had a picture of Jessica and Rachel being driven across a sleet-covered prairie, and somehow profiting from that had seemed obscene.

Yes, the Mormons were hated. But their property was also coveted. And the worthless land of the northern counties had now become rich and productive farmland. Greed had a wonderful way of fueling the fires of hate.

He stopped his pacing and turned to Caroline. "The point is, Boggs is a real Mormon-hater. Lucas too."

So was Joshua Steed. Once. But Caroline didn't say what was in her mind. Thankfully things had changed. There still was no deep affection for the Mormons per se, but now Joshua's family was involved. And that changed everything.

Joshua was still talking. "The old settlers up north are stirring things up." He shook his head. "That talk we heard on the Fourth of July isn't helping any. I warned Joseph that it was gonna mean trouble. And that affidavit signed by that man from Daviess County. I'm sure Boggs has seized on that and the Indian problems as an excuse to do whatever he wants."

"You can't go," Caroline said quietly.

Joshua's head came up slowly.

"You can't, Joshua," she said, standing now too. "How can

you be part of something in which you end up fighting against your own family?"

"You think this is a matter of choice?"

"I don't care whether it's a matter of choice or not. You can't do this, Joshua."

This was the very thing that had hit him the hardest when he had first read the letter to General Atchison. He walked over and took her by the shoulders. "Caroline, you don't understand. I hold a commission in the militia. If the governor activates that militia, no one is going to ask me if I feel all right about it. I am duty bound to comply."

"Figs on your duty!" Caroline cried. "This is your family, Joshua. You can't do it!" Suddenly her eyes brightened as a thought struck her. "Go on a trip, Joshua. Go to St. Louis." Her mind was racing now. "Or better, take that wagon train to Santa Fe you talked about. I know I told you I didn't want you to go, but I've changed my mind. Take it. It's the perfect excuse. And by the time you get back, hopefully it will all be over."

He gripped her shoulders more tightly. "Caroline, listen to me. You weren't here in '33 and '34. You don't know how deeply the feelings against the Mormons run. And now, everyone in town knows about my family. If I leave . . . If they think I'm running out on them . . ." He let her go, stepping back, shaking his head.

"What?" she asked, already sensing what he was saying.

"You wouldn't be safe."

That shocked her deeply, but almost instantly she knew he was right. Down deep—and it terrified her to know it—she knew he was exactly right. "Then we'll all go to Savannah," she burst out in a rush again. "You need to check on the cotton crop for next year. It's been a long time since—"

"It's too late for that now, Caroline," he said sharply. Then more gently, "And you know it."

She took his hands now, looking up into the bleakness of his gaze. "How can you, Joshua? How can you possibly do this?"

His shoulders sagged, and the lines around his mouth were

deep. "General Atchison is friendly to the Mormons. He and Alexander Doniphan are both lawyers. Doniphan holds a general's commission too. They defended Joseph Smith and the Church during the Jackson County troubles. Maybe I can get assigned to one of their divisions."

Finally he looked at her. "I think Joseph and the Mormons"—he took a quick breath—"and my family are going to need all the friends in the militia they can get."

Chapter Notes

The two documents cited in this chapter—the affidavit signed by William Peniston and the letter activating units of the Missouri militia—are quoted almost exactly as given in Joseph's record (see *HC* 3:60–62, 65).

Details about the actual troubles in Indian Territory are not given in the historical records, so the mention of the burning of the trading post and the death of an agent is the author's creation. But we do know that the Missourians were very sensitive about the dangers of living that close to the Indians and that Governor Boggs capitalized on that fear to call out the militia against the Mormons.

Chapter Ten

Under date of Saturday, September 1, 1838, Joseph Smith, Jr., President and prophet of The Church of Jesus Christ of Latter-day Saints, had his scribe make the following entry in Joseph's journal history: "There is great excitement at present among the Missourians, who are seeking if possible an occasion against us. They are continually chafing us, and provoking us to anger if possible, one sign of threatening after another, but we do not fear them, for the Lord God, the Eternal Father is our God, and Jesus the Mediator is our Savior, and in the great I Am is our strength and confidence.

"We have been driven time after time, and that without cause; and smitten again and again, and that without provocation; until we have proved the world with kindness, and the world has proved us, that we have no designs against any man or set of men, that we injure no man, that we are peaceable with all men, minding our own business, and our business only. We have suffered our rights and our liberties to be taken from us; we have not avenged ourselves of those wrongs; we have appealed to magistrates, to sheriffs, to judges, to government and to the President of the United States, all in vain; yet we have yielded peaceably to all these things. We have not complained at the Great God, we murmured not, but peaceably left all; and retired into the back country, in the broad and wild prairies, in the barren and desolate plains, and there commenced anew; we made the desolate places to bud and blossom as the rose; and now the fiend-like race is disposed to give us no rest. Their father the devil, is hourly calling upon them to be up and doing, and they, like willing and obedient children, need not the second admonition; but in the name of Jesus Christ the Son of the living God, we will endure it no longer, if the great God will arm us with courage, with strength and with power, to resist them in their persecutions. We will not act on the offensive, but always on the defensive; our rights and our liberties shall not be taken from us, and we peaceably submit to it, as we have done heretofore, but we will avenge ourselves of our enemies, inasmuch as they will not let us alone."

"Don't open them, Mother. Pa, make sure she keeps her eyes closed."

Benjamin was standing behind his wife, so he reached up and put his hands over her already tightly closed eyes. "All right, son, she can't see."

"What is it?" Mary Ann asked, laughing. "What are you doing?"

Matthew pushed the door open wider and nodded at Brigham Young. "You just wait a moment, Ma," he called, "then you can look."

Matthew and Brigham each took one end of the large chest, then lifted it up and walked it in quick little steps into the house.

"Over there, by the sink," Benjamin called.

There was a heavy thump as they set it down. "What in the world?" Mary Ann exclaimed. "What is it?"

"Just one more minute," Matthew said. He stepped back, eyeing the chest to make sure it was lined up straight. He looked to his mentor. Brigham smiled and nodded. "All right, Ma," Matthew said. "You can look now."

Benjamin dropped his hands and moved back. For a moment, Mary Ann stood there, blinking, trying to let her eyes adjust to the light again, then they flew wide open. "Oh," she said softly.

"Happy birthday, Ma," Matthew said proudly. "I know I'm about a month early, but I couldn't wait."

"Oh, Matthew, it's beautiful." The sunlight was coming through the window above the sink and lit the wood, making it gleam like satin. She walked over to the chest and ran her hand along the top.

Matthew was instantly at her side. "Look inside."

Smiling at his excitement, she lifted the top. He had counterbalanced it and it came up easily in spite of its weight. Again there was a soft "Oh." Inside, the chest had been partitioned off into a series of long, narrow compartments on one end. The other half had been blocked out into pigeonholes about three inches square.

"Your plates go here," Matthew said, pointing to the narrow slots. His hand moved to touch the other compartments. "And these will hold your cups."

She looked at him in wonder. "Matthew, this is wonderful. And you did this?"

Brigham nodded instantly. "He'll try and tell you I helped him, but all I really did was give him a suggestion or two here and there. This boy of yours did the rest."

Matthew dropped to one knee. The lower front of the chest had two drawers. He pulled the top one out. "And this one is big enough to hold your serving dishes." He pushed it back in and pulled out the second drawer, which was deeper than the first. "And you can put tablecloths or towels in this one." He moved the drawer in and out to show how smoothly it glided on its track.

Mary Ann reached down and took Matthew by the elbow and pulled him back up to stand in front of her. Looking up into his face, she shook her head in amazement. "I think that is the most wonderful dish chest I have ever seen," she murmured.

"Really?" he cried. "Do you really like it, Mother?"

She started to speak, then suddenly couldn't. She reached up and laid one hand on his cheek. "Thank you," she whispered. "Thank you, Matthew."

Brigham was standing on the porch putting on his hat as Benjamin stepped out to join him. Benjamin shut the door and said, "Thank you, Brother Brigham. That really is a fine piece of work. The ash turned out beautifully."

"It did," Brigham agreed. He gave Benjamin a piercing look. "I meant what I said in there about Matthew, Ben. He's got a gift."

Benjamin nodded. "I know. He sure didn't get it from his father."

Brigham was still pinning him with his eyes. "His heart's not in farming, Ben. You know that, don't you?"

Startled, Benjamin peered at his friend. "I . . . Maybe not, but he does well at it."

"Of course he does. Matthew is a fine young man. He'll do well at whatever he's asked to do. But his heart's not in farming. Not like it is in this." He shook his head, remembering. "You should see him when he's in that shop, Ben. It's like he's an artist, painting on a canvas."

Benjamin was silent for a moment, then finally conceded. "I know he loves it."

"I'd like to make him more than just my apprentice, Ben. Give me another year to help him develop his natural abilities, and then I'd like to make him a partner with me."

Benjamin made no effort to hide his surprise.

"But I know you need help with the farm too," Brigham said, "so I won't encourage him without your permission. You know that."

"I know. Thank you, Brigham."

"I don't need an answer now. You think about it. And talk it over with Mary Ann."

"I will."

Brigham stuck out his hand and Benjamin gripped it tightly. "Think about it hard, Ben. That's one fine boy you're raising there."

In 1833, during the trouble in Jackson County, Joseph Smith found two lawyers in Clay County who agreed to represent Joseph and the Church. David Atchison and Alexander Doniphan had proven to be not only fair and competent attorneys but also friends to the Mormons. That friendship had continued since that time, and Joseph was so grateful for the integrity of Alexander Doniphan that he named the son born to Emma on June 2, 1838, Alexander Hale Smith. Both Doniphan and Atchison were also generals in the Missouri militia, Atchison being the senior commander in northern Missouri. So it was not surprising that, on September second, Joseph wrote and asked if they would represent the Church as legal counsel once again. Both agreed, and Atchison immediately suggested that Joseph and Lyman Wight submit to trial in Daviess County to answer the charges filed by William Peniston. Atchison also promised he would do all he could as a military officer to disperse the mobs and protect the Saints.

Joseph agreed, and the trial was set for September seventh. Wary of being trapped by the same mob spirit that had flared on election day in Gallatin, Joseph asked that the proceedings be held at the home of a nonmember who lived just across the Caldwell-Daviess county line. He then stationed a company of the brethren just south of the line, with instructions to be ready at a moment's notice should trouble erupt.

Austin King, the same one who had taken the original deposition from William Peniston, sat as judge. Peniston and Adam Black came into the court with the wildest concoction of lies and exaggerations ever heard. Joseph countered with a series of defense witnesses who refuted their testimony.

When the testimony was finished, Judge King ordered the two defendants bound over to be tried before the circuit court, then released them on five hundred dollars bond. Privately he told Joseph and others that there was not enough incriminating evidence to convict them of any wrongdoing, but he feared the reaction of the citizenry and did not dare acquit them. Not surprisingly, this waffling did nothing to satisfy the Mormons, and only infuriated the Missourians all the more.

"Maybe we should have waited," Derek said in disgust. "By spring I could have done something with this."

"Derek Ingalls, you stop that!"

He didn't look at Rebecca. Morosely he let his eyes sweep around the small room. This was the third day of incessant rain, and the sod roof was now leaking muddy water in nearly a dozen different places. Some of the leaks were slow drips, others steady streams. They didn't own enough jars, pans, and buckets to catch them all, and several places on the packed dirt floor were becoming muddy slicks.

He shook his head. "Mice in your bed, water coming through the ceiling like it wasn't there, moldy corn bread to eat. What in the world was I thinkin' of, bringing you here now?"

Rebecca's lips pressed into a tight line. She couldn't remember a time when she had been so miserable. Though it was still only mid-September, the rain had brought a cold spell along with it and she was constantly chilled. Their bedding was damp. Their clothes were damp. The firewood was soaked and seemed to put out no heat at all as it sputtered and smoldered in the fireplace. The night before, just after they had gone to bed, she felt something crawling across her feet. She had jumped up screaming. Even the mice were looking for somewhere warm to sleep.

The tiny hut with its dirt walls and dirt floor and dirt ceiling seemed to shrink with every hour that the gray and gloomy weather persisted. With the fields a mud bog and the roads not much better, there had been no getting away from it either. She longed for some sunlight. She longed to be warm. She longed for a pot of her mother's hot chicken dumpling soup. She longed for a bath and a chance to let her hair dry enough to brush it out straight again. She would give anything for a chance to sit across a table and talk with her mother or Lydia or Mary Fielding Smith. Any feminine voice. Anyone who knew her and could make her laugh again.

"You didn't bring me here against my will, Derek," she said, with a little more tartness to her voice than she had intended. "I wanted to come. I didn't want to wait until spring."

"I know, but—" He stopped, so glum it was almost laughable. "I'm just glad your parents can't see what I've brought you to."

Suddenly the thought of Mary Smith she had had a moment ago filled Rebecca with shame. Mary Fielding had married Hyrum Smith at the very height of the apostasy in Kirtland. In one day she went from single woman to mother of five children, including a six-week-old baby. Within less than a month they were fleeing westward across the frozen plains of Ohio and Illinois, driven out by those who sought the lives of Joseph Smith and any who stood by him. Now she was seven months pregnant. She was due in November, which meant she would have two babies barely a year apart. And yet Rebecca had never seen her the least bit cross. Around others Mary was always teasing or cajoling them until they were laughing out loud and their troubles were forgotten.

Rebecca looked around. If Mary were here, how would she deal with this? That thought was enough to cheer her a little. She wasn't sure what Mary would do, but she was sure of one thing: Mary wouldn't be standing here moping around like a kicked dog. A thought popped into Rebecca's mind and she turned around. "Derek, where's the Book of Mormon?"

Her voice seemed to startle him. "What?"

"Where's the Book of Mormon?"

He gave her a strange look. "In the chest. Why?"

She didn't answer. She walked quickly over to the small chest they kept at the foot of the bed, opened it, and found the book lying on the top of some other papers. She sat down on the bed, blew on her fingers for a moment, then began thumbing quickly through the pages of the book. It took her a minute but finally she found what she was looking for.

Rebecca gave her husband a fleeting smile. "This is in the book of Alma. It's one of Mother's favorite passages." She looked down and started to read. " 'I would that ye should be humble, and be submissive . . .' " She let her eye drop a few lines. " 'Always returning thanks unto God for whatsoever things ye do receive.' "

He stood there, looking at her as if she were daft.

She closed the book. "I'll bet I can think of more things to be thankful for than you can."

"What?"

She giggled a little, warming up to the game even more now when she saw his bewilderment. She leaned over, touching the bucket of water that was catching the heaviest stream of water from above. "I would like to return thanks to God for the fact that we have rain barrels inside the house as well as outside."

"Rebecca!" He was clearly exasperated.

"And I'm grateful that mouse didn't bite my toes last night."

He smiled in spite of himself.

"That's two to zero. I'm ahead." She jumped up quickly and went to him. She reached up and touched the scar on his forehead. "And I'd like to return thanks to God for giving you a head harder than any piece of wood ever made."

He grabbed her hand. "I beg your pardon."

Laughing, she pulled away. "And I'm grateful he broke your left arm and not the arm you hold me with." She cocked her head impishly at him. "That's four. You're falling behind, Mr. Ingalls."

He gave her a sharp look, then finally smiled. "All right. I'm

. . ." He looked around. "I'm grateful that we don't have to worry about the water warping the boards on our floor."

She squealed with delight. "Bravo! Four to one. And I'd like to return thanks to the Lord for having the grass on our sod roof only grow upwards. Otherwise, we'd have to cut our ceiling."

Derek roared. Rebecca tried to keep a straight face, but couldn't hold it and started to giggle again.

He spun around, his eyes darting. "Oh, and I'm grateful that the Lord didn't bless you with a stronger pair of lungs, or Peter and I wouldn't have any eardrums after you saw the mouse last night."

She slapped at his good arm. "Not true!" she cried.

"Five to two," he said. "And I'm also grateful for . . ."

Five minutes later when Peter opened the door and stepped inside the hut, shaking the water off the umbrella, he stopped dead. Derek and Rebecca were sitting on the edge of the bed, convulsed with laughter. The sight of his face only set them off again and they fell back, holding their stomachs.

"What is going on?" Peter said when they finally subsided a little.

Both of them just shook their heads as they sat up again. Finally, Derek got control of himself enough to speak. "It's a long story. We were just talking about being thankful, that's all." He chuckled to himself as he reached out and took Rebecca's hand. Then he looked back at his brother. "Was there any mail today?"

Peter reached inside his coat and withdrew a letter. He was beaming. "Yes, I got a letter from Jessica."

Rebecca stood up. "Really? How nice."

Peter tossed the umbrella to one side and opened the envelope quickly. "She and John are going to Father Steed's on Saturday the twenty-ninth. They're going to stay over for Sunday services in Far West." He paused for a moment; then excitement filled his voice. "She wants to know if we could come down too. She says if we do, she could give me my first school lessons. Can we go, Derek? Please, can we go?"

By the middle of September, rumors among the Missourians as well as the Mormons were flying as thickly as a plague of locusts, and it became increasingly difficult to discern truth from story. Di-Ahman was going to be attacked. The Mormons were arming themselves under the banner of "the Armies of Israel." The mobs were taking prisoners and torturing them. The Mormons were in a state of uprising and were looting and pillaging the countryside. The call to arms went out in every direction.

And with increasing frequency, rumor fueled reaction. A wagonload of arms was sent north to the citizens of Daviess County. The Mormons learned of it, intercepted it, and took two prisoners. The very men who had sent for the illegal weapons now screamed foul. Though the prisoners were released a few days later and the arms eventually returned to General Atchison, the word that the Mormons were in open rebellion was sent to Jefferson City with desperate cries for help from Governor Boggs. Roving bands of both Mormons and Missourians covered the countryside, often coming together to shout insults and threats at one another. By day and by night, the situation deteriorated. Cattle were rustled, stock shot, hogs run off, haystacks fired. On the twenty-fifth of September, General Parks, not known as being a friend to the Saints, wrote a report to Governor Boggs: "Whatever may have been the disposition of the people called Mormons, before our arrival here, since we have made our appearance, they have shown no disposition to resist the laws or of hostile intentions. There has been so much prejudice and exaggeration concerned in this matter, that I found things entirely different from what I was prepared to expect. When we arrived here, we found a large body of men from the counties adjoining, armed and in the field, for the purpose, as I learned, of assisting the people of this county against the Mormons, without being called out by the proper authorities."

There is no record of any reply from Governor Boggs to this report.

General Atchison—commander of the militia in northern Missouri, and Parks's superior officer—twice wrote to the governor. "Things are not so bad in [Daviess County] as represented by rumor," he wrote in one letter, "and, in fact, from affidavits I have no doubt your Excellency has been deceived by the exaggerated statements of designing or half crazy men. I have found there is no cause of alarm on account of the Mormons; they are not to be feared; they are very much alarmed."

He requested that the governor come north and view the situation for himself. There was no reply.

He wrote a second letter asking Boggs to come and review the situation personally. There was no reply.

"I don't feel like playin' this afternoon, Mama."

Caroline let out her breath. "Olivia, we've gone over this again and again. When your father left to go with the militia, you promised him you would practice an hour a day."

Olivia's head was down and her hands were in her lap. "I know, Mama," she said in a low, pleading voice. "I . . . I'll practice two hours tomorrow."

"That's what you say about half the time, Livvy. And you never do. Now, you sit here and get it over with. Then you can go out and play."

Olivia shook her head stubbornly. "I can't, Mama. Not today. Besides, I don't want to go out and play."

Caroline stood up, totally exasperated. "Your father brought this piano all the way from New York City, Livvy. Do you know what that cost him?" When Olivia didn't answer but only tucked her chin in more tightly against her chest, Caroline's frustration only went up. "Do you know how few girls west of the Mississippi have a piano in their home? Do you know how hard I had to look to find someone who could give you piano lessons?"

Olivia turned for just a moment, her long auburn hair swishing across her back. The green eyes that were so like her mother's were dark and stricken. In November she would turn eleven, but at that moment she looked like she was thirty. "Please don't make me, Mama."

Caroline threw up her hands. "You are so stubborn!" she exploded. She walked swiftly to the door of the small parlor, then decided to try another tack. "Livvy, Mrs. Harwood says you are doing very well. You have a natural talent for it. But if you don't practice, that talent is not ever going to be developed."

Olivia was staring at her hands, and there was no response.

"Well," Caroline snapped, "then you can just sit there until you do feel like playing." She left the room and shut the door hard, rattling the glass in the windows. She started down the hall, thoroughly angry now. Why were her children so stubborn? They were good children but as hardheaded as Missouri mules. Will had always driven her to the point of distraction with his independent nature and free-spirited approach to life. And Olivia had that stubborn streak that no amount of coaxing or threatening could bend.

She shook her head, and a smile came to her lips in spite of herself. And then there was Savannah. At eighteen months, Caroline's youngest was already putting the other two to shame. More social than an East Coast society matron, Savannah was at her happiest when she was around people. She was not in the least intimidated by adults and would come up to perfect strangers, tug on their dress or coattails, and then, with soft flirtatiousness, look up at them and say, "Hi." It melted the hardest almost instantly. As saucy and impudent as her fiery red hair, she was a tiny, totally adorable and completely irresistible little tyrant, bending everyone to her will with ridiculous ease.

Caroline stopped, feeling the anger melting away. She loved her children and was fiercely proud of what they were. With the emotions calming now, she turned back and looked at the door. What was the matter with Olivia? This was not like her. She loved the piano, took to it as naturally as a water bug to the swamp.

Puzzled now, Caroline tiptoed back to the door and opened

it softly. What she saw brought a quick intake of breath. Olivia still sat on the piano bench, but her face was buried in her hands and her shoulders were shuddering convulsively.

In four steps Caroline was to her and took her in her arms. "Livvy," she said in alarm, "what's the matter? What is it, honey?"

Her daughter stood up and threw herself against her mother. For almost a minute, the sobs were too great for Olivia to speak. Caroline just patted her and stroked her hair. Then gradually she got control of herself, and the racking sobs began to subside. Caroline put a finger under her chin, lifting her head. "What is it, Livvy? What happened?"

It came out in a torrent, the words tumbling like stones in a flood. "Elizabeth . . . she said she hates me. And Kathy and Mary. They say they are never going to play with me again." That brought a new burst of tears.

"But why?" Caroline soothed. "What caused all this?"

Now that the gate had been opened, Olivia couldn't stop. "They were so hateful, Mama. Elizabeth wouldn't let me come in the house. She said her mother didn't allow no Mormon-lovers in their house. They hate me, Mama. They hate me! Mary even threw some dirt at me as I left."

Caroline had gone cold. "Mormon-lovers?" she whispered.

"Yes," Olivia cried. "They know about Grandma and Grandpa and all of Papa's family. They said they're Mormons, and that means we must love the Mormons. They won't play with anyone who's a Mormon-lover."

Caroline's mouth had tightened into a thin line. She held her daughter tightly, staring over her head out of the window, not seeing anything. "It's all right, Livvy," she murmured. "It's all right."

Jessica and John Griffith arrived at Benjamin Steed's cabin a little before ten o'clock on the morning of September twenty-ninth. Derek, Rebecca, and Peter, who had left even earlier because they had about twice as far to go, arrived just after noon. Mother Steed had a full dinner on the table waiting by then, and there was little chance for Peter to talk with Jessica. But the moment the meal was finished and the dishes done, he came to her. She was ready for him. She brought out some books and papers, and they spread them out across the table and plunged in. As an only child of one of Palmyra's wealthier families, Lydia McBride, now Lydia Steed, had received the finest of schooling as a child. So she joined them and quickly became a second tutor to Peter, filling in where Jessica could not.

Peter soaked up knowledge the way a dry field takes a stream of water. He read eagerly, peppered his two adopted sisters-in-law with question after question, and took whatever they could fire at him.

About an hour into their session, the door to the cabin opened. Nathan was standing in the doorway. "How's it going?" he asked.

Jessica smiled, then reached out and laid a hand on Peter's arm. "I've never seen one quite like this," she said.

"He's wonderful," Lydia agreed. "He's very bright and has a marvelous feeling for words."

"Good," Nathan said matter-of-factly. "I thought as much, based on what Jessica had said earlier." He turned to the boy. "So Peter, I have a surprise for you."

Peter was taken aback. "You do? What is it?"

Nathan stepped inside the room, holding the door open. "Come in, brethren."

There was a little exclamation of surprise as Joseph Smith entered the room. "Peter," he said, stepping across the room in three strides. "How are you, young man?"

"I'm fine, Brother Joseph." Peter was a little dazed. A second man had entered the cabin now too. He was finely dressed and had a stack of books under one arm.

"How are the newlyweds doing?" Joseph asked cheerfully, looking around.

"Great," Lydia answered. "Mother Steed has taken Rebecca

in to buy her some things for their house. Derek is out with Matthew and Father Steed doing something or other."

"Peter," Nathan said, "this is Brother John Taylor. He's one of the new Apostles the Lord named to fill the vacancies in the Twelve."

John Taylor smiled at Nathan. "Well, I've been called, but I've not actually been ordained as yet."

"You will be, Brother John," Joseph said easily. "Otherwise how can you leave on that mission next spring?" He turned back to Peter. "He'll probably be going back to your native land."

That surprised everyone except John Taylor. "England?" Lydia said. "Really?"

"Well," Joseph explained, "the Lord didn't actually specify England in the revelation. All he said was that the Twelve were to leave on their missions 'over the great waters' come next April twenty-sixth. Along with Brother Taylor, the other men called were Wilford Woodruff, John Page, and Willard Richards. And as you know, Peter, Brother Richards is still over in England, serving as the president there. So I just think the Twelve will be headed back to England again."

"That's exciting," Peter said. "I always liked Brother Richards."

"Everyone likes Brother Richards." Joseph walked over to the table and looked down at the books. He nodded in satisfaction. "Nathan tells me of your interest in learning, Peter."

"Yes, Jessica is teaching me my letters and some arithmetic."

Jessica laughed. "This boy already knows his letters better than many twice his age."

"That's wonderful, Peter," Joseph said. "Remember what the Lord said. 'The glory of God is intelligence, or light and truth.' So the more knowledge and intelligence we get, the better off we will be."

Peter nodded gravely. "One of my favorite scriptures in the Doctrine and Covenants is the one that tells us to learn about all kinds of things—things in the heavens and in the earth, and all that."

"Good for you," Joseph said. "The Lord wants us to learn all about this wonderful world he has given us."

John Taylor stepped forward and laid the pile of books on the table. He smiled at Peter and spoke for the first time. "There's another scripture about learning in that same revelation," he said.

Peter looked up in surprise. John Taylor spoke with a British accent. He seemed to read Peter's thoughts, for he smiled and nodded. "Yes, I'm from England too. My wife and I came to Canada though. That's where Nathan and Parley Pratt found us."

"Oh, that's right," Peter said. "I remember now Nathan telling us about that."

"But as I was saying, there is another related passage from that same revelation. Do you know it? The one about good books?"

Peter's face twisted a little as he thought. "I don't think so."

" 'Seek ye out of the best books words of wisdom,' " Brother Taylor began quoting softly. " 'Seek learning even by study, and also by faith.' "

"I remember it now."

Brother Taylor reached out and laid a hand on the pile of books he had brought. "The scriptures are the best of all books, Peter. Are you reading them regularly?"

"Yes, sir. Every day, sir."

"Good for you. But there are other good books too. I too have loved to read since I was a boy. And I know that good books are hard to come by out here on the frontier. So when Nathan told me about you and how much you like to read, I thought I would share some of my books with you."

Peter was staring at him; then he looked down at the books. His eyes were filled with awe. "Really, sir?"

"Yes, really. Will you take especially good care of them?"

Peter's mouth was half-opened. "Of course. Yes. Yes, I will. Very good care of them."

Joseph laughed and then sobered almost immediately. He

leaned down and put his face close to Peter's. "I didn't have much chance for schooling when I was a boy, Peter. I am an unlearned man. It is something I very much wish I had. But Brother Taylor is a man who has much learning and much faith. You will do well to emulate him."

"I will, Brother Joseph." He looked to John Taylor. "Thank you, Brother Taylor. Thank you very much."

The newly chosen Apostle smiled broadly now. "You're welcome, and when you're through with those, bring them back and we'll get you some more. I think a boy who loves to read should have as many books as possible."

Chapter Notes

The Prophet's journal entry for September first is found in his history, as are the letters written by General Parks and General Atchison saying that the Mormons were not in a state of rebellion (see *HC* 3:67–68; 84–85).

The passage from the book of Alma that Rebecca cites can now be found in Alma 7:23.

John Taylor and the other three Apostles named were called in a revelation given to Joseph Smith on July 8, 1838. They replaced the four Apostles who had left the Church during the apostasy in Kirtland. In that same revelation, members of the Quorum of the Twelve Apostles were told that they were to take their journey over the great waters, leaving from Far West on April 26, 1839. (See D&C 118:4–6.)

The Lord's statement to which Joseph refers is now D&C 93:36; the scripture referred to by Peter is now D&C 88:78–79; and the scripture quoted by John Taylor is now D&C 88:118.

Chapter Eleven

Even though the weather had turned considerably cooler, during the last week in September 1838 it turned warmer again and Indian summer came to Missouri. With as many people as there were in Far West, when the weather turned bad there were too many branches of the Church to all meet in the school-courthouse building. So some met in their homes, while others met in stores or other public buildings. But with the weather turning good again, larger groups could meet together outside. On this Sunday, even though Joseph had ridden out to visit outlying settlements, the people all gathered to the public square for worship services, and Hyrum Smith and Sidney Rigdon, the other two members of the First Presidency, preached to them.

When the services were finished, several people came over to the Steeds to say hello to the family members who had come into Far West to visit. As one group gathered around Jessica and John, and another, even larger, began talking with the newlyweds, Nathan sidled up to his mother. "Mother, Lydia and I are going to go on ahead and put the baby down for a nap."

Mary Ann turned to him. "All right. Dinner won't be for at least an hour or so."

Lydia, who was right behind Nathan, had Elizabeth Mary in one arm and held on to little Nathan with her free hand. "That'll be about just right," she said.

"Let the children come home with us," Mary Ann suggested. "They're anxious to get as much time as possible with their cousins before they leave again tomorrow."

"That's fine," Lydia said.

Nathan reached down and held out his arms to his son, but Nathan, who would turn three in a couple of weeks, darted around him and burrowed into his grandmother's skirts. "I wanna stay too, Mama."

"No, Nathan," his father said. "You need to take a nap too, young man. Then we'll go to Grandma's and play."

Nathan ignored his father and looked up at his grandma. Joshua and Emily were as dark-haired as their mother, but Nathan had broken the trend. His hair was so blond it looked almost white. "Oh, please, Grandma," he cried, clutching at her leg, "please let me go with you." His eyes were large and of the palest blue color. Now they were so filled with imploring hope that Mary Ann had no will to resist.

She reached down and swooped him up. "Of course you can go with me, darlin'." She looked at Lydia and gave a helpless shrug. "How can I turn that down?" she said. "He'll be fine."

Benjamin was standing with Heber Kimball, Parley Pratt, and Derek and Rebecca. When he saw his wife talking to Nathan and Lydia, he excused himself and came over to join them. "You leavin'?" he asked Nathan.

"Yes. Lydia wants to feed the baby and give her a quick nap."

"All right. We'll see you in a while."

"Pa?"

"Yes?"

"Lydia and I have a request."

"What's that?"

"After dinner today, once things settle down a little . . . well, we'd kind of like to have a family meeting."

One eyebrow lifted slightly as Benjamin looked at his son. "A family meeting?"

"Yes," Lydia answered for Nathan. "A family council. While we've got everyone here. Well, not Joshua and Caroline, of course, but the others."

"Is something wrong?" Mary Ann asked.

"Oh, no," Lydia responded quickly. "It's just that Nathan and I have an idea. We've talked a lot about it."

Nathan was nodding. "We'd like to talk to the whole family about it."

Benjamin shrugged. "All right. Let's do it right after dinner."

When the time finally came and the children were settled into various corners—the smaller ones given something to keep them quietly occupied, the older ones placed so they could fully participate—Nathan seemed quite nervous. He was standing at one end of the room. Lydia was seated next to where he stood and watched him fidgeting. He had a copy of the Doctrine and Covenants in his hand and kept turning it over and over as he waited for everyone to get settled in their places. When they finally quieted and all the faces turned to look at him expectantly, he cleared his throat.

He looked first at his father, then at his mother. "Thank you for letting us have this time." He paused again, fingering the book. Mary Ann could see now that he had small pieces of paper stuck into it as page markers.

Lydia jumped in. "We first got this idea just after everyone was here last time, for the wedding. Nathan and I have talked a lot about it. And the more we've thought about it, the better we like it."

"We thought about waiting until Joshua and Caroline come

up again," Nathan said, "but with Joshua called into the militia that could be a long time. So we decided it might be best to go ahead today while we are all together. Then, if we all agree, we can write to Joshua and Caroline and tell them about it."

He looked down at his wife. She smiled her encouragement up at him.

"I'd like to start with some things the Lord has said to us." He brought up the book and opened it to the first marker. But he did not look down at it immediately. "One of the things I find most appealing about the church we belong to is that it is practical as well as spiritual. It's not all just focused on the hereafter. It gives us principles and concepts to bless our daily lives here."

Matthew raised a hand. "Brother Brigham says that if a church can't help its people in this life as well as save them in the next, it's not good for much."

"I agree," Nathan said heartily. Now he glanced down at the book of scripture. "In the revelation that Joseph called the law of the Church, the Lord gave some important commandments—spiritual commandments, if you will—don't kill, don't lie, don't steal. But immediately following those, he gave some very practical commandments too—remember the poor, be good stewards over the property you have been given, don't take your brother's garment without paying for it."

Benjamin was nodding thoughtfully. Without thinking, he reached out and put his hand through Mary Ann's arm.

"And," Nathan went on, "right in the midst of those practical commandments, the Lord said this." He started to read. " 'Thou shalt not be idle; for he that is idle shall not eat the bread, nor wear the garments of the laborer.' "

The adults were all listening carefully, but, surprisingly, so were most of the children. Young Joshua was especially intent on what his father was saying.

Nathan found his next marker. "In another place he says, 'Verily I say unto you that every man who is obliged to provide for his own family, let him provide and he shall in no wise lose his crown. . . . Let every man be diligent in all things.' And then again he says, 'And the idler shall not have place in the church, except he repents and mends his ways.'"

He was getting into it now, and his nervousness was pretty well gone. "One more, and then I'll make my point." He turned to the last page he had selected. " 'A commandment I give unto you, to prepare and organize yourselves by a bond or everlasting covenant that cannot be broken. . . . Behold this is the preparation wherewith I prepare you, . . . that through my providence, notwithstanding the tribulation which shall descend upon you—' "

He stopped and let his eyes run across the faces of those in the room. "Did you note that?" he asked. "I suppose you could say that what Derek went through up at Gallatin, and what Joseph's going through being charged with rioting and disorderly conduct and who knows what else, and what our people have been going through with mobs riding the countryside and threatening them—all that could be called tribulation."

This time almost every head in the room, except for the youngest child's, was nodding soberly.

"But . . ." He held up one finger and he found his place again. "It says that if we organize ourselves, then God's providence will be with us even through tribulation. Then he continues, 'That the church may stand independent above all other creatures beneath the celestial world.'"

He closed the book and handed it to Lydia. "I'm not sure what that all means. I know that things are starting to look more and more frightening. We are all starting to feel a great deal of concern."

Rebecca suddenly thought of the liberty pole and the feeling of despair that had settled upon her when she had learned it had been shattered by a bolt of lightning. She reached out and took Derek's hand. She loved Di-Ahman, but the Saints weren't as secure in Daviess County. It worried her a great deal.

There was not a sound in the room. Finally, Nathan smiled. It was brief, but it let them know that he was not trying to frighten them. "I don't know what all's going to happen, but I do know this: We have a wonderful family. We have a growing family." He looked around the room and smiled again. "We can barely fit us all in Grandma's house right now and we have five who are not here with us." He looked at Rebecca and Derek, and now the smile broadened, and there was a sudden teasing note in his voice. "I expect that the family will grow even larger in the next little while."

Rebecca blushed deeply as soft chuckles filled the room. Derek just bobbed his head up and down, beaming proudly. There were no announcements yet, but they hoped there would be by the next time they came to Far West.

"And if Matthew would pay even a little bit of attention to that Miller girl who's just dying to get one of his winning smiles, we might see our family grow even more."

Matthew didn't blush easily, but Nathan had caught him totally off guard, and his face flamed. Derek roared and the rest of them hooted. "And before we can turn around," Nathan went on quickly, "Peter will find him some lovely young lass. And then Will and Olivia will be old enough to marry. Rachel will grow up. Emily will get old enough to break the heart of every young man within a hundred miles."

"We're gonna have to rent a livery barn to have our family dinners when we get to that point," Benjamin said dryly.

"Yes," Nathan said, as the others laughed. "And then instead of having twenty-three mouths to feed and five different families to house, we'll have eight or ten families and forty or fifty people to keep fed and clothed."

Mary Ann looked suddenly depressed. Nathan noticed it immediately. "Mother, what's wrong?"

She shook her head. "I was just thinking that there should be six more added to the count. What about Melissa?"

That sobered them all. Melissa and her husband, Carl Rogers, were still in Kirtland. There was very little chance they would ever see them again. Mary Ann looked at Nathan. "I'm sorry. There's nothing we can do, of course. I was just thinking about them."

Nathan nodded. Then, brightening again, he turned to his wife. "Lydia, tell them what we've been thinking."

As she stood up, he moved over and sat in her chair. Lydia plunged right in, her dark eyes sparkling with excitement, her black hair bouncing on her shoulders as she began to pace back and forth while she talked. "Nathan read the Lord's commandment that we not be idle. We are very fortunate that no one in this family is lazy. We don't have any idlers. John and Jessica are running a good farm in Haun's Mill, and Jessica teaches school. Derek and Rebecca and Peter are under way with another fine piece of land. Father Steed has wheat and corn. Matthew's working with Brigham Young. We are all working hard. But . . ." She paused for effect, then lowered her voice. "But are we working as wisely as we could?"

"How do you mean that?" John Griffith asked.

"Well, Benjamin Franklin once said of the American colonies, 'We must all hang together, or assuredly we shall all hang separately.' I think the same principle applies to our family. As the children and then the grandchildren grow up and marry and form their own families, we can hang together, or we can go our separate ways."

"So," Jessica spoke up, "what are you suggesting?"

"We're suggesting that we organize ourselves as a family, just like the Lord counseled us to do. Maybe that way we can become independent and care for our own even if hard times do come. Instead of each of us going our separate ways, what if we decided to work together?"

Nathan couldn't stand it. He was up beside his wife now, his hands waving back and forth as he spoke. "What if we made a covenant as a family, just as we do in the law of consecration, that we will stick together and help each other no matter what? What if we planned out everything?"

"Like what?" Peter said.

Lydia whirled to face him. "Planned to do just what you and Jessica are doing now. Jessica has a wonderful ability to be a teacher. So what if we let her teach all of our children?" She spun to face Benjamin. "Father Steed, I know you've farmed much of your life, but in Kirtland we saw another side of you. You have a natural ability for business, for managing things. Brother Joseph saw that in you. That's why he asked you to be on the building committee for the temple."

"Are you saying I should stop farming?"

"Not at first, Pa?" Nathan answered for her. "Not right away. But John is a natural farmer. I like to farm. Derek, you say you're thrilled to have your own land to farm. So what if the three of us farm, and Pa, you manage the business end of things for all of us?"

Nathan was getting even more excited now. He turned to Matthew. "As our family keeps growing, we're going to need houses, furniture, tools. And right here in Matthew we have a natural carpenter. A fine builder. So let's not only encourage him to take his apprenticeship under Brother Brigham; maybe in a few years we can pool our money and help him start his own carpenter shop. Then not only could he make a living for his family, but he would be a great blessing to all of us."

"I see what you're saying," Mary Ann said. "It's not just helping each other when there's a need; it's planning how to work together as a family to help everyone."

"That's right, Mother Steed," Lydia said. "We decide now what some of our needs will be, and then we go to work to meet those needs in a long-range way." She stopped to get her breath. Her eyes were alive with excitement. "For example, right now Joshua is probably the best off financially of any of us."

"That's for sure," Rachel sang out. "He's rich."

"Yes, he is," Lydia agreed. "And what if he puts up enough money for us to start our own dry goods store here in Far West?"

As Rebecca made a soft sound of surprise, Lydia turned to face her. "Yes. I grew up in my father's dry goods store in Palmyra. I worked in Newel Whitney's store in Kirtland. I know how to run a store. Rebecca has a very quick mind. She could help. Peter is wonderful with books and learning. He could do a lot. Joshua and Will could freight in all our goods and build up their freight business in this part of the state as well."

Nathan looked at his mother. “I’d be willing to write to Melissa and Carl and tell them what we’re doing, see if they would ever be interested in joining with us. But . . .” He didn’t finish.

“But there’s not much chance of that,” his father finished for him.

“I know,” Mary Ann said, “but I think we need to at least try.”

Emily raised her hand. Lydia turned and smiled down at her daughter. “Yes, sweetheart?”

“Me and Joshua could tend baby Elizabeth while you’re at the store.”

Mary Ann reached over and hugged her granddaughter. “How sweet, Emmy.”

“Emmy’s got the idea,” Lydia rushed on. “Everyone helps. We pull together as a family. We cooperate with each other. We help each other.”

Nathan jumped in again. “Eventually it might mean that we would all move here, so we are closer together.”

“I would like that,” Mary Ann piped in, bringing a smile from her children.

“That doesn’t mean someone gets stuck doing something they don’t want to do,” Nathan continued. “We don’t say to Peter, ‘Peter, you’ll be a cooper because we need someone to make barrels for us.’ We let Peter decide what he wants to do, but then once he decides, we let it bless the whole family and not just his own wife and children.”

Derek punched his brother on the arm. “Congratulations, mate. It’s a fine family you have now already.”

Peter pulled a face at him, but then he turned back to Nathan. “Could I ever do something with writing, Nathan?”

Nathan stopped, thinking quickly. “If that’s what you like. What about a printing shop? Or better yet, how about something like a newspaper? How’d you like to run a newspaper someday, Peter?”

Peter didn’t have to answer that. His face said it all.

Benjamin was slowly nodding. "We organize rather than just let things happen."

"Exactly."

Mary Ann looked up at her son and daughter-in-law, her eyes filled with admiration. "I think this is the most wonderful idea. What are families for, if not to help one another?"

"When would all this start?" Rebecca asked.

Nathan and Lydia had talked about that a great deal. Nathan looked first at his wife; then, when she smiled her support, he turned to his sister. "It may take years to get it fully under way, but I think we ought to start right now—by making a covenant and a promise with one another that we are a family, and that we will always work together for the good of the family."

Benjamin stood and walked over to stand beside his son. To everyone's surprise, he put an arm on Nathan's shoulder, then reached out and took Lydia's hand, drawing her to him as well. "As the patriarch of this clan"—he looked around, smiling wryly—"which seems to grow larger every time we get together, I'd like to thank Nathan and Lydia for what they've suggested to us today."

He stopped, and for a long moment the room was silent. When he finally spoke, he spoke in a low voice. "I, for one, think it is an inspired idea. And as patriarch I would like to be the first to make that covenant with all of you."

By early October, the situation for the Latter-day Saints was becoming increasingly grim. In DeWitt—a small Missouri river town located about seventy miles southeast of Far West and sixty miles downriver from Independence—the influx of Mormon emigrants began to tip the balance of power in favor of the Mormons. The old settlers reacted with typical alarm. On the twentieth of September, somewhere between a hundred and a hundred and fifty armed men rode into DeWitt and told the Mormons to leave or be killed. The Mormons begged for some semblance of reason. They had property, homes, livestock, and crops. After some discussion, the mob relented and gave them until the first of October—a full ten days to put their affairs in order and be gone. But George M. Hinkle, the leader of the Saints in DeWitt, who was himself a colonel in the Missouri militia, defiantly refused to leave and promised to resist any attempts to force them out. He and the other leaders wrote a hasty letter to the governor, explaining the situation and asking him to intervene.

There was no reply.

With the Mormons refusing to run, the mob element gathered at DeWitt sent out a call for help. The timing could not have been worse. General Atchison had dispersed a whole body of armed Missourians in Daviess County when he found out the Mormons were not in uprising. Now those men were lusting for action. They immediately headed south to join the forces surrounding DeWitt. Terrified now, the Mormons dug in and began to build barricades.

In a matter of days, the mobs ringed the Mormon portion of town. The Saints in DeWitt were under siege.

In Far West, things also began to deteriorate. Some months earlier Joseph had sent out a call, saying it came by the word of the Lord, for those living in isolated settlements and the smaller communities to come into Far West and Di-Ahman where there were larger bodies of Saints living. When all seemed peaceful, few paid attention to the counsel. But now, as the "Mormon War" began to escalate and reports of depredations against isolated Mormon families circulated almost daily, family after family decided perhaps it was time to heed the voice of their prophet. Refugees poured into Far West, usually fleeing their homes and bringing only the scantiest of provisions—if that—with them. In a short time the resources of the Saints were taxed to the limit. Every home was filled to capacity. Tents and wagons and lean-tos and open campsites lined every street.

And as if that weren't enough, on October second the Kirtland Camp rolled into Far West.

When Kirtland fell into the control of the enemies of the Church in late 1837 and early 1838, many of the Saints, like the Steeds, immediately left for Missouri. But there were hundreds who were too poor to make the journey on their own. Rather than just leave them to their own devices, the leadership of the First Quorum of the Seventy covenanted to pool what little resources they had and to leave no one behind who wanted to go. On July sixth, the Kirtland Camp, as these Saints called themselves, started west. The roster said there were over five hundred people, twenty-seven tents, fifty-nine wagons, ninety-seven horses, twenty-two oxen, sixty-nine cows, and one bull in the company. Some stopped along the way. One group had pulled out at Haun's Mill to fix their wagons and let their teams rest. But after nearly three months on the trail, the main body arrived in Far West, exhausted, sick, destitute, and frightened. And suddenly Joseph and the brethren had several hundred additional people requiring food, housing, and medical attention.

"Brother Joseph!" Benjamin raised his hand and waved to the horseman cantering toward him.

The man on the horse was about thirty or forty yards from where Benjamin was digging the last of the carrots from the garden. He reined up, peering at Benjamin. Then as recognition came, he waved, turned the horse's head, and trotted forward to where Benjamin was.

Joseph Smith swung down from the saddle. "Brother Benjamin, how are you?" He laughed easily. "I was so preoccupied, I didn't even see you here."

The day was sunny, but the temperature was hovering in the mid-forties, and both men wore coats against the chill. Joseph's cheeks were touched with color, but as usual his eyes were filled with cheer and good humor.

He stamped his feet for a moment, then looked down. "You got a good crop of carrots this year, Ben."

"I did. And some fine potatoes as well. Maybe not all we need to get us through the winter, but every bit helps."

A quick shadow passed over Joseph's face. "I fear that with all the mouths we have to feed now none of us are going to have enough to see us through the winter."

Benjamin's face was grave. "Was that what you were preoccupied with?"

There was a moment's hesitation, then a long sigh. "I ride a lot these days, Brother Ben. It seems like that is the only time I have to myself to wrestle with the problems that beset us like flies around spoiled meat."

Benjamin laughed. "Who are the flies and who is the spoiled meat?"

Joseph looked startled for just a moment, then laughed heartily. "Ah, Ben, it is good to be with a man who can make me laugh. You are a good friend."

"And I treasure your friendship, Brother Joseph."

There was a sound behind them, and they both turned. Mary Ann was coming from the house, wrapping a shawl around her shoulders. "Hello, Brother Joseph."

"Good afternoon, Mary Ann. How good to see you."

"I saw you ride up. We just finished some soup and there's hot bread out of the oven. Would you come in and partake?"

He shook his head. "No, thank you kindly anyway. But I promised Emma I'd be coming home hungry." He shook his head again, looking duly contrite. "My wife says every time I go out, someone invites me in to eat. She never knows when I'll be home for supper. So I promised her today—no food except at Emma's table."

Mary Ann smiled. Emma was a wonderfully patient wife. She had to be. Joseph was beloved of his people, but that worked considerable hardship on his wife. When he was not gone off to supervise this task or that, or visit some branch of the Church here or there, his home was the center of constant activity: people with problems, newcomers wanting to meet the Prophet, priesthood leaders seeking counsel, overnight guests—there were few times when Joseph and Emma had the luxury of time alone.

"Are these problems we can help with?" Benjamin asked. "We'd be happy to do whatever we can."

"How thoughtful of you to ask," Joseph said warmly. "But no. I'm afraid with some of these things, there's not much that anyone can do."

"Well, we stand ready if you need us."

Joseph reached out and laid a hand on Benjamin's arm. "I know, Brother Ben. I know." As his hand dropped to his side again, he got a faraway look in his eyes. "You know, it's not the huge problems that trouble me as much. It's when . . ." He shrugged. "Sometimes it's the little things which prove to be of greatest consequence."

"How true," Mary Ann said. "Even in our own lives."

Joseph had seemed about to change the subject, but Mary Ann's response spurred him on. "The writer of Proverbs summed up one of the most common of human weaknesses. 'Pride goeth before destruction, and an haughty spirit before a fall.' " There was a soft sound of discouragement. "Human nature can be a thing of such tenderness—and a thing of such unbending toughness! And pride has a way of nursing the totally unimportant into something unbearably significant."

Benjamin was watching him closely, listening, yet was not sure what Joseph meant. But with that natural intuition which was part of her gift, Mary Ann took a shrewd guess. "Thomas B. Marsh?" she asked softly.

Joseph nodded, the pain now darkening the clearness of those blue eyes. And then Benjamin understood. While the fires of war were raging across the countryside, a smaller battle had erupted in Far West. At first it went unnoticed by any except the principals involved. Two women were neighbors to each other. One was a Sister Harris. Benjamin knew her only very slightly. The other was the wife of Thomas B. Marsh, who was President of the Quorum of the Twelve Apostles. She and Sister Harris were desirous of making cheese, but since neither of them possessed the requisite number of cows, they agreed to exchange milk. To be sure to have justice done, it was agreed that they should not save the strippings—the milk that comes at the end of a milking and that is richer in cream—but that the milk and strippings should all go together. Small matters to talk about in a time of war, to be sure, two women's exchanging milk to make cheese. But things don't often work as reason would suggest.

Sister Harris, it appeared from the reports Benjamin had heard, was faithful to the agreement and carried to Sister Marsh the milk and strippings; but Sister Marsh, wishing to make some extra-good cheese, saved a pint of strippings from each cow and sent Sister Harris the milk without the strippings. Understandably upset, Sister Harris confronted her neighbor and asked that she stop the practice. Sister Marsh angrily and haughtily denied the accusations and refused to make any change or reparation.

Sister Harris decided to follow the counsel given by the Lord. She went to the priesthood quorum where her husband was a member and asked them to help her settle the matter. By now, of course, the matter had become public knowledge, and people began to take sides. But after a careful examination of the matter, it was determined that Sister Marsh had saved the strippings, contrary to her promise not to do so, and consequently had cheated Sister Harris. Thomas B. Marsh's wife was asked to make restitution.

"Is that matter still not settled?" Benjamin asked Joseph.

There was a slow shake of his head.

"I spoke with Sister Marsh last week," Mary Ann said. "She is a proud woman. She absolutely refused to admit that she had done anything wrong and said she will not pay Sister Harris anything. And she was really angry at the quorum leaders. She said she is the wife of the President of the Twelve. As Aaronic Priesthood holders, she says, they have no right to rule on her actions."

Joseph was quiet for a moment. "It's not just Sister Marsh.

Thomas was furious. As you know, Brother Benjamin, from meetings you've sat in, he already thinks that I do not pay sufficient attention to his counsel or treat him with the respect his office deserves."

"Is it true that they appealed the case to Bishop Partridge?" Benjamin asked.

"Yes. Like his wife, Thomas said the teachers quorum had no right to sit in judgment on an Apostle. So the bishopric heard the case. A regular Church trial was held. After listening to both sides, the bishopric upheld the decision of the quorum leaders. Thomas did not consider that the bishop had done him and his lady justice. He immediately appealed to the high council. 'Surely they would side with an Apostle,' he said." There was a faint irony in Joseph's voice now. "Especially with the senior Apostle! He made a desperate defense of his wife and her character, but the high council finally confirmed the bishop's decision. Sister Marsh was in the wrong."

Benjamin was staring at Joseph in disbelief. "And he won't accept that counsel?"

"No." For a long moment Joseph looked out across the prairie, which was dry and bleak now that the cold weather had come. "Brother Marsh said he had been betrayed. He demanded that the case be brought before the First Presidency."

"No!" Mary Ann said, deeply shocked now.

"Yes. That does seem a little ironic, doesn't it? Here we are in the midst of a war. The last word we got from DeWitt is that the Saints are being increasingly threatened. Closer to home, men are being taken out and whipped. Women are driven from their homes in the middle of the night. Haystacks are burned. Cattle stolen or shot. The whole of Missouri is howling for our blood." There was a soft laugh of derision. "And with all that, the First Presidency has to stop and sit in judgment over a pint of milk strippings."

"And how did you rule?" Benjamin asked after the silence had stretched on for a time.

Joseph looked up. "Oh, there was no question. Sister Marsh

was in the wrong. Sister Harris had to be made right." He looked at Benjamin, his eyes filled with a great sadness. "What would common sense dictate in such a case? Does one who is called as an Apostle—a supposed model of spiritual justice and commitment to gospel principles—stand by his wife, or does he accept the correction and counsel of the First Presidency?"

"What will he do?" Mary Ann asked, almost whispering.

Joseph turned to her. "I don't know. It is a hard choice for a proud man. But I fear that it will prove to have lasting and terrible consequences for him." He looked away. "And for the rest of us."

On the fifth of October, Joseph Smith and some of the other brethren rode to the southern part of Caldwell County to look for a site for a new settlement. To their surprise they were met by a rider from DeWitt on his way to Far West to summon help. The report was not good. The Saints in DeWitt were under siege. They were greatly outnumbered. Provisions were low, and any incoming or outgoing was prohibited by the mob. Movement of anyone inside the barricades was drawing fire. One of the attacking groups had sent to Jackson County for a small cannon and powder and shot. Petitions had been sent to the governor, but there had been no answer.

Joseph immediately changed his plans and accompanied the harried messenger back to DeWitt. It was not an easy task. It took them the rest of that day and most of the night to slip inside the city. The main roads were heavily guarded, and only by traveling the least-frequented paths and forging through wooded areas did they make it through the siege lines. They arrived early the next morning.

The reports had not been exaggerated. The Saints were desperate. They had few arms. Food supplies were critically low. Small children were on the verge of collapse. Men and women walked around in a stupor, faint from hunger. The weather was turning colder now, and many of the Saints were emigrants who had stopped in DeWitt, contrary to Joseph's counsel, and made temporary camp. They were living out of wagons or tents or nothing at all.

Joseph immediately called on some of DeWitt's more respectable citizens and asked for their help. None were Latter-day Saints, but being honorable men, they deplored the actions of the mobs and agreed to write affidavits attesting to the perilous situation and the mistreatment that the Saints were receiving. A Mr. Caldwell volunteered to take the documents to Jefferson City and present them to Governor Boggs. Joseph and the Saints hunkered down to wait for relief.

Three days later, Caldwell returned. The governor's answer was short, blunt, and unmistakably final. "The quarrel is between the Mormons and the mob," he said. "Let them fight it out."

Joseph was not willing to do that. On October eleventh, the Mormons gathered up about seventy wagons, loaded them with what little goods had not been consumed in the siege or looted by the mobs, and moved out. Though the Missourians had promised to let them go in peace, as the wagon train moved slowly northwestward, the Mormons were continually harassed and occasionally fired upon.

That night, camped in a grove of trees a short distance off the road, the Saints huddled together for protection and against the cold. The sisters hovered around a woman who had given birth to a baby earlier in the day. Their ministerings were not sufficient. The next morning, she was buried in the soft dirt beneath the trees—there was no lumber for a coffin—and the company moved out again. Weakened by starvation, exposure to cold, and a week of relentless terror, several more brethren died that day and were buried along the wayside.

On the afternoon of October twelfth, the ragged, tragic company from DeWitt came slowly into Far West.

Chapter Notes

The details concerning DeWitt and the deteriorating situation in Far West are taken from Joseph's record and other contemporary sources (see *HC* 3:77–86, 149–60; *Persecutions*, pp. 202–12; and *CHFT*, pp. 195–97).

The story of the Kirtland Camp is filled with many accounts of faith and sacrifice and dedication, but a full treatment of it was not within the scope of this novel. For those wishing to read the full account, Joseph Smith's history includes the daily journal of the company's travels (see *HC* 3:87–148).

The story of the problem between Sister Harris and the wife of Thomas B. Marsh, including the response to the rulings of the various Church courts, is told by Joseph in the novel. But the details, and much of the exact wording, are taken from the account given by George A. Smith in general conference after the Saints arrived in Utah (see *JD* 3:283–84).

Chapter Twelve

Joshua reined in and stood up in the stirrups, staring at the silent barricades and the ragged buildings behind them that marked the outskirts of DeWitt. His hand rested on the butt of his pistol as his eyes darted here and there, searching for trouble. But there was no one hiding behind the wall and no one out in front preparing to assault it.

Which was probably just as well, he thought. The wall was obviously hastily built. Boxes and crates were the mainstay, buttressed with nothing more substantial than a plank here, a broken chair there. It wouldn't have taken much to breach it.

His eyes dropped. The grass was heavily trampled, and the dirt of the road was a mass of hoof and boot prints where man and animal had crossed and crisscrossed a hundred times. He lifted his head a little, letting his gaze take in a wider arc. Even without the barricades, it was obvious that an army had camped here. And not a very tidy one. Charred scars in the prairie sod marked the sites of now cold campfires. The place was littered with trash. Pieces of paper, empty boxes, wet and chewed cigar butts, scraps of food, stripped chicken bones, piles of horse droppings thick with buzzing flies—it was as though a glacier had swept through the garbage dump of a large town, then left its detritus here when it finally melted.

So the siege was over. The Mormons were gone. Joshua felt a tremendous sense of relief. As he nudged his horse forward and passed around the barricades, he kept scanning the ground for any signs of blood. He saw none, and felt the relief even more keenly than before. He kicked his horse into a trot and entered the main street of DeWitt.

"I'm Captain Joshua Steed, adjutant to General David Atchison of the Missouri militia in Richmond, Ray County. We heard there was trouble here. The general asked that I come and survey the situation."

The look on the face of the woman behind the counter went from suspicious to respectful in one flicker. "General Atchison, eh?" She peered at him over the top of her glasses, the one lens of which was cracked right down the center. "Heard about our war with the Mormons?"

Joshua had to pull his eyes away from staring at the broken lens. How did that affect her vision? *Are you seeing two of me?* He gave a little shake of his head. "Yes. They're gone, then?"

She chortled with glee. "Gone like whipped dogs." She turned and spat toward the corner spittoon. She wasn't chewing tobacco, but her action was a perfect imitation of the men who did. It made her look all the harder and repulsive to Joshua. "Sorriest bunch of devil worshippers you ever did see. They had their tails 'twixt their legs, I'm tellin' ya, and their Mormon prophet, old Joe Smith, with 'em."

That bought Joshua's full attention. "Smith was here?"

"Yup. Snuck in a few nights ago. Saw that he and his were about to be massacreed and led the whole kit and caboodle out of here yesterday afternoon. And on the run, I might add."

"Massacred," Joshua corrected her absently, his mind racing. So a confrontation had been avoided. All the better. "Where have the men gone? Your men, I mean. Not the Mormons. Did they go after them?"

"No," she said, shutting one eye—the one behind the cracked glass—and squinting at him with a frown. "But they're planning on it. Goin' after them today sometime. They're meetin' at ten o'clock down at the churchyard. Why you askin'?"

But Joshua barely heard the last question. He glanced at the clock on the wall at the end of the store. It was five minutes of ten. He spun on his heel and was out the door and moving toward his horse.

Joshua dismounted and edged to the back of the large and angry group of men. As he did so, a man in a long black coat and top hat walked up to the front porch of the church and raised his hands for silence. Joshua nudged the man in front of him. He turned. Joshua held out his hand. "Joshua Steed, from Richmond. Heard I missed all the fun yesterday."

The man shook his hand enthusiastically. "You sure did."

"Who's this?" he asked, gesturing toward the man who stood before the crowd.

"The Reverend Sashiel Woods."

Joshua nodded, not really surprised. During the Jackson County war with the Mormons five years earlier, Joshua had once convinced his commanding officer to take along two ministers who were rabid Mormon-haters. Joshua cared no more for their religious twaddle than he did for the Mormons', but he knew they could be useful, lending an air of respectability to the mobbings and stiffening the will of the Missourians by filling them with a towering sense of self-righteousness.

For the first few minutes it was all bombast and braggadocio. Woods reminded them of their victory as the men shouted and cheered him on. Joshua smiled grimly. He knew the technique well. It took a while to get a group of men with limited courage to the point where they were convinced they were invincible.

But then the reverend began to talk about the job not being finished. The Mormons were gone from DeWitt, sure enough, but they were only gone back up to Caldwell and Daviess counties. And the good people of that part of the state were being terrorized by the depredations of the Mormons. It was time for the good men of Carroll County to ride north and put an end to the Mormon scourge once and for all.

That sobered the men somewhat, and Joshua sensed there was some hesitation. But the parson had preached more than one sermon to a shaky audience and knew where the heart of his congregation lay.

"Brethren," he shouted, "you know what time of year it is?"

Several heads came up. What did the calendar have to do with anything?

"I'll tell you what time of year it is," he answered. "Before long it's gonna be land sales time. Do you hear me, men? Land sales time. Do you know what that means?"

Even Joshua was a little puzzled by this sudden turn of the speech. But again the Reverend Mr. Woods answered his own question.

"You ever heard of preemption? A man farms a piece of ground, it's his. But if he should leave it for any reason, the land gets preempted and sold in the land sales."

Now they had it, and Joshua did too. A murmur of excitement swept through the crowd.

"Now, we know the Mormons are horse thieves and lowlifes of every kind," Woods continued, "but they do have some mighty purty farmland up there. Mighty purty. If we were to go up and help our good brothers in Daviess County drive them Mormons clear out of the state, you know what would happen next?"

"Their land would be preempted!" someone shouted.

"Amen, brother! You got that exactly right. Now, the old settlers up north are gonna drive them Mormons out, with us or without us. We don't get ourselves up there, they're gonna be havin' that land all to themselves."

"I heard the old settlers agreed to sell out to the Mormons," another man called.

The reverend swung on him, smiling as if he were real pleased. "Thank you, John. That's exactly right." He paused, and then a wolfish grin stole across his face. "And when the Daviess County boys drive the Mormons out of the state, they'll have that land back *and* the money they was paid for it."

Laughter and applause swept through the group.

"Now, do you want to be part of that or not?" Woods shouted, suddenly angry. "Do you want them boys to have it all to themselves?"

"No!"

Woods let his voice drop to a conspiratorial whisper, but made sure it was loud enough to carry to the back of the crowd. "And you know what else? We here in DeWitt know something those boys up there don't know yet, don't we?"

"What's that, Reverend?"

"We know the government ain't gonna be botherin' us none while we drive those Mormons out of here. Now, don't we know that for a fact?"

As the crowd began to whoop, his voice rose to a shout. "You heard Governor Boggs. He said it's between us and the Mormons. 'Let them fight it out,' he said."

Now the roar was like a howl of triumph.

"So what do you say, boys? Do we ride north or not?"

As the crowd exploded, Joshua turned and walked swiftly to his horse. It was a long ride back to Richmond, and he was going to have to push his horse hard to make it before midnight.

General Atchison was never at his best early in the morning, tending to grumpiness until he had a couple of cups of coffee and an hour out of the bed. This morning he had had neither, and he was like a rumpled old bear who had been kicked out of his den too early in the spring. "What time did you get back, Steed?" he grumbled.

"About one-thirty, sir."

"And? What is the situation in DeWitt?"

Joshua gave him his report quickly. "I assume they're on their way north by now," he said as he finished.

Atchison swore. "Just what we need is another four or five hundred hotheaded idiots riding around up there with guns in their hands and greed in their hearts."

"And their bellies full of whiskey," Joshua added dryly. "But it's more than that, sir." He shook his head. His trip back had been delayed when he heard another rumor passing through a town west of DeWitt. "The name Cornelius Gilliam mean anything to you?"

Atchison's eyes narrowed. "Neil Gilliam? Of course. Is he in on this too?"

Joshua nodded wearily. "Gilliam is raising a group of men from Platte and Clinton counties. They're joining Parson Woods somewhere north of here." Joshua knew Gilliam well. When the Mormons had come from Ohio in 1834 in what they called Zion's Camp, Gilliam had led a party of men to the Fishing River to intercept them. Joshua had been with him. They were filled with hard liquor and empty boasts. And then a storm had hit their camp. It still gave Joshua the creeps when he remembered it. He had never seen anything to match the likes of that, not before, not since. The Missourians had been scattered, and the Mormons attributed it to divine intervention. He looked at Atchison. "Near as I can tell, they'll have about eight hundred men, all told."

Atchison swore again, this time bitterly. And then the qualities that made him a natural selection to be a general officer in the militia took over. He yelled for the man who served as his personal aide, and dictated a quick letter to Governor Boggs. He turned to Joshua. "I want you to take this personally to Governor Boggs in Jefferson City. Tell him the situation is deteriorating rapidly." His voice was suddenly sarcastic. "See if you can't persuade him to get His Excellency's royal body up here and evaluate the situation before this turns into all-out warfare."

"Yes, sir."

"On your way out of town, get General Doniphan over here too. We'd better have a war council."

"Yes, sir."

"And you get yourself back here in a hurry, Captain. We may be headed north too."

Joshua kept his face impassive. "Yes, sir." He turned and started out, but at the door he stopped. "Sir?"

"Yes?"

"Independence is only a little bit out of the way, sir. I haven't seen my family in almost a month now. Tomorrow is Sunday. Would you mind if I swung by there on my way back, just to see if everything's all right with them, sir?"

Atchison started to shake his head, then changed his mind. "Why not?" he growled. "One more day isn't going to see the end of this." He nodded now. "Permission granted. But don't dally, Steed. A short visit, then right back here. We've got things to do."

"Yes, sir. Thank you, sir." And Joshua was out the door, feeling a deep sense of foreboding as he tucked into his pocket the letters he had been given and strode out of the building.

By mid-October, Far West was like a burlap bag filled with too many potatoes. The fabric was stretched to the limit and the seams were starting to unravel. In addition to the refugees pouring in from the countryside now—up to thirty teams a day were coming—the city had had to absorb the five hundred of the Kirtland Camp and then another two hundred of the weak and starving who had survived the siege of DeWitt.

With the brethren spending half their time running here and there to protect themselves, any building of new homes had virtually ceased. Less than thirty homes had been built since the beginning of September, and in that same time the population had swelled by three or four hundred families. Families now were housed in rooms rather than individual residences. Extended families like the Steeds, where parents and married children lived in separate homes, moved in together and turned their vacant homes over to the newcomers. Nathan and Lydia and their children were now living with Benjamin and Mary Ann and Matthew. Two young families shared Nathan and Lydia's one-room cabin. But even that was not sufficient. Every vacant lot was jammed with wagons, tents, crate shacks, and open campfires.

Even before the troubles had started, the infrastructures of Far West had been taxed to the limit. In just over two years the site had gone from being a desolate, windswept ridge on the prairie to a city of nearly five thousand people. And now that population was up by another fifteen hundred or more. Even in the best of circumstances it would have been a logistical nightmare, but with civil war threatening to engulf the countryside the movement of goods and services into Caldwell County virtually came to a standstill.

"Provisions are low," wrote one man in his journal, phonetically spelling some words as best he could. "Here corn is 20 cts per bushel, beans 1.00, wheat 87 1/2 cents. Wood is $2.00 per cord. Soap is the hardest necessary to be got. Bar soap is worth 18 3/4 per pound, soft soap is from 7 to 10 cents per pound which is about 1.00 per gallon. Salt is 12 1/2 cts per quart. Milk is nothing but is getting rather skirse. Pumpkins and squash are quite low. Verry little of domestic fruit is raised within 20 miles. Medical herbs are reather scirce. Bring on Lobelia, Babary Rasbury, slipery Elm, Composition, bitters, & Hot drops. Peneroyal is plenty. Clothing is twice as high hear as at the East, shoes also. 3 Months since 1 per cent would insure goods from St Louis to this place but now is thought worth 25 per cent. Indeed perilous times have verily come, and it is at the Risk of our lives that we go to the landing for our goods."

With his characteristic flair for practicality, Joseph decided to capitalize on the already existing Mormon militia. The brethren had been organized into "companies" of tens and fifties and hundreds, which were quickly dubbed the "armies of Israel." Some of the companies were given assignments that were of a military nature. One was asked to monitor the movement of the mobs and any opposing militia. Another set up a runner system to deliver messages quickly between Far West and Di-Ahman or among the scattered settlements. And in case of open warfare, the companies would provide defense for the city.

But the vast majority of these companies were given the task of helping the Saints to better prepare for whatever eventualities were coming. One of Joseph's favorite scriptures came from the book of James. " 'Pure religion and undefiled before God and the Father,' " he was fond of quoting, " 'is this, To visit the fatherless and widows in their affliction, and to keep himself unspotted from the world.' "

With the flood of incoming refugees there were many poor and not a few widows trying to survive with their children. And while the situation was becoming more and more desperate in Far West, Joseph was not one to sit about and wring his hands. So the "army of Israel" was put to work. One company was assigned to build cabins for those without shelter. Another was sent to help get in the crops. Cutting wood, fixing wagons, mending fences, stockpiling bedding and clothing—wherever there was a task or need that was too much for an individual family alone to do, Joseph sent one of the companies to help. Widows were specifically targeted, and the "army" was told to make sure these widows had sufficient shelter and food for the winter.

If any of the brethren started to grumble about the extra work they were assigned, Joseph would gently chide them. "Now, Brother Brown," he would say, "how can you expect to keep yourself unspotted from the pollutions of the world if Sister Green and her fatherless children, who live just two doors away from you, are in want? How would you face your Savior and hold your head up high in such a case?" And even the crustiest of the Saints could not resist such persuasion.

Not only was it a brilliant strategy in terms of making sure the Saints were better prepared, but also it took otherwise idle people and put them to work. Instead of standing around bemoaning their lot, they were actively engaged in productive service. This boosted morale in a time when the grim realities of the situation they were facing could have created unmanageable tension and anxiety.

On the afternoon of Saturday, October thirteenth, the day after Joseph had returned with the group of Saints from DeWitt, a letter arrived from General Alexander Doniphan. When he had been briefed by General Atchison, Doniphan sent an express to Joseph and told him that a body of eight hundred armed men were headed for Di-Ahman, or Wight's Town, as he called it.

Doniphan authorized Joseph Smith to activate the Mormon militia under the command of Lieutenant Colonel George M. Hinkle, who was a fully commissioned officer in the Missouri militia. It was what the Saints had prayed for. They had official permission to resist and to protect themselves from their enemies. Later that same day Joseph called for all the Saints to meet at the public square immediately following worship services the next day.

By one o'clock on that Sabbath afternoon, the public square was packed solid. There was a high overcast, and it was a cool day, but not unpleasantly so. The Steeds stood together not far from where the makeshift podium had been set up for Joseph. Young Joshua had been left behind with the other children. This was not a meeting for children.

After opening the meeting with prayer, Joseph explained the situation about the approaching army. It didn't come as much of a surprise. Word of the news from the south had swept through Far West like a flash flood down a narrow canyon. What hadn't spread as quickly was the word that Colonel Hinkle had authorization to call out the armies of Israel. A murmur of excitement rumbled across the group as Joseph explained that. Hinkle was a proud man who, like Thomas B. Marsh, felt that Joseph did not give him enough honor and recognition, but he was also courageous and a natural leader. It had been he who had resisted the demands of the mob in DeWitt and held out until help had come. So the people welcomed the news that he would be leading an official group of militia against their enemies.

Then, to Mary Ann's surprise, Joseph reached to where a Bible was set on the podium in front of him. He picked it up, every eye on him, and turned pages slowly until he found his place. Then he looked up. The blue eyes that were so clear and so often filled with gentle amusement were now clouded and grave. "Brethren and sisters, I should like to read something to you," he began. "It comes from the book of John, the fifteenth chapter, the thirteenth verse."

There was a pause as he let his eyes sweep across the assembled men and women, their faces as grave and filled with concern as his. "This took place in the upper room, on the night before Jesus was crucified. So it was a grim time for them as well. Jesus had been teaching his disciples about love and what it meant to love one another. Then he said . . ." His eyes dropped to find the verse; then he read it slowly and with great emphasis. " 'Greater love hath no man than this, that a man lay down his life for his friends.' "

He shut the book. Not a sound came from the assembly. A great hush even seemed to lie upon the surrounding countryside, as if all of nature were holding its breath to see what the Mormons would do now. Then Joseph began to speak again in slow and measured tones. "Brethren and sisters, as you know, these are perilous times. Our enemies prowl about us like wolves following the scent of an injured stag. We are told that a large body of men are marching from the south against Di-Ahman. Well, I have friends in Di-Ahman. And you have friends in Di-Ahman. These are not only friends in the normal sense of the word, but friends in the gospel sense of the word. These are fellow disciples of Christ. And Christ said that no man can have greater love than to be willing to lay down his life for his friends."

Nathan Steed watched Joseph closely. They had been friends since the spring of 1827, more than eleven years now. They had been through some glorious times together. They had also seen times that would cause hell to throw back its head and howl with glee. And through it all, Nathan could not remember seeing Joseph quite so somber. He felt a little shiver run up his back. In the case of Nathan Steed, some of those "friends" in Di-Ahman consisted of his younger sister, her new husband, and his fourteen-year-old brother, Peter.

"We shall be leaving from this square tomorrow morning. All of you brethren who wish to join me and Colonel Hinkle in riding north to save our friends from harm, please assemble at eight o'clock."

That was it. Joseph laid the Bible down and stepped back. There were no dramatics. No histrionics. No passionate appeals for action. He had read a scripture, then quietly called for a response from men of faith. The very quietness of the request infused it with more drama and power and passion than anything else Joseph could possibly have done.

Nathan and Benjamin hung back, waiting for the throngs of men to shake Joseph's hand and pledge their support. Mary Ann and Lydia had left immediately to start preparing food for their men to carry on the march north.

"Hello, Brother Ben. Hello, Nathan."

They both turned. Brigham Young and Heber C. Kimball had come up to stand beside them.

"Good afternoon, brethren," Benjamin said. Nathan greeted them, and they shook hands all around.

"You'll be going?" Brigham asked without turning his head. He was watching the men surrounding Joseph.

"Yes." Nathan and Benjamin spoke as one.

"Matthew?"

Benjamin shook his head. "Matthew's with the express company."

"Oh, that's right. I knew that."

Because of his age, Matthew had been assigned to the company of militia that set up a series of relay posts at two- or three-mile intervals between Far West and Di-Ahman so that word could be passed between the two communities quickly. He manned the second post north of Far West from dawn till dusk each day.

"Are you going?" Nathan asked.

Brigham shook his head. "Joseph has asked that Heber and I stay behind and make sure all is in readiness in case something develops here."

"That's the first sensible thing I've heard all day," a sarcastic voice behind them said.

The four of them turned. Thomas B. Marsh had walked over to join them. He was scowling in the direction of Joseph and the gathering of men. "He loves the glory, doesn't he?"

Brigham glanced quickly at Heber, then back to Marsh. "What makes you say that, Brother Thomas? Joseph is just listening to the men making their pledges about coming tomorrow."

Heber was looking at Marsh from beneath his heavy eyebrows. There was a hint of warning in his eyes. "I didn't see Joseph asking for much glory today," he said shortly.

Marsh blew out his breath in disgust. "Oh, no? Well, where's the Twelve in all this?"

Heber grinned suddenly. "Brigham and I are right here. David Patten is waiting his turn to see Joseph. You're right here too."

"Don't be clever," Thomas snapped. "You know what I mean. We're the Council of the Twelve. Were you consulted in this decision? Were any of us asked if sending an army with Hinkle is the best course of action?"

"Why are you so angry, Thomas?" Brigham said cautiously. "Joseph is the prophet."

"And I'm the senior Apostle!" Marsh shot right back. "And I don't even get so much as a fare-thee-well. That's why I'm angry. And it makes me angry that you and Heber sit here and let it happen without getting angry too."

Brigham Young was not a tall man, no more than about five foot ten. He was a good two inches shorter than Marsh, but now he straightened to his full height and looked every bit as tall as Marsh. "Are you the leader of this church, Brother Thomas?" he asked softly.

For a moment Marsh spluttered; then he finally shook his head. "No," he admitted.

"Then why don't you leave it alone?" Brigham said, with equal softness.

For several moments, Marsh just stared into those steel gray eyes, as if he had been struck speechless.

"Thomas," Heber broke in, "you are the senior Apostle. You have a right to revelation. Why don't you ask God about the matter?"

Finally the spell was broken and Thomas B. Marsh nodded curtly. "I shall do just that," he said, and turned and stalked away.

Brigham watched him go for a moment, then let out his breath slowly. "I don't know, Brother Heber. He's a proud man."

Heber nodded. "The fact that Joseph ruled against his wife is still a piece of grit stuck in his craw."

"I know," Brigham said. Then he brightened and took Benjamin's and Nathan's arms. "Come on, you two. It looks like Joseph is about done. Let's go tell him the Steeds shall be riding with them."

But David Patten, who had also been hanging back waiting for the crowd to disperse a little, saw his chance and stepped forward, reaching Joseph just before the four of them did. In the original Quorum of the Twelve, seniority was determined by age and not by date of ordination to the apostleship. At the time of the organization of the Twelve, Thomas B. Marsh was thought to be the oldest and was therefore first in seniority. David Patten was second, and Brigham was third. Therefore, Patten was next to Marsh in the leadership of the quorum. But unlike Marsh, David Patten was humble and completely teachable. He was a man of quiet but firm integrity and was admired and loved by the Saints.

"Brother David," Joseph said, taking him by the hand and squeezing his arm. Nathan and Benjamin and their two companions were close enough to hear the interchange.

David Patten shook Joseph's hand vigorously. "Brother Joseph, thank you for that speech. For that scripture. That has special meaning to me."

"It is a wonderful concept."

Patten grew suddenly very serious. "You should know that I have prayed earnestly to the Lord that he will give me the privilege of dying the death of a martyr."

Nathan gasped a little. His father and the two men with him were gaping. But Joseph saw none of that. His eyes were locked with Patten's, and he reached out with his other hand and placed it on his arm. "Dear Brother David," he said gravely, "that sorrows me deeply, for when a man of your faith asks the Lord for anything, he generally receives it."

Patten murmured something that Nathan did not hear. Joseph pulled him forward and there was a quick embrace, then Patten stepped back. He nodded a silent greeting to the four of them, then started away. Nathan was barely aware of his father stepping forward and starting to speak to Joseph. He couldn't take his eyes off of David W. Patten's back as the man walked slowly out of the public square of Far West.

Joshua buried his face in Caroline's hair and breathed deeply. The scent of her, so familiar and so wonderful, knifed into him more sharply than he had thought possible. When they were first married, he was gone from her a lot, out with this wagon train or on this trip to St. Louis or on that journey to New Orleans. But in the last months, more and more he found himself wanting to stay at home. More and more he found himself resenting having to miss important things when he was away—Savannah's taking her first step, Olivia's winning the spelling bee at school, Will's harnessing six span of oxen without a single error.

Caroline's arms were around him, holding him tightly. Finally she stirred. "Do you really have to leave again so soon?"

He sighed wearily. "General Atchison almost didn't let me come. I pushed him pretty hard to get a couple of hours."

She straightened and smiled up at him. "Then I shall not say another word. I don't want the general to be unhappy with you. You worked too hard to get that assignment on his staff rather than a field assignment."

Joshua still felt a little guilty about that. Other men in Jackson County were begging for field commands so they could ride against the Mormons. But Joshua had called in a favor from a longtime business associate in Richmond. That got him the appointment to meet with Atchison. Then Joshua had shamelessly laid out his credentials. With his business experience and substantial freighting capability, he was a natural to serve as adjutant, and Atchison had bought it almost immediately. Joshua felt guilty but also tremendously relieved to avoid any possibility of being sent against members of his own family.

He cleared his throat. "Things are not looking good, Caroline. I may still have to go north. Atchison is talking about going up there and monitoring the situation directly."

"No!" she cried. Then instantly she was contrite. She had worried and thought about this almost constantly for the last month. "But you'll still be working with the general?"

He shrugged. In war, things remained pretty fluid, and he knew down deep in his gut that war was imminent. Not the little skirmishes and show confrontations that were going on now. Real war. It was inevitable. And that could change everything.

Caroline was watching his face anxiously. "Is it bad, Joshua?"

His shoulders lifted and fell again. "Governor Boggs was instrumental in driving the Mormons from Jackson County. His feelings haven't changed. He's not going to be satisfied until he's driven them from the state. The people aren't going to be satisfied either." He was suddenly quoting with soft mockery something he had once heard Boggs say. "And Lord knows a man has got to be true to his constituents."

He took her hands. "This isn't going to go away, Caroline. Inflammatory letters are coming into Jefferson City every day. The Mormons did this, the Mormons did that. Boggs has enough depositions and affidavits to send the Mormons to hell and back using any jury in the land."

"I came to that same conclusion," she said quietly. "That's why I wrote your father."

One eyebrow lifted. "You what?"

"I wrote Benjamin. I told him things are not looking good. I begged him to take the family and leave. At least for now. So if something happens and you do have to go . . ." She couldn't bring herself to actually say it. "It'll be better this way."

"When?"

"When what?"

"When did you write Pa?"

"Three days ago."

He gave a short, mirthless laugh. "There are men up there stopping the mail now. It won't make it."

She was startled at that and started to protest, but he put a finger to her lips. "Just as well. You know they're not going to leave, Caroline. Not unless Joseph Smith takes them all out. I understand your wanting them to, but it's not going to happen. You know that, don't you?"

She pulled away, her eyes glistening now. "Yes," she whispered.

He pulled her against him, forcing a smile. "It will be all right. Now, how about getting a soldier some real food before he has to leave again?"

Caroline didn't move. "Joshua?" she finally said.

"What?"

"Before we go back in with the children, there's something you need to know. About Olivia."

"Joshua!" Obadiah Cornwell stepped through the front door of his home, his hand extended. "I didn't know you were home."

"Just rode in for an hour or two on my way back to Richmond from Jefferson City."

His partner sobered instantly. "I hear things are getting very difficult."

Joshua nodded, his eyes hooded.

"Have you heard anything from your family up north?"

"No."

"Look, if you want me to go—"

Joshua took his arm, cutting him off. "Obadiah, I need to talk with you. There are some things I need to have you do."

Lydia drew close to Nathan's chest, pressing her face against the roughness of the skin beneath his nightshirt, feeling the faint but familiar horror at the welts that crisscrossed the chest and back beneath the material.

"It's going to be all right," he whispered into her ear. There was no sound in the cabin, and Nathan was pretty sure his parents were asleep along with the children, but he didn't want to take any chance of waking them.

"I know," Lydia whispered back to him. It was said bravely, but sounded terribly unconvincing.

"Really," he said. "They're gonna turn tail and run when they find out we're not going to take it lying down." When she only barely nodded, he went on quickly. "Remember how frightened you were when I went on Zion's Camp? And everything turned out fine then too."

She scooted up further in the bed, so her face was next to his. She kissed him softly. "I'm going to be all right, Nathan," she murmured. "Just hold me. Just hold me tight for a minute."

On Monday, October fifteenth, promptly at eight a.m., about one hundred of the brethren assembled with Joseph Smith at the public square in Far West. Shortly thereafter Colonel Hinkle gave the order and they marched out. It was a solemn group, but they tried to look brave for their weeping women.

Rumors that the Mormon army was coming leaped from house to house and from town to town across Daviess County. The reported number in the group jumped with each telling, and by the time the Reverend Sashiel Woods and Cornelius Gilliam and the other men they had linked up with heard the report, they made a hasty decision to abandon any designs on Di-Ahman. They scattered, leaving the field to the Mormons.

They scattered, but they did not leave. They spread across the prairies, looking for anything or anyone that might give them a chance to vent their frustrations and their lust for action. Led by the old settlers of Daviess County who knew the territory, they went straight for those homesteads and small settlements where the Latter-day Saints had not yet heeded the call to gather. Hay and grain stacks were scattered and trampled. Cattle, sheep, and hogs were sent stampeding through fields waiting to be harvested.

Bolstered by the eight hundred men from the south, and realizing that the Mormon army was camped at Di-Ahman, the plundering mob grew more brazen. Now the haystacks were torched. Stock was shot outright or run off to dress some Missourian's table. Men were caught and tied to trees, whipped unmercifully with hickory withes, and left naked and half-dead.

On the morning of the seventeenth, a south wind was blowing, and great, dark clouds began to gather in the west. By late afternoon the wind shifted around until it blew straight out of the north. The temperature plummeted, and the first snowstorm of the season came slashing in. So did the marauders.

Between the towns of Di-Ahman and Millport, Sister Agnes Smith lived in a simple cabin with her two small children—one an infant just a few months old. Wife of Don Carlos Smith, youngest brother of the Prophet Joseph, she had not gone to Di-Ahman or Far West, because she had no man to help her make the move. Don Carlos had been called on a mission to Tennessee some time before. He knew nothing of the precarious position his wife was in. The men from the armies of Israel in charge of collecting the unprotected families and helping them gather in had not yet gotten to her.

And so, as a blizzard raged across the Great Plains, the men from DeWitt and the men from Platte and Clinton counties, armed and mounted on horseback, rode up and surrounded the cabin of Don Carlos Smith. Here was prey that wouldn't shoot back. Drunk and hooting like a pack of wild dogs, they drove her out of her home. It was past bedtime, and she was barefoot and clad only in her night clothing. She had a screaming baby in one arm and a whimpering, terrified child clinging to her skirts. As she stumbled away into the night, the men who outnumbered her by twenty or thirty to one, went through the home, smashing, looting, desecrating. And when they were finished they kicked over the kerosene lantern and tossed a match into the spreading liquid.

It was three miles to Di-Ahman, and the Grand River lay between Agnes and safety. Shivering violently, feet so numbed with the cold she could not feel the lacerations, terrified that her tormentors would come for her when they finished their work at the cabin, she had no other choice. She told her oldest to hang onto her neck; then, holding the baby high, she plunged into the waist-high, icy black water. Half an hour later she reached the home of Derek and Rebecca Ingalls and collapsed on their doorstep, barely coherent enough to tell them what had happened.

It was around this time that General William Parks arrived from Richmond with a company of militia. He was at Lyman Wight's cabin on the eighteenth of October with Joseph and the other Mormon leaders when the report of Agnes Smith's experience and other similar cases started coming in. Incensed that the mob had chosen to attack women and children, Parks ordered Lyman Wight into active duty. Wight held a commission in the Fifty-ninth Regiment of the militia. He was to put the mobbers down and stop the depredations, using whatever force was necessary.

Lyman Wight was known throughout all of northern Missouri to Mormon and non-Mormon alike as a man of relentless courage and implacable determination. As he marched out of Di-Ahman the next morning, the word of his commission and Parks's order outraced him. This time the old settlers knew they had no choice but to flee.

Furious at the Mormons, and equally furious with General Parks and General Doniphan for thwarting their plans, the mobbers hit on a stratagem for turning the tide back in their favor. Stripping their cabins and outbuildings of anything of value, they put them to the torch. When Lyman Wight arrived in Millport, he found only a dozen or so burning buildings or smoldering ruins.

As Woods and Gilliam and their Daviess County allies headed south for Richmond and the protection of General Atchison's militia, they sent runners in every direction with the news. The Mormons had "riz" and were laying waste northern Missouri. They were looting, burning, pillaging. They were killing with unchecked abandon. If the government didn't take immediate and drastic action, there wouldn't be an old settler left north of the Missouri River.

Chapter Notes

The meeting in DeWitt in which the Reverend Sashiel Woods goads the men into riding north to plunder the property of the Latter-day Saints is documented in Joseph's record (see *HC* 3:161).

Joseph Smith did preach a sermon based on John 15:13 on Sunday, October fourteenth, in connection with his call for the brethren to march with

Colonel Hinkle to Di-Ahman (see *HC* 3:162). However, the exact time that David Patten told Joseph he had prayed for the privilege of being a martyr is not known (see *CHFT*, p. 200). It is the author's device to place it on the same day as Joseph's sermon.

In the novel the conversation between Brigham Young, Heber C. Kimball, and Thomas B. Marsh is also placed on the day of Joseph's sermon. The conversation did take place as given (see *American Moses*, p. 65), but may not have been at that meeting. Ironically, Marsh did take Heber's challenge to pray about the matter. He went directly to his office and later reported that the Lord gave him a revelation in answer to his supplications and he wrote it down. The Lord told him to sustain Brother Joseph and to accept what Joseph said. But his pride and his stubbornness were in the way and he could not do it. (See *American Moses*, p. 65.)

Seniority in the Quorum of the Twelve was at first determined by age, as noted in this chapter. David Patten was placed second to Thomas B. Marsh because at the time the quorum was organized Patten was not sure of his exact birth date. However, it is now known that he was actually about a year older than Thomas B. Marsh. (See *CHFT*, p. 154.)

The story of Agnes Smith, wife of Don Carlos Smith, has been fleshed out for purposes of the novel, but is based on the accounts given by Joseph and others (see *HC* 3:163; *Persecutions*, pp. 214–15).

Chapter Thirteen

"Pa, I'm telling you, I don't trust the man."

Benjamin looked at his son as they walked briskly along toward the meeting place. "Neither do I."

Nathan barely heard him. "Sampson Avard is a conniver and a glory seeker whose pride is exceeded only by his sense of self-righteousness."

Benjamin looked at Nathan in surprise, then laughed shortly. "You don't feel strongly about this, do you?"

"You better believe I do."

"There are some men in Far West who would disagree with you about that."

Nathan made a noise as if he had just bitten into something very foul.

"No, I'm telling you. There are some people who are quite taken with Dr. Sampson Avard. He's a smooth talker."

"That's for sure. Ask John Taylor on that one."

"Brother Taylor? Why him?"

Nathan peered at his father. "You never heard that story of what happened in Canada?"

"Having to do with Avard? I guess I haven't."

"That's right. You and Mother had come to Missouri by then." He paused a moment, collecting his thoughts. "He was stripped of his license to preach by the high priests quorum last October."

"What happened?"

"Well, as you know, when Parley finished his mission up there he ordained Brother Taylor to preside over the churches in Upper Canada. Then, a short time later, the Taylors and the Fieldings and others came to Kirtland. That's when they visited us."

"Yes."

"Well, before they got back, Avard showed up in Toronto. And he had papers with him saying he was to be the presiding Church officer in Canada. The papers were totally fictitious, of course. The dissenters in Kirtland wanted somebody besides Brother Taylor in charge up there because, as you know, John Taylor had been fearless in his defense of Joseph."

"So what did Brother Taylor do when he got back?" Benjamin had slowed his pace and was watching Nathan closely now. This was a story that might just confirm some of the deep misgivings he had about what was happening.

Nathan wagged his head in disgust. "Elder Taylor was still so new in the Church, he assumed the papers were for real. He stepped aside and let Avard take over. I guess it was awful. The Saints said Avard was arrogant and overbearing. He nearly undid all the work we had done up there. When Joseph and Sidney went to Canada last August they discovered what was happening. Joseph was furious. He publicly rebuked Avard and reinstated Brother Taylor. When they got back to Kirtland, Joseph reported the incident to the high priests and they took Avard's license away."

"Well, that is probably what's happening again right now." Benjamin stopped and half turned. "Taking authority when he has none. Convincing people he's acting for the leaders of the Church." He was quiet for a moment, considering, then made up his mind. "Nathan, there's something you ought to know before we get there."

"What?"

"I can't tell you how I know this. The brother who told me was terrified. Made me swear never to tell anyone where I got the information."

Nathan's eyebrows lowered. "Terrified? Terrified of what?"

"Evidently our Sampson Avard has been holding meetings."

Now Nathan was puzzled. "I know that. He's been setting up companies of tens and fifties and hundreds just like Joseph has instructed us to do. I'm a captain. You're a captain. We've been holding drills. Isn't that what this meeting today is about? It's for all the captains. Why is that so surprising to you?"

"I don't mean those meetings, Nathan," Benjamin said quietly. "I mean secret meetings. Meetings where everyone comes heavily armed. Meetings where they post a guard outside so that no unwanted intruders can interrupt them. Meetings where you have to show a secret sign and where you give secret passwords."

Nathan's jaw dropped and he gave his father a questioning look.

"That's right. I'm talking about meetings where only those who have sworn a blood oath are welcome."

"A blood oath?" The words were being heard, but Nathan's mind couldn't keep up with the implications of what his father was saying.

"That's right," Benjamin said grimly. "An oath that goes something like this: 'In the name of Jesus Christ, the Son of God, I do solemnly obligate myself to keep the secrets of this society called the Daughters of Zion—' "

"The Daughters of Zion?"

"Yes. That's one of their names. It comes from Micah, where it says something like, 'Arise and thresh, O daughter of Zion, for I will make thy hooves like brass, and thou shalt beat in pieces many people.' They also call themselves the 'Big Fan,' from the idea of using a fan to separate the wheat from the chaff." He blew out his breath, glad he was finally sharing this with someone. "They also call themselves the 'Destroying Angels,' and another name they've chosen is the 'Danites.' "

He started walking again and Nathan fell into step. "But occasionally we call ourselves the Danites. Joseph once said that the armies of Israel are Danites."

"That's right. And do you remember why?"

Nathan shrugged. "Sure. He took the name from the book of Daniel. Daniel prophesied that in the last days the Saints would rise up and prepare the world for Christ's second coming. Since we're the Latter-day *Saints*, Joseph thought Daniel's words applied to us."

"That's right!" Benjamin said wearily. "Joseph calls our militia the armies of Israel, but you and I both know he's not just talking about arming ourselves for defense. We're called to care for the poor. There are companies who watch out for the widows and the weak. That's what it's all about. Not just trying to protect ourselves, but to be *Saints* while we do it, like Daniel saw. Right?"

"Right."

"Well, that's not what Avard's saying. He says the name comes from the tribe of Dan. They were the most warlike of the twelve tribes. They were famous for striking against their enemies with swift harshness."

Nathan's countenance had turned very grim. "That's not quite the same thing as Joseph had in mind, is it?"

"No. You think about those names this group is using. Everyone of them carries the idea of vengeance and retribution . . ." He looked away. "And violence."

"You're starting to frighten me, Pa. This man who told you this—you believe him?"

Benjamin nodded slowly. "I've never seen a man so terrified in my life. Let me finish telling you the kinds of things they're doing, and you'll see why. As I said, in their oath they invoke the name of God or Christ. Then they say, 'I do solemnly obligate myself to keep the secrets of this society and swear never to reveal them. Should I ever do so, I hold my life as forfeiture. I will even commit perjury and suffer the pains of death rather than reveal these secrets. May my body be shot and laid in the dust if I do otherwise.' "

He let out his breath in a long, slow exhalation, as if the pain of keeping it inside was gone now. "It *is* frightening, Nathan. They say they'll pursue a man five thousand miles and kill him if he ever breaks the oath."

Nathan gave a low whistle. "Does Joseph know any of this?"

"Not yet. I'm telling you, Nathan, Avard is a smooth one. He puts on a good face. And, of course, the oath works! Avard and those who are supporting him swear Joseph has given his approval. But because of the oath, no one dares to ask Joseph if that's true." He looked away, the frown deepening. "The brother who told me all this this morning said he thinks that's why Thomas Marsh and Orson Hyde fled to Richmond."

Nathan's chin lifted with a quick snap. "What?" The two Apostles had disappeared two days ago. Everyone knew that Thomas Marsh had never gotten over the bitterness he felt over the incident involving his wife. But Orson Hyde had left a note with a friend telling him they could no longer abide with the conditions in the Church. Two members of the Quorum of the Twelve, gone. It had shaken the members in Far West deeply. "What did Avard have to do with that?"

"This man says the Daughters of Zion threatened them. Since they were no longer faithful, either they left immediately or the Destroying Angels would kill them. He says Avard told his band they weren't going to tolerate any more apostasy, especially not among those who are called to be Apostles."

"Are you going to tell Joseph all this?" Nathan asked slowly.

"You bet I am!" Benjamin said, his voice heated. "That's one reason I agreed to go today. I want to see what Avard has to say. But if any of this is true, and word of it gets out to the Missourians, they'll have the perfect excuse to come against us."

Nathan grabbed his arm. "And if Avard and his men find out you know . . ." He peered into his father's eyes. "You've got to be careful, Pa. Real careful."

Benjamin sighed, and he sounded very much like a tired old man. "Believe me, Nathan, I've already thought of that."

The place Avard had chosen for his meeting with the captains of the armies of Israel was in a grove of trees along the creek that ran just to the north of Far West. Nathan saw immediately why he had chosen it. Once they entered the trees, they were totally secluded from the eyes of the world.

Avard was a dynamic man, handsome and a touch dashing. He wore a neatly trimmed beard and had flashing dark eyes that were never still—and never met a direct gaze for more than a moment or two. Today he was agitated and excited. There was also some evident nervousness. He barely waited until the last man had sat down on the ground in front of him before he launched into his speech.

"Brethren," he said, "I have called you here today, as the captains of the various companies of the Danites, because the situation grows worse with every passing moment. It is time for us to act." He looked around, his face lengthening with studied gravity. "I met with President Sidney Rigdon last night and received authority from him to proceed."

Nathan jerked around to give his father a questioning look. "I doubt that," he whispered.

Benjamin raised one eyebrow. "Sidney is just enough of a hothead to give him encouragement," he whispered back. "But I also think Avard is an outright liar. You don't know what to believe."

Benjamin turned and looked at Avard, suddenly angry. "Brother Avard?" he called out. "I have a question. What about Brother Joseph? Does he know what we are doing here?"

For an instant there was open anger on Avard's face. Then it was quickly masked, and Avard smiled broadly. "Brother Rigdon represents the First Presidency. We act with their blessing."

Several of the men looked at each other and began to whisper, so Avard went on swiftly. "My brethren, as you have been chosen to be our leading men, our captains to rule over this last kingdom of Jesus Christ—and you have been organized after the ancient order—I have called upon you here today to teach you, and instruct you in the things that pertain to your duty, and to show you what your privileges are, and what they soon will be.

"Know ye not, brethren, that it soon will be your privilege to take your respective companies and go out on a scout on the borders of the settlements, and take to yourselves spoils of the goods of the ungodly Gentiles?"

At that, there was a ripple of surprise as numerous heads came up.

Avard rushed on, more loudly and adding force to his words. "That's right! For it is written, the riches of the Gentiles shall be consecrated to my people, the house of Israel; and thus you will waste away the Gentiles by robbing and plundering them of their property; and in this way we will build up the kingdom of God, and roll forth the little stone that Daniel saw cut out of the mountain without hands and roll forth until it filled the whole earth."

"No," someone muttered, loud enough for everyone to hear, "that's not right. That's not what that scripture says."

"Yes it is!" Avard thundered. "This is the very way that God destines to build up his kingdom in the last days. And there is no need to fear. If any of us should be recognized, who can harm us? For we will stand by each other and defend one another in all things."

Now the bewildered looks were giving way to dismay and outrage. Avard could tell he was losing them, and he rushed on, desperation making his voice rise in pitch. "If our enemies swear against us, we can swear also. Why do you startle at this, brethren? As the Lord liveth, I would swear to a lie to clear any of you; and if this would not be enough, I would put an enemy under the sand as Moses did the Egyptian. In this way we will consecrate much unto the Lord, and build up his kingdom; and who can stand against us?"

Benjamin stood up. "I stand against you," he said calmly.

Avard's eyes narrowed as there was a rumble of agreement with Benjamin. Avard's voice went cold. "Brother Steed, we have made solemn promises to each other, and if any of us transgress, we will deal with him amongst ourselves. And if any one of this Danite society reveals any of these things of which we speak now, I will put him where the dogs cannot bite him."

Nathan was on his feet, one fist raised and shaking at Avard. "Are you threatening us?" he shouted. "This is not what Joseph wanted when he called us Danites. What you are suggesting is in open violation of the laws of our country. If we rob and steal and plunder from the Gentiles, we would be robbing our fellow citizens of their rights. That is not according to the language and doctrine of Christ, or of The Church of Jesus Christ of Latter-day Saints."

Several men were on their feet now, but Avard did not back down. "You are wrong, Nathan Steed," he said tightly. "The laws of our country were not executed in justice. How else would we at this very time be surrounded with mobs and armed thugs? I care not for the laws of this country. This is a different dispensation. This is the dispensation of the fulness of times. The scriptures tell us that in this dispensation the kingdom of God is going to put down all other kingdoms. Then the Lord himself will reign, and no laws but God's laws will be in force then."

"God does not set up laws that condone stealing and killing," a man behind Nathan shouted. "He never has and he never will."

"Nor does God tolerate secret combinations," Benjamin said. "The Book of Mormon tells us that secret combinations are a most abominable thing in the sight of God. He does not approve of them, and they cannot exist in the true Church of God."

Suddenly Avard realized he was not going to win this one. He raised his hands, the unctuous smile reappearing as if by magic. "Brethren, brethren," he said, "I can see you are not ready for such teachings. Perhaps it is best if we drop the subject for now, although I say again, I have only been acting on the authority of Sidney Rigdon."

Nathan was still very agitated. "Just like the authority you had when you were in Canada?" he exclaimed.

Avard swung around, his eyes filled with cold fury. "Watch your tongue, young man. You may not like the consequences of being rash."

"And you may not like the consequences of having us check with Brother Rigdon to see if what you say is true."

"And with Brother Joseph," Benjamin said darkly. "I think Brother Joseph will be very interested in what we have learned today."

As Joshua walked briskly along the main street of Richmond, the county seat of Ray County, he could barely believe what he was seeing. The streets were packed with people, mostly men and most of those bearing arms.

When word had spread that the Mormons were in a state of general uprising following the torching of their homes by some of the mob, panic had sent virtually every old-time settler in northern Missouri fleeing to Richmond. And with them came the Reverend Mr. Woods and Cornelius Gilliam and the eight hundred wild, undisciplined, and nearly uncontrollable men they called an army.

Joshua pulled a face. At least the Mormons were safe for a time. He wasn't so sure about the good citizens of Ray County though, what with this much weaponry on display and this much liquor being consumed and this much bragging and boasting going on.

He turned up the walk and entered the courthouse, where General Atchison had set up his headquarters. As he entered the room where the general's aide was, Joshua saw that the door to the inner office was open. General Atchison was behind his desk. Across from him sat General Parks. "Ah, Captain Steed,"

Atchison said when he saw him. "Good. Come in. I want you to hear this."

Joshua stepped into the office. "What is it, sir?"

"How well do you know the Mormon leaders, Steed?"

That startled Joshua.

Parks was watching him closely. "I understand your family are Mormons living in Far West. That true?"

Joshua nodded curtly. He had told Atchison about his parents first thing, so there would be no surprises. He wasn't sure why Parks was bringing it up now.

"So, do you know their leaders very well?" Parks asked.

Joshua shook his head slowly. "I know Joseph Smith, of course. We lived in upstate New York, not far from him. I might recognize one or two, but that's about it."

"The name Thomas B. Marsh mean anything to you?" Parks asked.

Joshua thought for a moment. "It sounds familiar. My sister got married in August. I was there. A lot of the Church leadership was there."

"He claims to be the chief Apostle. They have twelve Apostles, you know. Claim they're just like Christ's church when it was on earth. Marsh claims he's the leading Apostle."

Joshua's head began to go up and down slowly. "Yes, I think I did meet him that day."

"So you'd recognize him?" Atchison broke in.

"Probably. Yes, I think so." Joshua hesitated. "What's this all about, if I may ask, sir?"

General Atchison picked up a sheet of paper from off his desk. "Marsh came to Richmond about a week ago. Said he's fed up with the Mormons. Another Apostle, name of Hyde, was with him. Anyway, Marsh went before a justice of the peace this morning and swore out this affidavit." He handed it across to Joshua. "This is bad. I was hoping the Mormons would be restrained and that we could find a solution to the conflict." He gave a weary sigh. "Now I don't know anymore. Go ahead, Captain. Sit down."

Joshua took the paper and sat down. His eyes dropped to the bottom of the paper, where the signature of Thomas B. Marsh was over the signature of Henry Jacobs, justice of the peace, Ray County. "What does it say?" he asked, looking across at his commanding officer.

"Read it. First couple of paragraphs just state who he is and so forth. Start about the third paragraph."

Joshua's eyes dropped and he scanned quickly. Then, as he began to read more slowly, he felt a chill settle in upon him.

> I hereby testify that the Mormons have among them a company, considered true Mormons, called the Danites, who have taken an oath to support the heads of the Church in all things that they say or do, whether right or wrong. Many, however, of this band are much dissatisfied with this oath, as being against moral and religious principles. On Saturday last, I am informed by the Mormons, that they had a meeting at Far West, at which they appointed a company of twelve, by the name of the "Destruction Company," for the purpose of burning and destroying, and that if the people of the town of Buncombe came to do mischief upon the people of Caldwell, and committed depredations upon the Mormons, they were to burn Buncombe; and if the people of Clay and Ray made any movement against them, this destroying company were to burn Liberty and Richmond. . . .
>
> Their prophet, Joseph Smith, accepts this notion, and it is believed by every true Mormon, that Smith's prophecies are superior to the laws of the land. I have heard the Prophet say that he would yet tread down his enemies, and walk over their dead bodies; and if he was not let alone, he would be a second Mohammed to this generation, and that he would make it one gore of blood from the Rocky mountains to the Atlantic ocean.

Beneath the signatures of Marsh and the justice of the peace there was a brief statement, which read: "Most of the statements in the foregoing disclosure I know to be true; the remainder I believe to be true." It was signed by Orson Hyde and likewise attested to by the justice of the peace.

Joshua swallowed once, then again, then finally looked up, handing the paper back. "I don't believe that, sir."

Atchison leaned forward, his mouth pulling into a line. "You don't?"

"No, sir. I think Joseph Smith is a deluded and misled man. I think the Mormons, including my own family, are foolish for following him in religious things. I think the whole idea of Mormonism is a fraud. But . . ." He took a quick breath. "But I know Joseph Smith. I know the Mormon people. They are not out to bathe this country in blood. I do not believe for a minute that they will try to burn us out. I don't know why this Marsh and Hyde have decided to say these things, but I don't believe them."

He sat back, trying not to let his breathing be too heavy. Atchison and Parks were both watching him closely, and he felt a tiny bead of perspiration begin to form on his lower lip.

A noise in the outer office drew their attention. The general's aide was standing there with a well-dressed and fine-looking man. Atchison looked up for a moment, then to Joshua. "Is this man Thomas B. Marsh, as you remember him?"

Joshua studied the man's face for a moment. Marsh did not look at him. Finally, Joshua nodded. "Yes, sir. It is the man I remember."

Atchison tossed his head slightly and the aide led Marsh away again. He turned back once more to Joshua. "Thank you, Captain. That will do. You're dismissed."

Chapter Notes

There has been much controversy about Sampson Avard and the Danites. Many non-Mormon authors have used the Marsh statement and later testimony by Avard himself to try and discredit Joseph Smith and the Church. However, two excellent articles in *BYU Studies* reveal several important points: (1) Sampson Avard was keenly opportunistic and a known liar. (2) The companies of the armies of Israel organized in Far West were not commonly called the Danites by the Mormons. Joseph Smith occasionally used that term because Daniel the prophet had talked about the Saints in the last days. Joseph did not take the name from the warlike members of the tribe of Dan. This is confirmed by the only known eyewitness account actually written at the time the events were happening. (3) The companies organized under Joseph's direction were far more than military groups and filled the function of caring for the Saints as outlined in this and the previous chapter of the novel. (4) The oaths and secret signs and death threats were part of Avard's way of keeping his true purposes hidden. (5) Once Avard's true colors were discovered, he was excommunicated from the Church. (See Leland H. Gentry, "The Danite Band of 1838," *BYU Studies* 14 [Summer 1974]: 421–50; and Dean C. Jessee and David J. Whittaker, eds., "The Last Months of Mormonism in Missouri: The Albert Perry Rockwood Journal," *BYU Studies* 28 [Winter 1988]: 5–41.)

An interesting footnote to Sampson Avard's life: After the fall of Far West, Avard was found hiding in a thicket and was arrested. In an attempt to turn blame away from himself, Avard testified that Joseph had authorized the secret society and sent them on a mission to kill and plunder. (So much for his sacred oath never to reveal the secrets of the society, even at the risk of his own life!) Though others testified as to his lack of integrity and that his testimony was perjured, the Missourians never punished Avard for his actions against them prior to his defection.

The bulk of Avard's speech to the captains as presented in the novel is taken virtually intact from Joseph's record, as is the affidavit signed by Thomas B. Marsh (see *HC* 3:180–81, 167). John Taylor later noted that it may be possible the enemies of the Church embellished Marsh's statement to make it worse than it was. However, he also notes that it was still a very terrible thing Marsh and Hyde did. (See *HC* 3:167–68n.)

It should also be mentioned that Orson Hyde was ill with a violent fever at the time of his defection and may have been more susceptible to Marsh's persuasions. Hyde returned to the Church a few months later, asked forgiveness, and was reinstated to the Twelve in June of 1839. Thomas B. Marsh was out of the Church until 1857 when he came to Utah and publicly confessed his error and was rebaptized into the Church. (See *CHFT*, p. 199; see also Lyndon W. Cook, " 'I Have Sinned Against Heaven, and Am Unworthy of Your Confidence, But I Cannot Live Without a Reconciliation': Thomas B. Marsh Returns to the Church," *BYU Studies* 20 [Summer 1980]: 389–400.)

Chapter Fourteen

Lydia lurched up into a sitting position, one hand at her throat, the other clutching at the empty air, trying to find something to steady her. The cabin was pitch black, and for a few terrifying seconds she thought she had been buried alive and was smothering. Then, as suddenly as she had come awake, she came to awareness. They were in her mother-in-law's cabin, sleeping in Rebecca's old bed. She and Nathan had moved in with Nathan's parents and given their cabin to other families. The baby slept in a small bassinet beside them. Her other children were just through the curtain from her.

Reaching out in the darkness, she felt Nathan's bulk beneath the blanket. She lay back down slowly, the pounding in her chest gradually slowing now. *It must have been a nightmare.* She had not slept well since she and Nathan had moved their family—

Her head jerked up again and cocked to one side. And then she knew what it was that had awakened her. The sound was faint, having to come through thick log walls and narrow window openings, but it was unmistakable. Somewhere from the direction of the courthouse someone was sounding a trumpet. "No," she whispered. "Oh, dear Lord, no. Please no!"

There was silence for just a moment. Then the hauntingly beautiful and coldly terrible sound started again, carrying in the stillness of the night across the whole of Far West. Now it was joined by a deep booming sound. The signal drum. Then a rifle fired. Then another. Then another. Three shots!

Suddenly her hands felt as cold as if they had been packed in snow, but she knew what she had to do. She leaned over and shook her husband roughly. "Nathan! Wake up!"

"Huh? What?" He was mumbling as he half turned.

"Nathan, listen!" she hissed. "They're sounding the call to battle."

There were almost a hundred men on the public square when Nathan, Benjamin, and Matthew arrived. It was just after the hour of midnight. The twenty-fifth day of October 1838 had just begun. The trumpet was still now, but someone on the far side of the square was still beating the big bass drum with slow, heavy beats. The sound was both forlorn and ominous at the same time. The brethren milled about, some talking in quiet whispers, others standing motionless, hugging themselves against the chill, looking grim-faced and a little numb.

As the Steed men joined the crowd, Nathan saw his good friend Parley Pratt. "Parley," he called.

Parley turned, peering at them in the darkness. "Ah, Nathan." He came over, sticking out his hand. "Hello, Father Steed. Matthew."

"What's happening?" Nathan asked.

"Two more men came in from the south a short time ago," Parley explained. "There's more trouble."

Nathan felt his heart sink. Just after sundown a rider had come in from the southernmost part of the county. The report he brought sent a shock wave through Far West. For the past several days a band of about thirty Missourians from Jackson County—under the command of a Reverend Samuel Bogart, one of the Mormons' most bitter enemies—had been patrolling the line between Ray and Caldwell counties. The group was a unit of the militia and supposedly was there to make sure the Mormons and Missourians didn't clash. But this morning Bogart had taken his unit across the line into Mormon country.

They quickly reached an isolated settlement and began to terrorize a man by the name of Thoret Parsons, a member of the Church who lived there with his family. Brandishing weapons, Bogart and his men told Parsons he had better be gone by ten o'clock the following morning or he would be shot. Bogart also bragged that Cornelius Gilliam was on his way from DeWitt to bolster Bogart's forces. Gilliam was bringing a small cannon, and they would give Far West "thunder and lightning" by noon of the same day.

Parsons dispatched a rider to Far West to warn Joseph and the Saints. Joseph had immediately put the whole city on alert. It was decided that the sound of the trumpet, the drum, and three rifle shots would serve as the call to battle. So the men of Far West went to sleep with their clothes on and their weapons close at hand.

Parley looked around, as if he was expecting to see someone; then when he didn't, he turned back and began to explain. "This morning, two of our brethren saw Bogart's men out and about again inside the county line. They decided to follow them at a safe distance and see what they were up to. Those are the two brethren who rode in just a short time ago."

"What did they say?" Matthew asked eagerly. "Is Bogart still coming?"

Nathan looked at his younger brother and shook his head. Supper at the Steeds' had been a tight-lipped affair. Nathan and his father could not shake a heavy sense of dread. His mother and Lydia had barely held back the tears. But there was none of that in Matthew. After Lyman Wight's militia had frightened the mobs out of Daviess County, things in the north had quieted down somewhat, and Matthew had been pulled off the communications relay line. That had been three days ago. He had chafed under the interminable waiting. He was hungry for action and was almost dancing now in anticipation. "Did they find Bogart?" he pressed.

Parley nodded slowly, staring at the ground.

"Well?" Benjamin said.

"Eight of Bogart's men went to the Pinkham place, in the same general area as the Parsons farm. They threatened him, same as Parsons, but they also stole four horses, some food, and Brother Pinkham's firearms." He let out his breath in a long, pain-filled sigh. "What's worse, they took three prisoners."

"No!" Benjamin exploded.

"Yes," Parley went on grimly. "Pinkham's boy and two other men. As they rode away, they told Pinkham they'd all be dead by morning."

Matthew whistled softly. "Then we've got to go after them."

Nathan laid a hand on his brother's arm, still looking at Parley. "Do they know where they've taken them?"

"We think so. The two brethren followed Bogart until he seemed to be making camp. That was on the ford of the Crooked River, about twelve miles from here. The prisoners were still with them and alive at that time, near as they could tell."

"Where's Joseph?" Nathan asked, looking around now too.

"He took the two messengers to Judge Higbee. He wants them to give their report to the judge. As you know, he's the highest civil authority in the county. And a crime has been committed."

"What good will that do?" Matthew demanded. "We've got to go save those men."

"Joseph wants to—"

But just then someone called out. The crowd of men went instantly quiet as they turned. Joseph was coming with two brethren whom Nathan didn't recognize. They were accompanied by several of the Church leaders. The men stepped back, opening a place for them in the center of the crowd. Joseph waited until they closed in again, then lifted his hands. Now all noise stopped.

"Brethren,"—he held up a paper and waved it back and forth—"we have what we need. After hearing the testimony of Brother Holbrook and Brother Juda, two brave men, Judge Higbee has ordered Colonel Hinkle to call out the militia."

The crowd erupted into a ragged but triumphant cheer.

"That's great!" Matthew nearly shouted into his father's ear. "It's about time we did something besides stand around letting the mob have their way with us."

Joseph continued, "We are asking for about seventy-five volunteers to help us carry out Judge Higbee's order to disperse the mob and rescue the prisoners." As the excitement began to sweep across the group again, Joseph spoke more loudly. "I remind you brethren, we go not out as a mob or as an unauthorized body of men. Brother Hinkle is a lieutenant colonel in the Missouri militia. Now the ranking, duly elected official in Caldwell County has given Colonel Hinkle power to activate the militia. You go now with full legal authority." He turned and motioned for a man on the front line to come up. "Colonel Hinkle."

Hinkle stepped up to stand by Joseph, raising his hands for silence. In a moment he had it. "Brethren, the danger to our city has not lessened. Bogart told Parsons we will have thunder and lightning by noon today. We must take that threat seriously and be prepared to defend our city. So I am hereby calling two companies of men, one to be under the direction of Captain David Patten, the other under the command of Captain Charles C. Rich. Captain Patten will have overall command."

Elder David Patten, now the senior Apostle since Thomas B. Marsh's desertion, was near Joseph too. He called out in a clear voice. "I accept that commission, Brother Hinkle."

"Good. Brethren, we are calling for volunteers. Please line up in front of Captains Patten and Rich to enlist."

Nathan hesitated. The first thing that popped into his head

was the image of Lydia, holding Elizabeth Mary. Then he thought of Joshua, and Emily, the little miniature of her mother, and three-year-old Nathan. The thought of maybe not seeing them again was like acid in his bowels. And yet in that same instant came thoughts of the three prisoners, probably bound and gagged, in the hands of men like those who had whipped Nathan until his back was a bloody mass. Those prisoners would be desperately hoping that their brethren had not abandoned them.

Matthew was staring at his father, face hopeful. But Benjamin too was lost in his own thoughts. "Pa?" Matthew finally said.

Benjamin pulled out of them with an effort.

"I want to go."

Nathan's stomach lurched, and then instantly he knew Matthew was right. He stepped forward. "Matthew and I will ride with Captain Patten, Pa. You need to stay here and make sure Mother and Lydia and the children are all right."

Parley nodded vigorously. "I agree, Father Steed. We need some wise heads to stay here and get the city prepared. Joseph could really use your help."

Benjamin hesitated only for a moment. Something in his heart cried to push that suggestion aside. His blood ran as hot as Matthew's when he thought of the three men facing possible execution. What if one of them were Matthew? Or Nathan? Or any one of his family? And yet he was past fifty now. War was a young man's affair. And Nathan was right about Mary Ann and Lydia. If Bogart and Gilliam came against Far West, his family would be without a man if he went with the group tonight.

Finally, he nodded slowly at Nathan and Parley. Then he turned and looked at his youngest son, this fair-haired, blue-eyed son he had come to love so much. Benjamin's eyes were filled with deep gravity. "Your mother is going to ask why I didn't make you stay home too."

Matthew's face fell. "Pa, they need me. I'm eighteen now. I want to be with Nathan."

There was no answer as his father searched his face. Then finally, Benjamin's shoulders lifted and fell in resignation. "I know," he murmured. With a quick step, he was to Matthew and gave him a fierce hug. "You be careful, son. This isn't going to be a party."

Matthew nodded, a lump suddenly in his throat. "I will, Pa. I promise."

Benjamin turned to Nathan. "He's a man now, Nathan," he said in a husky whisper, "but he's also our last born. If anything happens to him, your mother is never going to forgive me or you."

Nathan nodded slowly, touched by his father's emotions. "I know, Pa. I'll stay with him. Close. Tell Mother. I'll watch him. I promise."

Benjamin started to turn, his mind made up now. "I'll go and tell your mother and Lydia." He stopped, then lifted one hand. "Go with God," he said softly. Then he turned.

The column of riders was barely discernible in the darkness. There was no moon, but the sky was clear and a thousand stars filled the sky above them. About three a.m., a meteor shower began. Pinpoints of light went streaking across the sky until they disappeared in one final, blazing flash. Some were bright enough to make Matthew gasp inwardly. It was an awe-inspiring sight, and his neck grew sore from his staring upwards, for he did not want to miss a single one.

But if the heavens filled him with awe, the great prairie fires to the north of them left him with an eerie and uneasy feeling. The group of Mormon men was miles away from those fires, but even from this distance Matthew could see the flickering dance of the flames and the immense columns of smoke rising upward in awful majesty before they disappeared into the night sky. Vast areas of the grasslands of northern Missouri were ablaze with wildfires. Were they accidentally set, or was this the result of the mob's torching some Mormon's hay and grain stacks?

Matthew didn't know. Fires were not uncommon once the grass died in the fall, and in some ways they were welcomed by the farmers because they seared off the thick tangle of dead grasses and brush that choked the prairies. But either way, Matthew kept feeling a little chill crawling up and down his back. It seemed as if the very fires of hell were marking their path, holding out the promise of some coming consuming inferno.

Matthew rode just behind Nathan and Parley Pratt. There were riders ahead and behind, about sixty or seventy in all. No one spoke, not even in whispers. The only sound in the night was the soft thudding of the horses' hooves and the occasional rattle of a sword against a saddle or the even softer chinking of a bridle chain. The breathing of men and horses sent out from their nostrils little clouds that hung white and ethereal for a moment, then almost instantly dissipated.

Matthew turned his head slightly, so that he looked directly east. Squinting, he peered at the point where land met sky. At first he wasn't sure, but as he swung his head to the right, checking the horizon due south, it was more evident. The eastern sky was just starting to lighten. Dawn was no more than half an hour away now.

He felt his pulse quicken a little. And then the solemn voice of his father rang in his mind. "*You be careful, son. This isn't going to be a party.*" A crawling sensation moved up and down his back. Subdued, Matthew pulled his coat more tightly around him and hunched deeper in the saddle.

About two miles from the river, David Patten raised a hand and brought the column to a halt. Speaking in hushed whispers, he gave the instructions. A few men would be left with the horses. The rest were to follow him on foot. There was to be absolutely no talking, no noise of any kind. They marched in silence for the next twenty minutes. Now the sky to the east was becoming noticeably lighter.

The Crooked River ran through Caldwell and Ray counties

in a diagonal line from northwest to southeast. Over the centuries it had cut a deep, meandering path through the prairie land. But at one point, near the county line, there was a place where the stream was shallow enough to provide a ford. A road had been cut down the side of the bluffs to provide access to it.

It was at the top of the bluff that Patten stopped again and raised his hand. The men moved in as closely as they could. "We're at the river," he whispered, pointing. "The ford should be right below us."

Matthew turned and stared into the darkness. They were looking west, and the line of trees was only the tiniest shade darker than the land beyond it.

Still talking very softly, but with authority now, David Patten began giving his orders. "Brother Rich, you take your division and go to the left. Captain Durphey, I want you to take another group. You go straight on down. My division will go to the right. Remember, the signal for attack will be, 'God and liberty.'"

Matthew jumped as a hand was laid on his arm.

"Sorry, Matthew," a dark figure next to him whispered. "It's me, Patrick O'Banion."

"Oh." Matthew felt like a fool for being so jittery. "Hullo."

Patrick O'Banion was not a member of the Church but was one of those few of the old settlers who were friendly to the Mormons. Because of O'Banion's knowledge of the countryside, Captain Patten had asked him to serve as their guide. He was just a year or two older than Matthew. The Steeds had had the opportunity to get to know Patrick some, and both Matthew and Nathan liked him.

"Would you mind if I stuck with you and your brother?" O'Banion asked.

Nathan was right next to Matthew. He smiled warmly and clapped the young man on the shoulder. "Love to have you, Patrick," he whispered.

"All right," Patten commanded, "move out."

To take the right flank, Patten's unit turned so that they

were moving almost directly west now. Even before they reached the bottom of the gentle hill, they were starting into the first of the low underbrush that marked the wider flood channel of the stream.

Nathan stepped close to Matthew. One hand came up to grip Matthew by the neck. He pulled Matthew's head over until it was close to Nathan's mouth. "I don't like this," he whispered. "We can't see a thing ahead of us. But we're backlit against the dawn. If they're waiting for us . . ." He shook his head. "Stay low. And be careful!"

Matthew nodded, swallowing hard. His mouth was as dry as a dirt road in August. He swallowed again, trying to force some saliva onto his tongue. He was also aware of the painful thudding inside his chest and of the fact that even though the stock of the rifle barrel was cold in his hands, his palms were sweating.

He turned to O'Banion, wanting to pass on the warning that Nathan had given, but just as he reached out to touch O'Banion's arm, Matthew's head jerked back to the front. A movement just ten or fifteen yards off to his right had caught his eye. He leaned forward, peering, bringing his rifle up. Something moved again. It was a man! In the brush.

Matthew swung around to warn Nathan, but at that instant a voice shouted out just in front of them. "Who goes there?"

It came out more as a frightened croak than as a shout of challenge. But the sentry didn't wait for an answer. "It's the Mormons!" he screamed. There was a brilliant flash and the crack of a rifle. After a night of silence the explosion sounded like a cannon. Men screamed, and dove for cover. A rifle just behind Matthew fired, nearly deafening him.

Matthew was frozen in place, so stunned that for a moment it didn't register that something was pulling at his sleeve, dragging at his arm. Then the weight became too much to ignore. He swung around and found himself looking into the stricken face of Patrick O'Banion. The young man's eyes were wide with shock. His face was twisted grotesquely. His mouth was working, but no sound came out. He stumbled a little, falling against Matthew.

"Patrick!"

There was a soft moan, and Matthew stared in stupefied horror as O'Banion's knees slowly collapsed and he slid to the ground, his hand dragging downward against Matthew's leg.

"Get down!" a voice said.

Matthew was distantly aware that someone had him by the collar and was wrestling him to the ground. He let his knees buckle and he dropped to the earth.

"Are you all right?" Nathan was lying beside him, his hand still on Matthew's collar. Nathan was shaking him and shouting into his face.

Matthew tried to answer, but his mouth wouldn't respond. Gunfire was blasting off all around them now. The acrid smell of gunpowder filled the air. Incredibly, amid the noise his ears caught the whip of a ball through the brush above him, and he felt a twig fall against his face.

"*Are you all right?*" Nathan repeated.

Matthew shook it off. "Yes," he gasped. "Patrick—" He nearly gagged. "He's been shot."

Nathan let go of Matthew's coat and leaped over him to kneel over the body of O'Banion. The young man was writhing and groaning. His eyes were wide open as he stared upward, seeing nothing. Nathan pulled O'Banion's coat together as best he could, then he was back with Matthew. "He's hit bad!"

"God and liberty! God and liberty!" Someone out ahead of them was shouting above the roar of the gunfire.

Nathan grabbed the front of Matthew's coat. "That's the signal. Come on, Matthew. We've got to stay with the others. We'll come back for Patrick."

They scurried through the brush, running in a half crouch, moving toward the line of men just in front of them. Matthew could hear David Patten shouting now. "Form up. Form a line. They're on the riverbank. There, by the campfires."

Directing his attention to something concrete was exactly what Matthew needed. He leaned forward, trying to see. The riverbank was in almost total darkness. But the campfires—two or three, maybe more—could be clearly seen now. Flashes were winking at him here and there, appearing simultaneously with the crackle of gunfire.

Then Matthew understood what Nathan had been trying to tell him. Against the dark background of the trees and the far bluff, they could see no one, only an occasional blur of movement and the flashes of the muzzles of their enemies. But the Mormons had the eastern sky directly at their backs, making them perfect silhouettes for Bogart's men to fire at.

"Charge!" It was Patten's voice, rising above the shouting and chaos like the roar of a lion. Nathan yelled something at Matthew and grabbed his arm. Only then did Matthew remember that he too had a rifle in his hand. He raised it to his shoulder, watched for a muzzle flash, adjusted quickly, and fired. He heard a scream, but wasn't sure if it came from the direction in which he shot. On the run now, he began pulling at the leather pouch that held his lead balls and powder.

Beside him, Nathan had his pistol out, holding it in his left hand. He also wore their father's sword in a scabbard. With the chilling sound of steel sliding against steel, he drew it out and raised it over his head, yelling like a banshee. To their right and left, men were running down the hill to join them, firing as they came. Captains Rich and Durphey had joined the battle.

Bogart was shouting at his men as wildly as Patten and his two captains were shouting at theirs. The Missourians were running from their campfires, forming a skirmish line along the riverbank. Suddenly it was too close for firearms and the battle was hand to hand. Though the Mormons were severely handicapped by having the light behind them, they outnumbered Bogart's men by about two to one. As they rushed forward, shouting, slashing with their swords, swinging rifle butts, the line broke. In a moment, a dozen Missourians were in the shallow ford of the river, racing for safety. It was a retreat but not a rout. The Missourians would run a few yards, then whirl and shoot, then fall back further to reload and fire again.

Matthew stopped at the edge of the water, still struggling to get his own rifle reloaded. He dropped to one knee, muttering angrily as he tried to jam another ball into the breech so he could fire again. Suddenly a shape loomed over him. The man was cursing. Both hands were high in the air, gripping something. Matthew saw the glint of light on steel. He threw himself to the side, tucking his rifle under him. There was the sickening sound of a sword slamming into empty ground and burying itself in the earth. It was close enough that sand was kicked up into Matthew's face.

Matthew grabbed his rifle by the muzzle and swung it like a club. It caught the man just at the knees. He howled in pain and went down hard. Scrambling like a man possessed, Matthew tried to get to his feet before the man could recover. But the man was coming up too, raising the sword again. Another figure came slashing in with blurring speed. He kicked hard at the man's arm. The man screamed and the sword went spinning away. A pistol rose and fell so fast that Matthew barely saw it. There was a heavy grunt and the cries instantly stopped.

Nathan dropped into a crouch beside Matthew and grabbed his arm. "Are you all right?"

"Yes." It came out in one strangled gasp.

Suddenly David Patten was standing over them. "Come on," he shouted. "They're crossing the river." He darted to the left, running along the riverbank, moving downstream from the two brothers.

Men were running everywhere now. Most of the Missourians were across the river and sprinting toward the opposite bluff. Nathan was up, heading straight into the river. He stopped and yelled something back at Matthew. Chagrined that he still did not have his gun loaded, and suddenly finding that his feet felt like great wooden blocks, Matthew waved a hand. "You go," he shouted at Nathan. "I need to reload. I'll be all right."

Nathan darted away. Matthew concentrated on the process of reloading again. His fingers were trembling, and the ball seemed three times larger than the opening it was supposed to fit in. A cry brought his head up with a snap. Two men had dashed out from the cover of the underbrush and were running hard for the river crossing. Patten and Captain Rich were in hot pursuit. Nathan, who was midway across the river, had heard it too. He swung around; then, seeing what was happening, he started splashing downstream to intercept them. In the half-light, the figures were almost like ghosts, phantoms flitting across a cloth screen in a dressing room. Matthew's hand stopped in midair as he watched the tableau unfold.

The Mormon officers were gaining on the two men. Patten was screaming at them to stop or he would shoot. Then, almost as if it were happening at half speed, the man closest to Patten wheeled around. There was no time to bring his rifle up—Patten was closing on him like a stag hound—so he fired from the hip, not ten feet away from the charging Apostle. Patten grunted as the ball caught him full in the body. He stumbled, his own rifle slipping from his grasp, then went down to his knees.

"No!" Matthew was on his feet. Then he was running. "No! No! No!"

Nathan was out of the river and coming fast now too. The first man had not stopped and was safely away now, but the man who had fired at Patten saw Nathan and Matthew coming. He raised his rifle, then realized it wasn't loaded. Swearing, he flung it away and clawed at the sword in the scabbard at his belt. Without breaking stride, Nathan raised his pistol and fired. The shot went wide, but it had the desired effect. The man dropped his sword and turned tail and ran.

The two Steed brothers and Captain Rich all reached David Patten at about the same moment. Patten was still on his knees, hands clutching at his bowels. With a soft groan, he looked up at them, eyes beseeching them for help, then he toppled slowly sideways and fell to the earth. Blood was pouring out from between his fingertips.

For a long, horrible moment, Matthew stared, not able to take his eyes away from the sight of the fingers digging at the stomach, trying to stop the pain, trying to stop the life from gushing out. And then something inside Matthew broke. He turned, hand over his mouth, and stumbled away, barely reaching the nearest bush before he started to retch.

What would become known as the Battle of Crooked River took place at dawn on the twenty-fifth of October. The Saints were successful in freeing the three prisoners whose abduction had precipitated the pursuit of Bogart's company, but not without cost. Three members of the Mormon company were mortally wounded. Brother Gideon Carter, a man of about forty who had a wife and children, was shot in the face and killed instantly. His face was so disfigured that at first the brethren did not realize he was one of their own.

Patrick O'Banion was not dead when the Mormon men came back to find him, but he died before they could get him back to Far West.

Elder David W. Patten, President of the Quorum of the Twelve, was placed on a litter by his brethren, and they started the return trek. But he was in such excruciating pain that finally he begged them not to take him farther. They stopped at the home of Stephen Winchester, who lived about three miles outside of Far West. By then, advanced riders had returned to Far West with the news. Joseph Smith, Heber C. Kimball, Lyman Wight, and several others came out to meet the returning brethren. Benjamin Steed was with them, and openly wept when he saw that both of his sons were not harmed.

Bathsheba Patten, David Patten's wife, was also with the group. Her weeping would be for another reason.

The group that gathered around the bedside of David Patten was a small one. The main body of those who had fought at

Crooked River went on home to Far West, to nurse the wounded and to let their families know they were safe. Parley Pratt, a fellow Apostle, stayed, as did Heber Kimball. As Nathan and Matthew mounted up and prepared to leave, Joseph surprised Benjamin by asking him to stay with him.

David Patten was made as comfortable as possible, and then Joseph administered to him, praying with great feeling for his recovery. Then they settled in to wait. Now, half an hour later, Sister Patten sat beside her husband, her eyes red and swollen, but she was no longer weeping. The others stood in a circle around the bed, watching their friend and brother slowly weakening. Joseph stood at the head of the bed, opposite Sister Patten.

"Brother Joseph?" It came out as little more than a croak.

The Prophet leaned down closer to the Apostle. "Yes, Brother David."

"Do you remember my prayer? That I might be a martyr for my Savior?"

There was a long pause; then with a trembling voice, Joseph answered. "Yes, David, I most certainly do. The Lord has granted you your wish."

"I know. Don't weep for me," David said, laboring to keep his voice steady through the pain. "If you wish to weep, weep for Brother Marsh. Weep for David Whitmer and Oliver, and all the others who have fallen from their steadfastness."

He raised his head from the pillow, looking around at the faces above him. "Oh, that they were in my situation!" he exclaimed. "For I feel that I have kept the faith, I have finished my course, henceforth there is laid up for me a crown."

Joseph dropped to one knee and took David's other hand in both of his. "You have indeed kept the faith," Joseph cried softly. "You have earned your crown, my dear brother."

"My time is nearly come," David said, falling back. His breathing was labored now, and his wife began to weep again. A glaze came over his eyes, and Benjamin realized that sight had now left him.

Heber Kimball leaned forward. "Brother David," he said softly, "when you get home, I want you to remember me."

"Is that you, dear Brother Heber?"

"Yes, it is me."

"I will remember you, and all the members of the Quorum."

The effort had exhausted him, and his eyes closed. For several minutes there was no sound in the room but the sounds of his breathing and his wife's quiet grief. Then he startled everyone when he spoke again. But he was not speaking to them. "Father, I ask thee in the name of Jesus Christ that thou wouldst release my spirit, and receive it unto thyself."

His eyes opened again and he looked around, though he saw no one. "Brethren," he whispered, "brethren, you have held me by your faith, but do give me up, and let me go, I beseech you."

Joseph was stricken, but as he looked around the circle, one by one they nodded. His eyes finally stopped on Sister Patten. She was looking at her husband. Finally, she too nodded, even as a silent sob made her whole body shudder.

Joseph straightened. He bowed his head, and everyone immediately followed suit. "Dear God, our Heavenly Father, we hear the request of our dear brother. We accordingly commit him into thy kind keeping, O Lord. Receive him unto thyself."

There was a great sigh, and a peaceful expression now settled over the pale and previously pain-filled face. It was only a moment or two later that he reached out, groping blindly for his wife. She grabbed his hand and pressed it to her cheek.

"Oh, my beloved Bathsheba, whatever you do else, oh, do not deny the faith."

His hand dropped. His eyes closed. And without another sound, Elder David W. Patten died, the first Apostle in the dispensation of the fulness of times to be martyred for the cause of Christ.

Chapter Notes

The description of the night march to the Crooked River comes from Parley P. Pratt's record (see *PPP Auto.*, p. 153). Three of those on the side of the Latter-day Saints were fatally wounded in the battle, and while there are conflicting reports, indications seem to be that only one Missourian was killed, though several were wounded.

David W. Patten had his prayers answered and became the first apostolic martyr of this dispensation. The novel's account of Patten's dying words is based on the account given in Heber C. Kimball's journal (see *LHCK*, pp. 213–14).

Chapter Fifteen

Samuel Bogart and his band clearly and decisively lost the Battle of Crooked River, making the Mormons the victors. But rarely has there been a more dramatic case of winning the battle and losing the war.

Richmond, county seat of Ray County, was already in an uproar. Many of the old settlers from the north had fled there to escape the "Mormon uprising." Along with them, some of those who had left the Church were also expressing horror at what the Mormons had done. A messenger had already been sent to Jefferson City with the affidavit of Thomas B. Marsh swearing that Joseph Smith was going to bathe northern Missouri in blood.

The reports from Crooked River arrived in Richmond later in the day on which the battle took place, and from there the rumors spread to other counties. That same night, word of the battle reached the town of Carrollton, Carroll County, and the ears of the Reverend Sashiel Woods, the fiery preacher whom

Joshua had heard in DeWitt. The next day Woods and the county clerk, Joseph Dickson, dashed off a letter to Governor Boggs.

"Sir: We were informed last night by an express from Ray County, that Captain Bogart and all his company, amounting to between fifty and sixty men, were massacred at Buncombe, twelve miles north of Richmond, except three. This statement you may rely on as being true, and last night they expected Richmond to be laid in ashes this morning. We could distinctly hear cannon, and we knew the 'Mormons' had one in their possession. Richmond is about twenty-five miles west of this place, on a straight line. We know not the hour or minute we shall be laid in ashes—our county is ruined—for God's sake give us assistance as soon as possible."

Carrollton was over thirty miles away from Crooked River—some distance to hear cannon shot! Bogart's forces were closer to thirty than to sixty. And one Missourian killed fell somewhat short of Woods and Dickson's "massacre." But, of course, truth wouldn't count for much in the events being played out now.

On October twenty-sixth, on the same day that Woods and Dickson were writing their letter, Governor Boggs ordered General John B. Clark to call out two thousand men and prepare them for battle. The next morning, two messengers from Richmond arrived in Jefferson City with letters and petitions as well as extremely exaggerated reports about what happened at Crooked River—the Mormons had killed ten, wounded many others, and taken prisoners, and they planned to sack and burn Richmond. That changed everything. Boggs drafted what would become the most infamous executive order in Missouri's history. It was addressed to General Clark.

"Sir: Since the order of the morning to you, I have received information of the most appalling character, which changes the whole face of things and places the 'Mormons' in the attitude of open and avowed defiance of the laws, and of having made open war upon the people of this State. Your orders are, therefore, to hasten your operations and endeavor to reach Richmond, in Ray County, with all possible speed. The 'Mormons' must be treated as enemies and *must be exterminated* or driven from the State, if necessary for the public good. Their outrages are beyond description. If you can increase your force, you are authorized to do so to any extent you may think necessary."

It was signed and sent by express rider. And with it went the last hopes of the Latter-day Saints in Missouri.

Caroline Mendenhall Steed was livid. Her chest rose and fell heavily as she sat on the sofa in the parlor. Her hands were still trembling. Her face was still flushed with the sheer effrontery of it all. She had been home for nearly five minutes now, but it was not going away. The longer she sat, the angrier she got.

There was a noise above her, and Olivia came to the top of the stairs. "Mama, Savannah is waking up."

Caroline looked up. "All right, Livvy. I'll be up in a moment."

Olivia was peering at her. "Are you all right, Mama?" She started down the stairs.

One hand came up sharply. "I'm fine, Livvy! Please don't come down."

Clearly dismayed, Olivia stopped, still staring at her mother. Caroline forced herself to give her daughter a quick smile. "Really, Livvy, I'll be up in a few minutes."

As Olivia turned and went slowly back up to the landing, shooting one last glance over her shoulder, the front door opened. Will came rushing in, with Obadiah Cornwell right behind him. Will was to her in three long steps and dropped to one knee in front of her.

"Mother, are you all right?"

She felt a flash of anger. She had hoped that word of the confrontation would not get out, especially to her own family. She had instinctively known that it was a futile expectation, but she had hoped it nevertheless. Then her mouth softened, and she looked squarely into her son's face. Will would turn fifteen in a few months. He was no longer a boy. He was doing a man's work at the freight yard, and since Joshua had been called into the militia Will had been the man of the house. She reached out and laid a hand on his. "Yes, Will, I'm fine."

Joshua's partner had come to stand over her, looking down at her with some anxiety. She took a quick breath and looked up at him. He motioned with his head, then looked at Will.

Caroline stood up and saw that Olivia had stopped on the landing above her and was watching now too, fear clouding her face. "Will, Savannah is starting to wake up from her nap. I want you and Olivia to go up and watch her while I talk to Obadiah."

"Mama, I—"

"Please, Will," she said firmly. "Don't fight me. Not now."

"All right," he said dejectedly. He turned and went up the stairs three at a time. "Come on, Livvy," he said.

When they heard the door shut, Obadiah turned back to Caroline. "I heard what happened."

The anger came back in a wave, darkening the green eyes and drawing her mouth into a tight line. "What infuriates me the most, Obadiah, is that this wasn't riffraff from the saloons. This wasn't the stable hands that sweep the horse droppings out of the barns. These were"—her voice became heavy with sarcasm—"some of Jackson County's finest women."

She was starting to tremble again. "They've been to my house for tea. They've sat around this very room, smiling and fawning up to me because my husband is the richest man in Independence. But when he leaves . . ."

She couldn't finish, and turned away, dropping her head.

Cornwell reached out and tentatively touched her shoulder. "Caroline, I need to tell you something."

She bit her lip, fighting to maintain her control, then slowly turned back to face him.

"That day Joshua was here last, when he only had a couple of hours before he had to get back to Richmond?"

"Yes?"

"He came and talked with me after he left you."

Her eyebrows lifted. "He did?"

"He was afraid something like this might happen. He had me get some things together. A wagon. Supplies. A good team. He said he wanted them ready at any moment."

She was looking at him incredulously. He went on doggedly. "Maybe you ought to consider going to St. Louis for a time, until—"

"No!" she said sharply.

"Caroline, this is only the beginning."

"No, Obadiah! This is my home. If they think they can drive me away, they're wrong."

He was shaking his head at her, getting a little angry himself. "Caroline, listen to me. Everyone's talking about this. There's a lot of emotion building. They know about Joshua's family. They know he asked to be on General Atchison's staff so he didn't have to ride against them."

He hesitated, trying to decide how to explain it to her. "You don't understand. When the trouble with the Mormons started here in Jackson County, Joshua was one of the leaders. He was in the forefront. No one did more to drive them out of here than Joshua, even though his wife was one of them. And now . . ."

"I know that, but that has all changed now."

"Exactly!" he shot back. "Joshua was a hero. Now they see him as a traitor. A coward." Her head snapped up, but he hurried on. "You know and I know what's really happened, but the town doesn't. The whole county is talking about this, Caroline. I think you ought to seriously consider—"

"I won't go, Obadiah."

He caught his breath, staring at her, exasperation twisting his face. Then finally he nodded. "I understand. But just know, that wagon is packed and ready. The team is stabled right next door. Anytime, day or night—"

"I won't go!" she said again in a fierce whisper. "I won't go!"

Many fourteen-year-olds were interested in possessing things. But Peter Ingalls had never been one to take pride in what he owned. What he wore. Where he lived. What belonged to him. They made little difference to him.

And then Derek and Rebecca had received a horse as a wedding present. And all of that changed.

Peter had always been fascinated with horses—the muscular and powerful dray teams that brought the huge bales of cotton to the textile mills; the leaner and finer carriage horses that carried the gentry and their ladies around town; or, most exciting because he had seen them only once or twice, the sleek mounts used in England by the wealthy as they hunted fox across the open countryside.

The horse that Rebecca and Derek had received was not that fine a breed. He was a sorrel gelding, about seven or eight years old. His winter hair was thick and shaggy, and he was not particularly swift. But Peter didn't care. He adored the horse, and brushed and curried it every morning. He begged the neighbors for every scrap of carrots or even their apple cores to feed to him.

So on the evening of October twenty-seventh, when Peter walked out to the small paddock behind their sod hut and saw that the horse was gone, it was instant catastrophe. For a moment, he stared in disbelief, then with a howl he turned and ran for the house.

"Peter," Rebecca said sternly. "You stay here until I can find Derek."

"Then hurry," he pleaded. "We've got to find the horse before it gets dark."

"I mean it, Peter," she warned as she pulled on her coat. "I'll get Derek, but you're not to go off looking alone." She wanted to say more but didn't; she just gave him one last severe look and left.

Peter waited for over five minutes at the window, holding the blanket back so he could see the road that led to Lyman Wight's place, where Derek was meeting with some of the brethren. His eyes kept lifting to scan the sky, which seemed to be growing darker at an alarming pace.

Finally he could bear it no longer. He checked to make sure his pocketknife was in his pocket, then pulled on his coat and went out the door and around to the corral. It took only a minute to find the problem. At one corner the rail was shoved away from it's supporting post. It didn't look to be a big enough opening for a horse to squeeze through, but as he looked more closely he could see tufts of red hair wedged in the grain of the wood. He stepped through the opening. They were faint, but they were there—the impression of hooves in the soft, grassy earth.

Head down, peering intently in the fading light, Peter began to follow the prints up the hillside toward the top of the bluff.

It would be some time before word of Governor Boggs's extermination order would reach Far West, but Joseph Smith didn't need any formal notice to know that the incident at Crooked River was a major turning point for the Saints. After returning from Stephen Winchester's home with the body of David Patten, he called a meeting of all major priesthood leaders and each of the captains responsible for home defense.

They started with prayer at Joseph's home, but immediately after that, Joseph took them out for a walking tour of the city. As they went they were besieged by anxious residents and the numerous refugees that filled every vacant lot and empty spot in the city. Rumor had now become a major combatant in the struggle, and anxieties were running high. The governor was activating every militia group within a hundred miles. Two thousand armed men were gathering at Richmond. Night riders were sweeping across the countryside in murderous revenge. Governor Boggs was out of the state and could not be reached to stop the coming carnage. The troops had mutinied against General Parks and were on their way northward.

Joseph seemed indefatigable in his patience. He soothed without being patronizing, encouraged without building false hope, chided where necessary but without giving offense. He was Brother Joseph, the prophet and seer. His people loved him, but more, they trusted him. It was as though the party were on a boat moving through roiling waters, but with their passage the waters smoothed and became calm again.

"I want two wagons ready to go in there," Joseph said, pointing to where there was an empty space between some cabins. George Robinson, the clerk of the Far West City Council, nodded, writing swiftly in a ledger book. Joseph turned to Brigham. "We may need some barricades there as well."

"I agree, Brother Joseph," Brigham said. "I've got some of the brethren gathering materials right now."

"Good." Joseph turned to Hyrum and Sidney. "What about the men we sent out to gather the last of the people in? Any reports?"

"Yes, Joseph," Hyrum answered. "We haven't heard how the gathering to Di-Ahman is going yet, but as you can see, they're coming into Far West in droves. I think they're finally convinced it's too dangerous out there."

"It's about time," Joseph growled. "What about Haun's Mill?"

Hyrum shook his head. "I don't think we've seen anyone yet from there."

Joseph threw up his hands. "What does it take? I guess I'm going to have to ride out and talk to Jacob Haun myself."

As one of the captains in the army of Israel, Benjamin Steed was part of the group making the rounds. He raised one hand to catch Joseph's eye. "But Jacob Haun is in town right now," he said.

Joseph stopped. "Are you sure?"

"I saw him not half an hour ago down by the courthouse. He came in last night to get some supplies."

"Haun's Mill is especially vulnerable," Joseph said gravely. "They're small—fifteen or twenty families—and they're right in the path of any force coming up from the south." He turned to his brother. "Hyrum, you finish with the brethren. Brother Ben and I will go find Jacob Haun. I want to talk to him personally."

Jacob Haun was a man of German stock—stubborn, hard-headed, independent. When the Church was first looking to come north to the mostly unsettled areas of northern Missouri, he had been one of the first to move. He founded a settlement on Shoal Creek in 1836 and built a small gristmill, hoping to provide milling service to the old settlers as well as the swelling population of Mormons.

Joseph and Benjamin found him at the store putting into the back of his wagon the last of some things he had purchased. Without preamble, Joseph laced into him, his voice showing some of his exasperation. But it made no difference. As Joseph spoke, Haun's jaw set and his eyes took on a hooded look. "Brother Joseph," he finally said, not unlike a father speaking to a child who didn't listen well, "I understand your worry, but we are fine. The local people have agreed that if we promise not to take arms against them, they'll leave us alone."

Joseph looked heavenward and rolled his eyes. "Brother Haun, after what happened at Crooked River we've got men gathering against us from a dozen counties. It is not just the locals we're worried about. Your settlement is not safe."

"We will be fine," Haun said obstinately. "We will post sentries and guards. We can use the blacksmith shop as a fort in case something does happen. It is made of logs. Very solid. But I don't think we will need it."

"Brother Haun," Joseph started, "I beseech you, for your safety and the safety of your community—"

But Haun cut him off. "I have worked very hard for these past two years to build a home on Shoal Creek. I have valuable property there. I will not abandon it. Now, if you will excuse me, I must get started so I can be back before dark."

As he climbed up in his wagon and snapped the reins, Joseph and Benjamin stepped back. They watched him swing the wagon around and head it eastward. Joseph said nothing, just watched Haun until he was gone, his blue eyes now almost gray with worry and sadness. Finally, he turned to Benjamin. "We'd better keep moving, Brother Ben. There is much to do."

"Brother Joseph?" Benjamin said.

The Prophet was deeply preoccupied as they walked back toward the group of brethren they had left earlier. He spoke without looking up. "Yes?"

Benjamin hesitated for a moment. Then, in spite of his reservations about bringing it up, he plunged in. "Why is all this happening to us?"

Joseph's step slowed, but he continued to keep his eyes on the ground.

"I know we haven't always been perfectly obedient," Benjamin continued, "but there are a great many of the Saints who are earnestly striving to do what God asks of them."

"Yes there are, Ben. A good many."

Benjamin shook his head slowly. "And if all of this trouble is punishment for our not being better people, what about those who are rising up against us? Compared to them, are we so bad?"

Joseph Smith stopped completely now, looking at Benjamin straight on, the wide blue eyes open and probing, the features laced with touches of pain. Finally, he gestured toward a rail fence. "Let's talk for a moment, Ben."

As they moved over and leaned on the split rails, Benjamin had second thoughts. "I'm sorry, Joseph. You have so much to worry about right now. Just ignore the ramblings of a worried old man."

Joseph chuckled. "How old are you now, Brother Ben?"

"I was fifty-three in May."

"Well, I'm just coming up on thirty-three in another couple of months. If I'm in as good a shape as you in twenty years, I'll be happy."

Benjamin did not smile back. He felt very old at the moment. More like he was seventy-three. Worry could do that to you.

One of Joseph's hands came up and removed his hat. The other followed, smoothing back his hair. He was staring out across the fields. To the south, about twenty-five miles, lay Richmond, where the armies were gathering. From the way Joseph's brow furrowed, it was as if he could see them coming. Finally, he put his hat back on, though he still kept staring out across the countryside.

"I wish you could have been with us when we first came to Missouri in '31, Ben. It was glorious. I'll never forget how excited we were when the Lord revealed that the center place of Zion was to be right there in Jackson County."

Yes, and within two years every last Latter-day Saint there was driven out of Zion at the point of a gun. But Benjamin didn't say that out loud. Joseph had enough troubles without having to explain everything to Benjamin Steed.

"And do you remember what he said at that time, Brother Ben?"

Benjamin knew the revelations that had been given during that time, but he wasn't sure what Joseph had reference to, so he shook his head. Joseph's eyes half closed as he began to quote, " 'You cannot see with your natural eyes, for the present time, the design of your God concerning those things which shall come hereafter, and the glory which shall follow, after much tribulation.' " His voice became very soft. " 'For after much tribulation cometh the blessings.' "

Benjamin felt a little thrill shoot through him as he often did when Joseph quoted the words of the Lord. Perhaps it was because Joseph had been the one to receive them, but he could quote them in a way that no other man could.

Joseph's eyes opened, and he turned to look squarely at Benjamin. "And we surely have seen the tribulation, haven't we?"

"Yes," Benjamin said. And now he couldn't resist adding, "And it isn't over yet."

"No, it isn't. So why? Why *are* these things happening to us? What is this design of God that we can't see with our natural eyes?"

Benjamin was almost too startled to realize that Joseph was asking him questions. He had read that passage many times—it was now in the Doctrine and Covenants—but he had missed the impact of that one word. *Design. And not just design. Divine design!* It had not occurred to him before to think of it in that manner.

But Joseph hadn't expected him to answer. He was musing now. "I have pondered this question too, Benjamin. Very often. Oh, there is no question but what we have not been fully faithful as a people, but we surely have tried to keep the Lord's commandments more than the men who are troubling us. So why isn't the Lord punishing them?"

"That's exactly it. It seems so unfair."

"Well, I don't want to dwell on this point—I want to get to the harder question—but I'd just like to remind you of something the Lord said on another occasion. 'For unto whom much is given . . .'?" He let his voice rise, making the statement into a question.

" 'Much is expected,' " Benjamin finished it for him.

"Ah, no, Ben. I hear the Saints quoting it that way, but that is not what it says. It says, 'For unto whom much is given *much is required;* and he who sins against the greater light receives the greater condemnation.' " He took a quick breath. "That is a very different matter indeed."

"So because we're Saints, we—"

"Not just Saints, Ben. We are the Lord's covenant people. The Missourians are not. We have made solemn covenants that we will live his law and serve him. And he has given us so much in return. The gift of the Holy Ghost. New scripture. The priesthood." His voice had risen with excitement; now it dropped to almost a whisper. "He has a right to require more of us." There was a long pause. "And he does."

Benjamin finally nodded. "All right, I can see that, but—"

Joseph raised one hand quickly, grinning now. "Let me get to your first question. How exactly did you say it again?"

"Why is all of this happening to us? Do you have an answer?"

The grin broadened, and there was a bit of a teasing look in Joseph's eye now. "I don't, but I think the Lord does."

Benjamin smiled back at him. "I'd accept the Lord's answer on this."

Joseph slowly sobered. "Well, for the past few nights I have been reading and rereading the revelations given during that time when we lost Jackson County. We seem to be in a similar situation again now, so I wanted to see if God had said anything that might give us some answers."

"And did he?"

"You judge for yourself, Ben. I can't quote it exactly from memory, but here is what the Lord said in '33, at the very time our people were starting into all the troubles with the Missourians. He said, 'Let your hearts take comfort, for all things work together for the good of them that walk uprightly, and to the sanctification of the church.' "

He stopped, letting Benjamin digest that for a moment. "Think about that, Ben. *All things*, it says, work for our good if we live right. Could he possibly mean persecution and hardship? Does 'all things' include the burning of homes and the driving of our women and children out in the midst of winter?"

"Do you think it does?"

"I think when the Lord says 'all things,' he means all things. And he also said that those things work for the sanctification of the Church." There was a soft sigh. "Think the Church could use some sanctification, Ben?"

There was only one answer to that, and Benjamin gave it with a sober nod.

Joseph smiled sadly. "And then the Lord said, and I think this is the key: 'I will raise up to myself a pure people, who will serve me in righteousness.' "

He brushed his hands back and forth together, as if dusting them off. "That's not easy doctrine, is it, Ben?"

"No." Benjamin thought of what Jessica had been through in Jackson County. "Not easy at all."

"Let me ask you something, Ben."

"All right."

"Tell me, where is Thomas B. Marsh right now?"

Benjamin's head came around and his eyebrows lifted sharply. But Joseph went on swiftly. "Where are the members of the Twelve who betrayed us in Kirtland? And where are Oliver Cowdery and David Whitmer and Martin Harris? Where have they all gone, Ben?"

"They left us because they weren't strong enough," Benjamin said slowly.

Joseph leaned forward, peering into Benjamin's face. "Strong enough for what, Ben? Strong enough for what?"

And now Benjamin Steed understood. "Strong enough to remain faithful when they lost all their money in the Kirtland Safety Society. Strong enough to ignore the ridicule and rejection and mockery of others."

Joseph was nodding with each answer. "We've lost quite a few. We lost some on Zion's Camp. We lost others when the Panic of '37 wiped us out financially. We lost some when the Prophet told them to do things they didn't agree with." A great sadness pulled at his mouth. "We lost one who thought it more important to please his wife than to accept the counsel of the First Presidency."

Ben felt a sudden surge of excitement. "And the Brigham Youngs and the John Taylors—they were strong enough, weren't they?"

"Yes. And the Fieldings and the Pratts and the Cahoons and the Woodruffs and the Kimballs." He paused for just a moment. "And the Steeds—Nathan, Mary Ann, Lydia, Jessica."

He reached out and gripped Benjamin's arm for a moment, and there was a sudden huskiness to his voice. "And I think I can still remember a man named Benjamin Steed who was beaten nearly to death one night because he wouldn't turn his back on Brother Joseph."

Benjamin straightened now, feeling like a new man. "If only easy things happened to us, Oliver and David and Thomas—they might still be with us, right?"

"Yes. That's part of the answer, Benjamin."

Benjamin's mind was alive with the implications of what Joseph was teaching him. And he wanted more. "What else?" he asked.

"The Lord said he would raise up a pure people. For what, Benjamin? Why does the Lord need a pure people?"

Benjamin stared into Joseph's steady gaze for several seconds; then understanding came with absolute clarity. "Because there is yet work to be done," he said in awe.

Joseph laughed softly. "That is exactly what I concluded last night. There is still much to be done. We have to establish the kingdom of God on the earth so that the kingdom of heaven may come. That takes men and women who have iron faith and steel in their commitment to the Lord." He put both hands on Benjamin's shoulders. "And if the Lord has to take us through the fires to find enough metal to do the job, then I say, let the fires begin. I, for one, am ready."

Chapter Notes

The infamous "extermination order" issued by Governor Lilburn W. Boggs on the twenty-seventh of October, 1838, is not given here in its entirety, but what is given is quoted from a published source (see *Persecutions*, 228–29; see also *HC* 3:175). The letter of Sashiel Woods and Joseph Dickson is also authentic (see *Persecutions*, 225; see also *HC* 3:168–69).

Jacob Haun's refusal to bring his settlement into Far West in spite of Joseph's specific request to do so is reported by Philo Dibble (see "Philo Dibble's Narrative," in *Early Scenes in Church History* [Salt Lake City: Juvenile Instructor Office, 1882], p. 90; see also *CHFT*, p. 201).

The scriptures cited by Joseph in his conversation with Benjamin are now D&C 58:3–4; 82:3; 100:15–16.

Chapter Sixteen

Benjamin called a family council as soon as he returned home. They asked a neighbor girl to take the children. The young ones of the city were frightened enough without making them sit through a council of war.

And so the five of them sat around the table—he and Mary Ann and Matthew and Nathan and Lydia. It was a somber group as Benjamin reported on his and Joseph's conversation with the mulish Jacob Haun. He blew out his breath in disgust. "I'm not sure that stubborn old fool will even tell his people that Joseph is asking them to come in."

"How can he simply ignore the Prophet?" Lydia burst out.

"Some people trust in their own wisdom more than they trust the counsel of the Prophet," Benjamin answered sadly.

Nathan stirred. "Then we have no choice. We have to go for Jessica and John ourselves."

The two women looked quickly at each other. Lydia's face was drawn. Mary Ann looked haggard. Their men had returned safely from Crooked River, but it could so easily have turned out otherwise. Just ask the families who would be having funerals tomorrow. And the Steed women knew full well it could just as easily be them weeping tonight and preparing bodies for burial. Mary Ann finally spoke for the both of them. "Is it safe? To be riding across the countryside right now?"

"Of course it's not safe," Lydia cried. "It's not safe for any Mormon anywhere in Missouri."

Nathan was sitting beside her at the table. He reached out and laid his hand over hers. "That's right," he said quietly, "including Jessica and her family. There are four children there too, remember."

Lydia looked away. "I know," she whispered. "And I know we have to try to bring them in. I'm just so frightened."

Mary Ann was staring at her hands, which were folded in her lap. Finally she looked up, her eyes catching her husband. "I want us to get Rebecca and Derek too," she said. "And Peter."

Benjamin's eyebrows rose. "But they're already in Di-Ahman. Joseph said to get everyone in to Far West or Di-Ahman."

"I know, but I want them here with us. I want to know they're safe. I want us to be together in whatever's coming."

Benjamin's head was nodding in assent even before she was finished. "Yes, you're right, Mother. Rebecca and Derek too."

"I'll go to Di-Ahman," Matthew said. He looked quickly at his mother, whose head had come up sharply. "We've still got the courier stations set up. It will be safer going north."

Mary Ann started to shake her head, then bit her lip and looked down again. "All right." It was barely audible.

"He proved himself well at Crooked River, Mama," Nathan said. "Matthew can do it."

"Can't you find some brethren to go with you?" Lydia burst out. "It is suicide to travel alone."

Benjamin sighed deeply, a sound of great pain and weariness. "Every man is looking to the care of his own family right now. I would go, but I've got to help get the city ready." He paused, waiting for a comment, but Lydia too knew the inevitable when she saw it.

"We don't have much choice," Benjamin continued. "So Nathan will go to Haun's Mill. Matthew will go to Di-Ahman." He looked at his sons. "I want you ready to ride at dawn. Brother Kimball said Matthew can borrow his horse again. Matthew, you can't make it that far and back in one day, so you stay overnight with Derek. Nathan, Haun's Mill is only twelve miles. I want you there and back by dark tomorrow. I don't care if Jessica and John have to leave everything behind. Just get them back here."

As Nathan and Matthew nodded, Mary Ann started to rise, resigned now to what had to happen. "Lydia and I will get some food ready."

But Benjamin held up his hand. "I would like to say something more."

As his wife sank back down again, Benjamin stood up. He reached down and touched the Doctrine and Covenants that lay on the table. A scrap of leather marked a spot near the end of it. "Joseph gave me a scripture tonight. I was asking him why all this is happening to us. He thought this was the Lord's answer."

He took his eyeglasses from his pocket and put them on, then opened the book to the place where it was marked. " 'Let your hearts be comforted, for all things shall work together for good to them that walk uprightly, and to the sanctification of the church; for I will raise up unto myself a pure people, that will serve me in righteousness.' "

He stopped and looked up. "That's where Joseph stopped. He taught me a great lesson, but I'll speak more of that later. Listen to what follows here, though. 'And all that call on the name of the Lord and keep his commandments, shall be saved; even so. Amen.' "

He closed the book and set it down again, then looked at the four of them. "I know that when the Lord says we will be saved, he may not mean saving us from sorrow and heartache here. Look at David Patten, for example. A more godly man never walked the earth, and now he's dead." He shook his head, still remembering watching David Patten die. "But the Lord says if we call upon his name and keep his commandments, we can expect him to hear us. Now, I know we Steeds aren't perfect, not by a long shot, but we've tried to be faithful. We've truly tried to keep his commandments."

Every one of them was watching him intently now, not sure exactly where he was going with all this.

He took in a breath, then let it come out again very slowly. "We are about to send our two sons off on a very dangerous mission. If there were a choice, we wouldn't do it. They're both so young and so—" His voice caught, and he had to look away.

There were wet streaks down Lydia's and Mary Ann's cheeks now. Nathan's eyes were blinking rapidly, and he kept having to swallow. Matthew's lower lip was quivering. "They are *so* important to us," Benjamin finished in a half whisper. "So I guess what I'm saying is that I'd like us to kneel and as a family call on God to watch over them. And to protect our family members who are out there in harm's way until Nathan and Matthew can find them and bring them back safely to us."

They knelt around the table. Lydia and Nathan held each other's hands. Benjamin was between Matthew and Mary Ann and reached out and took both of their hands in his. It was not a long prayer, nor was it particularly eloquent. Not in words, at least. But Benjamin Steed spoke the feelings of his heart. He spoke to God as if he had somehow been ushered into his presence. He spoke of the love they all had for each other. He mentioned the fact that Mary Ann and Nathan had accepted Joseph Smith and the work of the Restoration from the very beginning and had never wavered since that time. He pointed out that Nathan was the father of four small children and husband to a fine and faithful woman. It would be a terrible loss if he should be taken. He talked about Matthew's youth and all that was still ahead of him in life. Then, as a father and grandfather, he simply pleaded with his Father to watch over their children and give them his protecting care.

As they stood again, all were weeping openly now. Nathan took Lydia in his arms and held her tightly, not speaking. Mary Ann gathered in Matthew. He now towered some six inches above her and had to bend down to let her kiss his cheek as she clung to him. Then she turned to her husband and threw herself into his arms. "Thank you, Ben," she whispered. "You are such a good man. I love you."

Benjamin could not trust himself to speak. He merely nodded and held his wife tightly in his arms. Then suddenly his head came up. Mary Ann felt it and looked up at him. She gave him a quizzical look, but he did not see it. He was staring across the room. "What?" she finally asked. "What is it, Ben?"

Her voice seemed to startle him, and he finally looked down at her. Then, nodding, half to himself, he turned to Nathan. "Nathan, I don't want you and Matthew traveling separately."

Nathan dropped his arms from Lydia and turned in surprise.

"No," Benjamin said, more confidently now. "You and Matthew are to stay together. Don't leave each other for any reason."

"But what about Rebecca and Derek?"

Benjamin went on in a rush. "You are to go there first. Now." He nodded emphatically as all of them stared at him. "This evening. You need to leave as quickly as possible. Go to Di-Ahman first. Then you can go for Jessica."

By ten o'clock, Peter finally admitted that he was hopelessly lost. He had followed the trail of the horse up a dirt road for a couple of miles, moving rapidly because the prints were easy to see. Then the tracks had cut off across a patch of prairie. But they headed for the stretch of trees that marked the path of the Grand River, so Peter had taken off at a trot. But there was no clear ground there either. After a quarter of an hour, it was full dark, and any chance of seeing anything was gone. Heartbroken, discouraged, and starting to get a little bit frightened when he realized how far he had come, Peter set off to retrace his tracks.

Moving slowly in the darkness, he decided that once he found the road again it would be an easy thing to find his way back. But there was no road. By the time he had gone at least twice as far as the distance between the road and the river, he knew he had done something wrong. Fighting a rising sense of panic, he went back and tried again, changing directions slightly. There was no road anywhere.

Feeling more forlorn than he could ever remember, Peter pushed deeper into underbrush along the river and found a place where leaves covered the ground. Hugging his coat tightly around him, he sat down to wait out the night.

When the knock on the door came, Rebecca was not asleep. She was sitting in the rocking chair she had brought with her from her bedroom at home, slowly rocking back and forth, staring at nothing, willing the night to pass. The soft knock jerked her up with a start. She was on her feet and reached out and turned the lantern up to full flame. She took a step toward the door, then stopped, a little chill going through her. It must be somewhere around four a.m. "Derek?" she called. "Is that you?"

"Rebecca! It's Nathan. And Matthew."

"Nathan?" Stunned, she went to the door and unlatched it. For a moment she just stared, and then threw herself into her brother's arms.

By dawn the temperature had fallen to the low forties, and Peter was shivering violently as he came out of his cover. He jumped up and down, beating his arms against his body, trying to warm himself. He moved down to the river itself, feeling thirsty. But as he looked at the muddy water he couldn't bring himself to drink it.

Remembering, he dug into his trouser pockets and brought out the food he had scavenged for the horse the previous afternoon—two apple cores and an old dried up carrot. He had felt a little guilty then about having nothing better to offer the animal. Now he was grateful he hadn't been able to find him. He ate the apple cores, seeds and all, then devoured the carrot, wishing he had four or five more just like it.

The food wasn't much, but it cheered him greatly. The sky was overcast, but the light was full enough that he could see clearly. Cautiously he made his way to the edge of the trees and scanned the countryside around him. About half a mile away he could see the outline of the cabin. He felt a great surge of relief. He had passed that a short time before he had lost the horse's tracks. It had looked deserted—one of the dozens that had been abandoned by either Mormon or Missourian in the troubles that now gripped the county.

The sober realities of being alone and out away from Di-Ahman hit him hard now. And what was worse, he knew that Derek and probably other men from Di-Ahman would be out looking for him. That put them at risk too. It was a stupid thing he had done. Surveying the lay of the land, he decided he could find his way back easily enough, but being out in the open all alone made him nervous. He had basically gone upriver, so he could follow the tree line back almost to Di-Ahman and then come out more safely. Moving back into the trees, he began to walk, as swiftly and silently as was possible.

He had gone about half a mile when suddenly he stopped, his ear cocked to one side. Then he dropped into a crouch, looking around wildly. Just off to his left there was a soft moaning sound. It stopped. After a moment, he heard it again. Gingerly now, truly frightened but curious too, Peter straightened. Ready to bolt at the slightest sign of trouble, he made his way forward. And then as he came around a clump of hazel brush, he stopped again, but this time in shock and horror. He was at the edge of a small clearing. On the opposite side of it, tied to a small cottonwood tree, was a man. His boots were gone, and his shirt was down around his waist, torn into several pieces but still tucked in his waistband. But it was the man's back that Peter gaped at. It was one solid mass of red. Peter stepped forward slowly, at first not comprehending. Then he nearly gagged. The red was lacerated flesh. The man had been whipped severely. Holding one hand to his mouth, Peter moved forward very slowly.

"Brother Sterling?" Peter barely recognized the face. It was bruised and battered. One eye was dark purple and completely swollen shut. His nose had been bleeding but had dried now. His lips were puffy and cut in two places.

The eyes flickered open. There was a momentary flash of fear, and then they glazed over again. Peter knew him, though not well. The Sterlings were converts from Tennessee who had arrived in Di-Ahman just a couple of weeks before. They had started a simple hut about two miles outside of town.

"It's all right, Brother Sterling. I'll help you." Peter grabbed for his pocketknife and began sawing at the ropes. There was another moan. The bands had rubbed the wrists down to raw flesh. More carefully now, Peter finished cutting the ropes through, catching Sterling's weight as he did so. He lowered him slowly to the ground, face first so as not to touch his back to anything. For a moment Peter just stood there, wanting to vomit, horrified at what his eyes were registering, but knowing that this man was near death and that he had to do something.

Pulling a piece of the man's shirt loose, Peter ran to the river and thrust it into the water. Muddy water or not, he had to get something to bathe the flesh. With water dripping from the cloth, he darted back to the clearing.

"I've got some water, Brother—" He slid to a halt. Two men were standing next to the prone figure. Both carried rifles. One carried a coiled bullwhip in his left hand and was tapping it lightly against his leg. The man nearest Peter had a cold cigar butt clamped between his teeth. He shifted it enough to speak, suddenly grinning wickedly. The rifle came up, muzzle pointing at Peter's stomach. "Well, well. And what do we have here?"

"There's Derek!"

Nathan's head came up sharply and he turned to look where Rebecca was pointing. He and Matthew were out in front of the sod hut, saddling up again after grabbing an hour's sleep and a cold breakfast. He peered through the gray light of early morning to where the six riders were coming up the valley at an easy lope. "Are you sure?"

"Yes," Rebecca cried joyously. "It's Derek." She went up on tiptoes, leaning forward in her excitement. Then suddenly her face fell. She was counting the horses now. There were only six, the same number that had left last night. And now they were close enough that they could see that each horse carried a single rider. Peter was not with them.

Derek was off his horse and running toward them before the others had even reined up. "Nathan! Matthew! What are you doing here?" He grabbed Nathan's hand and pumped it up and down. "Am I glad to see you two!"

"You didn't find him?" Rebecca said.

Derek turned, the light going out of his eyes. "No, not a sign of him."

Lyman Wight dismounted and joined them. "There's no telling which way that horse went. It was too dark to track him. Peter could be anywhere."

"Daylight will help," one of the other brethren said, "but we thought we'd better come in for fresh horses."

"We'll find him," Derek said grimly. "We've got to." Then he turned back to his two brothers-in-law. "You're a welcome sight. What are you doing here?"

Nathan explained quickly. Lyman Wight nodded without hesitation. "I agree with Father Steed," he said. "You need to be together."

Nathan felt great relief. Wight was a rough-looking man, with full black beard and black eyes that were filled with life and energy. He was renowned for his fearlessness and his determination to protect his people. One of the first settlers in the valley of Adam-ondi-Ahman, he held a commission in the Missouri militia. So Joseph had appointed him to head the

Di-Ahman forces. For him to give his approval meant that Nathan wasn't going to have to try to persuade anyone about taking Derek and Rebecca back with them.

Wight looked at the other men. "Grab yourselves a bite to eat and some new mounts. We'll meet back here in half an hour."

"Our horses are rested," Matthew blurted to Nathan. "Let's you and me start now."

Wight had started to swing back up into the saddle. He stopped and turned. "I'm not sure that's wise. This isn't the time to be out away from the town in small numbers."

The thought of sitting around for another half an hour wasn't to Nathan's liking much either. "We'll be careful. We'll try and pick up the trail of the horse. Rebecca says it was still light when Peter left. He may have tried to follow it."

Wight considered that and then nodded curtly. "Tell Brother Ingalls here which way you're headed. We'll join you as soon as possible. Derek, we'll be back for you in half an hour or less."

"You ruined our ropes, boy. Why'd you go and do that, now?" The man with the whip was at the tree where Sterling had been tied. He was fingering the strands that Peter had cut.

Peter didn't answer. He wasn't sure whether or not the men had been drinking, but their mood was foul, and he knew they were very dangerous.

"You take pity on this idiot Mormon, did you?" The other man was standing next to the unconscious man. He reached out with the toe of his boot and kicked him lightly in the ribs. Sterling flinched and groaned.

"Leave him alone!" Peter said hotly. "Haven't you done enough to him already?"

The man turned about slowly. "Well, well, well." He looked at his partner. "You hear that accent? I think we've found ourselves a bloomin' Englishman." Rifle still held level and steady, he walked over and shoved his face close to Peter's. "Where you from, boy?"

Peter almost said Di-Ahman, then caught himself. "My brother and I are homesteading a small place south of here."

The eyes narrowed. "How long you been in America?"

"About a year."

The man with the whip came over now too. "I hear the Mormons sent some men over to England to preach their devil doctrine there."

The first man leaned even closer, and now Peter could smell the foulness of his breath and his body odor. "You a Mormon, boy?"

Peter's heart felt like it dropped into his boots. He stared at the man, his mind racing. And then suddenly a scripture popped into his mind. Brother Kimball had used it on more than one occasion in England. It was from the Apostle Paul. The words seared across Peter's consciousness. "*I am not ashamed of the gospel of Christ: for it is the power of God unto salvation to every one that believeth.*"

"Well, boy? The cat got your tongue? Are you a Mormon or ain't you?"

Peter looked straight into the bloodshot eyes. "No, sir, I am not a Mormon."

The man's eyes widened slightly. "Oh," he grunted, clearly disappointed.

Before he could say anything more, Peter went on calmly. "There is no such thing as a Mormon. That's merely a nickname people give us. But if you're asking me if I am a member of The Church of Jesus Christ of Latter-day Saints, then the answer is yes. I am that, and proud of it."

The man stepped back. For just a flickering moment, there was admiration in his eyes; then they turned ugly. "Turner," he snarled out of the corner of his mouth, "get some more rope. Our work here ain't finished yet."

"Them's Peter's boot tracks, sure as we're standing here," Matthew said excitedly.

Nathan went down into a crouch, looking at the marks in the soft earth of the roadside. "And they're over the top of the horse's trail. I think you're right, Matthew. This has got to be Peter." He stood, looking around. "It looks like they headed for the river." He blew out his breath, trying not to be too discouraged as he let his eyes run along the endless string of trees that stretched out in both directions. "It's a long shot, but it's a place to start."

"Nathan, look!"

He turned. Matthew was staring up at their horses. Both animals had turned their heads to the right, and their ears were cocked forward. They were listening intently.

Nathan grabbed for the reins. "Let's go!"

As they approached the tree line at a steady trot, suddenly a dark shadow moved among the brush at the edge of the line. Nathan stared, not sure if it was man or animal. Then there was a flash and a puff of smoke. "Watch out!" Nathan screamed. The sound of the rifle's explosion hit them a second later.

Nathan reacted instantly, dropping low over the saddle, knowing even as he did so that if the man hadn't fired hastily, there would be no reaction at all now. The shadow had dropped to one knee, and Nathan realized he was going to reload. He dug his heels into the flanks of the horse. "Let's go, Matthew! After him!"

Nathan raised his own rifle and fired, knowing there was no hope of hitting the man at this distance and from the back of a horse. But all he wanted to do was scare him off, and that he did. He saw the man leap up, spin around, and disappear into the trees.

Derek reined up sharply and stood up in the stirrups. "Did you hear that?"

Lyman Wight didn't have to answer. "No more than a quarter mile I'd say," he blurted. "Let's go!"

In an instant, six horses were stretched out, hooves pounding as they raced northward across the prairie toward the trees that lined Grand River.

When they reached the brush and trees, Nathan and Matthew pulled up sharply. They swung down, weapons ready, searching the undergrowth with anxious eyes. Both they and the horses were breathing hard. Suddenly there was a noise off to their left. They swung around.

"There they go!" Matthew shouted, pointing. About fifty yards away, two horsemen burst from cover. They were both low in the saddle and whipping the reins back and forth against their horses.

Matthew lowered his rifle, feeling his shoulders sag. "I don't think they want any more fight," he breathed.

"I think you're right," Nathan said, wanting to laugh with the relief that was suddenly hitting him. And then he had a thought. "Let's go see what those two were up to."

They had gotten only a short distance when Matthew stopped, holding up his hand. "Listen!"

They both turned and again the sound came. It was faint but unmistakable. "Help! Help!"

The cold was biting now, and Peter's teeth were starting to chatter. He was also shivering violently. He kept telling himself his trembling was only from the cold, but he knew better. He kept twisting around, in spite of the biting pain where the ropes dug into his wrists, trying to see what was happening. His captors had just gotten him stripped to the waist and tied to the cottonwood tree when one of them shouted something about someone coming. They had both grabbed their rifles and gone running off.

Then there had been two shots—one close, one more distant—followed by the sounds of men and horses running.

Suddenly he froze. Behind him, a twig had snapped. Instantly his pulse was pounding wildly again. His eyes were wide and frightened. He leaned forward against the tree, pretending he hadn't heard. There was the rustling of dry leaves. Closer now. He closed his eyes, not wanting to see.

"Peter?"

His eyes flew open and his head snapped around. The ropes bit hard into his wrists, but he was barely aware of them. He was staring in dumbfounded shock. "Nathan?" His knees gave way and he sagged downward, suddenly so giddy that he thought he would faint. "Matthew?" he whispered.

In three great leaps, Nathan was to him, whipping out his pocketknife. "It's all right, Peter. We're here. We're here."

Peter was half laughing, half crying. He felt the ropes bite deeper for a second and winced, but then he was free. His knees felt like rubber as Nathan dragged him up and threw his arms around him. Matthew was to them both, trying to get his arms around Peter and Nathan all together.

"How did you two—"

Nathan swung around as there was the crashing of someone coming through the brush. He started to grab for his rifle, then saw there was no need. He stepped back as Derek hurtled through the last stand of undergrowth and picked Peter up in a crushing bear hug.

When they finally pulled apart, the smile on Peter's face died. "Brother Sterling is right over there. He needs help."

They stopped where the wagon track from Daviess County joined the road running east and west between Haun's Mill and Far West. It was about half an hour before sundown, and the whole western sky was filled with the softness of muted sunlight. The heavy overcast was gone now, but there was still a high, thin layer of clouds that filtered the lowering sun.

Derek and Rebecca were on the wagon seat. Peter was sitting just behind them, next to the pitifully small pile of belongings they had taken from the sod hut. Matthew's horse—or better, Heber C. Kimball's horse—had been hitched to the wagon. Nathan and Matthew were riding double on Nathan's horse. No trace of Derek's horse had been found.

Matthew slid off, then Nathan swung his leg over the saddle and did the same. They stretched, letting the kinks from almost twenty-four straight hours in the saddle work themselves out a little. Then Nathan led the horse forward and tied the reins to the back of the wagon.

"You sure you don't want to keep him?" Derek asked.

"No," Nathan answered. "These horses are completely beat. It's only a few miles to Haun's Mill. Then we'll have John's team and wagon to come back."

Rebecca looked down at her brothers. She tried to smile, but she was so filled with gratitude that she was nearer to tears. "You both look as tired as the horses. Maybe you ought to come home first, then go back tomorrow."

Matthew shook his head. "Last night Pa said it was important that we leave immediately." He turned and grinned at Peter. "I think we all know why now. But we're not through until we have Jessica and John back with us too."

"You'll be all right now," Nathan said, the weariness showing in the lines of his face. "It's only an hour to Far West, and the mobbers haven't dared come this close yet. One of us would go with you the rest of the way, but Pa said me and Matthew are to stay together no matter what."

"We'll be fine," Derek said. His eyes softened, remembering the feelings that had swept over him when he saw Peter standing there, bare to the waist, with Nathan and Matthew trying to hug him. He also remembered what Brother Sterling's back and face had looked like and knew that Peter had come within minutes, if not seconds, of sharing in that condition. He swallowed at the sudden lump in his throat. "Really, we'll be fine."

Nathan nodded. "Tell Pa that we won't risk running into any Missourians tonight. We're going to hole up somewhere once it get's dark, then go the rest of the way in the morning.

So it will be late afternoon or early tomorrow night before we'll be back. Also, tell Mother and Lydia not to worry. Everything's going to be fine now."

"We will," Rebecca said. Then suddenly the tears she had held in since the moment she had returned to find Peter gone spilled over. She stood up, turned, and quickly climbed down from the wagon. Then with her head held high, not even trying to wipe at the streaks on her face, she walked to her brothers, reaching out her hands. She clasped Nathan and Matthew tightly, and for a minute they all stood there awkwardly, in a rough circle bound together by love. "Thank you," she finally managed. "Thank you both for coming for us."

"Yes, sir," Joshua said, standing at attention. "You sent for me, sir?"

"I did," General Atchison said. "At ease, Steed. Sit down for a few minutes."

Joshua did so, a little surprised. Atchison was usually very formal with him.

"Have you heard the news?"

Joshua's head came up. He knew about the clash at Crooked River, but that news had come in four days previously. And Atchison knew he knew about that. From the gravity he could see in the officer's eyes, Joshua sensed that this was not going to be good.

Softly, with obvious reluctance and open disgust, Atchison told Joshua of the news that had just reached Richmond. He did not have written confirmation, but the word was undoubtedly true: Governor Boggs had ordered the Mormons driven from the state or exterminated.

Joshua was stunned and sickened, not wanting to accept what Atchison was saying, but knowing full well it was true.

Atchison sat back and laughed in self-derision. "General Clark has also been given command of the militia."

Joshua's head came up at that. "But you're senior to Clark, sir."

Atchison laughed again, this time bitterly. "I've been what you could call 'dismounted.' I think His Excellency is afraid that I'm too sympathetic to the Mormons. Where Doniphan and I have served as legal counsel to Joseph Smith . . ." He didn't finish. There wasn't any need to. "Clark will have General Lucas with him. They'll have about two thousand men."

Lucas! Joshua had ridden with Lucas when they drove the Mormons from Jackson County. Lucas was unbendable when it came to the Mormon problem. He and Boggs were old cronies. Exterminate them or drive them from the state. It was the kind of order Lucas would relish. It made Joshua's stomach churn to think of what Lucas would say when he heard it.

He looked up, realizing Atchison was speaking to him.

"—understand how you feel, Steed. I've been willing to keep you out of the north so you wouldn't have to face it directly. But that's not possible anymore. The militia is headed for Far West. I won't be going as yet. But I want you to join Lucas's group."

"But, sir—"

Atchison raised one hand. "You go with Lucas. If you're going to do any good for your family, it's not going to be down here. Besides, I need someone I can trust. We'll do what we can to keep this thing from getting totally out of hand."

"I don't care what kind of agreement you've made with this Jennings," Nathan exploded. "John, it is not safe out here."

John Griffith was a short man, and quiet. Usually he was content to sit and listen at the family gatherings, speaking only rarely. But beneath that quiet exterior there was a firm-minded, unbendable will. He shook his head. "Colonel Jennings is the sheriff of Livingston County. He also commands the militia there. He and Brother Haun struck a deal. A treaty. As long as we don't take arms against the people around here, they'll leave us alone. He promised to do his best to prevent any hostilities."

"And you believe that?" Nathan shouted.

Jessica reached up and touched his arm. She and John were seated at the table. Matthew had collapsed in a chair. Nathan stood near the table, towering over them. "Nathan," she soothed, "we know your concern, but Mr. Jennings seems like an honorable man. He gave us his word."

Nathan threw his hands up, whirling away. "I can't believe this. I just can't believe it." He spun back, really angry now. "It's one o'clock in the afternoon. Matthew and me started at dawn this morning to try and get here. Do you know why it took until now? Because the whole countryside is crawling with men. Men with guns. Men with murder on their minds."

Matthew turned to Jessica. "We saw one group who had their faces all painted like Indians. Whooping and hollering like savages."

Neither John nor Jessica said anything.

Nathan decided to try a different tack. "And what about Brother Joseph?"

John turned, looking surprised. "What about Brother Joseph?"

"Didn't Brother Haun tell you?"

"Tell us what?" Jessica asked.

Nathan turned back, his mouth tight. "Day before yesterday, Joseph specifically warned Jacob Haun about your staying out here. He told him to bring you all into Far West until this is settled. Pa was there. He heard it all."

Jessica looked at her husband, the concern pulling at the corners of her mouth. "Did you know that, John?"

He shook his head. "Brother Haun said nothing."

Matthew jumped on that quickly. "Joseph's the prophet. Are you going to ignore the counsel of the prophet?"

John sat back, clearly troubled now.

Nathan put his hands on the table and leaned over until he was looking right into his brother-in-law's eyes. His voice went from anger to pleading now. "John, the whole countryside is aflame. I don't know if we can even make it back. But we've got to try. Please, come home with us."

John Griffith was staring at his hands. "Did you see those wagons and teams outside?"

"Yes."

"Some new families arrived about noon yesterday, right after church services. Joseph Young, one of the seven Presidents of the Seventy, is the leader. They barely made it this far. A mob stopped them and turned them back. They also took their weapons."

"That's no surprise," Nathan muttered.

"They want to rest up here a few days before pushing on to Far West." Nathan started to shake his head, but John finally looked up. "There was a meeting. It was decided that, for now at least, we'll all stick together and defend ourselves." Now his eyes were pleading for Nathan's understanding. "We were all party to this agreement. If I go now, it looks like . . ." He took a quick breath. "I can't just leave my brethren. If they're staying, I have to stay too. I'll talk to Haun. See if he'll reconsider."

"He won't!" Nathan said flatly. "John, I understand how you feel. But you've got to listen to the Prophet. And Mother and Father Steed are worried sick about you. Please come back with us."

John's head turned slowly and he searched Jessica's face. Finally, he spoke. "Why don't you and the children go with them? I'll see if I can't talk some sense into the others—"

She was shaking her head firmly. "I will not leave you, John. If you are staying, I'm staying."

Nathan felt like screaming. He and Matthew had had about four hours of sleep in the last thirty-six hours, and it was as if he were walking in a thick fog. He fought down the temptation to reach out and shake them both violently. Then suddenly he knew it was no use. And he knew they had to settle for second best. "Then let us take Rachel and the boys," he said quietly. There was no use asking for the baby. John Benjamin Griffith was just seven months old and still nursing.

Husband and wife looked at each other for a long moment, and something passed between them. Jessica stood up. "I'll get their things."

John stood now too. "I want you to take our wagon."

Nathan nodded, too weary to protest. "Matthew and I are going to try and get a few hours of sleep. We don't dare go until it's dark."

Chapter Notes

The tying of Mormon men to trees and flogging them was happening frequently during this period (see *CHFT*, p. 198).

There was a treaty struck on the twenty-eighth of October between a Colonel Jennings of Livingston County and the Saints in Haun's Mill (see *HC* 3:183). This seems to be part of what gave the members at Haun's Mill courage to stay where they were.

Chapter Seventeen

Jessica Roundy Steed Griffith stopped shucking corn for a moment and let her eyes sweep across the little settlement of Haun's Mill. It had been one of those late Indian-summer days. The sky was clear and blue, and the sun was warm—warm enough that many of the children were barefoot. But it had none of the oppressiveness of July or August. In the meadows across the creek, half a dozen horses and cows stood lazily in the sun, motionless except for the occasional twitch of their tails. Directly south of where Jessica sat, about a hundred yards away, two men were in a field digging potatoes. Further on, her husband, John, was in their cornfield. She could see the steady rise and fall of his arm as he slashed at the dried stalks with the corn knife. He was too far away for her to hear the crackle of the dry stalks, but just by watching him she knew that by tomorrow there would be several more bushels of corn to husk.

From the open door of the cabin a few yards away a woman was singing softly to herself. Down by the creek and the small millpond the children were playing some game or another, and their squeals and shouts provided a music of their own. Though pleasant, it brought a pang to Jessica. Missing was the voice of Rachel and the giggling of Mark and Luke. It had not even been twenty-four hours since they had gone with Nathan and Matthew, but she already missed them fiercely.

From another direction there was the steady ringing of the hammer and the anvil. Several of the families who had arrived two days earlier had problems with their wagons. So their menfolk had taken the wagons to the blacksmith shop for the repairs they would need before the families could continue their trek to Far West.

"Sure is a beautiful day, isn't it?"

Jessica looked up at Amanda Smith and smiled as she nodded. "Lovely. This is my favorite time of the year."

"Mine too."

As she tossed the bare ear into the wooden bowl and took another unhusked ear from the basket, Jessica reflected about the woman who sat beside her and the depths of their friendship that had developed in such a short time.

Jessica Roundy had grown up in a saloon. She had been around men—and certainly not the best of them—for her entire childhood and adolescent years. She had never had girlfriends. She had never sat around and giggled or whispered secrets or played house or talked about boys. And so as a woman she had found it somewhat difficult to make friends with other women. That was one of the reasons why the Steeds meant so much to her. Lydia and Rebecca and Mary Ann had been wonderful to her and for her.

She did much better now. She felt more comfortable with the women in the settlement, but there was none that she could really call a close friend. Then on Sunday the group of families led by Elder Joseph Young—an older brother of Brigham Young's, and senior President of the Seventy—had arrived in Haun's Mill. They had left Kirtland on July first, a few days before

Haun's Mill

the main body of the Kirtland Camp departed, but they took a longer route and had been delayed several times.

Jessica and John had gone down to meet the new families after dinner. They came across the Smith family just setting up their tent down near the gristmill. It was one of those times when there was almost instant bonding. John Griffith and Warren Smith were quickly immersed in conversation about the area, about the goodness of the land, and about the seriousness of the situation that was confronting them. And in what seemed like a matter of just moments, Jessica and Amanda Smith felt as though they had been friends and close neighbors for years. Jessica had never experienced anything quite like it, and before half an hour had passed, she and John had persuaded the Smith family to bring their wagon and tent to camp near the creek a short distance behind their cabin. The previous evening, after Nathan and Matthew had left with the children, the Griffiths and the Smiths had talked long into the night. They had agreed that as soon as the company was ready, Jessica and John would go with them to Far West. Then, once things were more settled, the Smiths would come back out to Haun's Mill and make it their home. The prospects were thrilling to Jessica, even more than she expected they would be.

Amanda looked up. "Looks like Warren has finished at the blacksmith's."

Jessica turned to follow her gaze and saw Warren Smith and his three young sons coming toward them. She started to nod, but a sound from behind cut her off. They turned. A man was running hard toward them from the direction of the creek. He was yelling and half turning to point behind him as he ran.

"Oh, dear Lord!" Amanda gasped. "Look!" She was pointing now too at something she saw across the creek and through the trees.

Jessica felt a sickening lurch. A large body of horsemen was coming toward them at a hard gallop, no more than a hundred yards away. It took only an instant to take it all in, and the images would ever stay frozen in her mind: Horses stretched to their limits, necks lathered, nostrils flaring. Chunks of dirt and sod flinging upward from the thundering hooves, then falling again like rain. Men bent low in their saddles, rifles in one hand, reins in the other, spurring their horses forward ever faster. The wild yells of two hundred men, rending the air with a chilling savagery. Startled children jumping up to stare, then shrieking with terror and scattering like baby chicks before the darting fox.

Jessica swung around, the shout tearing from her throat. "John!"

He was too far away to hear her, but he had evidently seen it too. The corn knife went sailing, the armload of cornstalks dropped at his feet. And then he was running hard toward her, joining the two men who had been digging potatoes. He was waving his arms frantically. And then his voice came to her, barely loud enough to hear. "Get the baby! Get the baby!"

The baby! She whirled around, darted inside, snatched the infant from his crib. John Benjamin instantly began to howl. Jessica barely heard it. She dashed back to the doorway and out onto the porch. In the large meadow around which Haun's Mill was built there was widespread pandemonium. Women were running, hair and skirts flying, shouting and screaming the names of their children. Children shrieked and howled. Men were dropping tools and racing back towards their families. Amanda was at the end of the porch, leaning over the railing, yelling at her two girls who were down by the creek playing. She turned back and shouted at her husband and sons.

Jessica's head jerked around and she looked toward the creek. The company of men had split into a three-square formation and the lead riders were just crossing the stream, sending out great sprays of water. With a sudden chill, she realized that many of the men had painted faces.

Her head whipped back around, eyes searching frantically for John. He wouldn't make it. Couldn't make it. The riders were moving too fast. Then she spotted him and felt a great rush of relief. He and the other men had concluded the same thing and changed directions. They were in a desperate sprint for the blacksmith shop. And they would make that.

Closer to her, Warren Smith and his three boys were frozen in midstride. Warren was staring—gaping—at the men who were thundering toward them. Behind him, from the blacksmith shop, Jessica saw Captain David Evans come running out. He was the commander of their home defense forces. He had his hat off and was swinging it back and forth wildly. "Peace! Peace!" he shouted. "Give us quarter!"

A rifle cracked sharply behind her. The dirt in front of Warren Smith kicked up, and there was the angry whine of a ricochet.

"*Warren!*" Amanda's cry was so shrill it was barely comprehensible. Her hands were clawing at the porch railing.

"Get back," Warren cried hoarsely. Then grabbing his two youngest sons by the arm, he started falling back toward the blacksmith shop again, half dragging them as he went. But Willard, at eleven the oldest of the three boys, stood rooted to the spot, petrified by the sound of gunfire that was crashing all around them now.

"Willard!" It was a scream of pure terror.

Amanda's shout got her husband's attention. He looked over his shoulder and realized what had happened. "Run, Willard!" he bellowed. "Run!" That broke the spell and the boy turned and raced after his father.

"Mama! Mama!" Amanda's two girls were screaming in terror as they came running to the house. In one leap she was over the railing and gathering them into her arms.

Rifle fire was resounding like ever-recurring claps of thunder now. Without thinking, Jessica dropped to a crouch, holding the wailing baby tightly to her breast. A bullet slapped into a log just above her head with a vicious thud. A rider went hurtling past, firing on the run. Somewhere back in her mind her eyes registered the savagery of the man's face—skin darkened with lampblack, eyes wild and filled with ferocity. And yet he was a white man.

An exclamation of relief was torn from her throat. John had reached the blacksmith shop and disappeared behind it on the far side, where the doorway was. Coming right behind him was Amanda's family. They too disappeared around the building, and Jessica knew they had made it. Amanda had seen it too. Dragging her sobbing girls with her, she came up on the porch. Jessica grabbed her arm. "Inside!" she hollered into her ear. "Hurry!"

"Run! Faster! Come on!"

John Griffith and Captain Evans stood at the corner of the log building, frantically waving at the men and boys who were darting and dodging from every part of the village towards them. It had been determined two days before that the blacksmith shop was the most solid structure in Haun's Mill, and that if an attack did come, the men would go there to defend the village. Now those who were anywhere in its vicinity were retreating toward it. Elsewhere, men, women, and children were bolting for the trees and brush that lined the creek and for the high ground beyond it. Horsemen wheeled off from the main party, trying to cut them off or ride them down. The gunfire was one continuous roar, and bullets were flying like a swarm of angry yellow jackets.

About twenty yards away, John saw a man run out of his cabin, hands in the air. He watched in horror as the nearest horseman reined around and fired at him from almost point-blank range. The man slammed backwards against the hitching rail, then went down. From inside the cabin a woman screamed.

With a start, John realized that Warren Smith and his three boys were coming toward him now. Ducking down, he ran out to meet them. He grabbed the youngest by the hand. "Run, Alma!" he blurted. "Come on, Sardius! Run!" He backpedalled now, pulling Alma with him. He swung the boy around and gave him a shove, propelling him toward the open doorway. Evans caught the boy as he nearly stumbled. He dragged him inside. Warren and Sardius were next. The father literally picked his ten-year-old son up and dove through the open doorway. Seeing that the last boy was right behind him, John darted inside the doorway.

"We've got to shut the door," Evans bayed into John's ear.

John stepped back. "This is the last one."

But as eleven-year-old Willard reached the door, his hands flew out horizontally, catching the two side beams and instantly arresting his progress. His mouth dropped open as he bounced back two or three feet. Again he dove for the doorway and again his hands flew out, stopping his entry.

"Willard!" Warren Smith screamed.

"Come on, Willard!" John urged.

The boy tried it a third time, but again it was as though he hit some invisible force at the doorway. John lunged forward to grab him, but Willard, terrified at the sounds of horsemen right behind him, gave it up. He leaped away, running hard for a woodpile a few yards away. He scampered behind it and disappeared.

"No!" Warren shouted as David Evans started pushing the door shut. "Willard!"

John caught Warren and dragged him back. Evans gave them both a hard shove. "Get out of the way! We have to shut the door!"

Warren Smith was flailing at both of them now, desperate to fight his way outside. Then he stiffened with a jerk. There was a heavy grunt. His head turned, mouth agape, and he stared at John Griffith for a moment. Then his knees buckled and he sagged downward, pulling free from John's grasp and sliding to the floor.

John was stunned. He stared down at Warren, not comprehending. Evans shoved John hard and slammed the door shut, dropping the latch.

"Watch out!"

John would never know who yelled the warning. Someone behind him. He swung around in time to see the muzzle of a rifle poke through a crack between the logs. There was a blinding flash, and simultaneously a searing pain ripped through his gut. He staggered back, smacking against the wooden cupboard that held the blacksmith's tools. As things spilled off the shelves he felt them bounce off his shoulders. Then slowly he dropped to his knees, clutching at his stomach.

He screamed in agony as his body took another ball, this time high in the shoulder. It felt like his arm had been torn out of its socket. He went down to the dirt floor, gasping in shock and pain, rolling over on his back and coming up against the east wall. Grunting as the waves of pain began to roll over him, he saw bright flashes directly above him. And then he realized what was wrong. The blacksmith's shop was a fortress, but it had one primary flaw. The gaps between the thick logs had never been chinked. Some were two or three inches wide. Now a dozen guns, maybe more, were jammed through the cracks and were pouring a withering fire into the narrow confines of the shed. The fortress had become a death trap.

No longer sure if the roaring in his ears was from the gunfire or the pain, John Griffith turned his head. A body lay just in front of him. Another man was hunched over the anvil, blood pouring from a wound in his head. "I am shot! I am shot!" he moaned over and over.

John blinked. He wanted to rub his hands over his eyes, clear his vision. But though his brain gave the command, nothing happened. With a curious sense of detachment, he realized he could no longer feel his hands.

John turned his head slowly, as the rifles kept exploding above him. Sardius Smith was huddled under the bellows, his face twisted with terror. Beside him, lying very still, was little Alma. The side of his trousers, up high near the hip, was a mass of blood. Dimly, and with a faint feeling of outrage, John realized that Alma had been shot. He wasn't sure if the boy was dead or unconscious, but his face was very pale and he wasn't moving.

"We've got to make a break for it, or we're dead men!" It sounded like Captain Evans's voice, but John couldn't be sure.

He saw the door flung open and dark figures race across the sudden brightness. And then, though he fought it back with frightened desperation, the blackness slipped across his line of vision, and John Griffith closed his eyes.

Young Willard Smith could hear men running behind him as he made a leaping dive for cover behind the small woodpile that belonged to the blacksmith. He burrowed in between the boards and logs, momentarily hesitating at the thoughts of black widow spiders, centipedes, or other horrible things that might be hiding in there. But those thoughts left him instantly. A bullet hit a board right over his head with a solid thwack. Splinters sprayed into his hair, some with enough force to sting his head. Another ball thudded into the split log right in front of his face.

Heart racing, Willard peeped out through a small opening. There were men everywhere. Most of them were running up and jamming their guns up against the wall of the shop—an action that struck him as being an odd thing to do. But two of the men had their rifles trained on the woodpile. A third joined them. One of the men pointed and the third one threw his rifle to his shoulder and fired directly at Willard.

Willard ducked as the ball hit just to the left of him. Dust flew, half blinding him. In terror, he backed out of his hiding place and scudded away, weaving in and out so as to make himself a more difficult target.

"There's the kid! There he goes!"

Willard's feet literally flew across the ground. The crash of rifle fire was steady, and though he knew differently, he felt like every bullet was aimed specifically at him. He saw a flash of movement by one cabin and kept running, headed for the cabins down by the millpond where there seemed to be fewer riders and gunmen.

The window in the back of Jessica's cabin was not meant to open. She dragged a bench over to it, then ran back to the line of hooks by the fireplace and retrieved a large black frying pan. Glass was a luxury on the frontier, and they had paid dearly for it. But she did not hesitate. One swing of the heavy pan and the window shattered. Behind her, Amanda was hugging her two daughters to her, trying to soothe them. Jessica's baby was on the bed, screaming so hysterically that he could barely get his breath. Gripping the frying pan with both hands now, Jessica hammered at the edges of the window, making sure there were no pieces of glass left to cut them as they went out.

She dropped the frying pan and spun around. "You go first, Amanda. I'll help the girls, then hand you the baby."

With her daughters wailing pitifully, Amanda gathered up her skirts and went out the window head first, kicking herself through until she dropped to the ground. Instantly she was back up and reaching her arms through the window. Jessica helped the younger girl up to the bench, then out into her mother's arms. The second followed.

"All right," Amanda cried. "Give me the baby."

Jessica pulled the blanket over the baby's face, kissed him quickly on the top of the head, and handed him out the window. As Amanda clasped the baby to her, her eyes flew open. She was staring over Jessica's shoulder. Then she screamed. "Jessie, watch out!"

Jessica whirled. The front door of the cabin had flown open and there was a man with a rifle standing in the frame. The only thing that saved her was the fact that the inside of the cabin was very dim compared to the bright sunlight outside. His head was swinging back and forth, trying to make out what was happening.

Without thinking, Jessica dropped to one knee and scooped up the frying pan. She grabbed the handle with both hands and sidearmed it across the room. It struck the edge of the door just a few inches above the man's head, but the force of the blow sent the door slamming into his rifle arm. He yelped in surprise and pain, and stumbled backwards. In two great leaps Jessica was to the door and slammed it shut in his face, yanking the catch that held the latch from being lifted from outside. There was a shout, then a stream of profanity. Then the man started pounding on the door with the butt of his rifle.

"Come on, Jessie!" Amanda screamed.

But Jessica knew the catch would not withstand the pounding it was taking if she let go of it. There was no way she could make it out the window before the man would be inside again.

The pounding on the door stopped, and she heard the man step back. Jessica leaned forward trying to hear. The clap of the rifle's detonation nearly deafened her. The Missourian had fired at the latch at a range of no more than two feet. The ball missed the latch entirely but pierced the door exactly where Jessica had pressed her left hand against it to hold it shut.

Her hand flew backwards, half spinning her around. Falling back two or three steps, she stared dumbly at the ragged hole that went in the palm of her hand and out the back. Blood was pouring out of the torn flesh. She felt her knees start to give way and felt her stomach heave.

"Jessie!" Amanda had seen it all and now screamed out her name with every ounce of strength she had.

It brought Jessica out of her near faint. Gasping as the excruciating pain hit her now, she stumbled to the cupboard where she kept her linens. Dizzy, pale as a new sheet of paper, she pulled open a drawer with her good hand and pulled out a dish towel. Leaning against the cupboard, she wrapped the cloth around her hand.

"Come on, Jessie! Hurry. Before he reloads."

And in that instant Jessica knew with perfect clarity that she and Amanda couldn't make it. Not with that man outside. She could still hear him, swearing as he fought to reload his rifle. She swung around, searching the floor in the dim light. Then she saw it. With her left arm cradled against her body, she picked up the frying pan. She moved quietly to the door, took a breath, then carefully removed the catch, leaving the outside latch clear. Then she stepped back.

In a moment, she heard the man's steps on the porch again and she saw the latch lift. The door flew open with a crash and the man jumped into the room. Amanda was still at the open window and the baby was still howling. The man's head jerked in that direction and the rifle started up. But he got no further than that. The heavy metal pan caught him right above the hairline of his neck. There was a loud clang, a soft explosion of air, and he went sprawling, the rifle clattering harmlessly to the floor.

Jessica didn't bother to check if he was out or not. She didn't have to. She pushed the door shut again, shoved the catch home, and walked swiftly to the window. "You'll have to help me, Amanda. I can't use my hand."

When they had first arrived in Haun's Mill, the Smith family had started to set up camp not far from the gristmill. There were two cabins there. One was Jacob Haun's. The other belonged to a Father McBride, an old man with nearly white hair. Brother Haun had introduced the family to McBride, and Willard Smith and his brothers had been awestruck. McBride had been born in 1776 and as a young boy had seen some of the revolutionary war. He had actually seen George Washington with his own eyes. That had won him the total hero worship of three young boys.

So when young Willard, running in blind panic from his hiding place in the woodpile, saw McBride's cabin, he veered toward it. Gulping breaths of air in huge, hungry chunks, Willard slid to a stop at the corner of the house and peered carefully around the corner. There was no one there. In three quick jumps he was across the small porch and through the front door.

Slumping back against a wall below one of the windows, Willard tried to get his breath. Outside, all hell was raging. He closed his eyes, trying to calm a heart that pounded so furiously that he thought he might die.

Suddenly his head snapped up. In one corner of the cabin there was a hole in the floor. It was a small root cellar, and the door was laid open. Then his eyes bulged a little. A red smear across the floor led right to the opening. Gingerly now, staying on all fours, he crawled over to the hole and peeked over the edge. Willard jumped nearly a foot. There was a body there. And the body's eyes were open.

Then the terror left him. It was Father McBride. A large red stain covered most of his shirtfront. He was wheezing, and his face was twisted with shock. Willard was up and in the hole almost instantly. He took the old man's hand and held it tight. "Father McBride, are you all right?"

Awareness came back into the eyes as McBride groaned. "Help me out," he whispered. "Get me out of here."

Frightened beyond reason, mouth so dry he could barely swallow, but filled with compassion for this wounded old man, Willard got his hands under McBride's shoulder. Crying out, wincing and twisting with agony, McBride helped as best he could until Willard had him laid out on the planking of the floor.

"Water."

Willard stared at him.

"I need water. Please."

Willard looked around. A tin cup sat on the wooden table. Not daring to stop and think about what he was doing, Willard ran to it, grabbed it, and dashed outside. The millpond was only a few steps away. But even as he darted out of the door, Willard was spotted. Three men were in front of a cabin thirty yards or so away. They shouted, wheeled around, and started firing. As Willard hunkered down at the water's edge, scooping up a cupful of water, bullets started pinging in the pond around him.

"Get 'im!" he heard one of the men shout as he flew back across the open ground to the cabin.

Willard ducked inside. In a moment he had McBride's head

cradled in one arm and was helping him drink. McBride finished and pushed himself up against a log stool. "Thank you, son," he said in a halting voice. "Thank you."

A window pane shattered, and Willard instinctively cringed. Another bullet whizzed by his head, coming through the open door, and thudded into the far wall. In one flash of understanding, Willard knew that if he stayed, the men would come for him and find McBride. "I've got to go," he said, reaching out to straighten the old man as best he could.

"I surrendered my gun to them." It came out as no more than a croak. There was no mistaking the bewilderment in his eyes. "And they still shot me."

"You'll be all right, Father McBride," Willard whispered. "I've got to go." Without looking back, he shot out the front door and was barreling across the small open space to the next cabin.

"I can't make it!"

"Yes, you can!" Amanda hissed in her ear.

"I can't, Amanda." Jessica's legs felt like rubber, and there were flashing lights in front of her eyes. She knew that shock was setting in. They were nearly to the creek, but it was not a straight run. A line of half a dozen men had spotted them as they had come out from behind Jessica's cabin. Some were on foot, some were on horseback. The opportunity to have four running targets in their sights, four targets that couldn't shoot back, was too good for the men to pass up. The two women zigzagged back and forth, half bent over, Amanda half dragging her screeching daughters, Jessica hugging the baby to her to shield him from any lucky shot. John Benjamin's cries were now little more than hoarse, exhausted gasps.

Amanda reached out and took Jessica's elbow. "Come on," she urged. "If we can get across . . ." She reached out and took the baby from Jessica. "I'll help you."

They had reached that point where the millpond was held

back by a small dam and the millrace. A twelve-inch-wide plank crossed over the race. Beyond it the banks of the creek rose sharply for several feet. Jessica saw instantly what Amanda was doing. If they could get across the plank and up the bank, the riders could not follow them. They slowed only enough to cross the board without falling off, Amanda hanging on to the baby and trying to herd her little girls as well. As they made the far bank and started clambering up the slope, Jessica tripped and went down. Without thinking, she threw out her left hand to catch herself. As it struck the ground, she screamed out, writhing in agony.

Amanda leaned over her. "Get up, Jessie!" she shouted. "Get up!"

A bullet slapped into the water just behind them. That galvanized Jessica into action. Sobbing now with the pain and terror, she stumbled to her feet and followed Amanda up the bank of the creek. But the effort was too much for her. She dropped to her knees, panting in huge, desperate gulps of air. "I can't. Oh, Amanda! Please! I can't. Save my baby."

Amanda looked down at her, her face stricken. Her younger daughter was shrieking, pulling at her skirts. "Mama! Mama!"

"*Please!*"

Amanda nodded, reached down and touched Jessica's face briefly, and then turned and ran into the brush, herding her two girls, clutching the baby tightly against her.

Another ball hit just to Jessica's left, kicking dirt into her face. The target was down and not moving. Driven by that same inner core of strength that had once taken her twenty-five miles across a frozen prairie with Rachel hanging onto her skirts, Jessica moaned and rolled over. Pushing herself up, she clambered up to the top of the small rise, using her knees, one hand, and her left elbow. About ten yards away there was a dead tree that had fallen to the earth many years before. It was nearly two feet high and over thirty long. Scuttling like a crippled crab, she reached it and, with one last cry of pain, heaved herself over and fell to the soft earth behind it.

There was a thud as a ball whipped into the softness of the rotting bark. Then another. But the log was nearly two feet thick and she knew they couldn't reach her. Half-faint with pain, soaked clear through, muddy, bruised, exhausted, and terrified that her attackers might come after her, Jessica Griffith lay behind her log. Incredibly, some distant part of her mind kept count as the bullets continued smacking into the log over and over. Just before she reached the count of twenty, her eyes slowly rolled up in her head, and, mercifully, she passed out.

Inside the cabin next to Father McBride's, Willard Smith bent over a chair, gulping in air hungrily. He looked around. The cabin was empty. He moved to the door to shut it, then froze. From this vantage point he could see the front entry to McBride's cabin. The door was still open and, to Willard's horror, McBride was standing in it, leaning heavily against the frame. Somehow he had managed to drag himself out and pull himself up to a standing position.

The three men who had been coming for Willard saw McBride and changed direction. As they drew closer, Willard noticed now that they had blackened their faces and put red cloths on their shirts and hats, so they looked like Indians. But they weren't Indians. They had white men's hair and beards and light skin. The one in the lead had something else in his hands besides his rifle. As the man ran, Willard saw in horror that it was a corn cutter, a knife with a wooden handle and a long, curved blade. McBride straightened and stepped out onto his porch. "Mercy!" he cried.

There was a laugh of derision, and Willard saw the corn cutter come up high as the man came at McBride on the dead run. Willard gagged, then slammed the door shut. He jammed his hands over his ears. It was not enough. There was a strangled cry, then a fiendish scream of triumph.

The slamming door had evidently caught the attention of the other men, for a rifle cracked and a hole suddenly blossomed in the upper panel of the door. Frantic now, Willard turned. His heart leaped. There was a back door! He started across for it, and then stopped in midstep. There had been a sound from the corner. Someone was crying. There was a double bed there. He saw a movement beneath it. In three steps he was to it and knelt down and lifted the valance.

There was a quick intake of breath. A white, very frightened face with large brown eyes was staring out at him. Stunned, Willard looked more closely. There was another face. And another. He dropped down flat on his belly. "It's all right," he soothed. He counted quickly. There were six of them. All of them girls. The oldest no more than ten. The youngest, three or four.

Willard didn't hesitate. Bullets were still hitting the front of the cabin. "Come on!" he said, reaching out for the closest hand. "You can't stay here."

As they crawled out, crying and wailing softly, he gave them a stern look. "Everybody take somebody's hand." They did so. "Whatever you do, don't let go." He forced himself to smile at them. "All right?"

Six heads bobbed simultaneously. "All right. Now, we're going out the back. When I say run, you run as fast as you have ever run in your life. *And don't let go!*"

He opened the back door, looked around quickly. There was no more time to make sure they understood. "All right," he said, tugging on the first girl's hand. "Run!"

They were out the door and scrambling toward the millpond. Willard headed for the narrow end of the pond, where the plank crossed over the millrace. Across the stream there was a cornfield. There was also a lot of brush and trees. If they could make that, they would have a chance.

If Willard had any hopes that the sight of little girls might deter the men coming after him, those hopes were soon shattered. A shout went up. He felt a whoosh of air go past his cheek. The pond looked like someone was throwing pebbles into it. But Willard didn't care anymore. Slowing just enough to make sure the girls could negotiate the board without falling off, Willard led his little parade in full flight away from the cabin.

As the last little girl jumped off the board onto solid ground, Willard's instructions were forgotten. Screaming and crying, the six of them scattered like prairie chickens, disappearing into the high corn or the thick clumps of hazel brush.

Stunned for a moment, not sure if he should go after them, the boy-turned-rescuer didn't move. Then there was a shout from behind him. Evidently children were not sport enough to draw the men across the creek. They had turned and were running off toward some other target.

For several moments, Willard Smith just stood there, chest heaving, staring at the disappearing forms of his tormentors. Then, looking around, he found a large tree and moved behind it. The undergrowth around it was thick enough to give him good cover but low enough that he could see over it and watch what was happening at the village. He sank down, feeling the rough bark against his back, trying to ignore the fact that his whole body was trembling violently now.

The pain was everywhere. In his mind. Throbbing at his fingertips. Behind his eyelids. In big fiery waves through the center of his body.

John Griffith was barely conscious of anything but the pain. But then it all came back in a burst of reality almost more intense than the physical pain. The blacksmith shop. The rifle muzzles firing. He realized with a start that, while he could still hear gunfire, it was now outside, distant, not exploding directly over his head.

He opened his eyes and turned his head slightly. The door to the shop stood open, and late afternoon sunlight flooded the room, revealing the horrors that lay around him. Sardius Smith was still lying under the bellows beside his younger brother. The boy saw John looking at him, but he was so terrified that it didn't seem to register. Alma's eyes were closed, but then one hand moved, and there was a soft groan.

John tried to raise his head, but the waves of pain washed over him, making him gasp. Turning some more, he could see the legs and feet of Warren Smith near the door. They were perfectly still. John fought back the pain. Clenching his teeth, he rose up on one elbow. He had to help these two boys. The image of his own sons swept before his eyes. Luke and Mark were younger than the Smith boys, but John knew what he would want someone to do for them in similar circumstances. But willpower wasn't enough. He couldn't do it. He fell back exhausted.

Then suddenly a shadow crossed the doorway, and there was the sound of men's voices. A man entered the shop, then another. "Damnation!" a rough voice cried. "We got 'em. Would ya look at this!"

"Watch it," another man growled. "See if there's any still alive."

A pair of boots came around the bellows, moving very cautiously. *Lie down! Play dead!* John's mind screamed at Sardius. But the boy just huddled there, watching the boots come around toward him.

With an oath, the man dropped to one knee. He had a rifle in his hand. Bending lower, his back to John now, he peered beneath the bellows. "Well, I'll be—"

"What is it?" someone else barked.

"We got a live one." There was a moment of silence, then a soft exclamation. "Hold it, Glaze! This is just a boy."

There was a harsh guffaw. "Nits make lice," the voice growled. "Leave him be and he'll grow up to be a Mormon." The rifle muzzle dropped, coming up against the boy's head.

No! Oh, dear God! The prayer burst out like a shout in John's mind. He turned his head against the logs and shut his eyes tightly.

In the confines of the shop, the explosion was like a cannon shot inside a barrel. John heard someone start to curse, his voice heavy with shock. And then suddenly John felt a lance of fire shoot through his side. Someone had nudged him with the toe of a boot. "This one's alive too," a voice above him said.

John didn't open his eyes. He didn't have to. He felt no fear. Just a deep, instantaneous sorrow that he would not get to hold his children one more time.

There was the scrape of boots on the dirt floor as the man stepped back. Metal clicked on metal as the hammer of the rifle was pulled back. John turned his head toward the wall. *Goodbye, dearest Jessie. I'll miss you.*

Chapter Notes

While the purposes of the novel require that the author place his fictional characters in the midst of the terrible events at Haun's Mill and provide some detail not given in original accounts, every effort has been made to depict the tragedy as it actually happened. The main events of the massacre come from several eyewitness accounts (see Joseph Young's account in *HC* 3:183–86; see also *HC* 3:186–87; *Persecutions*, pp. 234–37; *Restoration*, pp. 399–402).

Later reports of the Missouri militia indicate that there were 240 men in the group that attacked the settlement and that they were led by a man by the name of Nehemiah Comstock. Each man fired an average of seven bullets during the attack. This makes a total of almost seventeen hundred rounds fired against approximately thirty families. Eighteen people, men and boys, were killed, and thirteen other people (including at least one woman) were wounded, some of them critically. Only three of the Missourians were wounded.

The massacre in the blacksmith shop, including the shooting of the wounded and the brutal murder of Sardius Smith, are accurate, as are the mutilation of Father McBride with a corn cutter and the shooting at women and children. The killer of Sardius Smith later boasted about what he had done, showing the totally ruthless nature of some of the mob.

Willard Smith was one of the survivors and one of the heroes of Haun's Mill, even though he was not yet twelve. He wrote a little-known account of his experience, which gives some details not found in other sources. His hiding in the woodpile, the flight to the cabin of Thomas McBride (who was evidently first shot, then later killed with the corn knife), his getting the old man water from the millpond while under fire, and his daring escape with the six little girls are all based on his journal account (found in *By Their Fruits*, pp. 180–83).

There was an actual woman, named Mary Stedwell, who fled across the creek with Amanda Smith and who was shot in the hand. Amanda Smith later recalled, "One girl was wounded by my side and fell over a log, her clothes hung across the log [and] they Shot at them expecting that they were hitting her, and our people af[ter]wards Cut out of that log twenty bullets." (In *Redress*, p. 538; see also *HC* 3:186; *CHFT*, p. 203.) Rather than trying to introduce a new character so that the story of Mary's heroic escape could be told, the author has taken the liberty to have Jessica experience events similar to those Mary experienced.

Jacob Haun was wounded but recovered. Some time later, after the Saints reached Nauvoo, the Prophet Joseph said: "At Haun's Mill the brethren went contrary to my counsel; if they had not, their lives would have been spared" (*HC* 5:137).

Chapter Eighteen

A movement outside the window caught Mary Ann's eye. The glass panes were thick and wavy, and they distorted the image somewhat, but she didn't need clear vision to recognize the outline and the gait of her husband, or to see that he was coming at a swift trot, something Benjamin Steed didn't do much anymore.

"Your father is coming." She was peeling carrots at the cutting table. Rebecca and Lydia were at the main table deboning a boiled chicken and dropping the pieces of meat into the stew pot. Both of their heads turned to look at her. She set the carrot and the knife down, and turned slowly, trying to keep the fear out of her voice. "He's running."

The chicken was forgotten. Rebecca was on her feet, wiping her hands on her apron. Lydia swung around on the bench so that she was facing the door. There was no sound in the room except for the soft gooing of Lydia's baby from her cradle in the corner.

There was a clumping sound on the porch, then the door flew open. Benjamin took only one step inside. "Brigham and the men are coming in," he said.

"Derek?" Rebecca asked, holding her breath.

Benjamin nodded. "Fine. Nathan. Matthew. They're all back."

Relief flooded across the faces of all three women. That morning, word had reached Far West that a huge company of militia was on the march from the south, and Joseph had sent Brigham Young and Heber C. Kimball out with about a hundred and fifty men to scout the situation. Now it was five o'clock, and there had been no word. The worry had been weighing more and more heavily on their minds.

"Are you sure they're all back?" Lydia asked.

"Yes. They were chased by a large party of men as they tried to come in, but Brigham says he knew the lay of the land too well and easily eluded them."

"Thank the good Lord for that," Mary Ann half whispered.

Benjamin looked at his wife. "Where are the children?"

"Out back." With the worry lifted, she felt a need to let out her emotions. She smiled. "They're playing school. Young Joshua is the schoolmaster. Rachel is the teacher. The little ones are the pupils. Emily is—"

"I think you'd better get them inside."

Mary Ann's hands gripped her apron, her knuckles suddenly white.

"The army that chased Brigham's party are marshalling just south of town. There's another two thousand men—maybe more—camped down by Goose Creek."

Rebecca drew in her breath sharply. Lydia and Mary Ann both blurted out the same word at the same time. "No!" Lydia was on her feet now too, her greasy hands completely forgotten.

Benjamin nodded gravely. "Joseph is going to send out a flag of truce and see if we can talk with them."

"But—"

Benjamin hurried on quickly. "Our militia is forming a line

along the south edge of town. . . ." He didn't finish. He just looked at Mary Ann, trying to lessen the impact of what he was about to say. Then he shook his head. "It might be well if you begin gathering whatever valuables we can carry if we have to leave. You'll have to—" He shrugged helplessly. This was not the time for counsel about the need to travel light. "Don't come out until you hear something from us."

And with that, he backed out of the door and shut it quietly, leaving the women to stare at each other.

General Alexander Doniphan had command of the brigade of the right flank as the army marched northward. When he learned that a large party of riders was seen approaching Far West from the east, he sent word to General Lucas and asked permission to take his brigade and try to cut them off. Permission was granted, and Doniphan and his men rode off at a hard gallop.

The main body had reached Goose Creek by then, which was about a mile south of Far West, and Lucas gave the order to start camp there. But about half an hour later, a rider from Doniphan came tearing back to camp. Doniphan had chased the men, definitely a company of Mormon militia, but had been unable to intercept them before they reached the town. Now Doniphan had his men deployed about two hundred yards south of Far West and was waiting for further orders. Then the thoroughly frightened messenger added his own assessment of the situation, though Doniphan had not given him leave to do so. The Mormons were forming a line behind the barricades. He had seen them with his own eyes. There were over eight hundred of them, and they were heavily armed with rifle and cannon.

The messenger was about six hundred men too high in his estimate, but the damage had been done. Furious, and fearing a trap, Lucas ordered another brigade to march at full speed to link up with Doniphan.

When Joshua Steed got the news of the order to march, he

immediately mounted up and went to Lucas's tent. Lucas was inside, putting on his full dress uniform. Joshua went past the aide with barely a nod. Lucas had been furious. Now Joshua was trying to reason with the general.

"Sir, I've been to Far West. I know the lay of the land. I can help."

"No." He didn't even look up from pulling on his boots.

"But, sir, I am the captain of a mounted company. I—"

Lucas looked up, peering at him over the top of his spectacles. "Steed, I've already ordered General Graham's brigade forward. You are not part of that brigade."

"With all due respect, sir, I believe you're holding me back because of my family."

Lucas stood slowly, his face reddening. "You listen, mister," he said tightly, "I've got a war on my hands here, and I'll put you where I need you." He stopped, daring Joshua to contradict him. When Joshua didn't say anything, he went on. "If you're so all-fired anxious for something to do, you take your company and ride guard duty along the eastern flank."

"But, sir—"

Lucas overrode him heavily. "You patrol all the way up across the road that comes from the east. They already just got a hundred and fifty men back into town. I don't want them getting any more reinforcements."

Joshua's mouth opened to protest, but Lucas spun around and reached for his coat that hung over his chair. He didn't look back. "That duty will start immediately, Steed," he snapped. "Dismissed."

Too angry now to speak, Joshua turned on his heel and stalked away. Lucas finished buttoning the coat, brushing at the gold officer's braid on the shoulders, then turned, beckoning to his aide standing just outside the front of the tent. The man stepped forward smartly. "Sir?"

Lucas was buckling on his sword now. "Send a rider to Graham. Give him the word that I don't want to be caught in a trap. He's to get Doniphan and they're both to withdraw back to camp immediately. We'll wait until tomorrow for any engagement."

"Yes, sir." The aide started to pivot.

"Owens."

He turned back. "Yes, sir?"

"Find Lieutenant Carter. Tell him I want him to ride with Captain Steed."

There was a momentary flash of surprise, but he nodded immediately. "Yes, sir."

"You tell him I want him to stick by Steed every minute. He's to report to me personally if anything out of the ordinary happens."

The man saluted. "Yes, sir. I'll tell him, sir." And with that, he was away.

As the two brethren who had gone out with the flag of truce came walking back toward the barricades, the brethren nearest to Joseph pushed in close to hear their report. As a leader of the home defense, Benjamin Steed was right next to Joseph. Nathan, Matthew, and Derek were about fifty or sixty yards down the line, and all they could do was watch from a distance. The men huddled in a circle for two or three minutes, then they backed up a little as Joseph Smith began to speak to them. He waved an arm in one direction, pointing out things, then turned, doing the same in the other direction.

"Look, the army's leaving." Matthew was pointing at the long line of men down the rise from them. Just as the negotiations between the Mormons and Doniphan's brigade got under way, there had been a ripple of panic along the Mormon line when a second group, about the same size as the first, had appeared coming toward them at a hard march. But now there was no question about it. Both groups were retreating, moving slowly down the hill.

Nathan turned back and saw that Joseph's instructions were finished and that Benjamin was approaching them. As he came up, the men around Nathan and Matthew and Derek gathered in close so they could hear what was going on.

"What did they say?" someone blurted as Benjamin joined them.

Benjamin's mouth was drawn into a tight line. "Governor Boggs has issued an order to the militia. That's why they're here."

"What order?" Nathan demanded. "I thought they'd come to protect us."

Benjamin was staring at the ground. Slowly his head came up. "They aren't here to protect us."

There were cries of stunned surprise and horrified shock.

"But why?" Derek exclaimed. "We're not the aggressors here."

Benjamin was weary. "*Why* doesn't matter. The man read the order to our brethren. Their army is pulling back to Goose Creek for the night. Tomorrow . . . ?" His shoulders lifted and fell. And then he grew very businesslike. "Joseph wants the barricades strengthened. He wants every wagon, every spare table. These cabins along the edge of town, tear them down. Use the logs to strengthen the walls. Any unused lumber or logs, get them here as quickly as possible."

The men were still too stunned to protest. They just stared at him. Their obtuseness made Benjamin suddenly angry. "Move!" he shouted. "We've got no more than twelve hours to get ready."

They moved swiftly away, in groups of twos and threes. Benjamin watched them go, then turned back to his sons. "Derek, you and Matthew go home. Tell the women what's happened. Make sure they've started to pack our things. Tell them food will be important. Warm clothes for the children. Anything they can use for bandages."

Derek passed one hand over his eyes. He was dazed too. "Yes, Father Steed."

As they half turned, Benjamin spoke again. "Matthew?"

"Yes, Pa."

"There's a good chance they'll fire the houses. Move anything of value we can't carry with us outside. Far enough away it won't burn. Maybe we can salvage something once this is over."

"Someone's coming!"

Half a dozen men in Joshua's company saw the approaching horsemen at the same time. Rifles whipped up and everyone went on instant alert. But as Joshua squinted to try and see them better, he relaxed almost at once. It was a large party—more than two hundred, Joshua guessed—and they were raising a cloud of dust along the road. But even at this distance Joshua could see that many of them were painted to look like Indians.

He swore under his breath and raised one arm. "They're ours, boys. Stand easy."

Some of the lunatic fringe that was now part of Lucas's army had decided that they could convince the Missourians that there had been an Indian uprising—something that would strike terror in the heart of any Missourian. So they had put red on their clothes and painted their faces. If the sight hadn't disgusted him so much, Joshua would have laughed. Even at a distance they looked no more like real Indians than boys playing games in the school yard.

Joshua's men began calling and waving to the riders, and they cantered up to join them. As they approached, Joshua suddenly felt his stomach drop. The men were carrying the spoils of war. Some carried two rifles. One had a woman's dress draped across his saddle. Another had a small leather trunk between him and the saddle horn. Several were leading extra horses by their bridles or halter ropes. A boy not yet twenty was swinging a length of a woman's beads.

"Captain Joshua Steed," Joshua called to the man who was obviously in charge. "First Brigade, Third Division."

The man was grinning broadly. "Nehemiah Comstock and my boys from Livingston County." He leaned across his saddle, extending his hand.

Joshua started to reach out to take it, then recoiled in shock. The hand had dark red smears all across the palm.

Comstock looked down, then hooted. "Hey, boys, tell 'em what we've been doing." He looked at Joshua and cackled fiendishly. "We just come from Haun's Mill. We been killing Mormons."

"Lieutenant?" It took every ounce of the control Joshua had learned in a thousand poker games to keep the look of repulsion from his face and the nausea from his eyes.

"Yes, Captain." Lieutenant Carter owned a hat shop in Richmond. He was married and had a young family. Joshua saw, with some relief, that his face was nearly as gray as his coat. Some of the other men in Joshua's company were hollering and shouting out their regrets that they hadn't been part of Comstock's attack, but Carter had paled at what he was hearing. He had nearly fallen off his horse when one man, the front of his clothes stiff with dried blood, had told in graphic detail how he had hacked an old man to pieces with a corn cutter.

Joshua pulled himself out of his thoughts with a real effort. "Lieutenant, you and the men take Mr. Comstock and his men back to General Lucas. I'd like to ride on a little, make sure there're no Mormons out here."

Comstock roared with laughter. "Ain't no live ones, that's for sure."

Joshua ignored him. "Tell the general I don't think there's much—"

"Sir?" Carter cut in.

"What?"

"We can leave a detail out here to watch the road. I think you and me need to accompany Mr. Comstock back to camp."

Joshua wanted to scream out at the man, curse him for standing between him and getting to Haun's Mill. He had to know. He had to see with his own eyes if it was as horrible as Comstock said. He had to know if Jessica and Rachel were still there. But while those thoughts raced through his mind, he kept his face impassive. "I'll be fine. You ask the general to send out a relief for me. Then I'll come in."

Carter's hand came up and rested on the butt of his pistol. "Begging your pardon, sir, but I think it's best if you come back with us."

A sudden quiet fell over the men. They weren't sure what was going on, but they sensed the tension between their two officers.

And then, with a jolt, Joshua understood. Lieutenant Carter might be green when it came to military action. And he might be a little gray around the gills right now, but he was also totally loyal to General Samuel Lucas. And Samuel Lucas had sent him to watch Joshua.

Knowing he had lost, and almost physically sick at the thought of it, Joshua nodded, forcing his voice into a studied nonchalance. "Well, maybe you're right. Pick twelve men to stay here." He turned to Comstock. "Let's go. General Lucas is gonna want to hear what you have to say."

Willard Smith waited a full half an hour after the men had gone before he decided it was safe to move. And then he moved only with great reluctance. He was terrified that some of the mob had gone into hiding and that the silence was merely a trap to draw out any survivors. But, on the other hand, he felt driven to find his family. The sun had gone down now, and knowing that it would soon be dark was enough to frighten him even more deeply than the thoughts of a possible trap.

From his vantage point behind the tree, he had watched the mob wreak their final havoc on the village. The shooting had finally stopped, but then, whooping and wailing as if the very legions of hell itself had been unleashed, the men fell upon the now deserted dwellings. It was a race among thieves to see who could loot the most spoils, then vandalize what was left. In a frenzy, they ran from one cabin to another. Men snapped and snarled at each other like dogs fighting over a dead hare. Furniture was thrown out and smashed. Tents ripped to shreds. Wagons tipped over. Horses stolen. Cattle, hogs, chickens driven off or shot.

Willard stood slowly now, hugging himself against the chill that was settling in the air. Slowly, tentatively, head darting back and forth, eyes jumping nervously at every shadow, he made his way across the board that bridged the creek at the millrace. He averted his eyes as he walked past the cabin of Father McBride, not daring to look at the still form that lay on the porch. Somewhere off behind him, a dog was howling. Some of the cows that had been driven off had made their way back to the creek. Smelling the blood, they were lowing with long, mournful cries. But the village itself was so quiet it frightened him.

Not knowing where his mother was, knowing only that he had last seen his father and brothers going inside the blacksmith shop, Willard Smith made his way slowly toward the heavy log shed that was now so dark and silent.

Jessica's first awareness was that the sky was still light. Then the fiery ache in her left hand intruded, and the remembrance all came flooding back in an instant. Going rigid, she listened intently, not daring to raise her head. And then she realized that the mob sounds were gone. There were no gunshots, no shouting, no pounding of horse's hooves. She could hear a dog howling plaintively, and the mooing of some cows.

Carefully she reached up with her right hand, got a grip on the log, and pulled herself up enough to peek over the decaying wood that had served as her shield. She nearly fell back. Lights danced before her eyes, and the landscape began to weave. But she steadied herself, taking deep breaths, letting her head clear, and then with a groan, she went up into a full sitting position.

A movement caught her eye. A man— She peered more closely. No, it was a boy, and he was making his way slowly away from her, moving along the front of the row of cabins. She felt a quick jab of relief. The fact that he moved unimpeded was the best proof that their attackers had gone. And with that relief came the pounding anxieties. Where was her baby? Had Amanda made it to safety? And what about John? She stumbled to her feet, looking around. The last she had seen Amanda she was running toward the nearest cornfield. It was about thirty yards away.

Moving carefully now, constantly looking over her shoulder to make sure there was no one still around, she walked through the brush and to the cornfield. Then keeping her voice in a low, urgent whisper, she began to make her way slowly along the edge of the stalks of corn. "Amanda! Amanda! It's me. It's Jessica."

Jessica Griffith and Amanda Smith walked with heavy step. There had been another girl, a sixteen-year-old, hiding with Amanda. She was afraid to go back into the village this soon, and so Jessica had left the baby—finally so exhausted that he was sleeping in her arms—with the girl. Amanda also left her two girls behind. They were in a state of half shock themselves, and their mother knew they were not up to going back into the village yet.

The village green was a shambles—broken furniture; ripped bedding; clothes scattered every which way; bags of flour ripped open, leaving gaping trails of white. It looked like a tornado had struck the site. But that was not the most frightening thing. Twice Amanda and Jessica averted their eyes so they wouldn't have to see the bodies that were lying on the ground or sprawled across porches and steps. Just inside the open door of one cabin they could see a man covered with blood, lying on the floor, being cared for by his sobbing wife.

Amanda and Jessica moved on woodenly. They had last seen their men running for the blacksmith shop, and to the blacksmith shop they were going. But with each step the dread settled in more heavily upon them.

Suddenly Amanda's hand shot out and grabbed Jessica's arm. "There's Willard!"

Jessica stared. Coming around the corner of the log structure that belonged to the blacksmith, Willard Smith was staggering toward them. In his arms he carried the body of a smaller boy.

"Alma?" Amanda whispered. Then she was running, hair bouncing wildly on her shoulders, skirts flying. "They've killed my Alma!" she screamed.

Jessica followed immediately, running hard after Amanda.

"They've killed him!" Amanda cried as she slid to a stop in front of Willard and snatched her boy from the arms of her eldest son.

"No, Mama," Willard said. "He's alive."

Two wet streaks had drawn lines through the dirt and dust on Willard's cheeks, but he spoke calmly, and his voice had a curious detachment to it. As Jessica pulled up beside Amanda, she realized that this was a boy deep in shock. And then her hand flew to her mouth and she gasped. At the spot where Alma's hip should have been, the trouser fabric had been cleanly shorn away. All that was left of the spot where the hip had once been was a mass of mangled, bloody flesh. A section about the size of a small cantaloupe had been blasted from the boy's leg. Two jagged pieces of bone showed white against the redness.

With a sickening lurch, Jessica realized what had happened. As the men had fired into the blacksmith shop, one ball had hit Alma and blown the entire hip socket away. "Amanda!" she cried. "He's been shot!"

Amanda was staring at the wound now, but shock had hit her too. "Warren. I've got to find Warren," she mumbled. She started forward, haltingly.

Willard leaped in front of her, holding out his hands. "No, Mama. Papa and Sardius are dead. Don't go in there. Please."

Amanda stopped, staring with blank eyes past her son at the would-be fortress.

But Willard's words brought Jessica back to reality. She reached out and took the boy gently by the shoulders, wincing as pain shot through her left hand. "Brother Griffith?" she asked softly. "Did you see my husband, Willard?"

The boy nodded gravely. "He's dead. They're all dead! All of them. Please don't go in there."

For one blinding moment, Jessica nearly dropped to her knees. Her eyes were burning. A numbness swept through her body with such swiftness that she felt faint. And then she straightened. Earlier in this day a man had burst into her cabin with a rifle. She had been terrified, but she had fought it down and stopped the man. Now she did the same with the smashing waves of grief. The awful realities of their situation hit her just as hard. The majority of the men were dead. The village was helpless. There were still spoils to be taken. The mob had gone, but they might return.

With a terrible clarity driving her now, she reached out with her good hand and grabbed Amanda's elbow. "Alma is bleeding badly," she said firmly. "We've got to help him or he will die."

Slowly Amanda turned. She looked at Jessica, then down at her wounded son. Then she looked at Willard. "Are you sure they're dead?" she whispered.

One stifled sob shook the small boyish shoulders momentarily, then he nodded gravely. "I saw them, Mama."

Amanda turned to Jessica and nodded. "We must help Alma," she said.

Miraculously the Smith tent that had been pitched behind Jessica's cabin was still standing, though the main pole canted crazily to the left. Jessica had taken one step inside her cabin and immediately backed out again. It was a total shambles. The mattresses had been gutted and the feathers thrown everywhere. The table was overturned, chairs were smashed, broken pieces of crockery covered the floor. Her first thought had been of the man she had struck, but either he had recovered or his companions had found him and dragged him away. If he came back and found her . . . A little shiver ran up her spine.

So they carried Alma out back to the Smiths' tent. Here too the men had done their work. Their luggage had been kicked open and clothes strewn about. The Smiths had taken a thin, straw-filled mattress from the wagon box and put it in the tent for the boys to sleep on. Someone looking for hidden valuables had ripped the ticking from top to bottom, scattering the straw.

Jessica quickly dropped to her knees, smoothing out the straw with her good hand. "Willard, quickly, get me some of the clothing." The boy leaped to do her bidding. In a moment, Jessica had fashioned a rough bed. Amanda slowly went to her knees and laid Alma upon it. As he moaned with pain and began to twist and turn, Amanda went down on all fours, raking away the litter that surrounded them. A small box of sewing stuff had been turned upside down and the contents dumped out. She pawed through the pile, then turned, holding up a pair of scissors.

Moving carefully, telling Jessica and Willard to hold Alma's leg still, Alma's mother cut away the trouser leg from the wound. Alma jerked and his eyes flew open. For a moment he looked around wildly; then he saw his mother, and his movement stilled.

Amanda reached out and laid her hand on his cheek. "It's all right, son. We've got you. You're safe."

His face was laced with pain, but Jessica could see the comprehension and instant relief come into his eyes. "I hurt, Mama."

"I know, son. We're going to fix it."

He turned and found his brother's face. That jogged his memory. He looked back to his mother. "They shot Papa, Mama. And Sardius."

Amanda's eyes were shining. "I know, Alma."

"I pretended I was dead. A man grabbed me by the feet and dragged me across the ground. I wanted to scream, it hurt so bad. But I didn't. I kept my eyes closed and pretended I was dead."

"And that's why you're alive now, son." She reached down

and took his hand. "They shot away your hip, Alma." She bit her lip, then forced a wan smile. "Do you believe Heavenly Father can make you another hip?"

The brown eyes were large and frightened. "Do you think he can, Mama?"

She nodded. "Yes, I think Heavenly Father can do that if he wants to."

The eyes closed, and the small mouth tightened with determination. "Then I think he can too, Mama."

Amanda looked at Jessica, then up at her oldest son. "Willard, come closer. We are going to pray."

In a moment, they were kneeling in the straw around Alma's makeshift bed. Amanda bowed her head, and Jessica and Willard followed suit.

"Dear Heavenly Father," she began in a husky voice, "we kneel here around the bed of our son and brother, little Alma. And Father we supplicate thee for faith and guidance. This is a wonderful boy thou hast sent to our family, and we are grateful for his sweet and wonderful spirit. We dedicate his life to thee for thy service."

She took a breath. "We ask thee, O Father, that Alma be restored again and that he be made well and strong. We know thou canst do this if it be thy will. And if not—" Her voice caught and she had to swallow. Jessica felt the tears spill over her own eyelids and trickle down her cheeks.

"If this is not possible, then wilt thou take him in his innocence. Take him home to thee and keep him safe in thy care until we can see him again. We ask this of thee, in the name of our Savior, amen."

She rocked back on her heels, brushing at her cheeks with the back of her hand. Alma's eyes had closed now, and he was breathing deeply. Jessica started to get up, but suddenly the look on Amanda's face stopped her. Her friend was staring past her, her head partially cocked to one side, as if she were listening to something.

"What is it, Amanda?"

But Amanda waved her to silence. Then after a moment, she turned and reached out and grabbed Willard's hand. "Willard, you must do exactly as I say. Swiftly. Willard, get the ashes from the fireplace. I'll also need some water and a pan."

Jessica was up in an instant. "There's a pan in the house. I'll get the water."

"Pour the water over the ashes and into the pan. I need a mild lye solution. Then bring it to me."

In a few minutes they were back, crowding into the tent. In their absence, Amanda had torn a shirt into long strips. The moment Jessica set the pan of dark water down, Amanda dipped the first rag in the solution and began to cleanse Alma's wound. Jessica immediately took another strip of cloth and followed suit, taking turns with Amanda. It was a ghastly task, mopping out the pieces of bone and flesh. As they talked, Willard added to their horror as he quietly told them of his experiences in escaping the hands of the mob. But as they continued to work, to Jessica's amazement the bleeding stopped. The flesh began to bleach until it was as white as a chicken's breast.

Amanda tossed aside the rag she was holding and looked down at her son. Mercifully, he had fallen into unconsciousness again and was oblivious to their ministrations. She bowed her head for a moment, her eyes closed, then again the strange look crossed her face. Jessica watched her closely. After a moment, Amanda straightened. "Willard?"

"Yes, Mama?"

"I need some roots from the slippery elm tree to make a poultice. Do you know where there is some slippery elm?"

Willard seemed surprised by the question, but he was nodding almost immediately. "Yes, Mama. There's some down by the creek where it goes into the millpond."

"Good. Get a shovel, Willard. Go down and dig me some of those roots."

Willard stiffened. His head shot around and looked out the opening of the tent. By now it was full dark, and the thoughts of going out into the night clearly frightened him deeply.

Amanda reached out and took him by the hands, looking him in the eye. "Son, listen to me. Heavenly Father protected you today. Do you believe that?"

He nodded instantly. His escape had been too miraculous for him not to believe that.

"And he will protect you now. Everything will be all right. I need Sister Griffith here with me to help with Alma. You have to do it."

Jessica was watching him, her heart aching. He had faced so much this day. And now to be sent out to face the night alone . . . She stood. "Willard, I have a piece of hickory shagbark in the cupboard by the sink. I'll make you a torch so you can see."

Willard pulled back his shoulders, swallowing hard. "All right."

"Good boy."

Jessica got him the torch and got it lighted from the coals of the cooking fire. Then she went back to the tent to join Amanda. She knelt down beside her, watching her stroke her son's face for a moment. Then she couldn't hold back any longer. "Amanda, how did you know about the ashes?" She gestured towards Alma's still figure. "How do you know what to do?"

Amanda's head came up slightly, and suddenly her eyes were glistening again. "After we prayed?"

"Yes?"

"A voice began speaking in my mind. It has been telling me exactly what needs to be done to save my son's life."

Chapter Notes

Willard Smith was the first one to enter the blacksmith shop after the massacre at Haun's Mill. He carried his brother Alma out and there met his mother. Amanda Smith's prayer and the treatment of her son as directed by the Spirit are told in Willard's own account of that terrible day. (Found in *By Their Fruits*, pp. 182–83.)

Chapter Nineteen

Mary Ann moved slowly around the cabin, even the simplest task now draining what little reserves of energy she had left. Suddenly she felt an arm slip around her waist and she turned in surprise. Lydia was standing beside her. "Come sit down for a moment, Mother Steed," she said softly.

"No," she protested feebly. "I'm all right."

"The children will sleep for another hour or two. We can take time to rest for a moment." The seven children—four of Lydia's and three of Jessica's—were asleep on straw mattresses placed on the floor behind the blanket-curtain that partitioned off the one end of the cabin.

Rebecca put down the crock she was filling with corn flour and walked over to join them. "Mother," she said, taking Mary Ann's arm, "Lydia's right. We're almost done. Come sit down."

Mary Ann was too tired to protest further. The exhaustion seeped through every cell of her body. She let her daughter and daughter-in-law lead her to the sofa, and they all sank down heavily onto its threadbare cushions. The clock on the fireplace mantel showed ten minutes after five. It would start to get light in just over an hour. That meant they had been working quietly but steadily for almost eight hours.

Ever since the coming of the army to the outskirts of Far West the previous evening, the city had been in an uproar. The Steed men, including Peter, were out with the brethren. Barricades were being hastily thrown up all around the city to prepare for a siege. The women stayed at home, making their own preparations—packing up essentials, hiding valuables, consolidating meager food supplies, separating out needed clothing, folding enough bedding to see them through cold nights if they were forced from their homes.

"There's still so much to do," Mary Ann said, looking around the cabin.

"It can wait for five minutes," Lydia replied. Lydia's face was deeply lined too, though it was difficult to tell whether it was from weariness or worry. By unspoken agreement, they had avoided discussing what might be awaiting them with the coming of the sun.

Mary Ann stifled back a sigh, not wanting them to know how delicious it felt to be off her feet. She reached out and took their hands in hers. There was a fleeting smile. "I guess I'm getting old."

"We're all very tired, Mother," Rebecca said. "It's not just being up all night," she murmured. "It's the fear and the worry. It's being sick about Jessica and John not being here. It's . . . it's wonderin' if sometime today Derek is going to have to . . ." Her lip started to tremble and she looked away quickly.

Mary Ann squeezed her hand tightly. There was nothing to say to that. Putting words to the circle of pain in which each of them was enveloped only made it the more unbearable. From time immemorial, women had sat together like this, trying to comfort one another as their sons and fathers and husbands and brothers went off to war. So they sat quietly, shoulder to shoulder, content not to speak.

Five minutes later Mary Ann, Lydia, and Rebecca were still sitting together when the door opened. Peter and Derek came in first, rubbing their hands together to warm them from the cold. Benjamin followed, taking off his coat even as he came through the door.

All three women were up instantly. "Where's Nathan?" Lydia demanded.

"Him and Matthew are down with Parley Pratt, working on the last of the barricades," Benjamin answered. "They should be along in a few minutes." He hung his coat on a peg.

Mary Ann went to Benjamin. "How has it gone?"

There was a slow shake of his head. His face was smudged and his hands were dirty. "We've used about everything we could lay hand to. But if they've got cannon, like they say . . ." There was no point in finishing the statement.

"Come," she said, slipping one arm around his waist. "We've got half a dozen eggs. There's no sense trying to save them. We'll have some breakfast. It should be light in about an hour now."

But as she turned toward the fireplace, there was a heavy clunk on the porch outside. Even as they turned toward it, the door flew open. Nathan stood there. His eyes were wide and filled with horror. Matthew was beside him. In the lamplight, Mary Ann saw that there were streaks through the dirtiness of his face. He had been crying.

"What?" Lydia cried. "What is it?"

For a long moment Nathan just stared at them, his eyes moving from face to face. Then his gaze dropped and he stared at his hands. "A rider just came in from Haun's Mill."

Mary Ann was to him in three steps, grabbing at his shirt. "What, Nathan? What happened? Was there trouble?"

He looked up, his eyes stricken. "They were attacked yesterday afternoon. It was a massacre."

Mary Ann gasped. Rebecca's hand flew to her mouth. Lydia gasped and fell back a step.

"Half the men are dead. Even some children were killed. I guess . . ." He swallowed, and turned away, not able to finish.

Mary Ann reached out and took Nathan's shoulder, turning him back around to face her. "Jessica?" she whispered. "John?"

"The messenger doesn't know," Nathan answered. "There was so much confusion. He's not sure who—"

There was a scream from behind them. "Mama! Mama!"

They spun around. Six-year-old Rachel was standing at the edge of the curtain that sectioned off what served as a bedroom. Her hair was tangled from sleep. The large blue eyes that were usually so sober and thoughtful were filled with terror. "What happened to my mama?"

Mary Ann and Benjamin were to her instantly. Benjamin gathered her up in his arms, holding her tight to him as Mary Ann soothed her. "It's all right, Rachel. It's all right."

Nathan watched for a moment, then turned to his wife. Lydia had never seen a look of such terrible anguish on a man's face. Holding out her arms, she gathered him in. He crushed her to him, clinging to her desperately. Then great shuddering sobs began to rack his body. "I told them to come back with us," he cried hoarsely. "I told them. I told them. I told them."

"General Lucas isn't going to like this, Captain."

Joshua didn't even turn his head. He looked at the rest of the men. Fortunately they had no love for Lieutenant Carter and were grinning a little at the fact that their captain kept putting him in his place. But Joshua could also see that they were nervous about what he was about to do. "Keep the horses quiet," he said confidently. "If I need you, I'll fire one shot. Then come in quick and hard."

"Captain!" Lieutenant Carter's voice had risen to a whine. Joshua didn't glance back. He moved away in long strides, headed for the line of trees and undergrowth that marked the streambed of Shoal Creek. Beyond that line lay the village of Haun's Mill.

* * *

"There's a man coming!" "Who is it?" "It's a Missourian!" "He's alone."

Only gradually did the ripple of panic that was sweeping through the group finally register in Jessica's mind. Fighting for control, she finally looked away from the corpse that lay at her feet—the cold, gray body that until yesterday had been her husband. Women were huddling together nervously, pointing. Children started to whimper. A couple of the men ran for their rifles.

Jessica turned, looking to see what was causing the stir. And then she was leaning forward, staring. "Joshua?" She took one step forward. She rubbed at her eyes quickly, then slowly lifted a hand. "Joshua?" she said again, only then realizing that she had spoken in a bare whisper. She started waving. "Joshua!" she shouted. "Joshua! I'm here."

He broke into a quick walk, pushing his way through the gathered crowd. "It's all right," he said as he passed them, "I'm Joshua Steed. I'm her brother." He lied without hesitation. This was no time for a complicated explanation of relationships. He was focused on one thing, and one thing only, and that was getting Jessica and her family out of Haun's Mill.

* * *

They stood together, looking down at the body of John Griffith. Jessica wept silently while Joshua stared at the work of yesterday's mob. The bodies were lined up along the ground. A few feet away there was a pile of dirt and a hole where someone had started to dig a well. Then he understood. The well was to be the common grave for those who hadn't survived. There was no time for funerals or going to the cemetery with freshly made coffins. These people had no guarantees that the mob would not be back. And Joshua couldn't give them any either. He was nearly as frightened by the possibility as they were, not for himself but for Jessica.

He reached out and touched her shoulder, bringing her back to him. His eyes widened. For the first time now he saw her bandaged hand. He moved to her and took it gently. The rag that was wrapped around it was dirty and bloodstained. "What happened?"

"It doesn't matter. I'll be fine." She spoke woodenly, without looking at him.

He had to bring her out of her stupor. He shook her gently. "Where's Rachel?" he asked. "Where are the boys? Are they all right?"

Jessica's head came up. A momentary flicker of relief crossed her face. "Nathan and Matthew came day before yesterday. They took Rachel and the boys to Far West." She bit her lip. "They wanted me and John to go." Her eyes flooded with tears. "We didn't," she whispered. "We were going to but . . ."

Joshua closed his eyes for a moment, wanting to find a way to lessen the pain for her. But the time for solace was going to have to come some other time. "What about the baby?"

There was no answer.

He shook her more firmly. "Is baby John . . . ?" He couldn't bring himself to say it.

Her eyes finally focused and she shook her head. "He's all right. Amanda's children are watching him. Over at the cabin."

The relief washed over him, making him weak. "All right. Let's go get him."

As they crossed the board bridge that spanned the millrace, Joshua stopped and looked at Jessica. "Jessie?"

She was holding the baby tightly against her body, looking down into the bright eyes that looked out from the blanket.

"Jessie!"

Her head came up slowly, and when he saw her eyes he realized that she was still in deep shock.

"Jessie, I'm with some other men."

Her mouth rounded into an "oh" and there was instant fear.

"It's all right. I'm their captain. No one is going to hurt you."

She didn't answer, but he was pleased to see understanding register on her face. "Jessie, this is very important. They can't know we're related. They can't even guess that I know you. Do you understand?"

"Yes."

"Good. No matter what I say, don't let on."

"All right, Joshua." She turned and looked back toward the village. "I . . . Should I be leaving Amanda, Joshua?"

He grabbed her by the shoulders. They had gone over this three times already. "Jessie, you have children in Far West. Rachel is there. Mark. Luke. You've got to think about them now. John is dead."

"But Amanda—"

"She'll be all right. The men said they'll watch out for her."

"Why can't she come with us?"

"If she could, I would bring her. But she can't move that boy. Not with his hip like that." He shook his head, squeezing her shoulders with soft pressure. "She can't come with us, Jessie. You know that."

Finally she turned back. "I know, Joshua. I know."

Joshua swore bitterly, then grabbed Lieutenant Carter by the lapels of his uniform jacket. Even the uniform infuriated him. Most of the higher officers bought their own uniforms, but the lower officers and the enlisted men rarely had them. This was a state militia. It was activated only in times of emergency. But Lieutenant Carter had bought himself a uniform. It was so typical of his pompous arrogance.

Joshua shoved his face right up against Carter's. "You listen to me, Lieutenant. You can tell General Lucas any miserable thing you want. But we are not going to leave this woman here." He let go of Carter's jacket and gave him a little shove. The lieutenant, who was about four inches shorter and fifty pounds lighter than Joshua, stumbled backwards. The rest of the men stood in a half circle, watching their two officers closely.

Jessica stood just to Joshua's left, holding the baby, watching the whole thing impassively. It was as if she were an onlooker to something that had nothing to do with her.

Carter was sputtering as he caught his balance. "You can't do this! General Lucas will hear about this. He told you not to come here. He'll have you court-martialed."

Joshua decided to try a different tack. "You married, Lieutenant?" He knew the answer already.

Carter blinked. "Yes," he said guardedly.

"Children?"

"Yes, four."

"How old is the oldest?"

Carter was peering at him suspiciously. "He's twelve."

Joshua nodded and his voice dropped to a low rumble. "Well, this woman had a twelve-year-old son too. One of Comstock's men laid a rifle up alongside his head and blew it half away. A twelve-year-old, Carter! They just tossed him into a common grave. You want to be party to that?"

Carter's mouth opened, but Joshua bored in, not wanting to give him a chance to answer. "She had another son," he lied shamelessly. "I saw him too. He was eight years old. Eight! Half his hip is gone. Another one of Comstock's 'heroes' shot him at point-blank range." Now he lowered his voice, letting all the horror he was feeling pour into it. "Her husband's dead. She's been shot in the hand. All she has left now is this baby."

Joshua stepped forward, turning toward Jessica now, half whispering. "Look at her, Carter. She's in shock. She barely knows where she is." He turned to look at his men. "Is that what we stand for out here?"

Heads dropped or turned away. He saw two or three heads shake quickly back and forth. These men hated Mormons, but they weren't the lunatic types that rode with Neil Gilliam or Nehemiah Comstock. They had not come out to slaughter women and children.

Joshua stepped back. "This woman has family in Far West, and I say we take her close enough to the city that she can go the rest of the way in safety." He let his head swing slowly, staring down each of the men. "We're gonna drive the Mormons out of the state anyway. Doesn't this poor wretch deserve to be with them when we do? What do you say, men?"

Now he had them all, and Carter knew it. And it was also obvious that lumping Amanda Smith's loss with Jessica's had struck the mark with the lieutenant too. Carter straightened his uniform, not meeting Joshua's piercing glance. "I'm still going to have to report all this to General Lucas," he muttered.

"Report what you will," Joshua said. He turned to Jessica. "Come on, ma'am," he said gently. "You can ride with me."

By seven-thirty on Halloween morning, October thirty-first, 1838, Far West was like a town waiting for a tornado to strike. The Missouri militiamen camped to the south of them now outnumbered the Saints five to one, and more were coming in hourly. Word of the horror at Haun's Mill had ripped through the Saints like the bolt of lightning that had struck the liberty pole. Fear hung like a heavy fog over everything. The tension was as palpable as static electricity.

Shortly before eight, Colonel George M. Hinkle, the highest-ranking officer in the Mormon militia, sent a message to General Lucas requesting a meeting in which negotiations for some kind of truce might take place. Soon a message came back from General Lucas. He was too busy putting new troops into bivouac. He could not meet with the Mormons until 2:00 p.m.

And so the oncoming tornado was delayed for a time. It did little to change the mood in the town. The people knew that it was still coming, that it was headed straight for them with absolute inevitablity. But, for now at least, it stood off in the distance, dark, ominous, weaving sinuously back and forth, slowly driving everyone to the edge of madness.

Though no one knew it then, in actuality Hinkle had decided to take matters into his own hands. For some time now he had been chafing under Joseph's leadership. Hinkle had been the one who had led the Saints at DeWitt and defied the mobs. But in spite of that, Joseph had not given him full rein. There was not the slightest doubt in Hinkle's mind that the militia would roll over the Saints. Their poorly armed and virtually untrained home guard wouldn't stand a chance. But Joseph wouldn't listen. He was building the barricades, stiffening the will of the men. He was setting them up for a bloodbath. Being prophet was one thing, but this was war.

By quarter of two in the afternoon, the men and older boys from the city lined the barricades. A short distance away, on a small rise, the white flag fluttered on a staff along with the banner of General Lucas. He had kept his word and come to negotiate. Colonel George M. Hinkle rode out of town, moving toward the general's camp.

Benjamin, Matthew, Nathan, Derek, and Peter all stood together behind an overturned wagon. They watched somberly as the little party rode away from them. There was not a sound along the whole line.

Finally, unable to stand it any longer, Matthew turned to his father. "Pa?" he said softly.

Benjamin turned.

"What do you think is going to happen?"

Benjamin's shoulders lifted and fell. Nathan and Derek were watching him closely too. He wanted to unburden himself, tell them of the dark cloud of oppression that seemed to fill his own soul, but he knew they were looking to him for strength, for hope, for courage. But then he was spared the need for answering. Behind them, there was a cry. Turning as one, they saw Rebecca running hard toward them, coming up the street from their cabin.

"Papa! Papa!"

Her hair was flying. Benjamin felt a lurch of fear, and he leaped forward to see what was wrong. But then he realized her voice was joyous and triumphant. "Jessica's here! Jessica's here!"

Colonel George M. Hinkle held a commission in the Missouri militia from the governor. So as he walked up and saluted General Lucas, he moved with confidence and boldness. He knew what had to be done. There came a time when a man had to take the reins and put things in order.

They went through the formalities quickly, then Hinkle went straight to the point. "General Lucas, as senior officer in the Caldwell County militia, I am here to negotiate surrender terms. This insanity has gone on long enough."

General Lucas looked at him narrowly, then withdrew an envelope from inside the jacket of his uniform. "I think that is wise, sir, especially in light of the order we just received. It is signed the twenty-seventh day of October, just four days ago, by His Excellency, Governor Lilburn W. Boggs."

"Order, General?"

"Yes." Lucas took the paper out of the envelope and began to read, his voice hard and cold. Hinkle and his companions rocked back a little at the bluntness of the governor's order, but when Lucas read the words, "The Mormons must be treated as enemies and must be exterminated or driven from the state, if necessary for the public good," they went absolutely white. Hinkle barely heard the rest of what Lucas read to him.

Lucas stopped and folded the paper. "So you see, Colonel," he said, barely disguising his triumph, "it is a wise thing you have done to come now to negotiate. Actually, you have no choice."

"What terms do you require?" Hinkle whispered.

Lucas considered that for only a moment. "Four conditions. Number one, all Church leaders are to be given up for trial and punishment. Number two, the Mormons are to make an appropriation of their property for the payment of their debts and to indemnify the state for damages done by them. Third, the balance of the Mormons must leave the state. We will protect them with the militia, but they must leave."

Hinkle was deeply shocked. He hadn't expected warm terms, but there was no mercy here at all. "Immediately, sir?" he asked.

Lucas shook his head. "They can remain until I receive further orders from the governor." He looked at Hinkle sharply. "Fourth condition. Your people must give up arms of every description. These shall be receipted for."

Colonel Hinkle frowned. Lucas gave him a withering stare, and Hinkle immediately caved in. He began to nod. "And if I agree, there will be no attack upon our people?"

"You have my word, sir. And you will personally be treated as an officer should. There will be no incriminations of any kind against you."

Hinkle took a deep breath, then blew it out quickly. "Those terms are reasonable, sir. I can agree to them." Hinkle's lips pursed slightly. "It is already late in the day. I would suggest, therefore, that the surrender take place tomorrow."

"Agreed." Then a thought came to Lucas. "But I demand that you immediately bring to me hostages as pledge to guarantee your faithful compliance with these terms."

A little surprised, Hinkle leaned forward. "Hostages? Who, sir?"

Lucas was triumphant. He began to tick them off with his finger. "Colonel Lyman Wight of Daviess County. George Robinson of Far West. Parley P. Pratt and Sidney Rigdon." He paused, and a wicked grin pulled back his lips, revealing his teeth. "And Mr. Joseph Smith, Junior, of course."

For several moments Hinkle stared at the ground. Then he looked up. "Of course," he murmured.

"Be especially careful, Joseph." Hyrum Smith had been seriously ill for several days, and he looked drawn and tired. The thoughts of Joseph walking into the enemies' camp did little to help his weariness.

Joseph turned to his brother. "I will, Hyrum. Lucas just

wants to talk. I'm sure he wishes to set forth the terms of our surrender."

"And will you surrender, Joseph?" Benjamin Steed asked quietly.

Joseph turned to his old friend. "Benjamin, all this time we have thought that the militia was acting as a mob. But you heard the report. General Lucas is acting under direct commission of the state. He has an executive order from the governor."

"And that order says that we are to be exterminated or driven from the state," Nathan said hotly.

Joseph looked very tired too. His eyes were dark with sorrow. "It is still an order from the legal executive of this state."

Colonel Hinkle stepped forward. He was angry. "Enough of this talk. I have told you. The general only wishes to confer with Brother Joseph and our other leaders to see what can be done. They have pledged their sacred honor that you will not be abused or insulted."

Sidney Rigdon nodded. "We have no choice, Joseph."

Joseph looked at his couselor, then at Hinkle. Finally he nodded. "Yes, let us go." He quickly shook hands all around the circle. When he got to Hyrum they embraced. Parley Pratt stuck out his hand to Nathan. "Wish us luck, old friend."

"We'll be praying for you," Nathan said in return.

Joseph turned to Colonel Hinkle. "I'm ready," he said.

As they walked toward the gentle rise that led to Lucas's camp, Joseph and those with him could see the line of militiamen coming to meet them. It looked as though the whole of his army was marching to attack. General Lucas was in the lead. Directly behind him was a company of artillerymen. They had a four-pounder hitched behind a team of horses. On both sides of this group, infantry and cavalry stretched out behind them. There was at least a thousand men, maybe more.

Most chilling was the sight of one body of men. Led by Cornelius Gilliam—or Neil Gilliam, as he was more commonly known—they were dressed like Indians and had their faces painted black or red. Gilliam liked to fancy himself as the "Delaware Chief." He and his men had been terrorizing the countryside for several days. It was a sight to make the blood run cold.

The two groups closed quickly, and Lucas moved out ahead of his men. As they finally met, Joseph stepped out ahead of the others, extending his hand. "General Lucas," he said pleasantly, "we understand you wish to confer with us. It is late in the day. Would not tomorrow morning do just as well?"

But Colonel Hinkle stepped quickly up beside Joseph. "General Lucas," he said loudly, "here are the prisoners I agreed to deliver to you."

Joseph whirled around, staring at his leading commander in shocked dismay. Parley, Sidney, Lyman Wight, George Robinson—they all were thunderstruck.

Lucas raised one hand and instantly the soldiers nearest him leaped forward, surrounding the small body of Mormons, leveling their rifles. Like a battering wave of sound, a roar of triumph went up all along the line of Missourians. The company of artillerymen directly behind Lucas jumped up and down, waving their weapons and howling in jubilation. Neil Gilliam's men began to shriek wildly, spurring their horses and firing their rifles into the air. As Parley Pratt would later write, "If the vision of the infernal regions could suddenly open to the mind, with thousands of malicious fiends, all clamoring, exulting, deriding, blaspheming, mocking, railing, raging and foaming like a troubled sea, then could some idea be formed of the hell which we had entered."

Several hundred yards away, Benjamin and Nathan and the other brethren lining the barricades stood in stunned horror at the scene unfolding before them and the horrible shrieking that rent the air. After a moment, Nathan turned to his father. Benjamin was stricken to the core. "God help us now," he said in a hoarse whisper. "They've taken Joseph."

Chapter Notes

The surviving Saints at Haun's Mill were fearful that the mob would be returning and did bury their dead in the newly dug well (see *CHFT*, p. 204).

The treachery of Colonel Hinkle, the conditions set for the surrender, and the betrayal of Joseph and the other leaders is accurately portrayed in the novel (see *HC* 3:188–90 and *Mack Hist.*, pp. 272–73). Of this act, B. H. Roberts wrote, "So long as treason is detested, and traitors despised, so long will the memory of Colonel Hinkle be execrated for his vile treachery" (*Persecutions*, p. 243).

The quote from Parley P. Pratt can be found in his autobiography (see *PPP Auto.*, p. 160).

Chapter Twenty

"But, sir!" Lieutenant Carter was sputtering in his outrage. "The general asked me to report to him directly about Captain Steed. I demand to see him."

The man who served as the aide-de-camp to General Lucas was well aware of Carter's assignment. It made no difference. He had his orders too. "I will tell the general that you are back and wish to see him." He gave Carter a thin smile. "Or if you wish, you can give your report to me and I'll pass it on as soon as the general is free."

Carter stiffened. "The general said I was to report directly to him."

"Then you'll just have to wait until morning." The aide turned toward the tent door and waved his hand. Outside it was cacophony. Men yelling. Horrid shrieking. Occasional gunfire. "For heaven's sake, man! Can't you hear what's going on out there? We've got Joe Smith! We've got the Mormon leaders. The Mormons are going to surrender in the morning. General

Lucas has more important things on his mind right now than you and your Captain Steed."

Hyrum and Mary Fielding Smith had a modest home in Far West, but it was comfortably furnished and ample for the needs of them and their children. As Rebecca came up the walk, she could not see anyone in the lamplit windows. As she reached the porch, she stopped for a moment. A little shiver ran up and down her spine. The sounds of shrieking and yelling coming from the south of town carried faintly but clearly on the cold night air. Even though it was several hours later, the Missourians were still celebrating their capture of the Mormon prophet. It was enough to give you waking nightmares. Rebecca flinched as she heard a rifle shot, then another. Turning, she looked anxiously in that direction. Then she raised her hand swiftly and knocked on the door.

The door opened almost instantly to reveal Mary Smith. Now less than three weeks away from delivery, she was, as the scriptures say, "great with child." Her eyes were red and swollen, her cheeks tearstained. But when she saw who it was, her face lit up and she smiled. "Oh, Rebecca. Come in." As she stepped back, almost waddling, she braced her back with one hand and winced at a momentary flash of pain.

Rebecca followed her inside and shut the door. "I was hoping you would still be awake."

"How can we sleep with that?" She grimaced and flung one hand toward the window and the sounds coming to them from the far camp. Her face softened and she laid a hand on her belly. "And with this?"

"Are the children asleep?"

"Yes, thankfully." Mary sank down wearily into a chair. "Hyrum put them down before he went over to Joseph's house to comfort Mother and Father Smith. I tried to talk him out of it. He's so sick."

Rebecca shook her head. "How is Emma holding up?"

Mary frowned. "It's hard for her, of course, but Emma's strong. She's doing better than Joseph's father. When they heard all the shooting just after Joseph was taken, Father Smith was at the doorway to their home. He threw his arms across his chest. 'Oh, my God! my God!' he cried. 'They have killed my son! They have murdered him, and I must die, for I cannot live without him.' " Her eyes were glistening suddenly. "He collapsed and they put him to bed. He's barely moved since. He's so frail." She tipped her head back and massaged her neck.

Rebecca picked up a stool and set it down in front of Mary, then sat down to face her. "Are *you* all right? You should be in your bed."

"I'm fine," Mary managed. Then there was a smile in spite of it all. "If I could just get this boy to stop kicking me night and day."

Rebecca laughed. "You think it is a boy?"

"If it's a girl," Mary responded, "she's not acting much like a lady." Then she sobered. "It frightens me to think of having a baby with all this." She gestured again toward the south and the sounds that filled the air.

Rebecca had not come for this, in fact just the opposite. She clapped her hands together as if having a sudden thought. "I'm here to bring you some cheer."

Mary closed her eyes, the lines around her mouth softening slightly. "Now, that I could use."

Rebecca laid a hand on Mary's knee. "Forget about Missouri right now and all that's happening. Tell me about England. Is it really as beautiful as Derek says it is?"

Slowly Mary Fielding Smith's face smoothed out. She closed her eyes, and a quiet smile spread across her mouth. "Ah, yes, Rebecca. 'Tis a sight to behold, all green and lovely and. . . ."

Rebecca smiled and leaned back, pleased that her idea was working.

Joshua considered briefly trying to get to his horse, then decided against it. It was not much more than a mile to Far West, and he couldn't risk being caught by the sentries. He moved westward first. Far West was to the north, so the guards here were fewer and, as he hoped, much less alert. Once he was clear of the camp, he swung around to the north and broke into a jogging run, a black wraith moving swiftly through the rain and darkness of the early-morning hours of the first day of November.

Benjamin looked steadily at Mary Ann, feeling her grief as sharply as if it were his own. "There is no choice, Mother," he said firmly. He turned to his two sons. "Nathan, Matthew. Pack some things. You're going with the others."

There was a soft cry from Lydia, but she bit it back instantly. Nathan turned to her and held out his arms. Instantly she was into them and clinging to him in desperate longing. But when she spoke, it was loudly enough for everyone to hear. "Father Steed is right, Nathan. You've *got* to go. If they arrest you, we may never see you again."

Nathan turned to Joshua. "You're absolutely sure of this?"

Joshua threw up his hands. "Who's sure of anything out there? It's a madhouse. But yes, I heard one of Lucas's officers give the order. Any of the men who rode against the Missourians at Crooked River are to be arrested and taken south for trial."

"But how can they know?" Matthew said.

Joshua was grim. "You keep forgetting that some of your own people are with us, Mormons who have become bitter against you, men who are being offered money to finger the leaders and any others the militia wants."

Benjamin was very anxious. Joshua's arrival had been a pleasant surprise, but his news had spread alarm throughout the city. "The time for discussion is past. All those who they can find are gathering at the square in ten minutes. If you're not there, they'll leave without you. You've got to be long away before first light."

Mary Ann went to her youngest son, now eighteen and towering almost a foot above her. She put her arms around his waist. Neither could bear to speak. They just held each other, and Matthew patted his mother's shoulders awkwardly, and in great pain.

Joshua cleared his throat. "I've got to get back before anyone realizes I've gone."

Benjamin swung around. "Son—" His voice caught, and he shook his head, frustrated that his emotions rose up so easily.

In the lamplight, Joshua could see that his father's eyes were suddenly shining. He felt a great lump filling his own chest. He raised one hand. "You don't have to say anything, Pa. I'm just glad I found out about this."

Jessica had been sitting quietly in one corner of the room. She stood now and came to the man who had once been her husband. She stepped in front of him, her eyes large and filled with sorrow. She reached up and touched his face with her bandaged hand. He saw now that the bandage was new and clean. "This is twice in two days you've come to our aid, Joshua." She took a quick breath. "Whatever debts you may have incurred in the past, they're paid now. A hundredfold." She went up on tiptoes and kissed him on the cheek. "Thank you. Thank you for everything."

Joshua started to speak, but found himself too deeply moved to get the words out. He finally shook his head gruffly, turned, and spoke to his father and mother. "I don't know what's going to happen today. I'll try to come in with my troops, but . . ." He shrugged. Promises were cheap right now.

In two steps Mary Ann was to him, throwing her arms around him. "Oh, beloved Joshua, my son, my son."

They stood there for several moments, holding each other tightly. Then finally Joshua stepped back and turned to face Nathan and Matthew. "Be careful," he said, gripping Nathan's hand. "Don't stop until you're in Iowa Territory."

Nathan nodded, gripping his hand tightly. "We won't."

Joshua and Matthew hugged, then Joshua went to the door.

He looked at his father, then at his mother. There was a curt nod. Then he lifted one hand briefly, opened the door, and disappeared back out into the darkness of predawn.

They were seated around the kitchen table—all but Rachel, young Joshua, and Emily, who sat on chairs and held their breakfast plates in their laps. The meal was almost done, and tension had begun to fill the air. In less than an hour the brethren in Far West, the ones who had not fled before dawn, would gather in the central square, then march out of town to give up their weapons to the Missourians. It meant surrendering the only thing that gave them hope of holding the armies at bay. The thought of it weighed heavily on everyone's mind.

Then Derek cleared his throat and raised his hand. Benjamin looked up in suprise. "Yes?"

Derek cleared his throat again. For most of his youth and all of his adult life, Derek Ingalls had learned to keep his emotions to himself. He rarely spoke of feelings, even more rarely exhibited those feelings openly. So this did not come easy to him.

"Go on, Derek," Rebecca urged.

"All right." He looked around at the family. Even the children had stopped eating and were watching him. He cleared his throat a third time. "Peter and me? We . . . well, we never had any family. Not since we were little. We had to fend for ourselves. It wasn't always easy."

Peter was nodding soberly.

"But since we came to America . . ." He looked down, his hands and fingers twisting around each other. "Well, we found us a family."

"Amen!" Peter said quietly but fervently.

Derek looked at his father-in-law. "Father Steed, we just wanted you to know. No matter what happens today or in the days to come. We're Steeds now too. You can count on us to be here. No matter what."

"That's right," Peter said, more loudly now.

Derek looked over at Lydia, then to Jessica. "I know your husbands are not here, that you have children." His shoulders straightened. "But I want you to know, they are my children now too. You are my sisters. More dear to me than the sisters I lost when I was a young boy."

"And me too," Peter murmured bravely.

It was absolutely quiet in the cabin. Jessica, sitting directly across from Derek, was staring at him in wonder. Mary Ann was blinking her eyes rapidly. Benjamin was looking at him with open affection and admiration. But it was Lydia, sitting on the other side of Rebecca, who finally broke the silence, though her voice was very soft when she spoke. "Rebecca?"

"Yes, Lydia?"

"I have a favor to ask of you."

Rebecca looked surprised. "What?"

"I would like your permission to give your husband a great big hug, and maybe even be so bold as to kiss him on the cheek."

Rebecca smiled, then turned to Derek. She reached up and brushed a lock of hair back away from his eyes. "I think that would be most appropriate, Lydia. You have my permission."

This is madness! It can't work! Benjamin felt like throwing up his hands and screaming into the air. The time for praying had passed. The children had been sent behind the curtain to play school with young Joshua and Rachel. Now it was just the adults and Peter. In a few moments Benjamin and Derek would have to report to the square with the rest of the Mormon men and prepare to surrender their arms. And when they set out, there would be twelve women and children—two of them infants not yet a year old—left here with a fourteen-year-old.

Benjamin's shoulders lifted and fell. Weariness and worry etched deep lines into his face. His eyes were pinched and bloodshot. He had never felt so totally desolate in all his life. He stepped forward and took Peter by the shoulders. "Son?"

"Yes, Father Steed?" Peter's dark eyes were wide and intent, but there was no sign of fear.

Benjamin reached down and took the pistol from the waistband of his trousers. "I'm not going to surrender this one, Peter. You need to hide it. They'll probably search for other weapons. Hide it good, but you've got to be able to get at it quickly if you need to."

"Benjamin—" Mary Ann started, but he held up his hand, cutting her off, not moving his eyes from Peter's face. "Do you understand, Peter?"

"I understand."

"I . . ." He glanced over at Mary Ann, trying to reassure her with his eyes. Then he came back to Peter. "I don't want to do this, Peter. But you're the safest bet. The women are too . . ." He couldn't finish that thought. *The women are too vulnerable.* He took a quick breath. "The women need to hide with the children and keep them quiet. If the mob comes, they'll be looking for grown men. They shouldn't bother a boy."

"Yes, sir." Peter licked his lower lip, his mind flashing back four days earlier when two evil-smelling men had tied him to a tree and prepared to whip him into unconsciousness. The fact that he was a boy hadn't seemed to deter them. But he only nodded. "Don't worry, Father Steed. I'll be fine."

Benjamin straightened, the corners of his mouth pulling down. "I know. Colonel Hinkle says Lucas has promised that once our arms are grounded he'll let us return to our homes. So I hope we'll be back in an hour or two."

Derek came forward one step to stand in front of his brother. "The moment Father Steed and I are released, we'll come right back here."

Peter nodded, fighting to keep his eyes calm. He could already feel his pulse start to race a little at the thoughts of being alone, the only man left in the family, but there was no way he was going to show his feelings of nervousness.

Benjamin was very tired. He glanced at the front window. "Watch closely. If you see anything, Peter, any sign of trouble, you get everyone into the root cellar."

"I will, Father Steed."

"Good." Benjamin took Peter's shoulder, turning him around. He pointed to the large, round rug Rebecca and Mary Ann had woven from rags the previous winter. "That's big enough to cover the door to the cellar. Once everybody is inside, pull it over and put something on it. A chair, a table . . ."

"I understand. I will."

Benjamin slowly straightened, looking first at his wife, then at his daughter and daughters-in-law. "God be with you," he said softly.

At 8:00 a.m. on the morning of November first, the militia of Caldwell County—called by their enemies "the Mormon militia," and by themselves "the armies of Israel"—marched out of Far West under the command of Colonel George Hinkle. Not all the Mormon men were in the militia and a few remained behind, but there were about four hundred men, formed into companies, and this left the city largely unprotected. Benjamin and Derek were assigned to the company of Brigham Young and marched directly behind him and Heber C. Kimball. No one spoke. Ahead, about half a mile away, the prairie was black with men, four or five thousand of them, marshalled by companies of cavalry and infantry. Near the front, one brigade had formed into a large, hollow square—a prison compound of human flesh.

A ragged cheer went up and down the line as the Mormon militia marched into the square the Missourians had formed. Rifles were up and trained on the phalanx, but it was obvious that the Mormons weren't going to give them a fight. The battle was won. The day was theirs. It was a triumphant moment.

Colonel Hinkle raised his arm and the Mormons came to a ragged halt. "All right, men," he shouted. "Ground your arms. General Lucas has promised to receipt them. Put them into stacks and then stand clear."

There was angry muttering that broke out now among the Saints as they moved forward and began to stack their rifles together. It was bad enough that Hinkle had betrayed them, but to have him act as if this capitulation were all being done in perfectly legal fashion infuriated them.

They had just finished stacking their rifles, when one end of the square opened briefly and General Lucas rode in with a small entourage. He dismounted, then came over to the brethren, strutting arrogantly, nodding to the cheering troops as if he had single-handedly pulled off this entire coup. He walked around the stacks of arms, surveying them with satisfaction, then turned to Hinkle. "Good job, Colonel. You have met another of the conditions of our treaty."

Hinkle unbuckled the belt that held his sword and scabbard and a pistol. He handed them over to Lucas. "Thank you, sir. I promised we would not resist. May I release the men, then?"

Lucas gave him an incredulous look. "I say not, sir! They will be held here under guard for a time while I send my men to the city to look for additional weapons. Then I will march them back to their homes."

Hinkle was stunned. "But, General—"

Hinkle's cry of dismay went unheard. Lucas had swung around. "Men! Hear me! Those in the square will stay and act as guard, but the rest of you, listen good. The Mormons are disarmed. Go to the city. Search *every* house. Look everywhere. I want every rifle, every pistol, every weapon of any kind confiscated before we let these men return to their homes."

The roar of acclamation was instantaneous and thunderous. Men turned and darted for their horses. Those in the companies of infantry broke ranks and dashed forward, moving up the gradual hill that led to Far West, like the foul backwash belched up from some primeval swamp.

Peter was standing on the porch when he heard the roar go up. He went up, standing on tiptoes, but he was nowhere near the south edge of town. He couldn't see anything. A moment later, however, he heard closer cries and screams of alarm. A young woman came darting out from between two cabins, sprinting hard, her skirts billowing out and her hair flying.

"What is it?" Peter yelled at her. "What's happening?"

She barely broke stride. "They're holding the brethren prisoner and they've turned the militia loose on the city. They're coming! Run!"

Peter went white, then turned and darted inside the cabin, screaming for the women and children to get into the root cellar.

"He what!" Joshua yelled.

But the man had no time for some slow-witted militia captain. He pulled free from Joshua's grip, grabbed at the saddle horn, and leaped into the saddle as the horse bolted away.

Joshua had stayed back in the main camp, fearing that if he went out for the surrender of arms, General Lucas or Lieutenant Carter might see him. He had heard the animal roar from the crowd and had come out of his tent on the run. Now men were racing back toward their horses, shouting and jostling for the best position.

Joshua darted to the next man. This one was trying to mount his horse, but the animal was skittish from all the commotion. The man had one foot in the stirrup and was hopping frantically as the horse kept prancing around in a circle. He made it into the saddle just as Joshua reached him.

Joshua grabbed the reins, pulling the horse around. "Is it true?" he cried. "Has Lucas sent the militia into Far West?"

The man nodded ecstatically. "Yes, we're to look for any hidden weapons." He jerked the reins out of Joshua's hand and spurred the horse into a hard lope.

Joshua stared after him. *Or anything else you can lay your hands on!* He swore. What Lucas had really given them was a license for looting. And every man jack one of them knew exactly what he was being told he could do. Joshua swore again and turned and ran for his own horse.

As he reached his mount and started to untie the reins, a sharp voice cried out from behind him. "Oh no you don't, mister!"

Joshua jerked around to look into the muzzle of Lieutenant Jerome Carter's pistol.

"Get outta my way!" Joshua thundered. "I've been ordered into Far West."

"That's bull, Steed! I talked to Lucas. You ain't been ordered anywhere. I'm to arrest you and hold you for court-martial."

Joshua didn't even think. He lunged forward, half spinning away from the line of the muzzle. There was a tremendous blast, and he felt something pluck at his coat. Instantly he interlocked his fingers, forming a club with his two hands. Driven by all the pent-up rage he had felt toward this idiot-playing-soldier, he swung at Carter's arm. There was a sharp cry and the pistol went flying. Joshua raised his hands high again and chopped down viciously at Carter's neck. He caught him right behind the ears. Carter's head snapped sideways. He was thrown backwards against a tent pole. His legs tangled in the rope and he went down hard, face first.

Joshua didn't give him a second glance. He leaped for his horse and swung up. He dug his heels into the horse's flanks. "Go!" he shouted into its ear. "Go!"

Chapter Notes

Sometime during the night of October thirty-first or the early morning of November first, someone did come to Far West to warn the Saints that the men who had fought in the Battle of Crooked River would be arrested, though records do not say who it was. Some sources indicate that it was Hyrum Smith and Brigham Young who, having learned of this threat, spread the word. About twenty brethren fled north to avoid being taken. (See *CHFT*, p. 205.)

There is some discrepancy in the sources about exactly how long the men of the Mormon militia were detained by Lucas after they were forced to surrender their arms. Some say that they were released immediately. Lucas himself indicated that he placed them under guard to march them "back to Far West, and protect and take charge of them" (*HC* 3:198). Since it is difficult to imagine that the brethren of the Mormon militia were set free and were standing around in Far West while the Missouri militia ravaged the city, the author has chosen to have Lucas delay their return to the city until his men have done the damage, though allowance has been made to have *some* Mormon men in the city during the attack.

Chapter Twenty-One

"I'm tellin' ya, there ain't nothing here."

The smaller of the two men, bearded and filthy with mud, swung around on Peter. "Shut up, ya British brat!"

The man looked more ridiculous than frightening. Last night's rain and the sweat of today's looting had left his "war paint" streaked and grotesque. His buckskin shirt had large, ugly stains across the front. It was also too small and was barely able to cover the spread of his belly.

But Peter was not tempted to laugh. The glittering eyes, the naked lust for spoils that twisted the man's face were too terrifying. Peter looked away. "Well, there ain't," he mumbled under his breath.

The man leaped across the room, swinging his fist. Peter jerked away, deflecting the worst of the blow. But even then, it nearly knocked him off the chair and onto the large round rug on which the chair sat. He ducked his head, pretending to be cowed.

The larger man, dressed and painted in similar fashion, turned and looked only long enough to see that his partner was taking care of the situation; then he turned back and continued to systematically ransack the large chest that stood at the foot of Benjamin and Mary Ann's bed.

The cabin was a shambles. What dishes Mary Ann had not packed away and buried in preparation for this very eventuality had been hurled against the floor. The two men had fought over who got the dish cupboard Matthew had made for his mother, recognizing it as a valuable piece of furniture. But, like little children, when they couldn't agree on who would get it, or how they would get it out of the city on horseback, they fell on it in a fury. Now it was a shattered hulk in one corner. Clothing, rags, bedding, straw, feathers, and broken crockery, were strewn everywhere. The windows were all smashed out. Chairs had been hammered against the log walls until they splintered. Mattresses were ripped apart in the men's search for hidden valuables.

Peter had nearly died when the larger man, the one named Caleb, suggested they tear up the floorboards to see if there was anything hidden beneath them. But he had started in the corner opposite the root cellar, and when he saw that the boards rested directly on the packed earth beneath them, he abandoned the idea. Peter's heart was still pounding from that one.

Caleb finished his ruination of the chest and its contents. "He's right, Hugh," he snarled. He swung around and kicked bitterly at a pan with a large dent in it. It clattered across the floor. "The kid's right. There ain't nothin' here. Come on, let's find another place before all the good stuff is gone."

The small man's hand shot out and grabbed Peter's coat. He yanked him forward so that his face was right up against Peter's. His breath was foul and rancid, his teeth stained yellow, his tongue a dark brown from the wad of chewing tobacco in his cheek. "You stay here, brat!" he threatened. "You so much as stick your head out the door, and I'll blow it off. You hear me?"

"Yes, sir," Peter said meekly.

Swaggering with power, the man turned and strutted out the

door after his companion. "Let's see what's around back," he hollered.

Peter didn't dare move, but he could hear their progress. They were first into the toolshed and then in the smokehouse. He could hear the large man cursing and swearing. The Steeds had left very little of value in either of the two small buildings.

"Hey! What kinda contraption is this?"

Peter straightened. He could see nothing out the back window. There was an unintelligible reply, then the same voice said again, "What is this thing?" There was a solid crack as someone struck metal against wood.

Ducking down, Peter scooted over to the window, then came up slowly, peeking over the edge of the shattered sill. The big man named Caleb was standing in front of the McCormick reaper that Joshua had bought for his father. He had an ax in his hand. One of the paddle bars was already shattered. Caleb swung the ax again, and chips of wood flew. In a frenzy now, he fell upon the machine, swinging and cursing.

Suddenly, Peter jerked around. There was a soft knocking sound. It was coming from under the floor. "Peter!" It was muffled, but clearly heard.

In three leaps he was to where his chair sat on the large round rug. He kicked aside the debris from off one corner of the rug and dropped to a crouch. He lifted the rug up a few inches. "Be quiet!" he hissed.

"Have they gone?" He couldn't tell for sure whether it was Jessica or Lydia. Benjamin had been right about the root cellar being a safe place to hide, but it was just barely big enough to hold them all. It was not deep enough for the women to stand up in once the door was shut, so they had hunched over and the children had packed in around them. Peter knew it must be stifling and terrible down in the cellar, but it was also still very dangerous to be out of it.

He knocked softly on the door, putting his mouth right down against the crack. "They've gone outside," he whispered, "but they're still close by. Be quiet. I'll tell you when it's—"

A noise behind him made Peter jump. He whirled around so fast he lost his balance and went sprawling. As he scrambled up, the large man stepped inside the door. His teeth were pulled back in a huge grin that split the painted face. "Well, well, well," he leered. "Whaddya know about that?"

Hyrum Smith did not go out with the militia that morning to surrender weapons. He was sick. His wife was also sick—largely due to the terrible strain of what had happened and what was now happening, and to the fact that she was also eight and a half months pregnant. With the approval of the other leaders, it was decided Hyrum should stay behind, but he was to stay indoors and not come out.

But Hyrum Smith was in the First Presidency. He was now the senior Church leader in Far West. And the Missourians were eager that the Saints should be leaderless. Colonel George M. Hinkle thus completed the circle of his treachery. Sometime during the morning of November first, as the Missourians were beginning their rampage through Far West, an unarmed Colonel Hinkle arrived at the home of Hyrum and Mary Fielding Smith with an armed contingent of men. Ignoring Hyrum's weakened condition and Mary's advanced stage of pregnancy, Hinkle placed Hyrum under arrest and delivered him to the camp of General Lucas to be placed in bonds along with his brother Joseph.

Also arrested that day was Amasa Lyman, who was in the leadership of the high priests quorum.

Two years previous, Joshua Steed had gone to New Orleans to transact some business for his partners in St. Louis. He had arrived in the great river port three days after a hurricane had swept across the peninsula south of the city. He and a cotton factor had gone out to see how much damage had been done to the plantations. It had been a shocking experience to see what nature could do when fully unleashed.

When Joshua reached the outskirts of Far West he was met by a line of sentries posted to stop anyone from escaping from the city. Deciding he would be less conspicuous if he proceeded on foot, he left his horse in the care of one of the men and crossed through the lines. Now as he walked swiftly across the city, memories of that Louisiana hurricane came flooding back—only this time it was human nature that had been unleashed on a town, and it was more devastating than any wind could ever have been.

Cabins had been unroofed, rail fencing ripped apart, stores brickbatted. Men were running everywhere, pouring in and out of homes like ants on a foraging expedition. They carried bedding and clothing, pots, jars, dishes, boots, tools—anything that wasn't fastened down and that someone else had not already grabbed. Haystacks were torn apart as frantic men looked for treasure the Mormons may have hid. The front yard of virtually every house was littered with their leavings. Clothing had been slashed, linens trampled into the mud.

Joshua passed a dry goods store. Its door hung crazily from one hinge. The windows were smashed. Inside, men were fighting over the contents of the shelves, yipping and snarling and snapping at each other. Behind the store, three men were ripping at the railing of a fence. Puzzled, Joshua slowed his step, not sure why the fence should be a target. Then as the men finished their task, he understood why. With the fence down, they went after the five or six horses in the pasture, driving them through the opening they had made and into an adjoining cornfield. The men ran behind the horses, waving their hats and yelling at the top of their lungs. The cornfield, also fenced, was considerably smaller than the pasture, and the horses went wild in the confined space. In moments, the cornfield was a trampled, muddy mass of useless pulp, and the men whooped with glee at what they had done.

Joshua shook his head in disgust. This was even worse than the looting. At least there was some personal gain in that. This was just wanton, blind destruction. He moved on swiftly.

Joshua was nearly to his father's cabin when he pulled up

short. In the narrow space between a cabin and a shed, a man was on his knees in front of a small bench. He was sobbing uncontrollably over what looked like a rumpled piece of clothing. Cautious, but curious, Joshua changed direction and moved closer. And then his eyes widened and his jaw dropped. It was not a piece of clothing on the bench. It was a woman. In her late twenties, maybe. Her dress was torn. Her face was bloody. Her hands had been pulled above her head and lashed down tightly to the bench. Her feet had been tied to the opposite end.

Joshua felt suddenly sick. With terrible clarity he realized what had happened. He wasn't sure how many men there had been, but enough to kill her. And they had probably made her husband watch the whole thing at pistol point.

He fell back a step, horrified beyond anything he had ever felt before. The man must have heard him, for he jumped up, whirling around. His eyes were wild, and he raised his hands in front of his face. "No! Please!"

Joshua was backing up now. He raised his own hands, trying to calm the man. "It's all right," he said. "I'm a friend. I won't hurt you."

"Please. No. Oh, please." He was almost babbling.

Joshua turned and trotted away. Then, as the reality of what he had just seen hit him with its full force, he broke into a run. Faster and faster. Toward his father's house.

There was a third "Indian" in the Steed cabin now. He had been passing by just as Caleb and Hugh came back into the cabin and pulled back the rug that hid the root cellar. Sticking his head in to see what was going on, he instantly saw an opportunity too ripe to pass up. Now this third man had a pistol trained on Peter. But his eyes kept darting hungrily to where Lydia, Jessica, Rebecca, and Mary Ann stood wide-eyed and terrified. "I get the dark one, Caleb."

"Shut up!" the large man roared. "You'll get whatever Hugh and me say you get. We found 'em."

"Yeah," the little man with the dirty beard and the streaked war paint chortled. "We sure did."

The muffled screams and wailing of the children could be heard coming from beneath the floor. Caleb had made the women get out of the cellar, then had slammed the cover back down on the children. Only young Joshua had scrambled out to join the women. Now he stood beside his mother, clinging desperately to Lydia's skirts.

"Leave them alone," Peter shouted.

The newcomer swung around, his fist aimed at Peter's head. Peter jerked away, but the blow caught him on the back and shoulder and sent him slamming against the wall. He stumbled to one knee, gasping.

"One more word outta you, boy, and you're a dead Englishman. You hear me!" He swung a kick at Peter's ribs, but Peter saw that one and rolled away in time.

"*You hear me!*"

Peter dropped his head and nodded. "Yes."

The one called Caleb moved slowly across the room, his glittering eyes fixed on Rebecca. She shrank back with a sharp intake of breath.

"Come here, missy," he breathed heavily. "I like the young ones."

Suddenly young Joshua hurtled forward, arms flailing as he threw himself at the man's legs. "Leave her alone!" he screamed. "You leave my aunt alone!" It caught Caleb by surprise and stopped his forward progress.

"Joshua!" Lydia screamed. She lunged forward, but instantly the one called Hugh had his rifle up and pointed straight at her head. "Get back!" he yelled.

Sobbing, Lydia fell back. From the root cellar Emily started to scream. "Mama! Mama!"

Caleb swung down and corralled Joshua with ridiculous ease, then pushed him out at arm's length. "Lookee here, Hugh," he said over his shoulder. "This little Mormon mite has got some real spunk." He went into a half crouch, peering into Joshua's eyes. The boy was still trying to hit him, but his blows were going wild. "How old are you, boy?"

Joshua looked straight into the man's eyes but clamped his mouth shut.

Caleb's eyes narrowed dangerously. "I said, how old are you, boy?"

"He's seven," Lydia cried. "Please don't hurt him. Take me, if you must. But don't hurt my children."

Caleb gave Joshua a hard shove, and the boy stumbled back into his mother's arms. Lydia gathered him in with a sob, holding him tightly to her. Caleb leered at her. "Now, don't you get anxious, honey," he crooned. "You'll get your turn soon enough. First we're gonna get to know this one."

In one leap he was to Rebecca. His hand snaked out with lightning speed and he had her by the arm, dragging her toward him.

"No!" Rebecca screamed. There was the sound of tearing fabric and she pulled free, leaving most of her sleeve in his hand.

Mary Ann and Jessica leaped at him simultaneously. With a roar, Caleb swung around. His fist caught Mary Ann in the chest, knocking her backwards. Jessica was clinging to him, clawing at his face, the bandage on her hand totally forgotten. He reached up and grabbed her hair, yanking her head back. He smacked her across the side of the face with the pistol butt. There was a sickening thud and Jessica dropped like a sack of flour.

Rebecca and Lydia screamed. Young Joshua was shouting hysterically. But Peter kept quiet, hoping to seize an opportunity to make a move. The newcomer still had the pistol trained on him, but the man's attention was fixed on the action taking place across the room. Peter moved quickly, scrambling on all fours.

"Hey!" the man shouted. He swung up his pistol and fired. It was deafening in the confines of the cabin. But Peter was too quick. The shot buried itself in one of the logs where Peter had just been. By then Peter was at the fireplace, clawing at the two loose stones he had dug out earlier that day. Cursing wildly, the man leaped for the table, where Caleb's rifle lay. His pistol carried only one shot without reloading and was useless now.

Peter gasped in relief. The stones were free and the pistol lay in its hole beneath them. He yanked it out, rolling away as he did so. The man had the rifle up. There was a flash and another blast. The bullet whanged into the fireplace, flinging splinters of rock into Peter's face. But he was not conscious of the stinging barbs. He was up on his knees, clasping the pistol with both hands. He pulled the trigger, flinching as the pistol bucked in his hands.

The man who had come into the Steed cabin to share in the spoils slammed back against the table, his eyes wide and startled. Blood poured out of a small hole high in his left shoulder. The rifle clattered to the floor. He coughed once, then went down, clutching at his wound and moaning.

Peter heard a noise to one side and swung around to meet it, raising the pistol again. But this time he was far too slow. Hugh's boot came swinging in. The toe of it caught Peter right on the elbow, and the pistol flew out of his hands. "You stupid pup!" Hugh shouted.

The rifle butt came slashing in. Peter tried to throw up his arm, but it was like throwing a twig in front of a crashing log. There was a burst of flashing light and Peter went sprawling. He rolled to a stop and lay still.

"No!" Mary Ann was up on one knee. She was gasping. One arm was across her chest where Caleb had struck her. Her face was white, her mouth drawn back as she bit down on the pain. "Peter!" she cried. She began dragging herself through the debris on the floor toward him.

Caleb gave Peter's still form one contemptuous look, then whirled back around to face Rebecca. His eyes had narrowed to tiny slits. The pistol came up and steadied, not two feet away from Rebecca's face. "Now, missy!" he grunted. "You come to Caleb, or I'll blow your brains all over this—"

Behind them there was a tremendous crash as the back door

to the cabin burst open and slammed against the wall. Hugh and Caleb both whirled, weapons coming up.

"Don't do it!" Joshua shouted, waving his pistol at both of them. "Don't do it!"

Both men hesitated. The figure of a man was silhouetted against the outside light, and all they could see for sure was the shape of the pistol. Their hesitation was their undoing, and they knew it. Slowly Caleb lowered his pistol. In a moment, Hugh followed suit.

"Joshua?" Mary Ann was at Peter's side, but she clambered to her feet. There was a look of incredulous joy on her face. "Joshua, is that you?"

At the same instant, Rebecca gave a soft cry and dropped to her knees, burying her face in her hands. Great shuddering sobs began to rack her body.

Joshua didn't look at either of them. He jerked his head toward the two men. "Put your weapons on the table, then get over by the wall."

"Who are you?" Caleb snarled. But he complied as he did so. His partner did the same, his eyes darting back and forth between Joshua and Caleb.

Joshua stepped inside and shut the door. "Captain Steed, Third Brigade, Missouri militia. Serving under General Lucas."

"You're one of us?" Hugh exploded with relief.

Joshua's pistol never wavered. "What are you doing here?"

A lecherous grin stole across Caleb's face. "Whaddya think, Captain?" He leaned forward, the lust burning in his eyes. "And you're just in time. You can have first choice."

Joshua lunged forward, the pistol barrel whipping downward. The gunsight caught the big man high on his left cheek, instantly opening a three-inch gash. Caleb screamed and fell backwards. Joshua waded in, shouting at the top of his lungs. "That's my sister, you—" His hand lashed out again and again. "*That's my sister!*"

Caleb was shrieking now, his hands over his head. He went

down to his knees, then into a ball on the floor, trying to escape the blows raining down on him.

"Captain! Captain!" Hugh shouted. "Stop it! You're killing him!"

Joshua's hand stopped in midair, then gradually lowered. He stepped back, chest heaving. "Get outta here!" he said in heavy disgust. "Get outta my sight before I kill the both of you." He motioned to the man whom Peter had shot and who was now moaning and writhing on the floor. "And take this scum with you." The wounded newcomer needed no prodding. Lumbering awkwardly, trying to staunch the flow of blood from his shoulder with his other hand, he stumbled outside and disappeared.

Caleb reached up, groping for the table. He was a ghastly sight. His cheek was streaming blood. Another blow had cut open one eyebrow, and the blood pouring into his eye had closed it. He held his head in his hands, cowering as he started past Joshua. Joshua stepped back, turning away, afraid he might hit the man again. Then suddenly the big man lunged across the table, grabbing for the pistol he had laid there.

"Joshua, watch out!" Lydia cried.

Joshua rolled hard, shooting as he fell, his pistol firing a split second ahead of Caleb's. The bullet caught the Missourian square in the chest, smashing him backwards, jerking the muzzle of Caleb's pistol up sharply. The ball from Caleb's gun went straight up and into the ceiling of the cabin.

There was a crash as Caleb careened off a chair and then hit the floor. Joshua sprang up again, but the threat was over. Hugh was staring at his partner, eyes bulging from the midst of the streaked and washed-out war paint.

Joshua stepped forward, waving the pistol. Hugh cried out in terror and fell back scrambling. "You miserable cur!" Joshua said with low menace. "Get outta here!"

"I'm goin'! I'm goin'!" he squealed. He bolted through the front door and darted away, howling as he ran.

Joshua spun around. In three steps he was to Rebecca. Dropping the pistol, he gently took her by both elbows and pulled her up. He took her in his arms and pulled her to him. "It's all right now," he soothed, pressing her against him to steady her. "It's all right."

She looked up, still dazed. Then recognition dawned in her eyes. She threw her arms around him and buried her head against his shoulder. Mary Ann came over, crying now too, but with relief and joy. "I'll take her," she said, pulling Rebecca to her.

Joshua whirled back around. Jessica was getting up, holding her bandaged hand to the side of her head. Lydia was holding young Joshua tightly, sobbing uncontrollably. "Lydia!" he barked. "Jessica! Where are the children?"

They both turned and pointed. "In the root cellar," Lydia said.

He waved his hand in the direction of the dead man on the floor. "This is bad. Very bad. We've got to get out of here. Where can we take you?"

"To our house," Lydia cried. "There are two other families there, but it's a place where we can hide."

Joshua straightened. "Get the children. I'll get Peter. Come on! We don't have much time."

Joshua moved cautiously, pistol in hand, wishing desperately that it was night. He half laughed at his own irrationality. It was not even noon yet. There would be no covering darkness for him this time. He stopped at the corner of a barn and carefully peered around the corner. There were some men looting a home down the street about half a block away. He stepped back, wanting to be sure he could cross without being seen.

He would head west out of the city. Go four or five miles, enough to give Lucas's camp a wide berth, then head south. He had no plans to try and get back to his horse. That would be certain suicide. He would find a place to hole up, along a creek maybe, and wait until it was dark. Then he would head for Independence. Given half a break he might find a homestead. He'd buy a horse—or steal one if he had to. It was critical he get back to Independence and to Caroline, before the news could precede him. It would be close, but Cornwell had the wagon and emergency supplies all ready and waiting. They would go to St. Louis. Farther if they had to. He nodded at that. He suspected that anywhere in Missouri was not going to be safe for him now. Not for a very long time.

He cursed at himself. *I should have shot the other two as well!* That way there would have been no witnesses, no one to identify Captain Joshua Steed. But he pushed that thought aside almost as quickly as it had come. He couldn't just shoot a man down in cold blood. Besides, if he had shot them and gotten away clean, they would think the Mormons had done it. And there would be a heavy price to pay for that. A price that would fall on the heads of his own family.

He peeked around the corner again. The men were still at it, but they were running in and out of the house. He let out his breath, his mind racing, knowing it was dangerous to stand still too long. He had to move.

One more quick look. He jerked back, his heart pounding. A man had come out of a house just three buildings down. He was coming toward him. Joshua couldn't tell if he was Mormon or Missourian. With almost all the Mormon men still held outside of town under guard, it was probably a Missourian, but Joshua sure wasn't going to wait to find out. He started backing up, lifting his feet carefully so as to make no sound.

He never heard the sound of the rifle shot. He just felt the terrible blow to his back and the instant, searing pain that cut right through his entire body. He half fell, staggering, caught only by the wall of the building. Clutching at his chest, Joshua stared down at the blood splattered on the wall. *Someone's been shot!* It didn't register that it was his own blood he was seeing.

Dimly, through a roaring in his ears, he heard a voice shouting from somewhere behind him. "I got 'im! I got 'im!"

He turned slowly, his knees starting to buckle. *I know that voice!* The pain was making him gasp now, and he slid slowly downward until he was sitting down, his back against the barn. *Where have I heard that voice!* It seemed like a problem of immense importance. And then with a great sense of relief, he remembered. It was the voice of the man back at his mother's cabin. The little man. Joshua shook his head, vastly troubled. *But he left his rifle on the table. He doesn't have a rifle.*

Joshua let the pistol slide out of his fingers. He was glad he had talked to Cornwell. So everything would be ready for him and Caroline to quickly flee. There wouldn't be much time once he got there.

He was aware of the sound of running feet, but he couldn't make his eyes focus. The fire was blinding him as well as deafening him. He toppled over onto his side. Somewhere it registered that his face was in the wetness of prairie grass. "I'm coming, Caroline," he whispered. "I'm coming."

Chapter Notes

The surrender of the Mormon arms was the key to giving the Missouri militia and mob free rein to loot and pillage. Lucas made no effort to control or restrain them. (See *Persecutions*, pp. 243–45.) The descriptions of what followed as seen through Joshua's eyes are based on contemporary accounts of the fall of Far West (see *Persecutions*, pp. 243–45; *CHFT*, p. 206).

Chapter Twenty-Two

"No!"

Derek and Benjamin had come around the smokehouse, approaching the cabin from the rear just to be certain it was safe. There were still a few of the militia in town, and so the returning men were taking no chances. Lucas had marched the brethren back into town, then finally released them around noon, warning them that the city was surrounded and that no one was allowed to leave. But as the Mormon men raced homeward it was obvious they were too late to make any difference. Now as Derek and Benjamin rounded the cabin, they came face-to-face with the reaping machine. Benjamin stopped in midstride, gaping at the wreckage before him.

Derek was staring too. The wood panels that formed the sides were splintered and scarred. All but one of the crossbars on the paddle wheel were broken, some in three or four places. Even the seat had deep, ugly scars in the metal.

Half-dazed, Benjamin walked slowly to the battered and

broken machine. The place where his name had been burned into the wood had become a particular focus of the axman's rage, and only one or two letters were even legible. Shaking his head, he reached out his hand, gingerly, slowly, as if he were afraid to touch it.

Frightened now, both of them moved quickly to the back door of the cabin. They stopped, shocked by the shambles that lay before them inside. "Oh," Benjamin said. It was a low sound filled with immense pain.

Derek felt his stomach twist. "Look!" he whispered. He was pointing to a congealed reddish brown puddle on the floor near the table. Someone's boot had stepped in one edge of the puddle, then tracked across the floor.

In three steps Derek was to the root cellar. He yanked back the door that covered it. It came as no surprise that it was empty. Grimly, he turned to survey the room. But at that moment, they heard a child's cry. Both of them jerked around. It had come through the front door of the cabin.

"Grandpa! Grandpa!" The front door flew open and young Joshua burst into the room.

"Joshua?" Benjamin's cry was a strangled sob of joy.

The boy flew into his arms, nearly bowling him over. "Grandpa! Grandpa!"

"Joshua, where's Grandma? Where's your mother?"

The head tipped back and the dark eyes looked up. "At our house."

The rush of relief almost made Benjamin giddy.

"Are they all right?" Derek demanded. "What about Rebecca?"

"Yes. Everyone's there." He took his grandfather's hand. "Come on, Grandpa. They sent me to get you."

"What happened here, Joshua?"

A look of terror flashed across the young face. Then he shook his head. "Come home, Grandpa. Come home."

"If Joshua hadn't come . . ." Mary Ann shuddered and looked down at her hands. She took a deep breath, trying to compose herself. "But he did, thanks be to God."

Benjamin was standing over Peter. He had the boy's head tipped back and was examining the monstrous lump over his eye. It was brown and black and greenish blue. "You're gonna have a whoppin' headache for a while, son," Benjamin said softly.

Peter managed a fleeting smile. His face was still as pale as the bleached buffalo bones one found on the prairies. He looked very sick. Suddenly Benjamin reached out and pulled the boy to him, crushing him to his bosom with a fierceness that made Peter wince. "You were a man today, Peter. You . . ." He couldn't make his voice say it. He just shut his eyes against the burning in them and clung to his foster son. "Thank you," he finally whispered. "Thank you, dear Peter."

Benjamin stepped back and turned to Jessica. Rachel was standing next to her mother, holding Jessica's wounded hand as if to comfort her. Benjamin moved to her. She too had a dark lump, but hers was high on her left cheek. "As if you had not already been through enough," he seethed. "What kind of animal was he?"

"An animal," Lydia said simply. "And if Joshua hadn't come . . ." No one seemed to be able to finish that thought. The rest of it was too horrible to put into words.

"Did Joshua get away, then?" Derek said. He was on the small sofa, which had been ripped and slashed until the fabric barely hung together. Rebecca sat beside him, her head on his shoulder. He held her tightly.

Mary Ann's shoulders rose and fell in a quick shrug. "We hope so. He left here once he was sure we were all right. He said he was going straight back to Independence. He's going to get Caroline and the children and head for St. Louis."

"That may not be far enough," Benjamin said. "Not after what he's done to his own people here." He looked around the room. Nathan and Lydia's cabin was not nearly as vandalized as

Benjamin's, but it was still a mess. "We're going to have to let Joshua worry about himself right now. It will be dark in an hour. We'd better start straightening up, see if we can find any food, and enough bedding for all of us. And no one goes back to our cabin. No one!"

Suddenly remembrance dawned with Derek. "Where are the Haddocks and the Godfredtsons?" These were the other families who had been staying in Nathan and Lydia's cabin.

Lydia stepped forward. "We don't know. When we came back here, they were nowhere to be found. Brother Haddock came a few minutes ago looking for them. That's how we learned you were free."

Benjamin nodded briskly. If the other families came back, they'd worry about what to do then. Derek touched Rebecca's cheek softly. "I'm going to see if I can find any food they missed." He shook his head, the anger burning inside him as he looked around. "The city is sealed off," he said gently. "We're going to have to make do with whatever we have."

It was shortly past midnight when Hyrum Smith felt someone shaking his shoulder. He was lying on the cold, damp grass with nothing but his cloak for a covering, hugging himself tightly, trying to keep warm. His body was racked with chills and fever, and he felt very weak.

"Brother Hyrum!"

He sat up with a start, peering into the darkness. "Colonel Hinkle?"

"Shhh!" The colonel pressed a finger to his lips and leaned closer. "I don't want to alarm the guards."

"What? What is it?"

"I have some unfortunate news."

Hyrum was totally awake now. "What news?"

"I've just come from the court-martial."

"Court-martial? What court-martial?"

"For you and the other prisoners."

Hyrum stared. "But we're not in the army."

"Lyman Wight is." Then Hinkle waved the objection aside and went on. "Lucas called for a trial to determine what to do with you. We've been meeting for several hours now. There are a dozen or so officers, a judge, a district attorney, and a lot of other men. Lucas wants to have you all executed."

There was a gasp from behind them, and Hyrum realized that Joseph was sitting up now too, as were Parley Pratt and Sidney Rigdon. Hinkle looked around, irritated that they had awakened. "I can do nothing for Joseph, but I've tried to speak in your behalf." He shook his head. "But I fear I have not prevailed. I'm sorry."

"You're sorry, Colonel Hinkle?" Parley asked bitterly.

Ignoring that, Hinkle reached out and dug his fingers into Hyrum's shoulder. "I'm sorry, but I'm afraid you're all to be shot this morning."

And with that, he turned and hurried away, disappearing into the darkness. Hyrum felt as though he had been struck a blow. He turned and looked to Joseph, eyes wide and frightened. The other prisoners crawled closer, their faces white now too. Joseph looked at his brother, then at the others. "Brethren," he finally said calmly, "perhaps we should pray."

"General Doniphan, sir?" The aide spoke even as he stepped inside the tent. He clasped a piece of paper tightly in one hand.

Alexander Doniphan was on his feet instantly. "Ah, there you are, Johnson. What is it?"

"General, I've just come from the court-martial proceedings."

"What! Are they still holding that farce?"

"Yes, sir." The man licked his lips nervously. "There's been a verdict, sir."

"Verdict!" Doniphan exploded. "Confound it, man, how can there be a verdict? These men are all civilians except for Wight. They must be tried by a civil tribunal." Doniphan was a lawyer. On two different occasions now, he had represented Joseph Smith and the Mormons against the trumped-up charges filed against them. Lucas was a fool. A court-martial? It was pure lunacy.

"Sir," the man said, stepping forward and holding out the paper. "Here's an order. I was asked to deliver it to you."

"An order?" Frowning deeply, Doniphan took the paper. He half turned so that the light from his lantern would catch the paper more fully, and began to read aloud. "'Brigadier-General Doniphan. Sir: You will take Joseph Smith and the other prisoners into the public square of Far West, and shoot them at 9 o'clock tomorrow morning.'" He looked up, shocked. "It's signed, Samuel D. Lucas, Major-General, Commanding."

"Yes, sir," Johnson said in a trembling voice. "That was the decision of the court-martial, sir."

Doniphan was appalled. "They can't do that! There's been no trial. No formal charges. The prisoners have had no chance to defend themselves." He swore. "As if any of that matters to Lucas."

For a moment Doniphan stood there, fuming. Then rising to his full height, he turned to his aide. "Take a note."

The man jumped to the small table and sat down, reaching for the pen and inkwell. "Ready, sir," he said when he had the pen in his hand.

"To Samuel D. Lucas, Major-General, Commanding. Sir: It is cold-blooded murder. I will not obey your order. My brigade shall march for Liberty tomorrow morning, at 8 o'clock; and if you execute these men, I will hold you responsible before an earthly tribunal, so help me God."

The aide was looking at him in shock. Doniphan nodded grimly. "Sign it, A. W. Doniphan, Brigadier-General."

Matthew pulled back from his face the blanket of his bedroll, instantly feeling the chill of the night air against his cheeks. "What are you doing?" he whispered.

Nathan jumped, then turned around quickly, holding a finger up to his lips. Matthew tossed the blanket aside and rolled into a sitting position. Even though they had reached Iowa Territory now, they hadn't dared light a fire, and it was so dark he could barely make out Nathan's shape. Then Matthew jerked forward as he realized what Nathan was doing. "Where are you going?" he hissed.

Nathan gave the rawhide straps around his bedroll a hard yank, then crawled over to his younger brother and put his face close to his ear. "I'm going back."

"What?"

"Shhh!" he said, punching Matthew on the arm. "Don't wake the others."

Matthew grinned. "I'm going with you."

"No!" Nathan shoved his face up close to Matthew's. "I've got a wife and four children back there. I've thought about it all night. I'm going back."

"I'm going too," Matthew said stubbornly.

Nathan went up on his knees in front of him. He shook a finger under his nose. "You heard Pa! You'll be arrested. Tried for murder. Maybe even executed."

"And what about you? It's the same for you."

Nathan sat back on his heels. "I'm just going to have to be very careful. Stay low for a while. Maybe I can take Lydia and the children somewhere." Now it was *his* voice that turned stubborn. "I'm not running."

Nathan stood, wiping his hands on his pants. "Now, go back to bed. Tell the others in the morning. Tell them not to feel bad. It's right, what they're doing." He looked away. "Just not for me."

Matthew didn't move. "I mean it, Matthew," Nathan said menacingly. "Get back in your bedroll. Pa will be furious if I bring you back and you get arrested."

Reluctantly, Matthew crawled back in. He watched in the darkness as Nathan finished gathering his things, then pulled on his boots and stood up. He paused for one moment, looming over Matthew. There was a faint blur of white as he waved a hand, then he disappeared into the blackness.

Matthew counted slowly to thirty. Then, scrambling frantically, he was out of his blankets and rolling his things together. One minute after that, he had his boots on and stood up. He jumped as there was a soft rustle in the grass and a dark figure was at his side. "I knew it," Nathan hissed.

"I'm going!" Matthew droned stubbornly. Then it hit him what Nathan had done. "Why'd you come back?"

Nathan stood there for a long moment, then reached out and put his hand on Matthew's shoulder. There was a long sigh of resignation. "I came back to get you."

Matthew felt a shot of elation, but he just nodded soberly. "Good. Let's go. We've got about five or six hours till dawn."

Nathan didn't move. "This is crazy, you know," he finally said.

Matthew chuckled softly. "I've been accused of that before. But you, you're always the one who's so steady and logical." He punched him softly on the arm. "Welcome aboard."

Friday, November second, turned out cold and gray. Sometime during the night, the wind had shifted around and started blowing from the north, dropping the temperature ten or fifteen degrees. Now, about an hour after full light, the sky, from horizon to horizon, had no break. And the first drops of what promised to be a steady drizzle were starting to fall.

Derek stood on the porch, gazing out toward the west, forcing himself to keep his thoughts on something other than the day that awaited them. There was a soft noise behind him and he turned. It was his wife. "I didn't know you were awake."

She smiled and slipped her arm around his waist. "I was awake when you got out of bed."

He pinched her arm gently. "Faker. You could have fooled me."

She laughed softly. It was like music to him. He peered into her face. The haunted look was gone. The lines around her mouth had smoothed. The dimple that had that magical way of appearing in one cheek was back. Relieved beyond measure, he leaned down and kissed her quickly.

"What's that for?"

"Because I love you."

"Mmm. Do it again."

He complied. When he pulled back, the smile slowly faded. "I'm going to go see Mary this morning."

Derek immediately started shaking his head. "No, Becca."

She went up on tiptoe, letting her fingertip press the frown from his lips. "Yes, Derek."

"All the men have to be present to sign over our property. The town will be filled with Missourians. Until that's over, it's not safe. I don't want you out."

The brethren were scheduled to appear at the public square at eight o'clock this morning. This was another of the conditions agreed to by Colonel Hinkle in his surrender terms with Lucas. The Mormons would make "reparation" for the expenses of the war. It was a thin veneer for what would amount to a monumental grab of some of Missouri's prime farmland, along with livestock, homes, outbuildings, and anything else of value that was left from the previous day's rampage. Lucas had promised that if the Mormons cooperated, he would keep his men under control, but Lucas's promises had begun to ring a little hollow. Derek looked at his wife. "It's not safe, Becca," he repeated. "I don't want you out."

Rebecca's jawline tightened a little. "I'm not going 'out.' I'm just going over to help a dear friend whose husband has been arrested and taken prisoner, who has several children, including a year-old baby to care for, and who is ready to deliver a child, and who—"

"Becca!" Derek started, shaking his head. The fear in him raised his voice more sharply than he intended.

She clamped her hand over his mouth. "And who," she went on as if he hadn't interrupted her, "is very sick herself."

She took her hand away and kissed him quickly. "Now, don't you think with all that, Mary needs help?"

"Of course, but—"

She sobered, holding up one hand. "And what about Mary Ann Pratt? They tore her home to pieces yesterday. Ripped the roof right off it. Now she's in a ten-foot hovel that's barely fit for a litter of pigs, and no husband to help either. Mother is going to see if she can help her."

"No, Becca. No!" He spoke slowly, enunciating his words as if she had a hearing impairment. "*It . . . is . . . not . . . safe!*"

She stepped around so that she was directly in front of him. Reaching out, she took both of his hands. "Listen to me, Derek." Her eyes were instantly shining. "Yesterday? It was horrible. More terrible than you can ever imagine. But the Lord was there, Derek. The Lord answered our prayers. He protected us. If Joshua had been even a minute later . . ." She shuddered. One tear squeezed out and trickled down her cheek. "But he wasn't. And I'm all right today. I'm fine! And because I'm all right, I'm going to go and help those who weren't quite so fortunate as me. Do you understand?"

He began to nod slowly.

"This is my way of saying thank you to the Lord. And I can't wait until things are all wonderful again to do that." Her voice dropped to a small whisper. "Because even if I start this morning, and spend the rest of my life doing it, it won't be enough." She reached up and brushed away the tear with the back of her hand. "It won't be nearly enough."

General Doniphan's departure caused no small stir in the camp on Goose Creek. As his men formed up, Doniphan strode over to where the seven Mormon prisoners stood watching. The light rain had begun, and his boots made soft squishing noises in the prairie grass. One of the guards raised his rifle, as though to prevent him, but Doniphan shouldered it aside roughly, swearing at the man. He came directly to Joseph. There was no greeting, no salutation. His mouth was working, and it was clear that he was in a high state of agitation. "Mr. Smith," he began abruptly, "you and the others have been sentenced by the court-martial to be shot this morning. But I will be damned if I will have the honor of it or any of the disgrace of it. Therefore I have ordered my brigade to take up the line of march and to leave the camp as a protest. I consider it to be cold-blooded murder, and I shall do all I can to prevent it. I bid you farewell."

He spun on his heel and stalked away, glaring at the guards who were watching him. "Thank you, sir," Joseph called after him. "Thank you for your integrity."

Ten minutes later the sound of wagons brought the prisoners to the alert again. From the direction of the center of camp, two wagons were approaching. General Lucas and another man with general's stars walked just ahead of them. A full company of militia marched behind the second general. Joseph watched for a moment, then spoke without turning his head. "Do you know who that is?"

Sidney and Parley and the rest of the prisoners were staring, but it was Parley who spoke. "Moses Wilson."

"Exactly," breathed Joseph. "This is not good."

They knew Moses Wilson from Jackson County. Wilson had owned the store on the Big Blue River that had been the site of a major clash between the Mormons and the Missourians back in 1833. He often boasted of his role in driving the Mormons out of that county. He was only marginally behind Lucas in his hatred of the Mormons.

Lucas marched directly to the brethren. His mouth was pulled into a sneer. "All right, Smith," he said. "Into the wagons. You're being taken to Jackson County."

There was a momentary flicker of surprise. "I understood we were to be shot, general."

"You are. However, the court-martial has changed your sentence. General Wilson is going to take you to Jackson County. You will be tried and executed then."

"So Doniphan prevailed?" Parley said in amazement.

"General Doniphan will be dealt with," Lucas snarled. "He'll learn not to disobey a direct order."

Wilson leaned forward and grabbed the sleeve of Joseph's coat. "You'll be shot soon enough. Now, into the wagons."

"Sir," Joseph said, "two days ago we came here, thinking we were to only speak briefly with General Lucas. We brought nothing with us. We have no other clothes, no bedding, none of our toilet articles."

"What is that to us?" Lucas retorted. "You are prisoners."

Joseph ignored Lucas. "General Wilson, will you give us leave to return to Far West to bid our families farewell and get some of the supplies that we will need for this journey? If we can obtain our own supplies, your men will not have to give us any of theirs."

"Absolutely not!" Lucas shouted. "Do you take me for a fool?"

Joseph's face remained calm. Lucas was furious, but it was obvious that Wilson was wavering. Joseph went on earnestly. "And if we are truly to be executed, have we not the right to see our families one last time? Would you deny us that fundamental privilege?"

Wilson looked at Lucas. Lucas was staring at his fellow general in disbelief. Then he threw up his hands and snorted in disgust. "Do what you wish," Lucas said. "Just get them to Jackson County. Send me an express when they are all dead men." He spun on his heel and stalked away.

Wilson turned to Joseph. "All right, we'll go into the city, but only long enough to get what you need."

He swung around to the lieutenant who stood at the head of the company of men. "I want a heavy guard on every one of these men. They may go to their homes and get essentials only. See to it that they are not allowed to speak or say anything. Two minutes at their homes. Then I want them on their way immediately. Understood?"

"Yes, sir."

Wilson nodded and the lieutenant waved the first rank of

men forward. But as they approached the prisoners, there was a shout from behind them. Everyone whirled. "No! Kill them! Kill them all!"

Five men had broken from the back ranks of the surrounding troops. They raced toward the wagons, waving pistols. They were howling with rage now, breaking through the few men who stared at them in amazement.

Sidney fell backwards into the wagon. Hyrum Smith and Parley Pratt, already in the wagon box, threw themselves to the floor. Joseph had one foot on the rail that provided a step up. He was closest to the attackers. He threw up one arm and fell back against the canvas. There were screams, and some of the Missourians whirled away, seeing they were in the line of fire.

There was the snap of pistol hammers. The pistol pointed at Joseph's head flashed brightly, but there was no explosion. The powder had ignited in the flash pans, but the main charge in the chamber did not catch. Nothing happened. Every one of the five weapons misfired.

Swearing and cursing, the men fell back a step. Now Wilson sprang into action. "Seize those men!" he roared. The guards leaped forward, rifles high. In moments the five men were corralled. "Idiots!" Wilson screamed. "What are you trying to do?" He grabbed the nearest guard. "Put these men in chains and keep them there until tomorrow morning."

He stopped, his chest rising and falling, watching as the five men were shoved forward roughly and marched away. Wilson turned to Joseph Smith. "Fools!" he muttered. "No one's gonna cheat me out of the chance to march you up the streets of Independence. Now, get in the wagons, before I change my mind and shoot you myself."

Joseph nodded and climbed up into the wagon bed. He sat down between Hyrum and Parley. Sidney was white and shaking. Parley looked sick. In the next wagon they could see only Amasa Lyman, who had his head down and his eyes closed. Lyman Wight and George Robinson were not visible.

Joseph said nothing, just folded his manacled hands in his

lap. In a moment, the teamster climbed up into the wagon seat in front of them and snapped the reins. As the wagon lurched forward, Joseph's head came up. "Brethren," he said, speaking just loud enough for them to hear over the creaking of the wagon, "be of good cheer. The word of the Lord has come to me. Our lives are to be given us."

The heads of those who were in the wagon with him jerked up. His brethren stared at him in disbelief. He nodded and gave them a thin smile. "Whatever else we may suffer during this captivity, the Lord has promised that not one of our lives shall be taken."

Chapter Notes

Speaking of that day when the brethren were forced to sign over their property, Heber C. Kimball would later write: "We were brought up at the point of the bayonet and compelled to sign a deed of trust, transferring all our property to defray the expenses of this war made on us by the State of Missouri. This was complied with, because we could not help ourselves. When we walked up to sign the deeds of trust to pay these assassins for murdering our brethren and sisters, and their children; ravishing some of our sisters to death; robbing us of our lands and possessions and all we had on earth, and other similar 'services,' they expected to see us cast down and sorrowful, but I testify as an eyewitness that the brethren rejoiced and praised the Lord, for His sake taking joyfully the despoiling of their goods. . . . Judge Cameron said, with an oath, 'See them laugh and kick up their heels. They are whipped, but not conquered.'" (Quoted in *LHCK*, p. 219.)

There is no question that Alexander Doniphan's courageous refusal to obey the order of General Lucas saved the lives of Joseph and the others that morning of November 2, 1838. The note he wrote back to Lucas and the words he spoke to Joseph before his departure are quoted in the novel essentially as given in several sources (see *HC* 3:190–91; *CHFT*, 205–6; *Restoration*, pp. 405–6; *Mack Hist.*, pp. 274–75). Alexander Doniphan visited Salt Lake City in 1873. He was warmly received and shown every regard by Brigham Young. He was also welcomed in the streets as a hero by the Latter-day Saints. (See *HC* 3:191n.)

The story of the misfiring of the pistols comes from Hyrum's account of these events (see *Mack Hist.*, p. 275). Though weapons were much less reliable back then, to have all five pistols misfire at point-blank range is more than quite remarkable.

Joseph's prophecy that none of their lives would be taken is placed here in the novel to facilitate the narrative. In actuality, he uttered this prophecy about twenty-four hours later, while the prisoners were en route to Jackson County (see *PPP Auto.*, p. 164).

Chapter Twenty-Three

Hyrum Smith's first wife, Jerusha Barden, died in Kirtland eleven days after giving birth to a baby girl on October second, 1837. Hyrum was in Missouri at the time. He returned to learn of his wife's death and to face the formidable task of caring for five children, ages ten, five, three, twenty-three months, and a newborn just two months old. Joseph ached for his brother's loss and pondered how best he could help. A short time later he came to Hyrum with the answer. "Hyrum, it is the will of the Lord that you take the English girl, Mary Fielding, to wife without further delay." And so the day before Christmas of that same year, Mary Fielding became Mary Fielding Smith and an instant full-time mother.

Now she was less than two weeks away from delivering her own first child. Eight and a half months pregnant, five children to care for, her husband a prisoner, their home plundered along with everyone else's—just contemplating that kind of load was enough to make one reel and want to swoon. So Rebecca Steed Ingalls had come to Mary's house to help.

Rebecca had labored steadily for almost two hours, putting Lovina, now eleven, to work helping her. She let six-year-old John play with and watch the younger ones. Now finally the cabin was back into some semblance of order, and Rebecca was grinding some corn into cornmeal with a samp-mortar. It would be a meager meal that would be common to many families in Far West this day. Mary lay in her bed where Rebecca had insisted she stay. She was talking softly to baby Sarah, who lay beside her. The other four sat cross-legged on the floor, listening to whatever it was she was telling them.

Rebecca looked up. There was the sound of horses and a wagon outside. She leaned forward to where she could see out the window. She gasped in astonishment and fell back. Through the rain she saw a wagon pull up. Uniformed men jumped out, and then another man climbed down. He was shackled and in leg irons. "Mary," Rebecca cried. "It's Hyrum!"

"What?" Mary jerked up into a half-sitting position, then cried out and fell back down again, holding her stomach. Rebecca whirled. "Don't you dare get up, Mary Smith! Lovina, don't let her get up." She tossed the mortar aside and stood up fully now. "He's under guard." One hand came up to clutch at her blouse. The man behind Hyrum was prodding him forward with a bayonet.

"It's Hyrum!" Mary exclaimed. She closed her eyes. "I have feared for his life, and now shall I really see him? Oh, just to hear his voice and know that he is safe will be like the balm of Gilead to my soul."

"Children," Rebecca cried, truly frightened now but not daring to speak it. "Come over to me. Quickly!"

They all jumped to obey except for John, who had started for the door to meet his father. He cried out and jumped back as the door suddenly slammed open with a crash. There was no knock, no call to those inside. Two men with rifles plunged through the door, muzzles up, looking around quickly to assess the situation. Then the one seemed satisfied. He stepped to the door and waved those outside forward.

Hyrum stepped through the door, blinking in the reduced light after being outside. The man with the rifle at his back came right behind him. Another man, with officer's stripes, followed.

"Hyrum!" Mary cried.

"Papa!" Two of the children shouted it out together.

Hyrum's mouth opened, but instantly the guard jabbed him with the bayonet. "You heard me, Mormon! Not a word or your life is forfeit."

Hyrum's mouth clamped shut, and all he could do was look at his wife and children with eyes overflowing with anguish.

The officer stepped around him, glancing around the room and taking it all in. His gaze stopped on Rebecca. "Who are you?" he demanded.

Rebecca felt the terror rise in her throat. Yesterday, in all its horror, was back with paralyzing power. "A friend," she finally stammered. "I'm helping with the children."

"All right. Stay out of the way and you won't get hurt."

Little John was staring at his father, his lower lip quivering. "Papa?" he whimpered.

Rebecca started toward him, then stopped, giving the guard a beseeching look. He nodded. She hurried forward, her hands out wide. "Come, John, we will wait over here in the corner." Little Jerusha was crying now, and even Lovina was trembling with fear. And little wonder. There stood their father, chained and guarded, his clothes rumpled and mud stained, his hair plastered flat against his skull from the rain. More frightening was how pale his face looked behind the stubble of his whiskers and the hopelessness in his eyes.

The lead guard turned to Mary on the bed. "You his wife?"

"Yes."

"General Wilson said the prisoners can get a few things

before we move out. A change of clothes, a blanket, maybe a few personal things. You better hurry, the other prisoners are already at their houses."

Mary raised up on one elbow. "Where are you taking him?"

"To Independence," the man snarled. "Now, move!"

Mary moaned and fell back, her face etched with shock. "Independence?"

Rebecca stepped forward. "I'll get them for him."

The closest guard whirled on her as if she had pulled a gun. His rifle swung up to point directly at her stomach. Lovina shrieked, and John fell back, his hands over his eyes. The baby began to wail.

"I told you to stay out of the way!" the man shouted into Rebecca's face. In an instant his voice was a menacing whisper. "Now, don't you move."

Rebecca stared at him in disbelief. "But she's sick. And she's in the time of her confinement. Can't you see that?"

He looked over his shoulder. "She looks fine to me." His comrades cackled and hooted at that. He turned to glare at Mary. "Now, get up and get his things!"

Rebecca watched anxiously until the wagon pulled away from the house, then she grabbed her shawl. "Lovina, stay with your mother." Then to Mary, "I'll be back." She threw the shawl around her shoulders and was out the door. She ran hard, her hair bouncing as she jumped over puddles or darted around the debris from yesterday's looting. Twice she almost slipped, but caught herself and hurried on, ignoring the fact that the bottoms of her skirts were quickly getting soaked and filthy.

As she approached Father Smith's house, she could see the two wagons about a hundred yards ahead of where she was going. The street in either direction was packed with men. They bristled with weapons and were shouting and hollering, trying to get a glimpse of the famous prisoners.

Rebecca was up on the porch and pounding on the door. "Mother Smith! Mother Smith!"

There was a sound from inside, then the door opened a crack. Instantly it was pulled wide open. Joseph's mother was there, looking quite frightened. A moment later, young Lucy, Joseph's youngest sister, came up behind her.

"It's your sons, Mother Smith. In the wagons."

Her eyebrows shot up. "What?"

"Joseph?" young Lucy cried.

"Yes. Joseph and Hyrum. Come quickly if you wish to see them. They're taking the prisoners to Independence."

Mother Smith gave a cry of relief and despair. Lucy stepped back, then was instantly there again with a shawl in her hand. "Here, Mother."

"We've got to hurry," Rebecca said. "It looks like they're ready to leave."

They hurried down the walk and pushed into the crowd. The militia was the large majority of it, but the residents of Far West were coming out now too, craning their necks trying to see. For the first few yards, they were able to push their way through, but quickly the soldiers were packed in so tightly it was like a wall. They pushed and shoved, but to no avail.

Finally, Mother Smith threw back her head. "I am the mother of the Prophet! Is there not a gentleman here who will assist me to that wagon that I may have one last look at my children, and speak to them before I die?"

A large man, one of the Missourians, who was a good head taller than those around him, turned in their direction. There was a quick flash of pity, and then he moved to them, shouldering men aside. "Come," he said, taking Mother Smith by the hand. He started toward the wagons, shoving his way through the pack. Not knowing what else to do, Rebecca took Lucy's hand and plunged after them.

Many of the non-Mormons had heard Mother Smith's cry, and now they turned and began shouting at her group. This was

Joe Smith's mother. They couldn't pass up the chance to vent their feelings. Fists were shaken in Mother Smith's face and the faces of those accompanying her. Threats, insults, and vulgarities were hurled at the little group from every side. The onslaught was so vile and so venomous that it terrified seventeen-year-old Lucy.

As they reached the wagon, the man who had responded to the cry for help leaned around the canvas cover and looked inside. "Hyrum Smith," he hissed, "your mother is here. Reach out your hand to her."

The canvas cover of the wagon was fastened down tightly along the edge of the wagon box. There was a push against the fabric, and Mother Smith reached out for it. But the canvas was tied so tightly that Hyrum was barely able to get his hand through. As his mother grasped at it, one of the guards in the wagon turned and saw what was happening. "Hey! Get away from there!" He raised his rifle. "No speaking with the prisoners."

Mother Smith was moaning now, clinging to Hyrum's hand.

"Get back, or I'll shoot," the guard started shouting.

"Come," their benefactor said. "Quickly." He pulled Mother Smith around to the back of the wagon. Rebecca and Lucy followed, and the crowd pushed in around them again, cutting off the guard's view of them. The man who was guiding them put his mouth up against the canvas. "Mr. Smith," he called softly. "Joseph Smith. Your mother and sister are here and wish to shake hands with you."

The canvas had been tied together, so there was only a crack at the back, but it was not as tightly bound as on the side. Joseph's hand appeared immediately. Both mother and daughter grabbed on to it and clung to it with desperation. There was no sound from inside.

"Joseph," Mother Smith called pitiously, "do speak to your poor mother once more. I cannot bear to go until I hear your voice."

Through the heavy fabric came a strangled sob. "God bless you, Mother!"

Farewell at Wagons

Young Lucy was nearly hysterical. She leaned forward to kiss Joseph's hand. But then a movement caught Rebecca's eye. The guard was leaning out around the edge of the wagon and saw what they were doing. He swore loudly and yelled at the wagon driver. There was the snap of leather on horseflesh. "Hee yaw!" the driver yelled.

"Watch out!" Rebecca cried, grabbing for Mother Smith and pulling her back. The four horses lunged against their traces, startled by the unexpectedness and violence of the command. The wagon jerked forward, yanking Lucy's hand away from her brother's. "Joseph!" she screamed. "Joseph!"

But there was no answer that could be heard over the rattle of the wagons and the shout of the crowd as they saw the prisoners driven away.

Word spread through Far West like a lightning bolt that Joseph and Hyrum and the others had been taken south. There had been great fear for their safety before, but now? Jackson County! The Saints knew firsthand about that place. The very name left everyone filled with a deep sense of foreboding. It was a bitter blow indeed, and by the time night fell over the city on that evening of November second, the gloom descended with even greater thickness than the darkness.

The two babies—Jessica's and Lydia's—were so tired, the family decided to put them to bed first, then have supper. After supper, Benjamin suprised everyone by standing up abruptly. "All right," he said. "Who wants a story?"

There was an instant chorus of "I do's" from the children.

"Then get yourselves a pillow or a blanket and gather over there by the fireplace."

Mary Ann raised one eyebrow at him, not in question but in surprise. He shrugged. "The children don't understand all this," he murmured, waving his hand in a half circle, as though that could possibly define all that they were experiencing.

Mary Ann's face instantly softened. "Of course," she said. "They've had enough fear and terror. Thank you, Ben."

Lydia stood up now too. "It's a wonderful idea, Father Steed. As we cleaned the cabin yesterday, I found our book of *Grimm's Fairy Tales*. It's torn a little but still usable. Would you like me to read to them? You look tired."

He nodded. "I think they would love to hear you read, but I'm not too tired to join you." He looked around at the children, who were scrambling to get something to sit on and a place to put it. "Tell you what." He reached down and scooped a pillow out of young Joshua's arms. "How about Grandpa being the pillow?"

He moved a short distance beyond the fireplace where the wall was clear and there was open space on the floor. He sat down, placing the pillow behind his back, and leaned against the wall. "All right, now." He patted his legs. "Who wants to lie on Grandpa?"

There were squeals and shouts and a mad rush. Young Joshua sat right beside his grandfather, underneath his left arm. Emily and little Nathan curled up against Benjamin's hip on the same side. Rachel and her two stepbrothers, Mark and Luke Griffith, laid their pillows on his other leg and stretched out happily. They looked like a clutch of baby chicks gathering to the wings of the old mother hen.

The women watched with warm affection as each child snuggled in against this big and gentle man. Benjamin looked down at the place beneath his other arm, opposite where young Joshua sat. "I've still got room right here," he said to the children. "Anyone want it?" They all shook their heads. They had already gotten their first choices.

Rebecca was sitting with Derek on the bench. Suddenly she stood up. "I want it, Grandpa," she said shyly. She moved quickly and sat down beside him. Surprised, but deeply pleased, he enveloped her with his arm and reached down and kissed the top of her head. "This is *my* baby girl," he said to Emily. "Did you know that?"

Emily put her hand to her mouth and giggled.

Then a thought struck Benjamin. He looked at Peter and Derek. "We take children of all ages here," he said. Peter looked startled, but Derek laughed and in a moment was over sitting beside his wife. Peter moved over to sit by young Joshua. The moment Peter was settled, Emily, showing all the fickleness of a six-year-old, scooted over and sat on his lap.

"Come on, Mama," Rachel called. "Come sit with me and Luke and Mark. There's room."

As Jessica smiled at her daughter and complied with her wishes, Benjamin wiggled over a little, pushing Joshua over some more. He looked up at Mary Ann. "We even take beautiful grandmas."

Mary Ann laughed in embarrassment. "I'm all right. It's too crowded."

"No, Grandma, come on!" It came out as one chorus from the children. Laughing happily, she surrendered, stepped across the children, and snuggled in beside her husband.

"That's better," he said. Then he smiled up at Lydia. "All right. I think we're ready."

By nine o'clock, all of the children were asleep. Rebecca and Derek sat at the kitchen table, talking quietly as they held hands. Lydia, Mary Ann, and Jessica were working on patching a quilt that had been violently ripped open during the looting of the cabin. Peter was reading the fairy tale book to himself, and Benjamin was reading in the Doctrine and Covenants. It was the first quiet time they had had for nearly three days, and it felt wonderful to have a moment of peace.

When the knock came at the door there was an instant flutter of fear. They all looked at one another, then Benjamin rose slowly. Derek also stood and walked to the door with him. Every eye in the room followed them. For a moment, Benjamin hesitated; then he lifted the latch and pulled the door open.

"Brother Steed?"

Benjamin blinked in surprise. "Good evening, Brother Salisbury."

"I'm sorry to bother you so late."

"It's all right. We're still up. Come in."

William Salisbury lived across town, and Benjamin knew him only because they had worked on a building committee together a few months before. He was a small man, barely five feet six, and was of a quiet demeanor and an unassuming manner.

Benjamin shut the door behind them and quickly introduced him around the room. Then he motioned to a chair. Brother Salisbury swept off his hat, and they all sat down again. "I can't stay long. My wife is very nervous."

Benjamin nodded. Considering the past seventy-two hours, that wasn't surprising. "All right, how can we help you?"

"You probably can't. I only came because someone suggested your name." Everyone in the cabin was watching the man closely now, wondering what this was about. "A strange thing happened yesterday about midday."

Lydia gave him an incredulous look. Yesterday at midday was right at the height of the mobbing. *Only one thing was strange?*

"My wife saw a man get shot."

That brought a little involuntary intake of breath from both Rebecca and Jessica. Benjamin straightened a little. This wasn't what they had expected. Derek stepped forward. "Who was it?"

"Well, that's just it. He's at our home right now, but we don't know who he is. He's badly wounded, hasn't gained consciousness at all. I don't think he's one of us." He shook his head, clearly puzzled. "In fact, he looks like an officer in the militia. But that's what is so strange. It was two of the mob who shot him and—"

Derek shot to his feet. Salisbury looked a little surprised but went on. "My wife and children were hiding in the cornfield behind the barn. They saw these two men arguing with some other militiamen. The one was shouting and swearing at the others, said he had to have a rifle right now. He finally got one, then the two ran toward the fence and dropped down to hide. My wife says that pretty soon she and the children saw this other man coming, kind of sneaking along, and one of these two men who were hiding up and shot him. Then the two saw someone coming and got scared and ran."

Rebecca had one hand to her mouth. "Were the two men dressed like Indians?" she whispered.

Salisbury jerked around. "Yeah, they were. How did you know?"

Benjamin came up out of his chair now too, staring at Rebecca in astonishment. He spun back around to their visitor. "And you've no idea who this man is?"

"No. But somebody said you had a son who was in the—"

Derek's sudden movements cut him off. The young Englishman had whirled and gone to the door in two steps, grabbing his hat from the pegs that were on the back of it. Benjamin was right behind him. "Come show us," Benjamin said grimly.

Benjamin looked down at his son and shook his head gravely. "If we move him it's going to have to be very carefully. With a litter. I think even a wagon will be too much for him."

Sister Salisbury had a frightened look on her face. "We can't keep him here. What if the men who shot him come looking for him?"

Benjamin felt a flash of irritation, but it left him as rapidly as it had come. She was right. Someone had gotten the body of the man Joshua had shot out of Benjamin's cabin. That meant someone knew that a militia officer had shot and killed one of his own. So there was bound to be a search.

He turned to Brother Salisbury. "Do you have anything we could use to make a litter? We'll take him to our home." Nathan's home wouldn't be a solution for very long, but they had to get him away from the Salisburys'.

Salisbury considered that for a moment. "I can find something. And I'll get a couple of men to help. It's a long ways back to carry him."

As he hurried out, Benjamin turned and looked down at his son. His mind was racing. What did they do now?

It was about a half hour before dawn on the morning of Sunday, November fourth. The sky was overcast, and the night was pitch black. It had rained on and off for the past twelve hours, leaving the prairie wet and soggy, perfect for muffling the sounds of footsteps or crackling grass.

Nathan reached over and gripped Matthew's shoulder, slowing their pace even more. They were about a quarter of a mile north of the outskirts of Far West. It had been a shock when they arrived and saw the line of campfires. Far West was under quarantine. So they had settled down to wait. Then the rain had come, and the guards began to draw in to the fires, making only sporadic patrols. So Nathan and Matthew had decided to risk it.

Nathan had chosen a spot midway between two of the campfires, but that still left men on either side of them no more than thirty or forty yards away. He fought the temptation to look back and see if anyone had seen them and was coming. But he didn't give in. If they were sighted, they would hear about it soon enough. They were past the patrol line now, still close enough to be seen but moving closer to safety with every step.

"Hey! Who goes there?" The shout came from behind them and to their left. "Halt!"

"Go!" Nathan hissed. He ducked down and exploded into a run. He heard Matthew coming right behind him. There was a rifle blast, and now men were shouting.

"They can't see us!" Nathan cried. "Run!" Out of the corner of his eye he saw a flash, then another, followed instantly by the explosions. It only lent heels to their flight.

When they reached the tree line that marked the course of

Shoal Creek just to the north of the city, Nathan knew they had made it. He plunged into a thicket of elderberry bushes, ignoring the scratching and tearing at their clothing and faces. He dropped to the ground, pulling Matthew down beside him. Nathan turned to look back. He could see shadows milling back and forth in front of the nearest campfire. He held his breath, listening intently, trying to hear the sound of footsteps over the drizzling rain. There was nothing. He laughed softly. "I guess they don't care if Mormons come into the city," he said in relief. "Only if they try to get out."

"Then let's go home," Matthew said, panting heavily.

Nathan shook his head immediately. "Not until tonight."

"What? Tonight? Why not now?"

"It's going to be dawn in a little while. We don't know what's waiting for us in Far West. If the whole city is surrounded . . ." He let it go unfinished. "We'll hole up here until it gets dark again. Then we'll go in."

Chapter Notes

The depiction of Hyrum's being brought home under guard and the militiamen's heartless forcing of Mary to rise from her bed to get his things is based on true accounts. Similar scenes were repeated with the Prophet Joseph, Sidney Rigdon, and Parley P. Pratt. (See *MFS*, pp. 77–78; *PPP Auto.*, p. 162.)

It was after the prisoners were returned to the wagons from their various households that word came to the Prophet's mother that her sons were about to depart. The novel's detailed account of her attempt to bid farewell to her two sons at that departure is drawn from her history (see *Mack Hist.*, pp. 290–91).

Chapter Twenty-Four

The Mormon war is over!"

Caroline stared at Obadiah Cornwell blankly, his words not registering.

He smiled. "That's right. It's over, Caroline. The Mormons have surrendered. They're bringing Joe Smith to Jackson County right now. We just learned they're camped down by the river."

"Joseph Smith?"

"Yes. He and several others are in chains. Far West has surrendered."

She swayed a little, a mix of emotions washing over her. "Joshua? Is there any word from him?"

Joshua's partner shook his head. "No. It will be at least a week before they get things settled, but it's over. The war's over."

"Thank heavens." Then a thought struck her. "I'm going to go see him."

"Joshua?"

"No, Joseph Smith. Maybe he knows something about Joshua."

Cornwell was genuinely shocked. "That's not a good idea, Caroline."

"Why not? He knows us. He's good friends with Joshua's family." Suddenly her eyes darkened. "Oh, maybe he can tell me about Joshua's family. I'll bet it's weeks before we get mail from them."

"He's a prisoner, Caroline!" Cornwell exploded. "Don't you understand? They're bringing him here to execute him."

Caroline looked away, her mouth pulling into a stubborn line. "All the more reason to see him now. I'm going, Obadiah. Please don't stop me."

When Caroline and Will pulled up in the buggy, Caroline was surprised to see that they were not alone, not by any means. There were two dozen buggies or wagons out from town, and a crowd of people milling around the army wagons. She understood immediately. Joseph Smith would be a source of great curiosity to many. She tied the reins to a bush and, with Will in tow, hurried over to join the people, looking to see if she could spot Joseph.

As she came around the edge of the crowd, Caroline saw Joseph immediately, and he saw her. She saw one eyebrow go up in surprise, then a faint smile. But he immediately turned back to the people. He was speaking to a woman, or rather, she was speaking to him. Caroline recognized her. She was the wife of one of Jackson County's wealthier farmers. Caroline moved closer so that she could hear.

The woman was squinting at the prisoners, partly curious, partly in revulsion. "Sirs," she said, "which of you is the Lord which the Mormons worship?"

Joseph was startled. Then he laughed. "None of us, ma'am. I

am Joseph Smith, the prophet and President of the Church you call the Mormons. But none of us is the Lord."

"So you do not profess to be the Lord and Savior?"

Joseph clapped his hands. "Dear me, no. I am nothing but a man, and a minister of salvation, sent by Jesus Christ to preach the gospel."

"Oh?" the woman said. Caroline had to smile at the expression on the woman's face. The answer so surprised her that she was momentarily at a loss for words. "So you don't believe that you're Jesus Christ?" she finally stammered.

"Heaven forbid."

Her husband had come up behind her now. He tugged gently on her sleeve, embarrassed by her boldness. She ignored him. "But you believe in Jesus?"

"With all my heart and soul," Joseph answered.

Others were moving in closer now, wanting to hear and see the Mormon prophet. The woman's aggressiveness softened a little. "Do you believe in the Bible?"

"Most assuredly." Joseph was smiling now. His openness and obviously cheerful demeanor not only had disarmed *her* but were having the same effect on the rest of the crowd as well. Even the guards seemed interested more in what he was saying than in guarding him from escape. Joseph looked around at the circle of faces. "If you have a few moments, I could tell you what we do believe."

There were nods and murmurs of assent. Joseph looked to the guards, who shrugged. As the people pushed in closer, Joseph stood up on the wagon tongue. Caroline saw that Hyrum and the others had not expected anything like this. They were staring at Joseph in amazement.

Joseph spoke for nearly ten minutes, outlining in simple terms the doctrine of faith in the Lord Jesus Christ and repentance. He spoke of baptism and the gift of the Holy Ghost, quoting frequently from the book of Acts. When he was finished, the woman was quite pacified. She stepped forward and extended her hand. "Thank you, sir. I find you to be an honest man, and I shall pray that all will be well with you and your companions."

Joseph was clearly touched. "Thank you, madam." As he moved away, he turned immediately to Caroline. "Mrs. Steed, what a pleasant surprise."

"Hello, Mr. Smith."

"Joseph, please. How good to see you again." There was a fleeting, sad smile. "Would that it were under more pleasant circumstances."

"You remember my son, Will?"

"Of course," Joseph boomed merrily, shaking Will's hand firmly. "And how is your father?"

"But that is why we have come," Caroline explained. "We were hoping you had seen him."

Joseph's eyebrows narrowed, and then he snapped his fingers. "But of course, he was in the militia, Nathan told me. Was he up north?"

The disappointment was sharp. "Yes. You didn't see him at all?"

Will spoke up then. "He's an aide to General Atchison. But the general sent him up to serve with General Lucas."

"General Doniphan was there, but we didn't see Atchison or your husband," Hyrum said. "General Doniphan left Far West two days ago. He was coming down to Liberty."

"Really?" Caroline cried. Liberty was only a few miles north of the river in Clay County. If Joshua had come back with Doniphan to rejoin Atchison, he could easily slip home for a short time, even if he was not formally released. But then her face fell again. "And what of Joshua's family? Do you have any news of them?"

A great look of desolation swept across Joseph's face as he shook his head. "We"—he gestured at his companions—"were taken prisoner several days ago. We have no news from Far West except what the soldiers have told us. They boast of awful deeds. Our brethren were disarmed, and the mobs sacked the city. The reports have been terrible." He brushed a hand across his eyes. "Looting, pillaging. We have been told that some men and women were killed, though thankfully the numbers are small."

Will's head dropped. "Grandpa Steed? Grandma? Are they all right?"

"I don't know, son," Joseph whispered. "I'm sorry."

By nightfall of the Sabbath day, Far West was very quiet. Nathan and Matthew left the thicket about an hour after dark and moved quietly and cautiously into the town. But they saw no one. Many of the windows were covered and showed only slivers of lamplight. Others were totally dark, though they could see smoke coming from the chimneys. It was as if the city were under the equivalent of some massive house arrest.

"Look," Matthew whispered, pointing, "there's another one."

Nathan turned. Against the horizon he saw the skeleton of a cabin. The roof was gone. Several of the upper courses of logs had been pulled down or left hanging at a crazy angle. He looked more closely as they passed. The windows had only shards of glass, the door had been ripped from its hinges, the yard was littered with debris. And they had seen more than a dozen just like it. It was mute but powerful testimony to the forces that had been unleashed here.

And I was running away! I left Lydia to face this alone. Nathan shook his head, disgusted with himself, sensing what anguish he would feel if they returned only to find out something had happened to Lydia or the children.

"Shall we go to our house first?" Matthew asked.

Nathan shook his head. "Ours is closer. Then if they're not there, we'll go to Pa's."

As they stepped onto the porch a few minutes later, they could hear the murmur of voices through the door, but it went instantly quiet as one of the boards on the porch creaked loudly.

Nathan tried the door. It was fastened shut. He rapped on it sharply. For a long moment it was totally silent. Then they heard footsteps coming slowly toward the door.

"Who is it?" It was his mother.

Nathan grinned at Matthew and nudged him to speak. "Two hungry boys looking for something to eat," Matthew said in a high, falsetto voice.

There was a fumbling at the latch, then the door opened a crack. "I'm not sure you have—" There was a gasp, then the door flew wide open. Mary Ann hurtled through it and threw herself at her youngest son. "Matthew!" she cried. "Nathan!"

It took nearly ten minutes before the family settled down enough for the adults to talk. Nathan held the baby while young Joshua and Emily and little Nathan danced around their father, chattering excitedly, pulling at his sleeve, vying for his attention. Lydia's tears of joy were gone now, and she sat beside Nathan on the bench, one hand on his knee, smiling at her children.

After holding Matthew tightly for a considerable length of time, Mary Ann had finally surrendered him to Jessica's children, who were giving him the same treatment Nathan was getting from his. Then Jessica gave her baby to Peter, and she and Rebecca and Mary Ann began to cook johnnycake and some thin slices of ham, the best of what they had left in the house.

Benjamin sat quietly back, content after his initial welcome and embrace to watch it all. Though he was filled with rejoicing, worry lines pulled at the corners of his mouth too. It was obvious he was waiting for a chance to talk with his sons. Finally, Lydia noticed his expression. She immediately stood, taking baby Elizabeth from Nathan, and shooed Joshua and Emily and little Nathan aside. "Come children. Papa has to talk to Grandpa now. It is time to get ready for bed."

Jessica turned. "Rachel, Matthew needs to talk too. Will you get Mark and Luke into their nightshirts?"

"Yes, Mama," Rachel said reluctantly.

The men moved over to one corner. Derek motioned for Peter to come too, and Benjamin nodded his agreement. Peter had proved himself a man now, and would be part of any family decision making. He walked over and laid Jessica's baby in the small rocker crib, then joined them.

"What happened?" Nathan said in a low voice, once they were in a circle. "The town looks like it has been hit by cannon fire."

"Worse than that," Derek said bitterly. He and Benjamin took turns describing the events of the past few days. When they finished, Nathan whistled softly, no longer wondering at the destruction they had seen.

"That's not the half of it," Benjamin said. "There's more."

"Joseph? What about Joseph?" Nathan asked.

Benjamin shook his head. "Still a prisoner. They took him and the others—Hyrum, Sidney, Parley—they took them all to Independence. They say they're going to shoot them."

"They can't do that!" Matthew said hotly.

Benjamin reached out and touched Matthew's shoulder to calm him. "There are other things you need to know. About what happened here. To our family."

"What?" Nathan demanded.

Benjamin sighed. "You'd better see something first." He walked across the room to where blankets hung from ropes, dividing off the room into sleeping and living spaces. Mary Ann and the other women stopped what they were doing to watch. Their faces were grave. Benjamin took a deep breath, then reached up and pulled the blanket back.

For several seconds Nathan and Matthew just gaped at the figure on the bed. Then Nathan stepped foward and dropped to one knee. "Joshua?" he whispered. When there was no answer, he looked up at his father. "What happened?" he asked, his voice barely audible.

"He's lost a lot of blood," Lydia said. "We had Doctor Williams come look at him. The bullet went through one lung. He's very weak."

"I can see that." Nathan had been shocked by how gray Joshua's face was.

Benjamin held up one hand. What was pressing on his mind couldn't wait. "Today there was a company of militia searching for him. They came to the Salisburys and others around there. No one is telling them anything, of course, but it's obvious that what Joshua did has been reported. The Missourians are not sure if he was killed and the Mormons just stole the body, or if he's being hidden somewhere. But it won't be long before they learn that he had family here. Then . . ."

Nathan didn't need him to finish it. "We've got to move him."

"He'll die," Mary Ann cried.

"If they find him," Benjamin said bitterly, "he'll do more than die."

"We had an idea," Derek broke in. "But until now we didn't know how we could do it."

"What?" Nathan asked.

"We know a widow woman, a few miles out of Di-Ahman. She's not a member of the Church, but she's a fine woman. A real Christian. Peter helped her dig a well, and I helped her get in her corn crop. She's horrified by what is happening to our people. She said if we ever needed help—"

Mary Ann was aghast at the implications of what Derek was saying. "Di-Ahman is over twenty-five miles away!"

Benjamin took a deep breath. "We'll give him a priesthood blessing and ask the Lord to strengthen him enough to endure the journey. You'll have to change his bandages, Mother. Bind him up real tight." He wanted to say more, but it wouldn't come. "Real tight," he said again, very softly.

Tears began to flow down Mary Ann's cheeks. Her shoulders lifted and fell, and she spoke in a whisper. "All right."

Nathan was thinking quickly. "We'd have to rig up a travois, like the Indians use."

"Our thoughts exactly," Derek said eagerly. "We've already found two poles and some blankets."

"It will be rough. He might not make it. But"—His voice became more resolute—"it's the only chance. If they find him here, it won't be just Joshua that is shot."

"The town is surrounded by soldiers," Matthew noted with concern. "Nathan and I barely made it in. And we were on foot."

"That's why we didn't know what to do," Derek answered. "We think it will take at least three of us. One to go ahead and make sure the way is clear, one to guide the horse, and one to watch Joshua. So your coming is a godsend." He turned to Rebecca, his eyes dark with regret. "I—"

She cut him off instantly. "I know. But you go. I—*We* owe him everything. Do whatever it takes to save him."

Lydia looked sick. Her husband had not been home even an hour yet. But she didn't hesitate. "Yes, Nathan, go."

Matthew looked at his mother. He didn't have to say it. She bit her lip.

Nathan stood. "We'll have to leave immediately. There's no way we can get out of here in the daylight, and we can't risk waiting another day."

It took them ten minutes to get things ready. When they came out of the cabin, the horse and travois were ready. Four men stood beside it, waiting. Benjamin looked up in surprise. The nearest was Brigham Young. "You're going to need a diversion to get through that line," he said. "We're here to provide it."

Joshua had come out of his unconsciousness as they rebandaged his wound, then moved him outside. Now he lay on the bed, his eyes laced with pain and filled with dread. He motioned weakly at Nathan, who leaned over him and put his ear to his mouth. "We must warn Caroline," he whispered.

Nathan reared back a little.

"Yes!" Joshua said fiercely. "She is in danger."

Nathan immediately understood. When word reached Jackson County that one of their own had turned Mormon-lover, it could get very ugly. He nodded, then turned to his wife. She had come close and heard. "We'll get a letter off tomorrow, Joshua. I promise."

He lay back and closed his eyes.

"All right," Nathan said. "Dawn's coming fast. Let's get rolling."

On Monday, November fifth, another major blow befell the Saints in Far West. General John B. Clark had arrived at the camp of General Lucas with an additional sixteen hundred men on Sunday afternoon. Word quickly reached the city. Clark was the commander-in-chief of all militia forces in northern Missouri. He had come to see to the final disposition of the "Mormon problem."

First thing the next morning, an order was sent around the city commanding the Saints to gather at the public square at twelve noon. They came slowly and reluctantly, not daring not to show up but heavily fearful about what this new demand might mean. Mary Ann said nothing as she and her family moved along with the others, but she had a profound sense of foreboding and could barely force herself to put one foot ahead of the other.

Clark was already there, sitting astride his horse at the head of his troops, as imperious and arrogant as an Oriental emperor, sneering with barely disguised contempt at the assembly of the vanquished. His men stood in ranks along the streets, weapons at the ready, moving in behind the last of the Saints to form a circle around them. Mary Ann was disgusted. Clark had brought over a thousand men with him, as though the disarmed and demoralized Mormons were some kind of threat to be reckoned with. She started to say something to Ben, but there were soldiers close by and he warned her off with his eyes.

Precisely at twelve noon, Clark stood up in the stirrups and began, without preamble, to speak to the crowd in a loud voice. "I am General John B. Clark. I have been appointed by His Excellency, Lilburn W. Boggs, governor of the state of Missouri, as commander-in-chief of all militia forces in northern Missouri."

There was an undertone of angry rumblings at the mention of the governor's name. He it was who had issued the extermination order.

Clark's voice went up a note in shrillness. "The Mormon war is over. You are defeated. Several of your leaders are in jail awaiting execution. But . . ." His eyes swept up and down the lines of men, women, and children, who were watching him intently. "There are others who are likewise responsible for this outrage." He punched out every word now with harsh anger. "*And they must be punished too!*"

He spun around to the officer seated on the horse closest to his. "Major Crosby, you may proceed."

Crosby nodded, threw Clark a quick salute, and prodded his horse forward a few steps. "All men between eighteen years of age and fifty-five years of age, please step forward and form a line."

There were audible gasps. Then quickly these turned into angry mutterings, cries of alarm, moans, and the first whimpering cries of children. Husbands and wives stared at each other. Someone even had the temerity to shout at Clark and demand to know what was going on.

"Come on! Come on!" Crosby shouted. "Move forward or we'll drive you out of there at the point of a bayonet." Encouraged by their officers, the first rank of troops took a step forward, their weapons coming up slightly. Slowly at first, but then more rapidly as some of the other officers started shouting at them, the Mormon men moved away from their families and began to form into lines.

"Benjamin, no!"

Benjamin turned to his wife and grasped her hand for a moment. "Be strong, Mary Ann. It will be all right." He stepped out and joined the others.

Crosby watched until he was satisfied. Then he took a paper from his tunic. "The following men are under arrest. As I read your name, move foward one step."

"Arrest?" someone down the line from Benjamin shouted. "On what charges?"

Clark whirled as though a sniper were hidden in the trees and firing at them. "Put that man in chains!" he roared. Four soldiers leaped foward and dragged a struggling figure forward. Now the crowd was too stunned to do anything except stare.

Crosby let his eyes sweep across the assembled line of men. "Anyone trying to hide will be shot. Step forward smartly the instant I read your name. You will be taken to the camp tonight, and then taken by forced march to Richmond on the morrow, there to be tried for your crimes."

And so the "roll call" began. Women cried or dropped to their knees as their husbands' names were called. Children began to wail, and Major Crosby had to shout loudly now.

By the tenth name, Benjamin knew exactly what was happening. This was not a random list. Someone had furnished the Missourians with the names of the remaining leadership of the Church. And he thought he knew who had done so. He went up on the balls of his feet, trying to see beyond Clark and his officers to where a group of men were gathered in a tight knot behind them.

Then he came back down. "That's what I thought," he muttered out of the corner of his mouth to the brother standing next to him. "It's all of our old friends."

"Who?" the man beside him asked.

"William McLellin—all the old stalwarts." Benjamin's voice was heavy with sarcasm. The apostates would have their revenge now on their former friends and associates who had kicked them out of the Church.

"Quiet!" Crosby roared. "Or I'll have every one of you standing out here. Quiet!"

The noise dropped off sharply, though the children could not be totally quieted. Somewhat mollified, Crosby continued.

Benjamin Steed was twenty-first on the list. It came as no shock. What *did* catch him by surprise was that the name of Nathan Steed was thirty-seventh. Benjamin had hoped desperately that Nathan and Derek would be spared, since they were younger and weren't in prominent positions at the moment.

Crosby glanced up, then down again, ready to read the next name, but when no one stepped forward, his head snapped up. "Nathan Steed!" he said more loudly.

When nothing happened, Clark spurred his horse forward a step or two. "I'm warning you," he cried, "come forward now or risk being shot."

"Nathan Steed was one of those who fled north to Iowa Territory," a voice called.

A neighbor who lived a few houses down the street from the Steeds had been the one to call out. Benjamin gave him a quick look of gratitude.

"Nathan Steed!" the adjutant roared. "Step forward."

"He's gone," Benjamin said. "He's my son, but he's gone."

Suddenly McLellin was pushing through the crowd. He came to Clark's horse and said something up to him. Clark frowned, then nodded. The former Apostle walked swiftly down the line. Benjamin shot a quick glance over his shoulder. Mary Ann was white. Lydia had her hand to her mouth.

McLellin stopped directly in front of Benjamin. "Steed? You are known as being a man of integrity and honesty. I want you to look me in the face and answer two questions. Swear to them."

Benjamin did not answer.

McLellin took that as agreement. "Did your son Nathan Steed ride north with those who were at the battle of the Crooked River?"

"Yes, he did."

"And he is not here now? Not anywhere in Far West? Swear it!"

"I swear it," Benjamin said evenly.

The former Church leader stared at him for a long moment, then finally turned away. "His son is gone, sir," he called to Clark. "He's not here."

Chapter Notes

A few months before the fall of Far West in 1838, Joseph Smith prophesied in a public meeting that before the year was out, one of the elders of the Church would preach a public sermon in Jackson County (see *HC* 3:201; *PPP Auto.*, p. 165). The prophecy seemed incredible at the time, but it was fulfilled when Joseph preached in chains to the assembled crowd outside Independence.

Five days after Far West fell, fifty-six of the most prominent men of Far West were taken prisoner and marched off to Richmond. Contemporary accounts report that identification of the Church leaders was aided by former members of the Church. In addition to thus being enabled to satisfy old scores, some of the apostates were paid handsomely for the information. (See *LHCK*, p. 223.) The intent of General Clark was to strip the last vestiges of leadership from the Saints. But two notable and very important omissions from the list of prisoners should be mentioned: Brigham Young and Heber C. Kimball. Brigham was by then the senior Apostle, and with all the members of the First Presidency in bonds, he was the most important leader left to guide the Church. But his name was not on the list. Heber C. Kimball said it was because Brigham lived three or four miles outside of Far West and wasn't well known to the mob. Heber himself was the second in seniority in the Twelve, but he had been gone a year to England and had just returned to Missouri a few weeks before. So he too was overlooked. Heber said Colonel Hinkle came looking for him but could not remember him. (See *LHCK*, p. 222.) These oversights would prove to be of critical importance as Joseph Smith languished in Liberty Jail until April 1839 and the Saints were driven from the state of Missouri.

Chapter Twenty-Five

Will Mendenhall Steed came into the bathing room just as Caroline and Olivia were finishing Savannah's bath. "Oh, good," Caroline said when she saw her son. "Can you and Livvy finish with Savannah? I need to—" She stopped at the sight of Will's face and his heavy panting. "Will, what's the matter?"

"Mother, come quick. Mr. Cornwell needs you at the freight yard."

Caroline stood up, wiping her hands on her apron. "What is it? What's wrong?"

He gulped in air hungrily, gasping out the words. "He wouldn't tell me. Just said to fetch you real quick." He half turned. "Hurry, Mama. I've never seen him like this."

Joshua's business partner was waiting for Caroline and Will in the main yard. Caroline rushed up to him. "What is it, Obadiah? What's wrong?" He took her by the elbow, but to her surprise he did not start toward the office. Instead he steered her toward the long shed where they kept the wagons out of the weather.

"Caroline, there's been some news from up north."

She stopped dead. "About Joshua?"

He gently pulled her forward again. "There are two men in the office," he said slowly, obviously careful of what he was saying. "They've come down from Caldwell County just this morning."

"Do they know anything about Pa?" Will blurted, looking over his shoulder to see if he could see them through the window.

"Please," Cornwell said. "This isn't the place to talk."

Caroline's stomach was suddenly as tight as a bowstring, but she said nothing more and she and Will followed Cornwell into the shed. Obadiah stopped beside one of the big flatbed wagons they used to haul lumber. He was trying to meet her eyes, but he couldn't quite do it. "Has Joshua been hurt?" she asked.

His mouth opened, then shut again. Finally he looked away. "I'm sorry, Caroline. I'm so sorry."

It was more than a quarter of an hour later when the man called Hugh hurriedly stepped back from the window of the office. "Here they come," he said. He looked at himself quickly, to see if he was presentable. Any trace of the war paint he had worn just days before was now gone. He had changed the buckskin shirt and moccasins for white man's clothing. He had even trimmed his beard and spit out his chewing tobacco before he had come to the building that housed the company of Joshua Steed and Son, Freight and Portage.

He leaned forward again, peering at the three figures who had just emerged from the shed and were coming towards the office. He whistled softly. "Now, there's a looker!" But then he remembered what he was about and moved swiftly back against the wall. "You let me do the talking, Riley." He swore softly. "We'll teach that uppity captain not to mess with Neil Gilliam's boys."

The other man grimaced as he moved around the desk to join his partner. His left arm was in a sling, and his hand hung useless from out of it. "We already taught him one lesson," he chortled. "Best shot you ever made."

"Well, the debt ain't paid yet. Not by a long shot. So you just let me do the talking."

As the three of them stepped up to the porch of the freight office, Cornwell stopped and touched Caroline's arm. He spoke very gently. "Caroline, I'm not sure this is the best time for you. The men said they can stay until tomorrow if they have to."

Caroline's fingernails dug into the palms of her hands. She had finally mastered the tears, though she knew her eyes were red and puffy. She still felt as though huge waves of blackness were washing over her, but the trembling in her body had mostly stopped. Fighting the temptation to bite her lip, she turned to her son. "Will?"

He looked awful, as if he had been struck by some terrible force that had knocked the life from him. But instantly his shoulders straightened. "I want to talk to them, Mama."

She nodded and looked back to Cornwell. "Me too, Obadiah. I need to hear it for myself."

Cornwell started to say something else, then finally nodded. "All right." He opened the door and stood aside.

There were not many people that Caroline took an instant dislike to, but as they stepped into the office and the two men straightened, there was an immediate sense of revulsion. The first man was small, with a narrow face and tiny round eyes that glittered like those of a ferret or a weasel. His beard was trimmed and his clothes were presentable enough, but they weren't enough to overcome the evilness of his face.

"This is Mr. Hugh Watson," Cornwell said, "from over in Carroll County."

The man had his hat in his hand. He grinned, showing crooked teeth and a tongue brown from chewing tobacco. The smile was more like a grimace and only heightened the feral characteristics of his features. "Pleased to meet you, Miz Steed," he said. He had meant to keep his eyes downcast, but she saw that he was startled by her beauty and had to pull his gaze away from her with some effort. It only made her want to shudder.

Hugh turned to the man beside him. "And this is Mr. Riley—"

"Riley Overson," the other man said hastily. "I'm from Ray County, ma'am." He was bigger, fuller in the face, but also heavily bearded and with the kind of face that would make a woman shiver if she passed it on a dark night. She saw that his left arm was in a sling and that he was holding it with his other hand.

"How do you do?" she murmured.

Cornwell pulled out the chair for her, and she waved it aside. But Will took her by the arm and moved her to it. Too emotionally beaten to resist, she sat down. "Mr. Cornwell has told us that you were there when . . ." She fought back the surge of bile that rose in her throat. After a moment, she looked up again. "Will you tell us about it please?"

The one named Hugh stepped forward. He was twisting his hat in his hands as though he too were in pain. "Things were goin' just fine, ma'am," he said. "We had taken all the Mormon militia out south of town and had them surrender their weapons. General Lucas, he told us to go through the city, searchin' from cabin to cabin, lookin' just in case somebody had held some rifles back. There was three of us. Me and Riley here and a man named Caleb Scott."

He looked down, trying to muster some semblance of grief. "Suddenly some Mormons who had stayed in town and hid jumped out from a barn behind us. Weren't no warning at all. They just started shooting. Caleb took a ball right in the back. He was dead 'fore he hit the ground. Riley here swung around and took another one in the shoulder."

Riley kept his face impassive. He hadn't heard this version and was amazed at how smoothly Hugh could lie. He raised his damaged arm, just in case they hadn't noticed it before, to lend credence to Hugh's tale. Hugh stopped for breath, peering at Caroline with eyes that kept straying away from her face.

She watched him steadily, her face not betraying any emotion now. "Please go on."

"We started shootin' back, and they turned tail and ran. I was gonna go after 'em, but I had to look after my two friends. Weren't nothin' we could do for Caleb, of course, but Riley was hurt bad. Then those men started shootin' at us again. It was right then that your husband come runnin'. He'd heard the shootin'. He shot at them on the dead run. Hit one of 'em, too. Saw the man go flyin'."

He turned to Will, who was standing beside his mother, rigid as a steel beam and clenching and unclenching his fists. "Braver man ain't never been born. Even though there was still danger, he paid it no mind. No mind at all. You can be right proud of your pa, boy. Right proud."

"Get on with it," Cornwell said. This was a far more colorful version than he'd been told, and the man's fawning manner was starting to grate on him.

"Well, it was right then that it happened. The Mormons ran, but one of them must have stopped behind a nearby barn. We didn't see him, of course. Then just like the yellow-bellied cowards them Mormons are, the man took aim and shot your husband square in the back. Didn't give him a fightin' chance. Just shot him in the back, then turned and hightailed it away."

She thought she had steeled herself after hearing Obadiah tell her that Joshua was dead, but Hugh's words had both Will and Caroline openly weeping. Even Riley was moved. Hugh looked at Will and shook his head sadly. "It's a real shame, boy," he said. "Your pa was one brave man, and those Mormons shot him down cold."

Riley looked at his companion with open awe, then lifted the mug of beer in salute. "Best danged liar east of the Rocky Mountains," he toasted.

"Shut up!" Hugh snarled, looking around the saloon. But it was late, and the few men still inside were paying the two strangers little attention.

"Well, you are," Riley said sullenly, taking a deep swig of the dark brown liquid. "And it worked. You hear that boy start cussin' the Mormons, his ma trying to hush him up?"

"It ain't over yet."

Riley's eyebrows raised. "It ain't?"

Suddenly Riley was nervous. Neil Gilliam was Hugh and Riley's immediate superior officer, and it had been to him they had gone after finding and killing the arrogant Captain Steed. They had told him most of the story, leaving out only the minor detail that it had been their planned rape of the women in the cabin that had so infuriated Steed. Gilliam was seething by the time they finished their tale and was bitterly disappointed that Steed was beyond his reach now.

Then, while Riley and Hugh were taking a detail of men back to retrieve Caleb's body—hoping that the women would still be there—Hugh's plan had started to form. The humiliation they had suffered in the cabin was festering in him like a boil, and by the time they had returned to Gilliam, Hugh had devised a way to lance it.

Riley savored the idea of revenge too, especially as he saw how sweet and complete Hugh meant that revenge to be. But he couldn't get thoughts of Gilliam out of his mind either. Cornelius Gilliam was not a pleasant man when crossed. His fury could be murderous. He had agreed to their proposal to go to Jackson County and tell the Widow Steed in person how her husband had shamed her and every other Missourian. But, he said, as far as he was concerned, the Mormon war wasn't over yet, and there was still plenty yet to do before the Mormons were driven from the state. So Hugh and Riley were to get on down there to Independence, then get right back.

Now it was becoming obvious to Riley that Hugh's plan had grown more elaborate and that Hugh had no intentions of returning immediately.

Riley cleared his throat. "Look, Hugh, Gilliam said we was to get back real soon."

The small bearded man swung around on his companion, whispering fiercely. "You listen, Riley. All Gilliam cares about is seeing what else there is to loot up there. But it weren't Neil Gilliam who was in that cabin the other day." His eyes narrowed into tiny slits. "Steed came in there like he was God himself. He pistol-whipped Caleb, then killed him. He shot you down like a cur dog."

Riley thought about reminding Hugh that it was the English boy who had shot him in the shoulder, but he decided to let it pass.

Hugh was working himself up all over again. "We was right on the verge of gettin' some real action," he snarled, "but Steed stopped us from doin' that too. And them was good-lookin' women."

"Yeah," Riley said wistfully.

"Well, he's dead, and just shootin' him down and shamin' his name ain't good enough for me."

Riley looked around quickly, then leaned forward. "What if he ain't dead, Hugh? They still ain't found his body."

Hugh slammed down his glass of beer with a sharp crack. That won him a look from the other patrons of the saloon, so he held his tongue until they turned away. Then he shot Riley a withering look. "Not dead!" he exclaimed. "You was there with me. You saw him bleeding like a gutted pig. No man's gonna survive that kind of ball."

"Well," Riley muttered, "we still shoulda put another ball into him."

"Right," Hugh said in disgust, "with someone comin'! Whoever it was, we'da had to kill them too or have them tellin' Lucas or somebody that it was Missourians that killed one of their own officers."

"At least we'd be sure," the bigger man said, still worrying but fearing to make his partner angry.

"*I'm* sure!" Hugh snapped. "He's dead, and I don't want no

more talk about it being otherwise. And we can't make him pay any more, but his family's gonna pay. His family's gonna pay real good."

The other man set his beer down slowly. He licked his lips, suddenly nervous. "What're ya gonna do?"

Hugh was staring off into space, his eyes like two tiny points of ebony. "The name Sampson Avard mean anything to you?"

The other man looked blank.

"Never mind. He was a Mormon too. And let's just say Sampson Avard's going to give us a little helping hand in this matter. He won't know anything about it, but he's gonna be real helpful to us."

On Tuesday morning, the day after the arrest of the Church leaders in Far West, General Clark again ordered the Saints to assemble in the main square. He paraded the prisoners before them, then had them stand before their wives and children. And then Clark gave a speech. Though he himself had not been in the field until after the war was over, he had written a speech to the conquered. This time the Steeds had left the children at home, but Mary Ann, Lydia, Jessica, and Rebecca stood near the front row trying to get a glimpse of Benjamin. Peter stood farther behind, still half-fearful that additional arrests were going to be made and, in spite of his younger age, not wanting to be too conspicuous.

"Gentlemen," Clark said loudly, "we have the last of those who have committed crimes against the state under bonds now. And they shall be punished. But now I feel to show you some mercy. Those men whose names were not on our list, you now have the privilege of going to your fields and providing corn, wood, and so on for your families."

There were cries of surprise, and a murmur of excitement rippled across the group. Jessica turned to Mary Ann with a look of great relief. The loss of Benjamin had left the family stunned and shaken, but with or without Benjamin, food was becoming a critical problem. They had two babies, six other children, and five adults—counting Peter—to feed and, with the city under siege, no way to get more. Breakfast had been served only to the children. The adults were holding themselves to one meal per day. So this was at least one glimmer of good news.

"Those who are now taken will go from this place to prison. There they will be tried and receive the due merit of their crimes. But the rest of you are now at liberty, as soon as the troops are removed that now guard the place, which I shall cause to be done immediately. It now devolves upon you to fulfill the treaty that you have entered into."

Treaty! Jessica had to stifle a laugh of derision. They had been betrayed, deceived, and decimated. Only Hinkle had had the gall to call the betrayal a treaty.

"The orders of the governor to me were that you should be exterminated and not allowed to remain in the state, and had your leaders not been given up, and the terms of the treaty complied with before this, you and your families would have been destroyed and your houses left in ashes."

"Instead of just looted and left in ruins," Mary Ann muttered to no one in particular.

There were other voices now too, low and angry, protesting the blatant mutilation of the truth. Clark ignored them and went on loudly. "There is a discretionary power vested in my hands which I shall exercise in your favor for a season. For this leniency you are indebted to my clemency. I do not say that you shall go now, but you must not think of staying here another season, or of putting in crops, for the moment you do this the citizens will be upon you. If I am called here again, in case of noncompliance with the treaty made, do not think that I shall act anymore as I have done. You need not expect any mercy, but extermination, for I am determined the governor's order shall be executed.

"As for your leaders, do not once think, do not imagine for a moment, do not let it enter your mind that they will be delivered, or that you will see their faces again, for their fate is fixed, their die is cast, their doom is sealed."

Mary Ann gave a low, half sob, and Lydia and Rebecca both stepped up to her and steadied her.

"I am sorry, gentlemen, to see so great a number of apparently intelligent men found in the situation that you are; and oh! that I could invoke that Great Spirit, the unknown God, to rest upon you, and make you sufficiently intelligent to break that chain of superstition, and liberate you from those fetters of fanaticism with which you are bound, that you no longer would continue to worship a man.

"I would advise you to scatter abroad, and never again organize yourselves with bishops, presidents, etc., lest you excite the jealousies of the people, and subject yourselves to the same calamities that have now come upon you. You have always been the aggressors—you have brought upon yourselves these difficulties by being disaffected and not being subject to rule, and my advice is that you become as other citizens, lest by a recurrence of these events you bring upon yourselves irretrievable ruin."

He finished, folded the papers he had been holding, and put them back inside his jacket pocket. His mouth pulled back into a haughty smile. He looked up and down the line of Saints, daring anyone to contradict him. No one spoke. "If you were to come to your senses and disperse and become as we are, all would be well. In a word, renounce this ridiculous religion and you will be left alone. Otherwise, there is no choice. You must leave the state."

He wheeled his horse around. "Lieutenant!" he sang out. "Move 'em out."

As the guards leaped into action and the body of prisoners started forward, Mary Ann went up on tiptoes. "Benjamin! Benjamin!"

Other women took up the cry, calling out the names of their men.

And then Mary Ann saw him. He was in the far rank. His head was turned, searching for her. "Benjamin!" She screamed it out, waving frantically. "Papa!" Rebecca was crying. "Father Steed! Father Steed!" Lydia and Jessica were waving too.

And then he saw them. He lifted one hand, pulling up the hand of the man behind him as they were tied together with a sturdy rope. "Good-bye, Mary Ann! I'll be all right! Don't worry for me."

"I love you!" she shouted. "I love you."

A guard ran up to Benjamin and raised his rifle butt up to shoulder length. "No talking!" he shouted.

Benjamin barely glanced at him. There were tears in his eyes now. He tipped his head back. "I love you too, Mary Ann," he cried full throat.

The butt of the rifle slammed into the center of his back, knocking him forward. He went down on one knee, but being roped to the others saved him from falling.

"I said no talking!" the guard screamed at him.

Benjamin staggered to his feet. He turned and looked the man in the eye, staring at him balefully. The other brethren had turned now too. The guard looked startled, then suddenly a little frightened. Benjamin lifted his head again, not taking his eyes from the man. "Kiss the children for me, Mary Ann," he called.

The man raised the rifle again, but then when Benjamin turned and fell into line, he lowered it and stepped back.

From behind him, Benjamin could make out Mary Ann's sobbing cry. "I will. I will. God be with you, Benjamin Steed."

The hammering on the door brought Caroline out of the depths of sleep with a jerk. She looked around wildly, then gradually felt herself relax. It was as if she had been drugged. She had stayed up most of the night before, numbed and cold and staring into the darkness. Then the memorial service today—there would be a full funeral once Joshua's body was returned to Jackson

County—had been even more difficult than she had expected. She had gone through this once before, when Donovan died of yellow fever. She had loved her first husband fiercely. But Joshua she had loved deeply. His death tore at her to levels of her being she had not thought existed. It had exacted a heavy price on her, and she had finally fallen into an exhausted sleep this evening.

Bam! Bam! Bam!

She sat up straight, realizing now what it was that she was hearing. Throwing the covers aside, she groped for her robe. "I'm coming!" she shouted. Then she remembered that Savannah was asleep in the next bedroom. She had cried herself to sleep, begging for her papa. "I'm coming," Caroline muttered more softly, "I'm coming."

As she stumbled out into the hall, she saw Will's door open. "Mama? What is it?"

"I don't know, Will. You—"

Olivia's door opened and she came out, rubbing at her eyes.

"Will, stay here with Livvy," Caroline commanded. She walked swiftly down the hall and to the stairs. The pounding had stopped now, and as she reached the bottom of the stairs, she could see no one through the glass of the front door. Then she leaned forward. There was something there. A dark, square shape through the glass.

Cautious now, but also puzzled, she crossed the room to the door. She peered through the window. The porch was empty, but the dark shape was a piece of paper fluttering softly in the night breeze. Looking once more to make sure she was alone, she unlocked the door and opened it.

The paper had been tacked to the wood just above the glass. She tore it loose and stepped back inside.

"What is it, Mama?" Will and Olivia were both on the landing above her.

"I don't know. A note of some kind." She walked over to the table where a lantern filled the room with a barely discernible glow. She had almost turned it off before going to bed;

then, on impulse, she had left it on its lowest flame. She had found the total darkness more than she could face.

She reached down and turned the wick up slightly higher. The glow brightened, and she leaned over, holding the paper. It was crudely scrawled with large block letters.

MRS. JOSHUA STEED:

THREE DAYS AGO, YOUR HUSBAND KILLED SOME MORMONS IN FAR WEST. NOW YOU HAVE OUR PROPHET, JOE SMITH, IN YOUR JAIL. WE KILLED YOUR HUSBAND IN REVENGE FOR WHAT HE DID. BUT THAT IS NOT ENOUGH. YOU MUST PAY TOO. PREPARE TO DIE!

THE MORMON DANITES

She dropped the paper as though it were hot and the words seared into her hands. One hand came up to her mouth as she stared down at the hastily printed letters. The ink was smudged in one place. In another it had not been blotted properly and showed someone's thumbprint. Then, horrified but unable to help herself, she picked it up again.

"What does it say, Mama?" Will asked, starting down the stairs.

She whirled on him. "No, Will! Don't come down!"

The sharpness of her voice made him jump, and he backed up hastily. And then fear stabbed at Caroline's heart. She heard a sound coming through the kitchen from the back door. It sounded like someone was scratching at the window. Chills coursed up and down her back, and for one second she stood there, frozen into immobility. Then the sound started again.

Mobilized now, she jammed the paper in the pocket of her robe, whirled around, and grabbed for the lantern. She gave the wick control a hard twist and the room plunged into darkness. "Will," she hissed, "get the rifle."

Will had heard it too. He took the steps three at a time and raced across to the cabinet where Joshua's rifles were kept.

"Mama?" Olivia was at the top of the stairs.

"Livvy! Go in with Savannah. Don't come out until I tell you."

As Livvy darted back in, whimpering as she went, Caroline ran to join her son. "There's someone out back, Will."

He was fumbling with the weapon, trying to get the ball into the breech. Even in the darkness she could see he was trembling violently. She laid a hand on his shoulder, realizing that her own panic was terrifying him. "It's all right, Will," she said, fighting back the urge to scream. "It might be just—"

There was a crash against the back door. She jumped, then gasped. There was a dancing, yellow-orange glow lighting up the back windows. Even as she stared, the light doubled in brightness and size.

"Fire!" Will screamed. "Fire!"

Caroline whirled, took three steps toward the growing fire, then stumbled backwards again. Then she was to the stairs in two leaps. "Savannah!" she screamed. "Savannah!"

"They're both asleep," Mrs. Cornwell said. She shut the door carefully and came into the parlor where Caroline sat with Obadiah.

Caroline nodded gratefully. "Thank you, Emma Lou."

Cornwell's wife walked to the window. It was shortly after dawn now, and the smoke rose in a towering pillar from the south end of town. The neighbors had come first and formed a bucket brigade, but the watering trough behind the barn was emptied in a few minutes and the hand pump couldn't keep up with the need for more water. By the time the fire-fighters had come with the fire wagon, the fire had spread to both stories, front and back. There had been nothing to do but stand back and watch as the largest and most expensive house within a radius of a hundred miles, and everything in it, went up in flames.

The front door opened and closed, and in a moment Will had joined them. He had a valise in his hand. "Here's our clothes, Mama." He looked at Cornwell. "It was right in the wagon where you said it would be."

Cornwell had told Caroline about the emergency wagon Joshua had had him prepare for her, just in case. Part of that preparation had been a valise of clothing. Cornwell had sent Will for it so they would have something besides their nightclothes.

Caroline put her hands on the sofa and pushed herself up. "All right, Will. I'll go change."

"Caroline."

She stopped and looked at the man who had started out as Joshua's stable hand, then become his driver, then foreman, and then his business partner. Joshua had made him into a prosperous man, and Obadiah Cornwell would never forget it. "Can't you wait?" he asked. "There'll be a boat coming upriver in two or three more days. Then I'll go with you."

She shook her head.

Emma Lou Cornwell went quickly to stand beside Caroline. "Really, Caroline, you are exhausted. You are in shock. This is no time to be setting off for St. Louis."

Reaching into the pocket of her robe, Caroline drew out the piece of paper that had been tacked to her door. She held it out for Cornwell. He came over to her. "What is this?"

She didn't answer, just watched him as he read. Cornwell's mouth opened slightly, then slammed shut. Anger flashed across his face. He shoved it out for his wife to read. "Where did this come from?"

Emma Lou rocked back a step. "In the name of heavens!" she gasped.

"Someone tacked it to my door just before the fire broke out," Caroline said. "Their knocking is what woke us up."

"What kind of monsters would do such a thing?" Mrs. Cornwell cried in outrage. She was deeply shocked.

"I don't know," Caroline replied. She was too jaded to even feel anger anymore. "But I won't have my children waiting around here until they try again."

"They can't be . . ." Cornwell's voice trailed off to silence. He had been about to say "serious," but a few blocks to the south of them, a smoking pile of rubble bore silent witness to how serious they were. His shoulders lifted and fell. "I can't believe it. I've heard about these Danites. They're also called the Destroying Angels. But I never believed the stories. I—"

Caroline didn't want to think about them. She broke in quickly. "We'll let the girls sleep for an hour or so while Will and I get things ready." She stopped, suddenly realizing what the practical realities were going to be. "Obadiah, I would appreciate it if you could go to the bank and get out whatever money Joshua has there."

"All right. But you're not going alone. I'll go with you."

She was instantly shaking her head. "No."

"Caroline, don't be a fool. You can't possibly—"

She stood and walked to him. She took both of his hands. "You dear, dear friend. How Joshua trusted you. How I have come to depend on you. But no, Obadiah, I must go alone. Not even you must know where I am for a time." Her mouth tightened with a momentary flash of fear. "If they found us once . . ."

Will stepped forward. "We'll be fine, Mr. Cornwell. I can drive the team now."

"I know that, son," Cornwell said, the grief twisting at his face. "But—"

"We'll be all right," Caroline said. "I've got the money from the sale of my home in Savannah. Joshua made me put it in a bank in St. Louis. He wouldn't ever let me spend it." Tears were there again, burning at her eyes. "He used to tease me about it. 'You never know when you're going to tire of me,' he would say." She bit down on her lower lip. "'Keep your nest egg safe, just in case.'"

She fought back the hurt, not wanting to start crying again. "It will be enough to keep us comfortable."

"All right." He put an arm around her shoulder. "But you and Will sleep now too. It will take some time to get ready. I also want to get some more things for your wagon."

Her mouth opened to protest, but he went on quickly. "No one knows you're here. Wait until tonight. Then you can get out of the city without being seen."

Will was nodding. "That's a good idea, Mama."

She considered it, then surrendered. "Yes, that would be fine. I'm so tired."

"Yes," Emma Lou soothed, coming forward now too. "Just sleep, and we'll get everything ready."

Will waited until his mother had climbed up in the wagon, then he motioned for Cornwell to step aside. "Mr. Cornwell?"

"Yes, Will?"

"I'd like to ask a favor of you."

"Anything, Will."

"Mama wants you to have the freight business now, and so do I. But will you take a thousand dollars of my pa's share and hold it out."

Cornwell looked surprised. "Of course, but for what?"

Will glanced up at his mother, who was looking back at them now. He lowered his voice. "I want you to post a reward. I want you to find out who killed my pa. Find out who burned our home. If you need more, I'll send it to you when we get Mama's money."

Cornwell nodded, not without some sadness. "I understand, Will." He looked up to where Caroline was watching them curiously. Did she sense the hatred in her son? "I'll do it. But . . ." He blew out his breath. "What if it was the Mormons? What does that mean for you and Joshua's family?"

Will's eyes were hard. "You just find out who did it, Mr. Cornwell. I'll handle the rest."

Chapter Notes

General Clark's speech, given on November sixth, though not given in total here, is taken almost word for word from the written text, which was published some time later by the St. Louis National Historical Company (see HC 3:202–4).

Chapter Twenty-Six

The morning of November seventh was bitter cold. The line of prisoners from Far West rolled out of their blankets and immediately stood up. They began to dance lightly up and down, pounding their ribs to generate some warmth. They were a little more than halfway on the march to Richmond, Ray County. As they finished a miserable breakfast of cold, hard pieces of bread, the first flakes of snow began to drift out of the sky. Almost immediately the wind picked up, coming straight out of the north. By the time they were back on the road, the snow had turned to tiny, sharp pellets that came slashing in almost horizontally.

Benjamin jammed his hat down lower over his eyes, pulled the one blanket he had been given more tightly around his neck, and hunched his shoulders. They were still at least twenty miles from Richmond, and it was going to be a very long and miserable day.

It was about ten o'clock on the morning of November ninth when Joshua Steed finally came fully out of the haze of pain and hallucination and unconsciousness in which he had been lost for almost a week. For several minutes he lay there, so weak he could barely turn his head. He let his eyes move around the small room where he lay. It was a bedroom. A woman's or a girl's, judging from the few things he could see on the chest of drawers. The one window was opaque with frost, and he could see snow piled up in one corner of the glass.

There was a noise, and he turned his head with great effort. The door to his room was open, and he could see into the next room, the main room of the cabin. Two girls—one eleven or twelve, the other sixteen, maybe a little older—were seated at a table. His line of sight was too low to see what it was they were doing, and it wasn't worth the effort it would have taken to lift his head off the pillow to find out.

The girls were clearly sisters. Though the older girl's hair was a light brown and the younger's almost jet black, both had dark eyelashes over wide blue eyes and the same straight noses with just a touch of an upturn at the end. But then there were the older girl's freckles. She had just the lightest sprinkling of them across her upper cheeks and across the bridge of her nose. It gave her a distinctly impudent look that Joshua found quite charming.

He watched them, wondering who they were and where he was. He searched his memory, but could remember nothing that helped him answer either question. He remembered vaguely waking up, awash in pain, and knowing he was with his family and being prepared for traveling on a travois. Beyond that, there was nothing.

At that moment, the older one looked up directly at Joshua. Her eyes were startled for a moment. Then she dropped whatever it was she was doing and turned her head. "Mama, he's awake."

There was a murmur of a woman's voice and the sound of dishes being put down. Then a woman appeared in the doorway. She had an apron over her long dress and her hair pulled back in a bun. She was round and plump and looked like a kindly grandmother, though it registered in Joshua's mind that she wasn't really that old.

"Well, I'll be," she said, with a clear Irish lilt to her voice, "he is awake. Good mornin' to ya, Mr. Steed."

"Good mornin'." It came out as a ridiculous croak.

She came forward to stand by the bed. The two girls were now at the door behind her, peering in curiously at Joshua. "And it's a welcome sight to see you with your eyes open, I'll tell ya. You've had us worried for the past few days, I'll tell you that straight out."

"Where am I?" Joshua whispered.

She smiled and stuck out her hand, then realized he wasn't in shape to take it. She pulled it back and smiled all the more broadly. "You're in the home of the Widow Nancy McIntire and her daughters. We live about five miles north of the town of Gallatin in Daviess County." She half turned. "These are my two girls, Kathryn"—the younger one curtsied slightly—"and Jennifer, or Jenny." The older one smiled shyly at him and lifted a hand.

Mrs. McIntire looked at the older girl. "Jenny, go fetch Matthew and tell him his brother is awake."

She murmured a "yes'm" and hurried out.

Matthew? Joshua remembered that Matthew had been out with the horse while they loaded him. But so had Nathan and Derek. He was tiring quickly. "Nathan?"

"Went back home. Him and Derek both." She looked at the other girl. "Kathryn, fetch Mr. Steed some of that chicken broth."

"Matthew?" he asked. "Is he here?"

"He's out attending to some chores."

A jolt of fear flashed across Joshua's face. He tried to get up.

"Caroline! I must write my wife. She probably thinks I'm dead. She may be in danger."

Mrs. McIntire dropped to one knee beside him and pushed him gently back down. "You won't be remembering, I suppose, but you were insisting on writing to your wife before you left your father's. Nathan said to be sure and tell you that they wrote a letter and sent it."

He relaxed, stunned at how even that much physical exertion had sapped his strength. Caroline. It was important that she know. There could be trouble.

Mrs. McIntire was shaking him gently. "Now, don't ya be goin' back to sleep on us yet, Mr. Steed. You've got to have some nourishment or you'll not ever be gettin' your strength back."

He closed his eyes. He tried to say, "Yes, ma'am," but it came out as an unintelligible mumble.

Mrs. McIntire called out the door. "Hurry, Kathryn, we're losing him."

Jenny brought a large bowl of soup and half a loaf of bread and set it in front of Matthew. Her eyes were large with fear. "We were so afraid when we couldn't find you." Her eyelashes dropped a little. "I was praying for you," she said demurely.

"I'm sorry," Matthew said. He had not been in the barn when Jenny went looking for him, and it had taken her nearly an hour to find him. He blushed a little, embarrassed by her attention but pleased with her concern. "I didn't go far. I just wanted to get a feel for the lay of the land in case Joshua and me have to leave real quick." He turned to Mrs. McIntire. "I should have said something."

His brow furrowed. There were still a lot of men roaming the countryside looking for Mormons to harass. If someone came here and found him and Joshua . . . It might even put the McIntires at risk, and he didn't like that thought at all.

"Your brother was awake for a time."

Matthew blinked and looked at Mrs. McIntire. "He was?"

"Aye. I think he's passed the crisis. He's still very weak, but there was a clearness to his eyes, and he took nourishment."

Matthew started to push back his chair and rise, but Nancy McIntire quickly grabbed his hand and pulled him back down. "He's still sleeping now. Eat your dinner, then we'll speak with him."

"If we haven't heard by next week, I'm going down there."

Matthew was staring at him. "Are you crazy? Up until this morning we weren't even sure if you were gonna live. And besides that, you've already said that Jackson County will be dangerous for you."

Joshua ignored him. "You're going to have to help me, Matthew."

"I will, Joshua, but not before you're ready."

"No, I don't mean that." He looked at the bedroom door to make sure it was closed. "Even after I'm better, Matthew. You're going to have to go with me."

Now Matthew looked more closely at Joshua's face. It was now nine days since he had been shot. He had more than a week's whiskers, which were fast becoming a full beard. It only heightened the hollowness of his cheeks and the way his jawline had sunk in. It gave him a bit of a skeletal look, and now, with the hopelessness in his eyes, Matthew found it disconcerting. "What?" he asked slowly. "What are you talking about?"

Joshua closed his eyes, and Matthew saw the fingers of his hands clench together into a fist. "I can't feel anything in my left leg, Matthew."

Matthew rocked back. "What!"

"Not anything," he whispered. "Not in my leg. Not in my foot." He looked away. "Nothing."

Benjamin's cough started about midafternoon of the day after they arrived in Richmond. By then all of the brethren had been soaked through to the skin and were shivering so violently they could barely walk. The guards let them huddle around their fires for an hour or so to let them partially dry out, then herded them off to their temporary jail.

The courthouse in Richmond was still under construction, and the roof had not been put on it yet. It was really not much more than an open shell with rooms. But there were fifty-six prisoners from Far West and nowhere to put them, so the authorities had to improvise. A few additional blankets were found and passed among them, but they were pitifully few for the numbers who needed them. No fires were allowed inside the courthouse.

By the third night, Benjamin Steed knew he was seriously ill. His eyes burned, and his brow was feverish in spite of the cold air. Whenever a fit of coughing hit him, he had to clutch his arms around his ribs, trying to squeeze back the pain. It was sharp, as if a wood rasp were working up and down inside his lungs. When the coughing finally subsided again, he was spent and exhausted.

"That doesn't sound good, Brother Ben," his neighbor said, peering at him in the darkness.

Benjamin didn't answer. He just huddled down closer, cupping his hands over his mouth to warm the air a little before it went into his lungs.

"Brother Steed! Benjamin Steed. Can you hear me?"

Through the feverish haze, Benjamin was aware that someone or something was shaking his shoulder. With a tremendous effort, he pulled his head around and opened his eyes. The chills that had racked him violently through the night had now alternated back to the fire that felt like it was going to consume him. He wanted to throw off the blankets and let the cold air rush over him, but he was still in control of his mind enough to know that such a move could prove fatal. Somewhere it vaguely registered with him that it was just coming daylight.

"Benjamin, listen to me!"

He tried to focus on the dark shape leaning over him. Then finally he recognized the kindly face of Bishop Edward Partridge. He murmured an answer, but his ears heard nothing and he realized his lips had not moved.

"Brother Ben, you are very ill. You cannot stay here. It's too cold."

"Hot," Benjamin whispered.

"Yes, I know. You're burning with fever. We've talked to the guards. They've agreed to take you to where Brother Joseph and the other prisoners are being kept."

"Brother Joseph?" Benjamin repeated dully. "Brother Joseph is here?"

"Yes. They brought him and the others here from Jackson County last night."

Benjamin tried to bring his head around.

Partridge still had his hand on Benjamin's shoulder. "They're not right here. They've put them in an abandoned house. It's got one wall missing, but at least it's got a roof over it. Anything is better than being out in the open air like this."

"Thank you," Benjamin said, reaching up to pluck at the bishop's coat. "But not necessary. Others sick too."

"Not as sick as you, Ben. Not as sick as you."

"Brother Benjamin Steed . . ."

Benjamin felt himself relax under the weight of their combined hands. The chills were back now, and the warmth of their flesh on his head felt good. And Joseph's voice was like a soothing balm upon his soul.

"In the name of our Lord and Master, Jesus Christ, and by the power of the holy priesthood which we together hold, we lay our hands upon your head and give you a blessing in your hour of need."

There was a pause, and then Benjamin was aware of a deepening timbre in Joseph's voice. "We are in desperate times, O

Lord. We find ourselves in circumstances wherein we have been driven from our homes and from the bosom of our families and loved ones, and this through the hardness of those who do uphold the hands of Satan and who do carry forth his work.

"Before us lies one of thy choice sons, Benjamin Steed. His heart is full of integrity, O Father. His life has been one of faith and goodness. He has blessed the kingdom and been a pillar of strength to his righteous family. And now he lies stricken before us. Oh, bless him, Holy Father, bless him with the power of thy might. We rebuke the affliction that has come upon him, and we do so by the power of the holy priesthood. We command it to hold its destructive powers from ravaging him further."

There was the soft clink of chains as Joseph shifted his weight slightly. After being put in the house, the seven men who had been brought from Jackson County had been chained loosely together with two logging chains and several padlocks. They rattled every time one of them moved. Only six were participating in the blessing. Sidney Rigdon was on the far end of the chain and, like Benjamin, was stretched out on the floor, desperately ill and half-delirious.

"Dear friend, Benjamin," Joseph was continuing, "your mission in this mortal existence is not yet finished. There are things with your family and with others that yet require your able hand. You and they will be tried as the gold in the fire, but remain faithful, for the bounds the Lord has set cannot be crossed by evil men. Do not despair, for this time of sorrow and testing shall pass, and you shall yet be returned to the bosom of your dear family, in the Lord's due time. And this blessing we give to you in the name of our beloved Savior, even Jesus Christ, our Lord and Master, amen."

As the six brethren rocked back on their heels, Benjamin opened his eyes. He felt the scalding tears flowing out of the corners of his eyes, but he didn't care. "Thank you, Joseph. Thank you."

By Sunday, Joshua was sitting up in bed and eating solid food. By Monday, he was noticeably stronger—though he still tired easily—and a great sense of relief filled the McIntire home. The worst of the crisis was over. On Tuesday, Mrs. McIntire went to Gallatin. Joshua had dictated a letter, and he was very anxious to see if there was any word from Caroline. He slept through most of the morning after Mrs. McIntire left, but by afternoon he was so restless that he demanded that Matthew and Jenny help him out of bed and into one of the chairs in the kitchen. It had frightened them both a little, for by the time he was seated his face was an ashen gray. But his color gradually returned, and it boosted his spirits tremendously to be out of bed for the first time.

Kathryn was lying in front of the fireplace, reading a book. Matthew was across from her, working with two pieces of wood—whittling them down and trying to fit them together. Jenny sat at the kitchen table, sewing on a piece of needlepoint.

Joshua turned to watch her, for he had quickly sensed the attraction between this girl and Matthew. She would be seventeen in January, Joshua had learned, and, as was the case with many children who were the oldest in the family, she had matured beyond her years. Her hair—light enough brown to be almost blond—now had the sun coming through the window on it, highlighting it with just a touch of auburn, like Caroline's. Her eyes were a light blue, and though they were often sober and thoughtful, they could also dance with quick amusement or spark with a touch of Irish fire. But the freckles belied all of that maturity and made her look like a young girl. All in all, it was quite a charming combination, and Joshua was pleased with what he saw happening.

She looked up and caught him watching her, so he quickly turned to Matthew. "What is that, anyway?" Joshua asked. "You've been carving on it for two days now."

"Looks good, don't it?" Matthew took two more cuts with the knife in the notch that would hold the second piece at the top of the longer one, then shoved them together. Reaching across the table, he picked up a long piece of rawhide and dipped it in a small bowl of water. Then he propped the longer stick between his knees and began wrapping the rawhide around the joint holding the shorter crosspiece, as the Indians did when they tied a stone head to a stick handle to make a tomahawk.

Then Joshua's eyes narrowed and his lips compressed. "Is that for me?"

Matthew nodded without looking up. He stretched the wet rawhide tight so that when it dried it would shrink and bind the wood together into a joint strong enough to hold a man's weight.

Joshua's eyes were flashing. "I don't need no crutch."

Matthew rolled his eyes at Jenny, the way one parent does to another when a petulant child is being difficult. Jenny smiled and gave him a similar look.

"It isn't funny!" Joshua shouted angrily. "I am not a cripple. My leg just got banged up with all that bouncing on the travois. Now, put that thing away. Or better yet, throw it in the fire."

Kathryn put her book down, staring at him. She looked a little frightened. Jenny's smile slowly faded.

Good! Joshua thought. *I don't need any cuteness right now.*

Apparently not paying any attention to his brother, Matthew leaned back, examining his handiwork. The stick was not perfectly straight, but it was strong, and the piece that fit under the arm was big enough for a man like Joshua. Satisfied, Matthew set the crutch down on the table, an impish look now on his face. "You know what I think, Jenny?"

"What?"

"I think I may have to use this sooner than I thought."

One eyebrow came up, and there was a warning in her eyes. Joshua was still glaring at them.

"I think I might even use it tonight."

"Tonight?"

"Yes. I'm going to wait until my brother is asleep, then I'm going to break this over his head. It's hard enough, don't you think? His head, I mean."

A giggle burst out from Kathryn, but she instantly slapped a hand over her mouth. Jenny was staring at Matthew in amazement. Then she too had to suppress a smile.

"Matthew," Joshua growled ominously. "Stop it. I don't find this funny at all."

Matthew went on easily, still talking to Jenny, totally ignoring his brother. "Seems to me, a good hickory stick across the head is just what you give to a patient with such abominable manners. After all, we have been waiting on him hand and foot for over a week now. Not to mention the fact that three of us carried him twenty-five miles in the middle of the night through hostile bands of militia. Not to mention the fact that your mother is out right now risking her own safety to mail his letter and see if there is any mail for him. And what do we get for all that? The manners of a bear kicked in the rump in the middle of hibernatin' season."

Joshua had opened his mouth. Now it shut again. Matthew had met his gaze now and held it calmly but steadily. Then finally a fleeting smile appeared on Joshua's face, a smile that dissolved quickly into mock severity. "You're getting to be kind of an insolent little pup, aren't you?" he muttered softly.

"I'm eighteen," Matthew beamed, relieved that his tactic had worked. "Eighteen-year-olds have a natural gift for insolence."

On Tuesday, the thirteenth of November, the Mormon prisoners went on trial. Judge Austin King, one of the Saints' most bitter and dedicated enemies, was appointed to preside. There is an old Chinese proverb that states: "Where there is a will to condemn, there is evidence at hand." Judge Austin King may not have known the proverb, but he certainly knew how it worked. Within minutes of the opening gavel, he made it clear how things were to be. Witnesses were called and sworn at the point of a bayonet. Either they would give the testimony the court was looking for or their lives would be forfeit. One man, who dared to testify that it was the Mormons who had been wronged, had to jump out of the witness box, dive out the window, and flee for his life rather than be shot. No papers were read against the prisoners, and no formal charges were outlined.

Ironically, the first witness called for the prosecution was Sampson Avard, the man who had organized the secret society of the Danites in Far West to kill Missourians. Other disaffected brethren came in to swear against their former leaders and associates. Colonel George M. Hinkle; Reed Peck, Hinkle's adjutant and co-conspirator in the betrayal; John Corrill, a former counselor in the Presiding Bishopric—one by one they swore that Joseph and the leaders of the Church were intent on building a worldly kingdom, by conversion if they could, by bloodshed if they must. This was treason, the prosecution argued, if ever there was a case of it.

Benjamin came with the others each day. He moved slowly, and Parley Pratt supported him on one arm. He looked emaciated and drained, but he was walking. And he knew that that was no small thing. In the hours immediately following the blessing, he had stabilized. The fever was gone, as were the violent chills. The cough still felt as if it were ripping his lungs apart and left him trembling and hunched over, but he was alive, and that was nothing short of miraculous.

At one point, after days of false testimony and a continuous stream of invective aimed at them, Benjamin leaned forward to Joseph. "When did we leave the United States of America?" he whispered.

Joseph turned around, shaking his head. "There will be no justice here, Brother Benjamin. No justice at all."

On the afternoon of Tuesday, November thirteenth, Mary Fielding Smith had a baby. Still confined to her bed, with a serious illness, and still suffering from the shock of seeing her husband brutally torn from the family circle, she nevertheless gave birth to a healthy, squalling baby boy. Mary had already decided on a name for the baby, pending Hyrum's approval when she could get a chance to discuss it with him. She wanted to name the boy after her brother who was still in England on a mission.

When anyone asked about his name, Mary would manage a wan smile and say, "If Hyrum approves, we're going to call him Joseph Fielding Smith."

Chapter Notes

The two-day snowstorm discussed in this chapter struck while the prisoners from Far West were on the march to Richmond and greatly added to their suffering (see *HC* 3:204).

The details of the imprisonment at Richmond and the sham trial under Judge Austin King are documented in numerous sources (for example, see *Restoration*, pp. 410–11; *Persecutions*, pp. 255–60; *HC* 3:208–12). Before the trial began, Sampson Avard told Oliver Olney, a former member of the Church, that "if he [Olney] wished to save himself, he must swear hard against the heads of the Church, as they were the ones the court wanted to criminate; and if he could swear hard against them, they would not (that is, neither court nor mob) disturb him. 'I intend to do it,' said he, 'in order to escape, for if I do not, they will take my life.'" (*HC* 3:209–10.)

Joseph F. Smith, born to Hyrum and Mary Fielding Smith on November 13, 1838, later became the sixth President of The Church of Jesus Christ of Latter-day Saints.

Chapter Twenty-Seven

Caroline approached the boardinghouse wearily, almost too tired to take her usual precautions. She had been down by the Mississippi River docks most of the afternoon, working with one of Joshua's partners on business affairs. She always made the carriage driver drop her off in a different place—three or four blocks from where she and the children were staying—and walked the rest of the way. Then she could watch to make sure she was not being followed. It was a strain that wore her down, yet she was still too thoroughly frightened by what had happened in Independence to take any chances.

But it had been a long day, and she was anxious to be home and off her feet. She made one last check around to see if there were any strangers, then walked up the stairs and inside the rooming house.

"Hello, Miz Naylor." The landlord was always at the door of his own room, and monitored the comings and goings of his guests meticulously. He was a strictly conservative man and allowed only the most respectable of boarders to stay in his building. He would have been shocked to know this woman had given him a false name.

"Hello, Mr. Jenson."

He glanced toward the stairs. "The children are kind of restless."

She felt a flash of irritation. She was paying top dollar for this room and had specifically asked for one on the third floor where there were no other rooms. She didn't need monitoring. She started to say something to him, then bit back her retort, too tired to really care. She nodded again, perhaps a bit too curtly, and went up the stairs.

By the time she reached the third level, she knew what Jenson meant. She could hear Olivia's voice coming through the door and clear down the hall. There was the deeper rumble of Will speaking. The sound was angry and sharp. As she approached the door, she could hear Savannah crying.

Grimly Caroline started fishing in her purse for the key. But as she found it and reached for the door, her hand stopped. Olivia's voice had risen sharply. "Matthew's not that way."

"Matthew's a Mormon too."

"He is not. Not in that way." Caroline could tell that her daughter was on the verge of tears.

"He may be one of the better Mormons," Will said stubbornly, "but he's still a Mormon. And Mormons killed our pa."

"Grandma Steed's a Mormon!" Olivia cried. The anguish in her voice tore at Caroline's soul. "So is Grandpa. And Aunt Lydia and Uncle Nathan. Do you hate them too?"

There was no answer, and Caroline leaned forward, listening intently, so caught up in what was happening on the other side of the door that there wasn't even a thought about eavesdropping. Then finally there was a low, pain-filled voice. "They aren't really our grandparents."

"They are too!" There was a scuffling sound, then the sound of hands slapping against something.

"Stop it, Livvy!"

"They are too!" she sobbed. "You stop saying that!"

Caroline fumbled quickly with the key, feeling a sharp desolateness shoot through her.

"They're Mormons, Livvy!" Will shouted. "And Mormons shot our pa."

Caroline had the door unlocked and threw it open. Olivia whirled. Will's head came up with a jerk and his eyes flew open as he saw the look on his mother's face.

Livvy gave one strangled cry and hurled herself at her mother. "Oh, Mama! Mama!"

Caroline pushed inside and kicked the door shut with one foot. She held on to Olivia tightly as the girl sobbed against her. "It's all right, Livvy! It's all right." She leveled a withering glance at Will. "Are you proud of yourself?" she snapped.

Will's eyes dropped, unable to meet the piercing glare of his mother. "I just said they aren't our real grandparents," he muttered.

"Make him take it back, Mama! He's been saying awful things about the Mormons."

"I won't take it back!" he shouted at his sister. "*They killed our pa!*" Tears sprang to his eyes and he whirled, brushing angrily at the corners of his eyes. With a cry of rage or pain—Caroline couldn't tell which—he plunged across the room and into the bedroom where Savannah was crying.

The breath came out of Caroline in a long sigh of desperation. *What am I going to do? What ever am I going to do with him?*

Will sat with his head in his hands. Twice Caroline had asked him to look at her, but he had refused. That frightened her more than anything, for while Will had always been independent-minded, he had never been willfully disobedient.

She took a breath, wanting to weep for the pain he was nurturing down inside him. "Will, remember when we were in Savannah? Remember how folks always called the black people niggers?"

There was still no response, but she saw his eyes dart away from her.

"What did we say about that?" She waited a moment. "Didn't we say it was wrong to judge people just because they had dark skin? We talked about that, didn't we?"

He finally looked at her, but there was still defiance and bitterness in his eyes.

"Just because a few Mormons do bad things, doesn't make them all bad," Caroline said.

He leaned forward with a jerk, startling her a little. "You read them newspapers, Mama."

She sat back, the color draining a little from her face. "Yes, I did." Yesterday a riverboat had come into St. Louis from up the Missouri River. It brought papers from Ray County and news of the trials going on against the Mormon prisoners. The whole front page was filled with Sampson Avard's testimony about the Mormon Danite band. The Danite band! The very name had sent a chill up her back. It was the same name that had been signed to the note nailed to her door. It was the same name that had Caroline's own feelings of bitterness churning like a flash flood down a narrow gorge.

Avard's description of the Danites had answered all kinds of questions for Caroline. Why Joshua was dead. Why someone had come all the way to Independence to try and kill her and her family. And she was all the more frightened now, because one of the things Avard said was that these people swore with an oath that they would go to the ends of the earth to avenge themselves. And St. Louis was nowhere near the ends of the earth.

"Joseph Smith is their leader," Will said hotly. "He's the one who told them to go out and kill. And Matthew and Grandpa and Uncle Nathan believe in Joseph Smith. They think he's a great man."

"Will, we don't know for sure—"

"*Their own people are saying it, Mama!* You read it. It's not just their enemies. It's their own people."

Now Caroline looked away. Yes. She knew Joshua's family didn't condone it. But Will was right. By standing fast with Joseph, in a way that meant they were part of it. At least, they were not part of stopping it.

Will saw that his shot had hit home. He sat back, pouting, defiant, and a little triumphant. Finally, she looked up. She didn't know how to fight this cold core of anger and hatred and bile that had lodged somewhere deep in her boy. She had enough of a struggle fighting her own loss, her own growing bitterness towards the Mormons. "It isn't good to hate, Will," she said, with little conviction in her voice.

But before Will could answer, there was the sound of footsteps outside in the hall and then a soft knock on the door. Caroline turned her head, startled. It was nearly half past nine now. Will started across the room but she waved him back. "Go in with Livvy and Savannah," she said softly. "Make sure they're asleep."

She walked to the door, cautious now. "Who is it?"

"Mr. Samuelson."

There was a quick release of breath. Walter Samuelson was the business partner with whom she had spent the afternoon. She unlocked the door and opened it quickly. "Good evening, Walter. Come in."

He removed his hat and stepped inside. Will had gone to the bedroom door but had not gone in. Samuelson nodded a greeting to him, then looked back at Caroline. "I apologize for coming at such a late hour, Mrs. Steed, but I'm afraid I have some bad news."

She felt a sudden premonition. One hand fluttered nervously at the buttons on her dress. "What is it?"

His eyes looked away for a moment, then he shook his head. "I just learned that two men came in on the boat from upriver yesterday. They've been going around town asking questions about you." His head moved slowly back and forth in discouragement. "I thought I'd better warn you."

“Don’t wake Savannah up. Be as quiet as you can, but pack everything. I must write to your father’s family. I have put it off long enough. Now there is no choice.”

“Where will we go, Mama?” Olivia had not been asleep and had come out immediately after Samuelson had left. Now she was moved past her tears and was acting more like her mother—discouraged, tired, worried, but resolute and determined.

Caroline stopped emptying the small chest that held their few dishes and things. “There’s only one place far enough away that they can’t find us. Tomorrow is Tuesday. That means there is a boat going downriver, leaving at noon. Mr. Samuelson will pick us up at eleven tomorrow in a closed carriage and take us right to the boat. He’ll have other men with him to make sure we’re all right.”

“Why can’t we just arrest them?” Will demanded. “Mr. Samuelson said he knows which hotel they’re in.”

“Because we can’t prove anything.” The despair sank in on her heavily. “We don’t even know what they look like, Will. Until they do something . . .” She shuddered. “We’re not waiting for that. We’re going.”

“To Savannah.” Will didn’t make it a question. He already knew.

“Yes,” his mother said. “We’re going back to Savannah. We’ll go to the Montagues, see if we can stay with them on the plantation for a time.”

Without a word, Will turned and walked to the door of the second bedroom, where he and Olivia slept. When he reached it, he stopped. “Mama?” He spoke without turning around.

“Yes, Will?”

“I’ll see you and Livvy and Savannah safely to Georgia. Then I’m coming back.”

Caroline nearly dropped a knife. “You’re what?” she blurted.

"If those men can find *us*, then I can find them. You heard Mr. Samuelson. He's going to try and find out all about them. When I come back, he'll know something."

She laid down a dish very carefully, still staring at him in utter amazement. "He's doing that so he can send word to Obadiah Cornwell, Will. Obadiah will know what to do. These are dangerous men, Will. And you are only fourteen! Don't be insane."

His back only stiffened. "By the time my first father was fourteen, he had sailed back and forth to England three times."

"Will . . ." She couldn't finish. He had shocked her so deeply the words wouldn't come.

"Come on, Livvy," Will said quietly. "Let's get things packed." And with that, he walked into the bedroom without looking back at his mother.

"Jenny, I can't do that without asking your mother."

Her head bobbed back, the light brown hair bouncing softly. "My mother?" Her mouth twisted in puzzlement. "I just want to read your book, Matthew. Why should you ask my mother about that?"

Matthew looked over at Joshua for help. But he was not paying any attention to either of them. He was in a chair in front of the fireplace, his bad leg stretched out so that it caught the fulness of the heat. He had been staring steadily into the flames for the last ten minutes.

"Tell her, Joshua."

He looked up. "Tell her what?"

"She wants to read my Book of Mormon. I told her I can't let her do that without asking her mother."

Joshua frowned immediately. "That's right, Jenny."

"But why? I just want to see what it says."

Matthew blew out his breath. This dealing with a woman's mind was a new experience for him. So he started again, slowly and patiently. "Being a Mormon in Missouri right now is not a wonderful thing. And—"

"Oh, for heaven's sake, Matthew, I don't want to be a Mormon. I just want to read in your book."

"And," he continued stubbornly, "your mother has taken a great risk by taking us into her home. We owe her a great deal, and I won't be doing anything behind her back."

"Matthew's right, Jenny," Joshua said, coming fully back to their company now. "Your family is—"

She threw up her hands, blue eyes flashing angrily. "Oh, what's the use? I don't want to read your old book anyway." She stood and flounced angrily off into her bedroom, slamming the door behind her.

Kathryn stood up and sidled up to Matthew. "She really does," she said in the kind of conspiratorial whisper only a twelve-year-old was capable of. "She's just like that when she doesn't get her way."

Joshua reached down and picked up his crutch. He hauled himself up and hobbled over to the front door. He took his coat down. "I'm going to take another turn around the house," he said, "get some fresh air."

Matthew pulled his head around, wanting to deal with something he could handle. "You're getting pretty good with that," he smiled. "Are you getting any more feeling in your leg?"

Joshua reached down and rubbed his hand up and down his left thigh. "Maybe a little," he said hopefully. Instantly he sobered again. "Matthew? Don't ask."

Matthew's eyebrows lifted in surprise. "Don't ask what?"

Joshua spoke gently. "Don't ask Mrs. McIntire about the Book of Mormon. That's not going to help them. Not now. Not here. The McIntires are Catholics. They already have religion. You don't have to make them into Mormons."

Matthew watched him steadily for a moment, then finally nodded glumly. "I know," he murmured.

Putting on his coat, Joshua gave Matthew a nod, opened the

door, and stepped outside. He stood there for a moment, breathing in deeply the crisp afternoon air. One hand came up and rubbed at his beard. He would make ten circles around the yard and outbuildings today. Yesterday it had been six. Two days before that, only three. Day after tomorrow it would be exactly three weeks since he had been shot. And there was still no answer from Caroline. He couldn't delay much longer.

Benjamin looked down at the weevil floating on the top of the watery stew. With hardly a second thought, he began to dip out the ones he could see and toss them aside. He was too tired and cold and hungry to care much anymore. The bread tasted moldy, but there again, he hardly hesitated. For the past three meals there had been no bread, and right now it tasted wonderful.

He looked up and Joseph was grinning at him.

Surprised, Benjamin stopped what he was doing. "What?"

"You're becoming quite the expert at that, Brother Ben."

Benjamin looked down in his bowl, then at the spattering on the floor where he had been tossing the unwanted portions. "I guess I am."

"We all are," Hyrum said. He rubbed his thick whiskers ruefully. "Straining things out of my soup is a talent I never knew I had."

Benjamin didn't laugh. The battle against despair was endless now, and humor had little place in it. It was Tuesday, November twentieth. They had been in jail and undergoing "trial" for seven days now. They had spent another fruitless, spirit-crushing day before Judge Austin King and the mob that surrounded him. Now they were back in their "cell" in the vacant house. The guards were just outside, eating a decent meal brought by the townspeople. The prisoners welcomed the chance to talk freely.

They ate in silence for a time, then Joseph turned to Benjamin again. "Brother Ben, do you remember a conversation you and I had a few weeks ago, not long after Thomas Marsh left us?"

Benjamin lowered his spoon and nodded. He remembered it well, thought of it often. "Yes. I asked you why all of these things were happening to us. I also remember your answer. You said the Lord would have a pure people so that his work could be done."

Benjamin looked around. Here they were in a makeshift jail cell, without proper facilities, bound together by chains and padlocks. And their families were forty or fifty miles away, facing who knew what after going through a hellish nightmare. "Is this what it takes?"

There was a short, mirthless laugh. "I guess it is, Ben. I guess it is."

The guards assigned to watch the prisoners in the vacant house and also those in the unfinished courthouse building were under the direction of a Colonel Price from Chariton County. He and his unit had been picked by General Clark and Judge King because of their reputation. Some of the militia units who had fought against the Saints in Far West had been moved by the plight of the Mormons and tended to treat them more kindly. There was none of that in Price's company. They were merciless enemies of the Mormons in general and Joseph Smith in particular.

As the trial progressed, Price and his men quickly saw that Judge King was giving them license for mistreating the prisoners. The slightest hesitation in obeying the guards' commands—often deliberately vague or contradictory—brought a swift kick or a slap across the face. There was a stream of mockery, abuse, ridicule, profanity, and vulgarity. "Hey, Joe, I'm feelin' kinda poorly right now. How 'bout a healing?" Or, "Joe Smith, why don't ya get one of them angels to come in here and help you escape?" Or, "Ol' Joe, close your eyes and prophesy which one of us will be the lucky one who gets to shoot you dead."

But on this night, when the guards came back into the house after their dinner, things were especially bad. Even before

Benjamin smelled whiskey in the air, it was obvious that Price and his men had gotten a generous ration of liquor as part of their meal. They immediately forced the prisoners to lie down and warned them that one word would bring a rifle butt to the side of their heads.

There was no possibility of sleep. The alcohol made the men even louder and meaner than usual, if that was possible. Nine o'clock passed and they did not tire. Ten and eleven o'clock came and went, and they only got the more boisterous and ugly. There were obscene jests, horrid oaths, the most dreadful of blasphemies, and the filthiest language Benjamin had ever heard.

And then as the hour of midnight neared, the conversation took another, even more terrible turn. Price's men had been present at the fall of Far West. They began to regale one another with tales of their exploits there. Benjamin's disgust and revulsion now turned to something else—a sickness in his stomach that made him want to retch.

Murder, robbery, looting, destruction—each man tried to outboast the other, telling more and more horrible stories of what they had done. One bragged of smashing in the head of a young father with his rifle butt. It had fractured his skull but hadn't killed the man, so they had carried him about in the back of a wagon for two days until he died. Another one said he personally had killed a man while his young son watched.

Benjamin was between Lyman Wight and Parley Pratt. Wight was as rigid as a steel rod, and Benjamin could feel Parley's body trembling with rage and disgust. On the other side of Parley, Joseph Smith lay on his back. Benjamin raised his head. In the dim light from the one lamp that burned in a far corner, he saw that Joseph's eyes were open and that he was staring at the ceiling, his jaw clamped shut tightly.

"Well, you boys ain't done nothin' like me and Carl Thompson did," the next voice called out, cackling obscenely. "We came to this one cabin. Thought at first it was empty.

Then we found this woman hiding under the bed. She had a young'un, but we drove him out of the house screamin' and hollerin'. We took her outside and called a bunch of our comrades. She was screamin' and cryin' and beggin' for mercy."

"And I'll bet you were real merciful!" someone hooted.

"We were," he retorted seriously. "We tied her hands down to a bench so she wouldn't hurt herself thrashing around and all that. Then we—"

There was a sudden and sharp rattle of the chain, and Benjamin saw a movement out of the corner of his eye. His head came up just in time to see Joseph leaping to his feet.

"*Silence, ye fiends of the infernal pit!*"

It was like a clap of thunder, or the roar of a lion as it rides down its prey. The guards jerked around violently, stunned by what they saw before them. Joseph was facing his captors, hands out in front of him, fists clenched into hard balls, his eyes like a flame of fire.

"In the name of Jesus Christ I rebuke you, and command you to be still! I will not live another minute and bear such language. Cease such talk, or you or I die this instant!"

Joseph ceased to speak. He stood fully erect and in terrible majesty. Though he was chained and without a weapon, he was nevertheless unruffled and dignified as an angel.

A rifle clattered to the floor. Benjamin whirled. What he saw was as shocking as Joseph's sudden eruption. There was absolute silence in the room now. The guards had shrunk back. Their weapons were lowered—one had dropped his rifle completely—and they were quailing like children in front of a furious schoolmaster. Their knees smote together, and their eyes were wide and frightened.

The nearest suddenly dropped off his chair, falling to his knees a few feet in front of Joseph. "I'm . . . I'm sorry," he stammered. "Forgive me, sir." And with that, he jumped up and slunk out of the room, averting his face from his fellow keepers.

Joseph did not even look at him. He remained standing for

what seemed like a very long time but was actually less than a minute. Then he calmly lay back down again and continued to stare up at the ceiling.

One by one the others slunk away, going into the next room or outside to smoke quietly until the changing of the guard. But inside or out, there was not another word of revilement from those men for the remainder of their time of duty.

Chapter Notes

We are indebted to Parley P. Pratt for the account of the rebuke of the guards (see *PPP Auto.*, pp. 179–80). The account in the novel follows closely his description. Parley concluded: "I have seen the ministers of justice, clothed in magisterial robes, and criminals arraigned before them, while life was suspended on a breath . . . ; I have witnessed a Congress in solemn session to give laws to nations; I have tried to conceive of kings, of royal courts, of thrones and crowns; and of emperors assembled to decide the fate of kingdoms; but dignity and majesty have I seen but *once*, as it stood in chains, at midnight, in a dungeon in an obscure village of Missouri" (*PPP Auto.*, p. 180, italics in original).

Chapter Twenty-Eight

"Matthew! Matthew! Wake up! Quick!"

Matthew jerked up, looking around wildly, and nearly cracked his head on the low ceiling above him. The McIntire cabin had one small bedroom above the main room, and a tiny attic loft above that. With Joshua in the main bedroom where the girls usually slept, they now slept with their mother, and Matthew slept above them. The loft was barely long enough for his six-foot form. The ceiling sloped, so even at its highest point he could not sit up fully.

Jenny was kneeling at his side. She was in her long nightdress with a robe over it. Her hair was loose and hung down past her shoulders. It was obvious she too had recently been asleep.

He rubbed his eyes, fighting to come alert. "What is it, Jenny? What's the matter?"

"Mama says to come quick." She backed up and started partway down the ladder that led up to the loft. "Hurry, Matthew! Joshua's gone!"

As he came down the stairs three at a time, Matthew could see into Joshua's room. The bed had not been slept in.

He spun around again. "Where is he?"

Mrs. McIntire mutely held out her hand. There was a piece of paper in it. Matthew took the paper and turned to the lamp.

Mrs. McIntire—

How does one repay a gift of the heart? I know in your mind there has never been any expectation of repayment. That is one of the things that make the gift of such great value. I don't know how, or when, or where, but someday I shall return and say thank you in a proper manner. Until then, know of my great esteem and affection for you and your wonderful daughters.

Joshua Steed

Matthew lowered the paper and stared at Jenny and her mother. "That crazy fool! He's in no shape to—"

"Read the back," said Mrs. McIntire.

In surprise, he turned the paper over. There was Joshua's scrawl on that side as well.

Matthew—

I'm sorry to run out on you like this, but knowing what an insolent pup you are, I didn't feel like discussing it with you. Don't worry about me. I'm much stronger now. (I did sixteen rounds yesterday.) But strong or not, I have to go. It can't wait any longer. Go home. I shall write when I know something. Thanks for the crutch. I hate it!

Joshua

Mrs. McIntire sighed deeply. "I shouldn't have told him."

Matthew dropped the note on the table. "Told him what?"

She sighed again. "Yesterday, when I went to town? There were some men talking at the store. One of them said they'd been out riding past our place and had seen a man walking around my barns on a crutch."

Matthew drew in his breath sharply.

"I made up some story about it being a boy I'd hired." She crossed herself quickly. "Lord forgive me, when they pressed I just straight out denied it."

Matthew's mind was in turmoil. There was no question now about what had to be done. The fact that Joshua was gone made it easier in one way. It frightened him, but Joshua *was* stronger. Yet not strong enough to outrun men on horseback. He looked at Mrs. McIntire. "I'll get my things together."

"No!" Jenny stepped forward, her eyes pleading.

Matthew looked at her, started to say something, couldn't decide what could possibly help, and then looked helplessly at her mother.

Mrs. McIntire turned slowly, wearily. "Jenny, there's no choice. If the men come out here looking . . ." She shrugged and looked at Matthew. "Joshua's right, you know."

"About what?" Matthew asked.

"About going home." The kindliness of Mrs. McIntire's face was more evident than he had ever seen it before, and she had always been a wonderfully sensitive woman. "He's got several hours' head start on you, Matthew. And you don't know which way he went. Go home. Tell Nathan and your family."

Matthew started nodding even before she finished. "Yes. That's right." He felt a great relief. The thought of striking off to try and find Joshua in a countryside swarming with men out looking for Mormons was staggering to him. "Be sure there's no sign that we were here."

"I will," she said. She touched his arm. "You'd best hurry."

"Jenny, Kathryn, I'd like to speak with your mother alone for a moment if I could."

The girls looked a little surprised, but Jenny immediately shepherded her sister into the bedroom where Joshua had slept, and shut the door. Matthew turned slowly back around, letting the small valise with his stuff drop to the floor. "Mrs. McIntire, you've been so good to us. Derek was right when he said you were a Christian woman. I . . . well, just thank you."

There was a touch of mistiness to her eyes. "Actually, it is we who thank you. It's been marvelous to have your company. It gets pretty lonesome this far out." She looked toward the bedroom. "Especially for young people."

Matthew nodded; then, with time pressing him, plunged in. "Mrs. McIntire, I'd like to give Jenny a gift. But I don't want to do it without you knowing."

One eyebrow had come up. "I think that would be nice, Matthew."

He swallowed quickly. "I'd like to give her my Book of Mormon."

The eyebrow positively arched now.

"I know you have your own religion and all," he said hastily, "and I'm not trying to make her into a Mormon or anything like that. But, well, she said she wanted to know more about what we believe. And . . ." Now he was totally flustered. "The Book of Mormon is the most important thing I have with me right now. I'd like to . . . I'd like her to have it, if it's all right with you."

Nancy McIntire leaned back slightly, eyeing him very carefully. "Do you like her, Matthew? Do you like my daughter?"

He ducked his head, unable to meet her probing gaze. "Yes, I do."

She bored in more forcefully. "I think you know how I mean that?"

"Yes." He looked up quickly, then down again. "Yes, I do."

There was a sudden warmth in her eyes. "Then yes, I give my permission. You may give her your book."

He couldn't hide his surprise. "But—"

She smiled up at him. "It's been wonderful for Jenny to have you here. It's the most alive I've seen her in a long time. If you give her a present, it is going to mean a great deal to her. I just had to make sure it would mean as much to you as it will to her."

On the last day of November, the Steed family received three wonderful surprises. Over breakfast, Rebecca and Derek announced that Rebecca was with child. Then shortly after noon, a very weary Matthew Steed walked up the street toward his brother's cabin. Derek and Peter were out back cutting firewood. Peter looked up and nearly dropped the ax. Then with shouts to alert the house, he and Derek both raced to greet Matthew. This time the joy in the Steed household was tempered by the news that Joshua had left the McIntires' and was trying to make his way back to his family. During all that time he was there, Matthew had not dared to send a letter home from Daviess County. Any mail going to Far West would have instantly brought the McIntires under suspicion, so the news that Joshua's leg was partially paralyzed also came as a shock to them. That only added to the gravity of the situation. Nathan called for a family council right after they finished the midday meal.

But the third surprise, the most wonderful of all, came about an hour later, just as the family council got under way. Nathan had just opened up the discussion on what they should do, when they heard a noise outside.

Everyone turned toward the door. It was the noise of people, and it was swelling rapidly. People were shouting and calling out. Curious, Peter went outside. The rest of the adults followed. Half a block up the street there was a small crowd of people gathered in a circle. A woman gave a shriek of joy and started dancing around. Children were yelling, people were pouring out of their houses to see what was going on.

"What is it?" Lydia asked. "What's happening?"

A man broke loose and came running toward them. He was

waving his hat. "The brethren are coming! The brethren are coming! The rest of the prisoners have been released!"

On November twenty-fourth, Judge Austin King released twenty-three of the Mormon prisoners, stating that there was not sufficient evidence to sustain the charges. That had sent the Mormon community into a paroxysm of joy, for it proved what they had known all along—there was no foundation for the charges levied against the brethren. Rumors raced through Far West that Joseph and the rest would soon be released as well. Then on the twenty-eighth, after almost three weeks of false testimony and the most illegal of legal proceedings, Judge King made another ruling. Eleven prisoners would be held over for trial. Joseph, Hyrum, and Sidney Rigdon—all three members of the First Presidency—and three others would be tried in the spring in Daviess County for treason, and in the meantime would be held prisoner in Liberty, Clay County. Five others, including Parley P. Pratt, would remain in Richmond to be tried there for murder in connection with the Battle of Crooked River. The remaining twenty-nine prisoners were released and allowed to return to their homes.

Benjamin Steed was near the end of the column of men who trudged slowly up the long rise toward Far West. They could see silhouettes of some of the houses on the skyline, and a ripple of excitement swept up and down the line of returning men. But Benjamin was so exhausted that he could barely muster enough energy to raise his head. The two-day march and being outside in the winter weather around the clock had taken their toll on him. His lungs were on fire again. The cough ripped at his insides in regular spasms now and left him gasping and wheezing in agony. It took his total concentration to lift one foot and move it forward after the other one was put down.

It was only when he heard a great shout go up that he stopped and raised his head again. The column staggered to a ragged halt. He squinted, trying to make out what it was they were seeing against the late-afternoon sun. And then with a powerful, wrenching rush of relief he realized what it was. From out of the city streamed a river of humanity—men, women, children. They were running and shouting and waving their arms. Dogs ran alongside, barking wildly. They flowed toward the column in a great mass and then began to split as they reached the men. Only then did individual faces begin to come into focus for Ben. He recognized Reynolds Cahoon's wife as she came running down the line, crying out his name. Bishop Patridge was nearly bowled over by his oldest son, then swarmed down by his wife and other children. Benjamin felt a pang of sorrow as he recognized Parley Pratt's young wife, holding a baby, frantically looking for her husband. She had not yet been told that not everyone was returning. A man stepped out of line and whispered in her ear. She crumpled visibly and started to weep.

"Benjamin! Benjamin!"

He straightened with an effort, scanning the hundred faces that were running towards them.

"Papa!" "Grandpa!" "Father Steed!"

Now the voices took on shape and identity. He raised one hand, waving feebly. "I'm here!" he called, still not seeing them. And then he had them. Nathan was in front, holding Mary Ann's hand as they ran toward him. Matthew was on the other side of her, guiding her by her elbow so she didn't trip. Behind them came Lydia and Jessica, Derek and Rebecca and Peter. They were shepherding the children. Lydia and Jessica carried their babies. A great sob tore loose inside him and his knees almost buckled. It was his family. He was back with his family.

Nathan held Lydia's hand tightly as they walked slowly along, up the street away from their cabin. Neither of them spoke. They both knew what was coming, and both wanted to postpone it as long as possible. Finally he slowed his step. Lydia looked down at the ground, knowing the moment had come.

"You know it will be suicide if he tries to go into Jackson County," Nathan said.

"I know. If they think he's dead, his appearance will create a sensation. If they think he's still alive, then there'll be a price on his head." They still were not sure what the Missourians knew about Joshua.

"Exactly. That's why I've got to find him." Nathan looked down at his wife. He took her hands in his and peered into her eyes. For a moment he was struck again with his great fortune in loving and finally winning this beautiful, dark-haired woman who could have had any young man in all of western New York State.

He cleared his throat to speak, but she beat him to it. "You have to go, Nathan."

That took him aback.

She looked away, her eyes glistening. "Even saying the words leaves me sick, but you know and I know there is no choice. He's out there alone and crippled, desperate to find Caroline. But what I said before is still true. We . . . *I* owe Joshua a debt that cannot ever be repaid. And Caroline—what she must be going through by now!"

He lifted her hands to his lips and kissed them softly. "You know what this means?"

She looked away quickly. "More sharply than you can dream."

"If Caroline has left Independence, it could take weeks to find where she has gone. I . . . I don't know how long the militia is going to let us stay here. What if they make you leave the state before I get back?"

She put her arms around him. "That's why Derek cannot go with you. I'd feel much safer about it if he did, but with Father Steed so sick, we must have Derek and Matthew to be the men of the house."

"I know."

She pulled up tight against him and her hands began to rub his back, feeling the old welts and scars beneath his shirt. "It absolutely terrifies me to think of you going back into Jackson

County and . . ." She couldn't bring herself to say it. She changed the subject to make her mind go on to other things. "How will you ever find him? You don't even know which way he went?"

"I'll start in St. Joseph."

"St. Joseph? Why there?"

His brow furrowed. It was obvious he had thought this through already. "He won't head straight south. Not when the militia is all over the place. And St. Joe is only forty miles from Gallatin. It's the closest city. And remember, he takes freight there all the time. He'll have people there he knows, people who can help him. I'll go west from here, then take the road that goes up in case he's already started down."

She nodded. "He's got two days start on you, but Matthew says he can't move very fast."

He put his hand under her chin and tipped her head back. "Lydia, I love you. There is nothing else except my family that would make me leave you again."

She was crying openly against him now. "You must go immediately, Nathan. Every hour you are delayed will make it more difficult for you to find him."

He leaned down and kissed her very tenderly, but for a very long time. Then they straightened, turned around, and walked quickly back to the cabin.

Nathan left Far West within the hour of his farewell to Lydia. Late that afternoon, a fourth unexpected event occurred with the Steeds. A letter arrived from St. Louis from Caroline Steed addressed to Mr. and Mrs. Benjamin Steed. Unfortunately, Nathan had gone and was not there to know of it. The reading of it brought a great pall to the Steed household.

"But I don't understand, Derek," Rebecca said. "It can't be the Danites, can it?"

Derek shook his head. "No." It came out flat and hard. There was no question in his mind about that. "First of all, the group was disbanded the moment Brother Joseph learned what Avard was doing. Secondly, Avard has gone over to the Missourians. That sniveling coward wouldn't dare continue to function now."

"But the note that was on Caroline's door . . ."

That had really shaken Derek too. Caroline had sent the note along with her letter. It was her way of trying to tell the family why there were some bitter feelings in the Joshua Steed family right now toward the Mormons, why a fourteen-year-old boy was consumed with a desire for revenge. Derek had read it over several times.

"Did you notice anything peculiar about that note?" he asked.

Rebecca thought for a moment, then shook her head.

"One of the things it said was, 'You have our prophet, *Joe* Smith, in your jail.'"

Her eyes widened.

"That's right," he went on. "There's not a Latter-day Saint who doesn't know how strongly Joseph feels about his name. None of us call him Joe. Not even those who've left the Church. We just naturally call him Joseph."

"So . . ." Now her mind was racing. "If it wasn't one of us who wrote it, then who did?"

He shook his head in discouragement. "In Jackson County? It could be any one of a hundred people. Especially if they heard about what Joshua did for us."

"But they've followed her to St. Louis!"

"I know, and that's frightening."

"We've got to let Nathan know," Rebecca said with sudden determination.

"But how?"

"If he finds Joshua, they'll go to Independence, right?"

"Yes, but Caroline won't be there."

"So then where will they go? Very first, who would Joshua go see?"

Derek thought for a moment, then snapped his fingers. "To Joshua's partner, the one he asked to get a wagon ready for Caroline in case there was trouble."

"Right," she said, turning on her heel. "Let's go write a letter. We can tell Joshua's partner everything. If we send it immediately, it should get there before Joshua and Nathan do."

Joshua was staring into his mug of beer, deeply depressed. It was past ten o'clock. In a few minutes, the saloon keeper would come over, trying not to stare down at the crutch, and tell him it was time to close. Joshua would drag himself up, hobble out and across the street, and climb up the stairs to the filthy hotel, with its tiny room and blanket that reeked from having too many alcoholics sleep on it and cockroaches scurrying away when he lit the lamp. And then he would lie there all night long, just as he had the night before, trying to figure a way out of the mess he'd put himself in.

He slapped at his leg angrily. How was a man to function when he could barely hobble? The first night crossing over open countryside in the dark with his crutch had been an endless hell and showed him how low his reserves of strength were. He would have turned back if he hadn't been so afraid that there would be men waiting for him back at the McIntires' house. It took him all that night and all the next day to make ten miles, and then he had collapsed in exhaustion and pain. But on the second day he had pushed on and finally reached the main east-west road that cut across the state. He hitched a ride with a teamster headed west and reached St. Joe on the afternoon of the third day.

Trading his sixty-dollar watch for the driver's ragged overcoat and ten dollars in cash, Joshua got off the wagon on the outskirts of town. On the three-day trip across the state, he had come to the same conclusion that Nathan and Lydia had, and that was that he had an identity problem. Joshua did a lot of business in St. Joe and knew several people he could call on for help. But then it hit him that it was not totally unlikely that news of him had come this far north from Independence. If the word was that Joshua Steed was dead, his appearance would be a sensation, and Joshua wasn't interested in being a sensation. On the other hand, if word had come that he was alive, then there would be a price on his head. Frustrated, he had found this flea-infested hotel, and holed up while he tried to think of a way to solve his problem.

And so for the last twenty-four hours he had sat and temporized. He had no Obadiah Cornwell up here whom he could totally trust. And worse, with the crutch, he was as conspicuous as a pup in a litter of kittens. He drew stares every time he ventured out. He hated it. He hated the looks—the sickly pity in the eyes of the women, the openmouthed stares of children, the men who were embarrassed for him. But more than that, he knew people would remember him. And so he had spent most of his time holed up in the hotel, trying to figure out what to do, watching his tiny reserves of cash dwindling at an alarming rate.

He lifted the beer and drank deeply. *So much for the great Joshua Steed. Off to save his wife and children. Can't even get his own pants on without it taking half an hour.*

Suddenly his head came around. A man had appeared at the door to the saloon and was looking around. Joshua tensed as the man turned in his direction. Then Joshua swore under his breath. The man was coming toward him. His hat was pulled down low over his face, the collar of his coat turned up. Here was a man who, like Joshua, was not looking to be identified easily. Then suddenly Joshua jerked forward, staring.

Nathan came up to the table, stopped, and looked down at him with a sardonic smile. "I'd ask you to buy me a drink, stranger, but fortunately for you, I don't drink."

"All right, brother," Joshua said in a low voice. "You're in my country now. We see anybody, you just let me do the talking."

"Gladly."

They were just coming up on Independence from the south. Joshua had circled them around the outskirts to the west so that they didn't have to pass down Main Street. It was nearly midnight, and there were hardly any lights showing anywhere, but Joshua was in no mood to take chances. Nathan hadn't argued with him on that one.

"As you may remember, our house is one of the last ones on this side of town."

"I remember. And I also remember that it looked like it was the biggest one in town."

Joshua laughed briefly. "It's pretty big. I wanted Caroline to be happy."

"She was happy, Joshua," Nathan said softly. "You could see that in her eyes."

Joshua considered that and accepted it as true. He clucked softly and snapped the reins, moving the horse forward. Joshua stood up in the stirrup with his one good leg, peering carefully at every place that was big enough to hide a man. The moon was out and half full, and they made an easy target if someone was waiting for them. He reached down, letting his hand rest on the butt of the new Sharps rifle Nathan had purchased in St. Joe.

Getting the money had been shamefully easy, and Joshua realized that his physical state had affected his ability to think clearly. Once Joshua explained his fear about being a wanted man, Nathan had hit on a simple solution. At precisely nine o'clock the morning after his arrival, Nathan walked into the bank where Joshua did business in St. Joe. He introduced himself to the president as a business associate of Joshua's and asked if he was in town. He watched closely the man's reaction. No, the man said, he hadn't seen Joshua for over a month. There was nothing unusual in his reaction to the question. If word of Joshua had come north, this man hadn't heard it, Nathan was sure of that.

So Nathan had thanked him and left. Ten minutes later, Joshua walked in, told the man about having his leg crushed between two horses, and accepted his condolences. Half an hour later Joshua had walked out with five hundred dollars. By noon, Nathan had purchased two horses, two saddles, bedrolls, food, weapons, and ammunition, and they were on their way south.

The day-and-a-half ride had taken a toll on Joshua, but the excitement of being near to their goal had rejuvenated him. He was alert and poised for action. Then he reined in sharply, leaning forward in the saddle. "What the . . . ?"

Nathan peered into the darkness in the direction Joshua was looking. "What? What's the matter?"

But Joshua didn't answer. He kicked his heels into the horse's flanks and sent him trotting forward. Nathan drew the rifle from its scabbard, the hairs on his head suddenly prickling, then kicked his horse forward too.

Joshua stopped at a large pile of rubble that was barely visible in the dark. As Nathan reined up beside him he could smell the faint odor of burned wood. Confused, he looked around, then back to Joshua. "If I remember rightly, isn't your house close by? Why are you stopping here?"

Joshua swung gingerly down from the saddle. Only when he was down did he look back up at Nathan. "This was my house," he said flatly.

Cornwell was shocked to see Joshua at his door. And yet it was a great relief to him as well, for the letter from Derek Ingalls explaining about Caroline had left him deeply disturbed. He locked the door tightly behind them, then pulled down the blinds and lit a lamp. He let Joshua and Nathan read the letter.

It was a bitter blow. Nathan had feared they would have to go to St. Louis to find her. Now she wouldn't be there either.

There was a brief argument about Nathan's going back to Far West, which Nathan ended by finally yelling at Joshua that if he said another word he would kick his crutch out from under him. They rested through the day, not daring to let Joshua be seen, then rode out shortly after dark. They turned the horses east. Caroline was no longer in St. Louis, but that's where she had been last, and that's where they would pick up the trail.

Chapter Twenty-Nine

Caroline stepped up on the veranda of the big plantation house, removed her bonnet, and wiped at her brow. She had forgotten how wonderful the winters were in Savannah—bright sun, balmy days, the breeze off the ocean. And being out in it had been a wonderful tonic for her desolated soul.

She had not wanted to go out, had fought it even when Julia Montague insisted that she needed some sun. Her loss of Joshua was still searingly real, and the plantation carried too many painful memories for Caroline. It was here that she and Joshua had walked one night, and he had openly declared his intention to court her. Even now, a month after his death, the memory of that night brought pain so sharp it made her clutch at her throat.

Julia Montague knew all of what was going on inside Caroline but still had the wisdom to push her friend out of her shell. First she had asked that Caroline come to town with her and Abner, but that gave Caroline the chills. Though Caroline was almost certain that no one, not even Mormons driven by fanatical hatred, would follow her clear to Georgia, she had taken no chances. When she reached Savannah, she came straight out to the Montagues and asked for their help. The plantation was far enough outside of town that Caroline and her children could stay there for a time without anyone in town knowing about it. She felt foolish, felt like she was being too paranoid, but then she had also been sure that those who had killed Joshua would not follow her to St. Louis. And she had been wrong.

So when she refused to go into town, Julia had extracted a promise from Caroline that she would at least go out. Now Caroline was grateful she had agreed. The pain was still there, as it was almost every waking moment, but as she walked there came the sweetness of the memories as well, and she felt the first signs of healing. And that had felt so good, she had stayed out almost twice as long as she had first intended.

Behind her, the door opened and Olivia came out in a rush. "Mama! Mama!"

"I'm over here, Livvy. What is it?"

The face that looked so much like her mother's suddenly crumpled. "Will's gone, Mama!"

It was as though Olivia had slapped her. She fell back a step. "Gone?"

Olivia nodded, crying now. "He left a note. He said not to try and find him. He's gone back to look for Papa's murderers."

Caroline leaned back against a pillar, her knees suddenly going weak. "Are you sure?" she whispered.

"Yes, Mama. He's gone. I looked everywhere."

Caroline swung around, her mind racing wildly. If she had the servants hitch up the carriage, maybe . . . Then as quickly as the idea came, she rejected it. Her hands dropped to her side as she realized how carefully Will had planned this. Abner and Julia had gone to town to see off a packet ship loaded with their cotton and headed for the mills in St. Louis. It was to depart at one o'clock, more than half an hour ago now.

Then suddenly she straightened. "You go back in with

Savannah," she commanded Olivia. Caroline walked swiftly into the house and up the stairs to her bedroom. She went straight to the large chest of drawers in the corner and opened the bottom drawer. Pawing back the clothes, she uncovered the back corner. She stared for a moment, then sat back on her heels. It was gone.

A week ago she had hidden a small purse with one hundred dollars in it. Then she had told the Montagues about it. She was saving it for Christmas, she said. She had waited until she was sure that Will was in the next room within earshot. The decision to do it had come dearly, for in a way it was like giving him license. But nothing Caroline had said or done in the past days had lessened the iron-hard determination that raged inside her son. His desire to avenge his father's death was like a cancer consuming him. And if she couldn't stop him, then she decided it was better that he have some resources. A fourteen-year-old trying to make his way back to Missouri with nothing was as frightening as the thing that was eating at him. And so she had "hidden" the money.

She folded her arms around her knees and buried her head against them as the enormity of it all hit her. There was a stifled sob. "Oh, dear God," she cried. "Take care of my boy!"

The length of time that a candle burned was determined by how many times it was dipped into the hot tallow and allowed to cool and then dipped again. The stub that now sat in the small pewter candleholder near Mary Ann's elbow had been a thirty-six dipper, one of the thickest made. But it had already burned for nearly seventy hours, and there was no more than an inch left—maybe an hour, perhaps less.

The flame flickered slightly as a cold draft stirred the air in the cabin. Outside, the wind was blowing across the northern Missouri prairie, and she could hear the branches of the bushes rubbing against the cabin. She closed her eyes for a moment, feeling the tiredness behind the lids, reaching up with her fingers to massage them gently. Then, finally, she opened them again, picked up the quill pen, and dipped it into the ink made from lampblack, a touch of pine gum, and boiled water. She had only two sheets of paper, so she wrote slowly, keeping the letters small and the lines tight.

Dear Melissa, Carl, and children,

We received your letter dated November 4th just today. Mail service in Far West has been greatly delayed and is still spotty at best. I know not when I shall have another opportunity to reply, so am writing this while your father and the others sleep.

I wrote you of your father's imprisonment and his return in a previous note. I hope it has reached you. His health continues to improve, but he is still very frail. With our freedom of movement outside town still restricted somewhat, wood is becoming scarce. We keep a fire only to cook and the nights in the cabin become quite chilled, which seems to slow his recovery.

Things in Far West have settled down into a numbing routine. Food is very short and limited in both variety and quality. General Clark supposedly granted a few permits for some of the brethren to pass in and out of town freely for purposes of gathering food, but that is merely a fantasy. He has withdrawn almost all the militia forces now, leaving the countryside open to roving bands of ruffians who fall on any who are found away from town. Homes are still plundered. Stock is driven off or butchered. The only thing we have in any abundance is parched corn, and we try to find various ways to serve it to break the monotony of our diet. More and more it looks like the promise that we can stay until spring will not be honored. Many of our number—those with the means to do so—have already left. For those who have lost almost everything, such as ourselves, we do not know how we shall effect a trip across many miles of prairie in wintertime.

For now our destination seems to be eastward to Illinois. To the west there are vast tracts of land, but, as you know, that is Indian Territory. To the north is Iowa Territory. There is plenty of land there too, but very little timber, except along the scattered streams and rivers. Our numbers are such that this would never suffice for settlements. Going south means moving through countryside filled with our enemies. No one considers that an option. So that leaves the east. Many are finding safe refuge in Quincy and the people there are treating them kindly.

There is one bright spot in all this. With some families leaving the city, the housing shortage is not quite so critical as it has been. We have been able to move back into our cabin. We are still crowded but nothing like when we were all at Nathan and Lydia's. Jessica started a school for our family a week or so ago. Not only is this a blessing to the children, but it helps to keep her from grieving too much for John. Word has gotten out now and the neighbors beg Jessica to teach their children as well. They have promised her a cabin in which she can live and teach as soon as a family leaves next week. Lydia helps by teaching arithmetic, and our dear Peter Ingalls is their assistant. He loves it and will make a wonderful schoolmaster of his own someday.

I wrote you the whole story of what happened when Joshua saved us and ended up getting shot. We have learned since then that his one leg is crippled. Nathan has gone to help him find Caroline. Caroline has fled to St. Louis and farther. But they are going to look for her. That is a whole tragic story in itself but there is not time to tell it now. We pray for them night and morning and have faith they will have some success in reuniting Joshua with his family.

Rebecca has some wonderful news. She is with child. They will be expecting sometime in early summer. She and

Derek are filled with joy in spite of our dark circumstances. She promises to write the next letter, so I will let her tell you more then.

Well, enough about our lives. How are things with you and Carl? We were very pleased to hear that Carl's livery business continues to prosper. He is a hardworking and decent man. It is no surprise to your father and me that he does well. We miss the children fiercely and speak of them often. I fear by now they will have forgotten their "other" grandma and grandpa. Most painful is to know that we have a new granddaughter and can't even see her. Kiss little Sarah for all of us. Oh, how we wish we could see you all again! All our love. Write soon, my dearest Melissa. We love you and always will. God be with you.

Mama

She laid the pen down, then carefully folded the letter over into thirds and addressed the outside of the second sheet. There were no envelopes available and this would have to do. Then Mary Ann shook her head as she remembered something else. She opened the letter, picked up the pen, and added:

P.S. I am embarrassed that we have to send this to you without the postage being paid. Our cash money is practically non-existent here in Far West right now. We barter for almost everything we need, but could not do so for the postage needed to send this to you. Sorry.

As they walked down the wharf toward the Mississippi, Nathan let his eyes gaze across the river, here well over two hundred yards wide. The Missouri River came into it a short distance north of where they were, and it made an impressive sight. They were headed for the great riverboat tied up at the dock, black smoke pouring from its twin stacks. As they approached it,

Joshua slowed and then stopped. Nathan went on two or three steps before he realized it and stopped as well. He turned back. "Come on, Joshua. They'll be pulling the gangplank in a few minutes."

Joshua didn't budge. He leaned heavily on the crutch Matthew had made for him, his face lined with weariness. It was ironic that, although several business acquaintances in St. Louis had suggested he purchase a professionally made pair of crutches—tailor-made to fit his height, with padded cushions and hardened tips—Joshua flatly refused to even consider it. He was growing stronger each day, and he swore that more feeling was starting to return to his foot. It was as if he gave the credit for such improvement to Matthew's crutch and it had become a good-luck piece for him.

"Come on, Joshua. We're almost there. Then you can rest."

Joshua looked at his brother steadily for a moment. "I want you to go back, Nathan."

Nathan's jaw tightened stubbornly. He strode to his brother and took him by the arm. "We've gone over this enough, Joshua. I'm going with you."

"Your family needs you."

"I wrote to Lydia. I told her we're headed for Savannah."

"Christmas is only nine days away!" Joshua exploded. "Go home!"

Nathan's mouth softened and he looked his brother directly in the face. "Joshua, believe me when I say this—if Lydia were here, she would make me get on the boat with you. Now, stop being so blooming stubborn and let's go."

There was a deep, throaty blast of sound as the captain of the boat let steam through the boat's horn. Joshua didn't look up at all. "I know Caroline's in Savannah, Nathan. I can make it from here. All it takes is sitting on a boat for a few days and—"

Nathan shook his head and turned around. He started walking slowly toward the boat. "There's not another boat until day after tomorrow, Joshua. I'm going. If you're not, I'll write you from Savannah."

Joshua watched Nathan's back for a moment, then swore softly under his breath. Then he moved forward, hobbling quickly to catch up with his brother. "Stubborn, hardheaded fool!" he muttered as they reached the bottom of the gangplank together.

Nathan turned and grinned at him. "Guilty as charged." He punched Joshua lightly on the shoulder. "Care to guess who I learned it from?"

When Benjamin, Matthew, and Derek returned from the special meeting of the priesthood, the Steed women set aside their preparations for supper and gathered around them. A letter had been brought from Liberty Jail the previous evening by some of the brethren who had been able to briefly visit the Prophet Joseph and the others held prisoner there.

Anxious for any news and counsel from their prophet, the Steed family had gathered at Benjamin and Mary Ann's cabin to hear the report. It was still only midafternoon. The weather had warmed slightly, and the children were outside playing in the last hours of sunshine. They would leave them there while Benjamin told the adults what they had heard at the meeting.

"Well," Mary Ann said, "we are dying to hear. How are Brother Joseph and the others?"

Benjamin frowned. "In good spirits, considering the situation in which they find themselves."

"Is there any hope of an early release?" Rebecca asked anxiously.

Derek looked at his wife and shook his head slowly. "No. They say nothing about that in their letters, but Porter Rockwell has been able to visit Joseph two or three times. The Missourians still continue to talk about a trial, but no one is in any hurry to see it happen. Porter thinks the Missourians know they don't have enough evidence to get a conviction, and yet they are not anxious for an acquittal so that Joseph can go free."

"How are they?" Rebecca asked. "Are conditions there terrible?"

Derek nodded gravely. "According to those who've been there, it is more a dungeon than a jail. The walls are of stone and timber and nearly four feet thick. Guards stay in the room above them while they are kept in a single cellar room below. There are only two tiny barred windows for ventilation, and there is no place for a fire or heat of any kind. And with the severe winter we're having this year, you can only imagine what it must be like down there."

"The only way into that bottom room," Matthew added, "is through a hole in the ceiling and a rope. And Brother Rockwell says that the ceiling is not high enough for a tall man—like Joseph or Hyrum—to stand up straight. They must stay hunched over all the time."

Derek stood and began to pace. "The food is coarse and filthy, and only extreme hunger drives them to eat it. Porter has risked his life now several times to pass food into them, but for the most part they have to make do with what they are fed by the guards."

Benjamin reached up and began to rub his eyes. The report of those who had been to Liberty had shaken him deeply. "The guards torment and abuse them continually," he said slowly. "On at least two or three occasions now, large doses of poison have been put into their food."

"Poison!" Lydia cried in horror. "They're trying to kill them?"

"Yes," Derek said grimly. "Fortunately, the Lord watches over them. Their enemies have made the doses too large and their stomachs rebell. They become violently ill, vomiting over and over for two or three days. But their lives have been spared."

"That is horrible!" Lydia whispered, obviously shaken. "That will terrify Emma all the more."

Benjamin looked down at his hands, debating about whether to share the rest of it. He decided they would hear it

Liberty Jail

sooner or later. "Nor is that the worst that has been attempted," he explained.

To this point, Jessica had sat quietly. Now she looked up in alarm. "There is something worse than poison?"

Benjamin looked away. "Yes. Joseph doesn't mention this in the letter, but the brethren who have gotten in to see them say both Hyrum and Brother McRae told them something almost too horrid to utter."

"What?" Mary Ann whispered, not sure she wanted to hear and yet wanting to know what trials their leaders were enduring.

Benjamin took a quick breath. "Recently they were served a dish that seemed strange to them. It was a piece of roast meat, but it looked very dark, as though it had been burned. They said that Hyrum took the carving knife and fork to hand, but as he attempted to cut it, they fell from his hands. He tried again, and the second time the knife and fork fell from his hands. Then Joseph stood up. He said he felt a strong impression. 'Do not touch it,' he cried, 'for it is human flesh.' "

Jessica rocked back. Lydia gasped and threw one hand up to her mouth. Mary Ann was suddenly pale.

"It was true," Matthew spoke up. "Later the guards boasted that they had taken it from the body of a man who had died."

Mary Ann was staring at her hands. "Is there no limit to the depths of their depravity?"

Benjamin was overcome with that same sense of horror and outrage that he had felt when they had heard the reports in the meeting, but he didn't want to dwell on it any longer. "But, as usual, Joseph will not let things get him down. He actually was quite positive."

He took a small slip of paper from his pocket. "Listen to this. This so impressed me, I asked Brigham if I could copy it." He smoothed it against his leg and began to read. " 'Dear brethren, do not think that our hearts faint, as though some strange thing had happened unto us, for we have seen and been assured of all these things beforehand, and have an assurance of a better hope than that of our persecutors. Therefore God hath made broad our shoulders for the burden. We glory in our tribulation, because we know that God is with us, that He is our friend, and that He will save our souls. We do not care for them that can kill the body; they cannot harm our souls.'"

The room was completely quiet now as they contemplated the realities of what their prophet had said. Then Derek slowly straightened. He looked at his wife, and then at his father-in-law. "Amen!" he breathed softly.

All around him heads came up. Then there was an equally soft chorus of assent. "Amen!" they said. "Amen to that!"

"Jessica?"

"Yes, Matthew?"

"Can I ask a favor of you?"

She lowered the book she had been reading and laid it in her lap. "Of course. What is it?"

He hesitated a moment, then shoved one hand into his trouser pocket and drew it out again. It held a folded sheet of paper.

She smiled. "Oh, Mother Steed told me you got a letter from Jenny."

He colored slightly. "Actually, I wrote to her first."

"Good for you. I think that what the McIntires did for Joshua and our family was wonderful."

"Yes."

She laughed softly. "That wasn't the only reason you wrote, though, was it?" she teased.

He blushed more deeply. "Well . . ." That irrepressible grin that was Matthew's trademark flashed quickly. "Not entirely."

"So what's the favor?"

The smile quickly died and his brow furrowed. There was a quick sigh, then he thrust the letter toward her. She took it, opened it carefully, then spread it out on the book she held. Matthew moved quickly around behind her so he could read it with her.

Dear Matthew Steed.

Thank you for yur leter to me. After this long, I thot you wur not going to rite to me. It was a totle surpris for me and for Kathryn. We have mist you and Joshua sinc yur deepartur. We get lonesum so far away frum town.

I laffed at your leter. You cant rite wurs than me. I went to skul for 3 yers befor we came to Mizoori, but we wur to far away to go agin here. Mama trys to teech us sum, but she says she is no more lerned than we are. You said yur frend Peter helped you with yur leter. I wisht I had sum one like Peter to help me with my leter to you. I no it luks verry bad.

I half been reeding the Book of Mormon. I reed it to Kathryn. It is hard and I dont understan everry thing. But I beleeve it is a tru a count of a peeple who beleeve in Jesus. Mama has been reeding it to. She dont want me and Kathryn to no that. We dont have manny books out here so she reeds it at nite when she thinks we are a sleep. I dont no what she thinks abot it. But I like it a lot.

Thank you for riting. I was verry happy to here from you. Pleeze rite back.

Yur good frend,
Jenny McIntire

Jessica looked up at her young brother-in-law. "That's very nice, Matthew. And that's wonderful about her family reading the Book of Mormon."

"Yeah." His countenance was still fallen, and he looked suddenly morose.

"But?" she queried softly.

He shrugged, then looked away. "She don't spell very good." Instantly he looked ashamed at his disloyalty to her.

Now Jessica began to understand. "Well, I've seen worse. And from grown men."

"She don't talk like that."

"Like what, Matthew?"

He was struggling for the right words. "I don't know. She was very good at saying things. And she seemed really smart. She asked some questions I didn't even know how to answer."

Jessica set the book down and turned fully around. There was a gentle kindness on her face. "There's a difference between being unlearned and stupid, Matthew."

He flushed. "I didn't say I thought she was stupid."

"I know. But the reason why Jenny can't spell any better than she does is that she hasn't been to school very much. It doesn't mean that her mind is not very quick."

"Hmm!"

She was tempted to smile again. She had not seen Matthew quite so troubled over such an issue before, but she kept her eyes serious. "Brother Joseph is not wonderful at spelling. Haven't you ever heard him say that's why he uses a scribe all the time? He doesn't like to write. Neither does Brother Brigham. His spelling is not very good either."

Matthew's eyes grew thoughtful. "I hadn't thought about that. And they're really smart, aren't they?"

"Yes, they are."

He was still mulling over the implications of that in his mind, so Jessica went on quickly. "You know, Matthew, when Joshua and I were first married, I couldn't read."

"No!" he said in disbelief.

"Yes. That's true. And I felt very stupid."

"But you can read now. You're teaching school."

"Yes. I taught myself how to read and write."

His eyes widened and there was new respect there. Then his mind made the logical jump. "Could Jenny do that?" he asked eagerly.

Now she hesitated. "Well, it's a little harder for a young person. I was a married woman. Joshua had money, so I could get books and get people to help me if I needed to."

Suddenly Matthew shot to his feet. "Jessica! I have an idea."

She started to open her mouth, then smiled broadly instead. "I think it's a wonderful idea!" she said warmly.

"You do?" Matthew blinked. "But I didn't—"

She raised her hand. "You're thinking about having Jenny come down here to school, aren't you?"

He nodded eagerly. "What if they could—Kathryn too? Then Jenny could learn how to spell real good, like you and Peter can."

Jessica's mind was racing ahead, considering all the possibilities. "If Mrs. McIntire would let them, they could stay here with me. They could help me tend the children to pay for their board and room. And both of them could go to school."

Matthew nearly jumped in the air. "That's a wonderful plan, Jessie. Would you do that? That would be so wonderful."

Suddenly Jessica's face fell. Matthew saw it instantly. He leaned forward. "I'll write to Mrs. McIntire. I'll bet she'd be happy to have them come to school. And if she knows they've got a place to stay and all—"

Jessica was shaking her head. "But that's just it, Matthew."

"What?" he cried in dismay.

"We have to leave the state come spring—probably sooner. Then there won't be a house and a school and a place to keep them."

He stepped back, totally crestfallen. "Oh," he murmured.

She reached out and took his hand. "I'm sorry, Matthew. It is a wonderful idea, but it will have to wait until we see what happens, where we end up. Then we can write them."

"But then it will be too late," Matthew exclaimed. "Now we're just twenty-five miles away. Once we leave the state there's no way they can come that far."

Jessica wanted to weep for having to quench the joy she had seen in his face, and yet she couldn't try to soften it for him. The realities were too final. "I know, Matthew. But do you really think we can ask them to come here, when we're not even sure how long we'll be here?"

For a long moment he just looked at her, then his shoulders fell. He shook his head slowly, then turned and walked away.

Chapter Notes

The letter from Joseph discussed by Benjamin, Matthew, and Derek is found in Joseph's history (see *HC* 3:226–33). The conditions in the jail and the attempt to feed the prisoners human flesh are recorded by several sources (see, for example, *Restoration*, p. 423).

Chapter Thirty

Nathan kept his eyes on the dark line along the horizon off to the west of them. Somehow the Georgian coast—low and flat, but solid and unmoving in a world of constant movement—steadied his stomach. He got up out of his deck chair and walked to the rail. With brief stops in a couple of ports in Florida, they had been within sight of land for most of the way, which cheered him greatly. Seeing nothing but water stretching to the horizon in every direction left him with a deep sense of uneasiness. He peered at the coast. It was probably a mile or so away. But in an emergency a man could swim that far. . . . He shook his head, chiding himself for his foolishness.

This was their fifth day on the packet ship out of New Orleans, and Nathan thanked whatever fates there were that the weather had been almost perfect the entire time. Even then, he had lost his meals twice to the constant rolling motion of the ship, a fact which Joshua delighted in noting several times a day. Nathan shuddered as he considered the return trip that still had to be made. The chances of having good weather both ways were marginal, and his imagination was already working overtime in contemplating what it would be like.

He turned to where Joshua was stretched out in his chair, hat pulled down over his face to shade it from the early-morning sun. "How long would it take to go from Savannah to New Orleans overland?"

His brother didn't move, but there was a throaty laugh. "A lot longer than five days, you can count on that. It's seven, maybe eight hundred miles."

"Oh."

The laugh deepened, and Joshua reached up and pushed his hat back with his thumb. "Look, a man of faith like you should be able to get good weather going both directions."

"I was just wondering," Nathan said tartly, irritated that Joshua had seen through him so easily.

"What's today?" Joshua asked, sitting up.

"December thirtieth."

"I mean what day of the week?"

"Sunday."

Joshua got up and moved over to stand beside Nathan. "That's perfect. When I was last here, the packet ships sailed for New Orleans on Mondays and Thursdays at one p.m. I think you can make tomorrow's sailing easy. Won't be this ship, but one just like it."

Nathan turned fully from the railing now to look at his brother. "You're really sure they're here, aren't you?"

"They're here."

"I hope you're right."

"They're here!" Joshua said, a bit more snappishly.

"But you said that Savannah is a big town. We may not find them in one day. I may not make tomorrow's boat. And I'm not leaving until we know."

Joshua shook his head patiently. "I know right where Caroline is. I'll make you a wager that by midafternoon I'm holding her in my arms." Joshua set the crutch against the side of the ship and leaned on the rail. "You should be back home in a couple of weeks."

"Like I said, I hope you're right."

"You are the jolly one today, aren't you?"

Nathan looked up, surprised. Then he understood what he had been doing. "I guess your being this close to your family makes me miss my family all the more."

"Will they still be there?" Joshua asked softly.

After a moment, Nathan shook his head. "I hope so, but who knows? Originally the militia said we could have until spring. Now . . ." His shoulders lifted and fell. "I hope so."

Joshua reached down and massaged his leg slowly. "Can I ask you something without making you angry?"

Nathan's head reared back a little. "Angry? Why would I get angry?"

"I mean it," Joshua said, more soberly now. "I don't want to give offense."

Nathan laughed softly. "Which means this is about religion. Well, go ahead. You'll find we Mormons are pretty tough skinned."

Joshua nodded, but went on staring out across the water, deep in thought.

"Come on," Nathan teased, "I told you I can handle it."

"All right." Joshua's head came around. "Why don't you give up?"

That caught Nathan completely by surprise. "Give up? Give up on what?"

"You know what I mean. Joseph's in prison. So are the rest of your leaders. You've already dug enough graves on the prairie to fill a city cemetery. You've been kicked from pillar to post. The better part of the state of Missouri hates your guts. Now you're about to be kicked out again. All those farms and orchards and houses that you've worked so hard to get. You'll end up with nothing again, just as you did in Jackson County. So give it up. You've done enough, Nathan. Pa's done enough." He looked away. "Jessica has given more than enough."

For almost a full minute, Nathan stared down into the water that slid past the hull of the ship below them. Joshua watched him out of the corner of his eye, then finally looked down again. "Sorry," Joshua said. "It's none of my business."

"No," Nathan said slowly, "it's not that at all. I'm just trying to find a way to help you understand. I know that on the surface it must look absolutely crazy."

"It does," Joshua agreed instantly. "I used to think you were the devil's fools, you Mormons. Now I can't help but admire your courage. But is a courageous fool any less the fool?"

Nathan took a breath and straightened. "Let me ask you a question first."

"All right."

"When you came to the cabin and found those men with Mother and Lydia and Rebecca? From what they said, you never hesitated one moment. You just plunged in, even though you were outnumbered and outgunned. You really put your life at risk. Why?"

Joshua snorted in derision. "You know the answer to that as well as I do. And you would have done exactly the same thing."

"Probably. But that's my point. Why did you do that? Well, it comes down to one word, doesn't it? Love."

Joshua gave him a strange look. He hadn't thought of it in those terms.

"Doesn't it?" Nathan persisted.

Joshua nodded.

Nathan turned and leaned against the railing, his face pensive now. "Jesus said that a man has no greater love than this, that he lay down his life for his friends." He looked around again, his eyes soft with thankfulness. "And you came about as close to doing that as anyone I've ever met."

There was nothing to say to that. The crutch Joshua carried was evidence enough.

"Can you even begin to imagine how we feel about what

you did? Me? Derek? Pa? You saved our women from something so horrible it makes one shudder to even think about it. How can we ever repay that?"

"You're here with me now," Joshua said without hesitation.

Nathan smiled. Joshua had walked right into his trap. "Why?" he asked again softly.

There was only one answer. "To show your gratitude. Love."

"Of course." Nathan straightened now, choosing his words with great care. "And that's exactly how we as Latter-day Saints feel about the Savior."

Joshua looked openly dubious.

"Yes," Nathan said earnestly. "Don't you see? What Jesus did for us is all that you did for our family and infinitely more. He loved us so much, he gave his life for us on the cross. He suffered beyond description. Why? To save us from an eternal destiny too horrible to describe. And once you come to believe that—no, not just believe it, but accept it, live it, breathe it!—then you are willing to endure anything, do anything, give everything in return as your way of saying thanks to him."

He shook his head slowly, wanting so much to help Joshua understand. "You yourself are living proof of the power of love. Can't you see that, Joshua? Christ gave his life for all mankind. Can we as Saints do any less if we love him in return?"

Joshua was staring at Nathan. Nathan forced a quick smile, a little embarrassed by the passions that had stirred him to speak with such fervor. "You asked. That's the answer."

"I understand," Joshua said slowly.

"Do you, Joshua?" Nathan said. "Do you really?"

Joshua started to nod, but then suddenly the image of a row of bodies—men and boys—stretched out along the ground in Haun's Mill flashed into his mind. There was no looking down your nose at that kind of commitment, but in his heart Joshua still could not fathom feeling that strongly about God or one's church. He shook his head slowly. "No, I guess I don't, Nathan. I guess I never will."

Julia Montague took the stairs of the plantation house two at a time, even though the long, silken skirts dragged three steps behind her. As she burst through the door and into the sitting room, she had to stop and lean against the wall for a moment to catch her breath.

"My goodness, Julia," Caroline said, coming out of her chair in alarm. To see Julia walk briskly was enough to signal that something was terribly wrong. In nearly ten years of friendship, Caroline had never seen her run.

"Caroline," she gasped, "come quickly!"

Caroline walked swiftly to her and took her hand. "What is it, Julia? What's wrong?"

Julia's bosom rose and fell as she pressed one hand against it. "You have a"—there was a quick gulp for breath—"a visitor."

Now it was Caroline who lost her breath. She fell back a step. "A visitor?" she stammered. "But who—" Then her eyes widened. "Is it a man?"

"Yes."

"Oh, no," she cried. "Where are Livvy and Savannah?"

"They're out in the pecan orchard with Abner and the servants."

Caroline looked around wildly. "We must hide. Did you tell them I was here?"

Suddenly Julia understood. "No, no!" she exclaimed. "It's not those men who are after you. It's one man. And he says he is Joshua's brother."

Caroline's head stopped swinging and turned to stare at Julia. "Joshua's brother? You mean Nathan?"

Julia nodded, still trying to steady her breathing. "That's what he said. He said he must talk with you."

"Nathan?" Caroline said again, her mind not comprehending. "In Savannah? How can that be? Are you sure it's him?"

Julia gave her a quizzical look. "How would I know that? He called you Caroline and asked after the children."

Caroline's mind was racing. Nathan? All the way from Missouri? She shook her head. That was impossible. But what if the men who had followed her to St. Louis had somehow tracked her here as well? That seemed nearly as improbable, but then she remembered the newspaper articles about the Mormon Danites. They took a blood oath, it said, and would follow their enemies to the ends of the earth if necessary. Posing as Nathan might be just a ploy to get her out of the house.

"Julia, what did he—" Then she stopped. She realized she had never seen her would-be assailants. A description wouldn't help very much.

"I asked him to wait outside," Julia was saying. "It was very rude of me, but I was so shocked when he said who he was. He said it was most urgent that he speak to you." She wrung her hands. "Oh, Caroline, I'm sorry. I never thought that it might not be him. What shall I do?"

Caroline whirled and strode to the window that faced the front of the house. She slowed her step as she reached it, moved to the side, and then pulled the curtain back a little. There was a black covered carriage with a single horse. A man was standing at the door of the carriage, with his back to her. Then, even as she peered at him, he turned around and looked up toward the house. She dropped the curtain and fell back a step. "It *is* Nathan," she said, looking at Julia in wonder. She was instantly weak with relief.

Julia was at her side now. "Thank heavens," she gushed.

But then Caroline was jolted by another thought. How did Nathan know to come here? Suddenly she stiffened. She had gone to some effort to leave no trail of her movements. That meant that the men who had tracked her to St. Louis had reported back to the Mormons.

Slowly, bitterness welling up inside her like a boiling kettle, she moved over to the sofa and sat down. There was no other way that he could know she was here. And if he knew, then chances were that others knew as well—others like the men who had burned her house to the ground.

The disappointment was like a blow to the face. She had lost a husband and a son. She needed time to rest and heal. The thoughts of having to leave again—and go where?—were shattering. There were no more places of refuge. No other friends who might take her in and shelter her.

Julia had come toward her, puzzled and anxious at Caroline's sudden change in demeanor. "Shall I bring him up?" she asked tentatively.

Caroline's lips pressed into a hard line. "No."

Julia had started to turn toward the door. Now she jerked back around, staring.

Caroline made up her mind. "Julia, would you please tell him that I do not wish to see him. I appreciate him coming all this way to inquire about my health. But tell him that everything is fine and that I would prefer not to see him or anyone else of his faith."

"Are you mad?" Julia cried. "He's your brother-in-law. He's come two thousand miles—"

"Make sure he has something to eat and enough money for return passage, but under no circumstances will I—"

Caroline turned sharply. There was a sound on the stairway that Julia had ascended a few moments before. The sound was that of footsteps on the stairs. Caroline raised a hand, as if to shut the door from where she sat, but it was too late. A dark shape filled the frame.

"Hello, Caroline." His head turned. "I apologize for coming in uninvited, Mrs. Montague, but I saw Caroline at the window. I was afraid she might refuse to see me."

Caroline stood slowly, rigid as a brass bedpost. "I'm sorry, Nathan, but I would prefer not to speak with you."

"We got your letter. I understand how you feel."

"How could you?" she cried. "Your people killed Joshua, and now they're trying to kill me. And you've probably led them right to me."

He stepped inside the room and removed his hat. "I have something to tell you, Caroline."

She shook her head and turned away. "I don't want to hear it!" Then more softly she added, "Please, go away. Tell Mother and Father Steed I'm sorry. Maybe after some time has passed . . ."

She heard him cross the room toward her. She lifted her arms and hugged herself tightly. "Please, Nathan," she pleaded. "Don't make me fight you. Just leave me."

"Caroline, listen. It wasn't our people who shot Joshua. It was two Missourians, the same two men who came to your house and told you he was dead."

She half turned, her face registering her surprise.

"Yes, Obadiah Cornwell told us the whole story. But those are the men who set fire to your house. It wasn't Mormons. And those two men are also the ones who shot Joshua."

She turned slowly, anger starting to rise. "You're forgetting one thing. They left me a note, remember? And it was signed by your people."

"No, they signed our names, but it was those men who did that to you. It was those men who followed you to St. Louis." He took a breath and finished quietly. "It was those men who shot Joshua and left him for dead."

She was too weary to fight him. "It doesn't matter now, Nathan. It won't bring anything back. But I'm sorry, I can't feel the same toward you and your family anymore."

He brushed that aside as if she hadn't spoken. "They wanted to get even with Joshua because of what he did." Then swiftly, but quietly, he described that terrible day in Far West. He spared nothing. He talked about the mob let loose on an undefended town. He told of the Steed women and children put in a root cellar and Peter's terrified attempts to hold the men back when they discovered the hiding place. He described Jessica's being struck with the butt of a gun, Rebecca's terror as she became the target of the ugliest kind of lust.

In spite of herself, Caroline's arms slowly dropped to her side and she turned fully to watch him, a look of horror filling her eyes. It never entered her head to question whether he was telling her the truth. There was too much pain, too much revulsion on his face to have it be something made up to win her over. Julia stood frozen by her side, as shocked and horrified as Caroline.

"But," Caroline broke in, "those men never said anything about seeing Joshua in your father's cabin."

"Exactly!" Nathan answered grimly. "The whole story they told you was a pack of lies." He took a breath. "Joshua killed one of them, and drove the other two out of the cabin. He got Mother and the others to safety. Then he realized that once those men told the rest of the militia what he had done—that he had shot one of his own men, trying to protect the Mormons—they would come after him. He also knew that you and the children would be in terrible danger the minute word reached Independence. It was while he was trying to get out of the city and back to you that they shot him. In the back."

She jerked away, biting her lip. "Don't!" she cried softly.

He reached out and turned her so that he faced her, peering into her eyes. "It went clear through his body and out his chest."

Her head dropped and tears sprang to her eyes. "Please, Nathan!" she begged. "I can't bear it."

To her amazement, he smiled. It was soft and filled with tenderness and love. "It's no wonder they thought he was dead," he mused, half to himself. "He certainly looked dead. Even the family who found him thought he was."

Caroline's head came up slowly as her eyes widened. Nathan's smile broadened. "Should have been too. A ball through the lungs would have killed any other man."

"What are you . . . ?" She faltered, not daring to believe what her ears had just heard. "Do you mean . . . ?"

Julia Montague was gaping at Nathan now too.

"I mean, my dear Caroline," he said, taking her hand, "that those men who came and told you that Joshua was dead were wrong. Even they don't know that. But they were wrong. He was terribly wounded, but he did not die. Your husband is still alive."

Caroline's other hand shot out and grabbed Nathan's arm. Her fingernails dug deeply into the flesh. Her lips were moving but nothing came out as she stared up at him. Suddenly Nathan's eyes were filled with tears too, and he reached out and swept Caroline into his arms, pulling her to him in a crushing hug. "It's true, Caroline," he whispered into her hair. "We've been trying to find you now for almost a month to tell you."

She pulled free, brushing at her eyes. "But where?" she whispered. "Where is he?"

Nathan couldn't help but laugh aloud. "He's downstairs in the carriage. He was afraid that if he just showed up on your doorstep it might be too much of a shock for you. And I'm sure he's wondering what in the world is taking me so long to get you out there to him."

"In the carriage?" Caroline repeated dumbly. "Are you sure?"

Half laughing, half crying, he turned her around and gave her a gentle shove. "I'm sure. Now, get yourself down there and see for yourself."

It was evening now, and they were sitting around the great round table that filled the dining room of the Montague plantation. Savannah was snuggled into her father's arms, where she had been for the last hour, amazingly content to sit quietly, looking up from time to time into his face to make sure it was still her papa who held her. Olivia sat at Joshua's right elbow, her arm firmly through his. Though her eleven-year-old mind understood that he was safely back with them, like Savannah she seemed fearful that if she let him go he might disappear again.

Caroline sat between Joshua and Nathan, one hand resting lightly on Joshua's bad leg. Her fingers kept tracing small patterns on his trouser leg. Though her face was troubled now as they discussed what to do about Will, she was still radiant with joy at the wondrous thing that had befallen her. Abner and Julia Montague sat across the table, content for the moment to watch and listen as the family debated their options.

The afternoon had passed swiftly for Caroline and Joshua and dragged interminably for Nathan. Husband and wife had sat in the carriage together for nearly an hour, letting Caroline make the transition from numbing grief to stunning joy. Then they had set out for the great pecan orchards that lay behind the plantation house to find the children.

While they waited, Julia Montague told Nathan about Will. It was a crushing blow. The family had been found, but not reunited. The quest was not complete, and Nathan's frustration came back in one great rush. Thankfully, Julia left him to himself and went to see to dinner. He paced the house, restless to the point of distraction but unwilling to rush Joshua through the sweetness of being with his family again. However, the moment they had returned to the house, Nathan gathered them all around the table to discuss their course of action.

"He'll head for St. Louis," Joshua said flatly. "That's the last place the two men were seen, and that's where he'll try and pick up their trail."

"And what if he finds them?" Caroline asked, her face stricken. She was still torturing herself over whether she had done right in providing him the funds to leave.

"Those men will be long gone by now," Joshua said, trying to sound more confident than he felt. If Hugh and Riley had followed Caroline to St. Louis, there was a good chance they wouldn't quit as easily as he hoped they would. "The question is, how do we find Will?"

Caroline had thought this through already. "I think we all agree that he has gone to St. Louis. When he gets there, or he's probably there now, what will he do?"

"Go to Samuelson," Joshua said quickly.

"Who's Samuelson?" Abner Montague asked.

"One of my business partners in St. Louis," Joshua answered. "He helped Caroline when they were there. Will knows him too."

"And what will Samuelson tell him?" Caroline asked. "He'll tell him that you're alive. That you're not dead." The relief in her voice was heavy and obvious. The chase for revenge would be over. Her son could be healed, just as she was healed now. "He'll tell him that you and Nathan were coming to Savannah, and Will will turn around and come back here."

Julia's head bobbed up and down vigorously. "So all you have to do is wait here for him."

Nathan looked at Joshua. Their eyes locked for a moment, and something unspoken passed between them. Then Joshua nodded. He didn't have the heart to say it and was asking Nathan to lead out. Nathan cleared his throat. "It, uh . . . I'm sorry, Caroline, but it may not be that simple."

She whirled in dismay. "Why not? If we go looking for him, we might pass him on the river or on his way back here from New Orleans and not even know it."

Nathan sighed. "Caroline, I hope you're right. I hope Will got to St. Louis and is on his way back here right now. But what if he's not? What if something happened?"

"What could happen?" she asked in a small voice, wanting to know but not sure she could bear the knowing.

Now Abner jumped in to help Nathan. He understood. He had traveled to St. Louis on three different occasions. "There are a lot of gamblers and other riffraff that travel the boats," he said to Caroline. His wife was poking at him, but he moved away from her jabs. "Well, I'm sorry, but Joshua and Nathan are right. We have to face reality. Will had a hundred and fifty dollars with him."

Abner stopped at the surprised look on Caroline's face. "Yes, he took fifty dollars from my desk." He shook his head. "I thought he might, but like you I didn't want him going off without any money. Anyway, if Will isn't careful and lets anyone see that money, there's a good chance he could end up with a conk on the head and being left at one of those little river towns somewhere between New Orleans and St. Louis."

Joshua reached across Savannah and took Caroline's hand. "We're not talking about him being dead or anything, Caroline, but we have to face the possibility that he didn't make it to St.

Louis. Then the longer we sit here, the harder it will be to find him."

She looked away and tried to pull her hand free, but he held on to it and went on. "At least we've found you and the children now and know you're safe. So what if we leave you here? Nathan and I will take the ship tomorrow back to New Orleans. We'll ask around there if anyone has seen him. Then we'll take a boat north. Everywhere we stop we'll look for him. Riverboats are often at towns at the same time. We'll check every boat headed south. And if we do miss him, you'll be here waiting for him."

Caroline looked down at their hands, biting at her lip. Tears had welled up in the corners of her eyes. "I can't bear to have you leave me again." She drew in a breath. "And what if those two men know I'm here? What if they come looking for us?"

"I'm sure they've given up and gone back home," Joshua said again, but it sounded lame. Every adult in the room knew that what he said was a good possibility, but there were no guarantees.

"I'm going with Papa," Olivia said from her chair.

Joshua let go of Caroline's hand and turned around. "I'll be back, Livvy."

"I'm going with you," she said stubbornly. "I want to help look for Will."

"You can't, Livvy," Joshua murmured. "Papa will be back."

"No," Caroline said with sudden determination. "Livvy's right. Wherever you go, the children and I are going with you."

Joshua started to protest further, then nodded. It would greatly complicate their movements, but there had been too much separation in their family for them to part with each other again. "All right."

"Well," Abner said, "Julia and I will be here no matter what. If you do miss Will and he comes here, we'll turn right around and bring him to St. Louis. I'll accompany him personally to make sure he gets there."

"Thank you, Abner," Joshua said gratefully. He looked at Caroline. "Then it's settled. We leave tomorrow?"

She looked at him, then at Olivia, whose head was bobbing up and down vigorously. She turned back to her husband. "Yes, we'll leave tomorrow."

Nathan sat back, a great sense of relief washing over him. They still had to find Will, but tomorrow they would be heading back, back towards Missouri, back towards his family.

Will Mendenhall Steed was not on his way back to Savannah. Nor was he anywhere near to making that decision. In fact, it was not until the early evening of the thirty-first of December that he disembarked from the riverboat tied up at the docks at St. Louis, Missouri. The voyage from Savannah to New Orleans had been uneventful for him. There were several other passengers on board, and he had spun them a yarn about going to Louisiana to stay with an uncle. Once in the great river-ocean port, he had been forced to wait for three days for a boat going upriver all the way to St. Louis. So he holed up in a small hotel on the waterfront, more fearful of being found by those sent after him from Savannah than he was of any strangers.

The boat finally departed on the nineteenth of December, but they were only two days upriver when the first small chunks of ice started to appear in the muddy brown water. The steamers going downriver reported that way up north, in Iowa and Wisconsin territories, the winter had turned bitter cold and the river had frozen solid in places. With a warming trend, the ice had broken up and great blocks of it were now moving downriver. The ice blocks were nearly melted this far south, but farther north they could prove to be damaging to a boat's hull. So the captain docked in Natchez, Mississippi, and refused to budge for five days until there was no more sign of ice.

By then it was Christmas Eve, and the passengers had voted to spend another two days in Natchez rather than have the holiday on the river. Will had fumed under the delay but was totally helpless to do anything about it. They finally sailed again on the twenty-sixth. It had taken five more days to reach St. Louis.

Will suddenly realized he was shivering. In his haste to leave Savannah without being caught, he had not even thought about it being winter up north. He wore a light jacket and a woolen shirt, but the temperature was in the midforties, and his breath showed in the air. Shoving his hands in his pockets, he moved quickly down the gangplank and across the wharf. He stopped for a moment to get his bearings, then turned south, exactly opposite the direction of the warehouse and office where Walter Samuelson, his father's former business partner, worked.

Originally Samuelson had been in his plans. But Will had thought it through very carefully, and he knew that Samuelson's would be the one place his mother would think he would go. He didn't think it was likely that a letter from his mother had beaten him here, but he wasn't going to take any chances. If one had, Samuelson would hold him until Caroline came for him or else would send him back to Savannah. And that was not in Will's plan.

Brooding now, excited to finally be where he could take some action, Will moved along the street, beneath the misty circles lit by lampposts. He had scouted out this area during the time he and his mother were here in St. Louis. It looked different now at night, but he moved on steadily, watching closely for things he recognized. Then he grunted. There was the saddle shop, and across from it was the tobacco shop with the wooden Indian standing outside the door. Relieved, he turned up that street, walking more quickly now, fearing that the hour already might be too late. And then, as he rounded the next corner, he let out a sigh of relief. The lamp was still on in the window.

The shop owner peered at him over the top of half-cut spectacles. "Ain't you a little young to be purchasing a gun?"

Will looked insulted. "I'm sixteen, nearly seventeen," he said gruffly, trying to keep his voice as low as possible. "Man's got to have protection if he's joining a teamster caravan across Missouri."

The man was still skeptical, but let it pass. "That'll be twenty dollars for the pistol and three more for fifty rounds of ammunition." He made no move for the weapon in the glass case behind him, and Will suddenly realized that the man didn't think he had the money.

Will dug in his pocket and brought out his purse. He started to open it, then remembered the hungry look he had seen on a man's face when he had opened his purse on the boat. Will had stayed clear of the man after that, even though he had tried to befriend him. Now he turned his back on the shop owner and withdrew two ten-dollar gold pieces and three silver dollars. He counted quickly. That still left him almost sixty dollars, enough to keep him going for several weeks yet, if he was careful.

Closing the purse, he put it back in his pocket and turned around. He held the money out for the man to see but didn't put it down as yet. It gave him a perverse satisfaction to see the surprise on the man's face.

"All right, then." The man turned and got the pistol down, then reached under the counter and brought out a box and laid it beside the gun. Only then did Will give him the money.

"Thank you," Will said.

"You know how to use that thing?" the man asked.

Will looked disgusted. "Of course. My pa taught me."

"Oh."

Will started for the door, then stopped and turned around. "Can you tell me how to find the Riverbend Hotel?"

One eyebrow came up and the man squinted at him. "Yeah, it's down Water Street, about half a block from the river. 'Bout ten minutes from here."

"Thanks." Will started out the door.

The man watched him, then felt a touch of concern for the boy who was trying to act like a man. "You'd best be careful down that neighborhood. It ain't the best part of town."

Will raised one hand but said nothing. Before he and his mother and sisters had left St. Louis over a month ago, Samuelson had told them that the two men were staying in the Riverbend Hotel. It was a place to start.

He went out the door and shut it behind him. Face resolute, he turned left, retracing his steps back down to the waterfront. Shoving the pistol inside his trousers, he pulled his jacket around him and buttoned it so that the gun was hidden. Then hefting the box of ammunition up and down in his hand, he strode off, hunching down against the chill of the night.

Hugh Watson and Riley Overson had come to St. Louis driven by hate. Or rather, Hugh had been driven by hate, and Riley came because he did pretty much whatever Hugh told him to do. That hate had been partially slaked when they burned down the big fancy house that Steed had built for his wife in Independence. But Hugh was furious when he learned she had left town. He had plans for her, plans that involved getting his just dues. Steed had stopped them from getting at those Mormon women in Far West. So it was only fair that his wife should make up for it. And she was a beauty too. Hugh's dreams were filled with thoughts of her.

It took them a day to find out that her likely destination was St. Louis, then three more days to beg and borrow enough money from some of the most vigorous of the Mormon-haters to go after her. But by the time they followed the Widow Steed to St. Louis and tracked her down, she had eluded them again and gone south on one of the riverboats. By then they were totally out of money, and St. Louis in the dead of winter was not a hospitable place for men looking for work. The riverboat traffic was way down until spring. Nothing was going up the Missouri River to Independence. Freight was stacking up in the warehouses, and longtime stevedores were fiercely protective against anyone trying to muscle in on what little work there was. A few teamsters were braving the weather and headed west, but they had their own men and weren't willing to take on two more mouths to feed from provisions that took freight room from the wagons.

Riley was getting more and more ugly about the whole thing. They had moved out of the Riverbend Hotel the day after they learned about Caroline's departure. Now they spent their nights in an unheated, rat-infested hole beneath a cotton warehouse. Riley wanted to go home and fully expected Hugh to work out a way for them to do so. Typically they spent their days picking up an odd job or two, then spent the evenings in the saloons drinking away what little money they made, snarling and snapping at each other like two cur dogs trying to occupy the same narrow doghouse.

"Hugh. Hugh Watson."

Hugh set his beer down and turned around to see who was calling his name. The man was at the door, peering into the smoke-filled, half-lit room. Hugh raised a hand. It was Charlie Patterson, a man they had met while cleaning stables and who often teamed up with them in drinking cheap beer and moaning about the unfairness of life.

"Over here, Charlie."

"Blowhard," Riley grumbled. "Probably looking for a free drink."

"Shut up. I paid for yours, didn't I?"

Charlie came over, weaving his way through the crowd and around the few tables. He plopped down and grinned wickedly. "Got news fur ya, Hugh."

"What?"

"What's it worth?"

Hugh swung at him. "It's worth a lump on the jaw if you don't tell me."

Charlie jerked away, letting the intended blow whiz past his face. Now he laughed gleefully, knowing that what he brought was going to bless them all. "There's a kid looking for you, Hugh."

Hugh blinked. "A kid?"

"Yeah. Big kid. About fifteen or so. Big Mick O'Donnell pointed him out to me this morning, walking down near the river. I guess he showed up four or five days ago and started asking questions about two men from western Missouri who were at the Riverbend Hotel in mid-November." He looked at them archly. "Two men who were asking questions about a certain Mrs. Joshua Steed."

Hugh started at that. "Mrs. Steed? What the . . . ? How could a kid know about that?"

"Don't know," Charlie crowed, enjoying Hugh's sudden nervousness. "But he's willing to pay for information."

Riley swore. "What if it's the law?"

Hugh snorted loudly. "A kid? Don't be stupid."

Charlie smiled, revealing brown and crooked teeth. "You weren't listening very good, Hugh. Did you hear what I said?"

"No, what?" Hugh growled.

"Them that has seen him"—his tongue darted out and he licked his lips, his eyes narrowing hungrily—"they say he's got a purse full of money."

Chapter Thirty-One

"Matthew!"

Matthew had the ax poised above his head. When he saw his sister he swung it downward, burying the blade in the log they were chopping into firewood lengths. Derek and Peter, working together to split those shorter lengths, stopped as well.

"What is it, Rebecca?" Derek asked, wiping at his brow. It was cold enough that they could see their breath, but they were all sweating.

"Matthew needs to come to the house."

"What's the matter?" Matthew asked.

"You'd better come and see for yourself. You too, Derek."

As they wiped their feet at the door, Matthew gave Rebecca a quizzical look. She was smiling mysteriously, but when he looked at her she just shook her head and laughed softly.

She opened the door and stepped inside, holding it open wide for the three of them to follow. Matthew went first, taking off his hat as he entered. His hand froze in midair. His mouth dropped and his eyes flew wide open.

"It's not polite to stare, Matthew," his mother said, chuckling merrily. "Do come in and shut the door."

But Matthew didn't move. He just stood and gaped.

Derek stepped around him, as startled as Matthew. "Mrs. McIntire?" he blurted. "What are you doing here?"

Benjamin turned away from the table and hunched over, clutching at his chest, the coughs racking his body for several seconds. Mary Ann watched him anxiously, wanting to reach out and steady him but knowing he wouldn't like it. Finally he straightened and turned back. "Sorry," he murmured. "This cold air doesn't seem to agree with my lungs." He took a breath. "Mrs. McIntire, are you sure this is a wise thing you have decided to do? I mean, we think it is wonderful that you have read the Book of Mormon and feel it is true, but . . ." The lines of pain and weariness around his mouth and eyes seemed to deepen perceptibly. "But coming to Far West right now? Matthew should have been more clear when he wrote to Jenny. Things are not good here. The state still restricts our movements. We will probably have to leave sooner than expected."

"I'm aware of all that, Brother Steed," Nancy McIntire said evenly. "News of what is happening down here is common in Daviess County."

"But still you came?" Lydia said, not able to keep the awe from her voice.

"Aye," the robust woman said cheerfully. "We've decided that our lot is with the Mormons." She turned to her daughters. "Haven't we, girls?"

Jenny was looking at Matthew from beneath lowered lashes. "Yes," she murmured. Kathryn was nodding vigorously.

"We weren't able to sell the farm," Mrs. McIntire went on,

"but we've got a man to work it, and he says he'll do his best to find a buyer come spring."

"There won't be any buyers," Benjamin said bitterly. "Anybody looking for farms this spring will be taking whatever we leave. For nothing."

"Perhaps so," Mrs. McIntire agreed. "But wasn't it the Master who said, 'And whosoever forsakes houses or lands for my name's sake, shall receive an hundredfold, and shall inherit everlasting life'?"

Derek sat back, looking at this simple woman in open admiration. "Yes, that's exactly what he said." In a way that's what he and Peter had done when they left England two years before and came to America. They didn't own any property, but they left home and friends and occupation. And the Lord had repaid them four times over.

Mrs. McIntire turned to Benjamin, her eyes earnest now. "It's true, isn't it?"

Benjamin was taken aback.

"The Book of Mormon is true, isn't it?" she persisted.

"Yes, of course, but—"

"Then that's all that matters. We'll find a place to stay here and—"

Jessica spoke up quickly. "You and the girls can stay with me." She turned and smiled at Matthew for a moment. "In fact, Matthew and I had even thought about seeing if Jenny and Kathryn wanted to come to school. I teach it in my home. I could give you board and room if you would be willing to help with my children and around the house."

Mrs. McIntire clapped her hands. "Wonderful! Would you like that, Jenny?"

"Oh, yes," she cried. "I would love to go to school."

"Me too," Kathryn said eagerly.

Benjamin leaned back, smiling now and a little chagrined at his previous concerns. "You'll have dinner with us tonight, then," he said. "Won't be much, but we would be proud to have you at our table."

Mary Ann reached across the table and took Mrs. McIntire's hands. "Welcome—to our home, to Far West for however long we shall be here, and, most especially, welcome to the fold."

Jenny was watching Matthew, who was beaming like a mother with newborn twins. "What do we have to do to become Mormons?" she asked shyly.

"You have to be baptized," he said. "That's all."

"Can you baptize me?" She was blushing now.

He was startled, but recovered and grinned broadly. "Yes. I'm a priest in the Aaronic Priesthood. I can't confirm you and give you the Holy Ghost, but Derek is an elder. He could do that."

"I'd like that," Jenny exclaimed.

Nancy McIntire turned to Benjamin. "And would it be too much to ask that you baptize me, Brother Steed?"

"I—" Another cough rose up and he had to hunch over as it racked his body. When it was spent, he straightened slowly. There was a look of great respect on his face. "I would consider it an honor to baptize someone with faith like yours, Sister McIntire. An honor indeed."

"You the kid lookin' for the two Missourians?"

Will was slouched down on a stool in the tavern where he had found the least expensive rooms and meals along the waterfront. The remains of a meager supper still sat on the bar before him. He was instantly alert, straightening slowly. "Yes."

The man was filthy. Smears of dirt and coal dust streaked his face. His beard was matted and stiff, and the hair that showed beneath a battered felt hat was shaggy and streaked with gray.

"Charlie Patterson's the name," he said, and held out a gloved hand, the tips of each finger sticking out of the glove. There was a quick grin. It was meant to be a sign of amiability, but was in reality more of a hideous grimace. It revealed crooked, discolored teeth and flecks of tobacco at the corners of his mouth. Will shuddered inwardly, but took the hand briefly. "Do you know anything about them?"

Charlie cackled happily. "Dare say that I do."

Will had learned quickly that word of his willingness to pay for information had gotten around the waterfront and was bringing the hungry and the greedy out of their holes. "Do you know where they are right now? Are they still in St. Louis?"

"Right ya are on both questions, boy."

A thrill of exultation shot through Will. He had heard rumors that they were still around, had even talked to a man who had hired them as day laborers a week or so before, but so far no one had been able to tell him for sure if they were still here.

"Will you take me to them?"

Charlie looked aghast. "Are you crazy, boy? Them are two mean-lookin' gentlemen. I ain't about to get myself killed."

"I'm willin' to pay."

Charlie's eyes narrowed. "How much?"

"A dollar now. Four more when you show me where they live."

"Ha!" he shouted. Several men in the room turned and looked at them, and Charlie instantly dropped his voice to a hoarse whisper. "You think I'm gonna get myself killed for five dollars?"

Will considered that. He didn't trust the man, and yet he sensed that something about Charlie was different than the others. Charlie knew. He could feel it, and that both excited and frightened him. Will's determination to track down his father's killers was as strong as it had ever been—he burned with it, dreamed of catching them, weaved fantasies about dragging them to court, then watching them hang from the gallows. But the last week had also sobered Will tremendously. At the freight yards he had gotten used to being around toughened men, men with foul mouths and a way of life that was as rough as the roads they drove their wagons over. But even the teamsters didn't measure up to the seamy elements that inhabited the rabbit's warren of shacks and alleyways and saloons that lined the banks of the Mississippi. For the past two or three days, a voice in the back of Will's head kept crying out at him. It had started out as a persistent whisper. Now it was almost a shout. *Go home. Don't be a fool. You're swimming in deep water and swift currents.*

Charlie stood up abruptly, startling Will out of his thoughts. "See ya, kid. Sorry we can't do business." He wiped his mouth with the back of his sleeve, eyeing the empty dishes with a hungry look as he started away.

"Wait!"

Charlie was back in a flash, sitting down and grinning.

"All right," Will said, his heart pounding. "I'll make it five dollars now, and fifteen more when you take me there. But I have to see them. I have to know for sure it's them before you get your money."

Charlie was ecstatic. So what if the purse was twenty dollars lighter when Hugh and Riley got their hands on it? Who would be the wiser? The gloved hand shot across the table. "Done!"

Will didn't take the extended hand this time. Instead he reached in his pocket and, keeping the purse under the table where Charlie couldn't see it, found a five-dollar note and shoved it into the clutching fingers. It disappeared in an instant into a fold in the greasy shirt.

"I don't know where they are tonight," Charlie said, "but I know where they'll be for sure night after tomorrow. I'll meet you at the back entrance to the tavern here night after tomorrow at eleven o'clock. Then I'll take you to them."

"All right." Will stood up, wanting to get away from the creepiness of the man. "Night after tomorrow night, eleven o'clock."

Charlie cackled happily again, leering at him. "You sure you want to do this, boy?"

Will hesitated only for a moment, then his jaw tightened. "I'm sure."

The McIntires, mother and daughters, were baptized into The Church of Jesus Christ of Latter-day Saints on Tuesday,

January eighth, 1839, the third day after their arrival in Far West. Brigham Young was out in the countryside with a small group of men seeing to the needs of families in isolated homesteads, but Heber C. Kimball and John Taylor, both Apostles, were there, along with a hundred or so others. Normally converts were not an uncommon occurrence. But to have a family—and a Roman Catholic family, at that—join the Church at a time when the Saints were in such doleful circumstances was unusual, and many came out to witness it.

The baptism was held a short distance north of the city, where a place on Shoal Creek had been dug out so that it was deep enough to provide a baptismal site. It was determined that the services should be held first thing in the morning before any of their enemies might be out and about, and when the group arrived shortly after sunup there was a thin skim of ice across the top of the water.

Jenny McIntire was dressed all in white, as were her mother and sister. Rebecca and Jessica had found white dresses to borrow for Sister McIntire and Kathryn, but no one had something that would fit Jenny's slender form. So they had located some flour sacks made of bleached cotton, turned them inside out, bleached them even whiter with lye and soap, and then sewed them into a skirt. Lydia had furnished the white blouse to complete Jenny's baptismal dress.

As Matthew moved to the water's edge, Jenny removed her coat, then stepped out of her shoes onto the dry grass that lined the stream bank. Matthew watched her in open admiration. Her nose wrinkled slightly as the coldness of the ground hit her, and the freckles across the bridge of her nose almost melted together. She had pulled back her hair away from her face and woven it into a long braid that came to the center of her shoulder blades. In the early-morning rays of the sun, it was almost a strawberry blond rather than its usual light brown color. But it was her eyes he loved the most. Large and pale blue, they were filled with life and excitement and amusement and affection for him all at the same time.

"Are you ready?" he said.

Her head bobbed once, and she held out her hand to him.

Matthew gasped as he stepped into the water and the ice crackled and broke beneath his feet. Clenching his teeth, he turned and flashed her that disarming grin of his. "It's not that bad, Jenny," he managed.

"I don't mind at all," she said, smiling back at him with such pure joy that it made him ashamed he had even thought about the water temperature. When they reached the deepest part of the stream, Matthew stopped, then turned to Jenny. For a moment, their eyes locked. Then he reached out and took her wrist in his left hand. Very solemn now, he raised his right hand to the square, bowed his head, and closed his eyes. Immediately Jenny and all those looking on followed suit.

"Jennifer Jo McIntire," Matthew intoned, "having been commissioned of Jesus Christ, I baptize you in the name of the Father, and of the Son, and of the Holy Ghost. Amen."

He laid her back, letting her sink into the water, watching closely to make sure her hair went completely under with the rest of her. Then he pulled her up again. As she came out of the water, she was gasping from the cold, but her eyes flew open and a radiant smile filled her face. She wiped the water from her eyes, then touched Matthew's arm. "Thank you, Matthew Steed. Thank you."

Kathryn went in next, excited but anxious. She was twelve, and so much like Jenny in some ways—the blue eyes, the perky little upturned nose—and yet not like Jenny at all in others. Her hair was almost jet black, and she was much more serious of disposition. She made no pretense about how the water affected her, gasping and doing a little hop from one foot to the other as if that might somehow warm her a little.

Again Matthew positioned himself and the hand came up. "Kathryn Marie McIntire, having been commissioned of Jesus Christ. . . ."

As the women gathered around the two sisters, wrapping them in blankets and sitting them on chairs to get their feet off the ground, Nancy McIntire stepped to Mary Ann Steed and whispered something in her ear. There was a surprised look, then an immediate nod. Sister McIntire then turned to where Benjamin stood at the edge of the stream holding out his hand for Matthew.

"Brother Benjamin Steed," she said.

He turned. "Yes?"

"Considering your health and the condition of the water, perhaps it is better to have Matthew baptize me as well."

Benjamin frowned and shot Mary Ann a look.

"No, 'tis my idea, not your wife's. I have listened to your cough these past three days and have started to regret my haste in asking that you do this for me."

"Ben," Mary Ann said, "she's right. It's not wise."

He nodded thoughtfully, then looked back at Sister McIntire. "Do you remember the scripture you quoted to me the other night? About leaving lands and houses?"

"Yes, of course."

"And you would deny me the privilege of baptizing you because of a cough?" He sounded incredulous.

For a long moment she stood there. Then a slow smile spread across her face. "Of course not, Brother Steed. It was foolish of me to entertain such a thought." Half turning, and adding noticeably to the lilt in her Irish brogue, she spoke to Matthew. "Aye, laddie, out of the water now with ye. Let's see if a couple of old folk are as tough as you wee ones."

Nathan, Joshua, and Joshua's family had made near record time from Savannah, Georgia, to St. Louis, Missouri. In New Orleans, Joshua had found the captain of one of the smaller steamboats that hauled mainly freight up and down the river. The captain was waiting for a load of cotton to come in, but when Joshua offered him five hundred dollars cash if he would leave immediately, the load was forgotten.

After some discussion, they had decided to forgo any searching along the way. Though she had first wanted to watch for him, stopping at each town, even Caroline now felt a growing urgency to get to St. Louis as quickly as possible and start their search there. It took them eleven days—five to New Orleans, and with the captain making only occasional stops to resupply his wood and water needs, they made it to St. Louis in six more.

It was shortly after nine o'clock on the night of January tenth when they came down the gangplank and Joshua paid the captain the balance of his money. One of the cabin boys darted off to fetch a carriage, and as it rattled up a few minutes later, Joshua turned to Caroline. "Shall we find a boardinghouse first and get the children settled?"

"No!" She was exhausted and her face was drawn and gaunt, but there was no question in her mind. "Let's go to see Mr. Samuelson. We've got to know if Will is here."

"This is a most pleasant surprise," Walter Samuelson said, shaking his head as he opened the door to his large home and motioned them inside. "I didn't expect you back half so soon, Joshua."

"Have you seen Will?" Caroline blurted.

He looked surprised. "Will?"

"Yes, our son," Joshua said.

"But he went south with you," he said, looking at Caroline. "I saw you to the boat, remember?"

"He came back," Joshua said, crestfallen. "He's looking for the men he thinks killed me." The bitterness was so strong that he had to swallow it back or it would have choked him. "So you haven't seen him at all?"

Samuelson looked bewildered. "No, not since then."

Mrs. Samuelson stepped forward. Olivia was holding her mother's hand and leaning against her, looking as if she were about to fall over. Savannah had crawled into Nathan's lap as the carriage had started off and fallen instantly asleep. Now she was asleep over his shoulder. "Let me take the baby," she said.

"We can put her in the guest room." She reached out and touched Olivia's shoulder. "Would you like something to eat, my dear?"

Livvy looked up gratefully. "Yes, ma'am."

"You'll stay with us tonight," Mrs. Samuelson said to Caroline. "And I won't hear any argument about it."

Caroline looked at Joshua and shook her head in discouragement. "You go ahead," she said wearily. "I'll see to the children."

As the men moved into the sitting room, Samuelson went to a humidor on his desk and opened it. It was full of Cuban cigars. He extended it toward the two Steeds. "No, thank you," Nathan said. Joshua smiled briefly. "I've sworn off too, Walter. Caroline detests the things."

Samuelson laughed briefly. "Do you mind if I do?"

"Of course not," they both said at once. As he cut off the end of the cigar, then moved to the fireplace and reached down for a burning stick to light it, Joshua explained quickly to Samuelson all that had happened since he and Nathan had last been here.

"That is most puzzling," Samuelson said as he sat down in a chair, puffing the cigar into life until it glowed a bright red. "Surely here is the first place he would have come."

"That's what we thought," said Joshua.

Suddenly Samuelson snapped his fingers. "Wait a minute. That could explain the report I got yesterday."

Both Joshua and Nathan leaned forward in their chairs. "What report?" Joshua asked.

Samuelson inhaled deeply, then blew out the smoke over his head. "After you left, I decided I would try and find the two men who were looking for Caroline. I knew you'd want to find them as soon as you came back here." He blew out his breath in disgust. "We can't have them chasing after your family, and all that. So I talked to a local marshall I know and hired him to see if they were still around, and if so, to keep track of them."

"And are they?" Joshua asked eagerly. He had a score or two of his own that needed settling.

"Yes. Evidently they're out of money and trying to find some way back to the western part of the state."

"Where are they now?" Nathan asked.

"I don't know." Samuelson immediately held up his hand as he saw their disappointment. "The marshall found them, but I told him not to do anything that might scare them away. He'll know where they are."

Joshua stood up. "Let's go."

Samuelson waved him back down. "Not tonight. He's across the river in East St. Louis on some problem or another. He'll be back first thing in the morning. But in his last report to me he said there is word out along the riverfront that someone else has been asking questions about these same two men." He paused for a moment, then smiled triumphantly. "A young man."

"Will?" Joshua cried.

Samuelson nodded. "It just might be. I never thought anything of it, because I assumed . . ." He shrugged. "Well, we just might be in luck." Now it was he who stood. "Look, you're exhausted. Caroline has reached the end of her rope. Let's get you some supper, then a good night's sleep. We'll be at the marshall's house waiting for him the minute he gets back."

There was a deep sigh, a mixture of relief and frustration. Joshua turned to look at Nathan, who nodded. "He's right, Joshua. We'll start first thing in the morning."

As they crept along the pitch-black street, Will's hand kept straying down to touch the butt of the pistol stuffed in the waistband of his trousers. Will Steed was wet and cold and terribly frightened. Rain came down in a cold drizzle, running off his hat and down the back of his neck and into his eyes. By morning the rain would probably start to freeze on contact with the prairie grass and become one of the ice storms that Missouri was famous for. But the weather was only a small source of his misery. Will didn't trust Charlie Patterson. The greed in Charlie's eyes was open and wanton, and Will knew he wasn't going to be easily satisfied with just the fifteen dollars Will had promised to pay him.

You're over your head, Will, and headed for the cataracts. The voice in his head was a roar now as the realization that his bullheaded, blind craving for revenge was about to come to fruition. With every step, the stupidity of his plan hammered at him. True, he had a pistol, but he was going up against two men, men who without compunction had set fire to a house where people were inside, men who had killed.

Charlie had abruptly stopped, and in the darkness Will nearly bumped into him before he saw him. "All right. That's the place where they're staying. Gimme the fifteen bucks."

Will peered through the rain. He and Charlie were across the street from a small warehouse with a faded sign over the door. It was too dark to read the sign clearly, but one window was yellow with lamplight. Will gripped the pistol, swallowing hard, trying to get some saliva going inside his mouth. "How do I know they're really in there?"

Charlie started cursing under his breath. "You wanna get us killed?" he muttered. "All right, come on." He looked both ways to make sure they were still unobserved, then darted across the street. Will went after him, conscious now of the heavy thudding inside his chest.

"Look!" Charlie said. He was crouched beneath the window. He straightened for a moment, peering through the window, then ducked down again. "See fer yerself."

Moving cautiously now, Will reached the window. He took a quick breath, then peeked inside. Instantly he swung back, pressing himself against the clapboard wall of the warehouse. Inside, two men were sitting at a crate converted to a table. They were playing cards and had a bottle of whiskey between them. He had only a brief glance, but he saw that both were bearded and shabbily dressed. That fit what he had been told about them.

"Give me the money!" Charlie hissed. "That's them. And I'm gone."

"All right." Will stepped back, pulling the pistol out and holding it loosely on Charlie.

Charlie fell back a step. "Hold on!" he cried. "Is that thing loaded?"

"Yes," Will said grimly, "so just stay back." With his free hand he reached for his purse. Fumbling, watching Charlie closely, trying to get the money out one-handed, he finally managed to get the amount he needed. Holding the pistol more steadily now, he held out the money.

Charlie snatched it and stepped back again. His eyes were wide, but there was a new respect in them. "You're crazy, kid. What are you gonna do? Go in shootin'?"

And then in one flash of inspiration, Will had his answer. "No," he said slowly, feeling like a man who, standing before a firing squad, had received a governor's pardon at the last second. He started to back away from the building. "No," he said, his voice rising with excitement. "I'm gonna go find me a constable and have these men arrested. They killed my father and they're gonna pay for it."

"A constable!" Charlie cried. "Now, you listen, boy. You gotta promise to keep me outta this."

Will waved the pistol at him. "I won't say anything about you unless you try to warn them. Now, get!"

Charlie stared at him, his lips moving as he muttered something under his breath, but then he turned and walked away swiftly, back toward the river from where they had come. In moments, he disappeared into the darkness.

Will stood there for a moment, the relief washing over him with such power it made his knees weak. A constable. Why hadn't he thought of that sooner? But then he knew. If he had called the law sooner, Charlie Patterson wouldn't have come within a hundred yards of him, and he wouldn't know where the two men he had dreamed of for so long were staying.

Smiling for the first time in almost a month, Will shoved

the pistol back inside his pants and turned and started away at a trot. He wasn't sure where he could find a constable at this time of night, but he wouldn't stop until he had. By morning the two men could be gone.

Will was still marveling at the simplicity of his solution as he rounded the corner of the street that led down to the riverfront. He never saw the dark shape that lurked just inside a recessed doorway. As Will jogged past, Charlie hurtled out at him in a flying tackle. He caught him right at the waist, slamming him down against the cobblestones.

Will went down hard on one hand. He screamed. There was a snap and a searing pain in his wrist. Before he could move, he felt Charlie's hands fumbling at the front of his pants, and then the weight of the pistol was gone.

Charlie leaped back, straightening in triumph. "All right, Mr. Smart Kid. Now I've got the pistol." He was breathing hard, and smiling wildly through the misshapen teeth. He stepped forward. Will was writhing on the ground, holding his wrist and moaning. Charlie prodded him with the toe of his boot. "All right, boy. Up! There's a couple of men back there who are very anxious to meet you."

"Well, it's about time," Hugh Watson sneered as Charlie Patterson came through the door, pushing Will into the room ahead of him. "You're half an hour later than . . ." His voice trailed off and he was suddenly staring. "Well, I'll be a—"

"You!" Will had gone rigid, his eyes filled with shock and disbelief.

"Would you look at that," Hugh breathed. "It's the Steed kid."

Charlie jammed the pistol into Will's back, shoving him forward again. Will winced, cradling his crippled arm more tightly against his body. "You know him?" Charlie asked.

"Yeah," Riley said, stepping forward, peering out from watery eyes. "This is the son of that captain we killed. We met him and his ma when we went to Independence and told them it was the Mormons who'd done it."

Will started, stunned by the admission. "Then it was you who burned down our house too!" he cried.

Hugh came forward to stand in front of him. "That's right, sonny," he snarled. "And the only mistake we made was taking pity and scratching on the door to give you warning. We should have just let you all burn. Would've saved me and Riley here a whole lot of grief."

With a strangled cry of rage, Will leaped forward, his good hand coming up and swinging at Hugh's face. He moved so fast, Hugh had no time to react. Will's fist caught the Missourian square on the flat of his nose. Blood spurted and Hugh howled and fell backward. Riley was half-drunk and stared stupidly at his companion, but Charlie reacted instantly. He leaped forward, clubbing downward with the pistol. The butt of it caught Will in the square of the back, sending him crashing into some empty crates, then down hard, landing on his injured arm. He screamed, rolling back and forth in agony. Then he stopped and tried to get up, but as he came to his knees, Charlie was in front of him, the pistol pointing directly at his head. "Stay down!" he commanded. Will obeyed, sinking back to the floor.

Hugh was up on his feet again, holding his nose, staring at his bloody hand as he cursed wildly. Then, like a wounded bear, he lumbered around, groping towards the table. "Kill him!" he screamed. "Kill him!"

Charlie's eyes widened as Hugh grabbed something and spun back around. He had a pistol in his hands. "No, Hugh!" Charlie jumped in front of Will now, raising his own pistol.

"Get outta my way!" Hugh roared. "I'm gonna kill him."

"No!" Charlie's eyes were bugged out with terror.

Now even Riley realized what was happening. "No, Hugh," he said, jumping forward to grab at his partner's arm. Hugh threw him off, not even looking at him. His voice instantly dropped to a whisper. "Charlie, get outta my way." It was more menacing and frightening than any shout could have been.

Charlie was pleading now, his words tumbling out in near sobs. "Not murder, Hugh. You're getting outta here. But St. Louis is my home. We can't kill him." Suddenly he remembered something. He grabbed at his pocket. "Look, Hugh. I got his purse." Fumbling with one hand, he dumped the money out on the floor and tossed the purse aside. "This is what we came for. You can have it. I'll take him to that boat captain, like we said. He'll take him downriver to New Orleans and sell him off to one of them British ships. We'll never see him again."

"Charlie, if you don't move, I'm gonna blow your ugly head off."

Charlie Patterson had never used a gun. He was a coward at heart, living off what he could steal and pilfer without ever confronting anything that constituted a physical risk. But the thoughts of the gallows terrified him beyond anything else he could imagine. He stepped forward. "No, Hugh."

Hugh swung the pistol up, cursing and swearing. But Charlie already had his pistol leveled and pointed at Hugh's chest. He squeezed the trigger and the gun bucked in his hand. Hugh Watson stumbled backwards, the pistol flying from his hand, his eyes wide with shock and surprise. He crashed against the table, sending it sprawling. Cards flew, and the whiskey bottle shattered as it hit the floor.

"No!" Charlie screamed. He was gaping at Hugh, who now lay on the floor clutching at the spreading stain on his chest. "I didn't want to! I didn't want to! I didn't want to!" It was a wild, incoherent babble. He swung around to Will. "Come on, we've got to get out of here."

Will started to push himself up. His face was as pale as the dusty floor, half from the shock of his arm, half from the horror of seeing a man gunned down a few feet in front of him. Then suddenly he jerked his head around. "Watch out, Charlie!"

Riley Overson's brain had always moved slowly, and normally he took time to think things through or else trusted Hugh to help do it for him. But now Hugh was lying on the floor with a hole in his chest. Hugh was dead. Something snapped inside Riley and he dropped to his hands and knees and started across the floor toward Hugh's pistol, sobbing and cursing unintelligibly.

Charlie spun around. "Don't, Riley!"

Riley was oblivious to anything but the pistol. He reached it and picked it up, his back still to Charlie and Will.

"Don't be crazy, Riley!" Charlie screamed. "Put it down!"

Riley put one hand against the floor and shoved himself up. He turned slowly, thumbing back the hammer of the pistol in his hand. "You killed Hugh."

"No, Riley!" Charlie's drawn out cry was shattered by the nearly simultaneous explosions of both pistols. Charlie's ball struck first, jerking Riley backwards enough to deflect his shot upward. That round passed harmlessly over Charlie's head and buried itself in one of the wooden beams above them.

Riley hit the floor with a heavy thud and lay still. Suddenly the silence seemed more intense than the roaring of the pistols. Charlie seemed frozen, in suspension, as he surveyed what he had done. But then it hit him what all this meant. He leaped forward, dropping to a crouch and snatching at the money he had dropped. As he scrambled around for the bills and coins, he cursed God, he cursed Hugh and Riley, he cursed Will, and he cursed his own mother for ever bringing him into the world. Then he leaped up and whirled on Will, waving the pistol wildly. "Up!" he shouted. "We've got to get out of here."

Will jumped to his feet, trying to protect his bad arm. "What are you going to do with me?" he cried, the terror tightening his voice into little more than a croak.

Charlie stopped for a moment, his eyes darting back and forth as if the solution might be hidden somewhere in the warehouse. Then he shook his head. "I ain't gonna kill ya, boy. Not unless you try and fight me. But I can't have you hangin' around here tellin' the law what happened here tonight, now can I?"

"I won't say anything," Will half sobbed. He felt sick to his stomach and weak with fright.

Charlie grabbed him by the shoulder and shoved him towards the door. "Come on. We got someone waiting to meet you."

The marshall stopped at the door to the warehouse. "Mrs. Steed, I wish we could have you stay outside, but I'm afraid we need you to identify the bodies too."

She swallowed hard, but nodded immediately. She reached out and gripped Joshua's arm. "All right."

Motioning to them all to follow him, the marshall went through the door. As they came inside and paused for a minute to let their eyes adjust to the dimness, the officer spoke again. "It happened sometime last night. The owner of the warehouse wasn't here, but . . ." He shrugged and moved further inside. He stopped, then stepped aside. The two bodies were laid out on the floor near an overturned crate and a smashed bottle of liquor.

Taking a quick breath, Joshua moved forward and leaned over. After a moment, he straightened and stepped back. Nathan saw that suddenly his breathing was rapid and shallow. "That's them," Joshua said tightly. "That's the men who tried to kill me in Far West."

He reached back and took a hold of Caroline's arm. He pulled her gently forward. She stared downward, suppressing a gasp, then averted her head. "Yes, those are the ones."

"These are the men who came to you in Jackson County?" the marshall asked gently.

"Yes, and that same night my house was burned down. These are the ones. There is no question about it."

Samuelson looked at the marshall. "Then that's that," he said.

The man nodded slowly. "Yes, as far as that goes." He looked at Joshua. "They'll not be bothering your family anymore. But . . ." He turned and walked to a crate. He picked up something and brought it back over. "Do either of you recognize this?"

He handed a small money purse to Joshua. Joshua turned it over, then opened it up. It was empty. "No," he said. "It's nothing I've seen before."

But Caroline had gone rigid beside him, and there was a soft intake of breath. Joshua turned to her. "Caroline, do you know what this is?"

So slowly it was almost imperceptible, her head moved up and down. "That's the purse I left the money in," she whispered. "Will took it from my drawer."

The marshall looked away. He turned to Samuelson and shook his head. "I don't have any choice," he murmured. "I'm going to have to put out a warrant for the boy's arrest."

The door to the coal bin opened, letting in a flood of daylight. Will sat up quickly, blinking at the brightness of the light. A dark shadow filled the narrow frame.

"You all right, boy?"

Will pushed his back against the one empty wall, feeling the grit of the coal dust beneath his seat, but he didn't answer.

"How's the arm?"

Will lifted the splinted wrist without thinking and looked at it. "It's all right, I guess."

"Good." The man stooped and set a plate of food on the floor. "Eat up, boy."

"Where are we?"

The man turned to look out the door. "We'll shortly be docking at Cairo, Illinois, where the Ohio River comes in." He spoke more kindly now. "Wish we could let you off to stretch your legs, but we won't be stopping long. There's more ice coming downriver, and we've got to keep moving." Then abruptly he stepped back and shut the door. There was a metallic click as he put the padlock in the hasp.

Will could smell the food distinctly now, some kind of meat and beans, but he ignored it. He could feel the throbbing of the paddle wheels through the bulkhead and could hear the swishing of the water across the hull. Suddenly he dropped his head against his knees. Hot tears scalded his eyes, and his shoulders began to shake. "I'm sorry, Mama," he whispered. "I'm sorry."

Chapter Thirty-Two

When Jessica and her four children moved to the new cabin where she would teach school, the Steeds decided to once again realign their housing arrangements. Jenny and Kathryn McIntire moved in with Jessica to help with the children in payment for their enrollment in the school. Sister McIntire stayed with Benjamin and Mary Ann; Peter and Matthew were also still there. Rebecca and Derek moved over to stay with Lydia and Nathan.

Lydia was grateful for Rebecca's and Derek's company. Not only was Rebecca wonderful to help with the children, but she and Derek were both still so young and so in love and so perpetually optimistic and happy. Lydia desperately needed that right now. There had been no word from Nathan since the letter he had written from St. Louis almost a month before. And in that letter he had said that he had no idea how long it would take for him and Joshua to go to Georgia and look for Caroline, or where they would go if she wasn't there. But any way she figured it, it would be weeks at least, maybe a month or more.

And now their departure from Missouri loomed closer every day. That frightened Lydia more than she could bear to contemplate. She knew that she would have Derek and Matthew to help her. It wasn't that she felt abandoned, but it was not the same. She still felt that she was facing it all alone—trying to decide what to carry and what to abandon, crossing two hundred miles of open prairie in the depths of winter with a baby and three other children, the oldest only seven. She needed Nathan—to lean on, to complain to when she had to put on a brave face for everyone else, to snuggle against when there was no other safe place in all the world. Tears sprang unbidden to her eyes and she looked away, lest Rebecca should see them.

But Rebecca was dressing baby Elizabeth and finding her hands full in doing so. Elizabeth was eight months old now and had mastered crawling in the past two weeks. She was faster than a frightened kitten and could scoot out from under your grip in a flash. As Rebecca reached for her booties, she twisted away.

"She's getting away," squealed six-year-old Emily, giggling as she grabbed one of Elizabeth's legs and pulled her back.

"You little mouse," Rebecca laughed. "You're getting too quick for your own good."

"She not a mouse," little Nathan said. He had turned three in October and had mastered a glare that would freeze an avalanche in its path. He leveled it at Rebecca now.

Lydia laughed in spite of herself. She brushed at the corners of her eyes, then turned around. "No, Nathan, Elizabeth is not a mouse. Rebecca didn't mean it."

He looked at his aunt, still openly offended. Rebecca was appropriately contrite. "I'm sorry, Nathan. Elizabeth is not a mouse." She finished putting on Elizabeth's booties and turned her loose for Emily and Nathan to chase after. She stood up, looked at Lydia, then looked again more closely. "Are you sure you won't go visiting with Jessie and me?" she said.

Lydia hesitated. Normally being out with the other sisters was something she enjoyed. But Emma? Mary Fielding Smith? Sister Rigdon? All that would do is remind her all the more keenly about missing husbands and lonely women waiting for them to return. She shook her head. "No, I—"

There was a step on the porch, followed immediately by a knock at the door. Lydia turned. "Come in," she called.

It opened immediately and Jenny McIntire entered. She had a knitted scarf wrapped around her face and gloves on her hands, but her cheeks were still pink, which highlighted her freckles and her blue eyes and made her seem two or three years younger than her seventeen years. With a joyous shout, Emily and Joshua and Nathan leaped up and ran to her, nearly bowling her over. In the two weeks since the McIntires had come, Lydia's children and Jessica's children had fallen in love with Jenny and Kathryn. The two sisters were wonderful with the children, and the children adored them.

"Hello," Jenny said, laughing as she let them wrestle her to the floor.

"Emily," Lydia called, smiling. "Nathan. Let Jenny up, for heaven's sake."

Reluctantly they backed off for a moment, and Jenny stood. She unwrapped the scarf from around her face, then turned to Rebecca and Lydia. "Sister Lydia, Jessie sent me over to watch the children."

"She did?"

"Yes. She wants you to come right over. Amanda Smith and another family just got in from . . ." She hesitated, trying to remember the name.

"Haun's Mill?" Rebecca filled in.

"Yes, that's it. They just arrived. Jessica was so excited to see her, she dismissed school. But she wants you to come, right now."

Rebecca swung around. "Oh, Lydia, please come. Jessie says Amanda is the most wonderful woman."

Lydia nodded. She had never met Amanda Smith, but Jessica's accounts of Haun's Mill and what had happened there were filled with references to Amanda Smith. Lydia untied her apron and tossed it aside. "All right, let's go."

"Well, I'd not be a truthful woman if I told you it has not been a terrifying experience."

Jessica sat by Amanda's side on the sofa. With much of the furniture smashed or stolen by the militia, Mary Ann, Lydia, Rebecca, and Sister McIntire all sat in a half circle on the floor facing the sofa, listening intently to Amanda.

"The Missourians have been back a dozen times or more, telling us that if we did not leave the state immediately, they would kill us all."

"That's what they're saying to everyone," Mary Ann said.

"I know. We kept telling them we'd move as soon as we could, but there were three families of us with wounded men or boys who couldn't be moved. We had no choice but to stay. We told them that over and over. It made no difference to them."

"The fiends," Lydia said angrily. "Have they no heart whatsoever?"

Jessica knew the answer to that. Amanda's coming had brought back with searing sharpness the memories of that horrible afternoon. It made her sick even now—men on horseback, painted like savages, whooping and screaming, shooting down men and boys, firing at women and children as they scattered for cover. *Fiends* was a term that didn't half describe them.

"All I could do was show them my Alma," Amanda was continuing. "Obviously he couldn't be moved, not even enough to turn him over in his bed. Even the very little I had to move him to put cloths under his back so he wouldn't get bedsores made him scream out in agony."

"And they accepted that?" Rebecca asked, the horror making her voice almost a whisper.

"Yes, finally, but they continued to harass us. The leader, he came one day and said we could stay until we could move our wounded, but we were forbidden to do anything religious. We couldn't have any meetings, or even call the family together for prayers. They said they would shoot us if they caught us praying vocally alone."

Her lips tightened and her eyes were suddenly fierce. "I decided I could not—would not—stand this godless silence. So one day I went down into a cornfield and crawled into a shock of the corn which had been cut and stacked. You know where I mean, Jessica. Across the stream in the field next to Brother Haun's."

"Yes," Jessica said softly. "I know exactly where you mean."

"Well, after making sure no one could see me or hear me, I started to pray out loud. I raised my voice and prayed till my soul felt satisfied."

"Did they catch you?" Lydia breathed.

"No. But a most marvelous thing happened. As I left the shock of corn and started back toward the cabin where we were now staying, all of a sudden I heard a voice. It was a sweet and wonderful voice, and it sent chills through my whole body."

Sister McIntire's eyes were wide with amazement. "What did it say?"

"Do you know our hymn 'How Firm a Foundation'?" Amanda replied.

"No, I don't think so."

"Well, the voice repeated a verse from that wonderful hymn. The seventh verse, in fact, just as it is found in our hymnal."

"Which is . . . ?" Sister McIntire asked.

Amanda closed her eyes and leaned back, the memory softening her features. Then she began to quote softly. "'The soul that on Jesus hath lean'd for repose, I will not, I cannot desert to his foes. That soul, though all hell should endeavor to shake, I'll never—no, never, no never forsake!'"

Her eyes came open again and she looked around at the women's faces. "I can't begin to tell you what sweetness that brought to me. From that moment forth I had no further fear of the mob. I was so certain of God's protecting care that I went right home and gathered Willard and my two daughters around me. I told them that as long as they had faith and that if they would conscientiously do right, the Lord would shelter us from harm."

They all leaned back now, awed by the power of this simple woman and the story she had told them. Finally Jessica spoke. "And what of little Alma? How is he doing?"

Amanda sat up and clasped her hands together, her eyes shining with excitement. "You haven't heard?"

Jessica shook her head. "No. Heard what?"

Amanda laughed and turned. She and her children had been taken in by a family with whom they had come out from Kirtland. The family had gone out, leaving Amanda to visit with her friends. "Willard!" She cupped her hand around her mouth. "Willard, come here for a moment."

A moment later a young boy stuck his head into the room. "Yes, Mama?"

"Where is Alma?"

"He's in the bedroom, Mama."

"Will you fetch him for me?"

Lydia was shaking her head. She turned to Jessica. "Is that the boy you told us about? The one who helped those little girls who were hiding under the bed?"

Jessica nodded. "Yes, that's Willard."

Mary Ann felt her eyes burning. "You must be very proud, Sister Smith. I know you lost your husband and a son, but to have one like that . . ."

"Yes," Amanda said soberly. "I was very proud of Willard that day."

Just then there was the sound of footsteps and Willard came back in, this time leading a boy three or four years younger than himself. Amanda smiled. "Alma, these sisters would like to meet you."

Alma bowed slightly. "How'd ya do," he intoned. He was towheaded and slender, with an impish twist to his nose and mouth.

Jessica was staring at him, unbelieving. "But he's walking."

Amanda turned back and started to reply, then had to stop. Her lower lip was trembling noticeably now. "Yes," she whispered happily.

Jessica turned to her family, her mouth round with amazement. "But I saw his wound. The whole hip joint was gone." She turned back to stare at him. "I can't believe it."

Amanda motioned to her son. "Alma, turn so they can see your leg."

He turned and extended his leg so that it stretched the trouser material tightly over the skin. Now all the women gasped. At his hip there was a depression about the size of a man's fist beneath the material. It looked like someone had scooped part of the leg away.

Now Amanda began to speak again, not taking her eyes off her youngest son. "Alma lay in the same position for about five weeks while the wound was healing. But then one day—this would be in early December—I had taken a bucket to the spring for water. Suddenly I heard the children screaming back at the house. My heart nearly stopped. I thought the mob had returned."

She stopped, overcome for a moment. She held out her arms and Alma came over into them. "You too, Willard," she said. He came and stood behind the sofa, laying a hand on her shoulder.

"When I rushed inside the door, the children were all running around the cabin, with Alma in the lead, him crying, 'I'm well, Ma, I'm well!'" She pulled Alma tightly against her, for a moment too moved to continue. Finally, she sniffed back the tears. "Yes, I lost Warren and Sardius that day, but the Lord did not forsake me. He has given us a miracle, and I shall ever sing his praises for his glorious mercy and love for me and my family."

The others talked excitedly as they walked back toward their own homes, but Lydia lagged behind, not wanting to speak and break the wonder that filled her soul. Suddenly she dropped her head, staring at the ground. *Dear Lord, forgive me. Forgive my murmuring tongue. Forgive my foolishness that I should think I am tested beyond measure. I thank thee for reminding me of thy marvelous power and of thy wondrous love and mercy. I miss my Nathan fiercely, but I shall murmur no more. Be with him and Joshua in their task, then bring him home safely to us, if it be thy will. Strengthen my faltering heart and feeble knees, O Father. Help me to be strong. In the name of Jesus, amen.*

Opening her eyes fully, she raised her head, then moved forward more sharply. In three steps she was up to her mother-in-law and slipped her arm through hers. As Mary Ann looked at her in surprise, Lydia smiled happily. "Let's all have supper together tonight, shall we?"

Derek was waiting for Rebecca and Lydia at the front porch. He was grinning like a child with a secret too marvelous to share and too wonderful to keep. "Hello, dear," he said, kissing Rebecca on the cheek. "Hello, Lydia. You look well today."

Lydia looked up in surprise. "I *am* well, thank you. Very well. How are the children?"

He laughed in delight. "Better than they have been for many days." That puzzled Lydia even more, and she looked at him more closely. But his smile only broadened, sending the mischievousness spreading across his face. "By the way, we sent Jenny home."

"Oh?" There was something she was missing, but she wasn't sure what. "Is the baby asleep?"

"No."

"Oh. So Joshua's watching her?"

He was enjoying himself immensely. "No, I don't think so. Nor Emily either."

"Derek!" Rebecca said, getting exasperated. "Then who has the baby?"

He smiled, stepped to the door, and, with a sweeping bow, opened it. "I think she is in good hands, but why not go in and see for yourself?"

He pushed the door open wide. Thoroughly baffled now, Lydia started in, giving him one last quizzical look. But he merely gestured with his head for her to enter and chuckled all the more deeply. Then she was inside and turned to look for her children. She had lifted her hands to untie the scarf around her neck, but they froze in midair. Nathan was sitting in the rocking chair, Elizabeth in one arm, Nathan on his lap, and Joshua and Emily standing by his side.

"Hello, Lydia," he said happily.

"See?" Derek chortled. "I told you she was in good hands."

Lydia reached over and stroked Nathan's cheek with the back of her hand. "You must be exhausted."

He reached up and took her hand. "Actually, I'm so excited to be home again, I don't think I'll be able to sleep all night."

She laughed softly. "It's fine with me. I only have about a hundred million things to tell you."

He turned over on his side so that he was facing her. Now he took both of her hands in his and squeezed them. "I'm so sorry that it took so long, Lydia. I feel—"

She jerked one hand loose from his and clamped it over his mouth. "No!" she scolded. "Don't you say it." Then she went up on one elbow, removed her hand from his mouth, and kissed him hard. Still up, she stared at him in the dark and began to trace the shape of his lips with her fingertip. "I can't believe it. You're really here."

"Yes. I was going to write from Savannah, but we left the very next day. I figured we were going to beat any mail that could have been sent. When I left St. Louis it was the same thing. I figured I would make better time than the mail coaches."

"Hmm," she murmured, kissing him again. "This is much better than some dry old letter." Then her mouth turned down. "What will they do?"

Her sudden switch of thought caught him off guard. "Who? You mean Caroline and Joshua?"

"Yes. About Will. What can they do?"

"There's nothing now they can do. We spent two more days looking. He's gone without a trace. We found people who had seen him, but no one after that night. They're hoping he'll head south to Savannah, looking for his mother. If he does, the Montagues will ship him right back north again."

She shook her head. "It must be awful for him," she replied. "As far as he knows, his father is still dead."

"The problem is, if he comes back to St. Louis he's got that marshall waiting for him."

Lydia dropped back to the bed and put her hands under her head. "I can't believe that he really did it. Not Will. He wouldn't shoot somebody down just like that."

"That's what Caroline says. She absolutely refuses to accept the fact that Will shot them."

"What do you think?"

There was a pause, then a slow shake of his head. "I don't know. I don't think Will just walked in and shot them. There were signs of a struggle. A table was knocked over. And there was another pistol found at the scene as well. It had been fired once too."

Lydia's head came up sharply. "You didn't tell me that. Maybe Will is wounded."

"No, the only blood to be seen was around the two bodies." He shook his head again. "I don't know. Something went on in that warehouse, and we can't figure out what. What I can't believe is that Will had the courage to go against those two men. They were both animals. They'd shot his father. What in the world was he thinking of?"

"He's blind with grief and shock. He and Joshua were so close." Then Lydia didn't want to think about that anymore. It was too depressing. "And Caroline and the girls were all right?"

"Yes, fine. Wonderful. She wouldn't hear of not coming back with us to look for Will."

"And what will they do now? They can't go back to Jackson County?"

"No. Joshua has his businesses there in St. Louis with Samuelson and his other partners. Those two men are dead, so he thinks there'll be no more problems from what happened here."

"I'm so glad you stayed with him until you found Caroline," Lydia said, changing tracks again. "I missed you terribly, but I would never have forgiven myself if you hadn't gone."

"Nor I myself," he said. "Joshua's leg makes it difficult for him to get around without someone there to see to things."

They both lapsed into silence, occupied with their own thoughts. After a few minutes, his breathing began to deepen a little. She nudged him with her elbow. "See? I told you you were exhausted."

"Well," he admitted, "maybe more than I thought."

"That's all right, we'll have all day tomorrow to talk." She curled up against him, murmuring happily. "And the next day and the next and the next."

"Mmm."

She wasn't sure if that was agreement or not. She went up on one elbow again. "Nathan?"

"Hmm?"

"I don't care where we go now," she said with great soberness. "You're here. I can face anything. Thank you for coming home."

He didn't answer her, just reached out and put his arm around her and pulled her close to him. He extended his one arm and she snuggled into it, laying her face against his shoulder. This was her favorite place with him when they were together. "I love you, Lydia," he murmured.

"And I love you, Nathan Steed," she whispered, blinking back the sudden tears that sprang from nowhere. "Go to sleep, my darling. I'll be here when you awaken."

On January 16, 1839, the First Presidency, signing themselves as "prisoners for Jesus' sake," wrote from Liberty Jail a letter to Brigham Young and Heber C. Kimball, the two senior Apostles in Far West. "Inasmuch as we are in prison," they wrote, "for a little season, if need be, the management of the affairs of the Church devolves on you, that is the Twelve." Further on in this letter they stated: "If we live, we live; and if we die for the testimony of Jesus, we die; but whether we live or die, let the work of God go on." Also included were these words of encouragement: "Brethren, fear not, but be strong in the Lord and in the power of His might. . . . Neither think it strange concerning the fiery trials with which we are tried, as though some strange thing had happened unto us. . . . Rejoice in your afflictions, by which you are perfected and through which the Captain of our Salvation was perfected also."

The two Apostles had already taken much of the burden of leadership by default when the First Presidency had been arrested. With the arrival of the letter, they now had a mandate to act.

It was a sobering task. By this time, almost all of the Saints with any means to move had left Missouri. Wagons headed eastward almost every day. But there had been a massive gathering of Saints to northern Missouri during 1837 and 1838—some ten or twelve thousand—and even with hundreds of families already gone, there were still hundreds more to be moved.

Most of the remaining families were poor, some devastatingly so. As much as possible the Saints attempted to sell their lands and property to get enough cash or goods to make the removal possible, but they had little success. Much of their land had already been signed over at the point of the bayonet. Some Missourians did make purchases, but the conditions were not favorable to the Saints. Prime farmland sold for fifty cents an acre. One man sold forty acres for "a blind mare and a clock." Most of the old settlers realized that all they had to do was be patient and they would get almost all of it anyway.

The care of the poor was the direct responsiblity of the

Aaronic Priesthood, and therefore should have fallen under the direction of the Presiding Bishopric. But when Brigham tried to exercise the "management of the affairs of the Church" as asked by the First Presidency, he saw just how real the burden of leadership was. The Apostles called Bishop Edward Partridge in and asked how the Presiding Bishopric were going to see to the needs of the poor. Destitute himself, weary, and totally overburdened, Bishop Partridge hung his head. "I guess the poor are going to have to take care of themselves," was all he said.

With the situation growing more desperate almost daily, Brigham called for a general meeting of the leading elders of the Church who were still in Missouri. They met together in council at the schoolhouse on the twenty-sixth of January. Resolutions were passed having to do with assessing the extent of the problem. A committee of seven was appointed to find out how many families were unable to remove themselves from the state, and to survey what means were still left in the Church that could be used to help. All agreed that it was "the duty of those who have to assist those who have not."

On the twenty-ninth of that same month, the brethren reconvened.

Benjamin had been too ill to go to the first meeting, but he and Nathan and Derek were at the second. The meeting had barely gotten its first item of business over with when Brigham stood up. It was a somber occasion. Indications were that there were still hundreds of families needing assistance and very little available to provide it.

As Brigham stood slowly, the room instantly quieted. Everyone sensed in Brigham's countenance a solemnity far greater than anything they had seen to date. Brigham was not a particularly tall man, standing only about five feet ten inches, and his face, still without beard, had a certain boyish quality about it. But those who knew him did not consider him boyish in any way. In Kirtland, Brigham had been so courageous in defense of the Prophet that he had finally been forced to flee to escape assassination. Here in Missouri he had been passed over when the majority of the leading brethren had been arrested by the militia in November, because he was not well known to the enemies of the Church. But such was no longer the case. Brigham was now the most-wanted man in Missouri, and whenever he was away from the city, he traveled in disguise. But if he was frightened by any of it, he gave not the slightest sign.

Nathan watched him closely. No wonder Joseph had named this man "the Lion of the Lord." There had been a brief wave of panic when Joseph was taken. Who would lead the people through these terrible times? But those feelings had died quickly. Here was a leader who exuded confidence and who could build confidence in the Saints as well.

"Brethren," Brigham said, leaning forward on the table, "we know that our situation is grave. Therefore, I would propose a motion to the council."

No one moved. Every eye was upon him. He let his eyes sweep across the faces. "I propose that we resolve this day to enter into a solemn covenant to assist each other to remove from this state, and that we resolve that we will never desert the poor who are worthy."

"Second the motion!"

Nathan turned. He wasn't sure if it was Heber Kimball or John Taylor who had cried out, but there was a quick chorus of assent from all.

"Thank you, brethren," Brigham said, clearly pleased with the response.

Following some discussion, a committee of seven brethren was appointed to oversee the removal of the Saints from the state and the giving of assistance to those who needed it.

John Smith, uncle to the Prophet, had been assigned as chairman of the council. He stood now. "I propose that the secretary draft a document expressive of the sense of the covenant entered into this day."

Twenty minutes later the secretary handed a paper to

Brother Smith. He looked at it for a moment, seemed satisfied, then handed it to Brother Brigham. The Apostle read it carefully, nodding from time to time and making pleased rumbling sounds. "Very good," he finally said, standing again. "May I enter the following into the minutes, and may we then allow all those who wish to join in this covenant to sign it as witness of their intent, thus enabling the committee of seven brethren to carry their business into effect more expeditiously."

"Read it," someone called out.

"Yes, read it," Nathan joined in.

Brigham straightened, raising the paper in front of him. Again the room quieted until there was barely a sound. Then he started, his voice low and filled with pride. "'We, whose names are hereunder written, do for ourselves individually hereby covenant to stand by and assist one another, to the utmost of our abilities, in removing from this state in compliance with the authority of the state; and we do hereby acknowledge ourselves firmly bound to the extent of all our available property—'"

Brigham stopped. Then his voice rose majestically until it shook the room. "'Firmly bound to the extent of all our available property, to be disposed of by a committee who shall be appointed for the purpose of providing means for the removing from this state of the poor and destitute who shall be considered worthy, till there shall not be one left who desires to remove from the state.'"

Brigham lowered the paper and looked up. "It is dated Far West, Missouri, January twenty-ninth, 1839. There is a place for signatures of those who wish to subscribe to the foregoing."

Uncle John Smith was on his feet instantly. "As chairman, I propose we accept the covenant, and should like to be the first to sign my name to it."

Thirty-three men signed it at the meeting, including Benjamin and Nathan Steed and Derek Ingalls. Eighty more family heads signed it later the same day, and three hundred more the day following.

Chapter Notes

Amanda Smith's experiences at Haun's Mill were described in chapters 17 and 18 of the novel. Her later experience with prayer in the cornfield and Alma's wonderful recovery are given by her son Willard in his account of the events there (see *By Their Fruits*, pp. 182–83). Alma later walked across the plains to Utah with his family and also served a mission to the Sandwich Islands (Hawaii). Although he did pad his trousers to cover the hole caused by the missing flesh, he suffered no pain or discomfort in his leg after it was healed.

The letter written from Liberty Jail by the First Presidency to Brigham Young and Heber C. Kimball is given in its entirety in Heber C. Kimball's biography (see *LHCK*, pp. 237–39).

Brigham's actions following the First Presidency letter, including his call for a covenant to assist the poor, is historically correct. The covenant Brigham reads in the meeting is the actual covenant drafted during that January twenty-ninth meeting, though not all of the document is read here. (See *HC* 3:249–54.) Not all sources agree on the exact number of those who signed the covenant, though all put it at around four hundred. The numbers presented in the novel are as given by historian Leonard J. Arrington (see *American Moses*, p. 70).

Chapter Thirty-Three

In mid-January, Emma Smith and Mary Fielding Smith went to Liberty to see Joseph and Hyrum. It was a dangerous journey under the best of circumstances, but Mary had still not recovered from the serious illness that had dogged her since before the birth of her baby. She had been bedridden now for over two months. But Hyrum had never seen little Joseph Fielding Smith, and Mary was adamant about accompanying Emma. So they had made a bed in the back of the wagon for her and the baby, and she and Emma went south.

In spite of the hardships of the nearly one-hundred-mile round-trip journey, it had been a wonderful boost to the women's spirits, and they had returned much encouraged. While Emma and Mary were there, both Joseph and Hyrum had counseled their wives to leave the state as soon as possible. Also while they were there, a sympathetic sheriff had told them that as long as Emma was in the state of Missouri, Joseph's enemies would never release him. When the two women returned and reported this information, the Committee on Removal held a meeting on February first and determined that their first priority would be to get the families of the First Presidency and of the other prisoners out of the state.

Emma had accepted that with some difficulty. She was always one to put her needs and desires last, but she had finally given in. A neighbor who had been especially caring for her and the children was leaving and offered to travel with her. Also, Stephen Markham, one of Joseph's most trusted associates, said he would drive her wagon for her.

All this was going through Lydia Steed's mind on the night of February sixth as she walked across town toward Emma's home. Emma was supposed to leave in the morning, and Lydia had planned to be there to say good-bye. Then, just an hour ago, she had learned what had happened that day. Knowing Emma well, she knew Emma would be distraught, and so she had left the children with Nathan and come to see Emma. She walked swiftly, for it was nearly nine o'clock and Far West was still plagued from time to time with some of the bullies and local ruffians harassing the Saints, especially after dark.

Lydia shook her head. She wanted to be angry with the committee, but kept finding herself arguing in their behalf as often as she did Emma's. This was a time in Far West when about the only thing that was not in short supply was hard decisions. It was just too bad that it had to put the needs of Emma and her family in direct conflict with the needs of Joseph's parents. That would be especially hard on Emma.

This was the news Lydia had received a short time before. A few days ago, Joseph's parents had found a wagon to carry what little belongings they had and start east. It was about that same time when the committee made the decision to give priority to the families of those at Liberty Jail. The Smiths actually had the wagon loaded and ready to depart when the committee showed up. Apologetic, but determined to follow the counsel given them, they indicated that Sidney Rigdon's family was ready to leave and they needed the wagon the Smiths had gotten from the committee.

Disheartened, but taking it pretty much in stride, the Smiths unloaded the wagon and settled in to wait. That had been bad enough. But today there had been an exact repeat. They had found a second wagon, they had just gotten it loaded and prepared to leave, when once again the committee came at the last moment and said they needed the wagon—only this time the First Presidency's family they were giving it to was Emma and her children.

Lydia shook her head. "Dear Mother Smith," she said to herself. Four foot eleven and not tipping a hundred pounds, and yet she had enough spunk to fill a barn. But this surely must have been a bitter blow today. Father Smith's health was still poor. He had never fully recovered from the shock of thinking Joseph had been killed on that day he was taken prisoner. The Smith family was most anxious to remove the aging patriarch from this place, where the danger was still high and the conditions so poor. And then to have their departure delayed again. Lydia's lips compressed into a tight line. How could the committee have done that to her?

But almost instantly the other side of her began to answer. Joseph's parents had three of their own children—Don Carlos, Sophronia, and Catherine—and their families to help care for them. Emma now had no one. And as the Prophet's wife, Emma was in possible danger. It would be a crushing blow to Joseph if somehow his enemies could get to her. And then there was the news that perhaps Emma's removal would speed Joseph's release from jail. Would she have done any differently, given those options? Lydia wondered. Probably not.

As she turned up the path that led to Emma's cabin, Lydia stopped. Stephen Markham was on the porch. The door was open and he was speaking to someone inside. "Sister Smith," he was saying, "I know exactly how you feel, but you know there is no choice. Your things are loaded. Mother Smith is in total agreement with the committee. They are working on finding them something else. But you must go, and you must go now."

From inside, Lydia heard Emma reply, but couldn't catch the words. Markham nodded. "I'll be here first thing in the morning." He pulled the door shut and turned around, putting on his hat. Then he saw Lydia. He started a little. "Oh! Sister Steed. Good evening."

"Good evening, Brother Markham." She hesitated for a moment. "How is Emma? Will she go?"

His eyes were troubled but he finally nodded. "Yes. She feels awful about what has happened with Mother Smith. But, yes, I think she'll go."

"Good."

He forced a quick smile. "The Lord gave Brother Joseph a wife strong enough for a prophet. She is a woman of remarkable strength and courage."

"Yes," Lydia agreed instantly. "That she is. I will go in and sit with her for a time."

"I think she would appreciate that. Julia is with her, but the rest of the children are with the Holmans."

"Good." Julia, who would be eight in April, was the surviving Murdock twin whom Joseph and Emma had adopted when Emma's own twins died at birth back in 1831. But Julia could have been Emma's own, for there was a strong resemblance between them. She had stayed with her mother to help with the final packing. The Holmans were neighbors of Emma's who had been especially caring for her since Joseph's arrest. They would be going with her on the way east.

Markham tipped his hat and went past her. Lydia watched him for a moment, then went to the door.

By the time Lydia had been there fifteen minutes, Emma had cheered considerably. Lydia marveled. Emma was a beautiful woman, with her long black hair and flashing dark eyes. She looked too pretty, too elegant to have this kind of resilience. Yet in just moments after entering, it was Lydia who was drawing strength from Emma rather than the other way around. Emma would have vehemently disagreed with that assessment, for Lydia's coming and her quiet reaffirmation that what Emma was doing was the right thing had been sorely needed this night. But there was no denying it: Lydia had been blessed by her visit as much as the other way around.

But finally, reluctantly, Lydia declared that it was time for her to go. She stood. Julia and Emma stood too. Lydia and Julia hugged quickly, then Lydia turned to Emma. They pressed their cheeks together. "Good-bye, Emma," Lydia said. "We shall see you in a few weeks, if all goes well."

Emma was suddenly weeping. "Good-bye, dear Lydia. Will it surely be that long for you?"

"Yes. Father Steed is no better. Perhaps even worse. If we dare to leave now, it will surely kill him." She sighed. The Steeds had waged some verbal battles over this issue. "And he is determined to stay and help with the departures for as long as he is needed."

"And bless him for doing it. And Nathan too. Your family is such an inspiration to all of us." Emma drew a quick breath. "May God be with us both until we meet—"

She turned toward the door. A soft knock had sounded. "I'll get it," Julia said. She went to the door and opened it. "Oh, Sister Scott, good evening."

"Good evening, Julia. Is Sister Smith still—" And then she saw them. "Oh, hello, Sister Emma. And Sister Lydia, good evening."

Ann Scott was the sister of James Mulholland, who was Joseph Smith's personal secretary. She was a lovely young woman who had always been greatly concerned about Emma and her children.

"Come in, Ann."

She did so, and as Julia closed the door, Sister Scott came forward with some obvious anxiety on her face. She carried what looked like a simple pocket apron made of muslin, only it dragged heavily from her arm. "Here they are, Sister Emma. I have come as my brother instructed."

"Oh, thank you."

Looking more closely at the apron now, Lydia saw that the pockets were large and had been filled with something. Judging from the shape through the cloth, there was a book, or something similar, about a foot square and two or three inches thick in each pocket. The apron was heavy and quite bulky. The pockets had been sewn tightly shut around whatever they held.

Lydia understood immediately. When Joseph was arrested, Brother Mulholland had taken stewardship for many of Joseph's most important papers, including the only copy of the manuscript of his inspired translation of the Bible. When Far West fell, Mulholland had given the papers to his sister, hoping that the mob would be much less likely to search a woman.

Sister Scott stepped back as Emma took the apron and hefted it. "I can't tell you what a relief it is to give these over to your care," Sister Scott said. "I have not had a peaceful night's sleep since James gave them to me."

Emma examined the apron more closely, holding it up to the front of her now. Ann smiled at Lydia. "I designed it so you can tie it around your waist under your petticoats. It is hardly noticeable, especially with a full skirt."

"Thank you, Sister Ann," Emma said warmly. "How thoughtful and wise of you. Rest assured, when I leave tomorrow this shall be in place, and I shall care for these papers in the same conscientious manner that you have manifested while they were in your care." She reached out and took Sister Scott's hands. "I thank you in behalf of my husband, and in behalf of all the Church. Thank you."

"Are you sure, Caroline?" Joshua had stopped his work of tying down the canvas along the wagon box and was looking at her closely.

"Yes, Joshua. If I sit around here any longer with nothing to do, I shall go mad. Mrs. Samuelson is a wonderful woman, and both Olivia and Savannah adore her. They will be fine."

"And Will?"

"If Will goes to Savannah, which is the most likely thing, the Montagues will tell him the wonderful news about your being alive and will send him straight here. I think we will be back by then, but if not, then the Samuelsons will have him wait here with Livvy and Savannah until we return. If we get a letter from him, Mr. Samuelson will forward it to us. It will only take a few more days to reach us."

He stopped, watching her with admiration. "You have really thought this through, haven't you?"

She nodded, her eyes filled with gravity. "After what Nathan did for us, how can we not do this?" Her eyes took on a misty look. "And after the horrible things I said about the Mormons in that letter to your family . . ." She dropped her head. "I need to be there."

Joshua nodded. In his mind, there was no question about the necessity of what they were doing, although it raised some anxieties in his mind to be headed back to Far West. The Missourians thought he was dead, and he wanted it to stay that way. But they had to help his family. He had known that for over a week now. His main worry now was for Caroline and how she felt about leaving when there had still been no word of Will.

"If the thing with the marshall were still a question, I wouldn't go," she said.

"I know," he replied. "That's a great relief to me as well." Four days before, the marshall had come to their house. His news was good, though it did not solve everything. He reported that he had learned that a man by the name of Charlie Patterson, drunk to the point of indiscretion, had confided in some drinking friends that he and two Missourians had set up the robbery of a young lad with a purse full of money. Then something had gone wrong. The Missourians wanted to kill the boy, and Patterson had shot them while trying to stop it from happening. The marshall had gone after Charlie the day after he got that report, but evidently, upon sobering up, Charlie had realized that his loose tongue had put him in jeopardy, and he had fled the city. The upside of all that was that the marshall was satisfied now that Will had no blame in the matter, and he withdrew the warrant. The downside was, Patterson had given no clue as to what had happened to the boy after he saved his life.

Joshua tied the last knot, gave it a solid jerk, then turned to Caroline. "You ready, then?"

"Yes."

Joshua waved to the two men who would drive the second wagon and who were lolling around outside the livery barn. "All right," he called. "Let's move 'em out."

For nine bone-jarring, spirit-numbing, strength-sapping days, Emma Smith and her children, along with their neighbor Jonathan Holman and his family and Brother Stephen Markham, had made their way across the prairie. For the most part, the land was open and desolate. They would pass an occasional farmhouse or homesteader's cabin, but mostly it was just one vast expanse of rolling grassland, with thin strips of woodland along the creeks and rivers. Though they never saw one, at night they could hear the mournful howling of wolves off in the distance, or the eerie hooting of the great horned owl. When the nights were clear, the stars were beautiful, almost taking the breath away. But the clearest nights were also the coldest nights, and they preferred the overcast, even though it left the darkness so thick that one could barely move about with a light.

It brought back many memories for Emma, not all of them happy ones. It was almost exactly one year ago that she and Joseph, fleeing from Kirtland, had crossed this same stretch of country moving west. At the time, that journey had seemed impossible to bear. She had been five months pregnant with Alexander. But now this trip seemed no better. Alexander was eight months old. Frederick was just two and a half and could not understand the cold and the hunger and the jarring ride; he cried or whimpered almost constantly. Young Joseph the Third, a little over six, and Julia, a year and a half older, found it difficult but were taking it bravely.

There had been enough Mormons moving eastward now—literally hundreds of wagons—that the road had been churned into an endless morass of ruts and mud holes. Even in summer such ruts and holes would have been considered mankillers, but they were made worse than that by the February weather, which had turned on the refugees as if it too were one of the mobocrats determined to have one last shot at the Mormons before they escaped. During the day the rain alternated between steady drizzle and driving downpours. Half a dozen times a day the wagons would bog down. With backs bent and muscles straining until the veins bulged out on foreheads and arms, everyone would have to lend a hand to help the horses free the wagons again.

And as if that weren't bad enough, on the sixth day the temperature plummeted. The rain turned to sleet and snow that slashed in horizontally and felt like it would flay the skin off both man and beast. At nights, the roads froze into concrete ruts, and the following days the ride became so rough that it was almost impossible to stay seated. Clothing damp from dragging across muddy ground or through the endless puddles now froze stiff as boards. The children huddled around the meager fires, crying piteously either from hunger or from the cold.

It was late in the afternoon of February fifteenth, the ninth day of the journey, when the two wagons crested a low bluff. There below them were the river bottoms, a mile-wide tangle of marshes and high underbrush, with the silvery stripe of the Mississippi River snaking down the center of it. Sitting on the wagon seat beside Stephen Markham, holding Alexander in her arms, Emma shot to her feet. "Look, children," she cried. "We're here."

Stephen Markham stared down at the scene below them. From this perspective they could clearly see Quincy, Illinois, on the far side. That was their destination. It was a town of some means, with straight streets coming down to the river, and houses going all the way back to the low bluffs on the other side. His eyes began to pick out details. Streamers of smoke were wafting slowly upward from dozens of chimneys and open fires. There was the dock where the riverboats pulled in, though there were no boats now. Just to the north, where the houses petered out, he could see the thin line of the ferry rope that crossed the river. Squinting, he could make out the flat-bottomed ferryboat, pulled up on the shore on the far side.

And then he understood. There were no riverboats. There were no smaller craft—canoes, flatboats, rowboats—shuttling back and forth. The ferryboat was beached. And he didn't have to ask why. With the low sunlight on it, the river looked like a painting. It was not alive; it was not moving. There was no current, no muddy water swirling logs or debris in lazy circles.

And that also explained why, below them on this side, camped among the heavy undergrowth, there were dozens of wagons and tents and lean-tos and open camps. The Mormons who had gotten there before them were stopped, jammed up against the river like an army of ants run up against an obstacle that thwarted their onward progress.

"Is that Quincy, Mama?" Joseph was crying excitedly. "Is that where we're going to stay?"

"Yes, Joseph," Emma said, half laughing. "We're here. We'll cross the river and be there by nightfall."

Stephen Markham reached out and touched Emma's skirt. She looked down at him, her face radiant. Then she saw his eyes. "What? What is it, Brother Markham?"

He turned to stare. "Look at the river, Sister Emma," he said in a low voice, the discouragement so heavy it almost left him unable to speak. "We won't be crossing today. It's frozen solid."

"I'm going across," Emma said. "I will not have my children spend one more night out in the open."

Brother Markham blew out his breath, knowing that his words were going to make no difference but feeling compelled to say them anyway. They had come down to the camp where the Mormons waited. There had been a quick flurry of excitement to know that Emma had arrived, but the Saints also told them what Markham had already surmised. With the river frozen, the ferry hadn't run for two days. This morning, after the cold of the night, when the ice was the hardest, some wagons had started across. But the ice had groaned and creaked. Several had made it, but with the warming of the day, no one else would risk it. A few families, those with wagons furnished by the Committee on Removal, had emptied their belongings and carried them across on foot, leaving the wagons to return west for another load of exiles.

Markham looked at Emma. "You've heard what everyone is saying, Sister Emma. The ice isn't that thick. They don't think it will carry the weight of a loaded wagon now."

Emma shook her head, too weary to meet his gaze for more than a moment. "Then we'll not take it over fully loaded."

"But—"

"We'll unhitch the horses and put them in single file. One can pull the wagon if we're not in it. That way, the weight will be more evenly spread out. You can walk in front, leading the horse. That will help even more."

"But what about you and the children?"

Emma stepped to the edge of the river and tentatively moved onto the ice. She walked out about five feet, then stamped her foot down solidly. It thumped ominously, like hitting a hollow log with a stick. She looked at Stephen Markham, fighting hard now to keep any quaver from her voice. "I'll take the children and go first."

Markham started to say something, then thought better of it. He turned to Brother Holman and gave him a questioning look. Holman glanced briefly at his wife. She looked pale and frightened, and she shook her head quickly. Her husband turned back to Markham. "We have a much heavier load in our wagon than you. And there's no way we can carry it all across on our own. I think we'll wait here until it either breaks up or freezes more solidly."

Emma came back to the bank. She went to her neighbor and took his hand. "I understand, Brother Holman. Thank you for all you've done to help. We shall never forget it."

"Please, Emma—," Sister Holman started to say. But Emma quickly turned and smiled at her. "We are very much lighter than you. We shall be all right." She reached out and touched Sister Holman's shoulder briefly. "We'll see you when you come over."

Stephen Markham gave Holman a beseeching look. What would Joseph say if something should happen? But then he finally shrugged his shoulders. Emma was unbendable. Emma was emotionally and physically drained. She was going on pure willpower now. At this point no reasoning with her was going to make a difference.

"All right," he sighed, "give me a moment to get the horses ready." He gave her a stern look. "But if we hear one creak, one tiny cracking sound, we turn back. Agreed?"

Emma turned and looked east. This was the narrowest part along this stretch of the river, but it was still a good hundred yards or so of sheet ice they had to cross. Finally she nodded. "Agreed."

Markham worked swiftly now, determined to be done with it as quickly as possible. He unhitched the one horse and tied it to the back of the wagon with a fifteen-foot length of rope, then redid the harnessing so that the other one would pull the wagon. Finally, he led them down to where Emma stood waiting. "All right, I'm ready."

She took a quick breath. Julia was holding the baby and watching her mother anxiously. Emma reached down to her waist. Gripping through the skirts, she adjusted the apron with the manuscripts, making sure it was riding comfortably. She looked at Markham, who wouldn't meet her gaze, then let out her breath. Her heart was pounding and she felt a little dizzy.

"Mama?"

"It's all right, Julia. Give me the baby." She took Alexander from Julia and tucked him firmly in her left arm. Going down into a crouch, she reached for little Frederick. "Put your arms around Mama's neck, Frederick," she said in a trembling voice.

He nodded gravely, his eyes seeming more like those of a man than those of a boy not yet three, but he did as he was told. Emma straightened with an effort. Frederick clamped his legs around her body as she put her other arm beneath him to help hold him up. "Hold on tight," she commanded. "No matter what, don't let go of Mama."

"I won't, Mama." He shut his eyes and squeezed against her all the more tightly.

Joseph Smith the Third was Emma's fourth born, but the first of her children to survive for more than a few hours after birth. At six, he was already taking on a strong resemblance to his father. Emma looked down at him. "Joseph, you're to take ahold of my skirts here." She bobbed her head downward to her left side. "You stay right with me. You must not let go either. No matter what."

"Yes, Mama," he said. He reached out, grabbed a handful of material, and clenched his fist tightly.

"Julia, you do the same, here on the other side."

Julia had already moved into position and did as she was told. Finally, Emma looked at Brother Markham. "All right. Let's go." She smiled briefly, and wanly, at the Holmans, then turned and stepped out onto the ice. There was no hesitation now. She planted her feet carefully on the slippery surface so as not to fall, but moved steadily out and away from the bank. Little Frederick gave a slight whimper, and Emma saw that Julia's eyes were tightly closed. She could feel the girl's hands trembling through her skirts.

"It's all right," Emma said soothingly. "The ice is strong." She forced a light laugh. "It's like having our own great big ice-skating pond."

Brother Markham gave her about a twenty-yard head start, then tugged on the reins of the lead horse. "Giddyap, horse," he clucked. "Let's go."

"Go with God," Brother Holman called softly, standing rigid, holding his breath as he watched them move out into the full expanse of the river. From where he was, the hundred yards across looked like two miles.

"Don't look down, Joseph!" Emma cried in alarm. She was watching carefully where she placed each foot. Suddenly there was a patch where the ice was not clouded. She could see the muddy water moving slowly beneath it. A dizzying wave of vertigo swept over her, leaving her reeling.

"Mama, I'm scared."

Emma realized her mistake. "It's all right, Joseph." She smiled down at him, wanting to reach out and touch his hair, or lay a hand on his shoulder to steady him, but she had no hand free. She forced her mind away from what lay beneath her, what swirled beneath a thin sheet of flooring that could give way any moment. Her arms were starting to ache, and Frederick was clutching to her neck with such desperation, she could feel him pinching a nerve.

"Look," she said, as much for herself as for the children. "Look across the river. See where we're going? We're getting closer now. It won't be—oh!" Her foot had slipped on the ice and she jerked forward. Frederick squealed and Julia gasped. Emma caught her balance quickly. "I'm all right, I'm all right," she cried.

"Steady," Markham called from behind her. "Don't rush it."

They were halfway across now, right in the middle of the river where the water would be the deepest and the current the swiftest. The thought made her stomach turn over with a lurch. *Stop it, Emma! Stop it this instant!* She gripped Alexander more tightly and fixed her gaze on the houses on the opposite shore. "Look, Julia," she said in a forced voice. "Which of those houses do you think we'll stay in? Joseph, look at them! If you could choose any one as your house, which would it be?"

It worked. It worked for them and it worked for her. Even

Frederick opened his eyes and began to look for the houses that Julia and Joseph were calling out. Emma turned her head to glance back.

"I'm coming," Markham said. "It's going to be all right, Emma. We're going to make it."

But Emma wasn't sure. The weight of the manuscripts dragged at her waist. The arm with which she held little Alexander was on fire and starting to cramp. Frederick's arms around her neck felt like a blacksmith's vice squeezing tighter and tighter. Her knees felt like they were turning to water, and she was terrified now that she would collapse. Then the wagon and the horses and Markham would catch up with her, bringing all the weight together in one place. In her mind, she could hear the ice begin to crack beneath them, then give way with a sickening drop into the icy black chillness below.

She closed her eyes, staggering on blindly. *Oh please, dear God. Give me strength. Let me get my children to safety.*

Her eyes jerked open and she realized Joseph was tugging on her skirts. "Mama! Mama! We're almost there. Can I go ahead?"

She looked up. They were no more than ten or fifteen yards from shore. They had made it! She nodded weakly. "Yes, Joseph, you may go."

Julia released her grip too. Taking each other's hands, squealing and shouting with delight, the two children darted across the last stretch of ice and onto the land. They began doing a little jig, hopping and waving their arms.

With a great sob of joy and release, Emma set foot upon the shore. She went no more than two or three feet, then sank down to the frozen ground. Frederick released his grip, jumped off her lap, and ran to join his brother and sister, yelling lustily.

Now Markham was off the ice. He ran up the shallow bank, clucking at the horse, not letting the wagon wheels catch on the little rise where the ground met the water. Then in a moment he was at Emma's side. He too sank down to sit beside her. His face was pale, and he was breathing deeply. "We made it," he whispered.

Emma turned and looked down, pulling the blanket back from the face of her baby. Alexander had slept through the whole thing. Tears sprang to her eyes as she lifted her head and looked back across the river. Two small figures, the Holmans, stood there, waving their arms back and forth. A faint shout floated over to them. And then Emma looked up into the sky. "Yes," she said, half laughing, half crying, "we did, didn't we?"

On Sunday evening, February seventeenth, the Steeds gathered to Benjamin and Mary Ann's cabin, as was their custom. Of late there had been no large dinners, no apple pie and cold milk, but the tradition of gathering together carried on, and the warmth around the family circle had dimmed not at all. The babies were in bed now, but all the others were gathered for a family council. Even the smallest children were sitting on their parents' laps or at their feet. There was not much mirth on this night. Conditions were growing increasingly grim in Far West. Food was in short supply. There was no midday meal any longer, only a meager breakfast and a slightly more substantial dinner. Firewood was so scarce that they had started to use the logs from the walls of the toolshed. The smokehouse would be next. Their enemies, not satisfied with the hundreds of families that had already left, were becoming more and more brazen. It was time to make some decisions.

Rebecca sat beside Derek, listening but not saying much. From time to time she would look at Jessica, and something would pass between them. Finally, in a moment when the conversation lulled a little, Rebecca cleared her throat. One hand rose tentatively in the air to get their attention. "I have something I would like to say."

They all turned. Derek looked a little surprised.

"Yes?" Benjamin said.

"Mary Smith is leaving tomorrow."

Jessica nodded, but the others were a little shocked.

"Already?" Mary Ann blurted. "But she hasn't recovered

from her trip to Liberty to see Hyrum. I thought you said she was still in bed."

"She is," said Rebecca. "But she is the last of the First Presidency's families. The brethren feel strongly that she needs to leave immediately, just as Emma and Sister Rigdon did. She and Mercy have found two lumber wagons. They have made a bed for Mary and the baby in the back of one."

Sister McIntire leaned over closer to Mary Ann. "Who is Mercy?"

"Mercy is Mary's sister. Her husband was at the Battle of Crooked River back in October and had to flee for his life. So both women are without their men. Mercy has been wonderful to Mary. Mercy had a baby about five months old when little Joseph was born, so she has been nursing both babies all this time."

"Whew!" Derek exclaimed. "Between Mary's family and Mercy's baby— that's what, nine people? That's a lot. And with no man."

Now Jessica jumped in. "Amanda Smith is leaving in a few days."

Lydia and Derek spun around together. "But how can she?"

Jessica shrugged. "She has her own wagon. There's nothing here to keep her. She's decided to go now, maybe travel with Mercy and Mary."

Now Matthew was calculating. "So you add another woman and four children? How can they do that alone?"

Mary Ann was watching Jessica closely, her eyes wide with understanding. "No, you add two women and eight children."

Jessica jerked up.

"Am I right?" Mary Ann asked. "You want to go too, don't you?"

Jessica's head bobbed, and she colored deeply. She should have known Mary Ann would see it first. "Yes, I would like to go with Amanda."

"But—," Benjamin started, then he stopped. "I see," was all he said.

Jessica plunged in. She and Rebecca had rehearsed the whole thing, trying out their arguments on each other. "We've got to do something. We have too many people to feed here. The food is running out even more quickly than time is running out. We have too many people to move all at once. We can't keep waiting."

Rebecca jumped in to support her. "Matthew's right. They can't do it alone. Especially . . ." Her voice betrayed her and she faltered suddenly. She sniffed and raised her chin even higher. "Especially if Amanda and Jessica travel with them. So I have a proposal."

Now Derek finally understood. "You want me to go with them?" he asked in wonder.

Rebecca turned slowly and looked down at him. "Yes, you and Matthew." As there was the sharp intake of breath behind her, she raised her hands. "Now, listen. Hear me out." She didn't have to ask. There wasn't a sound in the room now. "Papa is too sick to go right now. But some of us need to go. Now, before it's too late for us. So Matthew and Derek could go with this group, then come back. By then Papa could be better. Then we'll still have our men with us to help when we go."

Nathan stood up. He had no knowledge of this, but the logic was compelling. "Rebecca's right. Our hopes now lie in getting to Illinois, where there is more food and shelter and where our enemies are not breathing down our necks."

Jessica thought she knew what he was going to say next, so she cut him off. "Nathan's been gone from his family enough already. He should stay and help with the preparations here. We'll send Amanda's wagon back, and that will give you a better chance of getting out of here."

Benjamin held up his hand, cutting off any further discussion. He turned to Derek. There was no need to speak; the question was in his eyes. Derek looked up at Rebecca and immediately nodded. "Of course I'll go. It makes sense. That way, when Matthew and I get back, we'll only have Nathan and Lydia's children. The rest of us will be older. It will—"

Again Benjamin's hand had come up, signalling that not

everything had to be said in full. Now he turned to Matthew. Matthew was nodding vigorously before Benjamin could even ask the question. "Yes, I'll go."

In the corner, Jenny shot to her feet. "So will I," she blurted.

Everyone spun around in surprise, no one more shocked than her mother. Jenny blushed deeply, which set the freckles off like rocks on a hillside. But she didn't back down. "How many children?" she demanded.

Lydia was half smiling, liking the spunk in this young Irish girl who was fast becoming a woman, liking the way she looked at Matthew with those sky-blue eyes and the way Matthew turned inside out when she did so. "I count four each for Jessica and Amanda," Lydia said, "six of Mary Smith's, counting the baby, and one baby for Mercy. That's . . ." She added quickly, but Jenny was quicker.

"That's fifteen children," Jenny said firmly, "two of whom are babies. And Sister Mary Smith isn't going to be able to help at all, not as sick as she is, and Mercy will be nursing and caring for two babies, and—"

Twelve-year-old Kathryn leaped up to stand beside her sister. "And if Jenny and I were along it would leave Derek and Matthew free to drive the wagons and care for the stock and—"

Jenny had whirled, her face flashing surprise and irritation, but instantly she saw the wisdom of it, and grabbed Kathryn's hand. "That's right. There'd be two of us to help." She turned to her mother, who looked as if she were reeling. "Oh, Mama, that would be two less mouths to feed here. Kathryn and I could stay in Quincy and help keep house and watch the children while Matthew and Derek come back for you."

Sister McIntire threw up her hands. "Hold on, lass. I'm drowning in your words. Give me a moment to catch my breath, please."

Jenny blushed even more deeply and stole a quick glance at Matthew. He was staring at her in wonder, but there was no mistaking the admiration in his eyes.

Then, shocking almost everyone, Benjamin turned slowly to

face the woman who had left her home because of the Book of Mormon and come to throw her lot in with the Saints. "There is some wisdom in what your daughter is saying," he mused. "What do you think of the proposition, Sister McIntire?"

She sat back, her eyes searching those of her two daughters. Kathryn nodded, her dark hair dancing as her head bobbed up and down. "Oh, please, Mama. We'll be all right."

Nancy McIntire turned slowly to Matthew. "Would you look after my daughters, Matthew? So I'd not have to be a-worrying overly much about them?"

"Aye," Matthew said soberly.

Derek leaned forward. "And I as well," he said. Then a smile stole across his face. "Though I'd probably have to spend most of my time watching out for Kathryn and leave the task of minding Jennifer pretty much to others on the journey."

Emily, Lydia's six-year-old, was staring up at her uncle. "Look!" she cried. "Matthew's embarrassed."

That broke the tension and everyone in the room laughed. "Come on, Emmy," Nathan chuckled, "leave Uncle Matthew alone. He's having a hard time of it right now."

As the laughter subsided, Benjamin turned and looked at his wife. "Mother? What do you think?"

Mary Ann held his gaze for a moment. Then she let her eyes go around the room, taking in Matthew and Jenny, Rebecca, Jessica, Derek. Finally she bobbed her head up and down slowly. "I think we don't have a lot of choices anymore."

Benjamin nodded back at her. "I agree." Then he looked to Derek. "I think you should try to be ready to leave day after tomorrow."

Chapter Notes

The delaying of the departure of the Prophet's mother and father is told by Lucy Mack Smith. They were able to leave a short time later, traveling with Don Carlos and with the Salisbury and the McCleary families (the families of Lucy's two married daughters, Catherine and Sophronia), and arrived safely in Quincy sometime before the first of March. (See *Mack Hist.*, pp. 294–97.)

Emma and Mary Fielding Smith did make a trip to Liberty Jail to see their husbands. Mary was still deathly ill, but felt compelled to try to see Hyrum before leaving the state. (See *MFS*, pp. 82–83.)

Emma's taking of the manuscripts and her incredible crossing of the Mississippi are presented in the novel virtually as they happened, though specific conversations and personal thoughts are the additions of the author (see Richard Neitzel Holzapfel and Jeni Broberg Holzapfel, *Women of Nauvoo* [Salt Lake City: Bookcraft, 1992], p. 10; *CHFT*, p. 213).

Mary Fielding Smith and Mercy Fielding Thompson did leave Far West as described here, as did Amanda Smith. Having them travel together and with the Steeds is the author's device. (See *MFS*, pp. 89–94.)

Chapter Thirty-Four

In the little party moving eastward across the bleakness of Missouri's northern plains, there were twenty-three people—two men, six women or older girls, and fifteen children, ranging in age from Amanda's Willard Smith, who would be twelve in May, down to Hyrum and Mary's little Joseph Fielding Smith, just barely three months old.

The weather was still cold, uncommonly so from what the old settlers were saying. The party had left Far West in a steady rain. Then about one o'clock, as they could see the tree line of Shoal Creek and the now deserted cabins of Haun's Mill off in the distance, the wind shifted around to the north, the temperature plummeted, and the rain turned first to sleet, then to a heavy snowstorm.

There were only three wagons, so all except the youngest children took turns walking beside the wagons. Of the three wagons, only one had been designed for moving people and goods. Amanda Smith's wagon had been purchased by her husband in Kirtland for the move to Missouri in the spring of 1838. It was not a large wagon. The box was no more than about eight feet long and four feet wide. Amanda's two little girls, Jessica's two youngest boys, and Jessica's baby, John Benjamin, would sleep in the wagon. The rest would make their bed beneath it.

The other two wagons had been designed as lumber wagons. Their wagon boxes were slightly wider and more than two feet longer than those found on normal wagons. This gave more room, but there were no springs and so the ride was considerably rougher in these wagons than in Amanda's. The first of these two wagons carried most of the goods that the two Fielding sisters had been able to bring. Those were shoved to the front, leaving room at the back for a bed for Mary and her baby. The second wagon carried Mary's other five children and Mercy and her baby, as well as the food and water for the trip. These two wagons had not been built with covers, so the families had had to find their own. But the canvas they had located was lightweight, and within an hour of their departure the rain was dripping through, wetting the blankets and other things inside. So in that sense, the snow was a blessing.

The snow also turned the prairie into something beautiful. The muddy wasteland quickly took on a mantle of white, and the sound of the wagon wheels grew muffled as the snow became an inch deep, then two, then four inches by late afternoon.

Jenny McIntire was out in front of the little train, walking along to scout the road. With the snow and the drop in temperature, the puddles were starting to freeze and cover over with snow. Her task was to spot the worst of the potholes and steer the party around them so that they didn't bog down and have to stop.

Derek was driving the lead wagon, the one with Mary Smith in the back. Kathryn McIntire sat on the wagon seat beside him.

Next came Amanda's wagon. She and Jessica sat together

on the seat, with Amanda driving. Willard Smith, Amanda's oldest, and Rachel, Jessica's oldest, slogged steadily alongside, their heads down, Willard's hat and Rachel's bonnet covered with white, making them look like angels who had lost something in the clouds and were peering downward trying to find it.

Matthew drove the third wagon with Mercy Thompson and Mary's other children. Like Willard and Rachel, Lovina, the oldest from Hyrum's first marriage, walked alongside. So did her aunt. Mercy's baby was sleeping at the moment, inside with the other children, and so Mercy had decided to lighten the load. At this point, not yet one full day out, the children were still in good spirits. They were cold, but they were playing some game inside the wagon, giggling softly so as not to wake the baby.

It was eerie in a way. There was no wind, and so the snow came straight down. The only sound was that of the wagons creaking along and the soft clopping of the horses' hooves. There were no other signs of life. They had passed some homesteads, abandoned now by their Mormon owners, but nothing moved. It was just one great, vast world of white silence, and they were momentary specks of blackness traversing their way slowly across it.

It was about a quarter to five and growing dark rapidly when Derek leaned forward, peering ahead through the falling snow. Ahead, barely discernible, he thought he saw a darker line against the whiteness. He raised a hand.

"Whoa!" he called, pulling on the reins. Behind him, the other two wagons pulled up too.

"What is it?" Matthew called forward.

"I think that's Tenny's Grove."

"What?" Jenny came back to the wagon, shielding her face from the falling flakes.

Derek pointed forward. "I'm pretty sure that's Tenny's Grove. That's our first stopping place." He turned and he shouted back. "We're almost there."

Amanda had stood up when the wagon stopped, trying to see beyond the lead wagon. When she heard Derek's call, she nodded and sank back down beside Jessica. Both of them were soaked through—coats, bonnets, shawls, dresses—and were totally miserable. Amanda looked over at Jessica. "I hope so," she muttered. Then she shook her head. "One day down," she said grimly.

As they pulled in under the trees, Derek saw that they weren't the only occupants of the grove. A horse, still tied to a small cart that was loaded and covered with a bedsheet, stood with its head down. Its legs were little more than sticks, and its sides looked like a half-finished barrel with the staves showing through. It didn't even lift its head as the wagons pulled in.

Three small children, the oldest no more than six or seven, stood around the cart. A man knelt on the ground nearby, trying to strike a fire but without success. Even here under the trees, which were nothing more than stripped, leafless branches mostly open to the sky, the ground was snow-covered. Any wood was long ago soaked through.

At the sound of the wagons, the man looked up, then jumped up. He strode quickly over to Derek. "Now, you're a welcome sight," he said, obviously greatly relieved. He stuck out his hand. "I'm Brother Eli Barton."

"Derek Ingalls," Derek said, shaking his hand. He waved a hand over his shoulders. "And a whole bunch of others." A movement caught his eye and he turned. A woman came out of the trees. She was dragging branches she had stripped off some of the underbrush. Her dress was soaked, and her hands were red and shaking. Her face was pale, and she looked to be on the verge of collapse.

Barton went to her, taking one elbow and steadying her. "This is my wife, Betsy."

Matthew got down, and he and Jenny came forward. Derek introduced them. Then Amanda and Jessica and Willard and

Rachel joined them. He introduced them as well. Derek glanced around. Mercy was checking on her own and Mary's family.

Jessica was watching Sister Barton. When the latter swayed slightly, Jessica jumped forward. "Here, let us help you."

Sister Barton surrendered the branches without protest, looking grateful. "Our little cart is not big enough even for my children to sleep in. I was hoping to find enough branches to get them off the wet ground."

"Are you traveling alone?" Derek asked.

Barton nodded, and his wife murmured a quick, "Yes." Derek fought to keep his face impassive. No wonder they were relieved to see someone! This close to Far West there were still plenty of the mob element out looking for Mormons to harass, especially any traveling in small parties.

"Bring your children to our wagon," Amanda said. "Let them get out of the snow for a while. You come too."

Eli Barton pushed his wife forward gently. "You go, Betsy. I'll bring the children." His eyes dropped to the wet stick he held. He let it slide out of his hands. "There'll be no fires tonight," he said glumly.

Derek nodded. He had come to that conclusion about three hours before.

As they turned toward the children, Barton looked beseechingly at Derek. "You wouldn't have any grease with you, would you?"

Derek was surprised. "A little, for the wagon axles. Why?"

The man looked stricken. "We didn't have enough money for shoes for everybody." He looked away, shame heavy in his eyes. "I barely had enough to buy two wagon wheels and enough lumber to make that small cart. There was nothing left after that."

Derek cocked his head slightly. Shoes? What did that have to do with building a cart or needing axle grease? Then, like a bolt, it hit him. His eyes jerked to where the children stood by the cart. Of the three, only the oldest, a boy, had shoes, and they were worn and scuffed and now wet from the snow. The other two did not; they wore heavy socks—two pair, Derek saw, as he looked closer. But surely they had not had to—

He glanced at the cart. There was no wagon seat. You didn't ride this cart; you led the horse that pulled it. His eyes moved backward. Underneath the sheet that they were using for a covering, Derek could see that the cart was filled. The wife had said there was no room for the children to sleep in it. As he looked at it, he doubted there was any room for the children to ride. Maybe one, stuck on the very back. But not three. And not a wife.

Next to him, Jenny drew in her breath sharply. "Oh!" she cried softly.

Derek looked away from the cart. The youngest child, a beautiful little four-year-old girl with long blond hair and large gray eyes that seemed to hold the sorrow of the world behind them, had started toward her father. She was holding out her hands, whimpering softly and hobbling painfully as she took two or three steps. But Derek's eyes had leaped to what Jenny had seen, and what he saw there made his stomach drop in a sickening lurch. Where the stocking feet had been planted in the snow, there were two large, round crimson stains.

Jenny was to her in an instant and swept her up in her arms. "Oh, you poor thing!" she cried. She pulled the girl in tight against her, burying her face in her hair. "You poor little girl."

The second boy—age five or six, Derek guessed—hadn't moved. He just lifted his arms toward his father. "Papa, help me," he implored.

His father moved to him and picked him up. He too left bloody imprints where he had been standing. Barton looked suddenly very old. "Betsy thinks if we could just grease their feet a little," he said faintly, "they might not crack so bad."

Derek swallowed hard, then nodded. "Yes," he said quickly, "we have plenty of grease."

Emma Smith went to the door fully expecting that it was another member of the Church with some request or another for help. In the week since she had arrived in Quincy, she had received a constant stream of people asking for help or advice, or wanting to know about family members still back in Far West, or sometimes simply coming by to let her know they had arrived safely in Illinois.

She opened the door. "Yes," she started to say. Then her eyes flew open and her jaw went slack. "Joshua? Joshua Steed?"

"Yes. Hello, Mrs. Smith."

He hopped back a little, making sure the crutch didn't slip off the edge of the porch. Caroline moved out from behind him. "Hello, Emma."

"We were originally planning to follow the road straight up the Missouri River from St. Louis to DeWitt, and from there to Far West. But then we heard that the exodus had already begun, and we didn't know if Father and the family had already left. We didn't want to miss them. They said everyone was coming to Quincy, so we decided to come here first, then move west across the trail."

Emma was nodding as Joshua spoke. "They haven't left yet. Or," she corrected herself, "they hadn't when I left."

"What day was that?" Caroline asked.

"We left on the seventh and got here on the fifteenth. But Lydia told me just the day before that your father was insistent on staying to make sure everyone got out."

Caroline's mouth softened into a sad smile as she looked at Joshua. "That's your father."

"But Nathan had arrived back home all right?" Joshua said.

"Oh, yes," Emma answered. "He got there a couple of weeks before I left." She glanced at the rough-hewn crutch that now lay on the floor at Joshua's feet. "Nathan told us everything. We're so happy that you found each other. I just know everything with your son will turn out all right."

When Joshua and Caroline just nodded, still finding too much pain to talk about it openly, Emma went on. "But this is an incredible coincidence. She never said anything about your coming. Did you have any idea you would be here at the same time?"

Joshua tipped his head, his eyes narrowing slightly. "She? Who is she?"

"Your sister."

Now both Joshua and Caroline shot forward. "My sister? You mean Rebecca?"

Emma's dark eyes widened. "No, Melissa."

Joshua rocked back, as stunned as if he had just been dropped from a cliff.

Emma's eyes widened even more. "You didn't know!" She clapped her hands. "What a wonderful surprise for you!"

"Melissa here?" He was reeling.

Emma laughed right out loud now. "Yes, she and her husband, Carl Rogers." She straightened as she remembered something. "But that's right. You never met Carl."

"No, I—"

"And they're here now?" Caroline asked. She too was totally flabbergasted.

"Yes," said Emma. "They arrived from Kirtland yesterday afternoon. Just like you. She said your mother had written and told them how bad things were in Missouri. So Carl suggested they do something to help."

Emma looked at Caroline. "Unless you know Carl, you don't know what a miracle that is. He doesn't think much of Mormons. But he's brought a wagonload of goods to take to your family. Just like you are doing."

Joshua scooped up his crutch and got to his feet, too excited to remain seated. "Do you know where she is?"

Emma's hand suddenly shot up to her throat. "Oh," she cried in dismay. "I totally forgot. They said they were going to try and cross the river this morning." Her hand fluttered downward. "Oh, dear. I don't know whether they made it or not. The ice is breaking up in the river, and sometimes the ferryman won't go out. I heard there were some who went over this morning, but only for a short time."

Joshua's mind was whirling. "Caroline, we'd better go. We'll have to get our wagons across the river too or we'll miss them. If they get a day's head start on us, we may never catch them." Then he remembered his manners. "Thank you, Emma. I'm sorry to be so abrupt, but we must hurry if we are to catch them."

"I understand." She stood now to face them. "Your family will be so thrilled to see you. The wagons and the supplies will be a godsend. Things are terrible in Far West."

Joshua barely heard her. "Melissa! After all these years. I can't believe it."

"Look, mister." The man was chewing on the wet stub of a cigar. He pulled it out of his mouth and pointed at the river with it. "I took my last trip across at noon. See them blocks of ice? This ain't no time to be trying to ferry wagons across. Come back in the morning and see if the river's froze solid enough to drive across."

"And if it's not?"

He shrugged, already losing interest. "Could be a day or two, could be a week."

Joshua reached in his jacket and pulled out his wallet. "Tell you what," he said briskly. "What if I buy your ferry?"

The man's head came up like that of a wolf catching scent of a wounded deer. He jammed the cigar butt back in his mouth, staring at the money Joshua was pulling out.

"'Course, that would leave a good man out of work, wouldn't it?" Joshua said. "So what say I just give you fifty dollars per wagon if you get me across in the next half hour. Then you can buy another ferry for yourself and become a rich man."

"A hundred dollars?" It came out as a hoarse croak.

"That's right. Best wages you'll ever see, I reckon." He

smiled at the look on the man's face. "I'm not playing with you, sir. I've got one hundred dollars cash money if you get us across now."

The man swung around. "Jacob!" he bawled. In a moment a young man, about fourteen or fifteen, stuck his head out of the hut built half into the riverbank behind them. "Get a pole, boy. One big enough to fend off them blocks of ice. We're going across."

Joshua walked back to where Caroline was standing with his two teamsters. She was shaking her head at him. "You're shameless."

He grinned at her. "I know." Then instantly he sobered. "This could be dangerous, Caroline. Maybe you'd better—"

She cut him off by striding past him toward the ferry. "I may keep my eyes shut all the way across," she called back over her shoulder, "but I'm going. What about you?"

It was getting close to dark by the time Joshua got his two wagons across the river on the ferry and up to the makeshift camp in the river bottoms. He was stunned at the numbers there. It was as if a miniature city had sprung up overnight. There were dozens of wagons of every shape and size. Horses, mules, oxen, and an occasional pig filled the air with their whinnying and braying and lowing and grunting. The approach of the ferry with Joshua's wagons created a near stampede as dozens of mud-splattered, exhausted-looking men ran down to see if the ferryman would take a load going back the other way. He refused. And Joshua didn't blame him. The boy was amazing with his pole and shoved most of the great blocks of ice aside, but when he couldn't or didn't, they slammed into the ferry with a sickening thud that shook the wagons and set the horses to pawing nervously. With no load, the ferry would be better able to speed up or slow down as needed. But the ferryman left a lot of disappointed men behind as he took off again empty.

As the two wagons moved into the camp, every head turned

to stare. Children whispered to their mothers; men pointed and spoke in low voices to each other. And then Joshua began to understand. It was not just that they were headed in the opposite direction of all these people. It was also the appearance of their wagons; the fineness of the two matched teams that pulled them; the fact that neither the horses nor the people had the gaunt, haunted look of the hungry. But perhaps more than anything it was the expensive cut and the absolute cleanliness of Caroline's dress.

It was all Caroline could do to keep from weeping. The children, most of all, nearly broke her heart. Filthy little waifs, often with tattered clothing and shoeless feet. But the women wrenched at her too—huddled around tiny, smokey fires, their dresses mud-stained up to their knees or higher, smoke and dirt and wagon grease on hands and arms and faces. She saw half-full pots of watery stew that would have to fill six or eight or ten empty stomachs. She saw blankets, wet and dirty, laid out on the ground and realized that this was where someone had slept the night before. Men had that grim weariness about them that comes from weeks of exhausting labor or endless strain or both.

Joshua asked three different people if they knew the whereabouts of a family named Rogers. In every case there was a blank look and a quick shake of the head. Then Caroline had an idea. The next time they stopped a man, she asked a different question. "Have you seen another wagon like ours come across today?" That brought an instant response. There weren't many wagons that were in that kind of condition and that were headed west. He pointed up the hill toward the edge of the camp. "They're up there," he said.

They found it immediately. The wagon had seen a lot of trail miles, but the canvas was heavy and well kept, and the horses were fat and strong and well curried. Joshua pulled in behind it, and motioned for his other drivers to do the same. As Joshua swung down, a man stepped from around his horses. His eyes were curious, but veiled and reserved. "Yes?"

"Carl Rogers?" Joshua asked, stepping forward.

There was a flicker of surprise. "Yes."

Joshua felt a rush of exultation. "Married to a Miss Melissa Steed?"

Carl was openly surprised now. "Yes."

There was a movement inside the wagon. The low sun was behind the wagon, and Joshua could see a dark shadow pass in front of it. Then a woman's head came out from behind the canvas. She didn't see Joshua because she was looking at her husband. "Carl, what is it?"

"Melissa?"

She leaned farther out and looked around to see who had spoken. "Yes?"

Joshua laughed in delight and moved right up beneath her. "Hello."

She came outside completely now, standing behind the wagon seat, looking somewhat puzzled and half-embarrassed that she did not know this man who obviously knew her.

She has gained weight, Joshua thought. *Nicely though. From having babies*, he guessed. Her hair was shorter now too, and pulled back. And her face was definitely older, more mature. A woman's face and not the girl's he remembered. Altogether it made her into a very handsome woman.

She was perplexed, peering down at him. "I—"

"Would you look at you?" he breathed. "You always were beautiful, but now?"

She blushed deeply. "I beg your pardon?"

Carl had visibly started at Joshua's boldness and moved toward him, half concerned, half angry. And then Joshua swept his hat off and turned his face full into the sun. "It's only been twelve years, Melissa. Surely you haven't forgotten me."

There was a shocked look, instantaneously followed by one of pure joy. "Joshua!" she screamed. She grabbed the small railing on the wagon seat and launched herself at him. Startled, he dropped the crutch and jerked up his arms to catch her. Down they went in a heap. "Joshua! Joshua!" she squealed, throwing her arms around his neck and squeezing him fiercely.

Suddenly she rolled away, jumping up. "Oh, I'm sorry," she cried. "I forgot about your leg."

Joshua hobbled to his feet, grinning widely. "You always were the impetuous one."

She stared at him for a moment, then came at him again, this time more carefully, throwing a bear hug around him and burying her face against his chest. "Oh, Joshua, I can't believe it."

Joshua saw Carl Rogers's face over Melissa's head. He was watching his wife, smiling faintly and yet hardly what anyone would call ecstatic. Joshua reached down and took Melissa by the shoulders. "Melissa, it is time for introductions." He turned her around. "I would like you to meet my wife, Caroline."

Caroline came forward and she and Melissa embraced, kissing each other on the cheek. "I'm so thrilled to meet you," Caroline said. "Joshua has talked about his favorite sister for so long."

Melissa touched Joshua's shoulder playfully. "I'll bet you never said that." Then before he could answer, she looked to her husband. "And Joshua and Caroline, I would like you to meet my husband, Carl Rogers."

Now the smile warmed a little, and Joshua could sense that the previous reserve was not any kind of resentment or reluctance but simply part of the man's nature. They shook hands firmly. "Carl, we are very glad to meet you. And no matter what Melissa thinks," he said with a wink, "you are married to my very favorite sister."

Melissa laughed happily and slipped her arm through Joshua's. "You haven't changed a bit."

"More than you think," Joshua exclaimed. "So come. Let's sit down. We have a lot of talking to do."

Melissa pulled away. "Oh no, not yet. We're not finished."

"Finished?"

"With the introductions." She slipped away from him and darted to the wagon. Joshua gave Carl a quizzical look, but Carl just smiled. Joshua turned the same look on Caroline, but she just shrugged. Then in a moment they understood. Melissa climbed back out of the wagon. In her arms she cradled a blanket and something inside it. Carl stepped quickly and helped her down again. As Joshua and Caroline moved to join them, Melissa pulled back the blanket. "Sarah Rogers, I'd like you to meet the handsomest uncle you'll ever have. Joshua, Caroline, this is Sarah. She's on her way to meet her Grandma and Grandpa Steed."

"Did you get my letter?"

Melissa rocked back on the small bench, holding one knee in her hands. "Oh, yes. I was so thrilled. When mother's letter came telling me you had found the family again, I wept. Then to hear from you. Oh, Joshua. It's been so long. It's so good to see you." She sat up. "Did you get my answer?"

Joshua looked at Caroline, who shook her head. "No," she said, "but we've been gone from Independence since early November."

"Oh, that's why, then." Melissa turned to Carl. "When did I mail it?"

He shrugged. "October probably."

Joshua watched Carl. He was definitely a quiet man, content to listen while they chattered on. But Joshua thought he was going to like him. He treated Melissa with respect and consideration, and he positively beamed when he took Sarah and held her. There was a thousand questions Joshua wanted to ask his sister. His mother had told him about Carl's opposition to the Church and how Melissa had finally given in to keep peace. Was she still a Mormon, then? If so, had things in Kirtland settled down at all? According to Nathan, there had been talk by some Saints about going back to Ohio now. How would that set with the ones who had stayed behind? But he didn't dare say any of this, so he and Carl talked livery stables and horses and freighting. For now, it was good enough, and from the pleasure shining in Melissa's eyes, he could tell she was pleased with what was happening.

"Oh, I wish you had your other children with you," Caroline said. "Mother Steed talks about how she misses them and how adorable they are."

"I know," said Melissa. "But coming this far with a baby at this time of year was hard enough. We left the rest with Grandma and Grandpa Rogers."

A movement caught Melissa's eye and she turned her head. The two teamsters who had come with Joshua were behind the second wagon, having a smoke. That would raise some eyebrows in this camp, she thought with amusement. But seeing them reminded her of another question. "So both of your wagons are filled with goods for the family too?"

Joshua nodded. "Like you, we thought we'd do what we could to help." Then he turned to Carl. "This is a fine thing, your coming this far to do this for our family."

Carl shrugged, a little embarrassed. "It's family. You don't leave family when they need help."

Melissa looked at Carl, letting him see her pride in him. "And it was Carl's doing too. I was sick with worry, but I didn't know what to do. Then Carl suggested it all on his own."

Joshua was impressed. That said a great deal about the man. Maybe he had been bitter about the Mormons. Joshua had no trouble understanding that. But Kirtland to Far West was about eight hundred miles. And with a baby in the worst of the winter? Joshua could name more than one teamster who would have balked at the thought of that. Yes, he thought, Carl Rogers was earning some credit with Joshua Steed.

Joshua and Caroline walked along slowly. It was a beautiful night. Above their heads, the Milky Way was like some incredibly huge and beautiful diadem spread across the sky. The only other light came from the flickering campfires scattered around them or an occasional lantern still burning inside a wagon. With the sky cleared, it had turned very cold. Their breath hung in the air, dissipating only as they walked through it. There was five or six inches of snow, and the ground was slick. Joshua placed the tip of his crutch down with care lest it slip out from beneath his weight. Carl and Melissa had gone to bed, but Joshua was too excited to sleep. So when he said he was going to go for a walk, Caroline had come with him.

"What if we miss them, Joshua?"

"The family you mean?"

"Yes. What if they've left Far West already? It's been two weeks since Emma was there."

"We can't miss them. Carl said he wondered the same thing and asked around. The Mormons all come on the same trail, and that's the way we'll go. Even if they've left, we'll still meet them."

"Oh, good."

"In fact, it's really quite amazing. Carl learned that Brigham Young has established supply posts all along the way. They leave stuff there for those coming who have nothing. So I know they won't take another way."

"You like him, don't you?"

"Carl? Yes, I do. He's a good man."

"I know. Knowing how he feels about Mormons, and still he decides to do this. Coming here."

"I wonder if Melissa is still a Mormon."

Caroline nodded. "She told me she still reads the Book of Mormon and prays. There's no Mormon group there now that she meets with, but she still believes."

He turned and gave her a look of mild surprise. "She told you all that?"

There was a soft laugh. "Yes, silly. We talked a lot while you and Carl were seeing to the horses."

"You like her too, don't you?"

"Oh, yes," Caroline exclaimed. "She's everything you said and more. I feel like we've been friends for years and years."

Somehow that pleased Joshua more deeply than he expected it would. "Good," he said gruffly.

She stopped, turning to look up at him. The starlight caught in her eyes and flashed back at him. "I love your family, Joshua. All of them. Don't you know that?"

"Yes. And I'm glad."

"In fact . . ." Then she shook her head and turned away.

"In fact what?"

"Nothing."

"I hate it when you do that," he snapped, pretending anger. "Tell me."

"You'll laugh."

"No I won't."

"That or get angry."

"I won't!"

"Promise?"

"*Caroline!*"

"All right." She smiled up at him. "Remember, you promised."

He nodded. "I did. Now, what is it?"

As she took a quick breath, Joshua could sense her sudden nervousness. "Once Will comes back," she said, "how set are you on living in St. Louis?"

Joshua's chin came up. "What? That's where my business is. Where else would we live?"

"We lived in Independence and you had your business in St. Louis."

"What are you saying?"

Again there was the quick intake of breath, as though she were steeling herself. "I was just thinking. I still worry that someone from Jackson County will find out you're alive and living in St. Louis. We don't know where the Mormons will finally settle. Maybe here in Quincy, maybe somewhere else. But wherever it is, they're going to need food and building materials and supplies. I think a freight business might do very—"

"You want to move up here?"

"No," she said flatly, a little stung by the incredulous tone of his voice. "I want to live near your family. I want our children to have grandparents. I want them to sit around at night like they did at Far West, giggling with their cousins and running off to play games. I want to get to know my sisters-in-law, and my brothers-in-law. I want—"

He turned around abruptly. "We'd better be getting back," he said shortly. "It's late and we've got several long days ahead of us."

Her lips tightened, pressing together. *You promised you wouldn't get angry!* She nearly snapped it out at him, feeling a little betrayed. But then the wiser part of her nature took over. Patience had its own rewards. She slipped an arm through his as though there had been no conversation. "It was just a thought," she said pleasantly.

Chapter Thirty-Five

"Look, Melissa." Caroline had straightened from the campfire and was looking across the muddy track—now frozen as solid as rock—that separated them and the next campsite. The previous evening as they had talked, Caroline had let her eyes stray over there, watching the family prepare and eat their evening meal.

It was a large family, a husband and wife and five children. The thing that had first caught Caroline's eye was that the woman was pregnant—heavily so. She couldn't be very long from delivery. You could see it in the way she had to walk, holding her back or cushioning her stomach when she leaned over.

They were not wonderfully equipped, but Caroline could see that they were better off than many in the camp. The wagon looked sturdy. The horses were not the finest, but neither were they as pitiful as some she had seen. And she had seen that the family had enough to make a simple evening meal.

Caroline had felt guilty, knowing how much she and Joshua carried in their wagons, and had almost talked to Joshua about sharing it. But then she realized two things. There were far too many in this camp. Where would it stop? And wretched as their conditions were here, soon they would be across the river where they could find help. In Far West, from all reports, the conditions were worse, and from there Illinois was still two hundred miles and eight or nine days away.

"Melissa?"

Melissa poked her head out of the wagon. She had just finished feeding Sarah and had her wrapped tightly in a blanket and a small but heavy comforter. "Yes?"

"Look." Caroline motioned with her head toward the other camp.

Melissa did so, and then her eyes widened. "The wagon's gone."

"Yes. I thought I heard one go by late last night."

Melissa climbed down now and they stood together, half shielded by Melissa's wagon so that their staring wouldn't look quite so obvious. The place where the other family's wagon had stood the night before was empty, and the horses were gone as well. Near a dead log there were piles of furniture and goods, the obvious contents of the wagon. Next to where the wagon had stood there was now a low shelter. Stakes had been driven into the frozen ground, then long poles lashed to them with what looked like bed cords. Quilts and blankets had been hung around three sides, leaving one end open to the fire to catch some of the heat. Now the fire was crackling briskly. The woman was bending over it, stirring something in a big kettle that rested right in the flames. The oldest boy was beside his mother, watching her. The other four children sat in the front of their little shelter, holding their hands and feet out toward the fire.

"So that's what they were doing," Melissa said.

"What?"

"While you and Joshua were gone last night, Carl and I

heard hammering. It must have been them driving those stakes into the ground."

"But where is her husband? Where would he go in the middle of the night?"

Melissa shook her head. Caroline looked around. Joshua and Carl and the two teamsters had gone down toward the river, looking for men who could give them information about the conditions of the trail. Caroline couldn't see them returning, so she suddenly straightened. "I'll be back," she said, and turned and walked toward the other campsite.

"Good morning," Caroline said as she came up.

The woman turned around, a little surprised. "Oh, good morning."

"I . . ." Caroline felt suddenly awkward. She waved a hand back toward their wagons. "We're camped next to you."

"Yes. You're the ones headed west."

Caroline was surprised. "How did you know?"

The woman smiled. "Word gets around quickly in a place like this. What you are doing is wonderful. It will be a godsend to them."

Caroline nodded. Those were the same words Emma had used. "My husband has family there and . . ." She hesitated only for a moment. "I don't mean to pry, but where is your husband?"

The woman smiled again, but now it was not enough to hide the strain and worry showing on her face. "He left about midnight."

"But to go where?"

"You mean you didn't hear?"

"No, what?"

"One of the wagons that arrived last evening brought word from Far West. The militia has said that they are going to shoot every Mormon who isn't out of the city by April first."

Caroline was deeply shocked. "No!"

"Yes." It came out grim and determined. "We lived in a little settlement outside of Far West. We've seen what they can and will do. And what is worse, there are still many widows there.

And children." Her eyes were frightened and filled with concern.

"But if your people are leaving, surely that should satisfy them."

"It's not good enough. Not for some of them, anyway." She sighed. "So when we heard that, my husband and I discussed it and decided that he should immediately return to Far West with our wagon so that others can use it."

If Caroline was shocked before, she was stunned now. "He went back?"

The woman nodded. "We have been blessed to come this far as well as we have. We must help the others now."

"But you're not . . ." Caroline lifted her eyes and looked across the river to Quincy. "How will you get across the river? It could be days and days. You can't just stay out here like this."

The woman turned too, and her breath went out in a long, silent sigh. "I don't know yet," she said. "I just know Jonathan had to go back. He had to." And then that tiny spark of humor came back into her eyes. She turned and pointed at the newly erected shelter. "What queen ever had a finer bedroom than this? We slept very well, thank you."

Caroline shook her head, fighting her emotions. She didn't know what to do. Maybe Joshua and Carl could help the woman and her children across the river. But then she pushed that idea aside. If the report about the militia was really true, then it was important that they themselves get to Far West as quickly as possible to help Joshua and Melissa's family.

"We'll be all right," the woman said, grateful for the concern she saw on Caroline's face.

Caroline could not keep her eyes from dropping to the roundness of the woman's stomach. "How soon is your time?" she asked softly.

The woman looked down, and one hand lifted to rub her dress where it was tight against her body. "It could be any time now," she said.

"What will you do if it comes before you—"

Just then there was the crackle of footsteps in the snow from behind them, and a booming voice called out, "Sister Thomas!"

They both turned. "Yes," the woman called. "I'm over here."

A man was striding up the track from the direction of the river. As he came around a clump of undergrowth and saw them, he changed direction and came to join them.

"Good morning, Brother Wiswager." She turned. "This is . . ."

"Caroline Steed."

The woman smiled. "We're neighbors."

He nodded, giving Caroline only the briefest of glances. "Sister Thomas, I heard about your husband leaving."

"Yes, last night."

"Do you have a place to stay?"

She looked over her shoulder. "Only this."

"You're not to worry about a thing. Sister Wiswager and I have found a little hut across the river. It's not much, no more than twelve feet by twelve feet." He laughed shortly. "We have five children. You have five children. There'll be plenty of standing room for everybody."

Caroline watched them in amazement. As they began to talk about how they would get Sister Thomas and her family across the river, Caroline lifted a hand. "I've got to go," she murmured. "I wish you the best."

"Thank you," Sister Thomas said. "And may God speed you on your journey as well."

Joshua left Carl and the two men he had brought to drive his wagons. They were still asking questions about the trail, and Joshua decided to start back, since he moved a little more slowly than they did. The sky was still dazzlingly clear. The sun had been up for about half an hour now, and the snow glistened and sparkled. The rays were also rapidly taking the bite out of the cold. As he strode along as rapidly as he could, there was a commotion off to his right. He stopped, going up on the balls of his feet to see better. The noise was coming from the place on the riverbank near where the ferry landed, about ten rods from where he now was. There was a group of men there, maybe a dozen or so, clustered together. They were talking excitedly and pointing.

Curious, Joshua changed direction, moving as quickly as he could across the hard-packed snow. As he approached them, he saw again the awesome sight of the Mississippi River, now a vast sheet of ice a hundred yards wide that glistened in the sunlight. But it was not a smooth sheet. The great blocks of ice that had been such a threat to the ferry yesterday had been caught when the river froze. They were like discarded stones from some great building under construction, some mostly flat to the sheet ice, and others shoved up at sharp angles as if they were skyrockets about to launch.

And then amid the jumble, Joshua saw what it was the men were pointing at. About midway across the river he could see some figures silhouetted against the morning light—a man, a woman, several children. They were making their way across the ice, moving in and out around the upthrust blocks as though they were picking their way through a mountain pass.

"Who is that?" Joshua asked the nearest man.

The man glanced at Joshua. "It's the Hancock family. They're crossing the river."

"Oh." Joshua wasn't sure what all the excitement was about. He started to turn away.

"The locals say it's not strong enough, that once the sun hits it, it's going to break up."

"Oh!" Joshua swung back around, peering more closely now.

"I told them they ought to wait," one man said.

"You need two or three nights of hard cold before it's safe," said another, wagging his head.

That irked his neighbor. "That's why they went on foot. They didn't dare take a wagon across."

"They're out of food," the first man explained. "They can't just wait until the ferry starts running."

Joshua was only marginally aware of the comments around

him. He was staring at the small figures. At the rear, a boy, maybe eight or ten years old—it was hard to tell with the sun in back of them—was falling behind. He was having a hard time of it. He was trying to hurry, but staggered and slid like a drunken man. He went down on one knee, got up and tried to run, went bowlegged and then down again. Then Joshua raised a hand to shade his eyes, squinting into the sun. "The boy," he cried. "He's barefoot."

"That's right," someone answered. "Mosiah don't own no shoes."

Joshua couldn't believe his ears. Barefoot on that? In some places the ice was like a polished tabletop. In others it was as jagged as a saw blade. *Barefoot!* It was unthinkable.

Suddenly there was an ominous rumble. It was deep, low, as if the earth were groaning beneath their feet.

"Listen!" Whoever shouted it could have saved himself the effort. No one had to be told to be quiet. The rumble deepened; then there was a sharp crack, like a rifle shot. In the center of the river, about twenty yards behind the boy, a shaft of ice four feet long shot upwards from the smoothness of the surface. Right behind it a dark line opened up, revealing muddy water sliding below it.

"It's breaking up!" someone yelled.

But the family had heard it too. There were screams and shouts and they were scrambling madly across the ice now. The father turned. His son had started to dart forward, but his feet had gone out from under him and he slammed to the ice. Now he was up again, screaming, reaching for his father as he tried to get some grip with his feet.

There was a horrible shrieking noise, like a woman in travail. A fifty-foot crack in the ice opened up, more swiftly than a man could run. The river was tired of the weight that oppressed it and was shaking it off like a bear coming out of hibernation.

"Run, Mosiah! Run!" The father's voice came floating across to them.

"Run!" the men screamed. "Run!"

Blocks of ice were crashing against one another now with shuddering bolts of sound. The whole center of the river was churning, muddy brown water boiling up, ice shooting out of the water, then being sucked under again, the open water widening with every second, moving outward towards both banks, racing toward where a young boy scrambled frantically across the ice.

Suddenly Joshua realized he too was screaming. "Run!" he thundered. "Run, Mosiah! Run!" He nearly dropped his crutch as he went up on the balls of his feet to see better.

Then suddenly one of the men in front leaped up, punching the air with his fist. "They made it!" he shouted.

A ragged cheer went up. The mother and the other children were on the far bank. The father was to his boy now. He put one arm around him, and they slid and skated and slipped and crawled the last few yards. And then they were on land too and collapsed in a heap.

"Hoorah!" someone cheered. The men around Joshua shouted and pounded one another on the shoulders. After a moment, across the river the man stood, pulling his boy to his feet and sweeping him up in a great bear hug.

Joshua turned away, pushing back through the ecstatic crowd. He didn't want to stay and be part of the celebration. He felt a great wave of exultation and he wanted to go tell Caroline. Mosiah Hancock, this unknown boy, had made it. He had beaten the river.

Jessica Griffith sat down wearily on the wagon tongue beside Amanda. Immediately she shoved her hands up under her armpits to keep them warm. Amanda Smith was staring woodenly out across the prairie. She had a coat and a heavy shawl, but still shivered noticeably. It was going to be another clear, cold night. But it was also beautiful. The moon was in its third quarter, and with the snow and the air being so clear, they could see quite clearly. They carried enough wood to make a cooking fire, but not enough to keep a fire going through the night. The last timber they had seen was on a stream almost fifteen miles back. Their own body heat was the only fire they had to keep warm.

"The children are all asleep," Jessica murmured. "Even Willard and Rachel."

Amanda nodded slowly. "Thank you for checking on them. I don't know if I can lift my foot off the ground one more time."

"I know. I keep thinking about tomorrow. The thoughts of walking one more yard are almost more than I can bear."

"And it's not just tomorrow," Amanda muttered. "It's the day after that, and the day after . . ." She let it trail off, too discouraged to finish.

Jessica turned away, the thought of two or three more days of this so overwhelming that she couldn't bear to consider it. To her right she could see the outline of the Bartons' little homemade cart. There was no movement there, and she knew that the wife and children had fallen into an exhausted and fitful sleep. The faint cry of a baby started. She looked further on. Against the snow she could see Derek and Barton fussing at the back of Mary Fielding Smith's wagon. Between the jolting ride and the numbing cold, Mary was having a difficult time of it.

As Jessica looked more closely, she could see the silhouette of Mercy sitting on the wagon seat. "Little Joseph is angry because it isn't his turn to nurse yet," Amanda suggested. Mercy still continued to feed both babies as well as help care for Mary's other children.

Then off to her left Jessica saw two dark shapes approaching. Matthew and Jenny had gone out to check on the horses, hobbled a short distance away where the wind had blown the snow away and left enough grass showing to graze on. They were walking slowly, heads down, and talking earnestly with one another.

Jessica smiled in spite of herself. She poked Amanda and pointed. "Do you think they even know it's cold out here?"

Amanda laughed softly. "I don't think so. I don't think they notice much of anything besides each other."

"And that's wonderful," Jessica said, surprised how the very thought of those two warmed her.

"Yes," Amanda said. "Jenny is a beautiful young woman, and just perfect for Matthew. He needs someone who takes life a little more seriously."

"And she needs to laugh a little more," Jessica added. "Matthew will certainly help her do that."

The two young people had heard their voices and turned towards them. "Whoops, here they come," Amanda said, dropping her voice.

As they came up, Matthew let go of Jenny's hand, hoping the women hadn't noticed what he had been doing. "Are you two still up?" he said.

"Well," Amanda drawled, "we are sitting up, but actually that's only because we're frozen in this position and are waiting for you to tip us over and stack us in bed."

Jenny giggled at the imagery. "It is cold, isn't it?"

Jessica looked at Amanda, trying to hold a straight face. "I guess I was wrong about one of them, at least."

"But not the other," Amanda chuckled. "What does that tell us about the differences between men and women?"

Matthew and Jenny watched the interchange between Amanda and Jessica, looking a little puzzled.

"And what have you two been talking about?" Jessica asked, enjoying their little joke but not wanting to embarrass the two young people.

Matthew cocked his head. "Actually, we were just talking about Lehi's colony and how they had to flee from their homes."

That took Jessica by surprise. "Oh?"

"I've started reading the Book of Mormon a second time," Jenny said shyly. "I'm just to where the family has gone out in the wilderness."

"Like us," Matthew said.

"Somewhat like us," Jessica corrected him. "I don't think their weather was quite as temperate as this."

"Temperate?" Matthew asked. "What does that mean?"

Jessica waved it away. "I wasn't serious, Matthew."

Jenny sat down beside Jessica. Her eyebrows pulled down in concentration. "I thought about us this morning while I was reading. It talks about their women and children and how they did on the march."

Amanda nodded slowly. "That's right. I'd forgotten that."

"Yes, it says that the women were able to nurse their children and be strong and still have plenty of milk." She ducked her head, embarrassed to be talking about something so personal and feminine in front of Matthew, but wanting to make her point. "I thought about Mercy taking care of both babies under these kinds of conditions and still having enough milk for them."

Jessica nodded slowly. She hadn't tied the thought to the Book of Mormon, but she too had marveled at how Mercy Thompson was doing.

"And," Matthew broke in, "it says that after a time, the women were able to bear their journey through the wilderness without murmuring, so great were the blessings of the Lord upon them. They were even able to bear their journeyings without murmuring."

"Is this supposed to cheer me up?" Amanda said dryly.

"No, really," Jenny said, jumping back in to support him. "And the Lord told them they couldn't have any fires." She pulled a face and wrinkled her nose, making her look for a moment very much like a little girl. "They even had to eat their meat raw."

Jessica felt a little laugh bubble up. "Now, if they didn't murmur about that, that really is something." But then the reality of what she had just said sobered her. The previous evening Derek had shot a rabbit and they had roasted it over the fire, rejoicing over the fresh meat, even if each person barely got two bites' worth. In her mind's eye, she pictured Derek handing it to her after he had skinned and cleaned it. Her imaginary self then ripped off a leg and began to chew on it. The image brought instant humility. "That really is something," she repeated in wonder.

Amanda was contrite now too, the humor gone from her. "Yes, of course, Jenny. You're right. It was remarkable. And considering we have so many children with us, including two babies, yes, we have done very well too."

"Jenny and me," Matthew said, looking down at her proudly, "we decided we're going to make a special effort not to complain about things anymore. Not to murmur. We want to be more like Lehi's colony."

Jenny was nodding. "And I'm going to try and be nicer to Kathryn and help her more."

Both Amanda and Jessica were struck silent with that. The simplicity of their words, the pure sincerity of these two innocents had sent shafts of shame into their own hearts. What had they been doing at the very moment these two had joined them? Sitting together, joining together in a chorus of mutual murmuring. Finally, Jessica cleared her throat. "A worthy resolution," she said quietly. "Something we should all take to heart."

Amanda reached across Jessica and took Jenny's hand. "Yes," she whispered. "Thank you for reminding us."

Jenny seemed surprised, then blushed deeply. "I didn't mean that . . ." The thought that she had been trying to call them to repentance really flustered her now. "I wasn't suggesting that you were . . ."

"We know," Jessica said warmly, laying her hand on the both of theirs. "That's what makes it all the more meaningful." And then she didn't want to talk about it anymore. She wanted to be alone and think about the feelings this seventeen-year-old had created in her. She stood up. "Well, I suppose we ought to get to bed."

Jenny and Amanda stood too. All three of them were sleeping beneath Amanda's wagon. Matthew was over with Derek under Mary's. He nodded and tipped his hat. "G'night."

They watched him go. Then Jessica turned to Jenny, laying a hand on her arm. There was a great softness in her eyes.

"Don't give up on that boy," she said. "A little Irish blood is exactly what the Steed family needs right now."

Five minutes later, as Derek and Matthew were rolling out their blankets on the ground, Derek suddenly stood up, turning to look out across the prairie toward the east. The sound of horses' hooves and the rattling of wagons carried clearly to them.

Matthew backed out from beneath the wagon and stood by his brother-in-law. The approaching party was easily discernible in the silvery light against the snow. There were three wagons, each pulled by two horses. That was no cause for alarm. Derek and Matthew's group was well out of the area where their enemies were prowling, and also these wagons were coming from the east, meaning that it was likely some of their own people on their way back to get more Saints. That was a common thing now. In fact, they had seen Brigham Young the previous afternoon. He was leapfrogging across the prairie, taking his wife and family forward, leaving them in camp, then going back to pick up some of those less well-equipped, taking them back to his camp, then moving forward again with his family.

"Let's go see who it is," Matthew said. "They're traveling late. I'll bet they're ready to camp."

As they moved quickly out toward the wagons, they heard a man's shout. "Ho, the camp!"

"Yes!" Derek called back. "Derek Ingalls here. Come on in."

There was a muffled cry of joy and surprise—a woman's voice—then the man shouted again. "Derek. It's Joshua and Caroline."

Peter Ingalls and young Joshua, Lydia's oldest son, were in the back of Father Steed's cabin, digging through the garden, looking for any carrots or potatoes that might have been missed.

During the last two days the cold temperatures had softened enough that the ground had thawed. It wasn't likely they would find something, but there was nothing else to do, and even the small chance that there was something they had missed was worth the effort. It was late afternoon, and the sky was overcast. But it was high and thin and not threatening rain.

Peter stopped and cocked his head. Then young Joshua heard it too. There was the low rumble of voices—many voices—coming from the street that ran in front of their cabin. Sticking their shovels in the ground, they walked around the cabin to where they could see what was going on.

As they came out front, Benjamin and Mary Ann were coming out of the cabin onto the porch. Sister McIntire was right behind them.

"What is it?" Mary Ann called, raising one hand to shade her eyes.

For a moment, Peter wasn't sure. It was a crowd of people moving toward them from the eastern part of town. He could see the top of a wagon—no, three wagons, as he looked more carefully—and it was that which was creating all the excitement. Even as he looked, he saw people running out from their houses as the crowd reached them. And what was especially strange, he could see that many of the people were pushing around to the back of the wagon, calling and pointing to whatever was inside.

"It must be someone returning from the east," Peter said.

Benjamin had come down to stand by Peter and young Joshua now. Mary Ann and Sister McIntire were right behind him. Benjamin's eyes had narrowed to squint at the approaching group. He shook his head. "Those aren't any of our wagons." Wagons coming back from the east was a commonplace happening now; people didn't run out to greet them like returning royalty. And none of the Mormon wagons and teams looked as good as these that were approaching them.

All of a sudden, Mary Ann took three quick steps forward. She wasn't looking at the horses or the wagons. She was peering at the two men on the wagon seat, driving the lead team. One hand came to her mouth and there was a stifled cry of joy. "Ben, it's Derek! Oh, look! And Matthew! They're back!"

Now Benjamin was staring. "But how . . . ?" he started. It had been only thirteen days. The round-trip took closer to twenty. But Mary Ann wasn't there to answer. She was out the gate and hurrying toward the crowd. Benjamin started after her. Not running. That would set his lungs on fire. But he walked as swiftly as he dared.

And then suddenly young Joshua, who was following his grandmother, started jumping up and down, waving his arms. "It's Uncle Joshua!" he shouted.

"Glory be!" Sister McIntire breathed. "It *is* Joshua!"

Benjamin increased his step, frantically scanning the crowd. "Where? Where?"

"Driving the second wagon," Peter shouted over his shoulder. He had run and already caught up with Mary Ann.

Now the distance between the wagons and the crowd and the approaching Steeds had narrowed to about a hundred feet. Matthew had come to his feet and jumped down from the wagon, even as Derek reined in the horses. In moments he was to his mother and crushing her in a great bear hug. Derek was only steps behind him, searching the crowd for Rebecca. When he saw that she wasn't with her family, his face fell. But he brightened as he saw Peter and went to him swiftly.

The other two wagons had reined up too, and Joshua climbed down awkwardly, steadying himself against the wheel while he reached up for his crutch.

Joshua? But how? Benjamin's prolonged illness had slowed his ability to think clearly, and his mind was in a tumble of confusion as he moved as quickly as he could to meet his sons. Why were Derek and Matthew back so soon? And Joshua? Joshua was in St. Louis. How could he be here in Far West?

Before he could sort it out, Sister McIntire took his arm and they moved forward to where Matthew still held his mother and Derek was pummeling Peter on the arm. With a shout of greeting, young Joshua threw himself into his uncle's arms, nearly knocking the crutch out of his hand. His grandmother was right behind him now, holding out her arms.

"Hello, Mama," Joshua said, taking her under his free arm.

She brushed at the tears with the back of her hand. "Joshua, I can't believe it! What are you doing here?"

Joshua started to answer, but then he saw his father. He was shocked even as he stepped forward, with his hand outstretched. His father had lost fifteen or twenty pounds. There were dark circles under his eyes, and his eyes were not as bright as they had been when he had last seen him. "Hello, Pa," Joshua said, grasping Benjamin's hand. But Benjamin wasn't satisfied with a handshake. He pulled Joshua to him and pounded his back. "I can't believe it, Joshua. What are you doing here?"

Joshua laughed and looked at his mother. "That's just what Mama was asking me. Well, I—" He stopped. Matthew and Derek and Peter were all pressing in around them now, and Joshua saw a familiar and endearing face. "Ah, Mrs. McIntire."

"Hello, Joshua Steed."

"I met Jenny and Kathryn on the trail," he said. "They told me about your coming to Far West." He shook his head in mock exasperation. "I tried to warn Matthew not to give you that Book of Mormon."

She smiled cheerfully. "We'll be forever grateful that he did. And how are my girls?"

"Doing very well," he replied. Then he shook his head. "Well, at least Kathryn is."

A quick look of concern flashed across Sister McIntire's face. "But not Jenny?"

Joshua winked at her, then gave Matthew a severe look. "It was really hard to tell. Every time I tried to talk to her, all she could do was moon at this youngest brother of mine with those big blue eyes of hers."

Matthew blushed. "Oh, go on! It wasn't like that at all."

Mary Ann reached out and took Joshua's arm. "Did you find Will?"

The smile on Joshua's face instantly vanished. He shook his head. "Not yet." He sighed. "But it hasn't been that long, we—"

A shout from behind them cut him short. They all looked around. Nathan and Lydia and Rebecca were coming towards them with the children. Nathan had little Nathan in his arms, Lydia was carrying the baby, Rebecca was holding Emily's hand. Their cabin was another block or so further on from Benjamin's. They too had heard the noise and come out to see what was happening. As they drew close, Nathan saw Matthew and Joshua and gave a shout. He spoke to Lydia and they both broke into a run.

The others stepped back. Then Rebecca saw Derek and squealed in delight. She released Emily and came flying at him, hair bouncing, skirts swirling. She nearly strangled him as she threw her arms around his neck and clung to him with all her strength.

Nathan came up to Joshua and grasped his hand. "Did you find Will?" were the first words out of his mouth. Joshua shook his head, then smiled. He looked at his mother. "But I did find someone else."

"Who?" Mary Ann asked.

Joshua turned and pulled his father forward to stand by Mary Ann. "Mama, Papa, we have another surprise for you."

Matthew leaned forward, grinning. "Hold on, Mama! This is going to be a real shock."

"What?"

Joshua was ecstatic, enjoying this very much. He swung around, maneuvering his crutch around Nathan. "Come on." He turned. "You too, Nathan. Lydia. Rebecca. All of you. This is for everyone."

He brushed aside their questions and queries and moved back toward the wagons. At first, Mary Ann thought he was going to get something for her. But he didn't stop. They passed the first wagon, then the second. As they came around the second wagon, the third one came into view. A man was sitting on the wagon seat, the reins still in his hand.

Suddenly Mary Ann stopped, stunned into immobility. She was looking up at the driver, who was now smiling self-consciously down on the approaching family. It was a face Mary Ann had not seen for over a year. It was a face she had not expected to see again for years to come, perhaps never.

"Carl!" she cried.

Carl Rogers stood slowly. A quick smile flitted across his face. "Good afternoon, Mother Steed."

Joshua stood back, laughing and proud, as Carl jumped down and came to Melissa's parents. Mary Ann was weeping openly now, unable to believe what she was seeing. Benjamin was likewise bewildered. "But how?" he kept asking. "How did you get here?"

"Let's get out of the cold," Joshua suggested, "and we'll tell you the whole story."

Chapter Notes

In this chapter and the previous one, the details of the trek eastward from Far West are based on actual incidents from the experiences of the Saints. However, some of the incidents portrayed have been combined from the experiences of different families, and the events happened across a wider span of time than is depicted in the book. Also, in some cases fictional names have been supplied. Nevertheless, the story of the children with bleeding feet; the decision of the Thomas family to send the father back for others; the "queen's bed"; Brother Wiswager's offer of his "standing room" accommodations; Mosiah Hancock's crossing of the river—all are actual incidents. (See Richard Neitzel Holzapfel and Jeni Broberg Holzapfel, *Women of Nauvoo* [Salt Lake City: Bookcraft, 1992], pp. 8–13; *American Moses*, pp. 70–71; *Mack Hist.*, pp. 294–97; Gracia N. Jones, *Emma's Glory and Sacrifice: A Testimony* [Hurricane, Utah: Homestead Publishers and Distributors, 1987], p. 93; and *CHFT*, pp. 212–13.)

Chapter Thirty-Six

Inside Benjamin's cabin, the mood was one of exuberant joy. Mary Ann was still weeping unashamedly, not even trying to contain her happiness. She sat on the small sofa next to Carl, holding his hand. "And you brought Melissa?" she said.

"Do you think I could have kept her away?"

"The other children?" Lydia asked. "Are they with her?"

He shook his head. "They're with their Grandma and Grandpa Rogers. We didn't bring them this far. Besides, we had a wagonload already."

"And she'll be waiting in Quincy for us?" Mary Ann asked. "For sure?"

"Yes."

"With the baby?"

He laughed heartily, something Carl rarely did around Melissa's family. "Of course. She's nursing her and had to bring her. As if she would have missed the chance to let you see her!"

Joshua spoke up now. "Melissa and Caroline started west

with us. But when we met Matthew and Derek, we decided it would be best if Caroline and Melissa went back with Jessica and the others. They'll start looking for somewhere for you to stay."

"But who are driving the wagons?" Nathan asked. "If you brought Matthew and Derek back with you . . . ?"

"I brought two teamsters with me, so I just sent them back with Caroline. That way we could come straight here and save several days."

"Melissa was so anxious to see you," Carl added, "but it was very cold and we have been worried about having the baby out in it. She's done very well, but we thought this was better."

"I don't know if I can wait," Mary Ann said. "Melissa. I'll get to see Melissa."

"Oh, Joshua," Lydia said, "and I'm so anxious to see Caroline again. Is she all right now?"

"Yes, she's fine. Except for being concerned about Will, of course. But we're very optimistic about that too. She is worried about seeing you all again. After that letter she wrote, she's pretty nervous."

Being back inside had perked Benjamin up considerably now. He waved a hand to brush Joshua's comment aside. "You know that doesn't make a bit of difference to us." Then he turned to Carl. "And you brought a wagonload of supplies all the way from Kirtland?"

The man who had seen his relationship with his wife's family grow increasingly strained back in Ohio now colored slightly at the warmth he saw in his father-in-law's eyes. "When we got your letter, we knew we couldn't just stand by and do nothing. Melissa had been asking me to bring her west to see you in the summer anyway. This just made it a little more challenging."

Mary Ann squeezed his hand. "You will never know what that means to us, Carl. This is wonderful."

"Joshua had the same idea," Carl said, trying to turn the attention away from himself, "about bringing you help. It was a wonderful coincidence we happened to get to Quincy at the same time. But here we are, and with enough food and dry goods not only to get you back to Illinois but to see you through the rest of the winter."

Joshua pulled a face. "Except we've got this little problem. We're going to have to get some of that stuff out of the wagons, or there won't be room for anyone to ride." He laughed. "Maybe we'll have to just start eating tonight and not stop until we've made sufficient space to . . ."

His voice trailed off as a sudden, awkward silence filled the room. He looked around in surprise. "What?"

Nathan cleared his throat and looked at his father. Derek and Rebecca glanced quickly at each other, then turned to Benjamin. Mary Ann looked embarrassed. She too turned to her husband. When Benjamin saw that everyone was going to leave it to him, his shoulders lifted and fell. "You help me, Nathan. I may not explain this very well."

Now Carl was openly puzzled too. "Explain what?"

Benjamin took a breath, then began, speaking slowly and deliberately. "You have to understand something. Conditions here have been very bad. Many people came here poor. Many more have lost everything to the mobs. Those blessed with more of this world's goods have mostly gone now. Those of us who are left don't have much."

"Yes, we knew that," Carl said. "That's why we came."

Benjamin shook his head. "A few weeks ago, all of us made an agreement." He shook his head quickly. "It was more than an agreement. It was a covenant. A solemn and sacred covenant."

Joshua looked suddenly suspicious. "What kind of a covenant?"

Benjamin looked to Nathan, who stepped forward. "We agreed that we would all join together and pool our resources. We promised that we would not leave anyone behind just because they are too poor to make it on their own."

Carl looked up at Nathan. "Pool your resources? What does that mean exactly?"

Nathan went on doggedly. "It means that we share whatever

we have so that no one will suffer more than another. All will have equally or none will have."

Joshua shot forward, half coming out of his chair. "Do you mean . . . ?" He sat back, shaking his head. "We didn't bring all this to give it away, Pa."

Benjamin looked very sad. "I know that, and they are your goods. They are yours to do with as you choose. But if you choose to give them to us, then we are bound to share with others."

Carl, far more reserved than Joshua, looked disturbed, but held his peace. Joshua exploded. "Are you crazy? We have—what?" His head swung around, counting quickly. "Fourteen of us? Fifteen with Mrs. McIntire. Fifteen people to feed and two hundred miles of frozen prairie to cover. And that's not counting Jessica and her family when we get to Quincy. Good heavens, Pa, be realistic."

Mary Ann spoke quietly now. "Joshua, we have lived realistic since last November. We have people here who don't even have tents. They sleep under a bedsheet or a single blanket. There are children who are getting only half a bowl of cornmeal porridge a day, sometimes not even that. We have widows whose husbands were shot down or beaten to death and who have no one to provide for them. That's realistic. We can't just turn our backs on them because you and Carl have been so wonderfully generous and so marvelously kind to us."

Joshua looked to Lydia for support. She smiled faintly. "It was the family heads who signed their names to the covenant, Joshua. But we as women consider the covenant just as binding on us as them. These are our brothers and sisters. We can't simply ignore them."

He turned to Rebecca and Derek. They were nodding their assent to what had been said. Matthew, Peter, Mrs. McIntire—it was a united front.

"So you starve so that others may live?" Joshua asked.

"No," Nathan answered. "The covenant says that we are allowed to meet our needs first. All Pa is saying is that three wagonloads of food are a little more than we need."

"And three wagons," Benjamin came in. "We don't need three wagons. We can make it with one."

"For fifteen people?" Joshua was incredulous.

"All right," Nathan agreed, "two would be more like it. But we don't need three. Do you know what even one wagon and team will mean here? Four or five families will get out now. Then it will come back, and four or five more will be helped."

"I can walk," Benjamin said stubbornly. "All of the men can walk. We can do with one wagon."

Joshua hit his forehead with the heel of his hand. "I can't believe it." He turned on his mother. "Do you think Pa can walk, Mother?"

She turned to her husband and slowly shook her head. "No."

Joshua pounced on that. "Look at you, Pa. You're very sick. Even with a mattress and plenty of blankets in the back of the wagon, I worry about you. If we're not careful, you're not going to make it through that trip alive . . . Well, he's not," he cried, when he saw the shocked looks around him. "Somebody's got to face the truth."

Benjamin straightened slowly. "May I speak, please?" When there was no one to disagree with that, he went on. He spoke mostly to Joshua, but to Carl as well. "First let me say, as your mother did, that we are deeply touched. What you two have done is the highest expression of Christian love. You have left your homes, spent your resources, undertaken a difficult journey—and all because you care for us. I hope with all my heart that what we are saying now does not in any way make you think we are not grateful. We are, more than any meager words could possibly express."

He took a breath, his voice growing stronger now. "But let me see if I can help you understand. In some ways, our lives are like circles, circles in which we move and live and act. Some of us live longer and so we make wider circles than others. Some people are great and noble and famous. Their circles can become very large. We believe Joseph Smith is one of those. We believe his circle will embrace all of eternity."

Joshua had started fidgeting as his father began, looking for an opening, but he quieted, caught up in the intensity of Benjamin's words.

"George Washington, Columbus, the Apostle Paul—I could name hundreds of others who we know by name because their circles spread wide and touched many people. But for every one of those big circles there are a thousand unnamed and unknown people whose circles seem very small and insignificant by comparison. And yet, to God, they are not insignificant. To God, it is not how large our circle becomes, or how well known we are to the world. All that matters is how we—you, me, each and every one of us—fills that circle.

"Are we like our Savior and Redeemer? Are we following the example of the Master? Or do we care only about ourselves?" He stopped and peered into Joshua's eyes. "Do you understand what I'm saying, Joshua? If you and Carl can't bear the thought of seeing all that stuff you brought given away, I understand perfectly. And I will condemn you not, not in the tiniest way.

"*But*"—he lifted a finger for emphasis—"if you do decide to bring that food inside my tiny little circle, then I will keep the covenant I have made and I will share it with others in need."

Now he turned to his wife. Mary Ann was nodding as he spoke, her eyes shining with pride and love. "Otherwise," he continued, "my circle disappears, and I become nothing."

He sat back. The room was completely silent. Even the children seemed to hold their breath. There was a quick, fleeting smile. "That's all I have to say."

Joshua stared at his father for a long time. Then he slowly turned and looked at Carl. Something passed between them, though neither showed any expression on his face. Only their eyes spoke. Finally, Joshua turned back around. "Suppose Carl and I say, all right . . ." He turned and looked at Carl again. Carl nodded. "Suppose we say that all we will keep is two wagons and enough food and goods to get us back to Quincy and to get you established there."

He stopped, and there was a mixture of admiration and frustration in his eyes as he looked at his father. "Then will you ride in the back of that stupid wagon the whole way and not complain about it one time?"

Benjamin flinched as though he had been stung by a horsefly. "I . . ." He blinked a couple of times. "I'm not that sick. I can—"

"Benjamin!" Mary Ann said sharply.

"Mother, I'm fine. I—"

She cut him off again. "That's a definite yes," she said to Joshua.

Now Joshua turned to Nathan, ignoring the pained cry from their father. It was nearly lost anyway as the room rippled with laughter. "Derek told us that Pa plans to stay here until the last people are gone. If we agree, Carl and I, to participate in this covenant of yours, will you help me load this stubborn old man into the wagon tomorrow morning, hog-tie him to his bed, and then head out?"

"I will!" Nathan said without hesitation. Then, as Benjamin started to harrumph behind him, he added, "But I suspect it might take Matthew and Derek and Peter and Carl as well as you and me to do the job."

"And maybe Mrs. McIntire and me too," Lydia cried out, clapping her hands in delight.

Nathan quickly sobered, and now as he looked at his father, his eyes were misty. "I will do so, because I think our father's circle is far wider and has touched many more lives than he will admit, or even believes. And it won't diminish the size of that circle one tiny bit if he rides every foot of the way to Illinois."

He went to his mother and knelt in front of her, taking her hands. "Am I wrong, Mama? Can we take this hardheaded, wonderful old fool that you married and go see Melissa and Caroline and Jessica without displeasing the Lord?"

The tears welled up and spilled over as Mary Ann nodded vigorously. "I don't think there is much that this hardheaded, wonderful, glorious old fool can do that would displease the Lord."

Nathan stood up and swung around to face the family. "Then it's settled. All in favor?"

A thunderous "aye" shook the rafters.

"Any opposed?"

Benjamin started to lift his hand, but Mary Ann's hand shot out and pushed it back down again.

"Motion carried!" Nathan cried. "We leave in the morning."

Mary Ann pulled the canvas at the back of the wagon closed, then, stepping carefully over Emily's and young Nathan's sleeping forms, sat down beside her husband. She shivered slightly as she removed her coat and then quickly ducked under the big quilt Caroline had purchased in St. Louis.

They were in Tenny's Grove, the first stop on their journey to the Mississippi. They had gotten a late start by the time they got what few things they would be taking from their homes loaded on the wagons, but they made good time. It hadn't rained or snowed for two or three days now, and the roads were in reasonable condition.

As she snuggled up against Benjamin, he sniffed diffidently. "I thought only stubborn, old, hardheaded fools were allowed in this bed."

"They are," she said cheerfully. "My children said I qualify."

He wasn't in much of a mood for banter. "Well, I don't. I'm not going to ride in here for eight or nine days while everyone else takes their turn walking."

She reached out and found his hand. "Benjamin, I want to say something. And I want you to listen for a minute."

There was no answer.

"Will you?"

"I'm listening," he growled.

She lay back, putting her hands behind her head and staring up at the canvas.

"I said I'm listening," he finally said when she didn't speak. This time there was more softness in his voice. "Say it."

"I know," she said in a small voice suddenly tight with emotions. "I'm trying to."

She turned her head and wiped at her eyes with the corner of the quilt. Finally, she turned back. "Do you remember that night? Back in Palmyra?" She swallowed hard. "The night you and Joshua . . ."

There was a long silence, then, "Yes, of course."

"When was that?"

"September of '27," he said without hesitation.

"Eleven years ago now, coming up on twelve."

He nodded. That night had been relived so many times in his memory, it was still as vivid as if it had been the previous evening.

"Almost twelve years without having all of our children together." She came up on one elbow to look at him. "Have you thought about that? That we haven't had all of them together in that time?"

Actually Benjamin had thought about his children a lot, but he hadn't thought about it in those terms, that with Melissa staying behind in Ohio, even with Joshua's return there had been no having them together. Not all at the same time. He shook his head. "No, I guess I haven't."

"Do you know what this means to—" She had to stop, and her hand came up to her mouth. He could hear the tremor in her voice as she finally went on. "Do you know what this means to me? To see Melissa again? To see the baby? To have every one of my children . . ."

He reached out and took her hand and pulled it down against his chest. "Yes, I think I can understand that."

"Well, I want you there!" she exploded in a fierce whisper. "I want Melissa to see her father. I want Caroline to be able to know that you don't hold any feelings against her."

"I'm going to be there," he said, surprised by her passion, and strangely moved by her concern for him. "I'm fine."

"You're not fine, Ben," she said, in a voice that was now as small and hopeless as it had previously been filled with intensity.

"I watch you get weaker and weaker. I watch you hunch over in pain whenever you cough. And I get sick to my stomach. You are not fine."

She pulled her hand free from his and folded her arms on her chest. "And that's why, stubborn old fool or not, you are going to stay right here in this bed all the way across Missouri and onto the ferry and into Illinois. Do you hear me, Ben? That's the way it's going to be."

He didn't answer. He *was* a stubborn old fool. He had admitted that to himself long ago. And in these past months since his arrest and contracting the sickness in his lungs, he had also become honest enough with himself to admit that he was frightened. He could feel down in his bones what Mary Ann had only seen with her eyes. He *was* tired. He *was* weak. Something had gone out of him, and he sensed it was more than just the sickness. It was as if the cough had opened the floodgates for old age to come pouring in.

Down deep, he was secretly relieved that his sons had forced his hand, had carried him out to the wagon bed, not even letting him walk from the house, had covered him with quilts and blankets up to his chin. It galled him that it had to be so. It was a bitter blow, and he was finding it difficult to accept it. But he also knew that if they had let him have his way, had let him walk along with the others, he wouldn't make it. He was as sure of that as he was that his children loved him.

And now, after only one day on the trail, he wasn't even sure the bed would be enough. The pounding of the wagon had been brutal. It had sapped his reserves to dangerously low levels. And they were through only one day.

"Mary Ann?"

She turned her head.

"If I . . ." He shook his head and tried again. "If for some reason . . ." He couldn't finish it. "Will you tell Melissa for me? How much I loved her?"

Mary Ann was up instantly. "Stop it, Benjamin!"

"Will you?" he repeated quietly. "And Caroline?"

She leaned over and kissed him hard on the mouth. He tasted the saltiness of her tears on his tongue. "You tell them yourself, Benjamin Steed," she whispered with that same ferocity she had had in her voice earlier. "I won't do it." Her voice caught, and she fell back against the straw mattress. "I won't!"

By mid-March, one of the worst of the winters the Great Plains had seen in several years began to relinquish its grip. The snow melted, the rains came, and the roads turned to quagmires, but the temperatures started to rise. Occasionally a light frost would tip everything with white, but daytime temperatures were climbing into the fifties and low sixties. The vast inland ocean of prairie took on a green tint that deepened visibly almost every day. And most important to the grateful Saints who were still making their way eastward, the Mississippi had not seen ice for over a week, and the ferry was making continuous runs now, getting the Mormons out of the state that had refused to consider them as rightful citizens.

Every morning, Jenny and Kathryn McIntire and Rachel Steed walked down the main street of Quincy, Illinois, at quarter to eight. They would pass the still unopened shops and businesses, pass the blacksmith shop where the apprentice was just stoking up the fires for the day, and go on down to the street that ran parallel to the river. As soon as they could see across the river, they would go up on tiptoes and peer over to the camp on the other side. It was a hundred yards across here, and it was difficult to make out which wagons in the camp had not been there the day before, but they always looked. And then they would turn and walk up the street to where the ferryboat had its small dock.

The ferry did not start its runs until eight o'clock each morning, but the girls were always there five minutes early anyway. They would watch the ferryman check the lines. They would watch him and his boy start the first westward shuttle across the great river. When it reached the far side, they would begin to squirm and fidget in anticipation as the first wagons were loaded—with no ice in the river it could take two at a time—and people streamed aboard in the space that was left.

This morning was no different. As the ferryman and his son started pulling on the ropes, heaving together to move the heavy flat-bottomed boat across the muddy current, Jenny's eyes narrowed. She always imagined that Matthew would somehow be on that first wagon, sitting on the wagon seat, one hand up on the backrest, grinning as he saw her waiting for him. Now as the ferry approached, still only halfway back, she was up on the balls of her feet, squinting to see all the better.

"It's not him," Kathryn said. "It's an old man." With the typical myopia of a twelve-year-old, she thought she was being helpful.

Jenny came back down again. The second driver was not Matthew either. "I know that, Kathryn," she said with a little bit of reprimand in her voice. "There's not much chance they'll ever be the first ones across. There's too many people."

Now other people were coming up the street to join them—a man and his daughter, two women, an older woman with two young boys. By mid-March, some six or seven thousand Latter-day Saints had left Missouri and found refuge in Illinois. Many were in Quincy; many more were scattering up and down the river in nearby settlements. Not a few of these had left family or friends behind. So coming down to meet the ferry was a common practice.

The boat scraped to a stop on the muddy shoreline, and the boy sprang forward to release the front end of the boat, which served as a gangplank. The man driving the lead wagon snapped the reins and drove it off the ferry. Immediately the second followed. Then the people on foot swarmed in behind them. They carried valises and small trunks, cloth bags filled to bulging, packages tied with ropes, or trousers with the legs tied shut and stuffed with other belongings.

Those waiting on shore pushed forward and began calling out questions. "Have you seen the Levi Hatch family?" "Did any new wagons come in last night?" "The Judds? Anyone know anything about the Judds?"

Jenny fell in step beside the first wagon. Kathryn and Rachel moved in among the others. Jenny looked up at the wagon driver. "Good morning, sir."

He looked down and smiled. Inside the wagon she could see a woman's face and a child's. They were smiling too. They had made it. They were across the river. "May I help you?"

"Any new wagons come last night?"

"Yes. Half a dozen or so."

There was a quick leap of hope. "You wouldn't know if the Benjamin Steed family was among them?"

The man turned to his wife. "Benjamin Steed?"

She shook her head. Jenny felt like someone had thrown cold water in her face, the same way she felt every morning when it became obvious that they hadn't come.

The man saw it and felt bad. "They from Far West?"

"Yes."

"We're from Di-Ahman. Don't know a lot of people from Far West. Sorry."

Suddenly the woman was tugging at his shirt. "Wait a minute. Rebecca Ingalls? She married that English boy? Wasn't she a Steed?"

Jenny's head snapped up so quickly it made her hair bounce. "Yes!" she cried. "Derek Ingalls. His wife is Rebecca Steed."

The woman smiled. "Them we know." Her smile broadened even further. It was great to be the bearer of good news. "They came in late yesterday afternoon."

"Oh, yes, them," the man said. "There's a whole bunch of them."

Jenny was fairly dancing alongside the wagon now. "Are they coming over today?"

"Yep. They're ten, maybe eleven wagons back."

Jenny leaped into the air, then spun around and started running. "Kathryn! Rachel! Run home quick! Tell Jessica and Melissa and Caroline. They're coming! They're coming!"

Mary Ann was standing in the first wagon directly behind Joshua, Lydia, and Nathan, who rode on the wagon seat. They were still about thirty yards from the eastern shore, but she could see that there was close to a hundred people milling around waiting for the ferry to arrive. The sun was up about midway to noon, and it was difficult to look into it. The people were backlit and she couldn't distinguish faces.

Then she heard a familiar voice. "Grandma! Grandma! Grandma!"

Mary Ann's head came up. Lydia jerked forward. Joshua and Nathan had heard it too. "It's Rachel!" Lydia cried.

"Do you see her?" Mary Ann asked.

And then Lydia was pointing. "There! On the left. Right by the water."

Nathan laughed. "The one dancing like a banshee."

"And there's Caroline," Joshua exclaimed. He lifted his hand and started waving.

Matthew and Derek and Rebecca had walked onto the back of the ferry and were behind Carl's wagon. Now they pushed their way through the people and came alongside the lead wagon.

"Do you see Melissa?" Rebecca called up to her mother.

"No. There's Caroline and Rachel—and oh, there's Jessica! And the boys."

"There's Melissa!" Nathan said. "Right behind Jessica. She's holding up the baby."

The remaining fifty feet of water seemed like it took forever, but finally there was a lurch as the boat came up against the dock. The gangplank creaked down, then dropped with a thud. "All right," the ferryman bawled, "everybody off."

As Joshua picked up the reins, the man grinned up at him. "Hey, mister! I'm using that hundred dollars to buy me another boat. Then we can have one coming and going. Be the best danged ferry between here and St. Louis."

Joshua laughed and snapped the reins. "Good for you."

Joshua didn't even try and turn onto the street into the crowd. Holding the horses back as the people made way for them, he pulled the wagon over to the left, into the large grassy area that fronted the ferryman's home.

Caroline came up first, walking alongside the wagon, reaching up to hold Joshua's hand. And then as Joshua reined in the horses, the reunion began. Cousins screamed at the sight of other cousins and grabbed each other's hands. Jenny, suddenly shy, walked to Matthew. Not caring who saw them, he took her by the shoulders and kissed her soundly. The women were crying and laughing and hugging while the men stood back and watched. Carl smiled broadly as Melissa was mobbed. Oohs and aahs chorused as she lifted the blanket and revealed Sarah's sleeping face. Then Mary Ann and Caroline were in each other's arms, weeping and talking and telling each other that everything was going to be all right now.

Then suddenly they fell silent. Joshua had seen it first and called out to Caroline. That brought Derek and Rebecca and Mrs. McIntire around. They waved at the others to be quiet.

No one had noticed that Nathan and Lydia had left the group and gone around to the back of the wagon. Now they appeared again. Nathan had his father around the waist, supporting him. Lydia was on the other side, a hand out to steady him if he stumbled. He was trembling with the exertion of getting out of the wagon, and his face was pale. But the smile on his face split it nearly in two and made him look like the old Benjamin Steed again.

"Papa?" Melissa pushed around Emily and young Joshua, who was holding her baby now. She took two steps forward, hesitantly, then in a rush ran to him, stepping into his arms. "Oh, Papa!" she cried, kissing his cheek. "It's so good to see you."

"Dear Melissa," he whispered. "Thank you for coming. Thank you for Carl."

He stepped back, blinking at the tears that were burning his eyes. He tried to glare at Joshua. "I guess it's all right if I get out of that stupid bed now?"

Joshua slowly nodded, his Adam's apple bobbing as he swallowed quickly. "Yes, Papa, it's all right now. We're here."

As the noise started up again, Benjamin raised a hand. "I have a request."

Everyone went quiet again immediately. "Mother, come over here."

Mary Ann, looking a little surprised, complied. Nathan let go of his father and let Mary Ann take him instead.

"Now," Benjamin said, letting his eyes sweep around the group. "In order. Joshua, come here." He pointed to a spot beside him.

Joshua stepped forward, giving his mother a quizzical look. She just smiled at him, her face radiant now. She understood exactly what was happening.

"Nathan."

Nathan came around from behind his father and stood beside Joshua.

"Melissa."

Melissa was already there and just put her arm around her father's waist. Now everyone understood and the tears were flowing all over again.

"Rebecca."

She squeezed Derek's hand, then let go; and with a smile, she came forward. She went up on tiptoe and kissed her father on his forehead.

Benjamin turned. "And Matthew."

He had already left Jenny's side and walked over to stand behind Rebecca.

There they stood, not moving. As Benjamin looked at his five surviving children, his shoulders straightened and his voice rose. "Sister Steed?"

"Yes, Brother Steed," Mary Ann managed, wiping now at her eyes.

"It gives me a great deal of pleasure to present to you the children of Benjamin and Mary Ann Steed."

For a moment, nothing happened, then Caroline began to clap. Sister McIntire joined in instantly, then Jessica and Jenny and Kathryn. Then they were all clapping, standing there like an audience receiving a royal family. The people getting off the ferry and those who had come to meet them had turned and were staring at them with open curiosity.

They didn't care. The applause went out, striking the family, then rolling on to lose itself over the great Mississippi River.

WISCONSIN TERRITORY
LAKE MICHIGAN
IOWA TERRITORY
ILLINOIS
ADAM-ONDI-AHMAN
FAR WEST
QUINCY
INDEPENDENCE
Missouri River
Mississippi River
ST. LOUIS
INDIAN (UNORGANIZED) TERRITORY
MISSOURI
ARKANSAS
MISSISSIPPI
LOUISIANA
TEXAS (Independent from Mexico since 1836)
NEW ORLEANS
GULF